Southeastern Europe in the

Southeastern Europe in the Middl
important crossroads of trade and c
the spheres of influence of both the [illegible] Orthodox Church and Latin Christendom. This comprehensive and authoritative survey draws on historical and archaeological sources to illuminate 750 years of the region's history, covering Romania, southern Ukraine, southern Hungary, Croatia, Slovenia, Serbia, Montenegro, Bulgaria, Macedonia, Albania, and Greece. Exploring the social, political, and economic changes that marked the transition from Late Antiquity to the early Middle Ages, the book addresses important themes such as the rise of medieval states, the conversion to Christianity, the monastic movement inspired by developments in Western Europe and in Byzantium, and the role of material culture (architecture, the arts, and objects of daily life) in the representation of power.

FLORIN CURTA is Associate Professor of Medieval History and Archaeology at the University of Florida. He is the author of *The Making of the Slavs: History and Archaeology of the Lower Danube Region, c. 500–700 AD* (Cambridge University Press, 2001).

Cambridge Medieval Textbooks

This is a series of introductions to important topics in medieval history aimed primarily at advanced students and faculty, and is designed to complement the monograph series *Cambridge Studies in Medieval Life and Thought*. It includes both chronological and thematic approaches and addresses both British and European topics.

For a list of titles in the series, see end of book.

SOUTHEASTERN EUROPE IN THE MIDDLE AGES

500–1250

FLORIN CURTA
University of Florida

CAMBRIDGE
UNIVERSITY PRESS

CAMBRIDGE UNIVERSITY PRESS
Cambridge, New York, Melbourne, Madrid, Cape Town, Singapore, São Paulo

Cambridge University Press
The Edinburgh Building, Cambridge CB2 2RU, UK

Published in the United States of America by Cambridge University Press, New York

www.cambridge.org
Information on this title: www.cambridge.org/9780521894524

First published 2006

Printed in the United Kingdom at the University Press, Cambridge

A catalogue record for this publication is available from the British Library

ISBN-13 978-0-521-81539-0 hardback
ISBN-10 0-521-81539-8 hardback

ISBN-13 978-0-521-89452-4 paperback
ISBN-10 0-521-89452-2 paperback

To Ana and Lucia

CONTENTS

MAPS

ACKNOWLEDGMENTS

The debts incurred over the four years during which this book has taken – and changed – shape are numerous. In what follows I can only acknowledge a few specific and particularly important contributions. At the onset of this project is the work of many scholars in Southeast European countries, both historians and archaeologists. For all my efforts at synthesis, this book would not exist without their remarkable accomplishments and dedication. It goes without saying that I alone am responsible for the use that has been made in this book of their ideas and representations of the past.

Thanks for financial support are due to the Medieval Institute at the University of Notre Dame for the Mellon fellowship that made possible a valuable year of final research and first drafts. The Hilandar Research Library at the Ohio State University kindly opened its doors and provided the space and time for a brief visit before the manuscript entered its final stage. Recognition is also due to my students at the University of Florida, who first raised in seminars and senior colloquia some of the questions that I have tried to elucidate in the following pages. Among friends and colleagues who were particularly supportive of this work, I want to acknowledge Piotr Górecki, Maria Todorova, Jonathan Shepard, Roman Kovalev, Paul Barford, Cvetelin Stepanov, Joachim Henning, Alexandru Madgearu, and Paul Stephenson.

My largest thanks go to my wife, Lucia, for helping me see this book to completion, and to my daughter, Ana, for her patience and resilience.

NOTE ON TRANSLITERATION, NAMES, DATES, AND WORDS

The transliteration of personal and place names follows a modified version of the Library of Congress system. This is especially true for Bulgarian words: "Velbăzhd" instead of "Velbuzhd" and "Carevec" instead of "Tsarevets." As a consequence, and for the sake of uniformity, I have altered the standard transliteration for Ukrainian names, e.g., "Lenkyvcy" instead of "Lenkivtsi." In general, the geographical terminology closely follows the language in use in any given area. Commonly accepted equivalents are excepted from this rule. For example, "Cenad," "Durrës," and "Zadar" are favored over "Csanád," "Durazzo," and "Zara," but "Belgrade," "Bucharest," and "Corinth" are preferred to "Beograd," "Bucureşti," and "Korinthos." It is particularly difficult to be consistent about Greek forms, especially for names of emperors. In such cases, I have followed the established convention and used Constantine Porphyrogenitus and Andronicus, instead of Konstantine Porphyrogennetos and Andronikos. The same is true for several Slavic names. I have preferred Cyril to Kiril, John to Ivan, and Peter to Petar or Petăr. On the other hand, I strove to respect differing spellings, when anglicized versions have been long accepted as such. Thus the first Bulgarian emperor is Symeon, but his namesake, the first saint of Serbia, is Simeon.

Since all dates are from the medieval period, "AD" is not used unless necessary in the context. Where imprecise, years are given in the form "935/6" to indicate one year or the other, but as "1203 or 1208," when the options are separated by a longer span.

Certain terms are sometimes used in a technical sense, which is specific to the space and period considered in this book, not in their widely accepted meaning. Such is the case of the word "duke" to refer to a military commander or warlord. For example, the Croatian dukes of Bribir were local governors of that fortress and of the surrounding hinterland, but most importantly, local warlords. They should not be viewed as a part of a feudal hierarchy in the same sense as, for example, the Duke of Burgundy might be viewed. In much the same way, a Byzantine duke was a commander of troops, not a title referring to a position in the social and political hierarchy. The duke of Valona, for example, was a military governor appointed by the emperor. "Qagan" is the highest "imperial" title in medieval nomadic societies, while "khan" (qan) is a lesser title. I use "theme" in the sense of a (Byzantine) province, although the first attestation of the word in Byzantine sources seems to point to army units. "Roman" and "Byzantine" are used for distinct periods of time in the history of the Eastern Roman Empire, which has been arbitrarily divided by modern historians into an earlier and a later period, respectively, separated from each other by the reign of Emperor Heraclius (610–642).

CHRONOLOGY

499	Bulgar raid in the Balkans
502	Bulgar raid in Thrace and Illyricum
535	Emperor Justinian issued Novel 11 establishing the archbishopric of Iustiniana Prima; Gepid–Hunnic alliance for raids into the Balkan provinces of the Empire
536	Creation of the *quaestura exercitus* combining Balkan provinces with rich provinces in the Aegean and the eastern Mediterranean region
539	Bulgar raid devastated the northern and northeastern regions of the Balkans
545	First Sclavene raid of the northern Balkans
547	Gepids defeated by the Lombard and Byzantine troops
551/2	Gepids defeated by the Lombards
558	Cutrigur invasion of the Balkans that reached the Long Walls near Constantinople; Avar envoys arrived in Constantinople
568	Annihilation of the Gepid kingdom; the beginning of the Avar conquest of the Carpathian Basin
578	Avars raided the Sclavene settlements in Walachia
581–4	Four-year Sclavene invasion of the Balkans
582	Avars conquered Sirmium
583	Migration of three groups of steppe people (Tarniakh, Kotzager, and Zabender) into the Avar qaganate

586	Sclavenes and other barbarians besieged Thessalonica; Roman troops defeated the Avars near Adrianople
592	Avars conquered a number of cities on the Black Sea coast and defeated the Roman troops in the hinterland of Constantinople
595	Roman troops crossed the Danube against the Avars
596	Roman troops under Priscus defeated an Avar army in the southern region of the qaganate and killed the qagan's four sons
599–600	Byzantine troops devastated the southern regions of the Avar qaganate
601	Avar general Apsich attacked the Roman troops in the Iron Gates sector of the Danube frontier
602	Avar general Apsich attacked the Antes in the Lower Danube region; revolt of the Roman troops on the Danube frontier that led to the demise of Maurice and the rise to power of Phocas
610	Sclavene raid into Istria
615/6	Sclavenes besieged Thessalonica
617/8	Avars besieged Thessalonica
623	Avars ambushed Emperor Heraclius near the Long Walls of Constantinople
623/4	Samo led the rebellion of the Wends against the Avars
626	Avars besieged Constantinople
630	Rise of Great Bulgaria under Kubrat
631/2	Civil war within the Avar qaganate
c. 660	Khazars defeated the Bulgars; the collapse of Great Bulgaria
c. 670	Asparukh led the Bulgar migration to Oglos north of the Danube
677	Rynchines, Sagudates, and Drugubites besieged Thessalonica
678	Avar envoys brought gifts to Constantinople; Byzantine campaign against the *Sklaviniai* of southern Macedonia
680	Sermesianoi under Kouber moved out of the Avar qaganate and into the environs of Thessalonica

680/1	Bulgars under Asparukh defeated the Byzantine troops sent against them; the creation of the Bulgar polity in the Balkans
688/9	Byzantine troops defeated by Bulgars near Philippopolis; Justinian II settled the "Scythians" around the gorges of the river Struma
695	Leontius appointed first military governor of Hellas
705	Tervel, the ruler of the Bulgars, formed an alliance with Emperor Justinian II; Tervel proclaimed Caesar
716	Peace treaty between Byzantium and Bulgaria established the boundary in Thrace and regulated trade relations
723	St. Willibald stopped in Monemvasia en route to the Holy Land
725	Rebellion of the theme of Hellas against Emperor Leo III
740	Duke Boruth ruled over Carantania
745/6	Plague from Sicily spread to Monemvasia and the theme of Hellas; Duke Boruth died and his son, Cacatius, was recognized Prince of the Carantanians
752	Chietmar ruled over Carantania
755	Emperor Constantine V began fortifying towns in Thrace; Syrians and Armenians settled on the Byzantine frontier with Bulgaria
759	Constantine V campaigned in Macedonia; Byzantine attack on Bulgaria on both land and sea
761/2	Coup d'état in Bulgaria brought Telec to power
763	Byzantine invasion of Bulgaria; battle at Anchialos
764	Telec assassinated; Sivin sued for peace, but was overthrown; Paganos came in person before the emperor to sue for peace
765	Byzantine attack on Bulgaria; the Byzantine troops burned villages in northern Bulgaria and aristocratic courts on the river Ticha
766	Emperor Constantine V moved artisans from Hellas to Constantinople
769	Chietmar died; Carantanian rebellion against the Bavarians

772	Bavarian intervention in Carantania brought Waltunc to power
774	Byzantine campaign mounted against Bulgaria; Telerig sued for peace, but invaded Macedonia and killed the Byzantine agents in Bulgaria; Istria occupied by Frankish troops
783	Byzantine troops under Staurakios campaigned successfully in Peloponnesus
784	Empress Irene toured Thrace as far west as Philippopolis; Beroe rebuilt and renamed Irenopolis
788	Carantania within the Frankish kingdom
799	Akameros, the *archon* of the Slavs of Velzetia, supported Emperor Constantine V's sons against Empress Irene
c. 800	Creation of the theme of Macedonia
c. 802	Krum came to power in Bulgaria
805	Slavs of Peloponnesus attacked Patras
809	Krum attacked Serdica
810	A Byzantine fleet reestablished the Byzantine control over Dalmatia and Venice
811	Byzantine campaign against Bulgaria; Emperor Nicephorus I killed in a battle in a pass across the Stara Planina range of mountains
813	Krum was offered peace; the Bulgars conquered Mesembria and attacked Constantinople; battle of Versinikia
814	Krum died; Dukum and Ditzevg ruled Bulgaria; the beginning of the persecution of Christians in Bulgaria
816	Byzantine attack on Mesembria
818	Envoys from the Timociani and from Borna, the "duke of Dalmatia and Liburnia", appeared at the court of Louis the Pious in Herstal
819	Liudewit attacked Borna
820	Frankish armies devastated Liudewit's territory
821	Liudewit fled from Sisak to the Serbs; Omurtag intervened in the civil war between Emperor Michael III and Thomas the Slav

822	Two Bulgar embassies to Emperor Louis the Pious demanded the rectification of the Bulgar–Frankish frontier
826/7	Birth of Constantine-Cyril; Bulgar expedition against the Slavic clients of the Franks in the Lower Drava region
829	A Bulgar fleet of boats attacked Frankish estates on the Drava River
831	Omurtag died; Malamir became ruler of Bulgaria
832	Bulgar envoys brought an offer of peace to Emperor Louis the Pious; Prince Enravotas killed at the order of Malamir because of his Christian beliefs
836	Malamir died; Persian became ruler of Bulgaria
836/7	First Magyar raid in the Lower Danube region; Slavic rebellion against the Byzantine rule in the environs of Thessalonica
839	A Venetian fleet destroyed the encampments of the pirates on the Neretva
842/3	Constantine-Cyril arrived in Constantinople
846	Godescalc of Orbais arrived at the court of Trpimir, the duke of the Croats
852	First charter mention of Trpimir, the duke of the Croats; Persian died and Boris became ruler of Bulgaria
860	Constantine-Cyril and Methodius sent as Byzantine envoys to the Khazar court in Itil; Mutimir of Serbia defeated the troops sent by Boris of Bulgaria and captured his son Vladimir
863	Constantine-Cyril and Methodius' mission to Moravia
864	Byzantine troops landed at Mesembria; Boris accepted baptism with Emperor Michael III as his sponsor
865	Arab pirates besieged Dubrovnik; Bulgar embassies to Rome and Louis the German; Bishop Formosus of Porto arrived in Bulgaria
865/6	Rebellion of the Bulgar aristocrats against Boris's conversion to Christianity
867	Formosus returned to Rome; Grimuald, the bishop of Bomarzo, arrived in Bulgaria

869	Constantine-Cyril died in Rome; a papal embassy crossed Bulgaria on its way to Constantinople
c. 870	Creation of the theme of Dalmatia; the first archbishop of Bulgaria appointed by the patriarch of Constantinople; the expulsion of Grimuald from Bulgaria
871	Construction of the Church of St. John the Baptist in Athens completed
873	Domagoj mentioned in a letter from Pope John VIII
873/4	Construction of the Church of the Holy Virgin at Skripou completed
c. 875	Construction of the Great Basilica in Pliska completed
876	Domagoj died; Sedesclav became Duke of the Croats
876/7	Construction of the Church of St. Gregory the Theologian in Thebes completed
879	Branimir became Duke of the Croats
880	St. Elias the Younger arrived in Sparta; birth of St. John of Rila
881/2	On his way to Constantinople from Moravia, St. Methodius met a "king of the Hungarians"
885	The expulsion of Methodius' disciples from Moravia following his death; Clement, Naum, and Angelarius arrived in Bulgaria; Prince Oleg of Kiev attacked the Tivercians on the Dniester River
888	St. Elias the Younger and his disciple Daniel came to Patras; Symeon returned to Bulgaria from Constantinople
889	Boris abdicated in favor of his son Vladimir
890	Muncimir became Duke of the Croats; Vladimir launched a new persecution of Christians in an attempt to restore paganism
892	King Arnulf of Carinthia asked Vladimir to stop the sales of salt to the Moravians
893	The council of Pliska declared Vladimir deposed in favor of his brother Symeon; Clement of Ohrid appointed Bishop of Velika; Naum became Bishop of Ohrid

895	Construction of the church in Uzdolje near Knin completed
896	Battle of Bulgarophygon; beaten by the Pechenegs, the Magyars moved into the Carpathian Basin
897	Peace established between Byzantium and Bulgaria
c. 900	Khrabr composed *On the Letters*
901	Magyar raid into Carantania; Arab pirates sacked Demetrias
904	Arab pirates sacked Thessalonica
905	Naum, Bishop of Ohrid, died
913	Symeon received a crown from Patriarch Nicholas of Constantinople
916	St. Clement of Ochrid died
917	The Pechenegs' attack on Bulgaria failed; Peter, son of Gojnik, attacked Symeon together with the Magyars; battle of Anchialos
c. 920	Tomislav became King of the "province of the Croats and of the Dalmatian regions"
921	Milings and Ezerites rebelled against the Byzantine rule in Peloponnesus; Zacharias returned to Serbia with Bulgarian support
924	Symeon met Emperor Romanus Lecapenus in Constantinople
925	First synod of Split
927	Papal legates arrived in Croatia to mediate a peace between Croats and Bulgarians; the archbishop of Bulgaria elevated to the status of patriarch; Symeon died; Peter became Emperor of the Bulgars
928	Second synod of Split
930/1	Foundation of the Monastery of Rila
931	Časlav became ruler of Serbia and began to bring back the Serbian refugees from neighboring countries
c. 940	Emperor Peter of Bulgaria wrote to Patriarch Theophylact of Constantinople asking for advice about the outbreak of heresy in Bulgaria

941	Testament of St. John of Rila for his monastery
943	Magyar raid into Thrace
946	St. John of Rila died
948	Magyar chieftain Bulcsu baptized in Constantinople with Emperor Constantine VII Porphyrogenitus as sponsor
952	Duchy of Istria incorporated into Bavaria
953	First mention of the march of Carniola
958	Athanasios, the founder of the Great Lavra, arrived on Mount Athos
966	Bulgarian envoys arrived at Constantinople to collect the annual tribute; Emperor Nicephorus II attacked Bulgaria
968	Rus' troops of Prince Sviatoslav of Kiev blockaded Dristra and took Pereiaslavec
969	Peter died; Boris II became Emperor of the Bulgars
c. 970	St. Nikon the Metanoiete arrived in Sparta; the decree of Emperor John Tzimiskes for the monastic communities on Mount Athos (Tragos)
971	Byzantine campaign against Prince Sviatoslav and his Rus' troops in Bulgaria
972	Emperor Otto I granted Isola to the Venetian doge Peter Candiano IV
973	Emperor Otto II donated land near Kranj to the archbishop of Freising
976	Emperor Otto II separated Carinthia from Bavaria, with Istria as a march under Carinthian rule; Queen Helena of Croatia died; the revolt of the Kometopouloi in Macedonia; Samuel sacked Larisa and removed the relics of St. Achilleus
980	First mention of a count of Ptuj
985	Samuel took Larisa
990	Patriarch of Bulgaria moved to Ohrid
997	Samuel proclaimed Emperor of the Bulgarians; Bulgarians attacked Ulcinj and devastated the entire Dalmatian coast from Duklja to Zadar; Samuel transferred the relics of St. Tryphon from Kotor to Ohrid

1001	Emperor Basil II conquered Serdica and reoccupied Preslav, Pliska, and Pereiaslavec
1002	Byzantine troops took Vidin; Samuel attacked Adrianople
1003	Samuel defeated near Skopje
1004	Bled granted to the bishop of Brixen by Emperor Henry II
1009	Foundation of the bishopric of Alba Iulia
1014	Battle of Kleidion; Samuel died; Gabriel Radoslav proclaimed emperor as Romanus Symeon
1015	Romanus Symeon murdered by John Vladislav
1017	Byzantine embassy to the Pechenegs north of the Danube River
1018	John Vladislav died; the beginning of the Byzantine occupation of Bulgaria
c. 1020	Deacon Maio completed the Beneventan manuscript of the Zagreb Psalter; mosaic decoration of the Church of St. Luke at Steiris completed
1023	Foundation of the Abbey of St. Benedict on the island of Lokrum
1027	Constantine Diogenes defeated the Pechenegs
1028	Frescoes of the Church of Panagia ton Chalkeon in Thessalonica completed
1030	St. Gerald became bishop of Cenad
1032	Pecheneg raid into the Balkans
1034	Piraeus sacked by Harald Hardrada
1036	Dobronas, the governor of Zadar and Split, traveled to Constantinople; Pecheneg raid into the Balkans that destroyed Dinogetia
1037	First Greek-speaking archbishop appointed in Ohrid
1039	Ljutovid mentioned as ruler of Zahumlje
1040	Revolt of Peter Delian in Belgrade; Bulgarians occupied Demetrias
1043	Stefan Vojislav, ruler of Duklja, died; revolt of George Maniakes in Dyrrachion

1044	Foundation of the Abbey of St. Peter in Osor
1045	Kegen crossed the Danube with his Pechenegs
1046	Tyrach's Pechenegs invaded the Balkans
1048	Confraternity of the icon of the Holy Virgin in Thebes
c. 1050	Construction of the St. Sophia Cathedral in Ohrid completed
1053	Michael proclaimed King of Duklja; Byzantine peace with the Pechenegs of the northern Balkans
1059	Hungarian and Pecheneg marauders defeated near Serdica
1060	Provincial council in Split
1064	Foundation of the Abbey of St. John the Baptist in Trogir; Oghuz invasion of the Balkans
1066	Peter Krešimir IV proclaimed "King of Croatia and Dalmatia"; rebellion of the Vlachs in Larisa
1068	Pecheneg raid into Transylvania; battle of Chiraleş
1069	Foundation of the Abbey of St. Peter In the Village near Split
1070	Arab pirates sacked Demetrias
1071	Hungarians attacked and occupied Belgrade and sacked Niš
1072	Rebellion of Tatous, Sesthlav, and Satzas in Paradounavon
1073	Rebellion of George Vojteh in Skopje
1074	Amico of Giovinazzo invaded Dalmatia; coronation of King Zvonimir of Croatia
1075	Council of Split banned the use of Slavic in the liturgy
1076	Carniola and Istria granted to the patriarch of Aquileia by Emperor Henry IV
1077	Michael of Duklja obtained the banner of St. Peter from Rome in recognition for his royal title; Pecheneg raid into Thrace
1078	Revolt of Nicephorus Basilakes in Dyrrachion; revolt of the Paulicians in Philippopolis; first Cuman raid into the Balkans

1080	Foundation of the Monastery of the Mother of God of Mercy in Veljusa
1081	Robert Guiscard attacked Dyrrachion; Byzantine troops under Emperor Alexios I Comnenus defeated at Dyrrachion by the Normans
1082	Bohemond of Taranto occupied Pelagonia, Trikkala, and Kastoria and laid siege to Larisa; foundation of the Monastery of the Mother of God Petritzonitissa in Bachkovo
1083	Byzantine troops recovered Kastoria; Paulician revolt in Philippopolis
1087	Pecheneg–Cuman raid into the Balkans; Alexios I Comnenus attacked Dristra
1088	Battle of Markellai
1089	Anti-pope Clement III raised the bishop of Bar to the status of Archbishop of Dioclea
1091	Cuman raid into Transylvania; battle at Levunion
1092	Dukljan raid into Byzantine territories; Cuman raid into Thrace
1096	Passage through the Balkans of the pilgrims led by Walter the Penniless and Peter the Hermit
1097	Peter, the last Croatian ruler, defeated in the Kapela Mountains; passage through the Balkans of the crusading army led by Godfrey of Bouillon
1098	Passage through Croatia of the crusaders led by Raymond de St. Gilles
1100	Crusaders from Lombardy plundered the environs of Philippopolis
1105	Hungarian invasion of Dalmatia
1108	Treaty of Devol
1111	Mercurius first mentioned as "Prince of Transylvania"
1114	Cumans attacked Vidin; the Byzantine troops crossed the Danube to fight the Cumans in their own territory
1115	Venetian authority over the islands of the Kvarner Bay restored
1116	Venetian control established over Zadar

1122 Cuman invasion of Thrace; Emperor John II Comnenus attacked the Serbs

c. 1131 Korčula Codex completed

1135 Foundation of the Cistercian Abbey of Stična

1137 First Hungarian expedition into Bosnia

1147 Crusaders under Emperor Conrad III camped outside Philippopolis; the passage through the Balkans of the crusading army led by King Louis VII of France; Normans sacked Corinth and Thebes

1148 Cuman invasion of Thrace; Emperor Manuel I Comnenus attacked the Cumans north of the Danube

1149 Emperor Manuel I Comnenus attacked Uroš II of Serbia

1150 Battle on the Tara River; Byzantine troops devastated Frangochorion

1153 Andronicus Comnenus appointed duke of Niš and Braničevo

1154 Manuel I restored to power Uroš II; the bishopric of Zadar elevated to the status of archbishopric

1159 Ivan Rostislavich of Galicia crossed Moldavia together with his Cuman allies; first mention of a Venetian count of Zadar

1160 Foundation of the Carthusian Abbey of Žiče

1163 Stephen IV ruler of the southern region of Hungary

1164 Andronicus Comnenus captured by the Vlachs in Moldavia; Stephen IV established support in Sirmium

1165 Rabbi Benjamin of Tudela visited Thebes and Thessalonica; Stephen III of Hungary reestablished Hungarian control over Sirmium and Semlin, both retaken shortly thereafter by the Byzantines; Hungarian control reestablished over Zadar; Desa, the Serbian *zhupan*, tried in front of the emperor; Tihomir, Sracimir, Miroslav, and Nemanja appointed co-rulers of Serbia

1166 Byzantine attack on Transylvania; Nemanja attacked Kotor and Tihomir's domain in Serbia; construction of the cathedral Church of St. Tryphon in Kotor completed

1167 Treaty between Nicholas Kačić, duke of Omiš, and Kotor

1168 Foundation of the Benedictine Abbey at Sâniob

1169 Templars granted the Vrana Abbey near Zadar

1172 Manuel I attacked Nemanja, who was taken prisoner and paraded in Constantinople

1175 Raynerius, Bishop of Split, traveled to Constantinople; frescoes in the Church of St. Chrysogonus in Zadar completed

1176 First mention of the *voevode* of Transylvania

1180 King Béla III of Hungary occupied Sirmium and Frangochorion; Hungarian troops sacked Serdica and removed the relics of St. John of Rila

1181 Nemanja attacked Kotor and imposed his rule on the Dalmatian coast

1182 First mention of a Hungarian count of Dalmatia

1185 Normans sacked Thessalonica; revolt of the Vlach brothers Peter and Asen

1187 Byzantine army defeated near Beroe by the Cumans

1189 Passage of the crusaders under Emperor Frederick I Barbarossa through the Balkans; Nemanja and Peter established contacts with Emperor Frederick promising military assistance

1190 Emperor Isaac II Angelos attacked Nemanja

1191 First mention of the "Church of the Saxons" in Transylvania

1192 Conflict between Peter and Asen

1195 Asen took Serdica and transferred the relics of St. John of Rila to Tărnovo

1196 Nemanja abdicated in favor of his son Stefan; Asen and Peter died

1197 Ioannitsa (Kaloyan) became ruler of the Vlach and Bulgarian rebels in the northern Balkans

1198 Nemanja took the monastic vows and moved to Mount Athos

1199 Vlachs and Cumans raided Thrace; Nemanja-Simeon died

1200	Byzantine campaign against Ivanko
1202	Crusaders took Zara (Zadar); conflict between Nemanja's sons Vukan and Stefan
1203	Stefan restored to power in Raška with the assistance of Ioannitsa's troops
1204	Crusaders took Constantinople; Renier de Trith received Philippopolis as fief; Boniface of Montferrat began the conquest of Greece; Ioannitsa crowned king in Tărnovo by the papal legate
1205	William de Champlitte and Geoffrey of Villehardouin began the conquest of Peloponnesus; battle at Koundoura; William de Champlitte proclaimed Prince of Achaia; battle of Adrianople; Emperor Baldwin of Constantinople died in Bulgarian captivity
1207	Boniface of Montferrat killed by Cuman marauders; Ioannitsa murdered by his men under the walls of Thessalonica
1208	Foundation of the Carthusian Abbey at Jurklošter; Geoffrey of Villehardouin proclaimed Prince of Achaia; Bulgarian troops under Boril defeated by Emperor Henry of Constantinople
1209	Parliament in Ravennika confirmed the Latin lordships in Morea; Demetrius crowned King of Thessalonica
1212	Church synod in Tărnovo for the condemnation of the Bogomil heresy; a rebellion in Vidin against Boril caused the intervention of Hungarian troops from Transylvania; Teutonic Knights brought to Transylvania
1213	Michael Dukas of Epirus took Dyrrachion
1214	Michael Dukas died; Theodore Dukas became ruler of Epirus
1217	Templars granted the castle of Šibenik; Theodore Dukas of Epirus defeated and killed Peter of Courtenay; Stefan crowned first king of Serbia by the papal legate
1218	John Asen returned to Bulgaria and overthrew Boril
1219	Foundation of the autonomous archbishopric of Serbia
1221	Church synod in Žiča summoned by Archbishop Sava

1224 Theodore Dukas took Thessalonica

1225 Peter of Hum elected Prince of Split; Teutonic Knights expelled from Transylvania

1227 Theodore Dukas crowned emperor; the Cuman chieftain Boricius accepted baptism in Transylvania

1228 Creation of the bishopric of Cumania

1230 Battle at Klokotnica

1231 Hungarian troops occupy Niš and Braničevo

1232 Creation of the Hungarian march of Severin

1234 Construction of the monastery church at Mileševa completed; foundation of the Cistercian Abbey of Kostanjevica

1236 John Asen and John Vatatzes besieged Constantinople

1237 Theodore Dukas released from Bulgarian captivity; John Asen attacked the Nicaean troops in Tzurullon; a plague outbreak in Tărnovo forced John Asen to make peace with John Vatatzes; Archbishop Sava of Serbia died

1238 John Asen allowed the crusaders recruited by Baldwin II to pass through the Bulgarian lands on their way to Constantinople

1241 John Asen died; Mongol invasion of Hungary

1242 Serbia and Bulgaria devastated by the Mongol troops of Kadan

1243 Uroš I crowned king of Serbia

1244 Matthew Ninoslav, *ban* of Bosnia, was elected Prince of Split; privilege of King Andrew II of Hungary in favor of the Saxon "guests" of Transylvania (*Andreanum*)

1246 Nicaean troops occupy Thessalonica; Michael II Dukas seized Ohrid

1247 John Plano Carpini appointed Archbishop of Bar; charter of King Béla IV of Hungary in favor of the Hospitallers mentioned Vlach polities between the Carpathian Mountains and the Danube

1249 Conquest of Peloponnesus completed after Monemvasia was taken

ABBREVIATIONS

AAASH	*Acta Archaeologica Academiae Scientiarum Hungaricae*
AB	*Archaeologia Bulgarica*
ABSA	*Annual of the British School at Athens*
AEMA	*Archivum Eurasiae Medii Aevi*
AMS	*Annual of Medieval Studies at the CEU*
BF	*Byzantinische Forschungen*
BHR	*Bulgarian Historical Review*
BMGS	*Byzantine and Modern Greek Studies*
BS	*Balkan Studies*
BZ	*Byzantinische Zeitschrift*
CA	*Cahiers Archéologiques*
CCM	*Cahiers de Civilisation Médiévale Xe–XIIe Siècles*
EB	*Etudes Balkaniques*
EBPB	*Etudes Byzantines et Post-Byzantines*
GSU	*Godishnik na Sofiiskiia Universitet "Kliment Okhridski." Istoricheski Fakultet*
H&M	*Histoire et Mésure*
IAI	*Izvestiia na Arkheologicheskiia Institut*
IIBI	*Izvestiia na Instituta za Bălgarska Istoriia*
INMV	*Izvestiia na Narodniia Muzei Varna*
JOB	*Jahrbuch der österreichischen Byzantinistik*
MGH	Monumenta Germaniae Historica. Scriptores rerum Germanicarum in usum scholarum separatim editi
MGH Epist.	Monumenta Germaniae Historica. Epistolae

MGH Poet.	Monumenta Germaniae Historica. Poetae Latini Medii Aevi
MGH SS	Monumenta Germaniae Historica. Scriptores
MGH SS rer. Germ.	Monumenta Germaniae Historica. Scriptores rerum Germanicarum
PG	Patrologiae cursus completus. Series Graeca
PL	Patrologiae cursus completus. Series Latina
REB	*Revue des Etudes Byzantines*
RES	*Revue des Etudes Slaves*
RESEE	*Revue des Etudes Sud-Est Européennes*
RRH	*Revue Roumaine d'Histoire*
RVM	*Rad Vojvodanskih Muzeja*
SCIVA	*Studii şi Cercetări de Istorie Veche şi Arheologie*
SEER	*Slavonic and East European Review*
SG	*Studi Gregoriani*
SL	*Starobălgarska Literatura*
SP	*Starohrvatska Prosvjeta*
T&M	*Travaux et Mémoires du Centre de Recherches d'Histoire et Civilisation Byzantines*
VV	*Vizantiiskii Vremennik*
WMBHL	*Wissenschaftliche Mitteilungen des bosnisch-herzegowinischen Landesmuseums*
ZFF	*Zbornik Filozofskog Fakulteta. Beogradski Univerzitet*
ZLU	*Zbornik za Likovne Umetnosti*
ZRVI	*Zbornik Radova Vizantološkog Instituta*

INTRODUCTION

This book is an attempt to explore the fundamental dimensions of the medieval history of Southeastern Europe from *c.* 500 to 1250, broadly the period between the last century of Roman power in the Balkans and the Mongol invasion of Eastern Europe. The primary aim of the book is to provide an overview of the historical developments that characterized a region of Europe about which there is generally little knowledge outside a small number of scholars with specific, often narrowly defined research interests. In the last few decades, the study of medieval societies in Eastern Europe has moved in new and significant directions. The successful use of interdisciplinary approaches, the growth of medieval archaeology, the revived interest in the history of the Church, the development of gender studies, and the encouragement to engage with comparative history have all informed research into the medieval past of Eastern Europe. The following chapters will make extensive use of the results of these new lines of research, in the process delineating a general conclusion that is worth stating plainly from the very beginning: medieval Southeastern Europe was in many ways similar to other parts of Europe, to a degree far greater than most scholars have so far been willing to admit. The secondary purpose of this book is therefore to relate to each other developments in the southeastern region of the European continent and to consider their implications for our understanding of the Middle Ages. The book is therefore concerned with moving back from the modern constructs and possible misconceptions deriving from attempts to draw lines of contrast against which either

"Western" or national medieval histories were defined. During the first half of the twentieth century, many historians in those countries in Eastern Europe that had either emerged or been enlarged at the end of World War I reinforced, rather than challenged, such misconceptions. A Polish historian, Każimierz Tymieniecki (1887–1968), first addressed the problem of the medieval history of Eastern Europe at the Sixth International Congress of Historical Sciences, held in Oslo in 1928. By Eastern Europe, Tymieniecki meant the regions east of the Elbe, namely Poland, to the exclusion of both Scandinavia and the Balkans. Scandinavia was still perceived as part of the "West," but the Balkans were not granted the status of a fully European region.

WHAT IS SOUTHEASTERN EUROPE?

While the idea of "Eastern Europe" originated in the intellectual milieu of the Enlightenment, Southeastern Europe as a geographical expression has a much more recent history. During the first half of the nineteenth century, the preferred name for that region of the continent was "European Turkey," which included Greece (even after that country gained its independence in 1829), as well as the Romanian Principalities, Walachia and Moldavia, technically not part of the Ottoman Empire. Several other phrases have subsequently been coined, ranging from the "Greek–Slavic world" to the "Balkans," a name that proved remarkably resistant, perhaps because of its derogatory meaning introduced shortly before and during World War I. On the eve of the Congress of Berlin (1878), a new term appeared, "Southeastern Europe," which seems to have been initially used mainly by scholars interested in comparative linguistics, and especially in common elements to be discovered in such languages as Romanian, Bulgarian, Albanian, and Greek. In other words, the use of the phrase Southeastern Europe is linked to some of the earliest attempts at identifying what is now known as the Balkan linguistic unity, the world's most famous linguistic example of language contact.[1] The phrase was quickly adopted in Austria, especially by statesmen and

[1] A. Drace-Francis, "Zur Geschichte des Südosteuropakonzepts bis 1914," in *Europa und die Grenzen im Kopf*, ed. by K. Kaser, D. Gramshammer-Hohl, and R. Pichler (Klagenfurt and Celovec: Wieser, 2003), p. 277. For the Balkan linguistic unity, see now I. Sawicka, *The Balkan Sprachbund in the Light of Phonetic Features* (Warsaw: Wydawnictwo Energeia, 1997); J. Lindstedt, "Linguistic Balkanization: contact-induced change by mutual reinforcement," in *Languages in Contact*, ed. by D. Gilbers, J. A. Nerbonne, and T. de Graaf (Amsterdam and Atlanta: Rodopi, 2000), pp. 231–246.

diplomats, to refer to the region between the Carpathian Mountains, the Dniester River, and the Aegean, Black, and Adriatic Seas, a region of vital importance for the expansion of the Austrian–Hungarian Empire around 1900. Thirty years later, the phrase was similarly used to express Nazi political aspirations in that region.[2]

The first course of Southeast European history was offered at the University of Vienna in 1912 and was taught by a Romanian, Ion Nistor (1876–1962), later to become a renowned historian of the Middle Ages.[3] Following that appointment, another Romanian historian, Nicolae Iorga (1871–1940), founded in Bucharest an Institute of Southeast European Studies (1914), and later a periodical, *Revue historique du sud-est européen* (1922), dedicated to the study of the Balkan region, which hitherto both historians and politicians had excluded from Europe. Iorga's goal was to remove the stain of the derogatory meaning attached to the phrase "Balkans," while promoting a certain foreign policy at a time of growing Romanian influence in the region.[4] To Iorga, the history of the Southeast European countries revealed a number of similarities strikingly reminiscent of the Balkan linguistic unity.[5]

[2] M. Todorova, "Historische Vermächtnisse als Analysekategorie. Der Fall Südosteuropas," in *Europa und die Grenzen im Kopf*, ed. by Karl Kaser, Dagmar Gramshammer-Hohl, and Robert Pichler (Klagenfurt and Celovec: Wieser, 2003), pp. 227–252. According to Todorova, the Nazi use has completely discredited the phrase, to which one should now prefer the "Balkans," an idea for which see her *Imagining the Balkans* (New York: Oxford University Press, 1997).

[3] A. Pippidi, "Pour l'histoire du premier Institut des etudes sud-est européennes en Roumanie (I)," *RESEE*, vol. 16 (1978), p. 141.

[4] To be sure, in 1914 Iorga did not shy away from employing the phrase "Balkans," which he employed, however, in a positive sense, otherwise covered by the supposedly more neutral "Southeastern Europe." See N. Iorga, *Histoire des états balcaniques à l'époque moderne* (Bucharest: C. Sfetea, 1914) and *L'origine des idées d'indépendance balcanique* (Paris: J. Gamber, 1927). Moreover, to contemporary Yugoslav scholars, Iorga appeared as one of the most important historians *of the Balkans*. See M. Budimir and P. Skok, "But et signification des études balkaniques," *Revue internationale des études balkaniques*, vol. 1 (1934), p. 7.

[5] N. Iorga, *Cinq conférences sur le Sud-Est de l'Europe* (Bucharest: P. Suru, 1924) and *Le caractère commun des institutions du Sud–Est de l'Europe* (Paris: J. Gamber, 1929). For Iorga's attitude towards Romania's intervention in the Second Balkan War, see his *Notes d'un historien relatives aux événements des Balcans* (Bucharest: Charles Göbl, 1913). See V. Cândea, "Nicolas Iorga, historien de l'Europe du Sud-Est," in *Nicolas Iorga, l'homme et l'œuvre, à l'occasion du centième anniversaire de sa naissance*, ed. by D. M. Pippidi (Bucharest: Editions de l'Académie de la République Socialiste de Roumanie, 1971), pp. 157–249; Pippidi, "Pour l'histoire du premier Institut," pp. 147–156.

The study of Southeastern Europe survived both the dramas unfolding during World War II in that region and its subsequent political transformation. Institutes and associations for the study of Southeast European history now exist in many capital cities in the region, which have one after the other hosted the International Congress of Southeast European Studies. In addition, there is a journal entirely dedicated to that same topic, the *Revue des études sud-est européennes* published by the institute Iorga had founded in Bucharest. Despite the fact that few historians writing in English adopted this terminology, to which they seem to prefer the more popular "Balkans,"[6] the phrase "Southeastern Europe" is also used in the historiography of the region in Iorga's sense.[7] However, there is no consensus as to whether or not the phrase is more than a historiographical construct. What seems to be well understood, however, is that the "Balkans" do not include Hungary, Romania, Moldova, and the southern regions of present-day Ukraine. By excluding Romania from the Balkans, Iorga may have reacted to the political divisions of the pre-World War I period and to their underlying assumption of Ottoman cultural and political traditions. In doing so, his goal may have been to hint at a much deeper past, namely the period during which the region was supposedly unified under Byzantine, not Ottoman, rule. But during the Middle Ages that part of Europe had no sharp boundaries, especially to the north.[8] As a consequence, any serious analysis of the medieval history of the region cannot leave out those territories in the Carpathian Basin, as well as north of the Danube River and of the Black Sea, which have never been incorporated into the Byzantine Empire. In that respect, Iorga was right: the Balkans are a region defined by mountains, both etymologically and geographically. Geographically, the scope of inquiry in this book is limited to the area traditionally viewed as the Balkan Peninsula and comprised between the Adriatic and Ionian Seas to the west, and the Aegean and Black Seas to the south and to the east.

[6] See J. V. A. Fine, *The Early Medieval Balkans. A Critical Survey from the Sixth to the Late Twelfth Century* (Ann Arbor: University of Michigan Press, 1983); and *The Late Medieval Balkans. A Critical Survey from the Late Twelfth Century to the Ottoman Conquest* (Ann Arbor: University of Michigan Press, 1987).

[7] See P. F. Sugar, *Southeastern Europe under Ottoman Rule, 1354–1804* (Seattle: University of Washington Press, 1977).

[8] For the problematic northern border of Southeastern Europe, see F. Valjavec, *Ausgewählte Aufsätze* (Munich: R. Oldenbourg, 1963), pp. 37–38.

However, the northern limit, the most difficult one to establish, was moved beyond the Danube River and the Carpathian Mountains, to include Transylvania, as well as, occasionally, the eastern and southern regions of the Carpathian Basin now divided between Hungary and Serbia. The reasons for this rather arbitrary definition of the geography of Southeastern Europe are essentially historical and will hopefully become clear in the following chapters. It must be stressed that there is nothing unique in this approach to the geography of the region, although only archaeologists of the Bronze Age and political analysts of late twentieth-century developments customarily treat the area in this way. Similarly, to the northeast, the limit is pushed into the steppe corridor stretching from the Lower Danube to the Dnieper River, to include the forest-steppe belt across the modern states of Romania, Moldova, and Ukraine. Without the steppe lands to the northeast, an area from which the Bulgar, Pecheneg, Cuman, and Mongol invasions originated, very little could be understood in terms of both military and cultural history of medieval Southeastern Europe.

SOURCES FOR THE MEDIEVAL HISTORY OF SOUTHEASTERN EUROPE

Much of what we know about the history of Southeastern Europe comes from sources written outside the region and only later by authors in that region. This is certainly the case of the Byzantine, Rus', or Hungarian chronicles, the Byzantine saint lives, the acts of church councils, the letters or the panegyrics written by and for Byzantine authors, all of which have been the traditional sources employed to write the medieval history of Southeastern Europe. By contrast, only recently has the evidence of archaeology, numismatics, and art history been incorporated into the traditional narrative.

Writing and literacy were introduced to the region from outside as part of the "cultural kit" accompanying the conversion to Christianity.[9] Chanceries began to function in the tenth century in Croatia

9 See, for example, P. Štih, "Začetki in razmah listinskega pismenstva na ozemlju Slovenije do konca 11. stoletja [The beginnings and the spread of writing in the Slovene lands until the eleventh century]," *Zgodovinski Časopis*, vol. 55 (2003), pp. 279–290.

and Bulgaria and in the eleventh century in Hungary.[10] However, no charter survives from early medieval Bulgaria, although leaden seals provide clear evidence of large-scale use of writing for both official documents and private correspondence. The practice of sealing documents was of course adopted from Byzantium, but then quickly adapted to the needs of the Bulgarian society. Several seals are known from Symeon and Peter, in addition to seals of archbishops and bishops of Bulgaria.[11] After the Byzantine conquest of Bulgaria in the late tenth century, the volume of written documents in use by the Byzantine administration increased considerably, as illustrated by the extraordinary find in Preslav of an archive of more than 350 seals of various military and fiscal officials of Byzantine Bulgaria.[12] Since seals bear the names and, sometimes, rank and office of their owners, in the absence of any other written sources, they can provide valuable information, for example for the reconstruction of the administrative and military hierarchy of the Byzantine provinces in seventh- to ninth-century Greece or in late tenth- to eleventh-century Bulgaria.[13] Although not dated, seals have numerous ornamental and epigraphic attributes that lend themselves to a stylistic analysis, which in turn can be used to infer the date of specific specimens on the basis of comparison with known seals attached to dated documents. Identical seals have been found at great distance from each other, a testimony to the relations their owners have established by correspondence with various other individuals, but besides imperial seals, very few other

[10] G. Győrffy, "Die Anfänge der ungarischen Kanzlei im 11. Jahrhundert," *Archiv für Diplomatik, Schriftgeschichte, Siegel- und Wappenkunde* 30 (1984), pp. 80–96; E. Fügedi, "Ai confini tra l'uso orale e l'uso scritto. La pratica della cancellaria in Ungheria," in *Spiritualità e lettere nella cultura italiana e ungherese del basso Medioevo*, ed. by S. Graccioto and C. Vasoli (Florence: Olschki, 1995), pp. 377–387. There are to date no studies of the Croatian, Bulgarian, and Serbian chanceries during the early Middle Ages.

[11] I. Iordanov, *Pechatite na preslavskite vladeteli* [The Seals of the Preslav Rulers] (Sofia: Izdatelstvo na Bălgarskata Akademiia na Naukite, 1993); and *Korpus na pechatite na srednovekovna Bălgariia* [The Corpus of Medieval Seals from Bulgaria] (Sofia: Agató, 2001).

[12] I. Iordanov, *Pechatite ot strategiiata v Preslav (971–1088)* [The Seals of the Preslav Military Province, 971–1088] (Sofia: Universitetsko izdatelstvo "Sv. Kliment Okhridski," 1993); and *Corpus of Byzantine Seals from Bulgaria. Part I* (Sofia: Agató, 2003).

[13] F. Curta, "L'administration byzantine dans les Balkans pendant la 'grande brèche': le témoignage des sceaux," *Bizantinistica* 6 (2004), pp. 155–189; A. Madgearu, "The military organization of Paradunavon," *Byzantinoslavica*, vol. 60 (1999), pp. 421–446.

seals have been found outside the area of their owner's competence or power.[14]

Archives existed in several monasteries that often kept copies of charters issued on their behalf by rulers. The largest archives are those of the monasteries on Mount Athos, which preserve many chrysobulls (imperial charters with golden seals) granting land property or privileges to the monks.[15] While only seventy-five documents can be dated before the early eleventh century, the archives at Mount Athos are particularly useful for the later period, especially for the twelfth and thirteenth centuries, when the monks enjoyed the generosity not only of the emperors in Constantinople, but also of Serbian and Bulgarian rulers. Outside the archives of Mount Athos, the survival of official documents pertaining to the economic history of medieval Southeastern Europe has been only accidental, as in the case of the land-tax register known as the Cadaster of Thebes.[16] In the absence of such documents, *typika* (monastic rules) or the testaments of founders of Byzantine and Bulgarian monasteries often provide a wealth of information for social and economic history.[17] Several Benedictine monasteries in Croatia have extensive cartularies, containing copies of charters issued by Croatian and Hungarian rulers. A good example is the cartulary of the Abbey of St. Peter In the

14 For an excellent discussion of seal circulation, see C. Morrisson and J.-C. Cheynet, "Lieux de trouvaille et circulation des sceaux," *Studies in Byzantine Sigillography*, vol. 2 (1990), pp. 105–136.

15 *Actes de Lavra*, vol. I (897–1178), ed. by G. Rouillard and P. Collomp (Paris: Pierre Lethielleux, 1937); vol. II (1204–1328), ed. by Paul Lemerle (Paris: Pierre Lethielleux, 1977); *Actes d'Iviron*, vol. I (to 1050), ed. by J. Lefort (Paris: Pierre Lethielleux, 1985); vol. II (1050–1204), ed. by J. Lefort, N. Oikonomides, H. Papachryssanthou, V. Kravari, and H. Métréveli (Paris: Pierre Lethielleux, 1990); vol. III (1204–1328), ed. by J. Lefort, N. Oikonomides, and D. Papachryssanthou (Paris: CNRS Editions, 1994); *Actes du Prôtaton*, ed. by D. Papachryssanthou (Paris: Pierre Lethielleux, 1975); *Actes de Vatopédi*, ed. by J. Bompaire, J. Lefort, V. Kravari, and C. Giros (Paris: CNRS Editions and Pierre Lethielleux, 2001); *Actes de Hilandar*, ed. by M. Živojinović, V. Kravari, and C. Giros (Paris: CNRS Editions and Pierre Lethielleux, 1998).

16 N. Svoronos, "Recherches sur le cadastre byzantin et la fiscalité aux XIe et XIIe siècles: le cadastre de Thèbes," *Bulletin de Correspondance Hellénique*, vol. 83 (1959), pp. 1–166. See also L. A. Neville, *Authority in Byzantine Provincial Society, 950–1100* (Cambridge: Cambridge University Press, 2004), pp. 171–172.

17 A great number of foundation documents in English translation have been published in *Byzantine Monastic Foundation Documents. A Complete Translation of the Surviving Founder's* Typika *and Testaments*, ed. by J. Thomas and A. C. Hero (Washington: Dumbarton Oaks Research Library and Collection, 2000).

Village, a monastery founded by a wealthy citizen of Split in the late eleventh century. Known as the Sumpetar Cartulary, this is in fact a collection of documents pertaining to donations to the monastery, either of land or of moveable property (such as slaves). It also contains a list of books in the abbey's library, many of which had been donated by the founder. Besides such valuable information for economic and social history, cartularies sometimes contain unexpected documents of cultural history.[18] For example, the Cartulary of the Convent of St. Mary in Zadar (Croatia) contains documents from a long period between 1066 and 1236, including a church hymn known as *Sanctus*, one of the earliest pieces of polyphonic singing in Eastern Europe.

A relatively large number of notarial documents survive in the Venetian archives that pertain to the history of the cities on the Adriatic coast and in Istria, which were under Venetian rule beginning with the eleventh century. However, the number of those documents that could be dated before *c.* 1250 is rather small.[19] Similarly, in Hungary most chapters and abbeys served as notarial institutions, known as "places of authentication," but most contracts or authentic copies written by clerics date from the late thirteenth and early fourteenth century.[20] However, even before that date, and as early as 1200, chapters provided valuable service for laymen in Hungary, who often took oaths in front of the clerics or accepted ordeals to be administered by them. Although no records of such transactions have been preserved for the chapters of Arad, Alba Iulia, or Bač, the minutes of 389 ordeals held at the chapter of Oradea between 1208 and 1235 form the so-called Oradea Register, one of the most remarkable documents of social history in medieval Transylvania.[21] The quantity of surviving charters is only a fraction of what the royal chanceries of

[18] *The Cartulary of the Benedictine Abbey of St. Peter of Gumay (Croatia), 1080–1187*, ed. by E. Pivčevic (Bristol: D. Arthur and Sons, 1984). See also V. Novak, *Zadarski kartular Samostana Svete Marije* [The Cartulary of the Convent of St. Mary in Zadar] (Zagreb: Jugoslavenska Akademija Znanosti i Umjetnosti, 1959).

[19] R. Härtel, "Notariat und Romanisierung. Das Urkundenwesen in Venetien und Istrien im Rahmen der politischen und der Kulturgeschichte (11.–13. Jh.)," in *Notariado público i documento privado de los origines al siglo XIV. Actas de VII Congreso Internacional de Diplomática, Valencia 1986*, vol. II (Valencia: Conselleria de Cultura, Educaciò i Ciéncia, 1989), pp. 879–926.

[20] I. Borsa, "Die Beurkundstätigkeit der glaubwürdigen Orte in Ungarn," in *Forschungen über Siebenbürgen und seine Nachbarn. Festschrift für Attila T. Szabó und Zsigmónd Jakó*, ed. by K. Benda, T. Bogyay, and H. Glassl (Munich: Trofenik, 1988), pp. 143–147. Notaries appear in Hungary only after 1300.

[21] *Regestrum varadinense examinum ferri candentis ordine chronologico digestum*, ed. by J. Karácsonyi and S. Borovszky (Budapest: V. Hornyánszky, 1903). The *Regestrum* has

Croatia and Hungary produced between the tenth and the thirteenth century.[22] In Hungary, for example, while about 10,000 documents survive from the 1200s, there are over 300,000 for the entire period between 1300 and 1526. This has been estimated as about one or two percent of what had once been issued, for most archives were destroyed during the Ottoman conquest of 1526, as well as during World War II. Even greater must have been the destruction of royal and monastic archives in medieval Bulgaria, for which no charters survive that could be dated before *c.* 1200.

The deeds of the ruler were occasionally celebrated in ninth-century Bulgaria in inscriptions carved in stone, using the Greek alphabet and the Greek language. Much can be gleaned from the titles used in such inscriptions referring to ranks of the aristocracy that are otherwise unknown from contemporary written sources.[23] Foundation or funerary inscriptions in Greek are also known from Byzantine Thrace.[24] During the fifth to seventh centuries, Greek was used along with Latin for funerary inscriptions found in Bulgaria and southeastern Romania, while all known ninth- to eleventh-century

been reprinted in *Documente privind istoria României. C. Transilvania* [Documents regarding the history of Romania. Series C: Transylvania], ed. by M. Roller, vol. I (Bucharest: Editura Academiei Republicii Populare România, 1951), pp. 37–147. See also I. Zajtay, "Le registre de Varad: un monument juridique du début du XIIIe siècle," *Revue historique du droit français et étranger*, vol. 32 (1954), 527–562.

22 *Codex diplomaticus regni Croatiae, Dalmatiae et Slavoniae*, ed. by T. Smičiklas, vols. I–IV (Zagreb: Ex officina Societatis Typograficae, 1904); *Diplomata Hungariae antiquissima, accedunt epistolae et acta ad historiam Hungariae pertinentia*, vol. I, ed. by G. Győrffy (Budapest: Academia Scientiarum Hungarica, 1992). See also A. Marinović, "Le caractère juridique de la charte (diplôme) royale pendant l'époque de la dynastie nationale croate (vers 839 à 1102 a.)," *Folia diplomatica*, vol. 2 (1976), 7–16.

23 V. Beshevliev, *Die protobulgarischen Inschriften* (Berlin: Akademie Verlag, 1963); and *Părvobălgarski nadpisi*, 2nd ed. (Sofia: Izdatelstvo na Bălgarskata Akademiia na Naukite, 1992). See also V. Beshevliev, "Les inscriptions protobulgares et leur portée culturelle et historique," *Byzantinoslavica*, vol. 32 (1971), pp. 35–51 (reprinted in *Bulgarisch-byzantinische Aufsätze. Collected Essays of Veselin Beshevliev* [London: Variorum Reprints, 1978], Essay IX).

24 C. Asdracha, "Inscriptions byzantines de la Thrace orientale et de l'île d'Imbros (XIIe–XVe siècles). Présentation et commentaire historique," *Arkhaiologikon Deltion*, vol. 43 (1988), pp. 219–291; "Inscriptions byzantines de la Thrace orientale (IXe–XIe siècles). Présentation et commentaire historique," *Arkhaiologikon Deltion*, vols. 44–46 (1989–1991), pp. 239–334; and "Inscriptions chrétiennes et protobyzantines de la Thrace orientale et de l'île d'Imbros (IIIe–VIIe siècles)," *Arkhaiologikon Deltion*, vols. 49–50 (1994–1995), pp. 279–356.

inscriptions found in Croatia are in Latin.[25] Beginning with the tenth century, Old Church Slavonic was also used for inscriptions written in either Glagolitic or Cyrillic script. While Cyrillic inscriptions have been found mainly within the borders of medieval Bulgaria, Glagolitic also appears in inscriptions found on islands of the Kvarner Bay in the northern Adriatic region or in Istria.[26] Finally, a few inscriptions in so-called East European (or Turkic) runes have been found on bone artifacts from Avar burials, the most famous of which is the Szarvas awl.[27] But as a rule, inscriptions often pose difficult problems of reading (particularly runic inscriptions)[28] or interpretation

[25] V. Beshevliev, *Spätgriechische und spätlateinische Inschriften aus Bulgarien* (Berlin: Akademie Verlag, 1964). For Romania, see E. Popescu, "Die spätgriechische Inschriften aus Klein-Skythien," *Dacia*, vol. 11 (1967), pp. 163–176; and *Inscripţiile greceşti şi latine din secolele IV–XIII descoperite în România* [Fourth- to Thirteenth-Century Greek and Latin Inscriptions from Romania] (Bucharest: Editura Academiei Republicii Socialiste România, 1976). For Latin inscriptions in medieval Croatia, see V. Delonga, *Inscriptions des souverains croates du IXe au XIe siècle* (Split: Museum of Croatian Archaeological Monuments, 1997).

[26] I. Goshev, *Starobălgarski glagolicheski i kirilski nadpisi ot IX i X v.* [Old Bulgarian Glagolitic and Cyrillic Inscriptions of the Ninth and Tenth Centuries] (Sofia: Izdatelstvo na Bălgarskata Akademiia na Naukite, 1961); R. Mihaljčić, L. Steindorff, and M. Hellmann, *Namentragende Steininschriften in Jugoslawien vom Ende des 7. bis zur Mitte des 13. Jahrhunderts* (Wiesbaden: Franz Steiner, 1982); K. Popkonstantinov and O. Kronsteiner, *Starobălgarski nadpisi. Altbulgarische Inschriften*, 2 vols. (Salzburg: Institut für Slawistik der Universität Salzburg, 1994 and 1997). Glagolitic inscriptions: K. Popkonstantinov and Al. Medynceva, "Za glagolicheskite nadpisi ot X v. [On the Glagolitic inscriptions of the tenth century]," *Arkheologiia*, vol. 24 (1982), pp. 27–37; B. Fučić, "Glagoljski natpisi [Glagolitic inscriptions]," *Slovo*, vol. 38 (1988), pp. 63–73. Cyrillic inscriptions: Ph. Malingoudis, *Die mittelalterlichen kyrillischen Inschriften der Hämus-Halbinsel. I. Die bulgarischen Inschriften* (Thessaloniki: Association hellénique d'études slaves, 1979).

[27] A. Róna-Tas, "Problems of the east European scripts with special regard to the newly found inscription of Szarvas," In *Popoli delle steppe: Unni, Avari, Ungari. Settimane di studio, Spoleto 23–29 aprile 1987*, vol. II (Spoleto: Presso la Sede del Centro, 1988), pp. 483–511; I. Juhász, "A new Avar period runic inscription from Szarvas," in *Cultural and Landscape Changes in South-East Hungary I. Reports on the Gyomaendröd Project*, ed. by S. Bökönyi (Budapest: Archaeological Institute of the Hungarian Academy of Sciences, 1992), pp. 379–382. Many of the short inscriptions on bone artifacts found in Avar burials turned out to be Soghdian. See J. Harmatta, "Sogdian inscriptions on Avar objects," *Acta Orientalia Academiae Scientiarum Hungaricae*, vol. 48 (1995), pp. 61–65.

[28] See E. Tryjarski, "Alte und neue Probleme der runenartigen Inschriften Europas. Ein Versuch der Entzifferung der Texte aus Murfatlar und Pliska," in *Runen, Tamgas und Graffiti aus Asien und Osteuropa*, ed. by K. Röhrborn and W. Veenker (Wiesbaden: Otto Harrassowitz, 1985), pp. 53–80.

(especially inscriptions in Bulgar with Greek letters).[29] They are also notoriously difficult to date, unless there is a precise date given in the text. For example, an inscription mentioning Duke Branimir of the Croats gives the date as *anno Domini* 888, a quite novel practice for that time, as AD dates are not known before 800.[30] In an inscription on a column in the Church of the Forty Holy Martyrs in Tărnovo, the Bulgarian emperor John Asen II speaks of himself as ruling over much of the Balkans, leaving only Constantinople (characteristically called "Car'grad," the imperial city) to the "Franks" (i.e., the Latins). The inscription was written in Old Church Slavonic with Cyrillic script and dates from 1230, the *anno Domini* equivalent to *anno mundi* 6738 given in the text of the inscription.[31] Even when the inscription does not mention a specific date, an approximate one can occasionally be inferred from its content. The Baška Tablet, a Glagolitic inscription written in a Slavic idiom closer to present-day Serbo-Croatian than to Old Church Slavonic, was initially part of an altar screen in the church of the Benedictine Abbey of Jurandvor on the island of Krk. The text of the inscription contains no date, but refers to a donation of a certain king named Zvonimir, who is otherwise known to have ruled between 1075 and 1089.[32] Recently a great deal of attention has been paid to graffiti on church and rampart walls in early medieval Bulgaria. Many are short texts (of the type "Peter wrote this" or "I was here"), others are votive ("Lord, help thy servant Peter") or commemorative inscriptions ("On that date, at that time, Peter visited this place" or "Peter died in the year of the Lord so-and-so"). There are also insults, prayers, epigrams, and even obscenities. Such inscriptions give us little chronological detail, but have been turned into a gold mine of detail for social and cultural history.[33]

[29] K. Popkonstantinov and V. Popkonstantinova, "Die Inschriften des Felsklosters Murfatlar," in *Paleobalkanistika i starobălgaristika. Părvi esenni nacionalni cheteniia "Profesor Ivan Gălăbov,"* ed. by E. Dogramadzhieva and K. Popkonstantinov (Veliko Tărnovo: Universitetsko izdatelstvo "Sv. sv. Kiril i Metodii," 1995), pp. 111–134.

[30] M. Matijević-Sokol, "Latin inscriptions," in *Croatia in the Early Middle Ages. A Cultural Survey*, ed. by I. Supičić (London: Philip Wilson Publishers and Zagreb: AGM, 1999), pp. 242–243.

[31] Popkonstantinov and Kronsteiner, *Starobălgarski nadpisi*, vol. II, pp. 166–168.

[32] B. Fučić, "The Croatian Glagolitic and Cyrillic epigraphs," in *Croatia in the Early Middle Ages. A Cultural Survey*, ed. by I. Supičić (London: Philip Wilson Publishers and Zagreb: AGM, 1999), pp. 266–268.

[33] R. Kostova, "Lust and piety: graffiti from Bulgarian medieval monasteries," in *Disziplinierung im Alltag des Mittelalters und der frühen Neuzeit. Internationaler Kongreß,*

Another type of evidence that can go some way towards offering a glimpse into private life is letters. Byzantine letter writing was however a formalized subgenre of rhetoric shaped by a very elaborate style, which was designed to impose upon the addressee the impression of a highly educated sender. It is literary convention, rather than direct reflection of social and political events, that mattered most to authors of letters written in the "classical style" of ancient epistolography. This is true not only for letters whose recipients happened to be the rulers of Bulgaria, such as those written by the patriarchs of Constantinople, Photios (858–867 and 877–886) and Nicholas Mystikos (901–907 and 912–925), but also for letters written for less significant, albeit often highly educated, addressees, such as those of Theophylact Hephaistos, the late eleventh-century archbishop of Ohrid.[34] For example, when the archbishop complained in a letter about the "bumpkin lifestyle" in Ohrid, this is in fact a quote from Euripides, before being an accurate description of the conditions in Byzantine Bulgaria. Highlighting the literary value of these letters, recent studies have thus shown that despite his apparent hostility to anything Bulgarian, it is a mistake to take the archbishop's letters as evidence for the Byzantine administration's systematic effort at eradicating Old Church Slavonic culture and Bulgarian ethnic identity.[35] The risk of running into such misinterpretations of the evidence is apparently smaller with papal letters sent either to the Croatian rulers of the ninth to eleventh centuries or to Ioannitsa, the early thirteenth-century ruler of Bulgaria.[36] However, even in such cases, caution is recommended when attempting to reconstruct the thoughts or intentions of the rulers from the papal

Krems an der Donau, 8. bis 11. Oktober 1996, ed. by G. Jaritz (Vienna: Verlag der Österreichischen Akademie der Wissenschaften, 1999), pp. 233–254. For figural graffiti, see D. Ovcharov, *Bălgarski srednovekovni risunki-grafiti* [Drawing Graffiti from Medieval Bulgaria] (Sofia: Septemvri, 1982).

34 D. S. White and J. R. Berrigan, *The Patriarch and the Prince. The Letter of Patriarch Photios of Constantinople to Khan Boris* (Brookline: Holy Cross Orthodox Press, 1982); *Nicholas I Patriarch of Constantinople, Letters*, ed. by R. J. H. Jenkins (Washington: Dumbarton Oaks Research Library and Collection, 1973); M. Mullett, *Theophylact of Ochrid. Reading the Letters of a Byzantine Archbishop* (Aldershot and Brookfield: Variorum, 1997).

35 M. Mullett, "Byzantium and the Slavs: the views of Theophylact of Ochrid," *GSU*, vol. 87 (1994), pp. 55–70. For the reading of Theophylact's letters as evidence of anti-Bulgarian policies, see Fine, *Early Medieval Balkans*, p. 220.

36 M. Brković, "Il sovrano Branimir e la Croazia nelle lettere del papa Giovanni VIII," *Croatica christiana periodica*, vol. 27 (1991), pp. 171–172; B. Primov, "The papacy, the fourth crusade and Bulgaria," *Byzantinobulgarica*, vol. 1 (1962), pp. 183–211.

letters. At least in the case of Ioannitsa, we know that (some, at least, of) his letters were written in "Bulgarian" (Old Church Slavonic) and that they were translated in Rome into Greek and then into Latin. Much of the debate surrounding Ioannitsa's imperial title may therefore be based on misunderstandings caused by mistranslation or by the impossibility to render in one language the nuances available in another.

Native narrative sources are conspicuously absent for the early medieval history of Southeastern Europe. There is no Southeast European equivalent to Paul the Deacon or Bede. When they first appear, such sources are typically the work of men of the church, with a selective coverage and with an understanding of the events in the past that was deeply influenced by the interpretative framework of the Bible. The first known historical narratives are those of Bulgaria, but they appear only in the mid-eleventh century in the context of growing millennialist fears. Apocrypha written in Byzantine Bulgaria in Old Church Slavonic, but preserved only in much later Russian redactions, propagated not only an eschatological view of the future, but also a bright vision of the Bulgarian past, portraying the reigns of Boris, Symeon, and Peter as the glorious days long gone. One of them, entitled the *Vision of Isaiah* and dated to the 1070s, contains a brief historical narrative, now known as the *Bulgarian Apocryphal Chronicle*.[37] While the explosion of apocrypha extolling the Bulgarian past may well have been related to the political events of the

[37] I. Ivanov, *Bogomilski knigi i legendi* (Sofia: Pridvorna Pechatnica, 1925). A short passage from the *Vision* has been translated into English by T. Butler, ed. *Monumenta Bulgarica. A Bilingual Anthology of Bulgarian Texts from the 9th to the 19th Centuries* (Ann Arbor: Michigan Slavic Publications, 1996), pp. 173–184. See also V. Beshevliev, "Nachaloto na bălgarskata dărzhava spored Apokrifen letopis ot XI vek [The beginnings of Bulgaria according to the eleventh-century Apocryphal Chronicle]," in *Srednovekovna Bălgariia i Chernomorieto. Sbornik dokladi ot nauchnata konferenciia, Varna 1980*, ed. by A. Kuzev (Varna: Knigoizdatelstvo "Georgi Bakalov," 1982), pp. 39–45; T. Mollov, "*Bălgarski apokrifen letopis*: khronotop i struktura na teksta [The *Bulgarian Apocryphal Chronicle*: the chronotope and the structure of the text]," in *Studia protobulgarica et mediaevalia europensia. V chest na profesor Veselin Beshevliev*, ed. by V. Giuzelev, V. Tăpkova-Zaimova, K. Popkonstantinov, et al. (Veliko Tărnovo: Universitetsko izdatelstvo "Sv. sv. Kiril i Metodii," 1993), pp. 289–294; M. Kaimakamova, "Istoriografskata stoinost na *Bălgarski apokrifen letopis* [The historiographic value of the *Bulgarian Apocryphal Chronicle*]," in *Civitas divino-humana. V chest na profesor Georgi Bakalov*, ed. by C. Stepanov and V. Vachkova (Sofia: Centăr za izsledvaniia na bălgarite "Tangra" TanNakRa IK, 2004), pp. 417–441.

mid-eleventh century that brought the issues of imperial power and Bulgarian past glory to the forefront, the *Bulgarian Apocryphal Chronicle* can hardly be used as a reliable source for the early history of Bulgaria. The chronicler viewed "tsar Ispar," perhaps the same as Asparukh, as a biblical hero, ruling his people for no less than 172 years. Ispar was remembered as a builder of ditches and cities, primarily of Pliska, which, given the results of the recent research on that site, is a blatant anachronism. Moreover, he is also said to have expelled "Ethiopians" from Bulgaria and to have slaughtered great numbers of Muslims, before dying in battle against them "near the Danube."[38] Whereas the error of attributing to Ispar the works of much later rulers of Bulgaria may be excused as a matter of faulty chronology, Ispar's wars with the Muslims are a purely fictional detail, the invention of the chronicler.

Inconsistencies, obscurities, and fictional characters have also damaged the reputation among historians of the late twelfth-century *Chronicle of the Priest of Dioclea*, a work in fact written by Gregory, the archbishop of Bar.[39] Like the unknown author of the *Bulgarian Apocryphal Chronicle*, Archbishop Gregory was not interested in separating fact from fiction, but in writing a report of Dalmatian history that could support the claims to superiority of his see over that of Split, no doubt in the context of the reelevation of Bar to the status of archbishopric and of the Dukljan–papal contacts of the late 1100s. Long dismissed as a collection of fact and fiction, especially in relation to the coverage of earlier periods, the *Chronicle* is nevertheless an invaluable, if not the only available, source for more recent periods, such as, for example, the mid-eleventh-century history of southern Dalmatia. Much like the *Bulgarian Apocryphal Chronicle* in late eleventh-century Bulgaria, the heterogeneous collection of historical and literary materials to be found in the *Chronicle of the Priest*

38 Ivanov, *Bogomilski knigi*, p. 282. The account of Ispar in the *Chronicle* has been treated at face value by I. Duichev, "Edno legendarno svedenie za Asparukha [A legendary source on Asparukh]," *Vjesnik za arheologiju i historiju Dalmatinsku*, vols. 56–59 (1954–1957), 181–189.

39 V. Mošin, *Ljetopis popa Dukljanina. Latinski tekst sa hrvatskim prijevodom i "Hrvatska hronika"* [The *Chronicle of the Priest of Dioclea*. The Latin Text with Croatian Translation and the "Croatian Chronicle"] (Zagreb: Matica hrvatska, 1950). Fundamental for the understanding of the *Chronicle* as a medieval literary work is now E. Peričić, *Sclavorum Regnum Grgura Barskog. Ljetopis Popa Dukljanina* [Archbishop Gregory of Bar's *Sclavorum Regnum*. The *Chronicle of the Priest of Dioclea*] (Zagreb: Kršćanska sadašnjost, 1991).

of Dioclea may be seen as a different kind of historical source, namely as a remarkable gauge for the level of literacy and for the political implications of literary production in twelfth-century Dalmatia.

Serious questions of trustworthiness have also been raised in connection with the earliest surviving chronicle of Hungary, the *Deeds of the Hungarians* (*Gesta Hungarorum*), written by a former notary of a king named Béla, who called himself "Master P."[40] Although most certainly a man of the church, the author's goal with this work was to defend not the interests of the church or, even less, that of the "legitimate" dynasty of Arpadian kings, but those of the old aristocratic families of Hungary, the descendants of the pagan warriors who had conquered the Carpathian Basin around AD 900. Much ink has been spilled over the true identity of the author of the *Gesta* and of the king for whom he served as notary (no less than three kings named Béla ruled in Hungary between the late eleventh and the late twelfth century). However, much more controversial is the degree to which the account of the Hungarian conquest of the Carpathian Basin to be found in the *Gesta* can be trusted as a historical source written two to three centuries after the events narrated. Far from being a simple matter of source analysis, the debate has been complicated by the fact that the *Gesta* mentions both *Romani* and *Blachi* (Vlachs or Romanians) as inhabitants of certain regions of the Carpathian Basin before the arrival of the Hungarians, an issue that has received enormous importance in the context of modern territorial claims to Transylvania.[41] Nationalistic concerns aside, "Master P." has very little of significance to say about Transylvania proper, which he seems

[40] *Die "Gesta Hungarorum" des anonymen Notars. Die älteste Darstellung der ungarischen Geschichte*, ed. by G. Silagi (Sigmaringen: Jan Thorbecke, 1991). See also G. Győrffy, "Abfassungszeit, Autorschaft und Glaubwürdigkeit der *Gesta Hungarorum* des anonymen Notars," *Acta Antiqua Academiae Scientiarum Hungaricae*, vol. 20 (1972), pp. 209–229; L. Veszprémy, "Historical past and political present in the Latin chronicles of Hungary (12th–13th centuries)," in *The Medieval Chronicle. Proceedings of the 1st International Conference on the Medieval Chronicle. Driebergen/Utrecht 13–16 July 1996*, ed. by E. Kooper (Amsterdam and Atlanta: Rodopi, 1999), pp. 260–268. For the identity of "Master P.," see now K. Szovák, "'Wer war der anonyme Notar?' Zur Bestimmung des Verfassers der Gesta Hungarorum," *Ungarn-Jahrbuch*, vol. 19 (1991), pp. 1–17.

[41] Hungarian historians have the tendency to exaggerate the literary character of the *Gesta* to the point of treating its entire account of early Hungarian history as fictional. See G. Győrffy, "Formation d'états au IXe siècle suivant les Gesta Hungarorum du Notaire Anonyme," *Nouvelles études d'histoire*, vol. 1 (1965), pp. 25–155; G. Kristó, "Anonymus a 9. századi Kárpát-medence bolgár fejedelmeiröl [*Gesta*

to have known better from hearsay than from first-hand knowledge. There is no mention of Alba Iulia, which at the time of the *Gesta* was the most important power center of the province, the residence of the local governor (*voevode*) and of the bishop of Transylvania. If, as seems probable, "Master P." had been a notary of king Béla III (1172–1196), it is surprising to note that the *Gesta*, which is otherwise replete with allusions to twelfth-century events or situations, has nothing to say about the "guest" settlers brought from Western Europe by Béla's father, King Géza II.

The *Deeds of the Hungarians* exists only in one preserved manuscript, an indication that the work was not very popular during either its author's lifetime or the subsequent centuries. It may in fact have had but a limited circulation among some members of the thirteenth-century Hungarian aristocracy. A similarly limited circulation may be inferred for a work very different in terms of both genre and quality, namely the *Historia Salonitana* (The History of Salona) by Thomas of Spalato, which survives in only four medieval manuscripts, all of Dalmatian provenance.[42] A notary of the commune of Spalato (Split), canon of the cathedral, archdeacon, and candidate for the position of archbishop of that city, Thomas wanted to write a *gesta episcoporum*, that is a chronicle of the deeds of the archbishops of Salona and Split. In the process, however, he managed to produce a work of civic history much influenced by contemporary Italian models. As a consequence, one of the most salient features of his work is a strong feeling of urban patriotism, as well as the admiration that he

Hungarorum on the Bulgar princes of the ninth-century Carpathian Basin]," *Acta Historica*, vol. 113 (2001), pp. 11–19. By contrast, Romanian historians spared no efforts to emphasize the supposedly accurate, first-hand knowledge that "Master P." had of the late ninth- or early tenth-century developments in Transylvania, see S. Brezeanu, "*Romani* şi *Blachi* la Anonymus. Istorie şi ideologie politică [*Romani* and *Blachi* in the *Gesta Hungarorum*. History and political ideology]," *Revista de istorie*, vol. 34 (1981), pp. 1313–1340; Al. Madgearu, *Românii în opera Notarului Anonim* [Romanians in the *Gesta Hungarorum*] (Cluj-Napoca: Centrul de Studii Transilvane – Fundaţia Culturală Română, 2001).

[42] J. R. Sweeney, "Thomas of Spalato and the Mongols: a thirteenth-century Dalmatian view of Mongol customs," *Florilegium: Carleton University Annual Papers on Classical Antiquity and the Middle Ages*, vol. 4 (1982), pp. 161 and 176 n. 18. The edition of Thomas of Spalato's work most frequently cited by scholars is that published by F. Rački in Zagreb in 1894. Two other editions are now available, one by the Russian scholar O. A. Akimova (Moscow: Indrik, 1997), the other by the Croatian scholars O. Peric, M. Matijević, and R. Katičić (Split: Književni krug, 2003).

had for the republican government of the city, which in turn seems to have been the source for Thomas's rather dismissive, if not outright critical, views of members of other political or ethnic communities. The Slavs, Hungarians, and Mongols that populate the *Historia Salonitana* are either primitive and cruel or simply foreigners incapable of understanding the superior culture of Dalmatia. Archdeacon Thomas seems to have had access to numerous sources that are now lost, which makes his *History* a uniquely valuable source. However, since for earlier periods his information cannot be verified against any other sources, historians have much debated the value of this work for Dalmatian history.[43] By contrast, the information about the eleventh- to thirteenth-century history of Dalmatia is viewed as most trustworthy, even if it has been demonstrated that in many cases (e.g., the account of the Mongol invasion of Dalmatia), Thomas relied on oral testimonies, not on his own observations or on written sources.[44] Indeed, without the *History* of Thomas of Spalato, there would be very little to say about the complicated picture of Dalmatia between *c.* 1000 and 1250 that would not be tainted by the bias of the Venetian sources, such as the fourteenth-century chronicle of Andrea Dandolo (*Chronicon Venetum*).

For the first few centuries of Southeast European medieval history, only sources written outside the region are available, but they too have their problems. Most Byzantine authors, from Procopius of Caesarea to Niketas Choniates, wrote from the perspective of Byzantium as God's Empire and espoused a mixture of scorn and learned curiosity for the territories beyond its borders, which were inhabited by those whom they viewed as incorrigible barbarians. The degree to which they regarded the status of barbarian as ingrained in the nature of anyone born outside the Empire is illustrated by the use that these authors made of antiquated names to refer to contemporary peoples,

43 L. Katić, "Vjerodostojnost Tome Arcidjakona i posljedni dani Solina [The veracity of Thomas of Spalato's *History* and the last years of Salona]," *Vjesnik za arheologiju i historiju Dalmatinsku*, vol. 53 (1950–1951), pp. 99–120. Thomas had two Spalatan continuators, one of whom produced a new edition of Thomas's work to which he added some of the documents that the archdeacon had used for writing his *History*. The extended version of this work is known as the *Historia Salonitana maior* and has been published by N. Klaić (Belgrade: Naučno delo, 1967). See also L. Margetić, "*Historia Salonitana* i *Historia Salonitana Major* – neka pitanja [*Historia Salonitana* and *Historia Salonitana maior*: some remarks]," *Hilandarski zbornik*, vol. 47 (1994), pp. 1–36.

44 Sweeney, "Thomas of Spalato and the Mongols," pp. 160–161.

such as Procopius' "Massagetae" (for nomads in the steppe north of the Black Sea) or Niketas Choniates' "Mysians" (for the Vlachs or the Bulgarians in the northern Balkans). The stereotypical views attached to such labels considerably complicate the interpretation of these accounts, which are often the only ones that we have for key aspects of political and social history. For example, when Procopius of Caesarea described the Sclavenes as living "from of old under a democracy,"[45] what he meant was that in his eyes (as well as in those of any other subject of the Byzantine emperor), they, like all barbarians, lived in complete anarchy. Similarly, when the unknown author of a late sixth-century collection of questions and answers known as *Eratopokriseis* claims that the Sclavenes killed newborns by smashing them against rocks and consumed with pleasure "the breasts of women, full of milk," this can hardly be treated as anything other than stereotypes about barbarians in general, which resisted time with remarkable success and spread outside Byzantine culture to be found, almost word by word, in the late thirteenth-century description of the Mongols by Matthew Paris.[46] However, not all such accounts need to be interpreted as stereotypical. For example, the early ninth-century *Chronography* of Theophanes Confessor relates how, after the defeat of the Byzantine army by the Bulgars in 811, Emperor Nicephorus' head was cut and the skull covered on the "outside with silver" to be made a cup, from which the Bulgar ruler Krum drank together with his Slavic allies.[47] The same gruesome detail is reported in the

[45] Procopius of Caesarea, *Wars* VII.14.22. For the interpretation of this passage, see R. Benedicty, "Prokopios' Berichte über die slavische Vorzeit. Beiträge zur historiographischen Methode Prokopios von Kaisareia," *Jahrbuch der österreichischen byzantinischen Gesellschaft*, vol. 14 (1965), pp. 51–78. For Byzantine stereotypes about the Slavs, see G. P. Majeska, "The Byzantines on the Slavs: the problem of ethnic stereotyping," *Acta Byzantina Fennica*, vol. 9 (1997–1998), pp. 70–86.

[46] For the portrait of the Sclavenes in the *Eratopokriseis*, see R. Riedinger, *Pseudo-Kaisarios. Überlieferungsgeschichte und Verfasserfrage* (Munich: C. H. Beck, 1969), p. 302. The English translation is from J. Bačić, "The emergence of Sklabenoi (Slavs), their arrival on the Balkan Peninsula, and the role of the Avars in these events: revised concepts in a new perspective," Ph.D. dissertation (Columbia University, New York, 1983), p. 152. For the Mongol breast-eaters, see G. C. Guzman, "Reports of Mongol cannibalism in the thirteenth-century Latin sources: oriental fact or western fiction," in *Discovering New Worlds: Essays on Medieval Exploration and Imagination*, ed. by S. D. Westrem (New York: Garland, 1991), pp. 31–68.

[47] Theophanes Confessor, *Chronographia*, AM 6303, translated by Cyril Mango (Oxford: Clarendon Press, 1997), p. 674. This, of course, is in turn reminiscent of the story of how Alboin, the king of the Lombards, turned the skull of his rival, Cunimund, into a cup and forced his wife Rosemund, Cunimund's daughter, to drink from it (Paul the Deacon, *History of the Lombards* II.28).

twelfth-century *Russian Primary Chronicle* in relation to Sviatoslav of Kiev. He was ambushed in 972 on the banks of the river Dnieper by the Pechenegs, who "made a cup out of his skull, overlaying it with gold, and they drank from it."[48]

Byzantine sources pose different problems of interpretation when dealing with matters pertaining to those territories in Southeastern Europe which were under Byzantine rule. For example, Eustathius of Thessalonica's account of the Norman sack of the city, despite being delivered as a Lenten sermon in 1186, is nevertheless an objective account, which Niketas Choniates used for his section on the Norman invasion of 1185. Despite his ambiguous attitude towards the Vlachs, Niketas' account of the fighting going on in the late twelfth-century Balkans between the imperial troops and the Vlach rebels led by Peter and Asen is a reliable source, for Niketas participated in these campaigns as the secretary of Emperor Isaac II Angelos. Despite the commonplaces most typical of the hagiographical genre, there is no reason to raise doubts about the details about Sparta and the landed aristocracy in the surrounding countryside contained in the *Testament* of St. Nikon the Metanoiete.[49] This is also true of such works as the seventh-century *Miracles of St. Demetrius*, with its wealth of information about the hinterland of Thessalonica, or the tenth-century *Life of St. Blaise of Amorion*, with its rich detail about ninth-century Bulgaria.[50]

The earliest Western narrative sources to cover in some detail the southeastern region of the European continent are the annals of the Carolingian age reporting either on the Frankish–Moravian wars or, episodically, on conflicts with the Bulgars. Somewhat more detailed is the coverage of the ninth-century *Conversion of the Bavarians and the Carantanians*, which has nevertheless raised some questions of reliability and truth, despite being the most important source for the history of the eighth-century Carantanian polity. The value of such sources

48 *Russian Primary Chronicle* AM 6480, translated by S. Hazzard Cross and Ol. P. Sherbowitz-Wetzor (Cambridge, Mass.: Medieval Academy of America, 1953), p. 90.

49 *Testament of Nikon the Metanoiete for the Church and Monastery of the Savior, the Mother of God, and St. Kyriake in Lakedaimon*, English translation by A. Bandy in *Byzantine Monastic Foundation Documents*, pp. 313–322.

50 P. Lemerle, *Les plus anciens recueils des Miracles de Saint Démétrius et la pénétration des Slaves dans les Balkans* (Paris: CNRS Editions, 1979). See also V. Giuzelev, "Zhitieto na Vlasii Amoriiski kato izvor za bălgarskata istoriia [The *Life* of St. Basil of Amorion as a source for the Bulgarian history]," *GSU*, vol. 61 (1968), pp. 19–33.

for the history of Southeastern Europe is limited, as is that of the many chronicles of the Crusades, from Albert of Aachen to Geoffrey of Villehardouin. Limited in value is also the information provided by geographical sources, such as the sixth-century *Cosmography* of the Anonymous Geographer of Ravenna or the mid-ninth-century Bavarian Geographer.[51] Both show a rather vague understanding of the geography of Southeastern Europe, especially outside the borders of the Late Roman Empire. A somewhat more detailed knowledge of Southeastern Europe, including the steppe corridor in the northeast, is demonstrated by the twelfth-century map of the Arab geographer al-Idrisi, who lived and worked at the court of King Roger II of Sicily.[52] Much richer are travelogues of Jews from Muslim Spain, such as that of Ibrahim ibn-Ya'kub in the tenth century (preserved in the eleventh-century compilation of al-Bakri) and of Benjamin of Tudela in the twelfth century.[53] Contemporary Scandinavian sources,

[51] S. Čače, "Civitates Dalmatiae u 'kosmografiji' Anonima Ravenjanina [The *civitates Dalmatiae* in the Cosmography of the Anonymous Geographer of Ravenna]," *Diadora*, vol. 15 (1993), pp. 347–440. For the Bavarian Geographer, see *Descriptio civitatum ad septentrionalem plagam Danubii (t. zv. Bavorský geograf* [The So-Called Bavarian Geographer]*)*, ed. by B. Horák and D. Trávníček (Prague: Academia, 1956). For Carantania, see F. Lošek, *Die "Conversio Bagoariorum et Carantanorum" und der Brief des Erzbischofs Theotmar von Salzburg* (Hannover: Hahnsche Buchhandlung, 1997).

[52] *Géographie d'Edrisi*, ed. by P.-A. Jaubert (Paris: Imprimerie royale, 1840). See B. Nedkov, *Bălgariia i săsednite i zemi prez XII vek spored Idrisi* [Bulgaria and the Neighboring Lands during the Twelfth Century, according to Idrisi] (Sofia: Nauka i izkustvo, 1960); M. S. Kordoses, "Hoi dromoi apo to Dyrrakhio kai ten Aulona pros ten Anatole, symphona me ton Araba geographo Idrisi [The roads from Dyrrachium and Valona to the east, according to the Arab geographer Idrisi]," in *Istorike geografia. Dromoi kai komboi tes Balkanikes apo ten Arkhaioteta sten eniaia Europe*, ed. by E. P. Demetriades, A. Ph. Lagopoulos, and G. Tsotsos (Thessaloniki: Tmema arkhitektonon, Aristoteleio Panepistemio Thessalonikes, 1998), pp. 115–124.

[53] *Relacja Ibrāhīma ibn Ja'kūba z podróży do krajów słowiańskich w przekazie al-Bekrīego* [The Account of Ibrahim ibn-Ya'kub's Travel to the Slavic Lands Preserved in the Redaction of al-Bakri], ed. by T. Kowalski (Cracow: Gebethner i Wolff, 1946). Ibrahim ibn-Ya'kub did not travel to Southeastern Europe; instead he gathered information about Bulgaria from the court of Emperor Otto I, which he visited in the 960s. See P. Engels, "Der Reisebericht des Ibrahim ibn Ya'qub (961–966)," in *Kaiserin Theophanu. Begegnung des Ostens und Westens in die Wende des ersten Jahrtausends*, ed. by A. von Euw and P. Schreiner (Cologne: Böhlau, 1991), pp. 413–420; D. Mishin, "Ibrahim ibn-Ya'qub at-Turtushi's account of the Slavs from the middle of the tenth century," *AMS* (1994–1995), pp. 184–199. For Benjamin of Tudela's travelogue, see *The Itinerary of Benjamin of Tudela. Travels in the Middle Ages*, translated by M. N. Adler (Malibu: J. Simon, 1987).

such as sagas and runic inscriptions, also contain some information about the northern region of Southeastern Europe, especially about the Vlachs.[54] However, the richest body of information after that contained in Byzantine sources is that from Rus' chronicles. The *Russian Primary Chronicle* is the basic source for the reconstruction of the eleventh-century history of the Pechenegs, while the Hypatian Chronicle provides invaluable information about the twelfth-century expansion of Galicia into Southeastern Europe.[55]

MEDIEVAL ARCHAEOLOGY IN SOUTHEASTERN EUROPE

Despite the important contribution of such pioneering work as that of József Ujfalosi at Alba Iulia or Karel Škorpil at Pliska, medieval archaeology in Southeastern Europe only began to develop seriously some fifty years ago.[56] Much like in Western Europe, before about

[54] V. Spinei, "Informaţii despre vlahi în izvoarele medievale nordice [Informations about Vlachs in medieval Norse sources]," *Studii şi cercetări de istorie veche*, vol. 24 (1973), pp. 57–81 and 259–282.

[55] *Povest' vremennykh let*, ed. by D. S. Likhachev and V. P. Adrianova-Perec (Moscow and Leningrad: Izdatel'stvo Akademii Nauk SSSR, 1950), with English translation by S. Hazzard Cross and O. P. Sherbowitz-Wetzor (Cambridge, Mass.: Medieval Academy of America, 1953). See also D. Ostrowski, *The* Povest' Vremennykh Let: *an Interlinear Collation and Paradosis* (Cambridge, Mass.: Harvard University Press, 2003); Al. A. Shakhmatov, "*Povest' vremennykh let* i ee istochniki [The *Russian Primary Chronicle* and its sources]," *Trudy Otdela drevnerusskoi literatury*, vol. 4 (1940), pp. 9–158. The *Russian Primary Chronicle* contains unique information about tenth-century Bulgaria, see E. G. Zykov, "Izvestiia o Bolgarii v *Povesti vremennykh let* i ikh istochniki [The information about Bulgaria in the *Russian Primary Chronicle* and its origin]," *Trudy Otdela drevnerusskoi literatury*, vol. 24 (1969), pp. 48–53. For the Hypatian Chronicle, see *The Galician-Volynian Chronicle (Ipat'evskaia letopis')*, ed. by A. A. Shakhmatov (St. Petersburg: Tipografiia M. A. Aleksandrova, 1908), with English translation in L. L. Heinrich, "The Kievan Chronicle: a translation and commentary," Ph.D. dissertation (Vanderbilt University, Nashville, 1978). See also M. F. Kotliar, "Galicko-volynskaia letopis' [The Galician-Volhynian Chronicle]," *Drevneishie gosudarstva vostochnoi Evropy* (1995), pp. 80–165.

[56] J. Ujfalusi, *A gyulafehérvári székesegyház: alapittatásának 900-ik évfordulója alakalmból* [The Alba Iulia Cathedral at the 900th Anniversary of its Foundation] (Gyulafehérvár: Schäser Ferenc Könyvnyomdája, 1903). For Karel Škorpil's discovery of Pliska, see L. Doncheva-Petkova, "Karel Škorpil i istoriiata na prouchvaniiata na Pliska [Karel Škorpil and the history of research at Pliska]," in *Zwischen Byzanz und Abendland. Pliska, der östliche Balkanraum und Europa im Spiegel der Frühmittelalterarchäologie*, ed. by J. Henning (Frankfurt am Main: Johann Wolfgang Goethe Universität, 1999). Fundamental for the historical development of cemetery archaeology in the Carpathian Basin is J. Hampel, *A régibb középkor (IV.–X. század) emlékei Magyarhonban* [Monuments of the Early Middle Ages (Fourth to

1950, medieval archaeology was not recognized as a coherent discipline, separate from, yet fundamental to, the study of medieval history. Although many of its components, especially cemetery archaeology, have a much longer history of study, the main catalyst for this sudden rise of medieval archaeology was the post-war shift in emphasis from traditional political and constitutional to social and economic history. Unlike Western Europe, where explicitly Marxist approaches did not appear until the late 1970s and 1980s, in Southeastern Europe (with the exception of Greece), the rise of medieval archaeology coincides in time with, and was ultimately caused by, the imposition of Communist regimes under Soviet aegis, if not control. As a consequence, archaeology was organized along the lines of the Soviet school of "material culture history," and received a degree of institutional attention it had never experienced before. Considerable long-term investments, with no parallel in contemporary Western Europe, made possible large-scale explorations of several key sites, some of which resulted in total excavation, following the principles first championed by the Soviet school of archaeology.[57] By directing the attention of archaeologists to how ordinary people lived, the Marxist paradigm encouraged the development of settlement archaeology (as opposed to the excavations of cemeteries, which has until then been the primary focus of medieval archaeology). This led to large-scale horizontal excavations of villages such as Popina–Dzhedzhovi Lozia and Garvan in Bulgaria, Bucov and Dridu in Romania, Hansca in the Republic of Moldova, Bostanište in Serbia, or Mrsunjski Lug in Croatia, all of which are remarkable parallels to the more or less contemporary developments in Western Europe.[58] The growth in the 1960s and 1970s of cemetery

Tenth Century) from the Hungarian Homeland] (Budapest: Magyar Tudományos Akadémia, 1894).

57 F. Curta, "Pots, Slavs, and 'imagined communities': Slavic archaeology and the history of the early Slavs," *European Journal of Archaeology*, vol. 4 (2001), pp. 367–384. For the Soviet archaeology and its use of the total excavation of sites, see B. G. Trigger, *A History of Archaeological Thought* (Cambridge: Cambridge University Press, 1989), pp. 217–227.

58 The results of some of these excavations were published with remarkable speed shortly after the closing of the archaeological campaigns. Others had to wait for up to twenty years for a detailed publication, a delay otherwise attested for contemporary excavations in Western Europe (e.g., Feddersen Wierde in northwestern Germany). For Bulgaria, see Zh. Văzharova, *Slaviano-bălgarskoto selishte krai selo Popina, Silistrensko* [A Slavic–Bulgarian settlement near Popina,

archaeology, especially in Hungary and Yugoslavia, led to a quick increase in the volume of data, to such an extant that entire chronological gaps in the knowledge of the early Middle Ages have been virtually eliminated by 1990 primarily because of archaeological research. Without extensive archives, research in Hungary and what is now Croatia had to lean heavily on archaeological evidence, especially for the eighth and ninth centuries. This is not to be viewed as a weakness, because archaeology gives information of a character different from that provided by written sources. The Late Avar period (*c.* 700–800/820), for example, is devoid of written sources, yet can now be studied in detail on the basis of archaeological excavations of both settlements and cemeteries. Similarly, many of the changes to our perception of the eighth- and ninth-century Bulgar society have resulted from archaeological fieldwork.[59] History books published in the 1980s and 1990s on such subjects as the "material culture of the Old Croats" or the southern region of Hungary during the

district of Silistra] (Sofia: Izdatelstvo na Bălgarskata Akademiia na Naukite, 1954); *Slavianski i slavianobălgarski selishta v bălgarskite zemi ot kraia na VI–XI vek* [Slavic and Slavic–Bulgarian Settlements in the Bulgarian Lands from the Late Sixth to the Eleventh Century] (Sofia: Izdatelstvo na Bălgarskata Akademiia na Naukite, 1965); and *Srednovekovnoto selishte s. Garvăn, Silistrenski okrăg (VI–XI v.)* [A Medieval Settlement in Garvăn, District of Silistra (Sixth to Eleventh Century)] (Sofia: Izdatelstvo na Bălgarskata Akademiia na Naukite, 1986). For Romania, see E. Zaharia, *Săpăturile de la Dridu. Contribuţii la arheologia şi istoria perioadei de formare a poporului român* [Excavations in Dridu. Contributions to the Archaeology and History of the Romanian Ethnogenesis] (Bucharest: Editura Academiei Republicii Socialiste România, 1967); M. Comşa, *Cultura materială veche românească (Aşezările din secolele VIII–X de la Bucov-Ploieşti)* [The Old Romanian Material Culture (Eighth- to Tenth-Century Settlements in Bucov–Ploieşti)] (Bucharest: Editura Academiei Republicii Socialiste România, 1978). For settlements excavated in northern Serbia, see N. Stanojev, *Srednjovekovna seoska naselja od V do XV veka u Vojvodini* [Fifth- to Fifteenth-Century Medieval Rural Settlements in Vojvodina] (Novi Sad: Muzej Vojvodine, 1996).

59 G. Fülöp, "La basse époque avare en Hongrie," in *L'art des invasions en Hongrie et en Wallonie. Actes du colloque tenu au Musée royal de Mariemont du 9 au 11 avril 1979*, ed. by G. Donnay (Morlanwelz: Le Musée, 1991), pp. 151–154; U. Fiedler, *Studien zu Gräberfeldern des 6. bis 9. Jahrhunderts an der unteren Donau* (Bonn: Rudolf Habelt, 1992). One of the earliest books on the Avar qaganate was almost exclusively based on the archaeological evidence, and at least one archaeologist attempted to reconstruct the structure of Avar society on the basis of the archaeological evidence. See J. Kovačević, *Avarski kaganat* [The Avar Qaganate] (Belgrade: Srpska književna zadruga, 1977); G. László, *Etudes archéologiques sur l'histoire de la société des Avars* (Budapest: Akadémiai kiadó, 1955).

first century following the arrival of the Magyars were based almost exclusively on the results of archaeological excavations.[60]

On the other hand, the lead role taken by history in establishing national priorities for archaeological work provided the stimulus for the excavation agendas on such high-status sites as Pliska and Preslav.[61] To be sure, Pliska has been in fact discovered by Karel Škorpil on the basis of a thorough study and comparison of Byzantine sources. Similarly, the identification with Iustiniana Prima (Emperor Justinian's foundation) of the sixth-century city excavated since 1912 in Caričin Grad (Serbia) has been based exclusively on written sources, for no inscription was found that contains the name of that city. The tendency to use archaeology to illustrate what was already known from documentary history has also been a salient feature of the archaeology practiced in Southeastern Europe during the post-war decades. Despite the strong emphasis on the Marxist interpretation of history, archaeologists in the region have worked and continue to work within a "culture history" framework.[62] As a consequence, they have taken repeated assemblages of similar artifacts, burial rites, and building forms to be a reflection of cultural norms, in other words, of a shared culture. More often than not, cultures are equated with peoples, which means that any changes in culture are to be explained in

[60] J. Belošević, *Materijalna kultura Hrvata od VII do IX stoljeća* [The Material Culture of the Croats from the Seventh to the Ninth Century] (Zagreb: Sveučilišna naklada Liber, 1980); Cs. Bálint, *Südungarn im 10. Jahrhundert* (Budapest: Akadémiai kiadó, 1991). Even where written sources are available, the tendency has been to shift the emphasis onto the archaeological evidence, as in V. Spinei, *Moldavia in the 11th–14th Centuries* (Bucharest: Editura Academiei Republicii Socialiste România, 1986).

[61] R. Rashev and I. Dimitrov, *Pliska. 100 godini arkheologicheski razkopki* [Pliska, a Century of Archaeological Excavations] (Shumen: Svetlana, 1999); T. Totev, "Trideset godini arkheologicheski razkopki v Preslav [Thirty years of archaeological excavations in Preslav]," *Arkheologiia*, vol. 16 (1974), pp. 48–61; and *Great Preslav* (Sofia: Professor Marin Drinov Academic Publishing House, 2001).

[62] D. W. Bailey, "Bulgarian archaeology. Ideology, sociopolitics and the exotic," in *Archaeology under Fire. Nationalism, Politics, and Heritage in the Eastern Mediterranean and Middle East*, ed. by L. Meskell (London and New York: Routledge, 1998), pp. 87–110; K. Kotsakis, "The past is ours. Images of Greek Macedonia," ibid., pp. 44–67. See also the discussion in I. Rajterić-Sivec, "Oris arheološkega stanja in povojna raziskovanja zgodnjesrednjeveske arheologije v Albaniji [The state of post-war medieval archaeology in Albania]," *Arheološki vestnik*, vol. 25 (1976), pp. 552–561; F. Curta, "The changing image of the Early Slavs in the Rumanian historiography and archaeological literature. A critical survey," *Südost-Forschungen*, vol. 53 (1994), pp. 225–310.

terms of either diffusion of ideas (such as Christianity) or migration of people and replacement of one culture by another. The (ab)use of written sources has encouraged archaeologists to look for the material culture correlates of documented invasions of peoples or for the conversion of pagans to Christianity. The tendency to favor documentary over archaeological sources has sometimes led to a form of "text-driven archaeology" that is often associated with nationalistic concerns about territorial claims and racial purity. Particularly prone to this kind of interpretation is cemetery archaeology, with its emphasis on artifact typology and distribution maps of several "key artifacts," which could then be used to support the ideas of diffusion or migration. Needless to say, most practitioners of this kind of archaeology (of which there are still a great number in several Southeast European countries) have little understanding of or even interest in a critical reading of documentary sources. Nor have they been open to the ideas that during the 1960s have transformed the discipline of archaeology, primarily the concept of "culture as system" and the idea that, instead of being a direct reflection of social processes, material culture, like language, was used actively in the past to construct and categorize the world and, as a consequence, to negotiate and create cultural identities.[63] Such rather abstract issues had practically no echo in the medieval archaeology of Southeastern Europe, where most scholars continue to focus on data-gathering, hoping that by virtue of the simple accumulation of data, chronologies might be refined in order to allow a more sophisticated use of archaeology to write traditional history. This may also be the result of a lack of interest in the use of the new methods of precise and independent dating that have become available in the post-war period, especially tree-ring dating (dendrochronology).[64] By contrast, there has been a relatively early interest in the use of neutron activation

[63] See I. Mirnik Prezelj, "Slovenska zgodnjesrednjeveska arheologija med preteklostjo in sedanjostjo – pogled z 'Zahoda' [The medieval archaeology in Slovenia between the past and the present: a view from the West]," *Arheološki vestnik*, vol. 49 (1998), pp. 361–381. For a belated reaction to the concept of New Archaeology associated ever since the 1960s with the idea of "culture as system," see M. Stevanović, "'Nova arkheologija': da li ona ima buduchnost? [Does the 'New Archaeology' have a future?]," *Balcanica*, vol. 21 (1990), pp. 185–200.

[64] For a few remarkable exceptions, see E. Comşa, "Cîteva secvenţe dendrocronologice din perioada feudală timpurie din aşezarea de la Garvăn [Some dendrochronological sequences from the early medieval occupation phase in Garvăn]," *Peuce*, vol. 9 (1984), pp. 347–348; P. I. Kuniholm and C. L. Striker, "Dendrochronology

analysis (NAA) of pottery for the purpose of identifying composition elements that could be traced to known sources of clay.[65] NAA has also been successfully used for the study of medieval glass, primarily from Bulgaria.[66] Metallurgical science in the service of archaeology now includes a number of relatively low-cost methods of slag and phosphorus analysis, which have been used to trace the origin of the iron and to understand the technological process of production.[67] Meanwhile, much of the research done in skeletal analysis has been geared towards the quasi-racist identification of ethnic backgrounds,

and the architectural history of the Church of the Holy Apostles in Thessaloniki," *Architectura: Zeitschrift für Geschichte der Architektur*, vol. I (1990), pp. 1–26; B. Obelić and A. Sliepčević, "Correction of radiocarbon age of wooden beams from St. Donat's church in Zadar by dendrochronological method," *Vjesnik Arheološkog Muzeja u Zagrebu*, vols. 32–33 (1999–2000), pp. 197–206. Despite the extraordinary reliability of dendrochronology, recently there has been instead a revived interest in the use of radiocarbon dating, which, because of its large margin of error (plus or minus 140 years), does not present the same degree of chronological accuracy as tree-ring dating. See M. Guštin and G. Tiefengraber, "Oblike in kronologija zgodnjesrednjeveške lončanine na Novi tabli pri Murski Soboti [The forms and chronology of the early medieval pottery from Nova tabla near Murska Sobota]," in *Zgodni slovani. Zgodnjesrednjeveška lončenina na obrobju vzhodnih Alp*, ed. by M. Guštin (Ljubljana: Narodni Muzej Slovenije, 2002), pp. 46–64. There is to date no attested use of accelerator mass spectrometry (AMS) in the medieval archaeology of Southeastern Europe.

65 M. Comşa, "Die Keramik von byzantinischen Typus aus den Siedlungen von Bucov–Ploieşti," *Dacia*, vol. 24 (1980), pp. 323–339; M. Balla, "Provenance studies of Avar ceramics by neutron activation analysis," *Wosinszky Mór Múzeum Évkönyve*, vol. 15 (1990), pp. 131–133; J. Vroom, *After Antiquity. Ceramics and Society in the Aegean from the 7th to the 20th Century AC. A Case Study from Boeotia, Central Greece* (Leiden: Faculty of Archaeology, Leiden University, 2003).

66 I. Kuleff, R. Dzhingova, and G. Dzhingov, "Provenance study of medieval Bulgarian glasses by NAA and cluster analysis," *Archaeometry*, vol. 27 (1985), pp. 185–193.

67 Ş. Olteanu, "Procédés d'influence slave pour la reduction du fer à l'est des Carpathes, au VIe–VIIe siècles dans le contexte de la technologie traditionnelle des autochtones," in *Rapports du IIIe Congrès international d'archéologie slave, Bratislava 7–14 septembre 1975*, ed. by B. Chropovský, vol. I (Bratislava: VEDA, 1979), pp. 581–586; E. Stoicovici, "Unele caracteristici ale zgurilor din atelierele metalurgice daco-romane şi prefeudale [Some characteristics of iron slags from post-Roman and early medieval furnaces]," *Banatica*, vol. 7 (1983), pp. 239–247; J. Piaskowski, "Metallkundliche Untersuchungen antiker und frühmittelalterlicher Eisengegenstände," in *Iatrus-Krivina. Spätantike Befestigung und frühmittelalterliche Siedlung an der unteren Donau*, ed. by G. von Bülow and D. Schieferdecker, vol. IV (Berlin: Akademie Verlag, 1991), pp. 241–260.

with little, if any, research on diseases and malformations of medieval populations.[68] To date, no DNA sampling and analysis has been done on any skeletal remains from any medieval cemetery in Southeastern Europe, despite the considerable significance such research may have not just for trying to trace migrations and ethnic affiliations, but also for medical history and the anthropology of kin groups.

Zooarchaeology developed primarily in Hungary and Romania, with very little work done in any other country of Southeastern Europe. Scholars involved in this relatively new field of research have been quick in adopting a rather broad view of animal breeding as a strategy of survival in an economically complex environment.[69] Paleobotany, including pollen sampling and analysis, is a method of investigation that has so far been applied only sporadically to medieval sites, often with the purpose of reconstructing the paleoecology of the

[68] P. Lipták, "The Avar-period Mongoloids in Hungary," *AAASH*, vol. 10 (1959), pp. 251–279; Ž. Mikic, "Ein Beitrag zur anthropologischen Bevölkerungsgeschichte des Zentral- und Westbalkangebietes im 1. nachchristlichen Jahrtausend," *Starinar*, vol. 48 (1997), pp. 109–121. However, there has been some interesting work done, mainly by Hungarian and Bulgarian scholars, on the sexual dimorphism and life expectancy of medieval populations. See K. Éry, "Comparative statistical studies on the physical anthropology of the Carpathian basin population between the 6–12th centuries AD," *Alba Regia*, vol. 20 (1983), pp. 89–141; V. Ruseva, "Mortality patterns and life expectancy in medieval skeleton populations from Bulgaria (VIII–X c. AD)," *AB*, vol. 7 (2003), pp. 77–84.

[69] L. Bartosiewicz, "Az állatcsontok eloszálasi rendszere avar temetkezésekben [Patterns of animal offerings in Avar burials]," *Móra Ferenc Múzeum Evkönyve*, vol. 1 (1984–1985), pp. 77–95; M. Ş. Udrescu, "Vînătoarea şi creşterea animalelor în sec. VIII–XI în sud-estul României. Unele corelaţii între ocupaţii si condiţii ecologice [Hunting and animal breeding in southeastern Romania during the eighth to eleventh centuries. Some correlations between human occupations and ecological conditions]," *Revista Muzeelor*, vol. 17 (1980), pp. 56–60; L. Bejenaru, "Caracterele eto-ecologice şi de răspândire ale speciilor de animale sălbatice din România, în concordanţă cu evoluţia ambientului în prima parte a mileniului II e.n. [The eto-ecological peculiarities and the spread of wild fauna in Romania, in relation to the development of the medieval landscape during the first part of the second millennium AD]," *Arheologia Moldovei*, vol. 21 (1998), pp. 277–321; and "Date arheozoologice privind unele tipuri de animale domestice existente în evul mediu pe teritoriul României [Zooarchaeological data on some domestic animals in existence in present-day Romania during the Middle Ages]," *Arheologia medievală*, vol. 3 (2000), pp. 253–262; A. Powell, "The faunal remains," in *Byzantine Butrint: Excavations and Surveys, 1994–99*, ed. by R. Hodges, W. Bowden, and K. Lako (Oxford: Oxbow, 2004), pp. 305–320.

medieval landscape.[70] Landscape archaeology, on the other hand, an approach that employs several techniques to reconstruct economies of large areas and relate them to patterns of control, cult, and status, has yet to make its appearance in Southeastern Europe.

APPROACHES AND INTERPRETATIVE FRAMEWORKS

Only one book has ever been written in English on the medieval history of the entire region as defined above. This is Peter Sugar's *Southeastern Europe under Ottoman Rule*, from which the present book is different both in chronological and geographical scope.[71] The literature written in English has been dominated so far by John V. A. Fine's surveys with their primarily political and constitutional focus,[72] as well as by a relatively large number of studies, often translations of works produced in other languages, with narrowly defined topics ranging from archaeology to manuscript studies. No attempt has ever been made to incorporate the archaeological sources at a regional level or to use the many and extremely detailed art history studies to bring up issues of patronage and politics of culture. Within the region itself, there were substantial differences and divergent developments, with little interest for comparative approaches. For example, medieval Bulgaria is often compared to Byzantium, but not to Croatia, while the histories and archaeologies of Byzantine Greece and Bulgaria are rarely, if ever, viewed as the two sides of the same coin.

[70] M. Cârciumaru, "Analiza polinică a stratelor de la Bucov (jud. Prahova) [The pollen analysis of the medieval strata at Bucov, Prahova district]," *Studii şi cercetări de istorie veche*, vol. 23 (1972), p. 427; K. Borojević, "Analiza ugljenisanog semenja sa lokaliteta Svetinja [The analysis of charred seeds from the Svetinja site]," *Starinar*, vol. 38 (1987), pp. 65–71. See also E. Bozhilova and Iu. Atanasova, "Paleoekologichni usloviia i istoriia na rastitelnostta v raiona na Durankulashkoto ezero [The paleoecological conditions and the history of vegetation in the region of the Durankulak Lake]," in *Durankulak*, ed. by H. Todorova (Sofia: Bălgarskata Izdatelstvo na Bălgarskata Akademiia na Naukite, 1989), pp. 197–204.

[71] See Sugar, *Southeastern Europe*. The phrase "Southeastern Europe" is used also in the title of Georg Stadtmüller's *Geschichte Südosteuropas* (Munich: R. Oldenbourg, 1950). Like Sugar, Stadtmüller had little interest in a detailed examination of the earlier medieval period and jumped instead to the Ottoman and post-Ottoman periods.

[72] See Fine, *Early Medieval Balkans* and *Late Medieval Balkans*. There is to date no bibliography of the scholarship produced in English on medieval Southeastern Europe.

The research agendas and interpretative paradigms within which the history of different regions of medieval Southeastern Europe has been written have changed over time and vary nationally and even regionally. During the 1950s and 1960s the research agenda was tied to the new requirements of the cultural policies promoted by the Communist regimes and to the predominantly Marxist philosophy that inspired them. Economic and social issues were now to be preferred to any of the traditional topics, ranging from political to church history.[73] In addition, the new emphasis on economic and social history encouraged the use of the archaeological evidence, instead of, or in combination with, written sources. That evidence derived first and foremost from the excavation of cemeteries, the first archaeological sites to be published as monographs. Cemeteries were preferred because of the firm belief that the analysis of grave goods will produce conclusions about social structure, which could in turn serve for the writing of the new social history.[74] The use of archaeological sources also encouraged a shift in emphasis from the later to the early Middle

[73] G. László, *Etudes archéologiques sur l'histoire de la société des Avars* (Budapest: Akadémiai kiadó, 1955); P. Blaznik, *Zemljiska gospostva v območju freisinske dolenjske posesti* [Medieval Manors on the Estates of the Freising Chapter in Lower Carniola] (Ljubljana: Slovenska Akademia Znanosti in Umetnosti, 1958); A. Bartha, *A IX–X. századi magyar társadalom* [The Hungarian Society during the Ninth and Tenth Centuries] (Budapest: Akadémiai kiadó, 1968); D. Klen, *Fratrija. Feud opatije sv. Mihovila nad Limom u Istri i njegova sela (XI–XVII st.)* [Fratrija, a Fief of the Abbey of St. Michael above Lim in Istria and its Villages (Eleventh to Seventeenth Century)] (Pazin and Rijeka: Historijski arhiv, 1969); D. Angelov, *Obshtestvo i obshtestvena misăl v srednovekovna Bălgariia (IX–XIV v.)* [Society and Social Structure in Medieval Bulgaria (Ninth to Fourteenth Century] (Sofia: Partizdat, 1979). After more than forty years of total neglect, medieval economic history is now experiencing a remarkable revival in Serbia that parallels similar developments in Western Europe. See Z. M. Njegovan and M. Pantelić, *Agriculture of Medieval Serbia* (Belgrade: Economics Institute, 1998); S. M. Ćirković, D. Kovačević-Kojić, and R. Čuk, *Staro srpsko rudarstvo* [Early Serbian Mining] (Novi Sad: Prometej, 2002).

[74] See J. Korošec, *Staroslovenska grobišča v Severni Sloveniji* [Old Slavonic cemeteries in Northern Slovenia] (Celje: Tiskarna družbe Sv. Mohorja, 1947); J. Kastelić, *Slovanska nekropola na Bledu. Arheološko in antropološko poročilo za leto 1948* [The Slavic Cemetery in Bled. Archaeological and Anthropological Research in 1948] (Ljubljana: Slovenska Akademija Znanosti in Umetnosti, 1950); S. Stanchev and S. Ivanov, *Nekropolăt do Novi Pazar* [The Novi Pazar Cemetery] (Sofia: Izdatelstvo na Bălgarskata Akademiia na Naukite, 1958); S. Beslagić and Đ. Basler, *Grborezi, srednjovjekovna nekropola* [Grborezi, the Medieval Cemetery] (Sarajevo: Zavod za zaštitu spomenika kulture, 1964). The excavation and publication of settlement sites came comparatively later. In Romania, the sites first published as monographs were Byzantine forts in the Lower Danube region. See G. Florescu,

Ages, particularly the centuries of the so-called "Great Migration" or "barbarian invasions" which had been until then almost completely neglected.[75] However, the 1950s and 1960s also show the signs of remarkable continuity with the pre-war research agenda. This was a period of major importance for the publication of critical editions of sources or of collections of sources in translation, as well as for the publication of works of traditional political or even art history.[76] In Croatia and Hungary, this was also a period of interest in the

R. Florescu, and P. Diaconu, *Capidava I* (Bucharest: Editura Academiei Republicii Socialiste România, 1958); Gh. Ştefan, I. Barnea, M. Comşa, and E. Comşa, *Dinogetia I. Aşezarea feudală timpurie de la Bisericuţa-Garvăn* [Dinogetia I. The Early Medieval Settlement in Bisericuţa-Garvăn] (Bucharest: Editura Academiei Republicii Socialiste România, 1967). The first rural settlements identified by means of archaeological excavations were published in Bulgaria by Zh. Văzharova, *Slaviano-bălgarskoto selishte* and *Slavianski i slavianobălgarski selishta*, followed by the Romanian archaeologist E. Zaharia, *Săpăturile de la Dridu*. For the earliest attempts to write history exclusively on the basis of the archaeological evidence, see K. Horedt, *Untersuchungen zur Frühgeschichte Siebenbürgens* (Bucharest: Editura Academiei Republicii Populare Române, 1958); G. B. Fedorov, *Naselenie Prutsko-Dnestrovskogo mezhdurech'ia v I tysiacheletii n.e.* [The Population of the Region between the Prut and Dniester Rivers during the First Millennium AD] (Moscow: Izdatel'stvo Akademii Nauk SSSR, 1960).

75 J. Kovačević, *Varvarska kolonizacija južnoslovenskih oblasti od IV do početka VII veka* [The Barbarian Colonization of the Yugoslav Lands from the Fourth to the Early Seventh Century] (Novi Sad: Vojvodanski Muzej, 1960); D. Csallány, *Archäologische Denkmäler der Gepiden im Mitteldonaubecken* (Budapest: Akadémiai kiadó, 1961); V. Tăpkova-Zaimova, *Nashestviia i etnicheski promeni na balkanite prez VI–VII v.* [Barbarian Invasions and Ethnic Changes in the Sixth- to Seventh-Century Balkans] (Sofia: Izdatelstvo na Bălgarskata Akademiia na Naukite, 1966); I. Bóna, *A középkor hajnala. A gepidák és a langobardok a Kárpát-medencében* [The Dawn of the Middle Ages. Gepids and Lombards in the Carpathian Basin] (Budapest: Akadémiai kiadó, 1974).

76 The 1950s witnessed the launching of several multi-volume series of sources in translation: *Grăcki izvori za bălgarskata istoriia* [Greek Sources for the History of Bulgaria], ed. by V. Beshevliev et al., 11 vols. (Sofia: Izdatelstvo na Bălgarskata Akademiia na Naukite, 1954–1983); *Latinski izvori za bălgarskata istoriia* [Latin Sources for the History of Bulgaria], ed. by I. Duichev et al., 3 vols. (Sofia: Izdatelstvo na Bălgarskata Akademiia na Naukite, 1958 and 1965); *Vizantijski izvori za istoriju naroda Jugoslavije* [Byzantine Sources for the History of the Yugoslav Peoples], ed. by F. Barišić et al., 2 vols. (Belgrade: Naučna knjiga, 1955 and 1959). See also Mošin, *Ljetopis popa Dukljanina*; F. Barišić, Čuda Dimitrija Solunskog *kao istoriski izvori* [The *Miracles of St. Demetrius* as Historical Source] (Belgrade: Srpska Akademija Nauka, 1953); Novak, *Zadarski kartular*. In Hungary the publication of sources in translation, particularly of those written in Greek, continued to be a salient feature of medieval studies until very recently. See G. Moravcsik, *Az Arpád-kori magyar történet bizánci forrásai* [Byzantine sources for the history

political and cultural influence of Byzantium, a topic that caught the attention of Romanian and Bulgarian scholars only in the 1970s.[77] In both Romania and Bulgaria, this has coincided with a concern with the publication of inscriptions, both late antique and medieval.[78] In the course of the 1970s and 1980s, the first monographs dedicated to medieval coins were published in Hungary and Bulgaria, while a formidable explosion of studies on medieval architecture, sculpture, and painting was taking place in Yugoslavia, with no parallel in any other country in Southeastern Europe.[79] In Hungary and Bulgaria,

of Hungary during the Arpadian age] (Budapest: Akadémiai kiadó, 1984); S. Szádeczky-Kardoss, *Az avar történelem forrásai 557–töl 806-ig* [The Sources of Avar History, 557–806] (Budapest: Balassi kiadó, 1998). See also *Diplomata Hungariae antiquissima*; J. M. Bak, G. Bónis, and J. R. Sweeney. *The Laws of the Medieval Kingdom of Hungary, 1000–1301* (Bakersfield: Charles Schlacks, 1989). For the traditional political history, see S. Antoljak, *Samuilovata drzhava* [Samuel's State] (Skopje: Institut za nacionalna istorija, 1969). For church history, see I. Ostojić, *Benediktinci u Hrvatskoj* [The Benedictines in Croatia] (Split: Benediktinski priorat Tkon, 1963). For art history, see N. Mavrodinov, *Starobălgarskoto izkustvo* [The Old Bulgarian Art], 2 vols. (Sofia: Nauka i izkustvo, 1959 and 1966).

77 J. Ferluga, *Vizantijska uprava u Dalmaciji* [The Byzantine Rule in Dalmatia] (Belgrade: Naučno delo, 1958); G. Moravcsik, *Bizánc és a magyarság* [Byzantium and the Hungarians] (Budapest: Akadémiai kiadó, 1953). For Romania and Bulgaria, see I. Barnea, O. Iliescu, and C. Nicolescu, *Cultura bizantină în România* [Byzantine Culture in Romania] (Bucharest: Editura Meridiane, 1971); V. Tăpkova-Zaimova, *Dolni Dunav – granichna zona na Vizantiiskiia Zapad. Kăm istoriiata na severnite i severoiztochnite bălgarski zemi, kraia na X–XII v.* [The Lower Danube Frontier of the Byzantine West. On the History of the North and Northeast Bulgarian Lands between the Late Tenth and the Twelfth Century] (Sofia: Izdatelstvo na Bălgarskata Akademiia na Naukite, 1976); D. Gh. Teodor, *Romanitatea carpato-dunăreană şi Bizanţul în veacurile V–XI* [Byzantium and the Romance-Speaking Population between the Carpathians and the Danube, Fifth to Eleventh Century] (Iaşi: Junimea, 1981).

78 In Bulgaria, such concerns date back to the early 1960s. See Beshevliev, *Die protobulgarischen Inschriften* and *Spätgriechische und spätlateinische Inschriften*. See also Popescu, *Inscripţiile greceşti şi latine* and A. Medynceva and K. Popkonstantinov, *Nadpisi iz Krugloi cerkvi v Preslave* [The Inscriptions of the Preslav Rotonda] (Sofia: Izdatelstvo na Bălgarskata Akademiia na Naukite, 1984).

79 I. Iordanov, *Moneti i monetno obrăshtenie v srednovekovna Bălgariia* [Coins and Coin Circulation in Medieval Bulgaria] (Sofia: Izdatelstvo na Bălgarskata Akademiia na Naukite, 1984); L. Kovács, *Münzen aus der ungarischen Landnahmezeit. Archäologische Untersuchungen der arabischen, byzantinischen, westeuropäischen und römischen Münzen aus dem Karpatenbecken des 10. Jahrhunderts* (Budapest: Akadémiai kiadó, 1989). From among many art history studies published in Yugoslavia during the 1970s and 1980s, see especially S. Gunjača and D. Jelovina, *Starohrvatska umjetnost* [Old Croatian Art] (Zagreb: Grafički zavod Hrvatske, 1976); M. Zadnikar, *Romanika v*

the first biographies of medieval kings were published during this period, which also witnessed a revival of interest in church history.[80] An interest in medieval nomads is visible during these years in both Romania and Hungary, while Bulgarian and Yugoslav scholars were the first to publish monographs on medieval monastic sites.[81] In most

Sloveniji. Tipologija in morfologija sakralne arhitekture [Romanesque Art in Slovenia. The Typology and Morphology of the Church Architecture] (Ljubljana: Državna Založba Slovenije, 1982); J. Maksimović, *Srpske srednovjekovne minijature* [Serbian Medieval Manuscript Illumination] (Belgrade: Prosveta, 1983); Ž. Rapanić, *Predromaničko doba u Dalmaciji* [Pre-Romanesque Art in Dalmatia] (Split: Logos, 1987); M. Čanak-Medić and Đ. Bošković, *Arhitektura Nemanijnog doba* [The Architecture of the Nemanjid Era], 2 vols. (Belgrade: Republicki Zavod za zaštitu spomenika kulture, 1986 and 1989); and I. Fisković, *Romaničko slikarstvo u Hrvatskoj* [Romanesque Painting in Croatia] (Zagreb: Muzej za umjtenost i obrt, 1987). However, the 1970s and 1980s also witnessed the publication of some important studies on medieval architecture and decorative arts in Bulgaria and Greece. See T. Totev, *Preslavskata keramichna ikona* [The Preslav Ceramic Icons] (Sofia: Bălgarski khudozhnik, 1988); N. Chaneva-Dechevska, *Cărkovnata arkhitektura v Bălgariia prez XI–XIV vek* [Church Architecture in Bulgaria between the Eleventh and the Fourteenth Century] (Sofia: Izdatelstvo na Bălgarskata Akademiia na Naukite, 1988); P. L. Vokotopoulos, *He ekklesiastike architektonike eis ten dytiken sterean Hellada kai ten Epeiron. Apo tou telous tou 7ou mechri tou telous tou 10ou aionos* [The Church Architecture of Northwestern Greece and of Epirus (Late Seventh to Tenth Century)] (Thessaloniki: Kentron Byzantinon Ereunon, 1975).

80 G. Győrffy, *István kiraly és müve* [King Stephen and his Time] (Budapest: Gondolat, 1977); I. Bozhilov, *Car Simeon Veliki (893–927). Zlatniiat vek na srednovekovna Bălgariia* [Emperor Symeon the Great (893–927). The Golden Age of Medieval Bulgaria] (Sofia: Izdatelstvo na Otechestveniia Front, 1983). The genre remains popular in Bulgaria. See P. Pavlov, *Kniaz Presian vtori – posledniiat vladetel na părvoto bălgarsko carstvo i pretendent za vizantiiskata korona 996/997–1060/61* [Prince Presian II, the Last Ruler of the First Bulgarian Kingdom and Claimant to the Byzantine Throne] (Veliko Tărnovo and Stara Zagora: Zhivelev, 1993). For church history, see the reprint of J. Karácsonyi, *Magyarország egyháztörténete föbb vonásaiban* [The History of the Hungarian Church] (Budapest: Könyvértékesitö Vállalat, 1985) and T. Săbev, *Samostoina narodnostna cărkva v srednovekovna Bălgariia. Khristiianizatorski proces, osnovavane i văzkhod, avtokefaliia i mezhducărkovno polozhenie: cărkva i dărzhava, rolia i znachenie* [The Independent Popular Church in Medieval Bulgaria. The Process of Christianization, the Foundation and Progress of the Bulgarian Church, its Autocephalous Status and Position within the Universal Church: Church and State, its Role and Significance] (Sofia: Sinodalno izdatelstvo, 1987).

81 P. Diaconu, *Les Pétchénègues au Bas-Danube* (Bucharest: Editions de l'Académie de la République Socialiste de Roumanie, 1970) and *Les Coumans au Bas-Danube aux XIe–XIIe siècles* (Bucharest: Editura Academiei Republicii Socialiste România, 1978); V. Spinei, *Realităţi etnice şi politice în Moldova meridională în secolele X–XIII. Români şi turanici* [Ethnic and Political Realities in Southern Moldavia during

Southeast European countries, settlement sites were investigated during the 1970s and 1980s as part of regional or microregional studies, despite the popularity single-site monographs continued to enjoy in Romania and Bulgaria.[82] In both countries, there was a specific

the Tenth to Thirteenth Centuries] (Iaşi: Junimea, 1985); A. Páloczi-Horváth, *Besenyök, kunok, jászkok* [Pechenegs, Cumans, and Alans] (Budapest: Corvina, 1989); Cs. Bálint, *Die Archäologie der Steppe. Steppenvölker zwischen Volga und Donau vom 6. bis zum 10. Jahrhundert* (Vienna and Cologne: Böhlau, 1989). For the archaeology of monasteries, see P. Miljković-Pepek, *Veljusa. Manastir Sv. Bogorodica Milostiva vo seloto Veljusa kraj Strumica* [Veljusa. The Monastery of the Mother of God of Mercy in Veljusa, near Strumica] (Skopje: Fakultet za filozofsko-istoriski nauki na univerzitetot "Kiril i Metodij," 1981); T. Totev, *Manastirăt v "Tuzlalăka" – centăr na risuvana keramika v Preslav IX–X v.* [The Monastery in Tuzlalăka: a Preslav Center for the Production of Painted Pottery (Ninth to Tenth Century)] (Sofia: Izdatelstvo na Bălgarskata Akademiia na Naukite, 1982); S. Petković, *Morača* (Belgrade: Srpska književna zadruga IRO "Prosveta," 1986); N. Tuleshkov, *Arkhitektura na bălgarskite manastiri* [The Architecture of the Bulgarian Monasteries] (Sofia: Izdatelstvo na Bălgarskata Akademiia na Naukite, 1988).

82 D. Svoljšak and T. Knific, *Vipavska Dolina. Zgodnjesrednjeveska najdišča* [Early Medieval Sites in the Vipava Valley] (Ljubljana: Narodni Muzej, 1976); D. Gh. Teodor, *The East-Carpathian Area of Romania in the V–XI Centuries AD* (Oxford: BAR International Series, 1980); Đ. Janković, *Podunavski deo oblasti Akvisa u VI i početkom VII veka* [The Danube River Bank in the Environs of Aquis during the Sixth and Early Seventh Century] (Belgrade: Arheološki Institut, 1981); L. Szekeres, *Középkori települések Északkelet-Bácskában* [Medieval Settlements in Northern Bačka] (Ujvidék: Forum, 1983); S. Ercegović-Pavlović and D. Kostić, *Arheološki spomenici i nalazišta Leskovačkog kraja* [Archaeological Monuments and Finds in the Leskovac Region] (Belgrade: Arheološki Institut, 1988); N. Klaić, *Vinodol od antičkih vremena do knežova Krckih i Vinodolskog zakona* [Vinodol from Antiquity to the Lords of Krk and the Vinodol Statutes] (Pazin and Rijeka: Historijski arhiv, 1988). For single-site monographs, see S. Dolinescu-Ferche, *Aşezări din secolele III şi VI e.n. în sud-vestul Munteniei. Cercetările de la Dulceanca* [Third- and Sixth-Century Settlement Sites in Southwestern Walachia. Excavations in Dulceanca] (Bucharest: Editura Academiei Republicii Socialiste România, 1974); Comşa, *Cultura materială*; I. Glodariu, F. Costea, and I. Ciupe, *Comana de Jos. Aşezările de epocă dacică şi prefeudală* [Comana de Jos. Dacian and Early Medieval Settlements] (Cluj-Napoca: Dacia, 1980); S. Vaklinov and S. Stanilov, *Kladenci. Rannosrednovekovno bălgarsko selishte* [Kladenci, an Early Medieval Bulgarian Settlement] (Varna: Knigoizdatelstvo "Georgi Bakalov," 1981); P. Gatev, *Srednovekovno selishte i nekropol ot XII v. krai s. Kovachevo, Pazardzhishki okrăg* [The Twelfth-Century Medieval Settlement and Cemetery near Kovachevo, Pazardzhik District] (Sofia: Izdatelstvo na Bălgarskata Akademiia na Naukite, 1985). The publication of single-site monographs continued unabated through the 1990s and the most recent years. See I. Mitrea, *Aşezarea din secolele VI–IX de la Izvoare-Bahna. Realităţi arheologice şi concluzii istorice* [The Sixth- to Ninth-Century Settlement in Izvoare-Bahna. Archaeological Realities and Historical Conclusions] (Piatra Neamţ: Complexul Muzeal

interest in medieval cities and fortifications in the 1980s, in sharp contrast with the almost exclusive concentration of Yugoslav archaeologists upon cemetery sites.[83] The multiplication of approaches and the variety of sources now available to scholars interested in the Middle Ages prompted the publication, first in Yugoslavia and Bulgaria, of works of synthesis dedicated entirely to medieval history.[84] In Bulgaria, this increase in the number of publications dedicated to

Judeţean Neamţ, 1998); I. Dzhambov, *Srednovekovnoto selishte nad antichniia grad pri Khisar* [A Medieval Settlement near the Ancient City by Hisar] (Asenovgrad: Ekobelan, 2002).

83 D. Ovcharov, *Vizantiiski i bălgarski kreposti V–X vek* (Sofia: Izdatelstvo na Bălgarskata Akademiia na Naukite, 1982); R. Rashev, *Starobălgarski ukrepleniia na Dolniia Dunav (VII–XI v.)* [Old Bulgarian Fortifications on the Lower Danube (Seventh to Eleventh Century)] (Varna: Knigoizdatelstvo "Georgi Bakalov," 1982); M. Petrescu-Dîmboviţa, *Sisteme de fortificaţii medievale timpurii la est de Carpaţi. Aşezarea de la Fundu Herţii (jud. Botoşani)* [Early Medieval Defense Systems East of the Carpathian Mountains. The Fundu Herţii Hillfort] (Iaşi: Junimea, 1987); R. Rashev and S. Stanilov, *Starobălgarsko ukrepeno selishte pri s. Khuma, Razgradski okrăg* [An Old Bulgarian Hillfort near Khuma, Razgrad District] (Sofia: Izdatelstvo na Bălgarskata Akademiia na Naukite, 1987); M. D. Matei, *Civilizaţie urbană medievală românească. Contribuţii (Suceava pînă la mijlocul secolului al XVI-lea)* [Romanian Urban Civilization during the Middle Ages. Contributions (Suceava until the Mid-1500s)] (Bucharest: Editura Academiei Republicii Socialiste România, 1989). For cemetery archaeology in Yugoslavia, see D. Jelovina, *Starohrvatske nekropole na području između rijeka Zrmanje i Cetine* [Old Croatian Cemeteries between the Zrmanja and the Cetina Rivers] (Split: Čakavski sabor, 1976); G. Marjanović-Vujović, *Trnjane, srpska nekropola (kraj 11–početak 13. veka)* [Trnjane, a Serbian Cemetery of the Late Eleventh to Early Thirteenth Century] (Belgrade: Arheološki Institut, 1984); S. Ercegović-Pavlović, *Srednjovjekovna naselja i nekropole u Boljetinu i Hajdučkoj Vodenici* [Medieval Villages and Cemeteries in Boljetin and Hajdučka Vodenica] (Belgrade: Arheološki Institut, 1986); B. Marušić, *Starohrvatska nekropola u Žminju* [The Old Croatian Cemetery in Žminj] (Pula: Arheološki Muzej Istre, 1987); N. Stanojev, *Nekropole X–XV veka u Vojvodini* [Tenth- to Fifteenth-Century Cemeteries in Vojvodina] (Novi Sad: Arheološko društvo Vojvodine, 1989).

84 N. Klaić, *Povijest Hrvata u ranom srednjem vijeku* [History of Croatia during the Early Middle Ages] (Zagreb: Školska knjiga, 1971); G. Cankova-Petkova, *Bălgariia pri Asenevci* [Bulgaria under the Assenids] (Sofia: Izdatelstvo na Bălgarskata Akademiia na Naukite, 1978); V. Beshevliev, *Die protobulgarische Periode der bulgarischen Geschichte* (Amsterdam: Adolf Hakkert, 1981); P. Petrov, *Obrazuvane na bălgarskata dărzhava* [The Rise of the Bulgarian State] (Sofia: Nauka i izkustvo, 1981); V. Beshevliev, *Părvobălgari. Istoriia* [The History of the Bulgars] (Sofia: Izdatelstvo na Otechestveniia front, 1984); S. Antoljak and B. Panov, *Srednovekovna Makedonija* [Medieval Macedonia] (Skopje: Misla, 1985); M. Blagojević, *Srbija u doba Nemanjica. Od kneževine do carstva: 1168–1371* [Serbia during the Nemanjid Era. From Principality to Empire, 1168–1371] (Belgrade: TRZ "VAJAT" and

medieval history may have been prompted by the 1100th anniversary of Prince Boris's conversion to Christianity, an event conspicuously treated as a political rather than religious achievement. Similarly, the recent upsurge of monographs on early medieval Croatia and Nemanjid Serbia must be viewed against the background of the war in Yugoslavia in the 1990s. But this is no novel phenomenon: medieval studies in Southeastern Europe have always been a key area of confrontation for competing nationalistic discourses. In Greece, the "Slavs" became the national enemy during and after the Civil War. By 1950, those embracing the ideology of the right saw their political rivals as the embodiment of all that was anti-national, Communist, and Slavic. A strong link was established between national identity and political orientation, as the Civil War and the subsequent defeat of the left-wing movement turned Slav Macedonians into the Sudetens of Greece. As a consequence, much more was written on the "Slavic problem" than on any other topic of medieval history.[85] Conversely,

IRO "Beograd," 1989). The publication of works of synthesis on the "national" history during the Middle Ages gained in importance during and after the war in Yugoslavia, particularly in Croatia and Serbia. See S. M. Ćirković, *La Serbie au Moyen Age* (La-Pierre-qui-Vire: Zodiaque, 1992) and *Srbi u srednjem veku* [Serbians in the Middle Ages] (Belgrade: IDEA, IP Glosarijum, and Službeni glasnik, 1995); N. Budak, *Prva stoljeca Hrvatske* [The First Centuries of Croatian History] (Zagreb: Hrvatska sveučališna naklada, 1994]; I. Goldstein, *Hrvatski rani srednji vijek* [The Early Middle Ages in Croatia] (Zagreb: Zavod za hrvatsku povijest Filozofskog fakulteta Sveučilišta u Zagrebu, 1995).

85 D. A. Zakythinos, *Hoi Slavoi en Helladi. Symvolai eis ten historian tou mesaionikou Hellenismou* [Slavs in Greece. Contributions to the History of Medieval Hellenism] (Athens: Aetos, 1945); S. P. Kyriakides, *Byzantina Meletai VI: Hoi Slaboi en Peloponneso* [Byzantine Studies VI: The Slavs in Peloponnesus] (Thessaloniki: Hetaireia Makedonikon Spoudon, 1947). The interest in the "Slavic problem" was revived in 1991, at the time of the proclamation of the Republic of Macedonia (to this day not recognized by that name in Greece), and remains a controversial topic. See M. G. Nystazopoulou, *Slabikes enkatastaseis ste mesaionike Hellada: genike episkopose* [The Slavic Invasions into Medieval Greece] (Athens: Hidryma Goulandre-Chorn, 1995); Ph. Malingoudis, *He Thessalonike kai ho kosmos ton Slabon. Eisagogika dokimia* [Thessaloniki and the World of the Slavs] (Thessaloniki: Vanias, 1997); A. K. Iliadi, *Ta "thaumata" tou Agiou Demetriou hos istorikes peges. Epidromes kai slabikes epoikiseis enteuthen tou Dounabeos* [The Miracles of St. Demetrius as Historical Source] (Trikala: Vogiatzouglou Thrasyvoulos, 2003). For Vlachs and Slavs in Soviet Moldova, see V. D. Koroliuk, *Volokhi i slaviane russkoi letopisi* [Vlachs and Slavs in the Rus' Chronicles] (Kishinew: Shtiinca, 1971); I. A. Rafalovich, *Slaviane VI–IX vekov v Moldavii* [Sixth- to Ninth-Century Slavs in Moldova] (Kishinew: Shtiinca, 1972); G. B. Fedorov and L. L. Polevoi, *Arkheologiia Rumynii* [The Archaeology of Romania] (Moscow: Nauka, 1973).

there was a particularly strong interest in Romanian archaeology and medieval Vlachs in the 1970s, because of the Romanian nationalistic agitations in Soviet Moldova. Increased political tensions between Romania and Hungary over Transylvania were responsible for the obsessive preoccupation with the theory of Romanian continuity among Romanian scholars studying medieval Transylvania, as well as for the polemical tone of contemporary works published in Hungary on that same topic.[86] Finally, ever since the war in Yugoslavia there has been an increasing body of literature on ethnogenesis, which continues to grow as new identities are now forged out of old languages and historical traditions.[87]

During the last fifteen years, the predominant tendency was one of increasing particularism. Despite earlier and timid attempts at describing political and cultural interactions within the region,[88] studies of

[86] L. Bârzu, *Continuitatea creației materiale și spirituale a poporului român pe teritoriul fostei Dacii* [The Continuity of the Romanian People's Material and Spiritual Culture on the Territory of Formerly Roman Dacia] (Bucharest: Editura Academiei Republicii Socialiste România, 1979); N. Stoicescu, *Continuitatea românilor. Privire istoriografică: istoricul problemei, dovezile continuității* [Romanian Continuity: A Historiographic Perspective (History of the Problem and the Proofs of Continuity)] (Bucharest: Editura Ştiinţifică şi Enciclopedică, 1980); L. Bârzu and S. Brezeanu, *Originea și continuitatea românilor. Arheologie și tradiție istorică* [The Origin and Continuity of the Romanians. Archaeology and Historical Tradition] (Bucharest: Editura Enciclopedică, 1991). For a contemporary Hungarian response, see *Erdély története* [History of Transylvania], ed. by B. Köpeczi (Budapest: Akadémiai kiadó, 1986).

[87] A. Pleterski, *Etnogeneza Slovanov: obris trenutnega stanja arheoloških raziskav* [The Ethnogenesis of the Slavs. A Survey of the Current State of Archaeological Research] (Ljubljana: Filozofska fakulteta, Oddelek, 1990); I. Mužić, *Podrijetlo i pravjera Hrvata. Autohtonost u hrvatskoj etnogenezi na tlu rimske provincije Dalmacije* [The Origin of the Croats. Native Origins in the Croatian Ethnogenesis on the Territory of the Former Roman Province of Dalmatia] (Split: Zbornik Kačić, 1991); Đ. Janković, *Srpske gromile* [Serbian Burial Mounds] (Belgrade: Knijževna reč, 1998).

[88] M. Holban, *Din cronica relațiilor româno-ungare în secolele XIII–XIV* [Romanian–Hungarian Relations during the Thirteenth and Fourteenth Centuries] (Bucharest: Editura Academiei Republicii Socialiste România, 1981); R. Čuk, *Srbija i Venecija u XIII i XIV veku* [Serbia and Venetia in the Thirteenth and Fourteenth Centuries] (Belgrade: Prosveta, 1986); E. Mikhailov, *Rusi i bălgari prez rannoto srednovekovie: do 964 g.* [Rus' and Bulgars during the Early Middle Ages (to 964)] (Sofia: Universitetsko izdatelstvo "Kliment Okhridski," 1990). It is primarily in Bulgaria and Greece that this line of research has been followed in recent years. See E. K. Kyriakes, *Byzantio kai Boulgaroi (7os-10os ai.). Symbole sten exoterike politike tou Byzantiou* [Byzantium and the Bulgars. Contributions to the Study

the medieval history of Southeastern Europe have by now taken different paths in different countries, with little, if any, relation to each other. While the history of everyday life and women's history emerge as new lines of research in the literature written in Serbian, Christianity and the history of the Church have only now become a favorite theme of debate in Romania.[89] While church history is still a popular theme in Bulgaria, in addition to a revived interest in political symbolism, urban culture, and microregional studies, the most productive fields of research in that country have been literary studies, prosopography, and sigillography.[90] This diversity of experience,

of Byzantine Foreign Policy] (Athens: St. D. Basilopoulos, 1993); I. Bozhilov, *Bălgarite văv Vizantiiskata imperiia* [Bulgarians in the Byzantine Empire] (Sofia: Akademichno izdatelstvo "Prof. Marin Drinov," 1995); P. Antonopoulos, *Ho autokratoros Konstantinos Z' ho Porphyrogennetos kai hoi Oungroi* [Emperor Constantine VII Porphyrogenitus and the Hungarians] (Athens: Vasilopoulos, 1996); Kh. Dimitrov, *Bălgaro-ungarskite otnosheniia prez srednovekovieto* [Bulgarian–Hungarian Relations in the Middle Ages] (Sofia: Akademichno izdatelstvo "Prof. Marin Drinov," 1998); P. Angelov, *Bălgariia i bălgarite v predstavite na vizantiicite (VII–XIV vek)* [Bulgaria and Bulgarians through Byzantine Eyes (Seventh to Fourteenth Century] (Sofia: Lik, 1999).

89 G. Milošević, *Stanovanje u srednjovekovnoj Srbiji* [The Dwelling in Medieval Serbia] (Belgrade: Arheološki Institut, 1997); S. Marjanović-Dušanić and D. Popović, *Privatni život u srpskim zemljama srednjeg veka* [Private Life in the Serbian Lands during the Middle Ages] (Belgrade: Clio, 2004); L. B. Čelebić, *Žene srednjovjekovnog Kotora* [Women of Medieval Kotor] (Podgorica: CID, 2002). For Romania, see D. Gh. Teodor, *Creştinismul la est de Carpaţi de la origini şi pîna în secolul al XVI-lea* [Christianity in the Regions East of the Carpathian Mountains, from its Origins to the Sixteenth Century] (Iaşi: Junimea, 1991); N. Zugravu, *Geneza creştinismului popular al românilor* [The Rise of the Romanian Popular Christianity] (Bucharest: Editura Academiei Române, 1997); A. Madgearu, *Rolul creştinismului în formarea poporului român* [The Role of Christianity in the Romanian Ethnogenesis] (Bucharest: BIC ALL, 2001).

90 I. Venedikov, *Prabălgarite i khristiianstvoto* [The Bulgars and Christianity] (Stara Zagora: Izdatelstvo "Ideia," 1994); G. Petrova, *Cărkva i cărkovno pravo v srednovekovna Bălgariia* [The Church and Canon Law in Medieval Bulgaria] (Sofia: Sibi, 2005); C. Stepanov, *Vlast i avtoritet v rannosrednovekovna Bălgariia (VII–sr. IX v.)* [Power and Authority in Early Medieval Bulgaria (Seventh to Mid-Ninth Century)] (Sofia: Agató, 1999); R. Panova, *Stolichniiat grad v kulturata na srednovekovna Bălgariia* [The Capital City in the Culture of Medieval Bulgaria] (Sofia: Universitetsko izdatelstvo "Sv. Kliment Okhridski," 1995). For the new themes of Bulgarian historiography, see M. Kaimakamova, *Bălgarska srednovekovna istoriopis (ot kraia na VII do părvata chetvărt na XV v.)* [Medieval Historiography in Bulgaria (Late Seventh to Early Fifteenth Century)] (Sofia: Nauka i izkustvo, 1990); D. Petkanova, *Starobălgarska literatura IX–XVIII vek* [Old Bulgarian Literature (Ninth to Eighteenth Century)] (Sofia:

across time and between regions, will inevitably be reflected in the following chapters. Some topics have been researched thoroughly, but there are still many gaps in our understanding of the medieval history of Southeastern Europe. However, it has now become quite clear that diversity characterizes not only the quality and quantity of research, but also the history of the region. It is as an exploration of that difference and of the interactions between various areas in the region, across visible and invisible frontiers, that this book was written.

Universitetsko izdatelstvo "Kliment Okhridski," 1992); V. Tăpkova-Zaimova and A. Miltenova, *Istoriko-apokaliptichnata knizhnina văv Vizantiia i v srednovekovna Bălgariia* [The Historical and Apocalyptic Literature in Byzantium and Medieval Bulgaria] (Sofia: Universitetsko izdatelstvo "Sv. Kliment Okhridski," 1996); I. Bozhilov, *Familiiata na Asenevci (1186–1460): genealogiia i prosopografiia* [The Assenid Family (1186–1460): Genealogy and Prosopography] (Sofia: Izdatelstvo na Bălgarskata Akademiia na Naukite, 1994); Iordanov, *Pechatite na preslavskite vladeteli* and *Pechatite ot strategiiata.*

I

THE END OF LATE ANTIQUITY OR THE BEGINNING OF THE MIDDLE AGES (*c.* 500–*c.* 600)?

The idea of making the Danube the frontier of the Roman state goes back to Julius Caesar. For more than five centuries, the Roman power remained firmly entrenched in the Balkans and episodically (106–*c.* 275) expanded north of the Danube River into what is today western and southwestern Romania. A dense network of urban centers planted in the lowlands of the interior (especially in Thrace) or on the coasts sustained an administrative infrastructure that by and large remained unchanged from the late fourth to the late sixth century. The imaginary line dividing the Western from the Eastern Empire ran across the western half of the Balkan Peninsula, but the growing differences between the two political entities were barely visible in the region. The political developments associated with the rise of the Hunnic power in the Middle Danube region may explain, at least in part, why in the late antique Balkans the major contrast was north–south, not west–east. Nevertheless, despite the devastation brought in the early 400s to the northern provinces by the Hunnic raids, the natural and military borders continued to complement each other and to form an intricate matrix of Roman imperial self-definition. In the mid-sixth century, Procopius of Caesarea viewed the Danube as the "strongest possible line of defense" against barbarians, a line separating the "territory of the Romans, which is on the right" bank from barbarians living on its northern or left bank.[1] But by 500, both

[1] Procopius of Caesarea, *Buildings* IV.1, ed. by J. Haury with English translation by H. B. Dewing (Cambridge, Mass.: Harvard University Press, 1940), p. 229.

the Roman frontier and the Balkan provinces behind it began to change dramatically.

CITIES, FORTS, AND ECONOMIC LIFE

Perhaps the most visible sign of change was the transformation of the Roman cities. By 500, most, if not all, major cities in the Balkans had contracted and regrouped around a fortified precinct, sometimes located on the highest elevation available, but almost always dominated by a church building. In the northern Balkans, the process had started long before the sixth century. At Sirmium (Sremska Mitrovica, in Serbia), for example, the walls of the city had been leveled in the late fourth or early fifth century, and during the subsequent period most of the public buildings were abandoned, as the city disintegrated into small hamlets emerging in urban areas that had not been in use until then. After *c.* 400, the forum in Corinth (Greece) ceased to function as public square and no private houses were built any more around it. Large buildings, such as the Peribolos of Apollon, were transformed into small rooms subdivided by walls of stones bonded with clay. The hill just north of the Agora was now dominated by a small church with colored marble revetment erected in the late sixth or early seventh century. Archaeological excavations have revealed the extent to which the ancient street grid was altered by the transformations taking place during the fifth and sixth centuries. In Philippopolis (Plovdiv, in Bulgaria), a large church was built in the early 400s on top of two blocks of demolished houses in complete disregard of the access to the neighboring streets. Cities built anew in the 500s had no streets crossing each other at right angles and no public squares. This is the case of the city excavated on the Carevec Hill near modern Veliko Tărnovo in Bulgaria (perhaps the ancient Zikideva), as well as of the city erected in the early 500s in Caričin Grad, near Lebane, in central Serbia. The latter has been identified with Iustiniana Prima built shortly before 535 by Emperor Justinian on the site of his home village. It is on this site that the emperor established an important archbishopric and if we are to believe his novel 11 of 535, it is there that he intended to transfer the prefecture of the western Balkans (Illyricum). Whether Caričin Grad is Iustiniana Prima or not, it certainly represents an urban site of considerable importance, but with no history earlier than the sixth century. When built, it initially consisted of a fortified hill dominated by a large

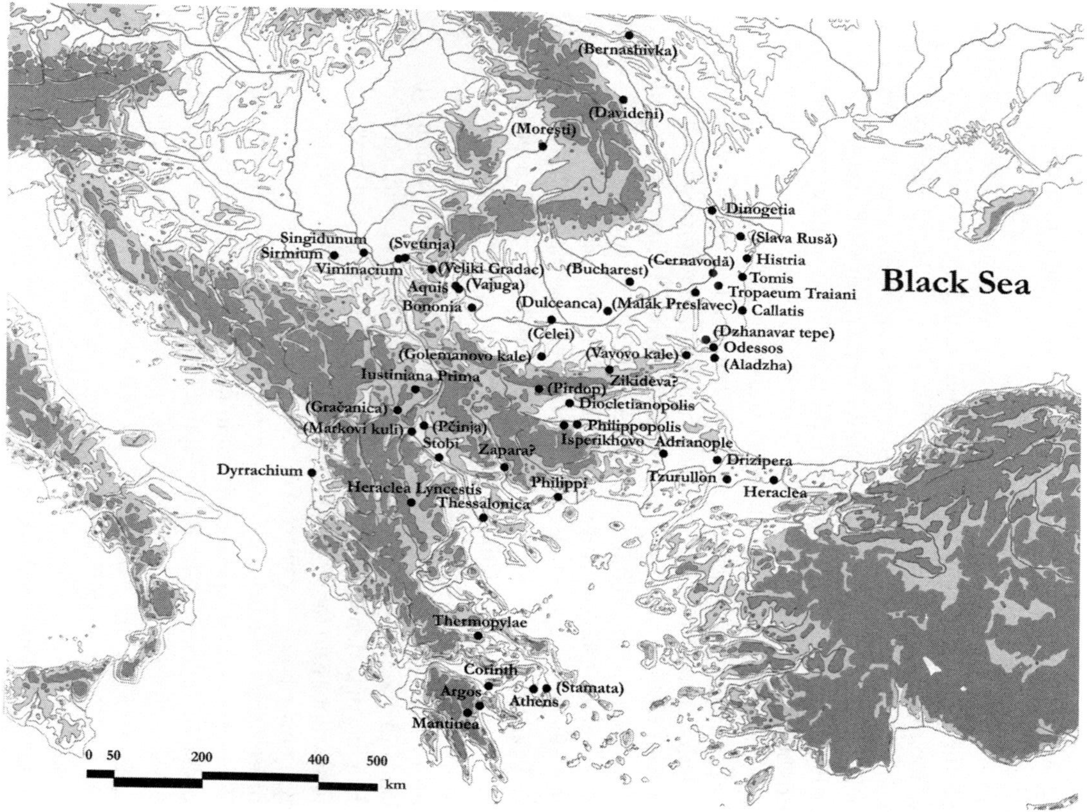

Map 1 Southeastern Europe in the sixth century. Location of the principal sites mentioned in the text by ancient or modern (in parenthesis) names.

episcopal church with a number of accompanying buildings, perhaps the episcopal residence. In addition to seven other churches, the site produced evidence of workshops, bakeries, storerooms, baths, and of course houses, but no public buildings or forum. Instead, the upper city underneath the episcopal basilica was divided into four unequal parts by two colonnaded streets meeting in a large, circular plaza surrounded by porticoes. No administrative buildings existed in or near this plaza. If Caričin Grad was Iustiniana Prima, it is not without interest that when describing the city in his *Buildings*, Procopius mentioned administrative buildings, but no civic administration. The same is true for the site on the Carevec Hill in central Bulgaria: no forum, no administrative buildings, and no streets crossing each other at right angles. Much like Caričin Grad, the site was dominated by a large church erected on the highest elevation available.

Such changes are visible on many sites, and archaeological remains of sixth-century cities suggest that the underlying reason had little to do with relative prosperity. Indeed, in many cases, contraction and encroachment into buildings once of public use are two phenomena that coincide with the construction of magnificent churches, which were now the new symbols of urban prosperity. At Philippi (Greece), the basilica called C for lack of a better name was restored during the second quarter of the sixth century, when it must have been equipped with stained-glass windows, judging by the large quantity of fragments of colored glass found during its excavation. In Sandanski (a site in southwestern Bulgaria tentatively identified with ancient Zapara), a large three-aisled basilica received a magnificent mosaic floor paid for by the city's bishop, as indicated in the accompanying inscription. A capital of marble from the island of Proconnesus in the Sea of Marmara, which has the monogram of Emperor Justinian carved on it, was found within one of the churches excavated in Caričin Grad, while an inscription recently found in Heraclea Lyncestis (Bitola, in Macedonia) specifically mentions the emperor's munificence. Both examples show that some church buildings in the Balkans may have benefited from very powerful and wealthy donors.

At Stobi (Pustogradsko, in Macedonia), large palatial residences with elaborate courtyards, decorated fountains, floors with pavements of mosaic, and walls covered with frescoes, were still in use in the early 500s. Elsewhere, archaeologists discovered aristocratic houses, often equipped with apsed rooms meant for entertaining. Such buildings found in Histria (on the Black Sea coast, in Romania), Diocletianopolis (Hisar, in Bulgaria), Caričin Grad, Butrint (Albania), or Mantinea (Greece) suggest that despite all change, a rich urban class was still in existence in the Balkans.[2] But the identity of that class is in itself indicative of change. The social group most frequently mentioned in late antique inscriptions in the northern Balkans is the military. Several inscriptions referring to new buildings or to repair and ornamentation of existing ones mention bishops, not representatives of the local land-owning aristocracy. In fact, at a closer look, the picture drawn from the enormous amount of archaeological evidence available for the sixth-century Balkans reveals a striking contrast between the multitude of forts and churches built all over the place and the absence of non-fortified rural sites. The economic infrastructure of the sixth-century Roman provinces in the Balkans differed substantially from that of the previous centuries. There were many rural estate villas (so-called *villae rusticae*) in the first- to fourth-century Balkans. However, after the middle of the fifth century, medium-sized estates completely disappeared. With just a few exceptions, mainly in the coastal areas of Greece and Dalmatia, rural villas are conspicuously absent from all surveys of the archaeological research pertaining to the sixth-century Balkans. The evidence of peasant settlements is also scarce. Procopius maintains that Justinian "made the defenses so continuous in the estates, that each farm either had been converted into a stronghold or lies adjacent to one which is fortified."[3] On the other hand, he describes local peasants in Thermopylae (Greece) suddenly changing their form of life, becoming "makeshift soldiers for the occasion" to keep the guard on the local defenses. Elsewhere, entire villages seem to have been abandoned. As the Cutrigurs invaded the Balkans in 558, they moved quickly through the northeastern provinces of Moesia and Scythia Minor, for all they encountered in their way were deserted villages.[4] The only evidence for the survival of a significant peasant population comes from the hinterland of the Empire's capital. Theophylact Simocatta mentions a populous village at about fifteen miles distance from Heraclea (Yeşilköy, in Turkey),

[2] See W. Bowden, "A new urban élite? Church builders and church building in late-antique Epirus," in *Recent Research in Late Antique Urbanism*, ed. by L. Lavan (Portsmouth: Journal of Roman Archaeology, 2001), pp. 57–68.

[3] Procopius of Caesarea, *Buildings* IV.1, p. 229.

[4] Agathias, *Histories* V.11, ed. by R. Keydell (Berlin: De Gruyter, 1967), p. 300.

which supplied the imperial armies with food.[5] Although it is true that archaeologists have a tendency to pay more attention to urban than to rural sites, the archaeological evidence for rural settlements after *c.* 500 is remarkably scanty: just a couple of single-room houses in those provinces that the Cutrigurs crossed in 558. This rarity of rural settlements is in sharp contrast to the evidence of flourishing rural communities in other parts of the Empire. It has been suggested that, faced with continuous barbarian raids, the inhabitants of the rural areas of the Balkans took refuge behind the strong walls of fortified cities. Archaeologists promptly pointed out the relatively large number of small houses with walls of stone and clay built in the 500s in every city of the region, often within the ruins of previously large buildings of public use or of aristocratic houses. Such buildings were hastily interpreted as evidence that the place of the rich may have been taken by the less well-to-do. The blame for this sudden rise in the number of poor inhabitants of Balkan cities fell on barbarian invasions forcing people to abandon their villages and to move into cities. However, the evidence suggests that the new occupants were not peasants. The absence of any significant number of agricultural tools from archaeological assemblages securely dated to the sixth century is in itself significant.[6] Whether or not houses hastily built in stone and clay were for peasant refugees from the countryside, the absence of rural settlements and evidence of agricultural production raises the problem of food supplies for the relatively numerous population of the sixth-century cities and forts.

At any rate, the rarity of rural settlements may be explained in reference to contemporary legal sources. In 505, a law of Emperor Anastasius acknowledged the difficulties of raising taxes in Thrace and introduced strong measures for compulsory collection. In 535, Emperor Justinian legislated again in an attempt to stop the rapid decline of the peasantry in two Balkan provinces, Haemimons and Moesia Inferior. To judge from this source, high-interest loan rates had forced peasants to forfeit their lands. Some had fled and others had died of starvation, the situation being described as worse than after a barbarian invasion. Another law of Justinian issued in 545

[5] Theophylact Simocatta, *History* VI.1.4, ed. by C. de Boor and P. Wirth (Stuttgart: Teubner, 1972); English translation by Mary Whitby and Michael Whitby (Oxford: Clarendon Press, 1986), p. 158.

[6] But see I. Popović, "Les particularités de l'outillage protobyzantin dans les Balkans du Nord," *Starinar*, vols. 45–46 (1994–1995), pp. 67–75.

made every farmer responsible for taxes from the abandoned land of his next-door neighbor. Justinian's successor, Justin II, twice granted tax exemptions for peasants in Moesia and Scythia Minor, in order to ensure that they would be able to provide food supplies for the armies stationed in these two provinces. Whether or not barbarian invasions contributed to the deteriorating situation depicted in these sources, the evidence suggests that in the Balkans the rural class was on the verge of disappearing. This conclusion is substantiated by recruitment shortages, which were particularly visible during Justinian's war in Italy against the Ostrogoths.

Why was the economic infrastructure of the Balkans crumbling at such speed? And if no rural settlements existed to provide constant supplies of food, who fed the soldiers and the inhabitants of the sixth-century Balkan cities? More to the point, how could a region under such economic stress sustain a military effort of the size suggested by the archaeology of early Byzantine forts? According to Procopius, Justinian built or renewed more than 600 forts in the Balkans, eight times more than in the entire Asian part of the Empire. A number of inscriptions from Greece and Albania reveal that responsible for the implementation of this grandiose program of fortification was Justinian's architect Victorinus.[7] The project, or at least its most important part, was probably completed in some twenty years. It was certainly completed in its basic lines when Procopius finished Book IV of his *Buildings*, in which he described three interrelated lines of fortification. Along the Danube and in the immediate hinterland, relatively small forts were built, each with less than 1 ha of enclosed area and a garrison no larger than 500 men. An estimation of the number of soldiers in the garrisons of forts in the Iron Gates area suggests that the entire sector may have relied for its defense on forces amounting to some 5,000 men. In the central Balkans, the program laid a stronger emphasis on mountain passes across the Stara Planina. Many forts in this region were comparatively larger (over 2 ha), each with an extra-fortified precinct in the middle. Finally, a third, less researched line of defense ran along the high ridges of the Yildiz Dağlari in the hinterland of Constantinople. The ubiquity of fortified sites in the northern Balkans, each perched above a cliff or on top of a

[7] D. Feissel, "L'architecte Viktôrinos et les fortifications de Justinien dans les provinces balkaniques," *Bulletin de la Société nationale des antiquaires de France* 1988, pp. 136–146.

steep-sided hill, is absolutely remarkable. Some of them may have been in existence long before Justinian, such as the small fort at Vavovo kale near Gradec, in Bulgaria, which was built under Anastasius. But all were equipped with similar facilities and produced evidence of similar fortification techniques, such as horseshoe-shaped towers or double enclosures. Inside the walls, houses were built in stone bonded with clay that are not unlike those found in contemporary cities in the region. No other buildings exist besides churches, which were sometimes built against the walls or blocking the main entrance into the fort. There is no sign of large-scale crop cultivation in the vicinity of any one of these forts, but samples of pollen and charred seeds collected from some of them indicate a shift from winter-sown cereal crops to garden cultivation of legumes, possibly within the very area enclosed by the walls. Consumption of cereal-based foods is clearly attested by relatively numerous finds of quern stones, often in special rooms that may have served as mills. But the specific composition of samples of grain seeds from Svetinja, a site located near Viminacium (Stare Kostolac, in northern Serbia), suggests that supplies of corn came from outside the small military settlement, no doubt on ships of the Danube fleet.

During the late fourth century, the army's supply system had largely depended upon the central government and the imperial administration. This was also true for the sixth century. In 536, Justinian created a new administrative unit in the eastern Balkans, the *quaestura exercitus*, by combining Balkan provinces with serious economic and military problems (such as Moesia Inferior and Scythia Minor) and rich provinces in the Aegean or the eastern Mediterranean region (such as Cyprus), all of which were ruled from Odessos (Varna, in Bulgaria) by a "prefect of Scythia." The only link between the various components of this administrative unit was the sea and the navigable Danube. The rationale behind the emperor's administrative measure was to secure both militarily and financially the efficient defense of the Danube frontier. But the *quaestura exercitus* was primarily designed to distribute the *annona* (regular supplies of food) to the army units stationed in Moesia Inferior and Scythia Minor. Finds of early Byzantine leaden seals, mostly commercial, delineate in the region the distribution network associated with the *quaestura exercitus*. This conclusion is further substantiated by pottery finds. Phocaean Red Slip wares (also known as "Late Roman C"), which were produced in western Asia Minor, appear on the Black Sea coast and in Greece, but are rare on, or altogether absent from, sites in the interior. Such sites, however, produced large quantities of amphora shards, an indication that the relative scarcity of Phocaean Red Slip wares should not be interpreted as lack of contacts with the more central provinces of the Empire. The most common amphora is the so-called "Late Roman 2" type, which was produced in the Aegean region and was used for the transportation of wine or olive oil. Such amphorae were found in relatively large quantities not only in coastal areas of Greece, Croatia, or Albania, but also in forts on the Danube frontier and in the central region of the Balkans. Elongated amphorae known as "Late Roman 1" were also a familiar presence on these sites. A third variant, known as *spatheion*, was produced in the east Mediterranean area and may have carried olive oil, fish sauce, or honey. Such amphorae are rare in Greece, but very common in the northern Balkans, and the only type of early Byzantine amphorae found on hilltop fortified sites in Bosnia, Dalmatia, and Slovenia.

By contrast, there is comparatively little evidence of amphorae produced in Palestine ("Late Roman 4, 5, and 6"), which appear frequently in the western Mediterranean region as carrying wine. Relatively large quantities of such amphorae were found in Argos (Greece) and several other coastal sites which also produced Phocaean Red Slip wares, but not on sites in the interior, where amphorae of the other types predominate. This may well point to different distribution networks, with "Late Roman 1 and 2" amphorae and *spatheia* indicating a system of state-run distribution of the *annona*. The archaeological evidence thus suggests that during the sixth century a formidable program of fortification was implemented in the Balkans, of a size and quality that the region had never witnessed before. But the project did not provide the expected solutions, because its implementation coincided with a deep crisis of the economic infrastructure of the region and a sharp decline of the rural population.[8] The project itself seems to have drained the last resources to the point of economic exhaustion. The analysis of hoards of early Byzantine copper coins found in Southeastern Europe has shown a decline in hoarding activity between 545 and 565, precisely at the time of the implementation of

[8] F. Curta, "Peasants as 'makeshift soldiers for the occasion': sixth-century settlement patterns in the Balkans," in *Urban Centers and Rural Contexts in Late Antiquity*, ed. by T. S. Burns and J. W. Eadie (East Lansing: Michigan State University Press, 2001), pp. 199–217.

Justinian's defense system. The increasing number of payments and other monetary transactions brought by this economic conjuncture had serious consequences on small savings, such as those represented by hoards of copper. Fewer coins were now withdrawn from circulation and the general liquidity seems to have drastically diminished. A certainly unintended consequence of this situation was the complete interruption of coin circulation north of the Danube frontier between 545 and 560.

SOCIETY AND CHRISTIANITY

In contrast to the generally gloomy picture produced by the archaeological evidence, sixth-century cities on the Black Sea coast display signs of prosperity and economic activity, though only for a relatively short period. The presence of merchants from the eastern provinces of the Empire is attested by inscriptions found in Constanța (Tomis) and Mangalia (Callatis). By the time Justinian established the *quaestura exercitus* with its headquarters in Odessos, one of the most important industries in that city was the preparation of hides, presumably for export. To judge from the evidence of inscriptions, wine was a major import in the area, with traders from as far as Alexandria supplying the major cities on the coast. In connection with this short-lived economic boom, a relatively large number of craftsmen and merchants appear in inscriptions, with no parallel in urban centers or military forts in the interior of the Balkan Peninsula. It is in the coastal regions of Greece and in Dobrudja that the most impressive funerary monuments of the age were built – large, single- or multi-room burial chambers with walls painted with quotes from the Psalms and with Christian symbols. To judge from the great number of skeletons found in each one of them, the chambers found in Corinth, Athens, Philippi, and Stamata (Greece), as well as in Cernavodă and Mangalia (Romania), may have served as family burial grounds. The associated gold pectoral crosses and jewelry suggest that these were wealthy families. Elsewhere, mortuary archaeology produced only evidence of stone-lined graves and burials with pitched tile covers, often in relatively large numbers grouped around a cemeterial church or chapel. Since in at least two cases (Vajuga, in Serbia, and Celei, in southern Romania), such cemeteries were associated with neighboring forts, the deceased buried there must have been members of the military. The same may be true for similar cemeteries found near such cities as

Heraclea Lyncestis and Iustiniana Prima (presumably Caričin Grad, in Serbia). Dress accessories and jewelry associated with such burials indicate the presence of women, perhaps wives of soldiers in the city or fort garrisons. But the general appearance of these grave goods is rather modest, especially when compared with the rich artifacts found in burial chambers. To be sure, the regions in the interior also produced extraordinarily rich assemblages, especially small hoards of gold artifacts, most likely collections of personal jewelry, such as found within the sixth-century forts at Markovi kuli (near Skopje, in Macedonia), Malăk Preslavec, and Sadovec (both in Bulgaria). A magnificent belt set of gold with incrusted gems has recently been found near Sirmium (Sremska Mitrovica, in Serbia) and may have belonged to a high-ranking officer of the army involved in defending the city against the Avar siege.[9] To the same military elite points the early sixth-century helmet found in a basilica excavated in Heraclea Lyncestis with its rim decorated with a coin-like punched ornament imitating the gold coinage of Anastasius and Justin I. Perhaps the most spectacular assemblage in this respect is the female burial found in Gračanica (Kosovo, in Yugoslavia), with a freshly minted gold coin of Justinian and a pair of Scandinavian brooches, for which the closest analogy is an early sixth-century fibula from Denmark.[10] The display of exotic artifacts and wealth was as important for the high-ranking female, perhaps the wife of a local officer of barbarian origin, as it was for her contemporary buried in northwestern Hungary, at Mosonszentjános, together with a Frankish bell-beaker and a wooden bucket with escutcheon mounts with anthropomorphic heads, both originating in the Rhineland.

Besides soldiery, no other social group appears with such prominence in the sixth-century Balkans as the high clergy. As in other parts of the Empire, bishops were taking over the urban administration during the sixth century, a process well illustrated in the contemporary

[9] I. Popović, *Zlatni avarski poias iz okoline Sirmiuma* [A golden Avar Belt Set from the Environs of Sirmium] (Belgrade: Narodni Muzei and Arheološki Institut, 1997); A. Kiss, "The treasure of a Byzantine gold belt from the Sirmium region," *AAASH*, vol. 50 (1998), pp. 251–258.

[10] M. Milinković, "Ulpijana kod Gračanice na Kosovu i gradina na Jelici kod Čačka u svetlu akulturacionih procesa u Iliriku VI v. [Ulpiana near Gračanica in Kosovo and the fort at Jelica near Čačak in the light of the sixth-century acculturation process in Illyricum]," in *Tretja jugoslovenska konferencija vizantologa. Kruševac, 10–13 maj 2000*, ed. by L. Maksimović, N. Radošević, and E. Radulović (Belgrade: Vizantološki Institut and Kruševac: Narodni Muzej, 2002), pp. 343–360.

legislation. Under Emperor Anastasius, bishops chaired local committees of landowners in charge of procuring grain for cities. Under Justinian, such committees had already replaced city council members (*curiales*) in the urban administration and had taken over their fiscal responsibilities. Justinian's novel 11 of 535, which created the archbishopric of Iustiniana Prima, also granted the bishop of Aquis (Prahovo, in Serbia) authority not only over the city but also over its territory, forts (*castella*), and churches erected outside city walls. In 594, before launching his campaign against the Slavs north of the Danube, the Roman general Peter brought his troops to a city near the Danube frontier called Asemus. According to Theophylact Simocatta, as soon as "the citizens learned that Peter was about to arrive, the garrison took up the standards and arrayed in armour, welcomed the general most gloriously." Peter immediately noticed the military valor of the local militia and tried to remove it from the city in order to include it amongst his own forces. When the soldiers, trying to escape him, took refuge in the city's church and barricaded themselves against Peter's own body of soldiers sent to expel the rebels by force, the general sent an imperial bodyguard to arrest the bishop of the city. But the citizens of Asemus "closed the gates and covered the general with insults." Peter had no choice but to leave Asemus and "proceeded to march forwards, escorted by the great curses from the city."[11] The episode clearly indicates that the bishop was blamed for the insubordination of the city's garrison. He appeared, at least in the eyes of Peter, as the most prominent political figure in the city.

By canon law, baptism was to be administered by bishops only, but by AD 500, perhaps because of the multiplication of the administrative tasks of the bishop, his presence at the baptismal ceremony was no longer a requirement. It has been noted that starting with Justinian's reign, there was an increasing number of baptisteries (baptismal fonts) in the Balkans, often built next to older basilicas. The presence of more than one baptistery in the same city, as in Stobi, suggests the performance of baptism by clergy other than the city's bishop. On the other hand, the multiplication of baptisteries betrays an increasing need of religious services. This growth also shows the concern of the Church and, we may presume, imperial authorities, for the conversion of a significantly larger number of people. Some scholars have interpreted this as an indication that large numbers of non-Christian

[11] Theophylact Simocatta VII.3.1–10, pp. 182–183.

soldiers of the Roman army, mostly barbarians, were now converted en masse. Others, observing that the correlate of the increasing number of baptisteries is their significant reduction in size, suggested that changes may have occurred in the ritual of service, with baptism being now administered chiefly to children. In the absence of contextual information from written sources, it is not possible to decide which one of these interpretations we should follow. Moreover, it is not impossible that both factors were at work in the Balkans. In any case, these architectural changes clearly point to an increasing concern with including larger numbers of people within the Christian community.

Such efforts for mass conversion were directed primarily towards the army, as indicated by the presence of baptisteries in or next to fort churches. At Veliki Gradac (Serbia), in the Iron Gates sector of the Danube frontier, a single-naved church was built with its vestibule blocking the fort's western gate. The gate itself became a narrow atrium, with a baptistery on the southern side. On the other hand, on many sites in the Balkans, much like on contemporary sites in the eastern Black Sea area or in Africa, churches were literally built as parts of the ramparts. Garrison churches were often built so close to the precinct that their apses were sometimes incorporated into the walls, as in Golemanovo kale (Bulgaria). Other churches were built within one of a fort's towers or just next to them, as in Dinogetia (Garvăn, in Romania) or Pčinija (Macedonia). In addition, the Balkans provide two examples of fortified churches built in isolated regions, apparently without any related settlements or cemeteries. In Dzhanavar tepe, near Varna, and in Pirdop (both in Bulgaria), local bishops may have been responsible for the decision to build churches that could easily be turned into strongholds.

During the sixth century, bishops had considerable control over local monasteries, at least since the Ecumenical Council of Chalcedon (451) had introduced the requirement of election and confirmation of abbots by local bishops. But monastic communities are conspicuously rare in the sixth-century Balkans. During Justinian's reign, a group of "Scythian monks," most likely from Scythia Minor, were zealous supporters of a formula attempting to reconcile adherents to Chalcedonian canons with the Monophysites. That doctrine, called Theopaschitism ("one of the Trinity suffered in the flesh"), was enthusiastically embraced by the "Scythian monks" who even went to Rome to win the support of Pope Hormisdas for their cause.

But the archaeological evidence of monasteries is meager. A fifth-century monastic site was found on the island of Majsan on the Adriatic coast: it was organized around two porticoed courtyards and included a small church with a reliquary containing the remains of St. Maximus. At Isperikhovo, near Plovdiv (Bulgaria), an early Byzantine monastery included a small single-naved church with a baptistery and a number of rooms built with stone bonded with clay. Tools for woodwork and agriculture suggest the existence of a group of monks who may have worked the land. A cave monastery existed not far from the modern monastery of Aladzha, near Varna (Bulgaria). Finally, at Slava Rusă, near Babadag (Romania), recent excavations have unearthed a monastic complex with two single-naved churches and three building phases, the last of which was dated to the late sixth century.

The evidence of monastic sites is remarkably small. Some have suggested that the invisibility of monasteries in the Balkans is due to the domination of the lavra system, in which monks living in individual hermitages would gather on feast days at a common center for services and meals. But even if all the known cases of monastic sites were lavras, it is still not enough to explain the absence of cenobitic sites. It is perhaps no accident that, although written sources mention either monks or hermits, none of them specifically refers to monasteries. The absence of monasteries can only be explained in reference to the absence of rural sites, as the association between the two is documented in cases of monasteries established elsewhere in the Empire. By contrast, the existing evidence suggests that in the Balkans monastic sites were associated with urban centers, such as Ibida (Slava Rusă) or Philippopolis (Plovdiv). The absence of monasteries may explain the absence of any mission to the barbarians beyond the river Danube, as many monasteries in frontier regions of the Empire were also centers of missionary activity. In all known cases, missions were directed towards protecting the Empire's frontiers through building alliances with neighboring polities. The *pax Romana* was equated with the *pax Christiana*, and the Empire's foreign policy became intimately associated with the missionary work of the Church. The absence of any information regarding sixth-century missions on the Danube frontier is puzzling, particularly in contrast with the 300s, when attempts were made to convert the Goths on the Danube frontier to the mainstream Christianity of Bishop Ulfila's days. In the early 400s, Theotimos, Bishop of Tomis, was well known to the Huns living north of the Danube, who called him "the god of the Romans." But no sixth-century bishop is known to have conducted such missions beyond that frontier, despite the increasingly prominent position bishops now occupied in the administration of the northern Balkans. No attempts are known to have been made for the conversion of any sixth-century group living north of the Danube. There is no indication of missions targeted at either Avars or Slavs.

BARBARIANS AND BARBARIAN RAIDS. "HUNS," LOMBARDS, GEPIDS, AND SLAVS

The sheer number of forts and military sites is a strong reminder that barbarian raids were the most prominent feature of sixth-century imperial politics in the Balkans. There is hardly any year within the first half of that century without a mention of raids by people whom the early Byzantine authors, writing as they did in the tradition of classical historiography, regarded as barbarians, without much concern for accurate or objective ethnographic description. For example, during the first decades of the century most raids were attributed to the "Huns," a generic term historians such as Count Marcellinus, Jordanes, or Procopius used for nomadic horsemen. At times, however, Bulgars (first mentioned in 480) and Cutrigurs are also mentioned, even along with the Huns, first allied with the Romans, then against them. Before 540, most raids targeted the eastern Balkans, especially Thrace and Moesia Inferior, an indication that they must have originated in the steppes north of the Lower Danube and the Black Sea. Exactly what was the area from which the horsemen came is difficult to establish, given that the steppe region in question has so far produced no archaeological evidence that could be dated to the first half of the sixth century. Marauding expeditions seem to have been the work of one or several chieftains working together, such as those intercepted, defeated, and killed in 539 after devastating Scythia Minor and Moesia Inferior. Despite all efforts, often surprisingly successful, directed towards intercepting and crushing marauding parties, "Hunnic" horsemen were at the same time recruited for Justinian's wars in Italy, most likely because of their extraordinary mobility. It was indeed mobility that enabled other Hunnic marauders of 539 to reach the western Balkans and even the outskirts of Constantinople. The result, to employ Procopius' bon mot, was a veritable "Scythian wilderness" that came to exist everywhere in the Balkans.[12] The frightful havoc wrought among the inhabitants of the Balkan provinces during this particular raid seems to have prompted Justinian to begin his project of fortifying the Balkans and the Danube frontier on a scale without any precedent.

Elsewhere, the emperor chose a different strategy. Ever since the Gepid occupation of Sirmium during the Gothic war in Italy, the Gepids had become the second most important problem in the northern Balkans after the "Huns," with whom they formed an alliance in 535 in order to raid Moesia. During the Gothic war, the Gepids were allied with the Franks and constantly threatened the Roman lines of defense in the northern Balkans. They were led by petty kings who ruled over most of the eastern part of the Carpathian Basin (the name commonly given to the lowlands on both sides of the Middle Danube region, between Vienna and the Iron Gates, roughly corresponding to present-day Hungary, in addition to various smaller territories in neighboring countries). Some of these kings ruled from Sirmium, others may have been their subordinates. In the late 400s, Thrapstila was "king" of Sirmium, followed at his death by his son, Thrasaric. During the reign of the last Gepid "king" of Sirmium, Cunimund (560–567), silver imitations of Roman and Ostrogothic coins were struck in his name in that city. Very little is known about the residences of these kings, and not much more about contemporary settlements in the Tisza plain north of Sirmium. Large sixth-century settlements were excavated in Transylvania, a region that also produced a number of fortified hilltop sites, one of which, Moreşti, was fully excavated and published.[13] None of the associated cemeteries can be compared in either size or wealth of grave goods with the large cemeteries of the Tisza plain. It has long been noted that high-status burials with costly grave goods dated to the mid- and late fifth century cluster in northwestern Transylvania, while sixth-century cemeteries primarily appear in the Hungarian Plain. This change may have been related to the reconfiguration of the social and political basis of power

[12] Procopius of Caesarea, *Secret History* XVIII.20–21, ed. by J. Haury with English translation by H. B. Dewing (Cambridge, Mass.: Harvard University Press, 1935), pp. 219 and 221.

[13] K. Horedt, "Befestigte Siedlungen des 6. Jhs. u. Z. aus Siebenbürgen," in *Siedlung, Burg und Stadt. Studien zu ihren Anfängen*, ed. by K.-H. Otto and J. Herrmann (Berlin: Akademie Verlag, 1969), pp. 129–138; and *Moreşti. Grabungen in einer vor- und frühgeschichtlichen Siedlung in Siebenbürgen* (Bucharest: Kriterion, 1979).

within the region inhabited by the Gepids, with retinues of warriors and wealth now controlled by a burgeoning aristocracy. This class of nobles maintained close relations with other aristocratic families in Scandinavia, Thuringia, Crimea, and the Baltic coast. Such long-distance contacts are well illustrated by artifacts associated primarily with female burials, such as Thuringian brooches, amber beads, or Scandinavian belt buckles. The need for displays of exotic dress accessories seems to have increased in the mid-500s, as the Gepids were in conflict with their western neighbors, the Lombards. The Lombards had moved into the Middle Danube region from the north in the early 500s and soon acquired the status of federates. Annoyed by Gepid depredations and by the impossibility of dislodging the Gepid king from Sirmium, Justinian agreed to give the Lombards the annual subsidies until then paid to the Gepids. In exchange, the Lombards became a permanent threat to both Sirmium and the neighboring Gepid settlements. The Gepids were defeated in 547 by an allied Lombard–Byzantine force, and then again, in 551 or 552, by Lombards alone.

Much like their Gepid counterparts, the Lombard kings entertained relations with distant potentates such as Merovingian kings and Scandinavian chiefs. Auduin, who ruled between 547 or 548 and 560 or 565, married the daughter of the last Thuringian king, Herminafred. Prestige objects, such as swords with damascened blades or Frankish glass beakers produced in the Rhineland, occasionally appear in cemeteries in western Hungary, while matrimonial alliances between Frankish and Lombard kings are well documented for the second third of the sixth century. The conflict that opposed the Lombards to the Gepids seems to have created a "no-man's-land" between the Tisza and the Middle Danube, with a clear distinction between the "Lombard" and the "Gepid" zones in terms of markers of ethnic identity, especially those associated with the female dress. During the Lombard–Gepid wars, the "no-man's-land" functioned as a political and military frontier region, which only political refugees could occasionally cross. For example, shortly after the Lombards and the Gepids agreed to a truce in 549, a candidate for the Lombard throne named Hildigis fled to the Gepids, followed by a multi-ethnic retinue, which he later took with him to Italy, where he joined the army of the Ostrogothic king Totila. By that time, however, the greatest danger for the Roman system of defense in the Balkans did not come from either Gepids or Lombard renegades. In 545, a great throng of

Sclavenes crossed the river Danube, plundered the adjoining country, and enslaved a large number of Romans. The Sclavenes, according to Procopius, lived on, and not far from, the left bank of the Danube.[14]

Generations of linguistically trained historians have chosen to ignore the evidence and sought the homeland of the Slavs in Podolia and Volhynia (now western Ukraine, near the Polish–Ukrainian–Belarusian border) or in the swampy area of the Pripet river basin (near the Ukrainian–Belarusian frontier). The migration of the Slavs to the Danube region where Procopius located them is said to have started because of the harsh climatic conditions in the north. The Slavs eventually succeeded in conquering most of Southeastern Europe, presumably because of their social organization in large families and egalitarian small-scale societies with no kings and no hierarchy. In fact, neither written sources, nor the archaeological evidence can support this interpretation. There is no need to posit a migration, which is otherwise not documented in contemporary sources, in order to explain the sudden appearance of the Slavs on the Danube frontier. Ethnogenesis, in general, and the Slavic one in particular, can rarely be explained in terms of migration. Nor are the "Slavs" mentioned in any source before *c.* 500. The Slavic "homeland," at least for the sixth-century authors who wrote about the Slavs, was north of the Lower Danube, not in the Belarusian–Ukrainian borderlands. To be sure, the raids of the Sclavenes (the name used by sixth- and seventh-century authors, which historians normally translate as "Slavs") in the 540s and 550s, some reaching as far south as Thessalonica and Dyrrachium (Durrës, in Albania), were particularly devastating. But after each one of them, the Slavic marauders returned "home," which was just north of the Danube River, not in the swampy Pripet valley of northeastern Ukraine and southern Belarus. There are about 100 sixth- to seventh-century settlement sites excavated so far in Romania, Moldova, and Ukraine, mainly located on the lowest river terraces, below the 200- or 300-meter contour, at the interface between everglades and higher ground, often on rich soils good for agriculture. Each settlement is no larger than about five acres, with a limited number of houses per habitation phase, ranging from ten to fifteen. This seems to indicate that most, if not all, sites had been occupied only for brief periods, then abandoned

[14] Procopius of Caesarea, *Wars* V.27.2, ed. by J. Haury with English translation by H. B. Dewing (Cambridge, Mass.: Harvard University Press, 1914–1928), p. 253.

and new settlements established nearby. This is particularly clear in the case of Dulceanca in southern Romania. The first occupation of that site had fifteen houses, and was abandoned in the early 500s. A new settlement grew less than a mile away. During the second half of the sixth century, this settlement moved to the south, but it was apparently much smaller (only nine houses), of briefer duration, and more dispersed. Finally, a seventh-century settlement appeared here after the third settlement was abandoned. Dulceanca, therefore, may well be viewed as a series of shifting hamlets, not a village properly speaking.

What caused this shifting of hamlets must have been the itinerant form of agriculture practiced by their inhabitants and requiring that lands under cultivation be left fallow after a number of years of repeated cultivation without manuring. Although most likely responsible for the ephemeral nature of almost all sixth-century settlement sites excavated in southern and eastern Romania, this phenomenon could hardly be called migration in the sense implied by the often-quoted phrase "the migration of the Slavs." On the contrary, itinerant agriculture may have encouraged mobility on a microregional scale, since no settlements as far away from each other as Ukraine and Romania produced matching elements of material culture that would support the idea of a fully-fledged migration. The standard building on settlements excavated in both Romania and Ukraine was the sunken-floored house, no larger than necessary for about five individuals, an indication that the social unit in each one of these hamlets was the minimal family. Much of what was found inside each house was by the oven, either of stone or of clay, built in one of the corners. By far the most common category of artifacts found on settlement sites in southern and eastern Romania is pottery, both hand- and wheel-made, often fired within one and the same kiln located on the fringes or in the center of the settlement. Sometimes, ceramic assemblages include fragments of clay pans used for baking flat loaves of wheat or millet bread. Metal artifacts typically include knives, flint steels, buckles, early Byzantine coins, and so-called bow fibulae (certainly of local production, as demonstrated by the artifacts found in a house of the settlement site at Bernashivka, in Ukraine). The classification of these brooches indicates that they were often inspired by artifacts of "exotic" provenance such as those found in Crimea or northeastern Poland, but were in "fashion" shortly before or after AD 600. Bow fibulae were highly visible dress accessories worn only by women of high status. Such artifacts indicate social rank, which means that the local society in the region where early Byzantine sources locate the Sclavenes cannot be treated as egalitarian. The intrasite distribution of artifacts suggests a much more complex picture. The houses of the small site on Soldat Ghivan Street in Bucharest (Romania) were arranged around an open area. A large building on the northern side produced all tools and weapons on the site. A bow fibula and a handmade lamp found in two houses on the southern side are in sharp contrast with the distribution in the northern part of the settlement. In Davideni (eastern Romania), two groups of houses located on both sides of a small creek produced different artifact distributions. In the north, houses were arranged around a central open area, occupied by some very small buildings, too small indeed to have been used as dwellings, but equipped with more than one heating facility. Many houses around this central area produced shards of clay pans. Four of them produced the majority of the tools found on the site, while another had a bow fibula and a double-layered comb. What does this distribution mean? The central area may have been associated with some industrial activities, such as smelting or the production of dress accessories, but it was also a place where some kind of ceremonies took place, which involved the consumption of special foods, such as flat loaves of bread. If bow fibulae were symbols of social rank and power, then the central open area may have also been an arena of social competition, the place where men of power competed with each other by means of dress accessories displayed vicariously by their wives, mothers, or sisters.

This interpretation of the archaeological evidence[15] is substantiated by the analysis of the written sources. In response to both the attacks of the "Huns" and the Slavic raids, Justinian began a massive program of fortification, of a scale the Balkans had never witnessed before. The results were remarkable: between 551 and 578, no Slavic raids are mentioned in an otherwise well-documented period, although in 558 a particularly devastating Cutrigur invasion managed to break through Justinian's lines of fortification and reached the Long Walls near Constantinople. When resuming in the 570s, the Slavic raids involved a much larger number of warriors, often under

[15] F. Curta, *The Making of the Slavs. History and Archaeology of the Lower Danube Region, c. 500–700* (Cambridge and New York: Cambridge University Press, 2001), pp. 297–307.

the leadership of just one chief, such as a certain Ardagastus who led a raid in 585 that, like the Cutrigurs' of 540 and 558, went as far as the outskirts of Constantinople. Unlike the raids of the 540s and 550s, those of the last quarter of the sixth century were much bolder enterprises, aiming at conquering large cities, as indicated by 5,000 Sclavene warriors storming the walls of Thessalonica at some point in the early 580s. Only the campaigns Emperor Maurice (582–602) launched in 592 into the Sclavene territories north of the Danube frontier eventually put a stop on the devastations perpetrated by the Sclavene warriors in the Balkans. Slavic raiding activity resumed during Heraclius' reign (610–641), when we have the first indication of Slavic settlement in various areas of the Balkans (near Thessalonica; in Bulgaria, not far from Constantinople; and in Dalmatia). The chiefs leading the successful raids of the late sixth century may well have been the men of power who competed with each other within the settlements excavated north of the Danube River. In any case, the associated archaeological evidence can certainly be dated to the same period.

So, who were the Slavs? Much like the "Huns," the "Sclavenes" appear in sixth-century sources as an umbrella term for a multitude of groups living north of the Danube frontier, which could not be classified as either "Huns" or "Gepids." The author of a military treatise written *c.* 600 and known as the *Strategikon* discussed the Sclavenes in an entire, fairly long chapter, which was separate from that dedicated to the Avars, because, in his eyes, the Sclavenes had radically different social and political systems and, as a consequence, different forms of warfare. To sixth-century authors, the "Slavs" were therefore a different, "newer" kind of enemy. As a consequence, Sclavene ethnicity may well have been an invention of (early) Byzantine authors, despite the possibility, which is often brought up by linguistically minded historians, that the name Sclavene was derived from the self-designation of a "real" ethnic group. "Invention," however, does not mean pure fiction: Byzantine authors seem to have used "Sclavene" to make sense of a process of group identification which was taking place under their own eyes on the Danube frontier of the Empire. The analysis of coin finds from the Balkans and from Romania suggests that between 545 and 565, precisely at the time the Sclavene raids stopped, there was an interruption of the coin circulation north and south of the Danube frontier. This interruption was accompanied by a sharp decline in the quantity of goods of Roman provenance, which may have until then been obtained by means of trade and used as prestige goods. This led to increased social competition within communities north of the Danube frontier and to the rise of leaders whose basis of power was now warfare. It is during this period of time that the first signs appear of particular styles of material culture that went beyond the boundaries of local communities. Leaders like Ardagastus or others whose names appear suddenly in written sources as having been known in Constantinople after *c.* 565 may have capitalized on such phenomena to draw boundaries of much larger communities. The mechanisms by which some of these leaders known from written sources may have reached power had to do with the orchestration of communal ceremonies, of assemblies, and feasts, such as signalized by the artifact distribution within sixth-century settlements like that on Soldat Ghivan Street in Bucharest. Prestige goods were available in abundance after *c.* 565, as long as predatory raids were successful. It is indeed prestige goods, such as gold, silver, horses, and weapons, that the Sclavene warriors of 581 were still seeking in 584 during their four-year devastation of the Balkan provinces. The evidence of amphorae found on sites north of the Danube frontier, many of which are from the second half of the sixth century, points in the same direction. Olive oil, wine, or fish sauce – the principal goods transported in amphorae – were as important for showing off as horses and weapons.

The rise of the local elites north of the Danube coincided in time both with the dissemination of specific material culture styles and with the sudden interest in "exotic," prestige goods to be obtained by plundering raids. But leaders rose to political prominence in contexts in which they also embodied collective interest and responsibility. Chiefs like Dauritas, the bold leader of the Sclavenes attacked by the Avars in 578, "created" groups by speaking and taking action in the name of their respective communities. When in the name of the qagan, the Avar envoys to the Sclavenes demanded tribute, Dauritas boastfully replied that "others do not conquer our land, we conquer theirs; and so it shall always be for us, as long as there are wars and weapons."[16] Political and military mobilization was a response to the historical conditions created by the implementation of the fortified frontier on the Danube. The identity represented

[16] Menander the Guardsman, *History*, frg. 21, ed. and transl. by R. C. Blockley (Liverpool: F. Cairns, 1985), p. 195.

by the material culture styles spreading amongst communities north of the Danube was therefore a reaction to developments leading to the isolation of those communities. If that group identity can be called ethnicity, and if that ethnicity can be called Slavic, then it certainly formed in the shadow of Justinian's forts, not in the Pripet marshes. "Sclavenes" is therefore the name chosen in the sixth century to define such political and military changes. In other words, the "Slavs" were the barbarians north of the Danube, different from, and requiring other strategies than those employed for, the "Huns" in the steppe lands north of the Black Sea or the "Avars" in the Carpathian Basin.

"THE FILTHY RACE OF LONG-HAIRED BARBARIANS": THE AVARS

The Slavic raids of the late sixth century were often associated with Avar raids and attacks against key points of Justinian's system of defence. In 582, the Avars conquered Sirmium after a long, drawn-out siege. To keep the Roman armies busy, the Slavs invaded Thrace and Thessaly in 581; they were still there in 584. But Slavic warriors also operated on the western border of the territory under Avar control. The Slavic raid of 610 on Istria, until then under Byzantine control, is mentioned in Paul the Deacon's *History of the Lombards* as following an Avar attack on northeastern Italy.[17]

The Avars first appear in the works of Agathias of Myrina and Menander the Guardsman. According to a later historian, Theophylact Simocatta, who wrote during the reign of Emperor Heraclius (610–641), the name Avar was a misnomer. They were not true, but "Pseudo-Avars," a group of fugitive "Scythians," who had taken over the awe-inspiring name in replacement of their original names Var and Chunni. The latter are otherwise known as names of Turkic (Ogur) peoples, a detail too hastily interpreted as indicating that the European Avars were remnants of the Juan-juan of Inner

[17] Paul the Deacon, *History of the Lombards* IV.40, ed. by G. Waitz (Hanover: Hahnsche Buchhandlung, 1878), p. 168. At this point of his *History*, Paul relied on information borrowed from the now lost history of Secundus of Trento. See K. Gardiner, "Paul the Deacon and Secundus of Trento," in *History and Historians in Late Antiquity*, ed. by B. Croke and A. Emmett (Sydney: Pergamon Press, 1983), pp. 147–154.

Asia mentioned in Chinese annals.[18] It is in fact quite likely that Theophylact's story is a distorted myth of barbarian origin. As such, the story was meant to underline the heterogeneity of the group of 20,000 horsemen in the steppe north of the Caucasus Mountains, in whose name an embassy was sent in 558 to Constantinople, where its members made a strong impression with their long, braided hair. Whatever the case, the numbers of those who would eventually move into the Middle Danube region were later greatly increased by repeated migrations from the steppe of separate, different groups. There were Cutrigur warriors among the rank and file of the Avar army, and in 583 or 584, three tribes named Tarniakh, Kotzager, and Zabender fled the steppes to escape the Turkic onslaught and joined the Avars. There is plenty of written evidence that a substantial number of Gepids had remained under Avar rule. During the campaign of 599/600 led by the Roman general Priscus in the Tisza region, the inhabitants of three Gepid villages were taken by surprise and massacred by the Roman troops. Perhaps as early as AD 600, but without any doubt during the early 700s, the Avars established in that region were very different, in both ethnic and social terms, from those who had sent the embassy to Emperor Justinian.

The Avars were quick in subjugating to the authority of their leader, the qagan Bayan,[19] all the nomads in the steppes north of the Black Sea, including the "Huns" and the Cutrigurs that had created so much havoc in the Balkans during the first half of the sixth century. Denied access to Scythia Minor (the border province on the Danube frontier closest to the steppes), the Avars made a surprise attack at the opposite end of the European continent, only to be defeated by Sigibert, the Frankish king of Austrasia. However, after 565 the focus of Avar raiding and political interest shifted to the Lower and, especially, Middle Danube region. Allied with the Lombard king

[18] Theophylact Simocatta, *History* VII.7.10 and VII.8.1, ed. by de Boor and Wirth, pp. 188–189. See also A. Kollautz and H. Miyakawa, *Geschichte und Kultur eines völkerwanderungszeitlichen Nomadenvolkes. Die Jou-jan der Mongolei und die Awaren im Mitteleuropa* (Klagenfurt and Bonn: Rudolf Habelt, 1970); W. Pohl, *Die Awaren. Ein Steppenvolk im Mitteleuropa 567–822 n. Chr.* (Munich: C. H. Beck, 1988), p. 35; S. Szádeczky-Kardoss, "The Avars," in *The Cambridge History of Early Inner Asia*, ed. by D. Sinor (Cambridge and New York: Cambridge University Press, 1990), pp. 206–207.

[19] Bayan is the only qagan known by name. His son and all his other successors were simply called Chagan (qagan) in contemporary sources. See T. Olajos, "La chronologie de la dynastie avare de Baïan," *REB*, vol. 34 (1976), pp. 151–158.

Alboin, Bayan defeated the Gepids and then forced the Lombards to migrate to Italy. No other event in the medieval history of the region was given more importance in historiography than the annihilation of the Gepid kingdom and the Avar conquest of the Carpathian Basin in 568. Some historians go as far as to regard that year as marking the beginning of the Middle Ages, an East European equivalent of 476, with Bayan conveniently replacing Odoacer as the first barbarian ruler after the end of Antiquity. In reality, the conquest of the Carpathian Basin was just an episode in a long process that resulted in the creation of the powerful Avar polity on the northern frontier of the Empire, and in its increasing involvement in both Balkan developments and imperial affairs.

From their newly established base in formerly Gepid or Lombard lands, the Avars constantly raided the Balkan provinces, as far as Constantinople and Greece, managed to capture some of the key fortifications of the Roman system of defense, and extorted enormous amounts of imperial gold nominally paid as stipends, but regarded by both Bayan and the critics of imperial policies as nothing less than tribute. In the words attributed by Menander the Guardsman to Emperor Justin II, it was indeed "more painful to be the friends of the Avars – nomads and foreigners – than their enemies, since their friendship was treacherous."[20] The history of Avar relations with Romans was indeed marked by a combination of deceit and military threat. In 578, "thinking to win favor" with Tiberius II, Bayan responded to the emperor's request of military assistance in his attempt to curb Slavic raiding in the Balkans. According to Menander the Guardsman, 60,000 Avar horsemen were transported on Roman ships down the river Danube, from the Iron Gates to Scythia Minor, where they crossed the river into Sclavene territory, which they laid waste. One year later, however, Bayan began a three-year siege of Sirmium, which eventually fell in 582, to the desperation of both the inhabitants of the city (many of whom migrated to Salona, where their presence is attested by funerary inscriptions[21]) and the imperial

[20] Menander the Guardsman, *History*, frg. 12.6, p. 141.

[21] See B. Gabričević, "Question de la datation du sarcophage de l'abbesse Jeanne," in *Disputationes Salonitanae 1970*, ed. by Ž. Rapanić (Split: Musée Archéologique, 1975), pp. 96–101. Another inscription illustrates the desperation of the citizens of Sirmium. During the final moments of the siege, one of them scratched on a tile with a shaking hand: "God Jesus Christ, save our city, smash the Avars, and protect the Romans and the one who wrote this." See R. Noll, "Ein Ziegel als

government, too preoccupied with the war against Persia to do anything about such a serious blow to the Roman system of defense in the Balkans. Throughout this period of complicated relations with the Empire, the annual stipends paid to the Avars increased steadily from 80,000 to 150,000 *solidi* (gold coins), i.e., from almost 900 to over 1,600 pounds of pure gold, over a period of thirty years. Very little of this large quantity of minted gold has survived in the otherwise well-documented archaeological record of the Avar presence in Hungary. Some fifty Byzantine coins found either as funerary offerings or as ornaments in rich male burials are better suited to underpin the entire chronological system of Avar archaeology than to illustrate archaeologically the wealth of the first generations of European Avars. It is more likely that a great part of the gold was melted to provide raw material for gold jewelry, which was found in great quantities in early Avar burial assemblages. The exact weight of some of the most popular earrings, for example, is equivalent to either eight or ten *solidi*, and provenance analysis may confirm that most, if not all, gold artifacts produced during this period within the area under Avar control were made of Roman gold. However, since the presence of gold artifacts is restricted to a few exceptionally rich burials, some of which may have indeed been the graves of qagans or of their family members, it is possible that during the first fifty years of Avar history a small elite headed by the qagan had exclusive control of the gold supplies from the Empire.

If true, this would substantiate conclusions drawn from literary sources that point to a highly stratified society in which power was almost exclusively in the hands of the qagan. Indeed, for the first, very well-documented century of Avar history, in spite of references to several Avar dignitaries (called *archontes*, "leaders," or *logades* by Menander the Guardsman), no mention is made in any source of any other position of power greater than that of the qagan. Even dignitaries seem to have been high-ranking persons rendering personal service to the qagan, rather than mere heads of ruling clans. It is this "class" of high-ranking, rich warriors that appears in the archaeological record of small, isolated groups of burials, many of which contain horse skeletons, but also rich grave goods and weapons. In imitation

sprechendes Zeugnis einer historischen Katastrophe (Zum Untergang Sirmiums 582 n. Chr.)," *Anzeiger der Österreichischen Akademie der Wissenschaften*, vol. 126 (1989), pp. 139–154.

of late Roman practice, the belt with multiple, secondary straps decorated with metal plates and strap ends, often made of bronze, but sometimes of gold or silver, seems to have been a symbol of social rank, although the exact significance of the belt deposition remains a matter of debate. A recent survey of just one small region in northern Serbia, near the Serbian–Hungarian border, brilliantly shows how small kin groups occupied distinct ecological niches along the valleys of some of the tributaries of the Tisza, while making extensive use of natural resources for their predominantly pastoral economy.[22] The existence of agricultural communities nearby, such as the three Gepid villages devastated by the Roman troops in 599, suggests that each aristocratic family may thus have controlled grazing fields in the vicinity of agricultural settlements under the family's control. Craftsmen enjoyed a privileged social status, to judge from the fact that, like rich warriors, they were often buried with their horses and weapons. Early Avar society was based on procuring prestige goods from the Empire and food supplies from small economic units, in the form of either direct production from family lands or tribute from subjugated population groups. It is indeed remarkable that, unlike Germanic federates of the previous centuries, the Avars neither requested nor received supplies of grain from the Romans. On the contrary, the Avars several times supplied Roman armies and populace with food, most importantly after the siege of Sirmium, when the conquering Avars fed the starving besieged with "bread and wine."[23] More often than not, the Avars chose to move the entire population of a conquered city or territory in the middle of the qaganate. The second book of the collection of homilies known as the *Miracles of St. Demetrius* describes one such group of Roman prisoners of war and other captives – men, women, and children – that were moved into

[22] M. Takács, "Einige Aspekte der Siedlungsgeschichte des südlichen Drittels des Donau-Theiss-Zwischenstromlandes von der awarischen Landnahme bis zum Ende des 11. Jahrhunderts," *AAASH*, vol. 51 (1999–2000), pp. 457–472.

[23] John of Ephesus, *Ecclesiastical History* V.32, ed. by E. I. Brooks (Paris: Typographeo Reipublicae, 1935), p. 256. However, Michael the Syrian (*Ecclesiastical History* X.21), in a passage undoubtedly inspired by John of Ephesus, reports that the Avars levied as much as half of the agricultural product from the inhabitants of two cities (most likely Singidunum and Anchialos) and several other forts in the northern Balkans, which they had conquered in 584. See N. I. Serikov, "Ioann Efesskii [John of Ephesus]," in *Svod drevneishikh pis'mennykh izvestii o slavianakh*, ed. by L. A. Gindin, S. A. Ivanov, and G. G. Litavrin (Moscow: Nauka, 1991), p. 288 with notes 38–39.

the Middle Danube region, where they were settled and forced to pay tribute to the qagan, though under separate organization and with their own leader in the person of a certain Bulgar named Kouber.[24]

During the 580s and the early 590s, as the imperial armies were engaged in war on the eastern frontier with the Persians, the troops remaining in the Balkans were no match for the Avars. Singidunum (Belgrade) was twice conquered and plundered, first in 584, when the army of the qagan swiftly moved across the Balkans from northern Serbia to the Black Sea coast. Only rumors of approaching Turkic horsemen convinced the Avars to withdraw. A year later, however, the Avars sacked a number of forts along the Danube frontier, from Bononia (Vidin, in Bulgaria) to Tropaeum Traiani (Adamclisi, in Romania). The war continued in 586, when the Avars inflicted a number of demoralizing defeats on the imperial armies. An army said to have been of 100,000 Sclavenes and other barbarians obeying the orders of the qagan appeared under the walls of Thessalonica on September 22, 586, but could not take the city under the protection of St. Demetrius.[25] When, in 592, the Roman defenses around the passes across the eastern Stara Planina range were left unmanned, the Avars invaded the Black Sea coast region and in only five days reached Drizipera (now Büyükkarıştiran, near Lüleburgaz in Turkey), just 90 miles away from Constantinople. Near Heraclea, they encountered the Roman army, which they attacked by night, and the remaining Roman forces locked themselves up inside the walls of Tzurullon (Çorlu, Turkey), a mere dozen miles from the Long Walls defending the capital city of the Empire.[26]

In the course of their confronting the Avars at various points during the last two decades of the sixth century, the Roman troops had learned how to beat the enemy at their own game. That much is shown by the recommendations of the late sixth- or early seventh-century military treatise known as the *Strategikon*, most likely written by a high officer or general who had participated in the campaigns against both Avars and Slavs. Besides pieces of equipment that were clearly borrowed from the gear of the Avar warriors, the Roman

[24] *Miracles of St Demetrius* II.5.286, ed. and translated into French by P. Lemerle (Paris: CNRS Editions, 1979), p. 228.

[25] *Miracles of St. Demetrius* I.13.117, p. 134. For the date of the attack, see Pohl, *Die Awaren*, pp. 104–105.

[26] Theophylact Simocatta, *History* VI.5.4–16, ed. by de Boor and Wirth, pp. 228–229; Pohl, *Die Awaren*, pp. 134–135.

troops were advised to employ tactics that were typical of the steppe horsemen.[27] The *Strategikon* contains the earliest reference to stirrups,[28] a device brought to Europe by the Avars, and the archaeological evidence shows that Roman troops garrisoned, for example, in Caričin Grad had already adopted stirrups imitating the Avar specimens that had turned out in great numbers in early Avar burial assemblages in Hungary. In 586, Drocton, the second-in-command appointed by Emperor Maurice to deal with the Avar threat, defeated the army of the qagan near Adrianople (Edirne, Turkey), "for by feigned flight his wing gave the enemy the impression of turning their backs, as though the Romans were afraid of the opposition; next he turned about in pursuit, came up behind the barbarians, and slaughtered those whom he encountered."[29]

It is therefore no surprise to see that, once the peace was signed with Persia, the Romans turned their attention to the Avar problem and, beginning with the mid-590s, successfully battled the nomadic horsemen within their own territory. Until Maurice's fall in 602, with some interruptions, the Roman armies incessantly campaigned north of the Danube River, sometimes against the Slavs, other times against the Avars. Among other generals, Priscus distinguished himself through a very aggressive approach. In 595, his troops crossed the Danube in the Iron Gates sector. To the envoys that the qagan sent to protest the action, Priscus replied that "the soil was Roman."[30] Two years later, Priscus crossed again the river near Viminacium and defeated a much superior Avar force in a series of encounters,

[27] For example, the feigned retreat (IV.2, ed. by G. T. Dennis and E. Gamillscheg [Vienna: Verlag der Österreichischen Akademie der Wissenschaften, 1981, p. 194]) or the night attack (9.2, pp. 306–310). See Samuel Szádeczky-Kardoss, "Der awarisch-türkische Einfluss auf die byzantinische Kriegskunst um 600 (Anmerkungen zum *Strategikon* des Maurikios)," *Studia turco-hungarica*, vol. 5 (1981), pp. 63–65.

[28] *Strategikon* I.2, p. 80. See Szádeczky-Kardoss, "Der awarisch-türkische Einfluss," pp. 66–69.

[29] Theophylact Simocatta, *History* II.17.9 and 11, translated by Mary Whitby and Michael Whitby, pp. 67–68. Drocton (Droctulf) was a Sueve brought up by the Lombards; his life and career are described briefly by Paul the Deacon, *History of the Lombards* III.18–19, pp. 124–126.

[30] Theophylact Simocatta, *History* VII.7.5, translated by Mary Whitby and Michael Whitby, p. 188. For Roman claims to territories long abandoned, see E. Chrysos, "Die Nordgrenze des byzantinischen Reiches im 6. bis 8. Jahrhundert," in *Die Völker Südosteuropas im 6. bis 8. Jahrhundert*, ed. by B. Hänsel (Berlin: Südosteuropa Gesellschaft, 1987), pp. 27–40.

killing almost the entire Avar army and the qagan's four sons at its command.[31] Priscus crossed a river that Theophylact Simocatta calls Tissus, a name probably referring to either Tisza or, more likely, the Tamis/Timiş river, an indication that the Roman army did not penetrate too deeply into Avar territory.[32] When, in 601, the Avars were "attempting to win control from the Romans of the place called Cataracts"[33] (the Iron Gates), the commander in chief was not the qagan in person, but his second-in-command Apsich, an indication that the defeats inflicted upon the Avars by Priscus in 595 and 597 had taken their toll on the prestige of the Avar ruler and the stability of his regime. By 602, when Apsich organized a quick campaign against the Antes in the Lower Danube region, "large numbers defected from the Avars and hastened to desert to the emperor,"[34] a clear indication of the deteriorating situation inside the qaganate.

For a long time, historians of the early medieval Southeastern Europe have associated Phocas' rebellion against Emperor Maurice that broke out in 602 with the crumbling of the Roman defense in the Balkans and a general invasion of the Peninsula by Slavs and Avars. But the Roman troops were still waging war successfully on both Avars and Sclavenes when Emperor Maurice's order to his army to

[31] Theophylact Simocatta, *History* VIII.2.2–8.3.7, ed. by de Boor and Wirth, pp. 285–288. See also Pohl, *Die Awaren*, p. 156, who places these military confrontations in the formerly swampy region of central Vojvodina, on the left bank of the Lower Tisza. For early Avar burial assemblages in this region, see S. Nagy, "Mečka – ein frühmittelalterliches Gräberfeld beim Dorfe Aradac," *Študijné zvesti*, vol. 16 (1968), pp. 165–174.

[32] Theophylact Simocatta, *History* VIII.3.11, translated by de Boor and Wirth, p. 288. The 4,000 men dispatched by Priscus to cross the Tissus remind one of the general's similar operations of 592/3 within the Sclavene territory in what is now southern Romania. In their pursuit of the Sclavene warriors, the Roman soldiers also crossed a river called Helibakia, most likely the Ialomiţa. The Tamis/Timiş, which flows into the Danube just east of Singidunum (Belgrade), and the Ialomiţa, which flows into the same river near Carsium (Hârşova, Romania) on the eastern border of the province Scythia Minor, delineate the theater of operations beyond the Danube frontier in which the Roman armies moved against Avars and Slavs *c.* 600. Broken in two by the then inaccessible Iron Gates sector, where the Danube crosses the Carpathians, that theater of operations included much of southern and southwestern Romania, the regions later known as Walachia and Banat, respectively.

[33] Theophylact Simocatta, *History* VIII.5.6, translated by Mary Whitby and Michael Whitby, p. 216.

[34] Theophylact Simocatta, *History* VIII.6.1, translated by Mary Whitby and Michael Whitby, p. 217. See also Pohl, *Die Awaren*, p. 161.

pass the winter in Sclavene territory sparked the mutiny that would eventually bring Phocas to the imperial throne. According to the seventh-century Armenian chronicle attributed to Sebeos, after overthrowing Maurice in 602, the army returned to the Danube front and continued to wage war "against the enemy."[35] Moreover, no evidence exists of raiding activity, by either Avars or Slavs, during Phocas' reign. By contrast, the raids resumed during Heraclius' early regnal years. Relying on information borrowed from an earlier source, Paul the Deacon mentions in a single breath the Avar conquest of Forum Iulii in Italy and the devastation of Istria by the Sclavenes.[36] In distant Spain, Isidore of Seville knew that at the beginning of Heraclius' reign the Persians had conquered Syria and Egypt, and the Slavs had taken Greece from the Romans.[37] Archaeology too indicates that occupation of most, if not all, forts in the northern and central Balkans ceased *c.* 620 at the latest, most likely due to Heraclius' final withdrawal of all troops from the Balkans to meet the dangers on the eastern frontier. For most of the seventh century, with the exception of a few coastal areas, the region remained without any troops until the first Byzantine theme was established in the Balkans.

[35] *The Armenian History Attributed to Sebeos*, English translation by R. W. Thomson (Liverpool: Liverpool University Press, 1999), pp. 80 and 196. The Roman army must have remained on the Danube frontier until Phocas concluded a treaty with the qagan in 605, in order to transfer troops to the Persian front.

[36] Paul the Deacon, *History of the Lombards* IV.40, p. 168.

[37] Isidore of Seville, *Historia Gothorum Wandalorum Sueborum*, in *Chronica minora*, ed. by Th. Mommsen, vol. II (Berlin: Weidmann, 1894), p. 497.

2

SOUTHEAST EUROPEAN "DARK AGES" (*c.* 600–*c.* 800)

Not much is known about the last decades of Roman (Byzantine) power in the Balkans. After 620, occupation ceased on most urban or military sites in the central Balkans (Ohrid, Caričin Grad, Bargala, Bitola, Pernik, and Veliko Tărnovo-Carevec), whose existence may have continued in one form or another into the early seventh century. In several cases, there are clear signs of destruction by fire at some point after AD 600, which was often interpreted as the archaeological trace of widespread raids of Avars and Slavs. To be sure, the little we know from historical sources about the first decades of Emperor Heraclius' reign seems to confirm this picture of devastation. Writing in the late 600s, the author of Book II of the *Miracles of St. Demetrius* knew that before attacking Thessalonica, the Slavs had devastated Thessaly and its islands, the islands of Greece, the Cyclades, Achaia, Epirus, and the most part of Illyricum, as well as parts of Asia.[1]

However, no precise date can be assigned to the first Slavic attack on Thessalonica recorded in Book II. It is only known that it must

[1] *Miracles of St. Demetrius* II.1.179, p. 175. Some Greek historians maintain that the Slavs could not have possibly reached the Cyclades on their canoes. But, apart from the testimony of the *Miracles of St. Demetrius*, Sclavene raids in the Aegean are mentioned in a compilation of various sources with different authors preserved in an eighth-century manuscript and known as *Liber Chalifarum*. According to the *Liber*, Crete and several other islands were raided by Slavs in the year 934 of the Seleucid era (AD 623). See M. V. Krivov, "Siriiskii 'Smeshannyi khronikon' [The Syriac Compilation]," in *Svod drevneishikh pis'mennykh izvestii o slavianakh*, ed. by S. A. Ivanov, G. G. Litavrin, and V. K. Ronin, vol. II (Moscow: "Vostochnaia literatura," Rossiiskaia Akademiia Nauk, 1995), pp. 517–518.

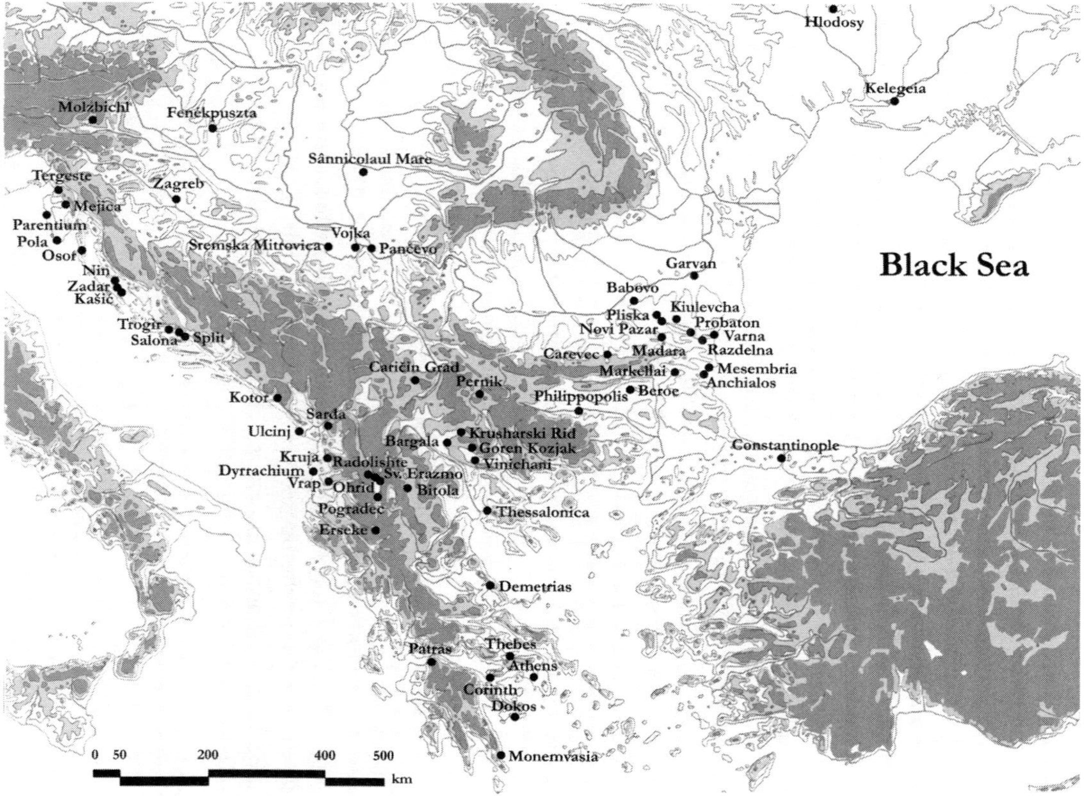

Map 2 Southeastern Europe in the "Dark Ages."

have taken place at a time John, the author of Book I, was still Archbishop of Thessalonica. The list of territories raided by the Slavs before they turned against Thessalonica fits well into the picture of Heraclius' first and very difficult years, snapshots of which are given by Isidore of Seville and George of Pisidia. In particular, the fact that the author of Book II specifically refers to maritime raids on canoes reminds one of what George of Pisidia has to say about the "Sclavene wolves."[2] It may well be, therefore, that the attack took place at some point during the first decade of Heraclius' reign. There is, however, a substantial difference between this siege and the attacks on Thessalonica mentioned in Book I. Unlike the marauders of the 580s, the Sclavenes of the early seventh century had brought with them families, for "they had promised to establish them in the city [of Thessalonica] after its conquest." This seems to indicate that, unlike those who besieged the city during Maurice's reign, the Slavs storming the city walls during the reign of Heraclius were not coming from afar. Indeed, the author of Book II used the term "Sclavenes" as an umbrella term for a multitude of tribes, some of which he knew by name: Drugubites, Sagudates, Berzetes, Baiunetes, and Belegezites.[3] Unlike Archbishop John, the author of Book I, the unknown author of the second collection of homilies dedicated to St. Demetrius knew a lot more about the current whereabouts of the Slavs. For example, the Belegezites are again mentioned in Book II as living in the region of Thessaly, near Thebes and Demetrias.[4] When did they establish themselves there? It is impossible to tell with precision, but it cannot have been earlier than the reign of Heraclius. On the other hand, it is hard to believe that the Belegezites and the other tribes mentioned in Book II were the perpetrators of the large-scale devastation of the islands of Thessaly, of the Cyclades, of most of Illyricum, and of parts of Asia. The list of territories plundered by the Slavs does

[2] *Miracles of St. Demetrius* II.1.179, p. 175; see also II.4.253 and 254, p. 214. For the "Sclavene wolves," see George of Pisidia, *Bellum Avaricum* 197–201, ed. by A. Pertusi (Ettal: Buch Kunstverlag, 1959).

[3] *Miracles of St. Demetrius* II.1.180, p. 175. For the multitude of tribes, see II.1.179, p. 175. For the location of the various tribes, see P. Lemerle, *Les plus anciens recueils des Miracles de Saint Démétrius et la pénétration des Slaves dans les Balkans. II: Commentaire* (Paris: CNRS Editions, 1981), pp. 89–90. For the question of names, see J. Koder, "Anmerkungen zum Slawen-Namen in byzantinischen Quellen," *T&M*, vol. 14 (2002), pp. 333–346.

[4] *Miracles of St. Demetrius* II.4.254, p. 214. The Belegezites supplied Thessalonica with food during the siege of 677.

not look at all like having been compiled on the basis of testimonies collected from refugees fleeing those territories to find shelter within the walls of Thessalonica. There are two other "lists of provinces" in Book II, one of which betrays an administrative source. It is therefore likely that, in describing a local event of relatively minor significance, namely the siege of Thessalonica by a coalition of local Slavic tribes, the intention of the author of Book II was to frame it against a broader historical and administrative background, and thus make it appear to be of greater importance. The impression one gets is that when all the other provinces and cities were falling, Thessalonica alone, under the protection of St. Demetrius, was capable of resistance. The siege itself did not last more than a week, although the Slavs were still bent on establishing themselves in Thessalonica. They now called upon the Avars for military assistance. An embassy was sent with rich presents for the qagan of the Avars, to whom the Slavs promised much more provided that he would help them capture the city. These Slavs were certainly not subjects of the qagan, for they were negotiating an alliance with him as equals. However, there were numerous other Slavs obeying the orders of the Avar ruler in the army he eventually brought under the walls of Thessalonica.[5]

Again, the Avar siege of Thessalonica does not seem to have been an event of any major importance. This time, even the emperor was ignorant about what had happened. The emperor in question is not named, but he must have been Heraclius, for the siege took place not long after the one described in the first homily of Book II. Indeed, two years after being offered the alliance of the Sclavene tribes that had failed to capture Thessalonica, the qagan marched against the city. The siege must have taken place in 617 or 618, at the latest, and lasted just over a month. In the end, however, the qagan could not take the city. Instead, he opened negotiations with the besieged, in order to obtain some form of monetary compensation for withdrawing his troops.

[5] *Miracles of St. Demetrius* II.2.197–198, p. 185. The Sclavenes attacked on the fourth day (II.1.185) and the decisive confrontation took place on that same day. See Th. Korres, "Some remarks on the first major attempts of the Avaroslavs to capture Thessaloniki (597 and 614)," *Byzantina*, vol. 19 (1998), pp. 177–183. For Avar–Slavic relations, see W. Pohl, "Die Beziehungen der Awaren zu den Slawen," in *Slovenija in sosednje dežele med antiko in karolinsko dobo. Začetki slovenske etnogeneze*, ed. by R. Bratož (Ljubljana: Narodni Muzej Slovenije, 2000), pp. 341–354.

Elsewhere in the Balkans, the situation is less clear. Historians have long maintained that Salona (Solin near Split, in Croatia) must have been conquered by either Avars or Slavs at some point between 619 and 626. Such assertions were based on information derived from much later sources, such as Constantine Porphyrogenitus, and from misdated funerary inscriptions. However, a coin hoard and finds of bronze vessels known as "Coptic bowls" clearly point to an occupation of the site continuing well into the early seventh century. At the same time, after partial destruction, parts of the large basilica at Manastirine, not far from the city, were turned into a smaller church. Similar evidence has meanwhile turned up in Kapljuč and comparable alterations were identified at the basilica at Marusinac, both in the city's environs. At Diaporit, near Butrint (Albania), an earlier Roman villa was reoccupied during the seventh century, with walls of stone bonded with clay dividing the available space into smaller rooms. A church built nearby at an unknown date before *c.* 600 was now modified and reused, much like the churches in Manastirine and Kapljuč.[6] In Athens, the old colonnade of the Stoa lost its original architectural integrity and was subdivided into rooms at some point during the seventh century. In room 6, hundreds of terracotta roof tiles recovered from the fallen debris of the house which was destroyed sometime in the 630s were piled in neat rows for possible reuse.[7] An early Byzantine fort identified on the island of Dokos in the Argolid Bay has two phases of occupation, one of which ends abruptly in the early 600s. To judge from the numismatic evidence, the site remained unoccupied until the late seventh century. An early seventh-century occupation is also attested on the western coast of Greece, for example on the island of Kephalos in the Ambracian Gulf. At Aphiona, on the island of Kerkyra, a group of houses with stone walls produced coarse ware jugs, amphora shards, and fragments of glass vessels, all of which may equally be dated to the seventh century.

In Greece, as elsewhere in the Balkans, the general withdrawal of the Roman troops is clearly visible in the numismatic evidence. After the early 580s, there is a sharp decline in the number of coins from Greek hoards, and new coins appear briefly only after 610. Stray finds

6 W. Bowden, *Epirus Vetus. The Archaeology of a Late Antique Province* (London: Duckworth, 2003), pp. 201–202.

7 T. L. Shear, "The Athenian Agora: excavations of 1972," *Hesperia*, vol. 42 (1973), p. 397.

seem to follow a similar pattern. A significant number of hoards of Byzantine copper or gold coins were buried during Phocas' reign, but especially during Heraclius' early regnal years. Hoard finds from the first two decades of the seventh century are in sharp contrast to those from the remainder of that century. Indeed, Greece has produced so far only three hoards, two of gold and one of copper, that could be dated after *c.* 630. After *c.* 630, gold finds disappear from the southern Balkans and copper coins of the last decades of Heraclius' reign are very rare. It has been suggested that responsible for the significant number of hoards closing in the early 600s were the Slavic invasions of Greece during Heraclius' first regnal years.[8] In fact, hoards of gold with a small number of coins may represent payments to the army known as *donativa*, which were still paid in 578 and perhaps as late as Heraclius' reign. Hoards of *solidi* may therefore be seen as an example of the correlation between mint output and hoarding, on one hand, and military preparations, on the other. Such hoards indicate the presence of the Roman army, not barbarian attacks. They were concealed and never retrieved not necessarily because of barbarian raids, but because their owners may have kept their savings in cash in a hiding place for lack of any specialized institutions such as banks. Though the notable presence of the military in Greece is certainly to be associated with the turbulent years at the beginning of Heraclius' reign, as well as with the increasing raiding activity of both Slavs and Avars, the hoards themselves are an indication of accumulated wealth, not of destruction. The cluster of closing dates for most hoards right before 620 strongly suggests that collections of copper were never retrieved because of the general withdrawal of Roman armies from the Balkans. There are indeed very few coins of Heraclius postdating the withdrawal of troops on any site in the region.

THE AVARS AND THE AVAR QAGANATE

Heraclius' transfer of the Balkan troops to the eastern front in 620 seems to have allowed the Avars a wider range of both raiding and control in the Balkans. Judging from the existing evidence, during the

[8] D. M. Metcalf, "The Aegean coastlands under threat: some coins and coin hoards from the reign of Heraclius," *ABSA*, vol. 57 (1962), pp. 14–23; and "Avar and Slav invasions into the Balkan peninsula (c. 575–625): the nature of the numismatic evidence," *Journal of Roman Archaeology*, vol. 4 (1991), pp. 140–148.

subsequent years they focused on the eastern regions of the peninsula. In 623, they ambushed the emperor himself near the Long Walls. Heraclius barely escaped alive, and the Avars got hold of the imperial treasury and of the emperor's escort before sweeping forward to the walls of Constantinople and carrying a great number of prisoners. Following this episode, Heraclius chose appeasement over retaliation and agreed to raise the tribute paid to the Avars to 200,000 *solidi* in addition to giving his own son as hostage. Three years later, the Avars laid siege to the capital itself. But the Avars were not able to establish an effective cooperation with the Persian armies on the other side of the Straits. The attack that the Slavs under Avar command launched on their canoes in the Golden Horn waters met the superior forces of the Byzantine fleet. The military failure grew quickly from debacle into disaster. Conflicts between Avars and Sclavenes seem to have followed the siege, and the subsequent decades witnessed some of the worst political and, possibly, social, convulsions in the two-hundred-year history of the Avar qaganate.[9] According to the chronicle of Fredegar, during the ninth regnal year of the Frankish king Dagobert (631/2), the civil war broke within the qaganate between an Avar and a Bulgar "party." The exact reasons for the conflict are not known, but it must have been a consequence of the considerable blow to the prestige of the ruling qagan brought by his defeat under the walls of Constantinople. The archaeological record is also quite explicit in this regard. A relatively large community of Christians had been thriving for almost a century around the basilica at Fenékpuszta, on the western shore of Lake Balaton (Hungary). Built in the mid-500s, the church was restored sometime around 600, and then destroyed, together with the adjacent settlement and cemetery, around 630. The Christians thriving under the qagan's rule must have been caught in the ongoing civil war and their community did not outlive the conflict. The serious crisis opened by the civil war is also reflected in the migration to Bavaria of 9,000 Bulgar families from the qaganate, no doubt supporters of the losing party. They would later be slaughtered at the orders of King Dagobert, and only 700 families eventually escaped to a certain Walluc, Duke of the Wends, who probably ruled

[9] George of Pisidia, *Bellum Avaricum* 197–201. For the siege, see J. D. Howard-Johnston, "The siege of Constantinople in 626," in *Constantinople and its Hinterland. Papers from the Twenty-Seventh Spring Symposium of Byzantine Studies, Oxford, April 1993*, ed. by C. Mango and G. Dagron (Aldershot: Variorum, 1995), pp. 131–142.

in what is today Austrian Carinthia and northern Slovenia.[10] Other, more belligerent Wends – the preferred name for Slavs on the western fringes of the qaganate – had by then established a powerful polity farther to the north or northwest. According to Fredegar, Samo, a Frankish merchant elected king of "those Slavs who are known as Wends," led their revolt against the Avars, after which he ruled them for thirty-five years. Samo's rise to power is dated by Fredegar to the fortieth year of King Chlothar's reign (623/4), but some have recently claimed that the episode of Samo cannot possibly be earlier than the defeat of the qagan under the walls of Constantinople. Even if Fredegar's chronology is correct, the possibility still remains that Samo took considerable advantage of that setback in order to consolidate his power.[11]

The troubles at the center of the Avar power reverberated also in the East European steppes. According to Nicephorus, "Koubratos, the nephew of Organas and lord of the Onogundurs, rose against the Chagan of the Avars and, after abusing the army he had from the latter, drove them out of his land."[12] Theophanes wrote of Kubrat as a ruler of the Bulgars, and his story may have originated in a "native," Danube-Bulgarian source. However, there is no reason to doubt that Kubrat's rebellion broke against the power of the Avars extending into the East European steppes. Kubrat may well have been that "Ketradates" mentioned by John of Nikiu as a staunch supporter of Empress Martina and her son Heraklonas, because of a long

[10] Fredegar IV.72. Walluc is not the actual name of the Wendish duke, but most likely the (Common) Slavic word for his position of power, *voldyka* (*vladyka*). See J. Mikkola, "Ein altslovenisches Wort in Fredegars Chronik," *Archiv für slavische Philologie*, vol. 41 (1927), p. 160; O. N. Trubachev, "Sclavania am Obermain im merovingischer und karolingischer Zeit: die Sprachreste," in *Central Europe in 8th–10th Centuries. International Scientific Conference, Bratislava October 2–4, 1995*, ed. by D. Čaplović and J. Dorul'a (Bratislava: VEDA, 1997), pp. 53–55. For Walluc, see also W. Fritze, *Untersuchungen zur frühslawischen und frühfränkischen Geschichte bis ins 7. Jahrhundert* (Frankfurt am Main, Berlin, and Bern: Peter Lang, 1994), p. 279.

[11] Fredegar IV.48, 68, and 87. For Fredegar's chronology, see S. Szádeczky-Kardoss, "Vernachlässigte Quellenangaben zur Geschichte des ersten awarischen Khaganates," in *Varia Eurasiatica. Festschrift für Professor András Róna-Tas* (Szeged: Department of Altaic Studies, 1991), p. 181. See also M. Eggers, "Samo, 'der erste König der Slawen'. Eine kritische Forschungsbericht," *Bohemia*, vol. 42 (2001), pp. 62–83.

[12] Nicephorus, *Short History* 22, ed. and transl. by C. Mango (Washington: Dumbarton Oaks Research Library and Collection, 1990), p. 71. Nothing else is known about Organa, and the Onogundurs are otherwise not known from earlier sources.

history of friendship between him and Emperor Heraclius.[13] If so, then his revolt against the Avars, which broke out in 631 or 632, could not have been better timed to serve the political and military interests of the Empire. According to Theophanes, Kubrat was the master of "the old Great Bulgaria" stretching from the Maeotid Lake (the Sea of Azov) to the river Kouphis, "where the Bulgarian fish called *xyston* is caught."[14] Historians have often interpreted this passage as locating Kubrat's Great Bulgaria between the Sea of Azov and the Kuban River, which was indeed known in other sources as Kouphis. However, the name was also used for other rivers, most importantly for the (Southern) Bug. Taking into consideration the geographic orientation of Theophanes' account, Kubrat's Great Bulgaria is therefore to be located in the steppes of present-day Ukraine, just north of Crimea, on both sides of the Lower Dnieper River.[15] This also dovetails with the archaeological evidence pertaining to the the seventh-century Middle and Lower Dnieper, especially with a number of exceptionally rich burials, such as Zachepilovki, Nove Senzhary, Voznesens'ke, Kelegeia, Hlodosy, and especially (Malo) Pereshchepyne. Besides weapons, exquisite dress accessories, as well as Byzantine and Sassanian silverware, the Pereshchepyne assemblage produced three golden finger-rings with monogram mentioning a certain *patrikios* Koubratos, a strong indication that, despite the absence of any skeletal remains, the Pereshchepyne assemblage may well be Kubrat's burial. Most similar burials were found in Left Bank Ukraine (east of the Lower Dnieper River), but the cremation burial from Hlodosy (near Kirovohrad), while sharing many features with the Left Bank assemblages, also displays a number of remarkable parallels with the most exceptional burial assemblages of the late Early Avar and Middle Avar periods in Hungary, which have been rightly interpreted as the graves

[13] John of Nikiu, *Chronicle*, ed. by H. Zotenberg with English translation by R. H. Charles (London: William and Norgate, 1916; reprinted Amsterdam: APA-Philo Press, 1987), p. 196. See V. Beshevliev, "Zur Chronik des Johannes von Nikiu CXX 46–49," *Byzantinobulgarica*, vol. 5 (1978), pp. 229–236. If the identification is correct, Kubrat may well been have a Christian at the time of the anti-Avar revolt.

[14] Theophanes Confessor, *Chronographia*, AM 6171, p. 498. See also H. Lauterbach, "Untersuchungen zur Vorgeschichte der Protobulgaren nach einem Bericht bei Teofanes," in *Die Araber in der alten Welt*, ed. by F. Altheim and R. Stiehl, vol. 1 (Berlin: De Gruyter, 1967), pp. 543–544.

[15] A. Róna-Tas, "Where was Khuvrat's Bulgharia?," *Acta Orientalia Academiae Scientiarum Hungaricae*, vol. 53 (2000), pp. 1–22.

of qagans or of close members of their families.[16] Dated to the second half of the seventh century by means of coins minted for the emperors Constans II (641–668) and Constantine IV (668–685), the group of assemblages in Ukraine to which Hlodosy belongs have been interpreted as princely burials of Kubrat's family. Judging from the archaeological evidence and from that of Nicephorus, Kubrat may thus have been appointed by the qagan of the Avars to govern a subject tribal union in the steppes north of the Black Sea. He seems to have taken advantage of the crisis of the Avar qaganate in the aftermath of the siege of Constantinople to strike on his own. Moreover, as the civil war broke in *c.* 630 within the western Türk empire (established in the Eurasian steppes in the mid-sixth century), two groups began competing for power and control over the steppes: the Bulgars, under the leadership of Kubrat, who was a scion of the Dulo clan, the leading group of the left division of the western Türk qaganate; and the Khazars, led by a member of the charismatic clan Ashina, which was associated with the right division. By 660 at the latest, the Khazars finally won over their rivals. In the words of Theophanes, "they subjugated the eldest brother Batbaian, chieftain of the First Bulgaria, from whom they exact tribute to this day."[17] According to the presumably native tradition reported by Theophanes, Batbaian was one of Kubrat's five sons, who divided Great Bulgaria among themselves at the death of their father. Another son, Asparukh, eventually fled across the Dnieper and the Dniester Rivers, and established himself and his followers just north of the Danube Delta, in a region called Oglos, "since he judged that place to be secure and impregnable on both sides: on the near side it is marshy, while on the far side it is encircled by the rivers."[18] The chronology of Asparukh's arrival and subsequent conquest of the eastern Balkans is still under debate, but it seems very likely that he was already in Oglos *c.* 670. Equally

[16] A. T. Smilenko, *Glodos'ki skarbi* [The Hlodosy Hoard] (Kiev: Naukova Dumka, 1965). For similar assemblages in Hungary, see E. H. Tóth and A. Horváth, *Kunbábony. Das Grab eines Awarenkhagans* (Kécskemét: Museumdirektion der Selbstverwaltung des Komitats Bács-Kiskun, 1992).

[17] Theophanes Confessor, *Chronographia*, AM 6171, p. 498.

[18] Theophanes Confessor, *Chronographia*, AM 6171, p. 498. See R. Rashev, "L'Onglos – témoignages écrits et faits archéologiques," *BHR*, vol. 10 (1982), pp. 68–79; A. Madgearu, "Recent discussions about 'Onglos'," in *Istro-Pontica. Muzeul tulcean la a 50-a aniversare 1950–2000. Omagiu lui Simion Gavrilă la 45 de ani de activitate, 1955–2000*, ed. by M. Iacob, E. Oberländer-Târnoveanu, and F. Topoleanu (Tulcea: Consiliul Județean Tulcea, 2000), pp. 343–348.

debatable is the possible association of his sojourn in the region north of the Danube with the three earthworks between the Prut and the Dniester known as the Bessarabian dikes.[19]

It is from this region that the Bulgars began raiding the regions in the eastern Balkans still under Byzantine control. Initially, because of the concomitant attacks of the Arabs who besieged Constantinople between 674 and 678, Emperor Constantine IV tried to ensure good relations with the new barbarians at the Empire's northern frontier. This, at least, is the most likely explanation for the presence of a large number of silver coins (hexagrams) minted for that emperor in isolated and hoard finds from the Lower Danube region, the latest of which are specimens of Constantine's third series dated no later than 681. Many of the specimens found in the Priseaca hoard are freshly minted and die-linked, which may indicate that they did not change hands much after leaving the mint. This remark substantiates the idea of such coins serving as bribes or gifts sent directly from Constantinople to some barbarian, most likely Bulgar, chieftain.[20] However, shortly after his victory over the Arabs, Emperor Constantine IV organized an expedition against the Bulgars, during which the Byzantine fleet seems to have sealed the segment of the Danube frontier of the Empire between the Danube Delta and the mouth of

[19] Recent excavations of the southern dike just north of the Danube Delta have produced evidence of a seventh- or eighth-century occupation in the form of sunken-floored houses built against the dike. See G. F. Chebotarenko and L. V. Subbotin, "Issledovaniia Troianovykh Valov v Dnestrovsko-Dunaiskom mezhdurech'e [The excavation of Trajan's Dikes in the region between the Dniester and the Danube]," in *Drevnosti Iugo-Zapada SSSR*, ed. by P. P. Byrnia (Kishinew: Shtiinca, 1991), pp. 124–145. However, as Rasho Rashev notes, it is still not sufficient evidence to link the dikes to Asparukh and his followers, for the earthworks could have as well been built after 680/1 as a barrier against Khazar raids from the northeast. See R. Rashev, "La plus ancienne période de l'état bulgare," in *Von der Scythia zur Dobrudža*, ed. by Kh. Kholiolchev, R. Pillinger, and R. Harreither (Vienna: Verein "Freunde des Hauses Wittgenstein," 1997), p. 50.

[20] F. Curta, "Invasion or inflation? Sixth- to seventh-century Byzantine coin hoards in Eastern and Southeastern Europe," *Annali dell'Istituto Italiano di Numismatica*, vol. 43 (1996), pp. 109–116; E. Oberländer-Târnoveanu, "La monnaie byzantine des IVe–VIIIe siècles au-delà de la frontière du Bas-Danube. Entre politique, économie et diffusion culturelle," *H&M*, vol. 17 (2002), pp. 176–177. For the Priseaca hoard, see B. Mitrea, "Un trésor du VIIe siècle découvert à Priseaca en Valachie," in *Actes du XIVe Congrès international des études byzantines, Bucarest, 6–12 septembre 1971*, ed. by M. Berza and E. Stănescu (Bucharest: Editura Academiei Republicii Socialiste România, 1975), pp. 212–213.

the Prut River. The campaign went awry when the emperor, having developed "an acute case of gout, was constrained to return to Mesembria" together with his retinue and a part of his fleet. A rumor spread that the emperor was fleeing, and in the debacle, Asparukh's warriors crossed the Danube and "came to Varna, as it is called, near Odyssos, and the inland territory that is there."[21] Following their victory of 680/1, the Bulgars remained south of the Danube, in Dobrudja and what is now northeastern Bulgaria, which they no doubt perceived as not only closer to the Byzantine territories, the target of future raids, but also as safely removed from any Khazar interference and pressure. Two Slavic groups in the region, the so-called Seven Tribes and the Severeis, were forced into submission and resettled as border guards, respectively, in the west against the Avars, and on the southern frontier, against the Byzantines. During the subsequent decades, most other Slavic groups in the northern and central Balkans were drawn into the orbit of the newly established polity, but there is no archaeological or historical evidence to support the idea of an early Bulgar control over the steppes north of the Black Sea.

BULGARIA DURING THE EIGHTH CENTURY

Visible as the presence of the Bulgars was in the archaeological record for the mid- and late seventh century through both princely graves in the Lower Dnieper region and finds of Byzantine hexagrams in the Lower Danube area, there is to date no archaeological correlate for the beginnings of medieval Bulgaria. In view of the notorious absence of metal artifacts with secured chronology from early medieval cemeteries in northeastern Bulgaria (Novi Pazar, Razdelna, and Babovo), recent attempts to date the beginnings of these graveyards to the time of Asparukh must be regarded with extreme suspicion. A horseman burial found within a prehistoric barrow in Madara, long considered to be the earliest archaeological evidence pertaining to the presence of the Bulgars in Bulgaria, has been recently shown to be of a much earlier date.[22] Similarly, and despite claims to the contrary, neither

[21] Theophanes Confessor, *Chronographia*, AM 6171, p. 499.

[22] U. Fiedler, *Studien zu Gräberfeldern des 6. bis 9. Jahrhunderts an der unteren Donau* (Bonn: Rudolf Habelt, 1992), pp. 319–320 and 321 fig. 113; and "Nochmals zur Datierung von Grab 5 im Hügel III von Madara," *Problemi na prabălgarskata istoriia i kultura*, vol. 3 (1997), pp. 125–140.

the "Outer Town" (a vast area enclosed within the earthen rampart), nor the immediate hinterland of the fortified palace compound at Pliska have so far produced any evidence of a late seventh- or early eighth-century occupation. To date, the earliest datable finds, mainly pottery remains, from the area inside the great wall of Pliska are of the late eighth century. Nothing is known about the residences or burial sites of the first rulers of Bulgaria, Asparukh and his successors.

Nevertheless, the Bulgar rulers played a prominent role in the history of the eighth-century Balkans. In 705, the second ruler Tervel, most likely Asparukh's son, formed an alliance with the Byzantine emperor Justinian II and helped him regain his throne in Constantinople. According to Theophanes, after receiving Justinian "with honor," Tervel "roused up the entire host of Bulgars and Slavs that were subject to him." Tervel was most likely following to its letter the peace treaty between his own father and that of Justinian, back in 680 or 681.[23] In return, he received the "imperial mantle" and was proclaimed Caesar.[24] Tervel displayed the symbols of his newly acquired position of power on a leaden seal most likely struck during his sojourn in Constantinople, as well as on a massive rock relief-carving (2.6 m high, 3.1 m wide) on a cliff in Madara showing the ruler on horseback trampling down a lion.[25] The accompanying inscriptions in Greek carved behind the horse mention the assistance, in both troops and perhaps gold, that the "slit-nosed emperor" received from Tervel. The latter appears as *archon*, a term frequently employed at the time for governors of such Byzantine cities as Mesembria or Chersonesus, or for Slavic chieftains operating as clients of the Byzantine military power in the Balkans (see below). The fact that Tervel recognized himself as a member of the Byzantine hierarchy of power clearly points to carefully regulated relations between his polity and

[23] Theophanes Confessor, *Chronographia*, AM 6171, p. 499. See V. Beshevliev, *Die protobulgarische Periode der bulgarischen Geschichte* (Amsterdam: Adolf Hakkert, 1981), p. 192.

[24] Nicephorus, *Short History* 42, p. 103.

[25] M. Nystazopoulou-Pelekidou, "Sceaux byzantins, improprement appelés protobulgares," *Byzantiaka*, vol. 11 (1991), pp. 17–18 (the seal of Tervel Caesar). The Madara relief-carving has been first published by K. Miiatev, "Madarskiiat konnik [The Madara Horseman]," *Izvestiia na Bălgarskiia arkheologicheski institut*, vol. 5 (1928–1929), pp. 90–126. Ever since, the literature on the "Madara Horseman" has grown considerably. For a quick orientation, see now R. Rashev, "Madarskiiat konnik – stari i novi văprosi [The Madara Horseman – old and new issues]," *Istoricheski pregled*, vol. 54 (1998), pp. 192–204.

the neighboring Empire. Indeed, despite a brief military confrontation in 708, Tervel dutifully fulfilled his obligations when sending 3,000 men to help Justinian quell the revolt of the fleet he had sent against Philippikos.[26] When Justinian was overthrown and assassinated, and Philippikos refused to pay the tribute, Tervel retaliated by raiding the outskirts of Constantinople, from which the Bulgar troops took many captives, as well as "much silver and a considerable number of utensils." After devastating many villages in Thrace, the Bulgars "returned home with innumerable cattle."[27]

Under Emperor Theodosius III, in 716, a peace treaty was concluded which, besides establishing the boundary between Byzantium and Bulgaria "at Meleones in Thrace," attempted to regulate the growing trade between the two countries by establishing a ceiling of no more than thirty pounds of gold worth of "vestments and (dyed) red hides," no doubt articles on a long list of goods produced in small quantities in imperial workshops in Constantinople and therefore not to be exported outside Byzantium without imperial approval. The treaty established an annual quota for such merchandise, which had to be sold to the Bulgars at a place where exports could be monitored and appropriately taxed by Byzantine authorities.[28] In the early 700s, that place could have only been Mesembria, where the imperial office of trade tax collection (*apotheke*) is attested on seals of affiliated officials (*kommerkiarioi*) as early as 690 and then, without interruption, during the subsequent decades until the joint reign of Constantine V and Leo IV (751–755). Until the mid-eighth century, the lucrative

[26] Nicephorus, *Short History* 45, p. 111. The Bulgar warriors crossed the Straits on Byzantine ships and joined ranks with the troops of the army of Opsikion. Nothing is known about them in the aftermath of Justinian's assassination by the *spatharios* Elias, but it is unlikely that they joined the other Bulgars Tervel sent to raid the outskirts of Constantinople in retaliation to Philippikos' coup d'état. They were probably recruited in the thematic army of Opsikion and never returned to Bulgaria.

[27] Nicephorus, *Short History* 47, p. 115; Theophanes, *Chronographia* AM 6204, p. 532. Theophanes' mention of the cattle serves a special purpose, namely to draw a parallel between Bulgars and Arabs, both "stealthily throwing themselves" upon Byzantine territories apparently with no other purpose than taking captives and cattle.

[28] Theophanes, *Chronographia* AM 6305, p. 681. See also N. Oikonomides, "Tribute or trade? The Byzantine–Bulgarian treaty of 716," in *Issledovaniia po slaviano-vizantiiskomu i zapadnoevropeiskomu srednevekov'iu. Posviashchaetsia pamiati Ivana Duicheva*, ed. by P. Dinekov, A. Dzhurova, G. Bakalov, et al. (Sofia: Centr dlia slaviano-vizantiiskikh issledovanii imeni Ivana Duicheva and Gosudarstvennoe izdatel'stvo imeni D-ra Petra Berona, 1988), pp. 29–31.

trade with the Bulgars seems to have mitigated any possible hostilities between Bulgaria and Byzantium and to have brought the two powers even closer to each other. During the siege of Constantinople by the Arab general Maslamah, the Bulgars allied themselves with Emperor Leo III and had an important contribution to the subsequent defeat and humiliation of the Arabs.[29] Tervel ultimately remained committed to his alliance with the ruling emperor, even after promising the deposed emperor Artemios "an army as well as 50 centenaria (5,000 pounds) of gold," in order for him to recuperate power in Constantinople. In the end, the Bulgar troops surrendered the rebel to Leo III and "returned home, duly rewarded by the latter."[30]

Not much is known about Bulgaria and Bulgar–Byzantine relations between *c.* 720 and *c.* 750. A second, but unfortunately damaged, inscription associated with the Madara Horseman mentions the *archon* Krumesis and gifts of gold, apparently from the Byzantine emperor, which the Bulgar leader redistributed to his warriors.[31] Judging by the existing evidence (or lack thereof), the peace established between Tervel and Leo III at the end of the Artemios incident may have continued into the reign of Tervel's successor, in fact outliving both the Bulgar leader and the Byzantine emperor. It is only during the reign of Constantine V that relations between the two polities became increasingly hostile. In 755, the emperor began fortifying some of the Thracian towns to which he moved Syrian and Armenian settlers transferred from the eastern frontier. The Bulgars reacted by demanding what Theophanes calls "tribute because of the forts that had been built" and Nicephorus calls "taxes" – no doubt remunerative compensations for what they saw as a breach

[29] Theophanes, *Chronographia* AM 6209, p. 546. See P. A. Yannopoulos, "Le rôle des Bulgares dans la guerre arabo-byzantine de 717/718," *VV*, vol. 55 (1994), pp. 133–153.

[30] Theophanes, *Chronographia* AM 6211, p. 552. According to Nicephorus, Leo had written to the Bulgars, asking them "to embrace peace and surrender his enemies." In turn, the Bulgars "apologized and asked for his forgiveness, promising to bring about peace." See Nicephorus, *Short History* 57, p. 127. Both accounts seem to put a spin on the events in an attempt to divert attention from Tervel's ability to maneuver between contenders, in order to maximize his profits. It is very likely that Tervel recuperated his gold, to which he now added the gifts received from Leo.

[31] Beshevliev, *Die protobulgarischen Inschriften*, pp. 99 and 111–122.

of preexisting agreements going back to Tervel's times.[32] When the emperor dismissed their charges, the Bulgars raided Thrace as far as the Long Walls. Only Nicephorus mentions a victory that Constantine apparently won against the Bulgar marauders. Following a brief campaign against the Slavs in Macedonia in 759, Constantine campaigned against Bulgaria on both land and sea, with a fleet of 500 ships. Theophanes' and Nicephorus' accounts of these events are contradictory to the extreme. Theophanes speaks of a defeat of the Byzantine army ambushed in the "pass of Beregaba" (perhaps the present-day Rish Pass across the eastern Stara Planina), while, according to Nicephorus, the emperor won a victory "at the so-called Markellai" (a fort on the Bulgar–Byzantine frontier, near present-day Karnobat) while his fleet entered the Danube through the Delta and set fire to the Bulgar lands. Sueing for peace, the Bulgars "delivered hostages from among their children," most likely of aristocratic clans.[33]

The burst of hostility seems to have taken a toll on the political stability of Bulgaria. According to Theophanes, in 761 or 762 the Bulgars "rose up, killed their hereditary lords and set up as their king an evil-minded man called Teletzes, who was 30 years old." Nicephorus equally blames the subsequent course of action on Telec's "rashness of youth." Historians have correctly interpreted this bit of information as evidence of a massacre of all members of the previous dynasty of rulers (the Dulo clan) and of the rise to power of a new and young leader with no connections with the previous regime and its commitments to peace. Telec's belligerant policies led to another conflict with the Empire. In 763, Constantine again invaded Bulgaria, both on land and on sea, and established his headquarters in Anchialos on the Black Sea coast, just south of the Bay of Burgas. Telec mobilized allies "from the neighboring nations" of the Slavs, whom he placed at

[32] Theophanes, *Chronographia* AM 6247, p. 593; see also Nicephorus, *Short History* 73, p. 145. Theophanes associates the transfer of the Syrian and Armenian population to the newly fortified Thracian towns with the transfer of population from Greece to Constantinople, "whose inhabitants had been reduced on account of the plague." However, he definitely does not see such measures in the rather positive light that Nicephorus sheds on the events, for Theophanes blames the iconoclast emperor's transfer of population to Thrace for the spread of the Paulician heresy.

[33] Theophanes, *Chronographia* AM 6251, p. 596; see also Nicephorus, *Short History* 73, p. 145.

key points in the mountains to guard the passes. On June 30, 763, the Bulgars attacked the imperial army outside Anchialos. In the ensuing battle, the Byzantines won a Pyrrhic victory, but managed to capture a great number of Bulgar aristocrats (who were later slaughtered by the circus factions outside the Golden Gate of Constantinople), while others deserted to their side during the fight.[34] The spoils seem to have been worth a parade in the hippodrome. Among them were "two golden basins that had been made in the island of Sicily, each one weighing 800 lbs. of gold." These had been most likely taken by the Bulgars in one of their previous raids in Thrace. Telec's main strategy seems to have been to capitalize on such possible gains by reversing the peaceful policies of his predecessors. His failure to secure the promised gains led to his demise and assassination by rival aristocratic factions.[35] The new ruler was Sabinos (Sivin), "the brother-in-law of their former lord, Kormesios" (Krumesis), which may be interpreted as an indication that Telec's assassins were members of a previously ruling clan.[36] Sivin sent envoys to the emperor and sued for peace, but the leading Bulgars "called a meeting and opposed him strenuously, saying, 'On your account Bulgaria is about to be enslaved by the Romans.'" Unlike his predecessors, Sivin ruled jointly with and under the control of a coallition of aristocrats who had brought him to power. Their opposition to the establishment of peaceful relations with a belligerent Byzantine emperor forced him to flee first to

[34] Theophanes, *Chronographia* AM 6254, p. 599; see also Nicephorus, *Short History* 76, pp. 149–150.

[35] Theophanes, *Chronographia* AM 6254, p. 599; see also Nicephorus, *Short History* 77, p. 151. Bulgarian historians speak of a "ritual killing of the divine king" of the Bulgars, but no such stretch of the existing evidence is necessary to explain what clearly amounts to factional strife within Bulgaria. See C. Stepanov, *Vlast i avtoritet v rannosrednovekovna Bălgariia (VII–sr. IX v.)* [Power and Authority in Early Medieval Bulgaria, between the Seventh and the Mid-Ninth Century] (Sofia: Agató, 1999), pp. 141–143.

[36] Theophanes, *Chronographia* AM 6254, p. 599; see also Nicephorus, *Short History* 77, p. 151. This could not have been the Dulo clan, for Kormisosh (Krumesis) was "of the Vokil clan," according to the so-called List of Bulgarian Princes preserved at the end of the fourth Book of Kings in a late fourteenth-century compilation known as *Letopisec ellinskii i rimskii* [The Greek and Roman Chronicle]. See Beshevliev, *Die protobulgarischen Inschriften*, p. 306. For this list, see O. Pritsak, *Die bulgarische Fürstenliste und die Sprache der Protobulgaren* (Wiesbaden: Otto Harrassowitz, 1955); T. Smiadovski, "Krumesis ot Madarskata skala i Kormison ot Imennika edno i săshto lice li sa? [Were Krumesis of the Madara inscription and Kormison of the List of Princes one and the same person?]," *Vekove*, no. 10 (1981), pp. 29–35.

Mesembria and then to the emperor.[37] While the Bulgars were kept busy electing their new ruler, Paganos, Constantine's "special ops" extracted Sivin's kinsmen and wives from Bulgaria and brought them to a safe place within the Empire.[38] The emperor was definitely bent on making as much use as possible of the ongoing factional strife in Bulgaria, as demonstrated by his reaction to Paganos who came in person to the emperor to sue for peace: "The emperor, having taken his seat and having Sabinos seated next to him, received them and reproved them for their disorderly conduct and their hatred of Sabinos."[39] Paganos was accompanied by his boyars (*boilades*), the first mention of the Bulgar name of the aristocratic class that seems to have controlled power in Bulgaria during the eighth-century prolonged conflict with Byzantium.

One year later (765), Constantine organized another expedition against Bulgaria. This time, his intentions were quite clear: to replace the ruler with another of his own choice, most likely a member of a pro-Byzantine clan. The Byzantines seem to have attacked mainly from the north, using their ability to move their ships up the river Danube. According to Nicephorus, the Byzantines burned many villages (*choria*), while the Bulgars "fled to the forests of the river Istros." Constantine's candidate, Toktos, was killed, perhaps in battle, while "another one of their commanders, whom they call Kampaganos," was assassinated by his slaves while attempting to escape to Varna and join the emperor.[40] Theophanes, on the other hand, only knows of a surprise attack from the south, as the emperor, "finding the passes unguarded because of the nominal peace," attacked the Bulgars as far as the river Ticha and burnt several "courts" (*aulai*),

[37] Theophanes, *Chronographia* AM 6254, p. 599; see also Nicephorus, *Short History* 77, p. 151. For Sivin as the Bulgarian form of Sabinos, see Beshevliev, *Die protobulgarische Periode*, p. 212. An aristocrat named Sivin is mentioned on a silver cup found in Preslav.

[38] Theophanes, *Chronographia* AM 6254, p. 599. Nicephorus, *Short History* 79, p. 153 has as Sivin's successor "a man called Oumaros," who is undoubtedly the Oumor of the List of Bulgarian Princes. See Beshevliev, *Die protobulgarischen Inschriften*, pp. 306 and 323. On the other hand, Beshevliev has proposed that Paganos is in fact a badly understood title, *qapqagan*, not a personal name. See Beshevliev, *Die protobulgarische Periode*, p. 216 n. 19.

[39] Theophanes, *Chronographia* AM 6526, p. 603; see also Nicephorus, *Short History* 77, p. 151. Nothing else is known about Sivin and his supporters. He may have remained in Constantinople and enjoyed the favors of the emperor.

[40] Nicephorus, *Short History* 79, p. 153.

before returning to Constantinople.[41] Despite their contradictory reports, both Nicephorus and Theophanes emphasize the surprise attack on Bulgaria, as well as the destruction brought in the process to either villages properly speaking or aristocratic palaces.[42]

However, two other campaigns ended in disaster in 766 and 774, when the strong fleets sent against the Bulgars were destroyed by storms on the Black Sea, while moving to the Danube Delta. By 774, when another campaign was mounted against Bulgaria with 2,000 ships entering the Danube, the new ruler Telerig quickly made offers of peace through a boyar envoy called *tzigatos*.[43] However, when Telerig began preparing to invade Berzitia (in Macedonia) in order to "transfer its inhabitants to Bulgaria," Emperor Constantine reacted with another attack on the border garrisons or guards, "whom he routed in a great victory." But the war of deception continued: Telerig duped the emperor into revealing the names of his agents in Bulgaria, who were all duly executed. When Constantine embarked on a new expedition in August 775, "he became sorely afflicted with carbuncles on his legs" and died while being transported back to Constantinople. Soon after that, however, Telerig himself "sought refuge with the emperor [Leo IV], who made him patrician and joined him in marriage to a cousin of his wife Irene."[44] Small skirmishes marked the long reign of Kardam (777–803), along with a number of pitched battles, such as those near the "fort Probaton" (present-day Provadiia) or the encounter near Markellai, in which St. Ioannikios the Great fought as a soldier in the Byzantine army.[45] It is only under Kardam's successor, Krum, that the confrontation with Byzantium shifted to large-scale engagements and Bulgaria became a major military power in the entire Southeast European region.

[41] Theophanes, *Chronographia* AM 6256, p. 603.

[42] For *aule* as palace, see the inscription of Omurtag (dated shortly before 822); Beshevliev, *Die protobulgarischen Inschriften*, pp. 247 and 254. Omurtag later built a palace on the Ticha river (inscription of 822; Beshevliev, *Die protobulgarischen Inschriften*, pp. 261 and 266).

[43] Theophanes, *Chronographia* AM 6257, p. 605; and AM 6265, p. 617. For *boilas tzigatos*, see Beshevliev, *Die protobulgarischen Inschriften*, p. 47.

[44] Theophanes, *Chronographia* AM 6265, p. 617; AM 6266, p. 618; AM 6267, p. 619; and AM 6269, p. 622.

[45] For skirmishes, see Theophanes, *Chronographia* AM 6281, p. 638; AM 6288, p. 646. For pitched battles, see Theophanes, *Chronographia* AM 6283, p. 641; and AM 6284, p. 643. For St. Ioannikios' participation in the battle at Markellai, see S. Vryonis, "St. Ioannicus the Great (754–846) and the 'Slavs' of Bithynia," *Byzantion*, vol. 31 (1961), pp. 245–248.

Judging by the great number of cemeteries, both north and south of the Danube, that could be dated to this period, the eighth century witnessed a substantial growth of population, despite written evidence to the contrary.[46] There were simply more people around than in the seventh century. In southern Romania and northeastern Bulgaria, some forty cemeteries are known to have been in existence during the eighth century. The chronology of most eighth-century mortuary assemblages is almost exclusively based on a few belt buckles, strap ends, and mounts with good analogies in Late Avar assemblages, but produced within territories under Byzantine control.[47] Equally important are two coins minted for Emperor Constantine VI (between 780 and 797), one of gold, the other of silver, that were found in a grave in Kiulevcha, the earliest coin-dated burial assemblage in early medieval Bulgaria known to date. Such finds are extremely rare, for like contemporary burials in Hungary, assemblages in Bulgaria produced very little evidence of sharp social differentiation. The prestige associated with such Bulgar rulers as Tervel was displayed on the Madara Horseman, not in any conspicuous deposition of grave goods. The same is true for the politically active aristocrats of the late eighth century, who do not seem to have used funerary displays to mark the social distinction separating them from the rest of society. The picture offered by the total excavation of contemporary settlements is not much different. On the multi-phased site at Garvan, near Silistra, some twenty-eight features – sunken-floored buildings and free-standing ovens – have been dated to the late seventh and early eighth century. With the exception of a fragmentary belt mount of gold, there are no other artifacts indicating social differentiation. No palpable trace of the lucrative trade with Byzantium regulated by the 716 treaty has so far been found on any site in Bulgaria and the neighboring regions. Archaeologists have yet to identify any of the "courts" which Constantine V set on fire in 765. The very beginnings of Pliska as a royal residence

[46] As a consequece of the usurpation of power by Telec in 761, a great number of Slavs fled from Bulgaria and sought refuge within the Empire. See Theophanes, *Chronographia* AM 6254, p. 599; Nicephorus, *Short History* 75, p. 149. Telerig intended to invade Berzitia in 772, in order to transfer its inhabitants to Bulgaria (Theophanes, *Chronographia* AM 6265, p. 617), apparently in order to compensate previous population losses.

[47] Fiedler, *Studien zu Gräberfeldern*, p. 270; and "Die spätawarenzeitlichen Gürtelbestandteile von Typ Vrap-Erseke aus Velino (Bez. Varna, Bulgarien)," *Germania*, vol. 74 (1996), pp. 248–264.

surrounded by an earthwork and a vast area of over twenty square kilometers enclosed by an earthen rampart some three meters high almost certainly postdate Emperor Constantine's wars with Bulgaria. It is only under Krum and his successors that the first palace, temple, and baths were built in Pliska. Similarly, the practice of glorifying royal deeds by means of inscriptions that had started with Tervel was only continued under the ninth-century rulers. The archaeological picture of eighth-century Bulgaria is in many ways similar to that of territories known to have been at that time under Avar control.

THE AVARS BETWEEN 630 AND 800. CARANTANIA

Judging from the evidence of a large-scale emigration of Bulgars from the Avar qaganate, the civil war that broke out in the early 630s ended in a victory for the Avar "party." Whether or not the dynasty established in the late sixth century by Bayan continued after that remains unknown. No names of qagans are known for the following 150 years, although Avar qagans episodically appear in written sources in 635, 662, 663, between 673 and 668, and in 678.[48] Assuming that the civil war had diminished the prestige associated with Bayan's successors, several historians have postulated a change of dynasty and the creation of another, different qaganate that remained in existence until the end of the eighth century.[49] However, between *c.* 630 and *c.* 660, the power center of the qaganate remained in

[48] S. Szádeczky-Kardoss, *Ein Versuch zur Sammlung und chronologischen Gliederung der griechischen Quellen der Awaren-Geschichte nebst einer Auswahl von anderssprachigen Quellen* (Szeged: JATE, 1972; reprinted in *Avarica. Über die Awarengeschichte und ihre Quellen* [Szeged: JATE, 1986]), pp. 93–95; Pohl, *Die Awaren*, p. 278. The qagan is mentioned again in 796, when he came to Pepin accompanied by his wife and dignitaries to sue for peace. A different qagan named Abraham accepted baptism in 805. See *De Pippini regis victoria Avarica*, ed. by E. Dümmler (Hanover, 1881; reprint 1997), MGH Poet. 1:116–7; Pohl, *Die Awaren*, p. 319.

[49] The idea of a first and second qaganate goes back to S. Szádeczky-Kardos and É. Csillik, "Az avar történelem forrásai IX. Az elsö avar kaganátus hatalma csúcsán (603–624) [The sources of Avar history IX. The power climax of the first Avar qaganate, 603–624]," *Archaeologiai Értesitö*, vol. 113 (1986), pp. 83–112. This idea found enthusiastic supporters among archaeologists whose work rests on the chronological division of burial assemblages into the Early, Middle, and Late Avar periods, particularly on a transition, *c.* 650, from Early to Middle Avar "cultures." See Cs. Bálint, *Die Archäologie der Steppe. Steppenvölker zwischen Volga und Donau vom 6. bis zum 10. Jahrhundert* (Vienna and Cologne: Böhlau, 1989), pp. 156–160.

the same region of central Hungary between the Middle Danube and Tisza Rivers. The qagan who quelled the Bulgar rebellion of the early 630s may well be the aged man buried in Kunbabóny with an amazing wealth and variety of accoutrements truly comparable to contemporary burial assemblages in the steppes north of the Black Sea.[50] During the last quarter of the seventh century, the center of power was still in the area between the Danube and the Tisza, which produced the richest finds of the Middle Avar period. Some of the best known monuments of this period, rich burials of the so-called Tótipuszta–Dunapentele–Igar group, which Hungarian archaeologists attribute to Bulgar immigrants from the steppes, were also found in this region.[51] There are signs of continuity in material culture between the Early and the Middle Avar periods, despite clear evidence of major cultural changes. The increasing number of weapons, including single-edged sabers, deposited especially with horseman burials, signals a society that was geared towards warfare perhaps more than during the previous period. The martiality revealed by burial assemblages may be a reflection of Avar belligerence during the Middle Avar period, which is certainly responsible for the expansion of the area covered by the material culture that was associated with this period to southern Slovakia or the region around present-day Vienna. By contrast, little is known about Avar involvement in Balkan affairs. In 678, an unnamed qagan "sent ambassadors and gifts to the emperor [Constantine IV], requesting that peace

[50] The Kunbabóny assemblage produced more than a pound of gold, about the same amount as that found in Hlodosy. See A. Kiss, "Zur Frage der Kontinuität bzw. Diskontinuität des awarischen Khaganats (567–796). Wieviele Khaganate hat es gegeben?," in *Ethnische und kulturelle Verhältnisse an der mittleren Donau vom 6. bis zum 11. Jahrhundert. Symposium Nitra 6. bis 10. November 1994*, ed. by D. Bialeková and J. Zábojník (Bratislava: VEDA, 1996), p. 86. For Kunbabóny, see Tóth and Horváth, *Kunbabóny*. Another burial assemblage found in that same area at Bócsa produced about three pounds of gold artifacts. See A. Kiss, "Goldfunde des Karpatenbeckens vom 5–10. Jahrhundert (Angaben zu den Vergleichsmöglichkeiten der schriftlichen und archäologischen Quellen)," *AAASH*, vol. 38 (1986), p. 113 fig. 5.

[51] Dated by means of coins minted for Emperors Constans II and Constantine IV, these burials have their closest analogies in the rich funerary assemblages of Ukraine (Malo Pereshchepyne, Hlodosy, and Zachepilovki). See G. Fülöp, "New research on finds of Avar chieftain-burial at Igar, Hungary," in *From the Baltic to the Black Sea. Studies in Medieval Archaeology*, ed. by D. Austin and L. Alcock (London: Unwin Hyman, 1990), pp. 138–146. For the theory of Bulgar migration, see Bálint, *Archäologie der Steppe*, p. 169.

and friendship should be confirmed with them."[52] Two years later, the qagan, no doubt the same one, could not prevent a group of rebel subjects under Kouber from leaving the qaganate and moving to the outskirts of Constantinople (see below). After 700 and until the Frankish attacks that led to its demise, the Avar qaganate completely disappeared from the radar of written sources. What we know about the last century of Avar history is therefore based mainly, if not exclusively, on archaeological sources.

Assemblages of the Late Avar period (*c.* 700–*c.* 800) are clearly distinguished from those of earlier periods on the basis of cast belt buckles, strap ends, and mounts, found in great numbers and variety. Floral patterns are the most typical elements of ornamentation employed by Late Avar craftsmen responsible for the production of such artifacts, but in fashion throughout the entire period were artifacts decorated with griffins, which made one historian call the entire period from 700 to 800 "the century of the griffin."[53] Despite clear evidence that the ornamental repertoire of the Late Avar period was of local, Avar origin, and not brought from the steppes north of the Black Sea, the griffin motif may signal a certain desire to revive the traditions of the steppes in a period of dramatic social and cultural changes. This tendency is also visible, for example, in the presence of richly adorned hair clips in sumptuous male burials, no doubt used for long braids, a fashion which has been associated with nomadic warriors ever since it had retained the attention of the inhabitants of Constantinople in 558 (see chapter 1). However, there are very few signs of nomadic life in the eighth-century material culture of the Avar qaganate. If anything, the Late Avar period has produced so far the greatest number of settlements known for the entire Avar history, and very large cemeteries in use for more than two or three generations, both categories of sites suggesting an advanced degree of sedentization. The particular cause for this profound economic and social change is not very well known, but it may have something to do with population growth. The Hungarian Plain is some 100,000 sq km large, but in the eighth century a great portion of that region was covered by water, especially in the flood areas of the

[52] Theophanes, *Chronographia* AM 6169, p. 496. See A. Avenarius, "Die Konsolidierung des Awarenkaganates und Byzanz im 7. Jahrhundert," *Byzantina*, vol. 13 (1985), p. 1024.

[53] Pohl, *Die Awaren*, p. 289.

Danube and Tisza Rivers and of their tributaries.[54] With 400 to 600 mm of annual rainfall, the Hungarian Plain is an ecological niche very different from the steppes north of the Black Sea, for which the only possible adaptation was seasonal nomadism of a kind attested by later sources referring to Cumans or Mongols. By contrast, the much more favorable climate of the Hungarian Plain encouraged nomadic communities to abandon nomadic pastoralism and to adopt more sedentary forms of economic organization, with much more room for agriculture. Pollen analysis even shows efforts to drain swampy areas and turn them into cultivated land.[55] On the other hand, the density of sites within the Hungarian Plain may in itself have been an obstacle in the way of nomadic, seasonal pastoralism. Eighth-century settlements excavated in Hungary produced a few agricultural implements, such as plowshares, and plenty of evidence for corn storage. Many more implements, especially sickles, have been found in funerary assemblages, along with a great quantity of domestic animal bones, most likely the remains of food offerings to the dead. At the same time, the overall number of weapons deposited in mortuary assemblages declined substantially, a clear indication that warfare was not any more the economic and political basis of Avar society. Settlements mushroomed in the Hungarian Plain, sometimes in networks of sites located only a few kilometeres from each other. This is particularly true for the southernmost district of the land between the Danube and Tisza Rivers, which is now in northern Serbia. Recent studies have shown that Late Avar cemeteries in that region cluster very close to the flood plains of the two rivers, often next to major fords.[56]

A number of cemeteries with horseman burials, some with weapons, are known from the neighboring "militarized frontier" of the qaganate in the Belgrade region (Sremska Mitrovica, Vojka, Pančevo).[57] Such burials signal the presence of Late Avar elites,

[54] Until the large-scale drainage works of the late nineteenth century, one-eighth of the entire Hungarian Plain was under water. Very large marshes existed near the present-day Serbian–Hungarian and Hungarian–Romanian–Ukrainian borders, respectively.

[55] K. J. Willis, P. Sümegi, M. Braun, et al., "Prehistoric land degradation in Hungary: who, how, and why?," *Antiquity*, vol. 72 (1998), pp. 101–113.

[56] Takács, "Einige Aspekte," p. 463.

[57] L. Trbuhović, "Avar finds from Sirmium and the surrounding region," in *Sirmium. Recherches archéologiques en Syrmie*, vol. IV, ed. by N. Duval, E. L. Ochsenschlager, and V. Popović (Belgrade: Institut Archéologique de Belgrade, Ecole Française

perhaps the *Tarcani* mentioned in late eighth-century Frankish sources as having been members of the qagan's retinue of warriors.[58] This is in sharp contrast with the large number of burials without any grave goods, a contrast that has been rightly interpreted as an indication of the increased polarization of Avar society. Moreover, with few exceptions, no gold finds are so far known for the entire Late Avar period. One of the few exceptions is a hoard of some 22 pounds of gold, with a chronology stretching back over a period of 120 years, which was found in 1799 in Sânnicolau Mare, near the present-day Romanian–Hungarian border. The collection includes two complete sets of liturgical, drinking, and washing vessels, some bearing inscriptions in Greek, others in Turkic runes. The hoard can help us picture the enormous treasure of the Avar qagan that the Frankish warriors plundered at will in 795 and 796. But the Sânnicolaul Mare find is not unique. The southern region of the qaganate has produced two of the five finds of gold dated between 700 and 800, one of which is a burial assemblage with nine Abbasid dinars minted between 762 and 794 or 799.[59]

Both finds of gold and horseman burials point to the existence of a center of power in the region of northern Serbia now known as Vojvodina. Rival centers had already appeared in various other regions of the qaganate where local elites had become de facto independent, long before the arrival of the Frankish armies. For example, a number of rich burial assemblages appear in the early 700s on the southwestern periphery of the qaganate, on both sides of the present-day border between Austria and Slovenia.[60] The men buried with Avar belts with multiple straps ornated with richly decorated mounts

de Rome, and the Research Foundation of the City University of New York, 1982), pp. 61–75. The phrase "militarized frontier" is that of Andreas Lippert, "Zur militärischen Westgrenze des Awarenreiches," *Mitteilungen der anthropologischen Gesellschaft in Wien*, vol. 100 (1970), pp. 162–172.

[58] *De Pippini regis victoria Avarica*, p. 117; Pohl, *Die Awaren*, p. 302.

[59] For the Petrovci burial with eighth-century dinars, see Kiss, "Goldfunde des Karpatenbeckens," pp. 119–120. Two other gold coins minted for the caliph Al-Mansur between 763 and 775 have been found in the environs of Novi Sad (Serbia). See N. Stanojević, "Naselja VIII–IX veka u Vojvodini," *RVM*, vol. 30 (1987), p. 143.

[60] E.g., burials of the so-called Grabelsdorf–Baardorf group. See E. Szameit, "Das frühmittelalterliche Grab von Grabelsdorf bei St. Kanzian am Klopeinersee, Kärnten. Ein Beitrag zur Datierung awarischer Bronzen im Ostalpenraum," *Archaeologia Austriaca*, vol. 77 (1993), pp. 213–234.

and Frankish weapons have been rightly associated with the Carantanians known from written sources as having successfully declared their independence from the Avars. Carantania was a federation of tribes of heterogeneous ethnic background, called "peoples" (*populi*) by the author of a source known as the *Conversion of the Bavarians and the Carantanians*. According to this text, a certain duke Boruth ruling over Carantania was attacked by the Avars *c.* 740 and, as a consequence, called for Bavarian assistance. The Bavarian duke Odilo (737–748) defeated the Avars, but in the process also subdued the Carantanians to his authority.[61] Once Bavarian overlordship was established in Carantania, Odilo took with him to Bavaria two hostages, namely Boruth's son (Cacatius) and nephew (Chietmar), who were baptized. As a consequence of this political arrangement, the Carantanians seem to have been forced to supply the Bavarian dukes with loyal troops. During the 743 conflict between Odilo, on the one hand, and Carloman and Pepin, on the other, Carantanian troops fought on the Bavarian side. The Bavarian domination also cleared the field for missions of conversion to Christianity sent by Virgil, the bishop of Salzburg (746–784). Many missionaries were of Bavarian origin, but some were Irish monks. To supervise their activity, Virgil appointed an "itinerant bishop" (*chorepiscopus*) of Carantania. Unlike Saxony, where Christianity had made progress only through the creation of bishops, monasteries, and churches, no such network existed in Carantania. There were no land donations to newly founded monasteries, no local saints, and no canonization of the mission members. The "itinerant bishop" Modestus built several churches, but created no see. Christianity was initially adopted only by a small group of Carantanian aristocrats, while many others remained staunchly pagan.

[61] *Conversio Bagaoriorum et Carantanorum* 4, ed. by F. Lošek (Hanover: Hahnsche Buchhandlung, 1997), p. 103. The *Conversio* cannot be classified as either chronicle or annals. Instead, it is a report written by an unknown author more than 100 years later than the events narrated, *c.* 870, in order to defend the position of the archbishop of Salzburg against the claims of the bishop of Pannonia. The Salzburg claims presented by the author of the *Conversio* are based on a carefully crafted, but strongly biased, account of the missionary work among Bavarians and Slavs (hence the conventional title). That work is attributed to Salzburg alone, to the detriment of other sees such as Aquileia or Freising, especially to St. Rupert (d. 716), the first bishop of Salzburg. See H. Wolfram, *Salzburg, Bayern, Österreich: die* Conversio Bagoariorum et Carantanorum *und die Quellen ihrer Zeit* (Vienna and Munich: R. Oldenbourg, 1995).

At Boruth's death (750), his son Cacatius returned to Carantania and was recognized as prince by the Carantanians. He ruled for only two years, before being replaced by his cousin Chietmar.[62] Chietmar's pro-Bavarian policies triggered two revolts organized by Carantanian aristocrats who had remained pagan. A third rebellion broke after Chietmar's death in 769, and lasted for three years, before being squashed by a Bavarian intervention. Carantanian autonomy was somewhat preserved under duke Waltunc, who was crowned in the presence of the Bavarian duke Tassilo, but the Bavarian domination secured a safe renewal of missionary activities, this time from monasteries founded in Carantanian territory, such as that recently excavated at Molzbichl in Austrian Carinthia.[63] Following Tassilo's defeat in 788, Carantania was incorporated, together with Bavaria, into the Frankish kingdom. These political changes are also mirrored by changes in material culture. Burial assemblages that could be dated to the time of Boruth's dynasty of dukes still combine late Merovingian or early Carolingian weapons and spurs with Late Avar belt sets. Shortly before 800 all belt sets disappeared in favor of exclusively Frankish fashions, before burial assemblages shrank in both size and quality. During the subsequent decades, graves moved from isolated locations or clan cemeteries into church graveyards, a development that reflects the progress of conversion to Christianity, as well as the incorporation of Carantania into the Carolingian Empire.

BYZANTIUM ON THE DARK AGE BALKANS

The situation in northern Greece is well documented in Book II of the *Miracles of St. Demetrius*. The fourth miracle is an extremely valuable source for the seventh-century Balkan Slavs and without this text there would be very little to say. The unknown author of Book II describes the powerful polity of the Slavic Rynchines led by

[62] Historians have correctly intepreted this chain of events as indicating the control of power by a single clan, a true Carantanian dynasty. See H. Wolfram, "Les Carantaniens, le premier peuple slave baptisé," in *Clovis, histoire et mémoire. Le baptême de Clovis, son écho à travers l'histoire*, ed. by M. Rouche (Paris: Presses l'Université de Paris-Sorbonne, 1997), p. 282.

[63] F. Glaser, "Das Münster in Molzbichl, das älteste Kloster Kärntens," *Carinthia*, vol. 179 (1989), pp. 99–124.

"king" Perbundos. Other groups of Sclavenes existed in the vicinity of Thessalonica. There were also Sclavenes in the Strymon valley by the time Perbundos was arrested and executed, and the Sagudates allied themselves with the Rynchines against Thessalonica. A third tribe, the Drugubites, joined the alliance. The ensuing siege of the city is to be dated to July 25, 677, because of a clear reference to "July 25 of the fifth indiction." The Sclavenes appear as militarily well organized, with an army of special units of archers and warriors armed with slings, spears, shields, and swords. In a long story most likely derived from an oral account, the author of Book II mentions a Sclavene craftsman building a siege machine. He also mentions Sclavene tribes living at a considerable distance and not taking part in the Sclavene alliance against Thessalonica. The Belegezites, who lived near Thebes and Demetrias, even supplied the besieged city with grain. The author of Book II also refers to Slavic pirates raiding as close to Constantinople as the island of Proconnesus. The emperor (whose name is not given) eventually decided to send an army to Thrace and to the "land on the opposite side," against the Strymonian Slavs. Since the siege can be dated to 677, and we are specifically told that prior to the siege the emperor was preparing for war against the Arabs, this expedition against the *Sklaviniai* of southern Macedonia must have been ordered by Constantine IV. The successful campaign took place in 678, shortly after the failure of the Arab blockade of Constantinople. As a consequence, it was possible for the archbishop of Thessalonica to participate in the Sixth Ecumenical Council in Constantinople (680/1), together with the bishops of Athens, Argos, Lacedaemona, and Corinth.

With Book II of the *Miracles of St. Demetrius* we come to the end of a long series of contemporary accounts on the Dark Age Balkans. None of the subsequent sources is based on autopsy and all could be referred to as "histories," relying entirely on written, older sources. Modern approaches to the history of early medieval Greece have been considerably influenced by one particular text: *De Thematibus*, a work associated with the emperor Constantine VII Porphyrogenitus. There is not much material relevant to the seventh or eighth century, but chapter 6 was long viewed as a crucial piece of evidence for the Slavic presence in Greece. According to Porphyrogenitus, during the reign of Constantine V (741–775) the entire country "was slavonicized and turned barbarian," as an indirect consequence of the plague of 746 that had wiped out the native population, thus making room for the newcomers.[64] Scholars paid less attention to another chapter, in which Emperor Constantine VII refers to measures taken by Justinian II in 688 or 689. Following his defeat by the Bulgars in a mountain pass near Philippopolis (present-day Plovdiv, in Bulgaria), Emperor Justinian II settled groups of "Scythians" around the gorges of the river Struma, thus laying the foundations of the Strymon *kleisoura*, later to become the theme (province) by the same name.[65] Many historians believed the "Scythians" to be either Slavs or Bulgars. To be sure, a tenth-century scholium on Strabo's *Geographia* does indeed refer to "Scythian Slavs."[66] However, it has been demonstrated that Constantine Porphyrogenitus often used "Scythians" in reference to steppe nomads, such as Khazars or Magyars. Judging from the existing evidence, the creation of a Bulgar polity shortly before 700 drastically altered the balance of power in the northern Balkans, while driving *Sklaviniai* into the orbit of the new state. Garrisoned outposts in the valley of the Lower Struma were thus designed to protect Via Egnatia, the major road across the Balkans from Constantinople to Thessalonica.

A similar system of defense existed at that time in Istria. Occupied by Roman troops during the Gothic wars in Italy at some point between 535 and 544, the peninsula remained under their direct control until the Lombard conquest of the mid-eighth century. Under the authority of the exarch of Ravenna, Istria was by the late seventh century a separate administrative unit, much like a *kleisoura*, with its own troops under the command of a local *magister militum*. As in contemporary Italy, a line of small forts stretching across the northern half of the peninsula was designed to control access from Lombard or

[64] Constantine Porphyrogenitus, *De Thematibus* 6, ed. A. Pertusi (Vatican: Biblioteca Apostolica Vaticana, 1952), p. 91. See A. Maricq, "Notes sur les Slaves dans le Péloponnèse et en Bithynie et sur l'emploi de 'Slave' comme appélatif," *Byzantion*, vol. 22 (1952), pp. 338–340.

[65] Constantine Porphyrogenitus, *De Thematibus* 3, p. 89. The gorges of the river Struma around which Justinian settled his "Scythians" are located near the modern Bulgarian–Greek border. See J. Karayannopoulos, *Les Slaves en Macédoine. La prétendue interruption des communications entre Constantinople et Thessalonique du 7e au 9e siècle* (Athens: Comité national grec des études du Sud-Est européen, 1989), pp. 689–690.

[66] *Geographi Graeci minores*, ed. by K. Müller, vol. II (Paris: A. Firmin Didot, 1861), p. 574. It has been suggested that the author of the scholium was either Photius or Arethas of Caesarea. See also A. Diller, "The scholia on Strabo," *Traditio*, vol. 10 (1954), pp. 43–44 and 48; P. Lemerle, *Le premier humanisme byzantin* (Paris: Presses Universitaires de France, 1971), pp. 218 and 233.

Avar-held territory to the north. The Istrian troops must have been relatively numerous, given that some of them participated in crushing the usurpation of imperial power in the aftermath of Emperor Constans II's assassination in Sicily (669). They were stationed in the forts on the northern frontier of the province, as evidenced by a number of cemeteries extending from the sixth to the eighth century. Many such cemeteries associated with neighboring forts produced stone-lined graves of men with weapons – short swords, axes, and arrowheads. Side by side with their burials, archaeologists found a relatively large number of child burials, as well as double burials, often including female skeletons. This suggests that the occupation of the northern Istrian forts was of a permanent character and that soldiers lived there together with their families. In Mejica, the excavated 260 burials, many of which were dated to the seventh century, point to the existence of about 60 individuals per generation. As many as six families with accompanying clients may have occupied the fort at any one time during that century.[67] Cemeteries were not associated with any funerary chapels or churches, but during the seventh and eighth centuries several churches were built in the countryside of Byzantine Istria. The province had three episcopal sees (Tergeste/Triest, Parentium/Poreč, and Pola/Pula), and the presence of the Istrian bishops is documented at the Lateran council of 649, as well as at the Sixth Ecumenical Council of 680/1. An early ninth-century source known as the *placitum* of Rižana describes the local Byzantine administration in existence before the Frankish take-over as consisting of consuls, tribunes, *domestici*, *vicari*, and *lociservatores*. According to the declaration recorded in the *placitum*, the central government in Constantinople used to exact taxes from the Istrian cities and their hinterland in the amount of 344 gold coins. Local bishops paid half of that amount and the incumbent duties, an indication of their power and influence.[68]

[67] M. Torcellan, *Le tre necropoli altomedioevali di Pinguente* (Florence: All'insegna di Giglio, 1986), p. 57.

[68] The *placitum* of 804 has been published with extensive commentaries by A. Petranović and A. Margetić, "Il Placito del Risano," *Atti. Centro di ricerche storiche – Rovigno*, vol. 14 (1983–1984), pp. 55–75. See also A. Guillou, "La présence byzantine dans les pays du nord de l'Adriatique. Un champ des mutations socio-économiques," *Byzantina*, vol. 13 (1985), p. 211; L. Margetić, "L'Istria bizantina ed alcuni problemi del Placito di Risano," in *Slovenia in sosednje dežele med antiko in karolinsko dobo. Začetki slovenske etnogeneze*, ed. by R. Bratož (Ljubljana: Narodni Muzej Slovenije, 2000), pp. 81–95.

For a short while between the mid-seventh century and Charlemagne's destruction of the Lombard kingdom in 774, Istria was controlled by the Lombards, but a letter of Patriarch John of Grado to Pope Stephen III describes the hostility of the Istrians towards Lombards and their loyalty to Byzantium. Following the implementation of Carolingian rule, the local aristocrats were also concerned with maintaining the social and political practices that have been in use during the Byzantine era, as clearly attested by the *placitum* of Rižana. It is only under Frankish rule, in the early ninth century, that the presence of the Slavs is first attested, a phenomenon linked to the appearance of a new group of burials in northern Istria, well illustrated by the cemetery at Predloka (near Koper, in northwestern Istria), with good analogies in late eighth-century burials in northern Slovenia and Carinthia. This suggests a migration from neighboring Carantania, perhaps of people fleeing the country in the circumstances surrounding the revolts of the local aristocracy during and after the brief reign of Chietmar.

The picture of Dark Age Istria is similar in many respects to that of the contemporary Dalmatian coast, Albania, and Greece, for which there is nevertheless less information from written sources. Beginning with the late sixth century, the western Balkans seem to have experienced a much earlier phase of that transformation of the settlement pattern known as *incastellamento*. With the complete abandonment of dispersed rural sites of Roman or pre-Roman origin, the population shrank to diminutive dimensions during the Dark Ages. Occupation was now restricted to a number of hilltop forts, such as Pogradec, Kruja, and Sarda in the vicinity of Dyrrachium (present-day Durrës, in Albania), with a layout and social structure very different from the previous urban and rural settlements.[69] However, such forts served a primarily military purpose, namely to monitor key passes through the mountains separating the coastal region from the interior of the peninsula. The system in existence in Dalmatia is described in chapter 29 of Emperor Constantine VII Porphyrogenitus' *De administrando imperio*: "For near the sea, beneath that same city [i.e., Spalato], lies a city called Salona, which is

[69] The Dark Age *incastellamento* in the Balkans may explain why in both Romanian (a Romance language) and Albanian (a non-Romance language) the term in use for fort (*cetate* and *qytet*, respectively) derives from the Latin word for city (*civitas*). See M. Pillon, "Sémantique et histoire de l'habitat: le *fossatum* proto-byzantin, le *fshat* albanais et le *sat* roumain," *Erytheia*, vol. 14 (1993), pp. 26–27.

half as large as Constantinople, and here all the Romani would muster and be equipped and thence start out and come to the frontier pass (*kleisoura*), which is four miles from this very city, and is called Kleisa to this day, from its closing in those who pass that way."[70] The *kleisoura* apparently closed access from across an unknown river, perhaps the neighboring Cetina. Like the *kleisourai* of Istria and the Struma valley, Kleisa may have been designed to prevent attacks on the coastal cities and roads by "Slavs on the far side of the river, who were also called Avars."[71] Constantine Porphyrogenitus' account has not been so far confirmed by the archaeological evidence, as excavations have revealed no substantial occupation of Salona during the eighth century. But Salona and Split did produce examples of seventh-century decorative stone-carving, the patronage of which could only have been ecclesiastical, pointing to the existence of a church organization in the area, no doubt under Byzantine aegis. There is also evidence that several other cities on the Adriatic coast or on the neighboring islands may have continued to exist throughout the Dark Ages. To be sure, the oldest inscriptions in this region are no earlier than AD 800: the dedicatory inscription from the Church of St. Tryphon in Kotor dated to the reign of Emperor Nicephorus I (802–811), and the dedicatory inscription of Guzma from Ulcinj mentioning Emperor Leo V and his son Constantine (813–820).[72] But the tomb chamber found beneath a modern hotel on the island of Lopud dates back to the 700s, as indicated by the associated silver reliquary. Similarly, and judging from the discovery of a coin of Emperor Constantine V within another tomb found on its southern side, the Church of the

[70] Constantine Porphyrogenitus, *De administrando imperio* 29, ed. by G. Moravcsik with English translation by R. J. H. Jenkins (Washington: Dumbarton Oaks Center for Byzantine Studies, 1967), p. 123. The mountain pass in question is Klis, near the present-day city by the same name.

[71] However, according to Emperor Constantine (or his source), Kleisa did not prevent the "Slavs and Avars" from sacking Salona in the disguise of Roman soldiers. See Constantine Porphyrogenitus, *De administrando imperio* 29, pp. 124–125. For forts in the vicinity of the Klis *kleisoura*, see N. Jakšić, "Constantine Porphyrogenitus as the source for destruction of Salona," *Vjesnik za arheologiju i historiju Dalmatinsku*, vol. 77 (1984), p. 324. Note that in the eyes of Constantine Porphyrogenitus, Salona itself was a simple fort, not a true city.

[72] J. Kovačević, "Aperçu historique et archéologique sur le rôle des villes de la Dalmatie méridionale dans l'expansion du christianisme parmi les Serbes," *AAASH*, vol. 17 (1965), p. 67; D. Dragojlović, "Dyrrachium et les évêchés de Docléa jusqu'à la fondation de l'archevêché de Bar," *Balcanica*, vol. 21 (1990), p. 202.

Holy Cross in Nin must have been built in the late eighth century. A date earlier than *c.* 800 could also be assumed, albeit only hypothetically so far, for a number of other churches, such as the Rotunda of St. Donat and the Church of St. Vitalis in Zadar, the St. Andrew Church in Zaton (near Nin), and a small church in the city of Osor on the island of Cres. On the basis of well-dated Italian analogies, a similar dating has been advanced for several sculptural elements found at different points in time within the perimeters of the present-day cities of Zadar, Trogir, and Kotor. Much like in the case of Salona and Split, the existence of decorative sculpture bespeaks the power and material means of the local churchmen, in itself an indication of a Dark Age occupation of these cities.

Unlike Istria, there are no cemeteries in Dalmatia extending from the seventh to the ninth century. Three cemeteries known so far begin in the seventh and continue into the eighth century, while two others existed only in the 700s. Among the earliest finds are the cremation urns from Kašić, near Zadar, pointing to the presence of a population with no traditions in the region. Whether or not this was a population of Slavs, "who were also called Avars," is still a matter of dispute. It is clear, however, that despite claims to the contrary, the influence of the Late Avar culture reached deep into Croatia, as far as the Zagreb region, which produced a number of cemeteries that can be dated to the late eighth century.[73] Another cemetery excavated in Kašić contained only inhumation burials, including some stone-lined graves similar to those of Istria and of the sixth-century fort cemeteries in the Balkans. Such graves also appear among those surrounding the Church of the Holy Cross in Nin, many of which can be dated to the early ninth century.

A few gold coin finds on the Adriatic coast may indicate direct relations with Byzantium during the reign of Emperor Constans II, but almost no coins of later emperors have been found. It remains unclear whether or not any of the Croatian cemeteries may be attributed to Byzantine garrisons at key points on the coast. Judging from the evidence of just one seal tentatively dated to the late eighth or early ninth century, an *archon* of Dalmatia was in existence by that time. His position of power was not different from that described on another seal

[73] For a recent association of the Middle and Late Avar culture with Dalmatian Croatia, see L. Margetić, *Dolazak Hrvata* [The Origin of the Croats] (Split: Knijževni krug, 2001), pp. 200–216.

of a certain Theodore, *archon* of Vagenetia, a coastal region behind the island of Kerkyra, in the Ionian Sea.

Given that the seal of Theodore is slightly earlier than the first mention, in the early 700s, of Byzantine military governors of the island of Kerkyra, he must have been a local chieftain in Byzantine service. If so, the same may be true for the *archon* of Dalmatia. Thus, the existing evidence strongly suggests that on the Dalmatian coast the Byzantine power relied on local elements coopted for the safeguarding of the sea lanes around the Balkan Peninsula, from Constantinople to Venice.

This conclusion is further substantiated by analogies between burial assemblages on the Adriatic coast and finds in the interior associated with the so-called "Komani culture."[74] Long viewed as the archaeological remains of the "first Albanians," the relatively numerous cemeteries of this group of finds point to a different interpretation. First, most of them are in the hinterland of Dyrrachium (present-day Durrës), a city that certainly remained in Byzantine hands throughout the entire period. Second, finds similar to those from burial assemblages turned up in at least two forts (Kruje and Sarda/Shurdhah) that were undoubtedly occupied at the time and controlled from Dyrrachium by the *archontes* of the city. Moreover, in at least three cases, the graves have been dug around, and even through the floor of, ruined churches, most likely because the sites were viewed as sacred. For example, in Sv. Erazmo (Macedonia), the cemetery was located both inside and outside the ruins of a Justinianic church. Elsewhere, the neighboring chapels may have been in existence concomitantly.[75]

[74] For the Komani culture, see now Bowden, *Epirus Vetus*, pp. 204–211; E. Nallbani, "Transformations et continuité dans l'ouest des Balkans: le cas de la civilisation de Komani (IVe–IXe siècles)," in *L'Illyrie méridionale et l'Epire dans l'Antiquité. IV. Actes du IVe colloque international de Grenoble, 10–12 octobre 2002*, ed. by P. Cabanes and J.-L. Lamboley (Paris: De Boccard, 2004), pp. 481–490.

[75] S. Anamali, "Le problème de la civilisation haute-médiévale albanaise à la lumière des nouvelles découvertes archéologiques," in *Actes du premier Congrès international des études balkaniques et sud-est européennes*, ed. by D. Dimitrov, H. Danov, V. Velkov, et al., vol. II (Sofia: Editions de l'Académie Bulgare des Sciences, 1969), p. 549. This is certainly true for the church found at Sarda between the two precincts. See G. Karaiskaj, "Të dhëna mbi arkitekturën dhe punimet e konservimit në kalanë e Shurdhahut (Sarda) [News on the architecture of the Shurdhah (Sarda) stronghold and the conservation work done on that site]," *Monumentet*, vol. 10 (1975), pp. 138–139.

A number of grave goods found on sites in Albania and the neighboring countries strongly suggest close contacts with Byzantium, possibly even the presence of speakers of Greek: belt buckles common for the Mediterranean area, both East and West; earrings with perforated pendants showing peacocks on either side of a tree; disc- and cross-brooches; finger-rings with dedicatory inscriptions in Greek. Moreover, two hoards of Byzantine drinking and washing silver vessels with Greek inscriptions, gold church candlesticks, and silver belt fittings were found in the vicinity of Dyrrachium, at Vrap and Erseke.[76] Like burial assemblages in Istria, those of Albania are often, if not always, associated with stone-lined graves, sometimes with several interment phases and multiple skeletons. This may be, and was indeed interpreted as, an indication that each individual grave may have been used for several members of the same kin group, in itself an indication that the soldiers in the garrisons of forts in northern Albania lived there permanently together with their families. That this was indeed a population of soldiers is shown not only by the relatively large number of associated weapons, but also by many such cemeteries, especially in Macedonia, located on or close to the main west–east artery across the Balkans, the Via Egnatia. Although this road was long believed to have been completely abandoned during the early Middle Ages, there is evidence that its central segment between Ohrid and Edessa/Vodena was repaired at some point during the eighth century. This is precisely the region with some of the most important cemeteries of the so-called "Komani culture" (Sv. Erazmo, Radolišta, Krušarski Rid, Goren Kozjak, and Viničani).[77] The same is true for the segment of the Via Egnatia running close to the present-day Bulgarian–Greek

[76] J. Werner, *Der Schatzfund von Vrap in Albanien. Beiträge zur Archäologie der Awarenzeit im mittleren Donauraum* (Vienna: Verlag der Österreichischen Akademie der Wissenschaften, 1986); É. Garam, "Über den Schatzfund von Vrap (Albanien)," *AAASH*, vol. 49 (1997), pp. 23–33; O. Minaeva, "On some peculiarities of the shape and decoration of the vessels from the Vrap treasure, Albania," *Problemi na izkustvoto*, vol. 1 (2001), pp. 13–22. The belt fittings of the Vrap hoard alone have a total weight of 694 grams (a little over 154 Byzantine gold coins), a considerable amount of money for that time.

[77] V. Malenko, "Ranosrednovekovnata materijalna kultura vo Okhrid i Okhridsko [The material culture in Ohrid and its hinterland during the early Middle Ages]," in *Okhrid i Okhridsko niz istorijata*, ed. by M. Apostolski, vol. 1 (Skopje: Sobranie na obshtina Okhrid, 1985), pp. 288–289 and 291–293; V. Popović, "Byzantins, Slaves et autochtones dans les provinces de Prévalitane et Nouvelle Epire," in *Villes et peuplement dans l'Illyricum protobyzantin. Actes du colloque organisé par l'Ecole Française de Rome, Rome, 12–14 mai 1982* (Rome: Ecole Française de Rome, 1984),

border in southern Thrace, where a number of cemeteries have been found showing striking parallels with burial assemblages in Macedonia and Albania.

On the other hand, a significant number of artifacts from both female and male burials – dress accessories, weapons, and belt fittings – have good analogies in Late Avar graves, as well as in assemblages from the steppes north of the Black Sea. Much like in contemporary Hungary, the mortuary assemblages in Albania display a sharp gender and status differentiation, often expressed through a great wealth of grave goods. Late Avar belt strap ends and mounts are the direct analogies for the belt fittings found in Vrap and Erseke, which seem to have been the source of inspiration for a wide variety of belt ornaments in Hungary and the neighboring regions. An eighth-century source known as the *Life of St. Pancratius* may give some substance to the Avar connection revealed by these archaeological parallels.

The apocryphal *Life* of the first bishop of Taormina was written around 700, shortly after the introduction of the thematic organization to Sicily (709/10). The author placed the life of Pancratius, a disciple of St. Peter who lived in the first century AD, in the context of his own lifetime. Pancratius' mission of conversion is thus set against the background of the first Arab attacks on Sicily, in the late seventh or early eighth century. One of Pancratius' converts was a local warlord named Bonifatius. Portrayed as the commander of the Sicilian troops, Bonifatius is said to have led several campaigns against barbarians abroad. At one time, he is described as organizing a seaborne expedition into the regions of Dyrrachium and Athens. Upon returning to Sicily, he was confronted by St. Pancratius, who claimed that his prisoners looked like Christians. Bonifatius assured him they were Avars who were to be distributed among his soldiers in order to be baptized, and were to be taught Greek and Latin, the languages in use at that time in Taormina. Through the intermediary of a

pp. 181–243. The westernmost segment of the road, between Dyrrachium and Ohrid, along the river Shkumbi, was abandoned sometime between the sixth and the ninth century, because the stretch across the Polis plateau required regular repairs that were just too expensive. However, alternative routes were in use along the rivers Mat (from Dyrrachium to Kruje, then to Dibër and Ohrid) and White Drin (from Shkodër to Kukës and then to Skopje, through Prizren). The important fort at Kruje was designed to monitor traffic on the Mat route and the associated cemetery produced some of the most significant finds of the "Komani culture."

translator, the prisoners eventually declared that they worshipped fire, water, and their own swords. It is hard to visualize the exact source for this story, but there is no doubt about its authenticity. Though the translator employed to interrogate the Avar prisoners may well have been a member of a Slavic community from Syracuse mentioned in another passage, the author of the *Life of St. Pancratius* clearly and carefully distinguished Avars from Slavs. It is therefore possible to see "Avars" in the population burying their dead in the cemeteries of the so-called "Komani culture" of Albania, which appear in relatively great numbers at a time of a general demographic decline in the Balkans.

Just how "Avars" could reach the central or western regions of the Balkans is shown in an episode of the second book of the *Miracles of St. Demetrius*. In *c.* 680/1, a conflict broke between the qagan of the Avars and a group of rebels led by a Bulgar named Kouber. The rebels were descendants of a group of captives brought to the Avar heartland from the Balkan raids of the early seventh century and settled in the environs of the former city of Sirmium. As a consequence, those following Kouber in rebellion called themselves *Sermesianoi*. The qagan allowed the Roman captives to have a separate organization with their own, specially appointed leaders. The revolt of one of them, Kouber, was eventually successful and the rebels crossed the Danube with the apparent goal of returning to their parents' homes. However, in the process Kouber managed to divert the return migration to Thessalonica and stage a coup to conquer the city, taking advantage of the situation thus created. His considerable army stopped somewhere in the vicinity of present-day Bitola, near the Greek–Macedonian border, where, at the order of Emperor Constantine IV, Kouber and his men received food supplies from the local Slavic tribe of the Drugubites. Many rebels left and moved on their own either to Thessalonica or to Constantinople; others joined Mauros, Kouber's henchman, who entered the city as a refugee but soon came to play an important role in local politics. His position was recognized by the emperor who bestowed upon him the military command over the *Sermesianoi* in addition to the title of *patrikios* shown on his personal leaden seal.[78] As *archon* of the *Sermesianoi* stationed in Thessalonica, Mauros was not different from contemporary

[78] *Miracles of St. Demetrius* II.5.292. For Mauros' seal, see Nystazopoulou-Pelekidou, "Sceaux byzantins," pp. 16–17.

archontes of Slavic tribes in or on the periphery of the Byzantine military district (theme) in existence at that time in eastern Greece.[79]

Shortly following the creation of the theme of Thrace in the 680s, a second theme must have already been in place when, in 695, Leontius, a former general of Anatolikon, was appointed military governor of Hellas.[80] Some historians have placed the theme in Peloponnesus, others in eastern and central Greece, with a northern extension into Thessaly. The evidence of leaden seals shows that the theme was an administrative unit, not just an army, despite considerable naval forces being concentrated in Hellas shortly after Leontius' appointment. Unlike anywhere else in Southeastern Europe, an unusually large quantity of copper minted for Emperor Philippikos (711–713) has been found in Athens, and most coins seem to have been specifically transported from Constantinople and "injected" into the circulating medium. Responsible for this phenomenon must have been the military, but the presence of low denomination copper coins bespeaks the existence of local markets of low-price commodities, most likely food in small quantities, serving a population that had direct access to both low-value coinage and sea lanes. The presence of small change suggests that oarsmen and sailors of either commercial or war ships could rely on constant supplies of fresh food at certain points along the coast. The fleet is indeed at the center of the early history of the theme of Hellas.

According to Theophanes, in 725 "the inhabitants of Hellas and the Cyclades" rose against Leo III and proclaimed a new emperor, Cosmas. The rebels sent a large fleet to Constantinople under the command of an officer of the theme named Agallianos.[81] Following the defeat of the rebels and the reorganization of the maritime themes, Hellas seems to have received land troops for the first time since its

[79] N. Oikonomides, "L'archonte slave de l'Hellade au VIIIe siècle," *VV*, vol. 55 (1994), pp. 111–118; W. Seibt, "Siegel als Quelle für Slawenarchonten in Griechenland," *Studies in Byzantine Sigillography*, vol. 6 (1999), pp. 27–36.

[80] Theophanes, *Chronographia* AM 6203, p. 514; G. Ostrogorski, "Postanak tema Helada i Peloponez [The creation of the themes of Hellas and Peloponnesus]," *ZRVI*, vol. 1 (1952), p. 65. For the creation of the theme of Thrace, see R.-J. Lilie, "'Thrakien' und 'Thrakesion'. Zur byzantinischen Provinzorganisation am Ende des 7. Jahrhunderts," *JOB*, vol. 26 (1977), p. 27. Thrace had been the basis for Justinian II's operations against Bulgars and Slavs, while interruption of communications between the theme and the city of Thessalonica prompted the emperor to create the military outpost on the Struma valley, later to become a *kleisoura*.

[81] Theophanes, *Chronographia* AM p. 560.

creation.[82] It is not clear what was the reason for this transfer of land troops to what had hitherto been an essentially maritime theme, but there is indirect evidence that in the early 700s the regions in the interior may have posed more serious problems than Arab sea raids.

In 723, Willibald, a western pilgrim en route to the Holy Land, sailed out from Syracuse and "reached the city of Monemvasia, in the land of Slavinia."[83] That Willibald traveled directly from Sicily to Monemvasia is a clear indication that in the early eighth century, communication lines between Constantinople and Sicily had been established along the coastal areas of southern Peloponnesus. The sojourn in Monemvasia does not seem to have been long, but the fact that the place was "in the land of Slavinia" is often interpreted as an indication of a Slavic presence in the hinterland. The Latin word *Slawinia* is a clear, though by no means unique, calque of the Greek form *Sklavinia*, which Theophanes used for the polities attacked by Constans II in 656 and by Justinian II in 688. As such, the word betrays a Constantinopolitan, not Peloponnesian, source for Willibald's account. By contrast, as we have seen, the *Life of St. Pancratius* that mentions the existence of Avars in the region of Athens may have employed eyewitness accounts.

That communications between Sicily and Peloponnesus have not been disturbed by Arab raids in the early eighth century is confirmed by other, independent sources. According to Theophanes, the plague of 745/6 "traveled like a spreading fire" from Sicily and Calabria to Monemvasia, Hellas, "and the adjoining islands," before reaching Constantinople. But the capital city seems to have been hit harder that any other region. Ten years later, Emperor Constantine V brought families from the islands, Hellas, and "the southern parts" to Constantinople, in an attempt to repopulate a city devastated by the plague.[84] In 766, he "collected artisans from different

82 J. Koder and F. Hild, *Tabula imperii Byzantinii 1: Hellas und Thessalia* (Vienna: Verlag der Österreichische Akademie der Wissenschaften, 1976), p. 57. Similar changes were taking place in the 740s in the theme of Thrace, as Emperor Constantine V began moving the troops that would sustain his successful campaigns against the Bulgars in the 760s and 770s.

83 *Vita Willibaldi*, ed. by O. Holder-Egger (Hanover, 1887; reprint 1992), MGH SS 15:93; English translation by C. H. Talbot, in *Soldiers of Christ. Saints and Saints' Lives from Late Antiquity and the Early Middle Ages*, ed. by T. F. X. Noble and T. Head (University Park: Pennsylvania State University Press, 1995), p. 145.

84 Theophanes, *Chronographia* AM 6253 and 6263, pp. 585 and 593. For the plague spreading along trade routes, see Il. Rochow, *Byzanz im 8. Jahrhundert in der Sicht*

places," and brought five hundred clay-workers from Hellas and the islands.[85] Apparently, by that time, a relatively large number of Slavs lived beyond, if not inside, the borders of the theme of Hellas, as well as in the vicinity of Thessalonica. In 783, an army led by the logothete of the Swift Course, Staurakios, moved from Constantinople to Thessalonica and Hellas, "against the Sklavinian tribes," and forced them to pay tribute to the Empire. According to Theophanes, Staurakios' army moved then into Peloponnesus and "brought back many captives and much booty to the Roman Empire."[86] The campaign is also mentioned by Syrian sources of a later date, such as Michael the Syrian and the thirteenth-century chronicle of Gregory Barhebraeus, who adds that Staurakios left a garrison in "the country of Peloponnesus." However, according to Barhebraeus, those conquered by Staurakios were "Arabs" (perhaps "Avars"), not Slavs.[87] If the reading of the corresponding passage is correct, this would confirm the testimony of the *Life of St. Pancratius* and give some substance to the most recent intepretation of the eighth-century cremation cemetery accidentally found in the 1970s in Olympia. Most analogies for both urns and a few associated finds point, again, to Late Avar burial and settlement assemblages in Hungary and the neighboring regions.[88]

During the late eighth century, at least three important Peloponnesian centers were already under imperial authority, as suggested by the participation of the bishops of Corinth, Monemvasia, and Patras in the Council of Nicaea that restored the cult of the icons (787).[89] But Staurakios' campaign had no impact on the *Sklaviniai* of northern

des Theophanes. Quellenkritisch-historischer Kommentar zu den Jahren 715–813 (Berlin: Akademie Verlag, 1991), p. 162.

85 Theophanes, *Chronographia* AM 6274, p. 608.

86 Theophanes, *Chronographia* AM 6291, p. 630. Staurakios celebrated his victory in January 784, during the hippodrome games, an indication that his campaign in the Peloponnesus may have lasted until November 783, most likely in order to force the Slavs out of the mountains. See N. Oikonomides, "A note on the campaign of Staurakios in the Peloponnese," *ZRVI*, vol. 38 (1999–2000), pp. 61–66.

87 See Barhebraeus, *Chronography*, ed. and transl. by E. A. Wallis Budge, vol. 1 (London: Oxford University Press, 1932), p. 120.

88 T. Vida and T. Völling, *Das slawische Brandgräberfeld von Olympia* (Rahden: Marie Leidorf, 2000).

89 Six other Greek sees (Athens, Monemvasia, Oreos, Skopelos, Zakynthos, and Nikopolis) were represented at Nicaea, along with the sees of Salona, Dyrrachium, and Kotor. In 787, Athens and Corinth were both metropolitan sees. See P. Yannopoulos, "Métropoles du Péloponnèse mésobyzantin: un souvenir des invasions avaro-slaves," *Byzantion*, vol. 63 (1993), pp. 395 and 398–399; R. Browning,

Greece. In 799, prompted by conspirators from the theme of Hellas, Akameros, the *archon* of the Slavs of Velzetia (eastern Thessaly) attempted to release Constantine V's sons from their exile in Athens (to which they had been confined by Empress Irene), and proclaim one of them emperor. The rebels were defeated and blinded and nothing else is known about the Slavic *archon*.[90]

Judging from the existing evidence, around the year 800, the most dangerous Slavs in Byzantine eyes were those of Greece, not those of Thrace, in the vicinity of Bulgaria. In 784, Empress Irene toured Thrace in the company of her troops. She rebuilt Beroe (modern Stara Zagora), renamed Irenopolis, and reached as far west as Philippopolis (modern Plovdiv), without encountering any opposition. Shortly following this visit, at some point after 790 and before 802, a third Balkan province was created in western Thrace, called Macedonia and centered on Adrianople. With this new military and administrative unit, the Byzantine Empire set a firm foot in the Balkans in preparation for the offensive to be launched in the early ninth century. Concomitantly, the northwestern Balkans witnessed a rapid expansion of Carolingian hegemony. Between West and East, the southeastern region of the Continent would find itself for the first time on the main stage of European history.

"Athens in the 'Dark Age'," in *Culture & History. Essays Presented to Jack Lindsay*, ed. by B. Smith (Sydney: Hale and Iremonger, 1984), p. 301.

90 Theophanes, *Chronographia* AM 6307, p. 651. See Oikonomides, "L'archonte slave," p. 117.

3

THE RISE OF NEW POWERS (800–900)

It has been persuasively suggested that far from being a response to the Arab conquest of Crete in 826 or to the beginning of the Arab conquest of Sicily, the creation of the fourth Byzantine theme in the Balkans, Peloponnesus, may be dated as early as the aftermath of Staurakios' expedition into Peloponnesus. The purpose of this theme created *c.* 800 must have been less the protection of the coasts against the Arab naval raids and more the protection of the Byzantine outposts on the coasts (mainly Corinth and Patras) against attacks from the interior. According to the much later testimony of Constantine Porphyrogenitus, in 805 the Slavs "who were in the province of Peloponnesus, decided to revolt, and first proceeded to sack the dwellings of their neighbors, the Greeks, and gave them up to rapine, and next they moved against the inhabitants of the city of Patras and ravaged the plains before its walls and laid siege to itself, having with them African Saracens also."[1] With the miraculous assistance of St. Andrew, the inhabitants of Patras were able to repel the attack, even if they lacked the support of the local military governor, who at the time was "at the extremity of the province, in the city of Corinth." Upon learning from the governor about the victory, Emperor Nicephorus I

[1] Constantine Porphyrogenitus, *De administrando imperio* 49, p. 229. The mention of Saracens may be a conflation of two separate events, the attack of the Slavs of 805 and much later raids by Arab pirates. For Muslims (pirates?) from Ifrikiyah, see A. G. C. Savvides, "Morea and Islam, 8th–15th centuries: a survey," *Journal of Oriental and African Studies*, vol. 2 (1990), pp. 48–49.

(802–811) "ordained that the foemen themselves, with all their families and relations and all who belonged to them, and all their property as well," should be transferred in perpetuity to the Church of St. Andrew in Patras. According to Constantine Porphyrogenitus, who most probably had in mind more recent revolts of the Peloponnesian Slavs, the source of this account were "the older and more ancient" who handed the information down "in unwritten tradition" to those who lived after them. However, he also mentions the bull (*sigillion*) of Nicephorus I concerning the Slavs of Patras.[2] To judge from his account, by the time of the Slavic revolt of 805, there was already a theme of Peloponnesus, with a governor residing in Corinth. The revolt was certainly not a singular event. In early 836 or 837, St. Gregory the Decapolite cut short his trip to the mountains north of Thessalonica as he miraculously predicted a rebellion of the *archon* of the local Slavs, no doubt a local leader, against the Byzantine administration of the region.[3] The revolt in Patras seems to have been caused by recent events threatening the independence of the local Slavs, namely the recent transfer of population from Sicily into Peloponnesus and the allotment of lands at their expense. The reopening of the axis of communication through the Gulf of Corinth gave Patras a strategic importance and the measures taken by the imperial administration against the rebels may have aimed at securing the safety of that line of communication. At any rate, in order to explain later revolts Emperor Constantine believed it was necessary to spell out the specific obligations imposed upon the defeated Slavs in the aftermath of their revolt. According to him, the Slavs "maintained like hostages the military governors and the imperial agents and all the envoys from foreign nations, and they have their own waiters and cooks and servants of all kinds for the table; and the metropolis interferes in none of these matters, for the Slavenes themselves collect the necessary funds by apportionment and subscription

2 Constantine Porphyrogenitus, *De administrando imperio* 49, pp. 230–231. For other sources on the 805 revolt of the Slavs against Patras, see N. Oikonomides, "St Andrew, Joseph the Hymnographer, and the Slavs of Patras," in *ΛΕΙΜΩΝ. Studies Presented to Lennart Rydén on His Sixty-Fifth Birthday*, ed. by J. O. Rosenqvist (Uppsala: Almqvist and Wiksell International, 1996), pp. 71–78.

3 Ignatius the Deacon, *Life of St. Gregory the Decapolite*, ed. by F. Dvornik (Paris: Champion, 1926), pp. 61–62. In the early 800s, the Chalkidiki Peninsula was still not completely under Byzantine control. A letter of Theodore Studites shows that the Slavic pirates of Kassandra frequently attacked incoming ships (*ep.* 3, ed. by George Fatouros [Berlin and New York: Walter de Gruyter, 1992]).

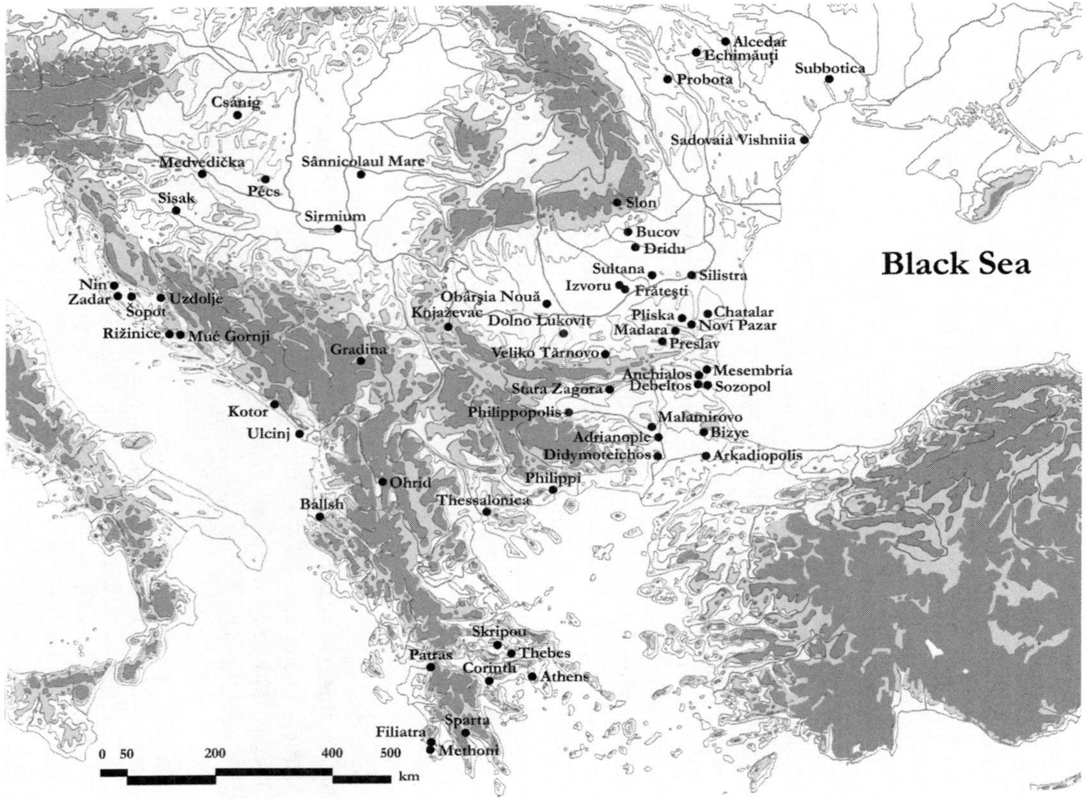

Map 3 Southeastern Europe in the ninth century.

among their unit."[4] Covering the substantial living expenses of all official travelers passing through Patras must have been an onerous task, but it is quite clear that the Slavs of Patras were subjects of the state, not of the local church. The events of 805–806 are also at the center of one of the most controversial sources for the history of the Slavs in Greece, the *Chronicle of Monemvasia*.[5] But instead of the heroic resistance put up by the inhabitants of Patras assisted by St. Andrew, the *Chronicle* mentions an expedition against the Peloponnesian Slavs ordered by Emperor Nicephorus I and led by an unnamed general of the theme of Armeniakon, a member of the Skleros family.

The chronicle survives in three late manuscripts. Only one of them, which is preserved in the Iviron monastery at Mount Athos and is dated to the sixteenth century, deals exclusively with the campaign ordered by Nicephorus I. The *Chronicle of Monemvasia* is not a chronicle properly speaking, but a compilation of sources concerning the Slavs and the foundation of the metropolitan see of Patras. Patras, and not Monemvasia, is at the center of the narrative. It has been argued, therefore, that this text may have been written in order to be used in negotiations with the metropolitan of Corinth over the status of the metropolitan of Patras. Since Emperor Nicephorus I is referred to as "the Old, who had Staurakios as son," the text must have been written after the reign of Nicephorus II Phocas (963–969). The author of the *Chronicle* explicitly refers to the death of Tarasius, the patriarch of Constantinople (784–806). He also calls Sirmium *Striamos*, and locates the city in Bulgaria, an indication that he wrote the *Chronicle* before the conquest of that city by Basil II, in 1018 (see chapter 5 below). The composition of the *Chronicle* must therefore fall within the second half of the tenth or in the early decades of the eleventh century. The Slavs only appear in the second part of the Iviron

[4] Constantine Porphyrogenitus, *De administrando imperio* 49, pp. 230–231.

[5] The standard edition is that of I. Duichev, *Cronaca di Monemvasia* (Palermo: Istituto Siciliano di Studi Bizantini e Neoellenici, 1976). For an English translation, see H. Kalligas, *Byzantine Monemvasia. The Sources* (Monemvasia: Akroneon, 1990), pp. 7–11. See also S. Turlej, "The so-called Chronicle of Monemvasia. A historical analysis," *Byzantion*, vol. 68 (1998), pp. 446–468; and *The Chronicle of Monemvasia. The Migration of the Slavs and Church Conflicts in the Byzantine Source from the Beginning of the 9th Century* (Cracow: Towarzystwo Wydawnicze "Historia Iagellonica," 2001); E. Kislinger, *Regionalgeschichte als Quellenproblem. Die Chronik von Monembasia und das sizilianische Demenna. Eine historisch-topographische Studie* (Vienna: Verlag der Österreichischen Akademie der Wissenschaften, 2001).

version of the text, which describes how Emperor Nicephorus I (802–811) conquered Peloponnesus and established the metropolis of Patras. This account comes very close to a scholium written by Arethas of Caesarea on the margin of a manuscript of Nicephorus' *Historia Syntomos* dated to 932.[6] The note is a comment made by Arethas while reading Nicephorus' work, and thus must be viewed as a text of private, not public nature. In some instances, Arethas repeats the *Chronicle* verbatim. Though the *Chronicle of Monemvasia* was clearly composed much later, it is very unlikely that its author derived his information from Arethas. Arethas was born at Patras in or around 850 into a rich family and his family's memories and stories may well have been the source for his knowledge of the resettlement in Peloponnesus of the Greek-speaking population of Reggio (Calabria, southern Italy) under Emperor Nicephorus I. By contrast, the author of the *Chronicle* mentions people from the themes of Asia Minor that were brought in to repopulate the central and southern regions of Peloponnesus.

The increasing number of new settlers contributed to further conflicts with the local Slavs. According to Constantine Porphyrogenitus, the Peloponnesian Slavs rebelled again "in the days of Emperor Theophilus and his son Michael." Following the former's death in 842, the military governor Theoctistus Bryennios led a campaign against the rebels and eventually subdued "all Slavs and other insubordinates of the province of Peloponnesus."[7] A second campaign was necessary in order to break the resistance of two tribes living on the slopes of Mount Taigetos, the Ezerites and the Milings. Both were eventually forced to pay tribute, but refused to accept "a head man at the hand of the military governor" or "to heed an order for military service under him." This seems to indicate that unlike the Ezerites and the Milings, subduing the Slavs living elsewhere in Greece had been a matter of accommodating the needs of their elites and providing incentives for their inclusion into the imperial administration, a policy confirmed by the evidence of seals of *archontes* (leaders) of the Slavs. By contrast, the Ezerites and the Milings of central Peloponnesus were apparently expected to provide troops for the Byzantine army to be included within units recruited from the theme. The Slavs

[6] L. G. Westerink, "Marginalia by Arethas in Moskow Greek Ms. 231," *Byzantion*, vol. 42 (1972), pp. 241–242.

[7] Constantine Porphyrogenitus, *De administrando imperio* 50, pp. 232–233.

in the Byzantine troops that participated in the conquest of Taranto in 880 had most likely been recruited from among the stubbornly independent Slavs of southern Greece.[8] By that time, the naval forces of the themes of Peloponnesus and Cephalonia had themselves received reinforcements from other regions of the Empire. The troops sent to Sicily in 876 to defend Syracuse against Arab attacks included Mardaites from Peloponnesus, who had been recently transferred to that province from the East.[9]

The growing military presence of Byzantium in the southern and southwestern regions of the Balkans is also indicated by seal finds. Military governors of Cephalonia, a theme created in the eighth century, are mentioned on five seals dated to the early ninth century, at the latest. Six military governors of the theme of Hellas appear on seals, one of them on no less than thirteen identical specimens. By contrast, only two military governors of Peloponnesus are known from early ninth-century seals.[10] One of them may have been a contemporary of the first military governor of Thessalonica, a city until then under the administration of its own eparchs, mentioned several times on late eighth- or early ninth-century seals. Particularly numerous are ninth-century seals of fiscal agents of Hellas and Peloponnesus, an indirect indication of the relative prosperity of the two provinces. Not much is known about the social structure of ninth-century Greece, but what we have suggests that the Byzantine provinces in the southern Balkans were centers of wealth and influence. Both Empress Irene and Theophano, Staurakios' wife, were born into rich families from Athens. By 850, the future emperor

[8] Theophanes Continuatus 5.66, ed. by I. Bekker (Bonn: E. Weber, 1838), pp. 305–306; Skylitzes, *Synopsis historiarum* 34, ed. by H. Thurn (Berlin and New York: De Gruyter, 1973), pp. 156–157. See also H. Ditten, *Ethnische Verschiebungen zwischen der Balkanhalbinsel und Kleinasien vom Ende des 6. bis zur zweiten Hälfte des 9. Jahrhunderts* (Berlin: Akademie Verlag, 1993), p. 262.

[9] Theophanes Continuatus 5.63 and 70, pp. 303 and 311. By the mid-ninth century, there were strong Armenian communities in Thessalonica, as well as in Philippopolis and Adrianople. See H. M. Bartikian, "He armenike parousia ste byzantine Makedonia [The Armenian presence in Byzantine Macedonia]," in *Diethnes symposio "Byzantine Makedonia, 324–1430 m. Kh.," Thessalonike 29–31 Oktobriou 1992* (Thessaloniki, 1995), pp. 35 and 38.

[10] One of them is that of Theoctistos Bryennios, who had crushed the rebellion of 842. See N. Zikos, "Molybdoboulla tou Byzantinou Mouseiou Athenon [Leaden seals from the Byzantine Museum in Athens]," *Arkhaiologikon Deltion*, vol. 32 (1977), pp. 86–87.

Basil I enjoyed the protection of a wealthy Peloponnesian widow named Danelis, who had made a fortune by raising sheep and employing slave labor for the production of cloth and rugs. An inscription recording the endowment of the Church of the Holy Virgin at Skripou erected in 873 or 874 refers to the estates of an imperial dignitary, the *protosphatarios* Leo, in the region of Orchomenos. Several military officers of the theme of Hellas were important enough to have their own seals and to become patrons of newly built churches.

Associated with such relative prosperity was a remarkable monetary growth, archaeologically visible during and after the middle third of the ninth century. The growth is most spectacular in Corinth, where the archaeological excavations carried on so far have produced just 2 coins of Michael II (820–829), but 157 of Theophilus (829–842), 280 of Basil I (867–886), and 957 of Leo VI (886–912). Though statistically less spectacular, finds from Athens, Thebes, and Sparta indicate a similar trend. The explanation most commonly advanced for this impressive monetary growth is the expansion of long-distance trade, especially at Corinth with its port at Kenchreai, which provided a much easier connection to the markets of northern Italy than circumnavigating Peloponnesus. In 832 or 833, on his way from Thessalonica to Rome, St. Gregory the Decapolite got a ship in Corinth and sailed to Reggio, and thence to Rome.[11] Even coastal sites in western Peloponnesus have produced archaeological evidence of contacts with faraway markets, such as a fragment of Chinese marbled ware recently found in Methoni.[12] On the other hand, there is yet no archaeological correlate of the monetary growth identified in Corinth. The idea has been put forward that the former Roman forum in that city was used for commercial purposes in the 800s, but no structures have so far been identified that could be associated with the growth of trade implied by the numismatic evidence. It has been therefore suggested that Corinth may have been a regional fair not unlike those of northern Italy, but future excavations in areas other than the Roman forum may show

[11] Ignatius the Deacon, *Life of St. Gregory the Decapolite*, p. 55. For the reopening of the Gulf of Corinth to both eastern and western travelers, see M. McCormick, *The Origins of the European Economy. Communications and Commerce, AD 300–900* (Cambridge: Cambridge University Press, 2001), pp. 531–537.

[12] N. D. Kontogiannis, "A fragment of a Chinese marbled ware bowl from Methoni, Greece," *Bizantinistica. Rivista di studi bizantini e slavi*, vol. 4 (2002), pp. 39–46.

otherwise.[13] Excavations in Sparta have so far indicated an expansion of the early medieval occupation beginning with the mid-800s, but nothing confirms the picture drawn on the basis of the *Chronicle of Monemvasia* and showing a massive repopulation with people from the themes in Asia Minor during the reign of Nicephorus I. In Athens, the Church of St. John the Baptist erected in 871 must have been built at about the same time as the earliest medieval structures in the area of the ancient Agora. None of these buildings produced evidence of long-distance trade and it is more likely that they served the growing administrative and military functions of the city, for Athens was the seat of the theme of Hellas, as indicated by an inscription on a column in the Parthenon concerning the death in August 848 of a military governor named Leo.[14]

At some point before the middle of the ninth century, the bishopric of Athens was elevated to metropolitan status, an indication of a growing number of episcopal sees within the theme of Hellas, a situation paralleled by similar developments in Peloponnesus and northwestern Greece. At the council summoned by Photius in Constantinople in 879, Greece was represented by twelve metropolitans and bishops, some from revived sees, such as Demetrias or Naupaktos, others from newly established ones, such as New Patras or Ezeros.[15] As the *Chronicle of Monemvasia* expressedly links the ecclesiastical rearrangements in Peloponnesus operated under Patriarch Tarasius (784–806) to the conversion of the local Slavs to Christianity, it has been suggested that the foundation of new bishoprics was directed towards converting the Slavs, but all known bishoprics in Peloponnesus were located in the east or on the coast, away from the troubled areas of the interior.[16] No church building still standing in eastern Peloponnesus can be safely dated to the ninth century. However, some of the earliest monastic communities in medieval Greece were located in western Peloponnesus, as indicated by the

[13] G. D. R. Sanders, "Corinth," in *The Economic History of Byzantium from the Seventh through the Fifteenth Century*, ed. by A. E. Laiou (Washington: Dumbarton Oaks Research Library and Collection, 2002), p. 650.

[14] M. Kazanaki-Lappa, "Medieval Athens," in *The Economic History of Byzantium from the Seventh through the Fifteenth Century*, ed. by A. E. Laiou (Washington: Dumbarton Oaks Research Library and Collection, 2002), p. 641.

[15] J. Herrin, "Aspects of the process of hellenization in the early Middle Ages," *ABSA*, vol. 68 (1973), p. 123.

[16] M. Dunn, "Evangelism or repentance? The re-Christianisation of the Peloponnese in the ninth and tenth centuries," *Studies in Church History*, vol. 14 (1977), p. 78.

monastery church of St. Irene in Patras-Riganokampo and the rock monasteries near Filiatra, not far from Methoni, all dated to the ninth century. A wave of monasticism is noticeable in Peloponnesus during the ninth century, as several monks came to the region, especially refugees from Sicily and the southern regions of Italy threatened by constant Arab raids. The *Life of St. Elias the Younger*, written at some point between 930 and 940, mentions the arrival of the Italian saint at Sparta in 880, where Elias and his disciple Daniel took shelter near a cave, in the ruins of an abandoned church. Both returned to Peloponnesus in 888, and resided for a short while in Patras.[17] Another itinerant saint from Italy, St. Elias Spaeleotas, also resided in the environs of Patras at some unknown date before 902, perhaps no later than 894. He chose a haunted tower as his dwelling, and remained there for eight years, after exorcising the place and gaining his reputation as holy man. Neither of these two saints encountered Slavs and no famous act of mass conversion is associated with their saintly glory.

If a connection may be proposed between the building of new churches and the Christianization of the Slavs, then the evidence to support such an argument is to be found only outside Peloponnesus. The earliest churches in the southwestern Balkan regions under Byzantine rule are those of Montenegro. The Church of St. Tryphon in Kotor was erected during the reign of Nicephorus I (802–811), that of Ulcinj during the reign of Leo V (813–820).[18] In Greece proper, the earliest medieval churches are those of the central region, not of Peloponnesus: the Church of St. John the Baptist in Athens, erected in 871; the Church of the Holy Virgin at Skripou, built in 873/4;

[17] *Life of St. Elias the Younger*, ed. by G. R. Taibbi (Palermo: Istituto Siciliano di Studi Bizantini e Neoellenici, 1962), pp. 40 and 56. For St. Elias Spaeleotas, see P. Yannopoulos, "La Grèce dans la Vie de s. Elie le Jeune et dans celle de S. Elie le Spéléote," *Byzantion*, vol. 64 (1994), pp. 198–199.

[18] Kovačević, "Aperçu historique," p. 67; Dragojlović, "Dyrrachium et les évêchés," p. 202. A date in the early 800s has been advanced, on purely stylistical grounds, for the Churches of St. Peter in Bijela (Boka Kotorska), St. Stephen in Grbalj and Dubrovnik, St. Michael in Ston, St. John in Lopud, and St. Mary in Budva. On the basis of a very similar plan, the Church of St. Demetrius in Katsoura (near Arta) has also been dated to *c.* 800. See P. L. Vokotopoulos, *He ekklesiastike architektonike eis ten dytiken sterean Hellada kai ten Epeiron (apo tou telous tou 7ou mechri tou telous tou 10ou aionos)* [The Church Architecture in Northwestern Greece and in Epirus between the Late Seventh and the Late Tenth Century] (Thessaloniki: Kentron Byzantinon Ereunon, 1975), p. 183.

and the Church of St. Gregory the Theologian in Thebes, built in 876/7. However, the donors of two of these churches were high-ranking officials with little, if any, concern for the conversion of any Slavs that may have lived in the neighborhood. Both church buildings and missions to the Slavs are conspicuously absent from the northern regions of present-day Greece that in the mid-ninth century were within the themes of Thessalonica and Macedonia. Local Slavs are a most notable presence in the *Life of St. Gregory the Decapolite* and its account of the saint's travels through the region of Thessalonica.[19] But they appear as rebels or pirates, not as submissive subjects of missions of evangelization. According to Constantine Porphyrogenitus, it was only under the reign of Michael III (842–867) that the Slavs in the region of Thessalonica were finally subdued.[20] And it is only at that time that a Byzantine mission was sent to the Slavs, which was led by two Thessalonians, Constantine-Cyril and Methodius, perhaps the most influential personalities of the early medieval history of Southeastern Europe.

So great is the significance of the Cyrillo-Methodian mission for Slavic cultural history that to some scholars the two brothers cannot have been but Slavs by birth. In reality, as Emperor Michael allegedly told Constantine himself before sending him on the Moravian mission, "all Thessalonians speak pure Slavic."[21] Much, if not all, of what we know about Constantine and Methodius, their lives and activity prior to their mission to Moravia, comes from their *Lives*, the only known biographies of Byzantine-born missionaries. Particularly useful is the *Life of Constantine*, a work composed in Old Church Slavonic by someone in the entourage of Methodius at some point between Constantine's death in 869 and December 885 (when we know the text was used in Rome), perhaps in 879 or 880.[22] The undeclared,

[19] Ignatius the Deacon, *Life of St. Gregory the Decapolite*, pp. 54–55.

[20] Constantine Porphyrogenitus, *De cerimoniis* II.37, ed. by J. J. Reiske, vol. I (Bonn: E. Weber, 1829), pp. 634–635.

[21] *Life of Methodius*, ed. by D. Bartoňková, L. Havlík, J. Ludvikovský, Z. Masařík, and R. Večerka, in *Magnae Moraviae fontes historici*, vol. II (Prague: Státní pedagogické nakl., 1965), p. 138; English translation by M. Kantor, *Medieval Slavic Lives of Saints and Princes* (Ann Arbor: University of Michigan, Department of Slavic Languages and Literatures, 1983), p. 111.

[22] *Life of Constantine*, ed. by D. Bartoňková, L. Havlík, J. Ludvikovský, Z. Masařík, and R. Večerka, in *Magnae Moraviae fontes historici*, vol. II (Prague: Státní pedagogické nakl., 1965), pp. 60–115; English translation by Kantor, *Medieval Slavic Lives*, pp. 25–96.

yet transparent purpose of the *Life* was to defend the Slavic writing and liturgy, both recently introduced to Moravia, by showing Constantine to have been a holy man and saint, an image Methodius and his disciples badly needed in their struggle with the Bavarian clergy.[23] Both because of its obvious political goals and of the late manuscript tradition (the earliest attestation of the text is that of a mid-fifteenth-century Russian manuscript), the text was long viewed, especially in the nineteenth century, as unreliable, but it is now appreciated as a first-rate source.

Constantine was born in 826 or 827, the son of "a certain noble and rich man named Leo in the city of Thessalonica, who held the rank of *drungarios*,"[24] a high-ranking Byzantine officer under the command of the military governor of the newly created theme of Thessalonica. His older brother Methodius had been appointed *archon* of the Slavs, perhaps the successor of one of those *archontes* mentioned on eighth-century seals as ruling on the northern and northeastern borders of the theme of Hellas.[25] He may have been married and with children, but he suddenly decided to leave his family and to take the monastic vows in a monastery on Mount Olympus (present-day Ulu Dağ, near Brusa, in Turkey). Meanwhile, his younger brother was entirely dedicated to learning and religious devotion. "Taking up his studies, he remained at home and committed to memory the writings of St. Gregory the Theologian."[26] Brought to Constantinople in 842 or 843, Constantine became a protégé of Theoctistus, the powerful minister of the regent empress Theodora. At the imperial academy at Magnaura, he studied "Homer and geometry with Leo [the Mathematician], and dialectics and all philosophical studies with Photius; and in addition to that, rhetoric and arithmetic, astronomy and music, and all the other Hellenic

[23] Fundamental for the history of the Byzantine mission to Moravia remains F. Dvornik, *Byzantine Missions among the Slavs. SS. Constantine-Cyril and Methodius* (New Brunswick: Rutgers University Press, 1970), pp. 160–193, esp. p. 182.

[24] *Life of Constantine* 2, English translation in Kantor, *Medieval Slavic Lives*, p. 27. Constantine's father may have been one of the first officers of the theme of Thessalonica, created by Emperor Nicephorus I in the early ninth century.

[25] *Life of Methodius* 3, English translation in Kantor, *Medieval Slavic* Lives, p. 109. Others believe Methodius' office must have been in some theme of Asia Minor, perhaps Opsikion. See A. E. Tachiaos, "Some controversial points relating to the life and activity of Cyril and Methodius," *Cyrillomethodianum*, vols. 17–18 (1993–1994), pp. 41–72.

[26] *Life of Constantine* 3, English translation in Kantor, *Medieval Slavic Lives*, p. 29.

arts."[27] After declining an offer to marry Theoctistus' goddaughter, he became a deacon (he was too young for a canonical ordination as a priest) and librarian (archivist) to the patriarch in Hagia Sophia. At the age of 24, Constantine was sent on an embassy to the caliph al-Mutawakkil, perhaps to negotiate an exchange of prisoners. While in Samarra, he engaged in a theological dispute with the Muslim ulamas and even cited a Quranic surah to support his arguments in favor of the Holy Trinity and against Muslim accusations of polytheism. Soon after his return to Constantinople, following the assassination of Theoctistus in 856 and the palace coup that drove Empress Theodora out of power, Constantine joined his brother in the monastery on Mount Olympus, where he remained until Photius was installed patriarch in 858. Shortly after that, the two brothers came to Constantinople and in 860 were sent to the Khazar court, perhaps to propose some joint Byzantine–Khazar action against the Rus' of Kiev, who had just attacked Constantinople in that same year. On their way to Itil on the Lower Volga, where the Khazar capital had moved in the early 800s, Constantine and Methodius stopped in Crimea, at Chersonesus. While in the city, Constantine discovered the relics of St. Clement, the second bishop of Rome, and wrote a sermon about the discovery, probably addressed to the local merchant community. He also "learned the Hebrew language and scriptures" and found "the Gospels and the Psalter written in Russian letters," which he was able to read and understand.[28] While the reference to the "Russian letters" betrays a later addition to the text and a contamination with much later sources, there is no reason to doubt that Constantine was in fact capable of learning Hebrew in preparation for his visit to the Khazar court, where the ruling class had recently adopted Judaism. Moreover, now capable of reading and understanding Hebrew, Constantine's arguments so impressed a "Samaritan" that he accepted baptism together with his own son. It is for the first time in the *Life of Constantine* that we learn about the saint's ability to convert people to Orthodoxy. Both disputation and conversion figure prominently in the account of the brothers' trip to the Khazar court in Itil, an account confirmed by tenth-century Khazar sources. Constantine used in a debate his newly acquired knowledge of Hebrew to draw a point about the distinction between image and idol.

[27] *Life of Constantine* 4, English translation in Kantor, *Medieval Slavic Lives*, p. 31.
[28] *Life of Constantine* 8, English translation in Kantor, *Medieval Slavic Lives*, p. 43.

Following the debate, "about two hundred of these people were baptized, having cast off heathen abominations and lawless marriages."[29] In addition, at Constantine's request, 200 Greek prisoners were released in order to be taken back to Byzantium. The mission returned to Constantinople, but on his way back, Constantine stopped again in Crimea after miraculously turning a salt marsh in the steppe into drinkable water, "sweet like honey, and cold."[30] This was most likely the same steppe from which Magyars had come before Constantine's departure for the Khazar mission and had fallen upon him "howling like wolves and wishing to kill him." Again, Constantine's "edifying words" miraculously persuaded them "to release him and his entire retinue in peace."[31]

The exact location of the encounter with the Magyars is not mentioned, but it cannot have been too far away from Chersonesus. The mention of a Magyar raid originating in the steppe north of the Black Sea is of great importance for the ninth-century history of Southeastern Europe. This piece of evidence substantiates what is otherwise known from a tenth-century Byzantine chronicle, namely that in 836 or 837 the Magyars raided the Lower Danube region as Bulgar allies in an attempt to prevent the intervention of the Byzantine fleet on behalf of the Byzantine prisoners that had been moved north of the Danube after the Bulgar ruler Krum had taken Adrianople in 813 (see below). In 881 or 882, on his way from Constantinople to Moravia, Methodius allegedly met a Magyar "king" somewhere in the Lower Danube region. But in the late 830s, when they controlled the steppe to the north and northwest of the Black Sea, the Magyars seem to have been newcomers to that region. They quickly established a firm control over the entire steppe corridor between the Don and the Lower Danube. As a consequence, Rus' envoys to Constantinople found themselves in the embarrassing position of not being able to return home through the steppes north of the Black Sea. They had to take a detour through Ingelheim on the Rhine, where they appeared in 839 together with an embassy from Emperor Theophilus. About the same time, the Khazars themselves apparently grew

[29] *Life of Constantine* 10, English translation in Kantor, *Medieval Slavic Lives*, p. 57.

[30] *Life of Constantine* 12, English translation in Kantor, *Medieval Slavic Lives*, p. 63.

[31] *Life of Constantine* 8, English translation in Kantor, *Medieval Slavic Lives*, p. 45. For barbarians howling like wolves as a literary motif, see L. Steindorff, "Wölfisches Heulen. Ein Motiv in mittelalterlichen slavischen Quellen," *Byzantinoslavica*, vol. 46 (1985), 40–49.

worried about raids from the western steppes and demanded assistance from the Byzantine emperor for the building of a fortress to control access across the Don from the steppe lands to the west of that river. In the region between the Dnieper and Lower Danube Rivers, the presence of the Magyars is signaled by the sudden appearance of fortified settlements, such as those erected at the border between the steppe and the steppe-forest belt, on the left bank of the Dniester River, at Alcedar and Echimăuţi (present-day Republic of Moldova). At the opposite, southern end of the steppe belt, all along the northwestern shore of the Black Sea, a number of settlements dated to the ninth and tenth century cluster behind the three dikes erected most likely at a much earlier date.[32] Despite the occasional presence on these sites of such steppe culture features as yurt-like buildings or clay cauldrons, there is so far very little archaeological evidence pertaining to the momentous political changes taking place in the steppe corridor north and northwest of the Black Sea in the aftermath of the Magyar migration into the region. All burial assemblages traditionally associated with Magyars that were found in that region (Probota, in eastern Romania; Sadovaia Vishniia and Subbotica, in southwestern Ukraine) cannot be dated earlier than *c.* 900 and thus have nothing to do with the Magyars whom Constantine and Methodius had met in the 800s. However, more recent research has revealed the presence of new styles (palmette decoration) and practices (hoards of silverware and jewels) that may have been associated with the rise of a new elite among the Magyars on the eve of their migration to the Carpathian Basin in the 890s.

THE PROBLEM OF GREAT MORAVIA

Only three years after their return from the Khazar capital at Itil, Constantine and Methodius embarked on another mission. According to the *Life of Methodius*, "the Slavic prince Rostislav together with Svatopluk sent emissaries from Moravia to Emperor

[32] V. Kozlov, "Zur Besiedlungsstruktur der Nordostprovinzen des ersten Bulgarenreiches," in *Zwischen Byzanz und Abendland. Pliska, der östliche Balkanraum und Europa im Spiegel der Frühmittelalterarchäologie*, ed. by J. Henning (Frankfurt am Main: Johann Wolfgang Goethe Universität, 1999), pp. 71–75. For the dikes in southern Moldova, see Chebotarenko and Subbotin, "Issledovaniia Troianovykh Valov," pp. 124–145.

Michael [III],"[33] asking for Byzantine missionaries to help him counteract the growing influence of the missionaries from Salzburg and Passau under Carolingian obedience. At the emperor's request, Constantine and his brother started the translation of religious texts into Old Church Slavonic, a literary language most likely based on the Macedonian dialect allegedly used in the hinterland of their hometown, Thessalonica. Constantine devised a new alphabet, later called Glagolitic, to render the sounds of the new language and to adapt it to the new conditions in Moravia. The two brothers seem to have initially translated only texts for religious instruction, such as the excerpts from the Gospels that were used in liturgy. This was apparently nothing new, for the Frankish missions to the Slavs of Carantania and the neighboring regions were already using Slavic for certain key aspects of their missionary work. The so-called Freising Fragments, a Latin manuscript written around AD 1000, contain a collection of formulas for confessions and baptisms, as well as an exhortation to penitence, all translated from Old High German into a language that is closer to modern Slovenian than to Old Church Slavonic.[34] It is only later, in Moravia, away from the supervision of either Constantinople or Rome, that Constantine and Methodius took the liberty of translating liturgical texts into Slavonic, namely the "matins and the hours, vespers and the compline, and the liturgy."[35] This translation program is best illustrated by two eleventh-century Glagolitic manuscripts from the St. Catherine Monastery at Mount Sinai, the so-called *Fragmenta Sinaitica* and the *Euchologium Sinaiticum*. The former is the earliest Slavonic translation of the Greek liturgy and shows that Constantine and Methodius employed the liturgy of St. John Chrysostom, to which they added a number of fourth-century prayers. The *Euchologium* contains several prayers for such non-liturgical occasions as harvest, baptism, or disease, but also such non-Eastern items as a prayer to St. Emmeram, the seventh-century

33 *Life of Methodius* 3, English translation in Kantor, *Medieval Slavic Lives*, p. 111.

34 *Brižinski spomeniki. Znanstvenokritična izdanja* [The Freising Monuments. A critical edition], ed. by F. Bernik and J. Kos (Ljubljana: Institut sa slovensko literaturo in literarne vede, 1993). See also V. Capkova, "The Freising monuments," in *Irland und die Christenheit. Bibelstudien und Mission*, ed. by P. Ni Chathain and M. Richter (Stuttgart: Klett-Cotta, 1987), pp. 461–470.

35 *Life of Constantine* 15, English translation in Kantor, *Medieval Slavic Lives*, p. 69. For the excerpts of the Gospels used in the liturgy, see C. Koch, "Tetra oder Aprakos? Zur Textgattung der ältesten slavischen Evangelienübersetzung," *Welt der Slawen*, vol. 44 (1999), pp. 27–62.

missionary to Bavaria.[36] The translation technique employed by Constantine and Methodius may be best described as an attempt to apply to the language spoken in Moravia the calques in use at that time among Slavs in the region of Thessalonica, who had been accustomed to the Greek liturgy. For example, the earliest translation of liturgical texts employed two words for "messenger," one used to refer to the heavenly messengers (*angel*), the other to more mundane envoys (*posăl*). Later, after the death of his brother in 869, Methodius continued the translation program on an even larger scale. According to the *Life of Methodius*, he "translated quickly from the Greek language into Slavic – in six months beginning with the month of March to the twenty-sixth day of the month of October – all the Scriptures in full, save Maccabees." In addition, before his own death in 885, Methodius translated a compendium of canon law known as the *Nomokanon* and, most importantly, wrote the *Court Law for the People* (*Zakon sudnyi liudem*), an adaptation of the lawcode of Emperors Leo III and Constantine V known as *Ecloga*.[37]

This impressive literary activity and program of translation, to which one should also add the first major original works in Old Church Slavonic, namely the *Life of Constantine* and the *Life of Methodius*, underscores the importance of the Moravian mission. But its significance for the history of Southeastern Europe is currently the subject of a lively debate. In the early 1970s, the American historian Imre Boba put forward the idea that the Moravia where the two brothers were sent in 863 was not the land along the river Morava

[36] I. C. Tarnanidis, *The Slavonic Manuscripts Discovered in 1975 at St. Catherine's Monastery on Mount Sinai* (Thessaloniki: Hellenic Association for Slavic Studies, 1988). See H. Birnbaum, "On the eastern and western components of the earliest Slavic liturgy: the evidence of the *Euchologium Sinaiticum* and related texts," in *Essays in the Area of Slavic Languages, Linguistics, and Byzantology. A Festschrift in Honor of Antonín Dostál on the Occasion of His Seventy-Fifth Birthday*, ed. by T. G. Winner (Irvine: Charles Schlacks, Jr., 1985), pp. 25–44.

[37] Kantor, *Medieval Slavic Lives*, p. 125. The manuscript of Methodius' Old Church Slavonic translation of the Bible was eventually lost, and the Bible was translated again in 1499. See F. J. Thomson, "Has the Cyrillomethodian translation of the Bible survived?," in *Thessaloniki Magna Moravia* (Thessaloniki: SS. Cyril and Methodios Center for Cultural Studies, 1999), pp. 149–163. The standard edition of the *Court Law for the People* is still M. N. Tikhomirov and L. V. Milov, *Zakon sudnyi liudem; kratkoi redakcii* (Moscow: Nauka, 1961), but the lawcode is now available in the English translation of H. W. Dewey and A. M. Kleimola, *Zakon sudnyi liudem. Court Law for the People* (Ann Arbor: University of Michigan, Department of Slavic Languages and Literatures, 1977).

separating present-day Slovakia from the Czech Republic and Austria, but the region on both sides of the river by that same name in present-day Serbia, south of the Danube.[38] His ideas have meanwhile been developed by advocates and sharply criticized by skeptics.[39] This is not the place for a detailed examination of the main arguments advanced by Boba and his supporters, but because the issue has some significance for the history of Southeastern Europe, it is worth summarizing the debate. The common opinion favored

[38] I. Boba, *Moravia's History Reconsidered. A Reinterpretation of Medieval Sources* (The Hague: Martinus Nijhoff, 1971); "The cathedral church of Sirmium and the grave of St. Methodius," *Die slawischen Sprachen*, vol. 8 (1985), pp. 5–19; and "Die Lage von Moravien nach den mittelalterlichen Quellen aus Bayern," in *Salzburg und die Slavenmission. Zum 1100. Todestag des hl. Methodius. Beiträge des internationalen Symposiums vom 20. bis 22. September 1985 in Salzburg*, ed. by H. Dopsch (Salzburg: Gesellschaft für Salzburgische Landeskunde, 1986), pp. 59–69.

[39] The literature on the location of early medieval "Great Moravia" has grown considerably over the last four decades. The most important advocate of Imre Boba's thesis is now C. R. Bowlus, "Die geographische Lage des Mährischen Reiches anhand fränkischer Quellen," *Bohemia*, vol. 28 (1987), pp. 1–24; "Imre Boba's reconsiderations of Moravia's early history and Arnulf of Carinthia's Ostpolitik (887–892)," *Speculum*, vol. 62 (1987), pp. 552–574; and *Franks, Moravians, and Magyars. The Struggle for the Middle Danube 788–907* (Philadelphia: University of Pennsylvania Press, 1995). An equally strong voice in favor of Boba's interpretations is M. Eggers, *Das "Großmährische Reich": Realität oder Fiktion? Eine Neuinterpretation der Quellen zur Geschichte des mittleren Donauraumes im 9. Jahrhundert* (Stuttgart: Anton Hiersemann, 1995); and "The historical–geographical implications of the Cyrillo-Methodian mission among the Slavs," in *Thessaloniki Magna Moravia* (Thessaloniki: SS. Cyril and Methodios Center for Cultural Studies, 1999), pp. 65–86. Among Boba's most important critics mention should be made of L. E. Havlík, "'He megale Moravia' und 'he chora Moravia'," *Byzantinoslavica*, vol. 54 (1993), pp. 75–82; H. Wolfram, "Moravien–Mähren oder nicht?," in *Svätopluk 894–1994. Materiály z konferencie organizovanej Archeologickym ústavom SAV v Nitre v spolupráci so Slovenskou historickou spoločnost'ou pri SAV. Nitra, 3.–6. október 1994*, ed. by R. Marsina and A. Ruttkay (Nitra: Vydavatel' Archeologický ústav Slovenskej akadémie vied, 1997), pp. 235–245; G. Birkfellner, "Methodius Archiepiscopus Superioris Moraviae oder Anmerkungen über die historisch-geographische Lage Altmährens (Vorläufige Stellungnahme zu jüngsten hyperkritischen Lokalisierungsversuchen)," in *Leben und Werk der byzantinischen Slavenapostel Methodios und Kyrillos. Beiträge eines Symposions der Griechisch-deutschen Initiative Würzburg im Wasserschloß Mitwitz vom 25.–27. Juli 1985 zum Gedenken an den 1100. Todestag des hl. Methodios*, ed. by E. Konstantinou (Münsterschwarzach: Vier-Türme Verlag, 1991), pp. 33–38; H. Birnbaum, "Where was the centre of the Moravian state?," in *American Contributions to the Eleventh International Congress of Slavists. Bratislava, August–September 1993. Literature, Linguistics, Poetics*, ed. by R. A. Maguire and A. Timberlake (Columbus, Ohio: Slavica, 1993), pp. 11–24.

especially in former Czechoslovakia and attacked by Boba maintained that the Moravia of Constantine and Methodius was the territory along the Morava north of the Danube River. This opinion was mainly based on the extraordinarily rich evidence produced by various archaeological sites in the region, mainly hillforts and large cemeteries showing clear wealth differentiation and status markers. The presence of churches (Staré Město, Sady, Mikulčice) and of clear signs of conversion to the form of Christianity favored within the Byzantine Empire (such as the pectoral cross with Greek inscription found in Sady) speaks strongly in favor of this opinion. By contrast, the arguments of Imre Boba and his advocates are exclusively based on written sources. They maintain that East Frankish sources should be preferred to Old Church Slavonic or Byzantine ones, because of being written closer to the main events of Moravian history. The idea that Moravia was south and not north of the Danube River is thus the result of a thorough analysis of the geographical indications of the *Annals of Fulda* and of ninth-century charters allowing the reconstruction of the itinerary of Arnulf's trip to the eastern marches in preparation for war with the Moravian prince Svatopluk (Zwentibald) in the 880s.[40] But the author of the *Annals* wrote at a considerable distance from the events narrated, and his concept of East Central European geography is at best approximate. Moreover, Arnulf's movements along the eastern border of the Empire may well have followed the movements of Svatopluk and his troops. What the charters cannot in fact tell is whether Svatopluk and his warriors were moving into Pannonia from Moravia in present-day Czech Republic or from their presumed headquarters around Sirmium, in present-day Serbia.

There are several reasons for rejecting Boba's thesis and not including Moravia into the present history of early medieval Southeastern Europe. First, the testimony of the earliest monuments of Old Church Slavonic literature should not be dismissed on grounds of late manuscript transmission. If the evidence of the *Life of Constantine* fits in well with what we know from independent sources about the history of the ninth-century Khazar qaganate, then there

[40] The most elegant presentation of these arguments is in Bowlus, "Imre Boba's reconsiderations." To date, these arguments have received no rebuttal. Essential to Bowlus's argument is the fact that the author of the *Annals of Fulda* employs the term Margus to refer to the river Morava. Bowlus maintains that Margus was the ancient name for the southern Morava River, while the northern one was always called Marus.

is little reason to raise doubts about the information the two biographies provide for the history of ninth-century Moravia. True, there is absolutely no indication in either the *Life of Constantine* or the *Life of Methodius* of just how the two brothers got to Moravia in 863. There is no itinerary, no place names, and absolutely no other kind of information about the trip itself. However, the *Life of Methodius* provides indirect evidence that Moravia in which he served as archbishop between 873 and 885 cannot have been the region of Sirmium. First, Methodius is said to have met a "Hungarian king" at some point during his trip to or from Constantinople in 881 or 882. The "king" had apparently "come to the lands of the Danube," where he received Methodius "with honor, solemnity, and joy" and showered him with many gifts.[41] Had Methodius been on his way to Constantinople from Sirmium, he would have had no need to travel along the Lower Danube, through a region that contemporary sources suggest was under the control of the Magyars. The easiest way for him to reach the capital of the Empire was to cross Bulgaria – in which the ruler had recently converted to Christianity and was therefore hardly hostile – from northwest to southeast along the old imperial road from Sirmium to Constantinople via Serdica (Sofia) and Philippopolis (Plovdiv). He would have left the Danube behind him, with little, if any, chance to meet a Magyar "king" on his way. By contrast, he could have certainly met the "king" if he was coming from farther north, across the Hungarian Plain, and needed to cross the Danube at some point in the Belgrade region. According to the *Life of St. Clement of Ohrid* (most probably written by Archbishop Theophylact of Ohrid [1050–1126]), this is exactly the route followed by Methodius' disciples Clement, Naum, and Angelarius, after their expulsion from Moravia in 885. They came to the Danube from the north, crossed the river at Belgrade, and continued their trip to Pliska, in northeastern Bulgaria.[42]

Second, the author of the *Life of Methodius*, in an attempt to show that "Methodius also possessed the gift of prophesy, for many of his prophesies came to pass," refers to a message that his hero had sent to "a very powerful pagan prince settled on the Vistula," who was apparently persecuting Christians. Methodius warned him that

[41] Kantor, *Medieval Slavic Lives*, p. 125.

[42] Theophylact of Ohrid, *Life of St. Clement of Ohrid* 16.47, ed. by N. L. Tunickij (London: Variorum reprints, 1972), p. 114.

it would be wiser to accept baptism willingly, than to be attacked and forced into baptism "as a prisoner in a foreign land."[43] Methodius' prophecy was apparently fulfilled, as the pagan prince was eventually attacked and captured by Svatopluk. The mention of the Vistula River is a strong argument in favor of locating Moravia not south, but north of the river Danube.

There is also a sharp contrast in the archaeological record of the two regions. The rise of ninth-century Moravia followed the destruction of the Avar qaganate by the Frankish armies through a number of expeditions, only one of which was led by Charlemagne himself, between 791 and 795. The conquest drove a sharp political edge in Central Europe and opened a long period of Carolingian intervention into the northern and northwestern regions of Southeastern Europe, with considerable consequences, both politically and religiously. However, in the aftermath of the collapse of the Avar qaganate, there was no wholesale occupation of the Carpathian Basin by the Frankish troops. Instead, the eastern and southern territories of the former qaganate may have fallen under Bulgar control. In addition, a number of peripheral regions in the northwest (Slovakia and Moravia), as well as the south (Vojvodina and northern Serbia) became practically independent, struggling to maintain that status between the main powers, which were now filling the political vacuum created after the destruction of the qaganate *c.* 800. The archaeological evidence that could be dated with some degree of certainty to the early ninth century points to dramatic changes taking place in the northwestern region, where Frankish fashions, weapons, and horse gear spread rapidly in an area previously controlled by the Avars. Spur finds cluster in the same region north of the Middle Danube River where the first strongholds appeared shortly before or after AD 800 (Mikulčice, Staré Město, Uherské Hradište, Pohansko). Carolingian swords found in male burials of the so-called Blatnica–Mikulčice group indicate a shift from the mounted combat tactics so typical of nomadic warfare to heavy cavalry equipment. The exquisite decoration of the sword hilt and pommel found in Blatnica (Slovakia) betrays a product of some Frankish artisan from the Rhineland. Much like his contemporaries in Carantania, the high-status warrior in Blatnica was buried together with his belt decorated with cast mounts in a style reminiscent of the fashions and social symbolism of

[43] *Life of Methodius* 11, in Kantor, *Medieval Slavic Lives*, p. 121.

the Late Avar period. The blending of traditions is also evident in the disappearance of cremation burials and the introduction of inhumation as the dominant rite pointing to strong influences from both Avar and Frankish burial rites. Present-day Czech Moravia also produced evidence of manors, economic and social units apparently modeled after Carolingian aristocratic courts. In Pohansko, near Břeclav, one such unit was included within the ramparts of a very large hillfort of some sixty-nine acres, which was located on an island surrounded by the meanders of the river Dyje. The manor had separate buildings for the lord and his family, on the one hand, and, on the other, for the workers, who lived both inside and outside the palisade separating the manor from the rest of the stronghold. In addition, the manor had a smithy and many storage facilities, as well as a church and a cemetery with more than 400 burials. In many aspects, but on a smaller scale, the situation in Pohansko reminds one of the large palatial complex erected in Pliska by the ninth-century rulers of Bulgaria.[44]

Such comparisons are not too far-fetched, as Moravia north of the Danube also shares with Bulgaria another puzzling feature of power representation. Thirty-five hoards of iron implements – agricultural and craft tools, horse gear, and weapons – are known so far from Moravia and the adjacent regions in Bohemia and Slovakia. Much like similar finds in Bulgaria, they were all found in or near important hillforts, sometimes in an archaeological context clearly marking their ritual significance. For example, one of the two hoards known from Mikulčice was found in a special pit dug under the apse of one of the ninth-century churches excavated on that site. Some hoards contain belt-strap ends and mounts, which are typically found in burial assemblages of the Late Avar period, *c.* 750–780. The presence of belt sets suggests that hoards were in some way related to social status, for the primary purpose of belts found with Late Avar burials was social rank representation. Late Avar connections are also revealed by the number and types of battle-axes found in both hoards and contemporary

[44] B. Dostál, *Břeclav–Pohansko. Velkomoravský velmožsky dvorec* [Břeclav–Pohansko. A Moravian Princely Manor] (Brno: Univerzita J. E. Purkyne, 1975); J. Macháček, "Břeclav–Pohansko," in *Europe's Centre around AD 1000*, ed. by A. Wieczorek and H.-M. Hienz (Stuttgart: Theiss, 2000), pp. 210–211; and "Pohansko bei Břeclav – ein bedeutendes Zentrum Grossmährens," in *Velká Morava meži východem a západem. Sborník příspevku z mežinárodní vedecke conference. Uherské Hradište, Staré Město, 28.9.–1.10.1999*, ed. by L. Galuška, P. Kouřil, and Z. Meřínský (Brno: Archeologický ústav Akadémie věd Česke Respubliky, 2001), pp. 275–290.

warrior burials. By contrast, no Carolingian swords were found in hoards, despite their relatively frequent deposition in such burials. The presence of multiple stirrups and bridle bits in each hoard suggests that such accumulations were thought of as the equivalent of burials with multiple horse skeletons, which were also typical of the Late Avar period. The kind of warfare represented in hoards was mounted shock combat. Other hoards contain slightly concave iron pans, believed to be some sort of standardized token, the intermediary stage between iron blooms and final products. Their standardized form and size, as well as the absence of any evidence of further processing of such pans into finished artifacts – tools or weapons – suggest a different interpretation. Iron pans may have played a role similar to that of axe-shaped bars, which also appear in great numbers in hoards. A study based on the factorial analysis of the main attributes of a large number of bars showed a strong correlation between length and weight, which suggests that bars were manufactured as standard units of raw material.[45] They were made in a restricted range of weights, usually equivalent to some division of the Roman pound. This further suggests that, like iron pans, axe-shaped bars served as a means of "storing" and displaying wealth, in other words as currency. Hoards of iron implements were thus more than simple collections of iron tools and weapons with intrinsic value. The items in these hoards seem to have been carefully chosen according to a predetermined set of beliefs. The symbolic value of several artifact categories is indicated by their extensive use in mortuary assemblages. Tools and weapons collected in Moravian hoards were symbols of wealth, power, and prestige. It has been suggested that the very "destruction" (i.e., burial and non-retrieval) of such hoards was a form of surrogate warfare known to anthropologists as "potlatch". The deposition of weapons in hoards played a role equivalent to the military posturing associated with fortified sites and to high social rank. The political turmoil and constant warfare which were typical of the ninth-century history of Moravia may have resulted in competitive accumulation and deposition of items in hoards, in order to reinforce prestige.

Nothing of the sort is known from the southern region of the Carpathian Basin along the Morava River, now in northern

[45] A. Tirpaková, D. Bialeková, and I. Vlkolinská, "The application of some mathematic-statistical methods in solving the possibility of exploitation of Roman measures in manufacturing of Slavic axe-shaped currency bars and pottery," *Slovenská Archeológia*, vol. 37 (1989), pp. 427–450.

Serbia, eastern Croatia, and northeastern Bosnia. As we have seen in the preceding chapter, several finds of gold, including the famous Sânnicolaul Mare hoard, indicate that a regional center of power certainly existed in this area during the Late Avar period. But no Avar cemetery excavated in the region continued into the ninth century and no Carolingian swords or any other kind of artifacts associated with high status have so far been found there.[46] The very few hoards of iron implements that could be compared to those of Czech Moravia were all found within early Byzantine sites briefly and sporadically reoccupied during the ninth and tenth centuries, an archaeological context that strongly suggests links with Bulgaria, in which many such forts were repaired to serve, perhaps, as regional centers of power. In other words, the hoards themselves and the archaeological context in which they were found suggest a presence of Bulgar social practices, not of Moravians. Several settlements excavated by Serbian archaeologists in northern Serbia can be dated with some degree of certainty to the ninth century, mainly on the basis of the associated pottery. However, unlike Czech Moravia, Vojvodina produced no evidence of hillforts, only rural, open settlements. The southern region of the Carpathian Basin was clearly not as sparsely populated during the 800s as the area between the Danube and Tisza Rivers in central Hungary, but there were no centers of power to be compared with the formidable hillforts of Czech Moravia. Moreover, the episcopal church in Sremska Mitrovica (Sirmium), too hastily identified by Boba and his advocates with the church in which Methodius' body was laid to rest in 885, proved to be an eleventh-century foundation.

During the 800s, the religious centers closest to the southern territories were those of the Slavic polity in the Balaton Lake region ruled by Pribina. Attacked and expelled from his homeland north of the Danube by a Moravian prince named Moimir, Pribina had fled to one of the border lords in the eastern marches of the Carolingian Empire, who presented him to King Louis the German. According to the *Conversion of the Bavarians and the Carantanians*, our main source for these events, Pribina received baptism, and after some adventures taking him to the Bulgars, and then to a Slavic principality on the Sava River, he was granted the lands near the Balaton Lake and "began to live there, to build a fortification in the forest and swamps on the Zala

[46] Z. Vinski, "Zu karolingischen Schwertfunden aus Jugoslawien," *Jahrbuch des Römisch-Germanischen Zentralmuseums*, vol. 30 (1983), p. 466 fig. 1.

river, to bring together people from the surrounding region, and to be enriched greatly in this land."[47] At Pribina's request, the archbishop of Salzburg consecrated a number of churches in Pannonia, among them that of Pécs in southern Hungary. Upon the death of Constantine in 869, his brother Methodius was appointed papal legate and sent to Pribina's domain, now under the rule of Pribina's son Kocel, in order to organize the church structure in Lower Pannonia. Kocel welcomed the prospect of an archbishopric as a bar to the archbishop of Salzburg's right to intervene in Pannonian affairs. It is in fact under such circumstances that an unknown author wrote the *Conversion of the Bavarians and the Carantanians* to support the claims of the archbishop of Salzburg against Methodius' claims of authority over Pannonia. It is also under these circumstances, specifically at the request of Kocel, that Pope Hadrian II appointed Methodius archbishop of the restored see of Sirmium. By such means, the pope seems to have planned the restoration of the see as it had existed in the sixth century, with full jurisdiction over the regions that were now under the archbishop of Salzburg. In other words, Methodius was now in charge of a wide area in the Middle Danube region, and not just of the see of Sirmium. In fact, it is unlikely that Methodius ever resided in Sirmium (Sremska Mitrovica), where, to judge from the archaeological excavations carried out so far on the site, no medieval church and settlement existed before AD 1000. Apparently, Pribina's efforts in the 840s had not resulted in the construction of churches farther south or southeast from Pécs.

CROATS AND CROATIA

Even before the collapse of the qaganate, Charlemagne's victories against the Avars had triggered internecine strife within the Avar polity. By the time the first Frankish troops entered the Carpathian

[47] *Conversio Bagoariorum et Carantanorum* 10 and 11, pp. 120 and 122. For Pécs during the ninth century, see F. Fülep, "Beiträge zur frühmittelalterlichen Geschichte von Pécs (Sopianae–Quinque basilicae–Fünfkirchen)," *AAASH*, vol. 25 (1973), pp. 307–326. Pribina's center was in the fortress of Mosapurc, now Zalavár, on the southwestern shore of Lake Balaton. See B. M. Szöke, "The Carolingian *civitas* Mosapurc (Zalavár)," in *Europe's Centre around AD 1000*, ed. by A. Wieczorek and H.-M. Hinz (Stuttgart: Theiss, 2000), pp. 140–142; and "Neue Ergebnisse der Ausgrabungen in Mosaburg–Zalavár (West-Ungarn)," in *Zwischen Byzanz und Abendland. Pliska, der östliche Balkanraum und Europa im Spiegel der Frühmittelalterarchäologie*, ed. by J. Henning (Frankfurt am Main: Johann Wolfgang Goethe Universität, 1999), pp. 23–26.

Basin, there were already Slavic leaders acting independently against the Avars, such as a certain Vonimir who participated in the campaign of 796.[48] The isolated warrior burials found in Medvedička (Croatia), on the right bank of the Drava river, and in Csánig, in western Hungary, may also be linked to the events leading to the collapse of the Avar qaganate. In both cases, the male skeletons were associated with long, Carolingian swords indicating the high status of the deceased, perhaps members of the local elites in the service of Eric, the Frankish margrave of Friuli, who had led the campaign of 796.

The Frankish involvement in the northern Adriatic region predates by a few decades the collapse of the Avar qaganate. At some point between 780 and 787, Istria had fallen under Frankish control, a situation first acknowledged by the Byzantines in 798. By 805, the Franks had also intervened in internal disputes in Venice in order to establish their authority in the entire north Adriatic region. Hostilities with Byzantium broke in 806. By 810, a fleet under the command of the military governor of Cephalonia entered the northern Adriatic waters and quickly regained Dalmatia and Venice for the Empire. Through the peace of Aachen (812), the Byzantines retained Dalmatia and Venice, while acknowledging Frankish control of the Dalmatian hinterland and of Istria, both adjacent to territories under Frankish rule near or within the former qaganate. Indeed, envoys from several Slavic polities emerging on the fringes of the former qaganate appeared in 818 at the court of Louis the Pious in Herstal. One of them was Borna, the "duke of Dalmatia and Liburnia," who ruled over the Guduscani, a Slavic tribe on the western border of the Avar qaganate, in what is today Gačka, the region of Croatia between the upper Kupa River and the Dalmatian coast.[49] Another Slavic duke, Liudewit, whom the author of the *Royal Frankish Annals* calls a "schemer and agitator," ruled over the southern region of the Carpathian Basin from his stronghold in Sisak on the Sava River. He seems to have been a Frankish client not much different from Pribina, and his fortress at Sisak certainly was as strong as

[48] *Royal Frankish Annals*, s.a. 796, ed. by F. Kurze (Hanover: Hahnsche Buchhandlung, 1895), MGH 6:98. See Bowlus, *Franks, Moravians*, p. 55.

[49] *Royal Frankish Annals*, s.a. 818, p. 149. Borna may have acceded to his position of power during the last decades of the qaganate. See N. Budak, "Die südslawischen Ethnogenesen an der östlichen Adriaküste im frühen Mittelalter," in *Typen der Ethnogenese unter besonderer Berücksichtigung der Bayern*, ed. by H. Wolfram and W. Pohl, vol. 1 (Vienna: Verlag der Österreichischen Akademie der Wissenschaften, 1990), p. 135.

Mosapurc.[50] In Herstal, Liudewit accused the Frankish margrave of Friuli of "brutality and arrogance." However, since charges were also levied against him by Borna, Emperor Louis eventually rejected Liudewit's claims. He rebelled against the Franks in 819 and attacked the neighboring territory of Borna. Two interventions by Frankish armies from Italy and Bavaria could not quell the revolt, particularly because the Carantanians had also rebelled against their Bavarian overlords, perhaps coordinating their efforts with Liudewit's. Liudewit managed to defeat the Guduscani, forcing Borna to withdraw, together with his retinue of warriors, into one of his strongholds on the Dalmatian coast, perhaps in Vinodol, opposite the island of Krk, where Croatian archaeologists excavated a cemetery, perhaps belonging to a center of power yet to be identified.[51] At any rate, both Borna and Liudewit seem to have ruled over territories that, much like contemporary Moravia, had a number of strong hillforts established at key points, either on the coast or at the confluence of major rivers. In Liudewit's case, instrumental for his ability to erect such strongholds was the assistance he received from Patriarch Fortunatus of Grado in the form of craftsmen and builders.[52]

In 820, Louis the Pious dispatched three armies from Italy and Bavaria, "in order to lay waste Liudewit's territory and curb his pretensions."[53] Liudewit withdrew to Sisak, and only new attacks in 821 and 822, respectively, eventually managed to dislodge him from his stronghold. He found refuge with the Serbs, "a people that is said to hold a large part of Dalmatia," but was later murdered under

[50] H. Wolfram, "Liudewit und Priwina (ein institutioneller Vergleich)," in *Interaktionen der mitteleuropäischen Slawen und anderer Ethnika im 6.–10. Jahrhundert. Symposium Nové Vozokany 3.–7. Oktober 1983*, ed. by P. Šalkovský (Nitra: Archäologisches Institut der Slowakischen Akademie der Wissenschaften, 1984), pp. 291–296. Unlike Pribina, though, Liudewit was under the tutelage of the margrave of Friuli.

[51] R. Matejčić, "Istraživanje dijela starohrvatske nekropole u Velom Dolu kod Križišča o Vinodolu [Archaeological excavation of the Old Croatian cemetery at Veli Dol near Križišča in Vinodol]," *Histria Archaeologica*, vol. 5 (1974), pp. 7–25; H. M. A. Evans, *The Early Medieval Archaeology of Croatia AD 600–900* (Oxford: BAR, 1989), p. 306.

[52] *Royal Frankish Annals*, s.a. 821, p. 155.

[53] *Royal Frankish Annals*, s.a. 820, p. 152; English translation by B. W. Scholz and B. Rogers (Ann Arbor: University of Michigan Press, 1970), pp. 106–107. For the routes followed by the Carolingian armies, see Bowlus, *Franks, Moravians*, pp. 63–69.

unknown circumstances by Borna's uncle.[54] Nothing is known about later developments within the region along the Sava River over which Liudewit had ruled for some years. By contrast, Frankish sources clearly show that in the following years Carantania was fully integrated into the duchy of Bavaria, with Frankish counts replacing the native princes under the reign of Louis the German.

Modern approaches to the history of the Balkans during the ninth century tend to focus attention upon two ethnic groups first mentioned during that period, the Serbs and the Croats. While the former appear several times in the Frankish annals, there is no mention of Croats in Carolingian or ninth-century Byzantine sources. The key source used by most historians to fill in this gap is *De administrando imperio*. The most important source for the early history of both Croats and Serbs is a series of chapters (29 to 36) written in 948 or 949, with the exception of the later interpolation of chapter 30, which was most likely composed by another author after Emperor Constantine's death in 959. As a consequence, the work remained unedited, with great discrepancies between chapters 29, 31, and 32, on the one hand, and 30, on the other, that are at the core of the great controversies surrounding the interpretation of Emperor Constantine's work as a source for the early medieval history of the Balkans. The basic problem is the presence of two substantially different accounts of the same event, the purported migration of the Croats. The version of events given in chapter 30 looks very much like a legendary account, which was viewed as, and may well be, a "native" version of ethnic history, perhaps collected by a Byzantine informant in one of the Dalmatian cities under Byzantine control throughout the ninth and early tenth century. Equally "native" seems to be the story of the migration of the Serbs, which may have originated in some Serbian account. All this is in sharp contrast with the other version of events given in chapter 31. Constantine's insistence in this chapter upon rejecting Frankish claims of suzerainty over Croatia raised early suspicions about political bias. Indeed, Constantine mentions the defeat of Prince Boris of Bulgaria by the Croats, but has no word for the major confrontation between King Symeon of Bulgaria and Prince Tomislav of Croatia, which happened in his own lifetime (926). This further suggests that the account in chapter 31 is biased against both

[54] *Royal Frankish Annals*, s.a. 822 and 823, pp. 158 and 161; English translation by Scholz and Rogers, pp. 111 and 113.

Frankish claims and Croatian independent tendencies, all in order to stress the Byzantine rights to the lands of the Croats. Many historians thus reject the version given in chapter 31 as Constantine's figment, while embracing chapter 30 as the only trustworthy source for early Croat history.

One of the most contentious issues raised by chapter 31 is the mention of Emperor Heraclius helping the Croats in settling in Dalmatia and ordering their conversion to Christianity. By contrast, the "Croat version" in chapter 30 has the Croats coming to Dalmatia as part of a story of five brothers (one of whom is appropriately called Chrobatos, "the Croat") and two sisters who fought their way to the new homeland, after defeating the Avars. The story is remarkably similar to the account of the Bulgar migration to be found in Theophanes and Nicephorus, and at least one historian has been tempted to identify Chrobatos as Kubrat (Koubratos).[55] Both chapters 30 and 31 place the homeland of the Croats somewhere in Central Europe, near Bavaria, beyond Hungary, and next to the Frankish Empire. In both cases, we are told that Croats, "also called 'white'," are still living in that region.[56] "White" Croatia is mentioned by several other, independent sources, such as King Alfred the Great's translation of Orosius' *History of the World*, tenth-century Arab geographers (Gaihani, Ibn-Rusta, and Masudi), the *Russian Primary Chronicle*, and Emperor Henry IV's charter for the bishopric of Prague. Since none of these sources, and no other information about Croats, could be dated earlier than the mid-ninth century, historians now tend to attribute the story of the Croat migration from White Croatia to an attempt to rationalize a political and ethnic situation in the light of what was known in Constantinople in the mid-tenth century about the geography of Central Europe. That *De administrando imperio* may contain the first record of a "native" version of the past is not easy to dispute. But there is little substance in the story that could have value

[55] H. Grégoire, "L'origine et le nom des Croates et des Serbes," *Byzantion*, vol. 17 (1944–1945), pp. 88–118. The parallel between the "Croat version" in chapter 30 and the account of the Bulgar migration in Theophanes and Nicephorus is discussed by W. Pohl, "Das Awarenreich und die 'kroatischen' Ethnogenesen," in *Die Bayern und ihre Nachbarn. Berichte des Symposiums der Kommission fur Fruhmittelalterforschung 25. bis 28. Oktober 1982, Stift Zwettl, Niederosterreich*, ed. by H. Wolfram and A. Schwarcz, vol. 1 (Vienna: Verlag der Österreichischen Akademie der Wissenschaften, 1985), pp. 293–298; Margetić, *Dolazak Hrvata*, pp. 200–208.

[56] Constantine Porphyrogenitus, *De administrando imperio* 31, pp. 146–147; 30, pp. 142–143.

for understanding the rise of medieval Croatia or the early history of the Croats.

The first mention of the name is in a charter of a duke of the Croats named Trpimir, which is dated to March 4, 852, but survives only in a copy of 1568. The charter mentions Trpimir's decision, taken in consultation with his noblemen (called *iupani* in the original Latin, most likely a corruption of *zhupans*) and court dignitaries, to build a monastery at Rižinice, not far from the old Roman city of Salona.[57] Although doubts could be, and were indeed, raised about the authencity of this charter, Trpimir's name is mentioned in a fragmentary inscription on a gable arch from an altar screen of the Rižinice monastery church.[58] Furthermore, a controversial theologian of the mid-ninth century, Godescalc of Orbais, spent some time at Trpimir's court between 846 and 848, after leaving Venice and before moving to Bulgaria. In his work, Godescalc describes Trpimir's accomplishments, especially his victory over a Byzantine *patricius*, perhaps an unknown *archon* of Dalmatia residing in Zadar. He also has some interesting comments about the Latin language in use in Trpimir's entourage, which apparently was closer to the Romance in use in coastal cities in Dalmatia than to the "learned" Latin Godescalc had come to master.[59] Trpimir's son, Sedesclav (Zdeslav), was deposed by a local nobleman called Domagoj and fled to Constantinople.

[57] *Codex diplomaticus regni Croatiae, Dalmatiae et Slavoniae*, ed. by T. Smičiklas, vol. 1 (Zagreb, 1967), pp. 4–5. The sixteenth-century copy of Trpimir's charter is now in the parish archive of Kaštel Sućurac in the diocese of Split. See J. Stipišić, "Croatia in diplomatic sources up to the end of the 11th century," in *Croatia in the Early Middle Ages. A Cultural Survey*, ed. by I. Supičić (London: Philip Wilson Publishers and Zagreb: AGM, 1999), pp. 287 and 288–289.

[58] M. Matijević-Sokol, "Latin inscriptions," in *Croatia in the Early Middle Ages. A Cultural Survey*, ed. by I. Supičić (London: Philip Wilson Publishers and Zagreb: AGM, 1999), p. 242. The inscription reads "PRO DUCE TREPIME [. . .]" which is taken as "pro duce Trepimero." The gable arch is decorated with so-called "egg-and-dart" motives, which are identical to those of other sculptural fragments found in various other places in Croatia, a possible indication of itinerant stonemasons. See I. Petricioli, "Sculpture from the 8th to the 11th century," in *Croatia in the Early Middle Ages. A Cultural Survey*, ed. by I. Supičić (London: Philip Wilson Publishers and Zagreb: AGM, 1999), p. 480.

[59] Godescalc of Orbais, *Responsa de diversis*, ed. by C. Lambot (Louvain: Spicilegium sacrum Lovaniense, 1945), p. 169. For his comments on the differences between Latin and Dalmatian Romance, see *De praedestinatione* 6, p. 208. A Saxon by birth, Godescalc had left his homeland and gone to Italy in 846. He was in Friuli for a while, then moved offshore to Venice. He then spent some time in Byzantine Dalmatia, perhaps in Zadar, before going to Croatia.

Domagoj seems to have been the organizer of a rebellion against the Frankish overlordship. Pope John VIII wrote to him in *c.* 873, complaining about the fact that the patriarch of Constantinople, Photius, had taken Bulgaria under his jurisdiction. The reason for the pope's sharing such concerns with a Croatian prince is that Bulgaria apparently bordered Croatia in some part of present-day Bosnia. One or two years later, the pope wrote again to Domagoj, asking him to curb the assaults of his pirates on Christian sailors, an indication of the growing power of the Croatian ruler not just on land, but also at sea. In another letter to the faithful living in the lands of the Slavs, John VIII complained about Domagoj ordering the execution of a conspirator, despite his promise previously given to a papal legate that he would spare his life. Apparently, by 875, the papacy was as present in Croatia through its delegates as in any other contemporary country. At Domagoj's death in 876, Sedesclav returned from Constantinople and briefly aligned Croatia to the Byzantine policies in the Adriatic region. Pope John VIII wrote to Sedesclav as well, asking him to provide assistance to his legate crossing Croatia on his way to Bulgaria. By that time, another local nobleman, named Branimir, had risen up against Sedesclav. Branimir (879–892) appears in no less than five Latin inscriptions. One of them was found in Nin and calls Branimir a "duke of the Slavs," while another from Šopot near Benkovac has him as "duke of the Croats."[60] A third inscription with Branimir's name was found in Muć Gornji near Split and contains the date of the consecration, AD 888.[61] Pope John VIII wrote to Branimir as well to thank him for returning the country to the Roman fold. Apparently, following his victory over Sedesclav, Branimir had sent a letter to the pope expressing his allegiance to Rome. In return, Pope John VIII acknowledged the independence of Branimir's principality and called him "a most excellent man." By 890, another son of Trpimir, Muncimir, suceeded Branimir as "duke of the Croats," a title mentioned in his charter of September 28, 892, which, like

[60] *Namentragende Steininschriften in Jugoslawien vom Ende des 7. bis zur Mitte des 13. Jahrhunderts*, ed. by R. Mihaljčić, L. Steindorff, and M. Helmann (Wiesbaden: Franz Steiner, 1982), pp. 7, 17, and 33. One of the inscriptions mentioning Branimir as duke of the Slavs was found in Ždrapanj near Skradin and was erected by a certain Pristina bearing the title of "iupanus" (*zhupan*). See I. Goldstein, *Hrvatski rani srednji vijek* [The Early Middle Ages in Croatia] (Zagreb: Zavod za hrvatsku povijest Filozofskog fakulteta Sveučilišta u Zagrebu, 1995), pp. 262, 264, and 266.

[61] Matijević-Sokol, "Latin inscriptions," pp. 242–243.

that of Trpimir, only survives in a sixteenth-century copy.[62] Among witnesses mentioned at the end of the 892 charter, there are several court dignitaries bearing such titles as court *zhupan* or princess's *zhupan*. Muncimir is also mentioned as the founder of a local church in an inscription on a triangular gable arch found in Uzdolje near Knin, which is dated to 895.[63]

It has long been noted that in the earliest "native" sources available (such as charters and inscriptions), the early dukes or princes refer to themselves as rulers of the people, not of the country. Given that one and the same duke, Branimir, was the ruler of both Slavs and Croats, some have concluded that the name "Croat" referred not to ethnic identity, but to an elite.[64] The "Croats" over whom Duke Branimir ruled at the same time as over the Slavs were the members of the emerging noble class, the people who are otherwise mentioned as *zhupans* in the charters. If true, this interpretation would dovetail nicely with the conclusions to be drawn from the analysis of the archaeological evidence. The material culture identified in the cemeteries of the so-called "Old Croatian culture" bespeaks the sudden affirmation *c.* 800 of a powerful elite in the political and military context of the Frankish encroachment in the northwestern part of the Balkans. This affirmation coincided in time with the spread of Christianity and the gradual conversion of the Croat aristocracy. Very little is known about the circumstances of the latter, except that, unlike all other neighboring regions of Southeastern and Central Europe, no evidence exists of a forceful imposition of the new religion. Most likely, in Croatia Christianity was willingly adopted as part and parcel of the cultural "package" introduced into the region by the Carolingian encroachment. Judging by the archaeological evidence, there seem to have been no significant differences in either rhythm or results between different regions presumably under the authority of the earliest Croatian dukes. At any rate, the process seems to have been completed by the mid-ninth century. Nothing is

62 Stipišić, "Croatia in diplomatic sources," pp. 289–290. Mutimir's charter mentioned that of Trpimir dated to 852.

63 V. Delonga, "Natpis župana Ivana iz Uzdolja kod Knina [The inscription of zhupan John from Uzdolje near Knin]," *SP*, vol. 25 (1998), pp. 7–42.

64 Fine, "Croats and Slavs," pp. 212–215. The argument gains weight in the light of Huw Evans's remarks about the absence of any archaeological evidence pertaining to the migration of any group of people into present-day Croatia between *c.* 650 and *c.* 800. See Evans, *Early Medieval Archaeology*, pp. 156–158.

known about its beginnings, although saint names appearing in early church dedications (St. Marcella, St. Anselm, St. Ambrose) suggest a strong influence of the see of Aquileia.[65] An early ninth-century silver incense burner from the ruins of a church near the headwaters of the Cetina River points to the Rhineland as a possible place of origin of the liturgical instruments brought by the earliest missionaries, but it remains unknown whether early missions came from Aquileia, from Salzburg, or some other see within the Empire. Benedictine monasteries appear very early in Croatia, as indicated by Duke Trpimir's charter of 852, as well as by the reference to a certain abbot Theudebertus in Branimir's inscription from Nin. Nin is also linked to the beginnings of medieval church architecture in Croatia. The plan of the Church of the Holy Cross, built shortly before AD 800, is very similar to centrally planned buildings in and around Ravenna, and to other Carolingian structures, such as the octagonal chapel of the palace in Aachen. The church must have been built at the order of the local ruler, though no dedicatory inscription survives. Elsewhere in contemporary Croatia, inscriptions testify to the role of local *zhupans* as patrons.[66] Often the church itself was located, like in Pohansko, in the middle of an already existing settlement, perhaps the very residence of the local ruler. Excavations carried out in the immediate vicinity of the Church of the Holy Cross in Nin have revealed parts of previous buildings, including sunken-floored features dated to the eighth century by means of an associated belt-strap end with clear parallels in Late Avar burial assemblages in Hungary.

Nin has also produced the largest and, to date, richest cemetery of the ninth century, situated on a small peninsula, called Ždrijač, protruding from the island into the sea. Over 400 burials have been found, many of which produced no grave goods whatsoever. By

[65] A baptismal font with a Latin inscription mentioning a certain duke Višeslav (Vuissasclavus) that was found in Nin in 1746 has long been viewed as the first piece of evidence pertaining to the conversion of the Croats. However, the date advanced for the inscription (early ninth century) was established only on the basis of the stylistical analysis of the sculpted decoration. As a consequence, not all scholars agreed with an early date for this Nin font. See Matijević-Sokol, "Latin inscriptions," pp. 240–241.

[66] E.g., *zhupan* Gastika mentioned in a dedicatory inscription from the ninth-century Church of Sv. Spas (St. Savior) near the headwaters of the Cetina River. See V. Delonga, "Donatorski natpis župana Gostihe iz crkve Sv. Spasa u Cetini (Vrh Riči) [Dedicatory inscription of the district prefect Gostiha, donor of the Church of the Savior in Cetina (Vrh Rika)]," *SP*, vol. 22 (1995), pp. 117–140.

contrast, others were exceptionally rich. The cemetery stands out from all others in Croatia by its richness and diversity of grave goods, many of which point to a date within the first half of the ninth century. Given the presence in one burial of a silver denar minted in Italy for Lothar I (817–845), the cemetery seems to have continued into the second half of the ninth century, but no later than *c.* 900. It represents therefore a community of "Croats" associated with the rising center of power at Nin, which was also the first bishopric of Croatia. The "Croats" were buried within the same graveyard as much poorer members of the community. To judge by the great number of burials with no grave goods, social differentiation must have been quite advanced in Nin, although the exact mechanisms whereby the "Croats" acquired their position of prominence remain unknown. The cemetery itself provides some hints, but the picture must have been much more complex. Prominent among the rich assemblages is a family burial, containing the skeletons of a male, a female, and a child. The male skeleton was buried with complete military equipment, including Carolingian sword and spurs, as well as with luxury items, such as two exquisite glass vessels of Syrian origin. The man buried together with his wife and child may have been a local chieftain, but what is remarkable about this burial is how similar the representation of power is to contemporary assemblages in Moravia. Moreover, a good number of Carolingian sword finds from Croatia, which cluster in the region between the Zrmanja and Cetina Rivers, away from the coast, were associated with spurs with damascened decoration reminiscent of the Blatnica–Mikulčice group of burials. A hoard of iron implements, including a Carolingian spearhead with damascened decoration, suggests that the representation of power may have taken forms very similar to those in existence in contemporary Moravia.[67] Much like in Moravia and Carantania, male burials in Croatia combine weapons of Carolingian origin with belt fittings or hollow containers of antler, both reminiscent of Late Avar fashions. As in Moravia, female burials are not as prominently equipped with symbols of power, though they are still rich in jewelry of Byzantine inspiration, if not origin. Byzantine coins, including gold coins struck for Emperor Constantine V, were also found in

[67] K. Simoni, "Skupni nalaz oruda i oružja iz Nartskih Novaka [A hoard of tools and weapons from Nartski Novak]," *Vjesnik Arheološkog Muzeja u Zagrebu*, vol. 15 (1982), pp. 251–266.

several assemblages, both in Nin and elsewhere. The martiality of the "Croats" was certainly not a mere pose. According to Constantine Porphyrogenitus, both Croats and "the other leaders of the Slavs" embarked in 870 on Ragusan ships to go to Italy and participate in the Byzantine conquest of Bari from the Arabs.[68] At that time, however, much like in contemporary Carantania, both weapons and accoutrements had disappeared from burial assemblages to make room for a more thorough phase of conversion to Christianity, associated with the abandonment of the old cemeteries and the beginning of church graveyards.

A number of churches were also erected at several points on the Dalmatian coast, which was throughout the ninth century under Byzantine control. Most prominent among them is the Church of St. Donat in Zadar, which was built over a part of the old Roman forum with many architectural and sculptural elements from the ruins of the ancient buildings it had obliterated. Built in the mid-eighth century, the six-conch church was soon imitated elsewhere on the coast in both plan and decoration. The amalgamation of architectural elements from both West and East is a feature typical of southern Dalmatia, but the Byzantine influence is most prominent in the modeling of the cupola and in the structural system with a cupola resting on four columns. The presence of Byzantium in the region was particularly strong during the second half of the century. Following the first raids of Arab pirates from Africa, who even besieged Dubrovnik (Ragusa) in 866, Emperor Basil I created a new theme on the eastern shore of the Adriatic Sea. The theme of Dalmatia, created in or shortly before 870, included all coastal towns and the islands along the coast. Its military governor resided in Zadar, a clear indication of the maritime orientation of the theme. There seems to have been little involvement in the hinterland of the coastal cities, many of which had to deal on their own with their Slavic neighbors. Pirates from the Neretva valley region had been very active in the Adriatic waters until a Venetian fleet destroyed their encampments in 839. However, when the theme of Dalmatia was created in 870, many local Slavic leaders quickly accepted the Byzantine overlordship and provided troops for the ongoing military operations in southern Italy. In exchange, according to Constantine Porphyrogenitus, Emperor Basil I allowed the Dalmatian towns to pay a part of the tribute initially sent to

[68] Constantine Porphyrogenitus, *De administrando imperio* 29, pp. 128–129.

Constantinople to the Slavic leaders (*archontes*) in the mountain region.[69] A mention is made of the rulers of Zahumlje and Trebinje, with their respective share of golden coins from the tribute formerly paid by Ragusa, but nothing more is said about the identity or political aspirations of the ninth-century elites in the interior.

Despite their early mention in Frankish annals, the ninth-century history of the Serbs is poorly understood. According to Constantine Porphyrogenitus, a chieftain of the Serbs named Vlastimir managed to defeat a Bulgar army at some point in the 840s. Although the emperor uses "Serbia" more than once in his *De administrando imperio*, it is altogether not clear where exactly was the chiefdom of Vlastimir. However, he is known to have married his daughter to Krainas, "son of Belaës, zhupan of Terbounia,"[70] an indication that his polity may have been in the hinterland of Trebinje, in the valleys of the upper Drin and Lim Rivers (southeastern Bosnia and southwestern Serbia). Vlastimir's sons, Mutimir, Strojmir, and Gojnik, defeated another Bulgar army sent against them by Boris, and even captured the son of the Bulgar ruler. Shortly hereafter, Mutimir took control of the chiefdom and pushed aside his brothers, who found refuge in neighboring Bulgaria. At some point during the first years of Emperor Basil I's reign, perhaps as a consequence of Bulgaria's recent conversion, Serbian envoys arrived in Constantinople requesting missionaries. When Mutimir became sole ruler, Gojnik's son Peter fled to Croatia, and so did his rival Prvoslav, Mutimir's son, when Peter defeated him in battle at some point in the 890s. That political rivals found it easier to move to Croatia than to Bulgaria is a strong indication that the Serbian polity may have also been a neighbor of the territory controlled by the dukes of the Croats. However, the absence of material culture correlates of power representation similar to those identified in Croatia makes it difficult to assess in similar terms whether "Serbs" is an ethnic or a social label. A number of eighth- to ninth-century cemeteries have been excavated in northern and northwestern Bosnia, just south of the Sava River, namely in the region to which Liudewit presumably fled after being dislodged from his stronghold in Sisak. Unlike contemporary mortuary assemblages in Croatia, there are no weapons associated primarily with the

[69] Constantine Porphyrogenitus, *De administrando imperio* 30, pp. 146–147.

[70] Constantine Porphyrogenitus, *De administrando imperio* 34, pp. 163–164. Terbounia is explicitly said to have stretched along the coast "as far as Ragusa" (Dubrovnik). See Constantine Porphyrogenitus, *De administrando imperio* 30, pp. 144–145.

representation of male power. However, much like in contemporary Bulgaria to the east, gender differences are particularly evident in the greater number and variety of grave goods, mainly dress accessories, found in female burials. At least one important hillfort has been identified in northwestern Bosnia at Vrbljani on the Sana River, and the finds from that site are in many ways comparable to those of the Dalmatian coast.[71] By contrast, no such finds are known from the eastern region of Bosnia and the central part of present-day Serbia. The ceramic assemblages from a number of settlements and cemeteries found around Knjaževac, near the Serbian–Bulgarian border, are remarkably similar to those of the better-researched region of the Danube valley to the north. Long-term excavations of the hillfort at Gradina near Pazarište, about six miles north of Novi Pazar, in southwestern Serbia, have revealed an early medieval occupation phase dated to the second half of the ninth century at the earliest. This is most likely the fortress of Ras on the western border of medieval Bulgaria, to which, according to Constantine Porphyrogenitus, Prince Boris was escorted after his defeat by Mutimir and his brothers in *c.* 860 AD.[72] Much like on contemporary sites in northeastern Bulgaria, the ninth-century inhabitants at Ras reused an early Byzantine hillfort by repairing some of its ramparts with drystone work and by adding palisades. The occupation consisted of a few houses scattered within the area enclosed by walls, mainly built against the ramparts. Besides locally manufactured pottery, the ceramic assemblages from Gradina include fragments of amphoroid jugs most typical of the region of Pliska and Preslav in northeastern Bulgaria. In the same direction point a few metal finds and potshards with Bulgar runic inscriptions. A neighboring hillfort at Gradina near Postenje has produced similar evidence of a ninth-century occupation. By contrast, at Gradina near Vrsenice, not far from the modern town of Sjenica (on the border with Montenegro), the ninth-century occupation phase

[71] I. Bojanovski, "Ranosrednjovjekovno utvrdenje u Vrbljanima na Sani [An early medieval hillfort in Vrbljani on the Sana River]," *Glasnik Zemaljskog Muzeja Bosne i Hercegovine u Sarajevu*, vol. 29 (1974), pp. 245–258. Besides Carolingian spurs, the site has produced a silver belt end with the Latin inscription "TETGIS FABER ME FECIT" ("Tetgis the artisan made me").

[72] Constantine Porphyrogenitus, *De administrando imperio* 32, pp. 154–155. For the Ras fortress, see M. Popović, *Tvrđava Ras* [The Fortress of Ras] (Belgrade: Arheološki Institut, 1999), pp. 139–161. The site was abandoned suddenly at some point before the end of the tenth century.

did not include any materials comparable to those of northeastern Bulgaria. From the distribution of ninth-century finds in the region, Marko Popović has drawn the conclusion that in the late 800s the region of Ras was a frontier district of Bulgaria, perhaps the seat of a local ruler controlling the upper course of the Lim River.[73] Gradina near Pazarište may thus be viewed as an archaeological illustration of the growing power of ninth-century Bulgaria reaching far into the central regions of the Balkans.

BULGARIA IN THE NINTH CENTURY

In the ninth century Bulgaria was a major European power, "the other Balkan empire."[74] However, historians are not willing to treat the polity of Krum, Omurtag, or Boris on a par with the mighty Carolingian or Byzantine states. The unstoppable Krum may well have moved freely in 813 under the very walls of Constantinople, "from Blachernai to the Golden Gate, exhibiting his forces," and without fear of any harm to himself or his troops.[75] The Bulgars may well have played more than an ephemeral role in Carolingian affairs.[76] Ultimately, the part in European history medievalists reserve for Bulgaria is still that of a second-hand power. A peculiar form of Orientalism may thus be responsible for the exclusion of pre-Christian Bulgaria from the medieval history of the European continent. On the other hand, the common opinion among Bulgarian historians is that from Krum to Boris, the Bulgar polity underwent drastic changes leading to its administrative, military, and political "modernization." In short, Bulgaria became a medieval state par excellence. The consolidation of power that accompanied these changes is commonly viewed as the result of Krum's successful implementation of a dynasty that would have no true contenders throughout the ninth century. No ruler is known to have been murdered after 814. Instead, the history of the

[73] Popović, *Tvrđava Ras*, pp. 400–401.

[74] J. Shepard, "Bulgaria: the other Balkan 'empire'," in *The New Cambridge Medieval History*, ed. by T. Reuter, vol. III (Cambridge: Cambridge University Press, 1999), pp. 567–585.

[75] Theophanes Confessor, *Chronographia*, p. 686.

[76] Much like the Vikings, the Bulgars accepted "bribes" from Charles the Bald "to move sharply against King Louis of Germany." See the *Annals of St. Bertin* a. 853, MGH 5:43, English translation by J. Nelson (Manchester: Manchester University Press, 1991), p. 77.

ninth century was marked by episodes of despotic behavior, such as Krum forcing his Slavic allies to drink from the skull of a defeated Byzantine emperor or Boris ruthlessly crushing the internal opposition to his conversion to Christianity. The building record of the ninth-century rulers is also interpreted as a sign of despotic power: "the Bulgar dikes [across Dobrudja] radiated the khans' glories across the cultural landscape they fashioned."[77]

However, the transformation of the Bulgar polity in the 800s was less about modernization and more about the (re-)"invention of traditions." A fragmentary inscription from an early Byzantine fort rebuilt in the ninth century on the right bank of the Lower Danube mentions the sacrifice Krum performed by the sea, perhaps the same "demonic sacrifices in the coastal meadow of the Golden Gate" that, according to Theophanes, Krum performed in 813 after moving under the walls of Constantinople, from Blachernai to the Golden Gate.[78] Whether he was acting on behalf of his entire army or just on his own, Krum's combination of military threat and manipulation of divine powers was certainly a novelty Theophanes thought worth mentioning in relation to what he viewed as the ridiculous behavior of the "new Sennacherib." Perhaps more important in this regard is that, according to Theophanes, following the raid on the Byzantine imperial palace at St. Mamas, Krum "loaded on carts the bronze lions of the hippodrome, the bear and the dragon of the fountain, as well as choice marbles," which he carried with him back home. It is not known where exactly Krum took the *spolia* from St. Mamas, but the conclusion seems inescapable that his intention was to reuse them in some other building of his own or, at least, display them as trophies. This is also a strikingly novel development, given that the only inhabitable structure in existence at that time at Pliska, where Krum may have had his more or less permanent residence, was the large yurt-like, circular wooden building discovered in 1981 in front of the stone

[77] P. Squatriti, "Moving earth and making difference: dikes and frontiers in early medieval Bulgaria," in *Borders, Barriers and Ethnogenesis in Late Antiquity and the Middle Ages*, ed. by F. Curta (Turnhout, 2005), p. 30.

[78] V. Beshevliev, *Die protobulgarischen Inschriften*, pp. 137–138 and 142–143; Theophanes, *Chronographia*, p. 686. This may well have been just a sacrificial killing of animals to an unnamed god (or gods), but a slightly later source also mentions human sacrifices. See Scriptor incertus, in Leo Grammaticus, *Chronographia*, ed. I. Bekker (Bonn: E. Weber, 1824), p. 342. See also I. Duichev, "Slaviano-bolgarskie drevnosti IX-go veka [Slavic–Bulgar ninth-century history]," *Byzantinoslavica*, vol. 11 (1950), pp. 16–17; Beshevliev, *Die protobulgarische Periode*, p. 375.

building otherwise known to Bulgarian archaeologists as "Omurtag's Palace."[79]

Krum came to power in unknown circumstances, perhaps in 802 or shortly before that. According to a late Byzantine source, a lexicon compiled around AD 1000 and known as the *Souda*, Krum was responsible for the collapse of the Avar qaganate, a story which many historians have interpreted as referring to the possible conquest by Krum's troops of the eastern and southern parts of the qaganate. In reality, all the information that we have about Avar–Bulgar relations in the aftermath of the collapse of the Avar qaganate refers to Avars joining the Bulgars, not to Bulgars conquering Avar territories. On the other hand, it is true that Krum's reign opened a period of more aggressive involvement of the Bulgars in the southern region of the former Avar qaganate, as well as in the neighboring areas, both north and south of the Danube River. However, in the early years of his reign, Krum's problems were elsewhere. In 807, Emperor Nicephorus prepared an attack on Bulgaria, but as soon as he reached Adrianople he learned of a conspiracy and had to return to Constantinople. One year later, the Bulgar troops fell on the Byzantine army stationed in the Strymon valley and seized the pay chest amounting to 1,100 pounds of gold. In 809, Krum attacked Serdica, which had been fortified and garrisoned by Nicephorus. A great number of civilians were killed, while a number of officers who had escaped deserted to the Bulgars. One of them was "the *spatharios* Eumathios, an expert in engines."[80] Like him, many would offer their services to Krum in the following decades. Emperor Nicephorus moved against Krum and retook the city, but faced with a revolt of the troops, returned quickly to Constantinople. He prepared for a new campaign in 811, this time apparently determined to destroy the Bulgar polity. A large army of thematic troops from Thrace and Asia Minor under the command of Nicephorus and his son Staurakios moved quickly across Thrace and the Stara Planina mountains in the direction of the "court" of Krum,

[79] R. Rashev and V. Docheva, "Iurtoobrazna postroika v Pliska [A yurt-like building in Pliska]," *Problemi na prabălgarskata istoriia i kultura*, vol. 1 (1989), pp. 291–313. For a second, slightly later yurt found in Pliska, see R. Rashev, "K rannei istorii prabolgar na Nizhnem Dunae [On the early history of the Bulgars in the Lower Danube region]," in *Novoe v srednevekovoi arkheologii Evrazii*, ed. by V. B. Kovalevskaia (Samara: Istoriko-kul'turnaia associaciia "Artefakt," 1993), pp. 185–186 and 190–191.

[80] Theophanes Confessor, *Chronographia*, p. 665.

most likely Pliska. The passes across the mountains were very poorly defended, but Nicephorus' army encountered some resistance on its way to Pliska. Following a number of Byzantine victories, Krum sued for peace, but Nicephorus rejected the demands. According to an eyewitness account of the campaign of 811, which was preserved in a Vatican manuscript, Pliska was not fortified and no Bulgars put up any resistance inside the ramparts that was worth mentioning. Krum himself had abandoned the site, leaving behind his entire treasure and cellars stacked with wine barrels. Nicephorus spent three days in Pliska, during which he ordered the massacre of "senseless animals, infants, and persons of all ages"[81] and began the distribution of the spoils to the soldiers. Krum's palace apparently had more than one story, as well as balconies, from which Nicephorus admired the view before setting fire to the compound, which was apparently made entirely of wood.[82] The emperor was looking for a decisive confrontation with Krum's army, without which no true success could be proclaimed. In the meantime, Krum had recruited Slavs and Avars and is said to have armed men, as well as women. He closed the passes across the Stara Planina and set a wooden barrier in one of them, perhaps the Beregaba (Rish) Pass. On July 25, 811, while crossing the mountains through that pass, the Byzantine army was ambushed and in the ensuing battle utterly defeated. Among the first to fall was Emperor Nicephorus himself, together with a great number of generals and high-ranking officers. The troops broke ranks and in the debacle entered into a mountain cul-de-sac, where they were slaughtered. The survivor of the 811 disaster who wrote the account of the expedition preserved in the Vatican manuscript describes in detail the barrier that the Bulgars had set in the pass, which was made of shafts tall enough to prevent anyone from climbing, with a deep ditch on the other side, into which many who did try to climb the barrier fell and shattered their bones. Those attempting to burn down an opening through the barrier floundered in the same ditch, filled with burning tree trunks, and perished miserably. The victory was complete and Krum ordered Nicephorus' corpse beheaded and his head hung on a pole to be exposed for a number of days. Later, the emperor's skull was turned into a silver-coated cup, from which the

[81] Theophanes Confessor, *Chronographia*, p. 673.

[82] I. Duichev, "La chronique byzantine de l'an 811," *T&M*, vol. 1 (1965), pp. 212–220.

Bulgar ruler drank together with the Slavic chieftains that had been on his side during the war. It was the first time since Valens' death at Adrianople in 378 that a ruling emperor had been killed on the battlefield while fighting against barbarians. The consequences for the morale of the Byzantine population of the eastern Balkans were disastrous.

When the new emperor, Michael I, rejected Krum's new offer of peace, the Bulgars stormed and conquered Debeltos, an important fort on the Bulgar–Byzantine frontier, near the Bay of Burgas. All the inhabitants of the city, together with their bishop, were taken into the interior of Bulgaria, where they would remain for at least another twenty years. The news of the fall of Debeltos triggered a revolt among the troops Emperor Michael was moving against the Bulgars. Krum's victories also spread panic among the inhabitants of the cities in Thrace and Macedonia. According to Theophanes, "at that time, the Christians abandoned Anchialos and Beroe and fled, although no one was pursuing them; the same at Nikaia, the castle of Probaton, and a number of other forts as also at Philippopolis and Philippi."[83] Even the settlers recently moved into the region of the Strymon valley by Emperor Nicephorus seem to have taken the opportunity to return to Asia Minor.

In 813, an envoy from Krum named Dargameros, most likely a Slav, came to Constantinople to bring Krum's offer of peace. The Bulgar ruler was asking for the renewal of the Byzantine–Bulgar treaty of 716, to which he now added new stipulations. One of them concerned the reciprocal agreement for the return of all refugees, "even if they had plotted against their own rulers." The other demanded that "those who traded in both countries be certified by means of diplomas and seals."[84] The offer was again rejected, probably because the first stipulation proposed by Krum would have implied the extradition of a number of Bulgars, no doubt Christians, who had taken refuge within the Byzantine Empire. In retaliation, Krum conquered Mesembria, the large center of the Byzantine–Bulgar trade since the early eighth century. Inside the city, Krum found "36 brass siphons and a considerable quantity of the liquid fire that is projected from

[83] Theophanes Confessor, *Chronographia*, p. 679. Of course, this does not mean that Krum occupied either Philippopolis or Philippi. See J. Karayannopoulos, "Wurde Philippoi von Krum im J. 812 erobert?," *GSU*, vol. 76 (1984), pp. 217–222.

[84] Theophanes Confessor, *Chronographia*, p. 681.

them" to produce the Greek fire, as well as much gold and silver.[85] Apparently, Debeltos was retaken at the same time. Late in the winter of the following year, learning that Krum was preparing for new attacks, Emperor Michael moved against the Bulgars, but Krum preferred to avoid the encounter. He made his move in June 813, when he encamped "at Versinikia, about thirty miles from the imperial army,"[86] which was stationed somewhere north of Adrianople. The organization of the Bulgar army is described in detail in an inscription found in Malamirovo, near the present-day border between Bulgaria and Turkey, perhaps the very spot of the battle. The fragmentary inscription, which is in fact an order of battle, mentions that the center of the Bulgar forces was under the command of Krum's brother. He was assisted by a general named Leo, no doubt a Byzantine renegade. The right wing reaching as far as present-day Stara Zagora was under the command of a nobleman named Tuk, who had the title of *ichirgu boilas*. His assistants were two generals named Bardanes and John. The left wing stretching along the Black Sea coast from Anchialos to Sozopolis was given to another Bulgar nobleman named Iratais, bearing the title of *boila kavkhan*. His assistants were the generals Kordylas and Gregoras, who, like the others, must have been of Byzantine origin.[87] After two weeks of facing each other in the heat of the summer, the two armies eventually engaged in battle on June 22, 813, and the Byzantines withdrew before losing too many men. Fearing an ambush, Krum did not exploit the victory, but eventually was capable of seizing the camp train. He later moved against the capital, but left his brother behind to besiege Adrianople. Under the walls of Constantinople, Krum moved freely in an attempt to humiliate the emperor, then "performed his foul demonic sacrifices in the coastal meadow of the Golden Gate."[88] The newly proclaimed emperor Leo V tried to ambush and kill Krum, but the Bulgar leader managed to escape unscathed. In retaliation, the Bulgar troops plundered the suburbs of Constantinople and the entire region of southern Thrace as far as Didymoteichos and Bizye. Krum returned to Adrianople, where his brother was still besieging the city. Together they broke the resistance of the besieged, and conquered Adrianople.

[85] Theophanes Confessor, *Chronographia*, p. 683.
[86] Theophanes Confessor, *Chronographia*, p. 684.
[87] Beshevliev, *Die protobulgarischen Inschriften*, pp. 220–229.
[88] Theophanes Confessor, *Chronographia*, p. 686.

In the absence of any other military or administrative representative of the emperor, Krum threw the local bishop, Manuel, to the ground and trampled upon his neck in a symbolic gesture of supreme humiliation. As in Debeltos, the inhabitants of Adrianople that had not been killed, including the parents of the future emperor Basil I, were transferred to the regions north of the Danube River.[89] In winter, a great number of Bulgar horsemen descended onto Arkadiopolis in Thrace, plundering the entire hinterland and taking many captives. As the thaw had meanwhile made impossible the crossing of the river Ergene, which was frozen when they had first arrived, the Bulgars spent two more weeks in Thrace waiting for the flood to recede. They eventually forced their captives to build a bridge and crossed unharmed back into Bulgaria together with their booty. The expedition seems to have been nothing but a raid, but Krum was preparing for a large-scale siege of Constantinople when he suddenly died on April 13, 814. The danger seems to have been so great that Emperor Leo V sent envoys to Louis the Pious asking for assistance against the Bulgars.[90]

Krum's successor was a man named Dukum, possibly his brother, but he too died a month or two after taking power. The next ruler, named Ditzevg, is known mainly for his large-scale persecution of both Christian prisoners of war and subjects of the Bulgar ruler who had embraced Christianity. Executed during this persecution were Manuel, the bishop of Adrianople taken prisoner after his humiliation in 813, and George, the bishop of Debeltos, who had been taken to Bulgaria, together with his flock, after the first Bulgar conquest of that city in 812. According to the early eleventh-century *Menologion of Basil II*, in charge of the persecution was a certain Tzok, perhaps the *ichirgu boilas* named Tuk mentioned in the Malamirovo inscription.[91] Moreover, among the victims were also Leo and John, the two

89 Leo Grammaticus, *Chronographia*, ed. by I. Bekker (Bonn: E. Weber, 1842), pp. 345–346; Symeon Magister, *Annales*, ed. by I. Bekker (Bonn: E. Weber, 1838), pp. 615–616. See also S. Brezeanu, "'La Bulgarie d'au-delà de l'Ister' à la lumière des sources écrites," *EB*, vol. 20 (1984), pp. 121–135.

90 Astronomer, *Vita Hludowici imperatoris* 23, ed. by E. Tremp (Hanover: Hahnsche Buchhandlung, 1995), pp. 352–354.

91 *Menologium Basilii imperatoris*, PG 117:276. For the illumination depicting the martyrdom of Manuel, George, and Leo, see *Il menologio di Basilio II (Cod. Vaticano Greco 1613)* (Turin: Fratelli Bocca, 1907), p. 345. The name Tzok is also mentioned in an inscription dated to AM 6328 (819/20). See Beshevliev, *Die protobulgarischen Inschriften*, pp. 209–214.

Byzantine generals assisting Krum's brother and the *ichirgu boilas*, respectively, who were mentioned in that same inscription. On the other hand, it would be a gross mistake to view the persecution as exclusively anti-Byzantine. A great number of martyrs in a long list of 377 individuals have Greek names, but there are also martyrs with Armenian and even Slavic names, an indirect indication that Christianity may have already spread among the local population of Bulgaria.[92]

Ditzevg too died shortly after the beginning of the persecution. His successor, Omurtag, was a son of Krum. He continued the persecution of Christians, especially during the Lent of 815, when he is said to have forced Christians to eat meat and killed those who refused. Unlike Ditzevg, Omurtag was concerned more with Christians from Bulgaria than with the anti-Byzantine dimension of the persecution. He was perhaps taken by surprise by Emperor Leo V's sudden attack on Mesembria in the spring of 816. Leo used a stratagem often associated with nomadic warfare: he encamped not far from the Bulgar army, then pretended to withdraw in fear of their superior forces, only to ambush his pursuers. The victory he obtained by such means was quickly followed by a devastating raid inside Bulgaria. A few months later, Omurtag agreed to a thirty-year peace, to be renewed every ten years. The peace was ratified by reciprocal oath-taking. According to the Byzantine sources, Emperor Leo V had to do such non-Christian things as pouring water on the ground, throwing saddles, and slaughtering dogs taken as witnesses to his faith and commitment to the treaty. In exchange, Omurtag may have taken an oath on the Bible.[93] The treaty stipulations were later carved on a marble pillar found in a village near present-day Novi Pazar, which, however, must have been brought there from Pliska.[94] The inscription mentions eleven articles

[92] E. Follieri and I. Duichev, "Un'acolutia inedita per i martiri di Bulgaria dell'anno 813," *Byzantion*, vol. 33 (1963), pp. 71–106. For Christianity in Bulgaria before the conversion, see P. Schreiner, "Das Christentum in Bulgarien vor 864," in *Das Christentum in Bulgarien und auf der übrigen Balkanhalbinsel in der Spätantike und im frühen Mittelalter*, ed. by V. Giuzelev and R. Pillinger (Vienna: Verein "Freunde des Hauses Wittgenstein," 1987), pp. 51–57.

[93] Ignatius the Deacon, *Vita Nicephori*, ed. by C. de Boor (Leipzig: Teubner, 1880), p. 207; Theophanes Continuatus, p. 31. For the interpretation of the pagan rituals forced upon Emperor Leo, see Beshevliev, *Die protobulgarische Periode*, pp. 377–380.

[94] Inscription no. 41 (also known as the "Suleyman Köy pillar"). See Beshevliev, *Die protobulgarischen Inschriften*, pp. 190–206. There is a second inscription with a similar content, repeating the first two stipulations of the treaty (no. 42, Beshevliev, *Die*

of the treaty, of which only five appear in the surviving part of the text. The first article dealt with the border between Byzantium and Bulgaria, which is described as a territory (*enoria*), not as a continuous line. The place names listed under this heading are dots on an imaginary map, and even the geographical features mentioned in the inscription, such as the river Hebros (Marica) and the Haemus (Stara Planina) Mountains, appear as zones, not as lines of demarcation. The fourth article dealt with the return of the Christian prisoners of war that had remained in Bulgaria ever since Krum's campaigns. Unfortunately, at this point, the inscription is damaged, but it is still clear that high-ranking officers of the Byzantine army were to be returned against ransom, while commoners were to be treated according to the principle "man for man."[95] Another stipulation regarding defectors, mainly Byzantine generals like those who fought on the Bulgar side at Versinikia, has not been preserved. Two other articles dealt with the "Slavs that were subject to the emperor," who were expected to remain where they were, as well as Slavs whom, not being his subjects, the emperor had to return to their abodes. The meaning of these apparently engimatic stipulations is without any doubt linked to the Byzantine practice of transplanting Balkan Slavs into other provinces of the Empire. In the early 800s, the practice may have been perceived as disruptive at least from a Bulgar point of view. The fact that such a stipulation appeared in a Bulgar–Byzantine treaty may indicate that Omurtag viewed the Slavs under Byzantine rule as an issue concerning Bulgaria. Omurtag's concern was not with population transfer per se, a practice in which the Bulgar rulers themselves had engaged in the past. At stake was not the protection of the Slavs, but the value of the lands they inhabited that could be considerably diminished if the entire population of a given territory was transferred to some remote area within the Byzantine Empire. The Slavs said to have been in need to return to their homes were from the coastal region (*paralion meros*), an indication that what Omurtag had in mind were specifically the *Sklaviniai* on the northern coast of the Aegean Sea from which the Byzantine emperors in the past had transferred the

protobulgarischen Inschriften, pp. 206–208). For the treaty, see W. Treadgold, "The Bulgars' treaty with the Byzantines in 816," *Rivista di studi bizantini e slavi*, vols. 4–5 (1985), pp. 213–220.

95 The expression in the original Greek is a direct quote from Leviticus 24.18: "And he that killeth a beast shall make it good; *beast for beast*." In addition, the phrase employed for the commoners is "the poor people" (*ptochos laos*).

largest number of Slavs. It is precisely in that region between Thessalonica and Constantinople that some of the most violent revolts of the Slavs against the Byzantines took place in the ninth century. Bulgar rulers often took advantage of the situation to intervene on behalf of the Slavs. Through the same region passed the easternmost segment of the old Roman road across the Balkans known as Via Egnatia, an overland route responsible for the reopening in the late ninth century of the "Balkan corridor" for communication between West and East.

It is not known whether or not the treaty of 816 obligated Omurtag to any military assistance to the emperor. In any case, in 822, Omurtag intervened in the civil war between Emperor Michael II and Thomas the Slav, who had led the rebellion of the thematic troops of Asia Minor. Crossing over into the Balkan provinces of the Empire, Thomas put Constantinople under siege in 821 by both land and sea. Besieged in Constantinople, with no real support outside the city walls, Michael asked Omurtag to attack Thomas's troops. When the Bulgar horsemen descended into Thrace, Thomas was forced to abandon the siege of Constantinople. In the ensuing battle, he was defeated and fled to Arkadiopolis, where he was besieged, then captured and executed. Omurtag ordered that his version of these events be carved on another marble pillar found in Chatalar, near Shumen. The inscription is about a palace (*aule*) that, while living in Pliska, Omurtag had built on the river Ticha, at a place where he had sent his army against "the Greeks and the Slavs."[96]

A memorial inscription for a certain member of Omurtag's retinue, a man called Okorsis "of the Chakarar clan," laconically explains that he had drowned in the river Dnieper, while on campaign.[97] If the date advanced for this inscription, *c.* 823, is to be trusted at all, it would imply that the Bulgar ruler was powerful enough to send troops as far as Ukraine, while at the same time battling Thomas the Slav in southern Thrace. Just who the enemy might have been against whom the troops presumably led by Okorsis had been sent remains a matter of debate. Some have seen the inscription as (the only piece of) evidence for a Khazar–Bulgar military conflict. Others

[96] Beshevliev, *Die protobulgarischen Inschriften*, p. 261, with commentary on p. 268. See also V. Beshevliev, "Nachrichten über den Aufstand Thomas des Slawen aus protobulgarischen Inschriften," *Byzantina*, vol. 8 (1976), pp. 339–342.

[97] Beshevliev, *Die protobulgarischen Inschriften*, pp. 281–285.

have rightly pointed out that the inscription, which cannot be dated later than 831, the year of Omurtag's death, is the "first clue" to the upheaval on the steppes created by the migration of the Magyars into the lands between the Dnieper and the Danube. In any case, at the same time as Omurtag's involvement in the civil war between Michael II and Thomas the Slav and, presumably, as the expedition into what is now Ukraine, the military presence of the Bulgars became prominent in yet another region of the Balkans. As early as 818, envoys of a Slavic tribe, the Timociani, had come together with those of Borna, the duke of the Guduscani, to the court of Louis the Pious in Herstal. The name of the Timociani apparently derives from that of the river Timok, a right-hand tributary of the Danube near the present-day Serbian–Bulgarian border, and they were said to have recently defected from their association (*societas*) with the Bulgars.[98] One of the goals of Louis's first expedition sent against Liudewit seems to have been to protect these Timociani, who were by now Frankish clients. A little later, another tribe, the Abodrites, "commonly called Praedenecenti," who "lived in Dacia adjacent to the Danube near the Bulgarian border," also complained to Emperor Louis the Pious about the Bulgars. Finally, in 824, a Bulgar embassy arrived in Francia, to the emperor's great surprise, as no relations had until then been established between the two states.[99] Omurtag offered peace and demanded that a common border be established by agreement between the two states. It is not clear what exactly was Omurtag's goal, but the insistent demand for a treaty on the common border is strikingly reminiscent of his preoccupation with the border between Bulgaria and Byzantium reflected in the Suleyman Köy pillar inscription. Perhaps Omurtag wanted a division of the areas of influence in the southern region of the Carpathian Basin, which would clearly assign Slavic loyalties in the region to either power. However, Emperor Louis was not willing to satisfy Omurtag's demand. Shortly before Christmas 824, another embassy of the Bulgars had reached Bavaria with demands for the rectification of the frontier.

[98] *Royal Frankish Annals*, s.a. 818 and 819, pp. 149 and 150; English translation by Scholz and Rogers, pp. 104 and 105. See V. Giuzelev, "Bulgarisch-fränkische Beziehungen in der ersten Hälfte des IX. Jh," *Byzantinobulgarica*, vol. 2 (1966), pp. 25–26.

[99] *Royal Frankish Annals*, s.a. 822 and 824, pp. 159 and 164–165. In 824, Louis dispatched a certain Bavarian named Machelm who returned to Bulgaria together with Omurtag's envoys.

Louis the Pious ordered the Bulgar envoys to wait in Bavaria until good weather. In the meantime, he received in Aachen the envoys of the Praedenecenti in order to hear their complaints about Bulgar aggression.[100] Finally, in May 825, Louis received the Bulgar embassy and sent a letter to Omurtag with the ambassadors. Dissatisfied with Louis's response, Omurtag sent the same envoys back with a letter threatening war if his demands were not met immediately. Since in the meantime rumors had reached Louis that Omurtag had been "either driven out or murdered by one of his nobles," the emperor decided not to reply. However, in order to verify the rumors, he sent his Count of the palace, Bertrich, to the "guards of the Avar border in the province of Carinthia."[101] Later in 826, Balderich, Margrave of Friuli, and Gerold, the prefect of the East, appeared before Louis in Mainz and assured him that no Bulgar threat was in sight. Other sources show that in the summer of 827 Frankish troops were in fact gathering in Bressanone, not far from the headwaters of the Drava River, ready to move quickly from Carantania into Pannonia. By that time, the Bulgars had already put together an expeditionary corps that entered the Drava on boats and attacked the Slavs of Pannonia who were clients of the Frankish Empire. That this was more than just a raid is shown by the fact that, according to the *Royal Frankish Annals*, the Bulgars replaced the local chieftains with their own governors (*rectores*).[102] The Frankish campaign against the Bulgars, which was put under the command of Louis, the young king of Bavaria, began

[100] *Royal Frankish Annals*, s.a. 824, p. 165. Since the Praedenecenti never resurfaced and no other source mentions them, their identity has been the subject of some dispute. The most controversial aspect is that the report of the *Royal Frankish Annals* seems to equate Praedenecenti with Abodrites, a Slavic tribe on the Frankish border with Saxony, east of the Elbe River and near the Baltic Sea. This has fuelled theories about a presumed migration of the northern Abodrites into the Carpathian Basin. To make things even more complicated, I. Boba has proposed that they were in fact Moravians, a hypothesis supposedly supporting his idea of a southern location of Moravia. See I. Boba, "'Abodriti quae vulgo Praedenecenti vocantur' or 'Marvani Praedenecenti'?," *Palaeobulgarica*, vol. 8 (1984), pp. 29–37. For an alternative explanation, see J. Herrmann, "Bulgaren, Obodriten, Franken und der bayrische Geograph," in *Sbornik v chest na akad. Dimităr Angelov*, ed. by V. Velkov, Zh. Aladzhov, G. Bakalov, et al. (Sofia: Izdatelstvo na Bălgarskata Akademiia na Naukite, 1994), pp. 41–46.

[101] *Royal Frankish Annals*, s.a. 826, pp. 168–169; English translation by Scholz and Rogers, p. 119.

[102] *Royal Frankish Annals*, s.a. 827, p. 173. For the 827 Frankish preparations for this campaign, see Bowlus, *Franks, Moravians*, pp. 95–97.

only in July 828, but nothing is known about the outcome.[103] At any rate, the Bulgars returned in 829, again using their boats, and put to fire a number of Frankish estates on the banks of the Drava River.[104] No Bulgar inscription makes any reference to these events, but it has been surmised that it was during one of the two military expeditions to the west that a certain military commander named Onegavonais drowned in the river Tisza, as mentioned on his memorial inscription found in Provadiia.[105] At any rate, much like in the case of the southern border with Byzantium, the frontier region to the west received additional fortification in the form of a dike now known as the "Great Roman Ditch," which was built across the southwestern part of Vojvodina closing the angle between the Danube River and the lower course of the Tisza. According to the *Conversion of the Bavarians and the Carantanians*, Pribina and his son Kocel fled to the Bulgars at some point in the early 830s, an indication that relations between the Franks and the Bulgars were still hostile.[106] However, the tensions on the Frankish–Bulgar frontier dissipated by 832, when according to one of the first entries in the early twelfth-century work of the so-called Saxon Annalist Bulgar envoys came to Emperor Louis bringing gifts and a message of peace.[107]

Omurtag's reign, significantly longer than that of Krum, was a period of major building programs. Although the exact chronology of the buildings within the Inner Town at Pliska is still the subject of scholarly dispute, there can be no doubt that the first walls made of stone were erected during the 800s, when Omurtag's Palace came into being to the east of the large yurt and on top of an older building inadequately called "Krum's Palace," which in fact postdates Krum's reign. To the north of both, there was a large precinct with three entrances, to the west a rectangular structure interpreted as a temple, mainly because of a three-aisled basilica erected on its ruins in the

103 *Annals of Fulda* a. 828, ed. by F. Kurze (Hanover: Hahnsche Buchhandlung, 1826; reprint 1963), MGH 7:25.

104 *Annals of Fulda* a. 829, p. 27.

105 Beshevliev, *Die protobulgarischen Inschriften*, pp. 285–287. As entering the river Drava by boat implies that the Bulgars also controlled the course of the river Danube in present-day Serbia, they must also have had access to the lower course of the Tisza River. It is precisely in this region that the Praedenecenti may be located.

106 *Conversio Bagaoriorum et Carantanorum* 10, p. 122.

107 *Annalista Saxo*, ed. by G. Waitz (Hanover: Hahnsche Buchhandlung, 1844; reprint 1980), MGH SS 6:574.

late 800s.[108] There were several rural settlements both inside and outside the Outer Town (the largest earthen rampart surrounding the palatial compound), all of which seem to have been designed to meet the exclusive needs of the Inner Town residents. Next to the palatial compound, recent excavations identified an industrial quarter, equipped with smithies, as well as with shops for the production of window glass. Much like the settlements with exclusively agricultural functions, this craft center was evidently meant to meet the demands of the nearby palace.

No pre-Christian burials have so far been found at Pliska, perhaps an indication that the palatial compound grounds were viewed as sacred. But a number of barrows of prehistoric origin on the western side of the Outer Town, outside the precinct, may have been used for sacrifices, as indicated by a twelve-meter deep sacrificial pit containing the skeletons of two horses, two dogs, and a cat.[109] Elsewhere in Bulgaria, cemeteries that had been in use since the eighth century continued into the ninth, while new ones began shortly after *c.* 800 and continued into the first decades of the tenth century. The latter group includes most cemeteries excavated in the region north of the Danube River now in southern Romania (Sultana, Izvorul, Obârşia Nouă, Frăteşti). Many of them produced a great number of female dress accessories, especially earrings, that are otherwise known from Moravian burial assemblages.[110] The beginning of several large settlements in this area (Dridu, Bucov) can also be dated to the ninth century. Ceramic assemblages typically include shards of amphoroid jugs that may have transported precious liquids (oil or wine) produced in or around Pliska. Tiles, bricks, drainage pipe segments, and other building materials strikingly similar to those from

[108] P. Georgiev, "Golemiiat ezicheski khram v Pliska [The Great Pagan Temple in Pliska]," *Problemi na prabălgarskata istoriia i kultura*, vol. 1 (1989), pp. 338–354. The Pliska temple may have been in fact a monument erected to commemorate Krum, as the surviving elements of the building are strikingly similar to a number of similar monuments erected for the Turkic qagans in present-day Mongolia. Four other similar structures have been found in Pliska, Madara, and Preslav, all of rectangular or square shape with a north–south or east–west orientation. For the architecture of the "pagan temples" of Bulgaria, see S. Boiadzhiev, "Arkhitekturata na prabălgarskite khramove [The architecture of the Bulgar temples]," *Problemi na prabălgarskata istoriia i kultura*, vol. 1 (1989), pp. 314–327.

[109] R. Rashev and S. Stanilov, "Kenotaf für einem Herrscher bei der ersten bulgarischen Hauptstadt Pliska," *Das Altertum*, vol. 44 (1998), pp. 67–72.

[110] Fiedler, *Studien*, p. 270.

Pliska have been found on several sites in the Walachian Plain. An even larger quantity of building materials comes from excavations at Slon, a stronghold in the Carpathian Mountains no doubt controlling access to a direct road from the Danube region to Transylvania.[111] A group of cemeteries around Alba Iulia bespeaks the presence in south Transylvania of a group of population with strong ties to the material culture of the Bulgar centers in the south.

That many, if not all, of the stone buildings at Pliska should be dated to Omurtag's reign (815–831) does not contradict what is known about his building record. In the text of an inscription on a marble pillar later reused in the Church of the Forty Martyrs in Veliko Tărnovo, Omurtag brags about building a "magnificent house" on the Danube, in addition to his old palace (possibly the one in Pliska). At mid-distance between the two, he erected a barrow (*toumba*) to mark the measurements taken across the land, themselves a symbolic appropriation of the landscape marked by buildings.[112] We have seen that the inscription found in Chatalar speaks of another palace, as well as a bridge over the river Ticha, which Omurtag built to commemorate his victory over Thomas the Slav.[113] Omurtag liked to be compared with his illustrious predecessors. He may have erected the so-called Great Temple in Pliska to honor his father, Krum. An inscription bearing his name was added to the already scribbled façade of the Madara cliff, next to the inscriptions of Tervel and Krumesis. However, unlike his predecessors, Omurtag was not satisfied with the mere title of "ruler" (*archon*). The Madara inscription calls him a "ruler from God" (*ek theou archon*). The phrase also appears twice in the Chatalar inscription and has been accordingly restored in the fragmentary inscription from a little church in Madara,

[111] M. Comşa, "Die Forschungen von Slon und ihre Bedeutung für das Studium der Entwicklung der Feudalbeziehungen südlich der Karpaten," in *Siedlung, Burg und Stadt. Studien zu ihren Anfängen*, ed. by K.-H. Otto and J. Herrmann (Berlin: Akademie Verlag, 1969), pp. 232–238. Settlements excavated in southeastern Transylvania have produced pottery with burnished decoration (the so-called Dridu B ware) with clear analogies on sites in the Lower Danube region. See Z. Székely, "L'aspect de la culture matérielle des VIIIe–Xe siècles dans le sud-est de la Transylvanie," *Mitteilungen des Archäologischen Instituts der Ungarischen Akademie der Wissenschaften*, vol. 1 (1972), 125–128.

[112] Beshevliev, *Die protobulgarischen Inschriften*, pp. 247–248 and 255.

[113] Beshevliev, *Die protobulgarischen Inschriften*, pp. 260–261. For an English translation of the text see S. Runciman, *A History of the First Bulgarian Empire* (London, G. Bell & Sons, 1930), p. 77.

which appropriately mentions Omurtag performing sacrifices to his god Tangra.[114] The ruler apparently offered thanks to the god who had appointed him. Moreover, in three memorial inscriptions from Pliska, Omurtag's name is preceded by the enigmatic phrase "kana sybigi." In four inscriptions (two of Omurtag and two of his son Malamir), the phrase appears together with the "ruler from God." The context in which this association takes place is always that of some public appearance of the ruler on behalf of all Bulgars or of only some of them, in order to perform sacrifices to God, to announce victories over the "Greeks," or to distribute food and gifts to the nobility.[115] By contrast, "kana sybigi" is mentioned alone only in inscriptions that publicize a rather personal relation, namely that between the ruler and a particular member of his retinue. "Kana sybigi" has been recently interpreted as a Bulgar translation of the Greek phrase "ruler from God."[116] But in inscriptions in which both phrases accompany the name of the ruler, the compound operates much like introductory formulas of Byzantine imperial edicts. If so, then "kana sybigi" cannot be a translation of "ruler from God," for the two languages (Bulgar and Greek) were clearly distinguished in other inscriptions.[117] Moreover, two inscriptions of Omurtag end with the following formula: "The name (*onoma*) of the ruler (*archon*) is Omurtag kana sybigi."[118] Apparently, Omurtag's "name" contained both his personal name and his title. Some have proposed that *sybigi* be translated as "lord of the army or commander," while others argued instead that the word meant "bright, luminous," hence "heavenly." By contrast, Omeljan Pritsak thought that *sybigi* meant "word" and that the phrase "kana sybigi" derived from Old Turkic and Old Mongolian introductory formulas with the meaning "The khan so-and-so (spoke the following) words."[119] Omurtag is represented on two gold medallions found in Belogradec (near Varna) and

[114] Beshevliev, *Die protobulgarischen Inschriften*, p. 149.

[115] Beshevliev, *Die protobulgarischen Inschriften*, pp. 149, 156, 260–261, and 277.

[116] C. Stepanov, "The Bulgar title KANASYBIGI: reconstructing the notions of divine kingship in Bulgaria, AD 822–836," *Early Medieval Europe*, vol. 10 (2001), pp. 1–19.

[117] See Beshevliev, *Die protobulgarischen Inschriften*, p. 261 ("boulgaristi," "grikisti").

[118] Beshevliev, *Die protobulgarischen Inschriften*, pp. 209 and 247.

[119] O. Pritsak, "The initial formula KANACYBHΓH in the proto-Bulgarian inscriptions," in *Studia slavica mediaevalia et humanistica Riccardo Picchio dicata*, ed. by M. Colucci, G. dell' Agata, and H. Goldblatt, vol. II (Rome: Edizioni dell'Ateneo,

Veliko Tărnovo. In both cases he is represented as a Byzantine ruler, carrying a cross-shaped crozier in his right hand. The accompanying inscription, "Cane sybigi Omurtag," is written in mixed Latin and Greek letters. The iconography on both medallions is strikingly reminiscent of that on gold coins struck for the Byzantine emperors, from Nicephorus I (802–811) to Theophilus (829–842), on which rulers were identified by name and title (*basileus*).[120] "Cana sybigi Omurtag" is therefore a Bulgar "translation" of the simplest imperial titulature that appears on Byzantine gold coins. While all such coins displayed the portrait of the senior emperor on the obverse and those of the co-emperors on the reverse, Omurtag's medallions have no image on the reverse, which in both known cases is completely blank. If indeed "kana sybigi" operates as the equivalent of "basileus," then Omurtag's intention was to point out that, while his Byzantine contemporaries associated their sons to power, he alone had exclusive, autocratic power over his subjects, which he did not share with anyone. The Bulgar "ruler from God" was an "emperor" uttering statements of political significance, even when using the language of the Byzantine imperial ceremonial and the imagery of the Byzantine emperors. Whether performing sacrifices to his god, Tangra, or displaying his generosity by distributing medallions marked with his image to his subjects, Omurtag was clearly striking imperial poses.

During the early ninth century, lofty titles were not the exclusive domain of the ruler. The Malamirovo inscription dated to Krum's reign mentions two high-ranking military commanders, the *kavkhan* and the *ichirgu boilas*. However, the Bulgar ruler whose name is associated with the largest number of inscriptions is Omurtag. Many of them were commissioned on behalf of members of his retinue, men

1986), pp. 595–601. Most scholars agree that the first element of the compound, *kana*, is the Bulgar version of the word for khan, despite the fact that the word appears in many other compounds associated with persons that were clearly not rulers (Beshevliev, *Die protobulgarischen Inschriften*, pp. 165–166 and 170–171).

[120] I. Iordanov, "Ednostranni zlatni moneti-medalioni s imeto na Khan Omurtag [One-sided golden medallions with Omurtag's name]," *Numizmatika*, vol. 10 (1976), pp. 18–34; P. Slavchev and I. Iordanov, "Zlatni medalioni na khan Omurtag (814–831) [Golden medallions of Khan Omurtag]," *Arkheologiia*, vol. 21 (1979), pp. 25–31.

bearing such titles as *zera* or *zhupan tarqan*.[121] They were members of aristocratic Bulgar clans (Kubiar and Kyrigir), whose rank was linked to military command, as confirmed by parallel attestations of the word *tarqan* for Turkic, Avar, and Khazar aristocrats. It has been suggested that no less than thirty-six hoards of iron implements and weapons found in Bulgaria, mainly in and around Pliska and Preslav, as well as in the neighboring regions north of the river Danube or in Macedonia, represent the material correlate of the military posturing of the Bulgar *tarqans* during ceremonies that may have emphasized their ritual connection with blacksmithing, as well as with state offices.[122] Moreover, a compound title such as *zhupan tarqan* is to be translated approximately as "(a) *tarqan* of (all the) *zhupans*." The title of *zhupan* is first attested by the inscription on one of the golden bowls found in the Sânnicolaul Mare hoard, but we have seen that some of the earliest inscriptions and charters in Croatia also mentioned *zhupans*, both as district prefects and as court dignitaries.[123] As there is more than one parallel to be drawn between ninth-century Bulgaria and Croatia, it is not impossible that the Bulgar *zhupans* too were district prefects. The early 800s were a period of administrative change in Bulgaria, as tribal–military institutions seem to have been converted into administrative state offices. As many as ten administrative units are mentioned during Boris's reign, but they may have come

[121] Beshevliev, *Die protobulgarischen Inschriften*, pp. 285–286 and 287–288. A third *tarqan* of Omurtag is commemorated by the Kalugerica inscription (Beshevliev, *Die protobulgarischen Inschriften*, pp. 294–295). One of his *zhupans*, a member of the aristocratic clan Ermiar, is commemorated by the Mogila inscription (Beshevliev, *Die protobulgarischen Inschriften*, pp. 290–291).

[122] F. Curta, "Iron and potlatch: early medieval hoards of implements and weapons in Eastern Europe," *AEMA*, vol. 10 (1998–1999), pp. 32–37. The hoards found north of the Danube River cluster in the region where written sources locate "Bulgaria beyond the Danube," to which the prisoners taken by Krum after the conquest of Adrianople in 813 were exiled. The region had its own local ruler, who enjoyed a certain degree of autonomy.

[123] The title is also mentioned three times by Emperor Constantine Porphyrogenitus, according to whom the Croats, the Serbs, and other Balkan Slavs had no rulers (*archontes*), but were simply led by their elders, named *zhupans*. Constantine Porphyrogenitus, *De administrando imperio* 29, pp. 124–125; see also 32, pp. 158–159; and 34, pp. 162–163. See also A. A. Gorsky, "On the origins of the institutions of zhupans among the Slavs," in *Acts. XVIIIth International Congress of Byzantine Studies. Selected Papers*, ed. by I. Ševčenko, G. G. Litavrin, and W. K. Hanak, vol. 1 (Shepherdstown, W.Va.: Byzantine Studies Press, 1996), pp. 232–241.

into being during the 820s or 830s.[124] *Zhupans* and *tarqans* may have played a role in these rearrangements.

Omurtag had three sons: Enravotas, Zvinitza, and Malamir. At his father's death in 831, the eldest may have already converted to Christianity. He was executed in 832 at the order of Malamir, for refusing to renounce his faith. Nothing is known about Zvinitza, except that two of the Bulgar rulers of the late ninth century, Presian and Boris, were his sons. Nor is there an abundance of information about Malamir. What we know about him comes primarily from an inscription on a marble column from Shumen.[125] The text clearly indicates that Omurtag's younger son ruled together with an official of the highest rank, the *kavkhan* Isbul. Shortly after Malamir acceded to power, the Byzantines seem to have broken the thirty-year peace, but their attack on unspecified territories in Bulgaria was repelled by Malamir together with Isbul, who managed to destroy two Byzantine fortresses on the frontier and devastated Byzantine Thrace reaching as far as Philippopolis. Isbul, who has been rightly compared with the eighth-century mayors of the Merovingian kings, continued to play a major role in Bulgarian politics during the 830s. Another inscription mentions a fountain which he had built and dedicated to Malamir, who, in return, invited the Bulgars to a feast and distributed gifts to the *boilades* and *bagaines*, the two "classes" of the Bulgar aristocracy.[126] At Malamir's death in 836, his successor Presian quickly responded to the call for assistance from the ruling Byzantine emperor. In 836 or 837, the Slavs under Byzantine rule rose in rebellion. This may be the revolt that St. Gregory the Decapolite had predicted in anticipation of his trip into the mountain region north of Thessalonica. In any case, the rebels received significant assistance from the Smoliani, a tribe on the lower course of the Nestos River (near the present-day Greek–Bulgarian border). Emperor Theophilus asked Presian to attack them. The expedition, which was again led by the *kavkhan*

[124] V. Giuzelev, "Allgemeine Charakteristik und Etappen der Errichtung der militärischen und administrativen Verwaltung des Ersten bulgarischen Staates (VIII. bis IX. Jh.)," *EB*, vol. 14 (1978), p. 77. The "counties" (*comitatus*) of Bulgaria are mentioned in the *Annals of St. Bertin* s.a. 866, p. 85. Even territories newly, albeit temporarily, conquered, such as those along the Lower Drava River, were under the command of specially appointed governors.

[125] Beshevliev, *Die protobulgarischen Inschriften*, pp. 156–163.

[126] Beshevliev, *Die protobulgarischen Inschriften*, pp. 277–280.

Isbul, is mentioned in a damaged inscription found during excavations in Philippi.[127]

It was at this moment in time that a new crisis broke within the Bulgar polity. The Byzantine captives moved by Krum into the region north of the Danube were under the command of a certain Kordylas, most likely the same general mentioned under the command of the *kavkhan* in the Malamirovo inscription. Kordylas seems to have established contact with Constantinople, asking for assistance for his plan to return the entire population under his command to the Empire. He organized and led a revolt of the Byzantine captives against the Bulgars, and the troops the *tarqan* of the northern region moved against the rebels were defeated. Unable to cross the Danube back into Bulgaria, the *tarqan* asked for assistance from the neighboring Magyars, an indication that the territory in question was located in the vicinity of the steppes north of the Danube Delta. While Magyars were attacking without much success Kordylas and his men, a Byzantine fleet appeared on the Danube, which quickly transported all the Byzantine captives to Constantinople.[128]

BORIS-MICHAEL AND THE CONVERSION OF BULGARIA

Very little is known about Presian's last regnal years, except that in 845 Bulgar envoys appeared in Paderborn to demand from Louis the German the renewal of peaceful relations that had been established since 832. It is also during Presian's reign that Godescalc of Orbais came to Bulgaria from Croatia. From Bulgaria he moved at an unknown date back to the Frankish Empire without difficulty, a sign that Frankish–Bulgar relations were peaceful.[129] Following Presian's death in 852, his brother Boris dispatched another embassy to Louis, but one year later Charles the Bald bribed the Bulgars into

[127] Beshevliev, *Die protobulgarischen Inschriften*, pp. 163–174. On the Smoliani, see also D. Cheshmedzhiev, "On the question of the localization of the Slav tribe Smoljani," *BHR*, vol. 25 (1997), pp. 89–93. Presian also offered assistance in the form of Bulgar troops that were sent to Asia Minor to participate in the war against the Arabs. See H. Ditten, "Herrschte 837 u.Z. Krieg oder Frieden zwischen Byzanz und Bulgarien?," *EB*, vol. 20 (1984), pp. 62–79.

[128] The account is in the continuation of the chronicle of George the Monk, which was published by G. Moravcsik in his *Studia Byzantina* (Amsterdam: Adolf Hakkert, 1967), p. 206.

[129] Godescalc of Orbais, *De corpore et sanguine Domini*, p. 325.

moving "sharply against the kingdom of Louis the German."[130] The attack must have targeted the eastern marches and moved along the Drava River, where the Bulgars could mobilize the local Slavs against the Franks. Boris also attacked unsuccessfully Croatia, with which Bulgaria now had a common border, as indicated by the accounts of the trans-Balkan trips of Godescalc of Orbais and of Pope John VIII's legates. Presian had campaigned without much success against a prince of the Serbs named Vlastimir, and Boris followed in his footsteps. His campaign met with serious resistance from the new ruler of the Serbs, Mutimir, who, together with his brothers Strojmir and Gojnik, defeated the Bulgars and captured Boris's son, Vladimir, together with twelve *boilades*.[131] According to Constantine Porphyrogenitus, Boris was thus forced to offer peace, but in the process of recuperating his son, he managed to obtain as hostages Mutimir's two sons, who accompanied Boris and Vladimir "as far as the frontier at Ras." Boris and Mutimir's sons exchanged gifts as a warranty for peace, but Boris chose to treat the Serbian gifts ("two slaves, two falcons, two dogs, and eighty furs") as tribute, perhaps because pairs of such items as falcons were symbolically associated with royal power.

By 864, Boris's relations with Louis the German improved considerably, as the latter was seeking his alliance against the Moravians under Rastislav. The new rapprochement was different from any other similar agreements between Franks and Bulgars. According to Hincmar of Reims, Boris had expressed his intention of converting to Christianity and Louis was obviously capitalizing on his need for a sponsor at the baptismal font.[132] The Frankish and Bulgar armies

130 *Annals of Fulda*, s.a. 845 and 852, pp. 35 and 42, English translation by T. Reuter (Manchester and New York: Manchester University Press, 1992), pp. 24 and 33; *Annals of St. Bertin* s.a. 853, p. 43, English translation by Nelson, p. 77.

131 Constantine Porphyrogenitus, *De administrando imperio* 32, pp. 154–155. See also J. V. A. Fine, *The Early Medieval Balkans. A Critical Survey from the Sixth to the Late Twelfth Century* (Ann Arbor: University of Michigan Press, 1983), pp. 109–112; S. M. Ćirković, *The Serbs* (Malden, Oxford, and Carlton: Blackwell, 2004), p. 15. The date of Boris's attack is a matter of dispute. See L. Maksimović, "O vremenu pokhoda bulgarskog kneza Borisa na Srbiju [On the date of the Bulgar prince Boris's invasion of Serbia]," *ZFF*, vol. 14 (1979), pp. 69–76.

132 *Annals of St. Bertin* s.a. 864, p. 72, English translation by Nelson, p. 118. Louis's advances are also mentioned in a letter of Pope Nicholas I to Bishop Solomon of Constance, *ep.* 26, ed. E. Perels (Berlin: Weidmann, 1925; reprint 1995), MGH Epist. 6:290–293.

were probably already moving against Rastislav, when a Byzantine expeditionary corps landed at Mesembria. Bulgar relations with Byzantium had deteriorated rapidly ever since the expiration of the thirty-year peace treaty. In the late 840s, the Bulgars had raided Thrace and Macedonia, and the Byzantines had responded with raids into Bulgar territories. The attack of 864 was not a raid but the first serious campaign against Bulgaria after the thirty-year peace treaty. Mesembria was reoccupied by Byzantine forces. Under circumstances that are not very clear,[133] Boris was forced into submission and had to abandon his newly established alliance with Louis, not long after Rastislav's envoys had arrived at Constantinople with demands for a Byzantine mission. More importantly, Boris was baptized with Emperor Michael III as his sponsor, and as a consequence took on the emperor's name. He also allowed members of the Byzantine clergy to enter Bulgaria and begin their missionary work. Boris's conversion is mentioned in an inscription found in Ballsh (Albania) that dates the event precisely to AM 6374 (865/6). The inscription also suggests that prior to his conversion, Boris (or his brother Presian) had extended the power of Bulgaria to the shores of the Adriatic Sea, in the vicinity of Dyrrachium.[134] Boris's second name acquired through baptism is also attested by his seal found in Pliska, as well as on the funerary inscription of a Greek monk.[135]

[133] According to Theophanes Continuatus, p. 165, Boris was filled with the fear of Hell after seeing a scene of the Last Judgment painted by a Byzantine monk on the wall of one of his hunting huts. He requested immediate baptism, right there in the hut. At least one source, the Chronography of Pseudo-Symeon, in Theophanes Continuatus, pp. 665–666 claims that Boris was actually taken to Constantinople and baptized there. He saw the Last Judgment scene only after returning from the capital of the Empire. All accounts of Boris's baptism have an air of legend, which may have been deliberately created for the purpose of distracting attention from the secret character of the baptism ceremony, away from the critical eyes of the Bulgar *boilades*. See L. Simeonova, *Diplomacy of the Letter and the Cross. Photios, Bulgaria, and the Papacy, 860s–880s* (Amsterdam: Adolf Hakkert, 1998), pp. 79–80.

[134] Beshevliev, *Die protobulgarischen Inschriften*, pp. 175–176. The inscription mentions that God had given to Boris his people to rule, apparently a variation on the theme of the "ruler from God" attested under Omurtag. In another inscription from Cherven, dated to 870, Boris appears as "God-loving *archon*" (Beshevliev, *Die protobulgarischen Inschriften*, pp. 328–329).

[135] R. Vasilev, "Oloven pechat na kniaz Boris-Mikhail ot Pliska [A leaden seal of Prince Boris-Michael from Pliska]," *Numizmatika*, vol. 25 (1991), pp. 3–6; Beshevliev, *Die protobulgarischen Inschriften*, pp. 328–329.

In a move meant to reassure his subjects that in fact he was not the first member of the dynasty established by Krum to have converted to Christianity, Boris ordered the building of the first Christian edifice in Pliska, a small *martyrium* erected next to Omurtag's Palace and most likely dedicated to his uncle Enravotas, killed at the order of Malamir in 832. Despite such gestures, Boris's momentous decision to convert to Christianity, which has been compared to that of King Aethelberht of Kent, did not go unchallenged. A group of notables, who had recently converted, rose in rebellion against him and after defeating the rebels, Boris had to order their execution, as well as that of their families and children.[136] This was the first time since the eighth century that a Bulgar ruler was facing the revolt of his own noblemen. The revolt may be responsible for the destruction of the Pliska *martyrium*, but judging from the violence of Boris's reaction, it is possible that the conspirators were less against his faith than against his poor political performance and his defeat at the hands of the Byzantines. They must have been disgruntled by what they perceived as Boris's excessively pro-Byzantine policies.

Whatever the case, Boris was already prepared for a change of tack. He had asked the new patriarch, Photius, to allow him to control the church in his country. Photius' response came in the form of a treatise on church history and dogma, as well as on Christian leadership.[137] On August 29, 866, an embassy headed by Boris's kinsman, a notable named Peter, arrived in Rome, asking for answers to a series of questions on church practices.[138] At the same time, an embassy from Boris was also sent to Louis the German in Regensburg, announcing

[136] *Annals of St. Bertin*, s.a. 866, p. 85, English translation by Nelson, p. 137. That the notables (*proceres*) were Christian and were executed together with their families results from Pope Nicholas's letter to the Bulgars, *ep.* 99, ed. by E. Perels (Berlin: Weidmann, 1925; reprint 1995), MGH Epist. 6:577.

[137] Photius, *Epistulae et amphilochia*, ed. by V. Laourdas and L. G. Westerink, vol. I (Leipzig: Teubner, 1983), pp. 5–15; English translation in D. S. White and J. Berrigan, *The Patriarch and the Prince. The Letter of Patriarch Photios of Constantinople to Khan Boris of Bulgaria* (Brookline: Holy Cross Orthodox Press, 1982). See also P. Odorico, "La lettre de Photius à Boris de Bulgarie," *Byzantinoslavica*, vol. 54 (1993), pp. 83–88; Simeonova, *Diplomacy*, pp. 112–152.

[138] *Liber pontificalis*, ed. by L. Duchesne, vol. II (Paris: E. Thorin, 1886–1957; reprint Paris: E. de Boccard, 1981), p. 164. For Peter as Boris's kinsman, see the letter of Pope John VIII's to Boris, *ep.* 192, ed. by E. L. E. Caspar and G. Laehr (Berlin: Weidmann, 1928; reprint 1993), MGH Epist. 7:154. According to the *Annals of St. Bertin*, s.a. 866, p. 85 (English translation by Nelson, p. 137), Boris also sent his own son (Vladimir?) together with the embassy to Rome.

the conversion of the Bulgar ruler and requesting missionaries. In November of that same year, a papal mission under Bishop Formosus of Porto came to Bulgaria, bringing Pope Nicholas I's response to Boris's questions in the form of an extensive letter, which is the most important document that exists on Bulgar social and religious practices before the conversion.[139] The letter addressed to the Bulgars, not to Boris, has 106 chapters, dealing with such common subjects as baptism, marriage, bathing, fasting, or the distinction between sin and crime. Nicholas's approach to conversion is clear: "We have told you that you must not use violence to make a pagan become a Christian."[140] On the issue of the independent Bulgarian church, his answer was less limpid: "Now concerning this we cannot give you a definite answer until our legates, whom we are sending over to your country, return and report to us how numerous and united the Christians among you are."[141] Instead, Pope Nicholas concentrated on specific concerns of Boris, whom he did not hesitate to compare to Constantine the Great. Knowing his military prowess, he encouraged him to "convert all these things into the battle gear of a spiritual preparation":

> We admonish you to turn the harshness of such a great severity into the practice of piety; so that, just as heretofore you diligently strove after that preparedness of arms and horses (checking whether it would suffice against visible enemies), so now let each of you strive to have spiritual arms (i.e., good works) prepared "against the principalities and powers, against the rulers of the present darkness of this world, against spiritual wickedness in high places."[142]

[139] Nicholas I, *ep.* 99, pp. 568–600. The standard edition of the *Responsa ad consulta Bulgarorum* is now L. Heiser, *Die Responsa ad consulta Bulgarorum des Papstes Nikolaus I. (858–867). Ein Zeugnis päpstlicher Hirtensorge und ein Dokument unterschiedlicher Entwicklungen in den Kirchen von Rom und Konstantinopel* (Trier: Paulinus Verlag, 1979). For an excellent commentary, see I. Duichev, "I Responsa di papa Nicolò I ai Bulgari neoconvertiti," *Aevum. Rassegna di scienze storiche, linguistiche e filologiche*, vol. 42 (1968), pp. 403–428. A complete English translation is available in S. N. Scott, "The collapse of the Moravian mission of Saints Cyril and Methodius, the fate of their disciples, and the Christianization of the southern Slavs: translations of five historical texts with notes and commentary," Ph.D. dissertation, University of California (Berkeley, 1989), pp. 222–299, which differs somewhat from W. L. North's translation available online at http://www.fordham.edu/halsall/basis/866nicholas-bulgar.html.

[140] Nicholas I, *ep.* 99, chapter 102; English translation by Scott, p. 296.

[141] Nicholas I, *ep.* 99, chapter 72; English translation by Scott, p. 280.

[142] Nicholas I, *ep.* 99, chapter 40; English translation by Scott, pp. 255–256. The quote is from St. Paul's *Epistle to the Ephesians* 6.12.

Current concerns can be gleaned from chapter 19, in which the pope offers instruction in what Boris "ought lawfully to do about people who have risen up to kill their king,"[143] no doubt a reference to the rebellion of 865–866. There is not much description of actual Bulgar practices, which can only partially be reconstructed from the pope's answers. Sometimes, the pope himself seems to have been annoyed by what he regarded as a terribly silly question (*supervacuum*): "What you seek to learn concerning trousers (*femoralia*) we consider superfluous. For we do not wish the external fashion of your clothing to be changed, but the morals of the inner man within you." However, Nicholas did address a question regarding linen turbans (*ligatura lintei*), because apparently Greek priests had forbidden the Bulgars to wear them when entering the church.[144] Chapter 7 indicates that there were specific beliefs in Bulgaria regarding ritual cleanliness, as Pope Nicholas answers in detail a question regarding "whether a clean person or an unclean person may carry or kiss the cross of the Lord and relics."[145] In chapter 42, we learn that the practice among Bulgars was that "when your king sits down to eat his meals it is your custom for no one, not even his wife, to dine with him." The king apparently requested that all his subjects "eat at a distance, seated in chairs on the ground level."[146] Bulgar oath-taking involved swords,[147] but nothing is said about the killing of dogs or about the libations forced on Emperor Leo V half a century before Nicholas's letter. Chapter 33 refers to the tail of a horse which the Bulgar ruler used as a military emblem when going into battle, while in chapter 35, Pope Nicholas blasts the "incantations, jests, verses, and auguries" that used to be performed by Bulgars when setting out for battle.[148] Equally strong are his words about the prohibition of incest, an indication that consanguinity may not have prevented marriage in pagan Bulgaria. Polygamy is equally prohibited in chapter 51.[149] Chapter 25

[143] Nicholas I, *ep*. 99, chapter 19; English translation by Scott, p. 246.

[144] Nicholas I, *ep*. 99, chapters 59 and 66; English translation by Scott, pp. 270 and 276.

[145] Nicholas I, *ep*. 99, chapter 7; English translation by Scott, p. 232.

[146] Nicholas I, *ep*. 99, chapter 42; English translation by Scott, p. 258.

[147] Nicholas I, *ep*. 99, chapter 67; English translation by Scott, p. 277: "Now we decree that not only is it unfitting for an oath to be made on a sword, but on anything created at all."

[148] Nicholas I, *ep*. 99, chapters 33 and 35; English translation by Scott, pp. 251 and 253.

[149] Nicholas I, *ep*. 99, chapters 39 and 51; English translation by Scott, pp. 255 and 265–266.

mentions Bulgar sentries posted on the borders "to keep watch," who are promptly put to death if found guilty of negligence, perhaps a reference to the tense atmosphere in the aftermath of the expiration of the thirty-year peace treaty with Byzantium.[150] A few answers to questions regarding such topics as the marriage of priests or the position of the hands during prayer indicate that Boris had already become aware of the differences in ritual between Western and Eastern Christians. In general, however, Boris was concerned more with practice than with doctrine. As a consequence, the general tone of Pope Nicholas I was moderation, as he allowed the continuation of some of the old customs and adopted a cautious approach to the conversion of Bulgaria.

Together with the mission to Bulgaria, Pope Nicholas sent another embassy to Constantinople to express as aggressively as possible the papal condemnation of Photius' election as patriarch. The envoys never made it to Constantinople, for they were stopped by the Byzantines at the border with Bulgaria. Unable to cross over into the Empire, they spent some time in Pliska before returning to Rome. Boris is said to have been very fond of the youngest member of the embassy, a subdeacon in Santa Maria Maggiore, whom he wanted as head of his church.[151] The fact that the papal legates were denied access to Byzantium was the result of the schism that by 866 had divided Constantinople from the church of Rome. Naturally, Patriarch Photius was well-informed about the arrival of the Roman mission and infuriated about the practices they were promoting in Bulgaria. At a church council in 867, he condemned the practices of the Roman priests, some of which had caught Boris's attentive eye and had provoked Pope Nicholas's lengthy explanations (celibacy for the clergy, fasting on Saturdays, use of unleavened bread in the Eucharist, and the *filioque* issue).

[150] Nicholas I, *ep.* 99, chapter 25; English translation by Scott, p. 248.

[151] It was probably from the former subdeacon Marinus who in 882 became pope that King Alfred the Great learned about the location of Bulgaria. On at least one occasion, when sending a relic of the True Cross to the king of Wessex, Pope Marinus was in direct contact with Alfred. According to Alfred's translation of Orosius, "to the east of Carendre land (Carantania) beyond the uninhabited district (*westenne*) is the land of the Pulgare (Bulgaria) and east of that is the land of the Greeks" (*Old English Orosius*, ed. by N. Lund, English translation by C. E. Fell in *Two Voyagers at the Court of King Alfred* [York: William Sessions, 1984]), p. 17.

Boris seems to have been enthralled with the two Latin bishops, Formosus and Paul, that Pope Nicholas I had sent to Bulgaria. After just one year of work, both had been highly successful in converting people, ordaining priests, and consecrating newly built churches. Boris now asked that Formosus be appointed his archbishop, something Formosus himself may have let him believe would be easy to obtain. However, shortly before his death, Nicholas had decided to recall Formosus and to send instead bishop Grimuald of Bomarzo and a few other priests. At the end of 867 or in early 868, Formosus returned to Rome, but in the meantime, Bishop Ermenrich of Passau, together with several priests and deacons, was sent to Boris by Louis the German, in response to his earlier request. As the Roman delegation was already in Bulgaria, they all returned home with Boris's approval. When a papal embassy crossed Bulgaria in 869 on its way to Constantinople to attend the synod called by Emperor Basil I and the restored patriarch Ignatius to settle the schism with Rome, Boris was pleased to receive their letters of greeting. However, on its way back, the papal embassy did not go through Bulgaria, for in the meantime Boris's envoys that appeared in front of that same synod had asked a much troubling question, namely whether they owed obedience to Rome or to Constantinople. Despite the protests of the papal legates, the restored patriarch Ignatius appointed an archbishop of Bulgaria who was promised considerable autonomy. By 870, the issue was settled in Boris's favor. Grimuald, the bishop of Bomarzo, who had arrived in 867, was expelled from Bulgaria, and the first Greek archbishop of Bulgaria arrived in Pliska. Nevertheless, the decisions of the church synod of 869/70 did not interrupt communication between Bulgaria and Rome. Pope John VIII wrote on more than one occasion to Boris, sometimes claiming that Bulgaria was under Roman, not Constantinopolitan, jurisdiction, other times encouraging him to flee the Byzantine errors.[152] He even sent legates: in 878, the bishops Paul of Ancona and Eugenius of Ostia, who were traveling from Constantinople; in 879, a priest named John, whom the pope also recommended to Branimir, the duke of the Croats, and asked for his protection on his way to Bulgaria.[153] Boris politely responded in both 878 and 879, when his envoy Functicus arrived in Rome with gifts

[152] *Epistulae Karolini aevi*, vol. v, ed. by E. Kaspar (Berlin, 1928), pp. 7, 66–67, 70, and 182–183.

[153] *Epistulae Karolini aevi*, vol. v, pp. 68, 69, 71, and 190–191.

for the pope.[154] Nothing came out of these exchanges of embassies, for during the 870s the Byzantine mission was firmly established in Pliska and in other places in Bulgaria.

In Pliska, construction had already begun by 870 on what is now known as the Great Basilica, which was erected near Omurtag's Palace on top of the former Great Temple and the *martyrium*. Finished at some point between 870 and 875, the three-aisled building of early Byzantine design is a strong reminder that the initial source of inspiration for the church architecture in Bulgaria was not Constantinople, where at that time the popular church plan was that of a dome over a cross-shaped ground plan. On the northern side of the church, there was an episcopal palace equipped with a bath, *scriptorium*, and other facilities. The discovery on the site of a seal of an archbishop George confirms that this was the episcopal church of Pliska.[155] A small cemetery behind the church contains the burials of the elite residing either in the episcopal or in the neighboring royal palace. An exquisite reliquary cross made of gold and covered with Greek inscriptions was found by the city's western gate in a pit together with potshards and animal bones.[156] Not much is known about the number and the location of the suffragan bishops, but a presumably episcopal church very similar in size and ground plan to the Great Basilica in Pliska has been recently found in Silistra on the Danube inside a stronghold that reused the ramparts of the late Roman and early Byzantine city of Durostorum. The conversion had an immediate and visible impact on burial practices. Burial assemblages in Bulgaria that can be dated to the late 800s produced a significantly larger number of dress accessories, such as finger-rings, beads, and earrings, but no grave goods such as pottery or tools, which were now abandoned in

[154] *Epistulae Karolini aevi*, vol. v, pp. 70 and 198. According to the *Life of St. Blaise of Amorion*, a Bulgarian bishop was traveling on pilgrimage to Rome in *c.* 874. Since the last bishop of the Roman church had been expelled in 870, this can only have been a member of the Byzantine clergy that came to Bulgaria after the appointment of the Bulgarian archbishop.

[155] R. Vasilev, "Novootkrit oloven pechat na arkhiepiskop Georgi v Pliska [The recently found leaden seal of Archbishop George of Pliska]," *Numizmatika i sfragistika*, vols. 1–2 (1992), pp. 26–29. For new finds of ninth-century episcopal seals, see S. Bilik, "Molivdovul na neizvesten episkop na Bălgariia ot IX vek [A leaden seal of an unknown bishop of ninth-century Bulgaria]," *Problemi na prabălgarskata istoriia i kultura*, vol. 3 (1997), 363–366.

[156] L. Doncheva, "Une croix pectorale-reliquaire en or récemment trouvée à Pliska," *CA*, vol. 25 (1976), pp. 59–66.

favor of Christian burial practices. The best example of a rapid transformation is that of a small community in northern Bulgaria, which had been using since the early ninth century the cremation cemetery excavated at Dolni Lukovit on the Iskăr River. Shortly before the end of that century, all cremation burials disappeared and new ground was opened for inhumations. Elsewhere, cremations remained in use, and the still incomplete character of the conversion is illustrated by such phenomena as an urn cremation burial from Preslav that produced an early tenth-century pectoral cross of the so-called Palestinian class.

The conversion was not exclusively the result of decisions taken at the top. According to the *Life of St. Blaise of Amorion*, the saint traveled at some point after 872 from Constantinople to Rome via Bulgaria, where he was sold into slavery by his wicked companion. Blaise's owner was a Bulgar nobleman, who released him, hoping that he would remain and guide him in leading a Christian life. Instead, Blaise boarded a boat traveling up the Danube, but was captured by pirates at a place where the river met "steep mountains" and terrifying "chasms," most likely the Iron Gates region. His captors thought that Blaise was a merchant transporting goods upstream, an indication that by 870 the Danube corridor had opened not only for communication with Rome, but also for trade.[157] The segment of the river course between the Iron Gates and the confluence with the Drava River was clearly in Bulgar hands, as indicated by the events following Methodius' death in 885 and the expulsion of his disciples from Moravia.

According to the *Life of St. Clement of Ohrid*, at least three of them – Clement, Naum, and Angelarius – managed to come across the Danube to Belgrade, where the *tarqan* of the region met and treated them with great respect. After they rested for three days, they were sent to Boris in Pliska, where they were received with great enthusiasm.[158] After a sojourn in Pliska, Boris sent Clement to the recently conquered region of Macedonia, where a religious center was established on the northern shore of Lake Ohrid. Boris "detached the

[157] V. Giuzelev, "Zhitieto na Vlasii Amoriiski kato izvor za bălgarskata istoriia [The *Life* of St. Basil of Amorion as a source for the Bulgarian history]," *GSU*, vol. 61 (1968), pp. 19–33. Blaise was abandoned by his captors in the middle of the wilderness, but miraculously managed to find his way back into Bulgaria, where he met a bishop going to Rome on pilgrimage, in the company of whom he eventually reached his final destination.

[158] Theophylact of Ohrid, *Life of St. Clement of Ohrid* 16, p. 114.

territory of Kutmichinica from that of Kotokios," and appointed a new governor for the new administrative unit in the person of a certain Dometas (most likely a *tarqan*), with Clement as "teacher" for that territory. In addition, Clement received three comfortable houses in Diabolis, as well as "places of rest" near Ohrid and in Glavinica.[159] Both Diabolis (the valley of the upper Devolli River, near the southern shore of Lake Ohrid) and Glavinica (between Berat and Valona) can be located with some degree of certainty in southern Albania, namely in that same region in which Boris's inscription of Ballsh was found. In Kutmichinica, Clement spent most of his time preaching to pagans, of whom there seem to have been a great number among the locals. Unlike the Greek clergy in Pliska, his efforts were aimed at the conversion of commoners, which may explain why the majority of Clement's works belong to the homiletic genre (sermons). The script in use must have been the Glagolitic invented by Constantine, but the thirteenth-century *Short Life* written by Archbishop Demetrius Chomatenos credits Clement with some improvement of Constantine's invention, as he "skillfully devised other shapes with a view to making them clearer than those which the wise Cyril invented."[160] Clement himself wrote extensively in the tradition of the Byzantine mission in Moravia, with a strong emphasis, among others, on *abrenuntiatio* (renouncing the devil), a theme prominently represented in the Freising Fragments. His sermons have a simple structure and often paraphrase an episode from the Old or New Testament to move quickly to teaching moral values. His eulogy of Constantine-Cyril is the first work to consecrate the image of an "apostle of the Slavs": when God decided to crown "the many-tribed Slavic people with the godwoven crown," He sent Constantine as His apostle.[161] Besides his literary activity, Clement created a monastery in Ohrid, which he dedicated to St. Panteleimon. After seven years of missionary work in Kutmichinica, he was appointed bishop of a see that the *Life of*

[159] Theophylact of Ohrid, *Life of St. Clement of Ohrid* 53 and 54, pp. 116–118; English translation from D. Obolensky, *Six Byzantine Portraits* (Oxford: Oxford University Press, 1988), p. 22.

[160] *Grăckite zhitiia na Kliment Okhridski*, ed. by A. Milev (Sofia: Izdatelstvo na Bălgarskata Akademiia na Naukite, 1966), p. 180; English translation from Obolensky, *Six Portraits*, p. 29.

[161] Clement of Ohrid, *A Eulogy to Saint Cyril*, English translation in T. Butler, *Monumenta Bulgarica. A Bilingual Anthology of Bulgarian Texts from the 9th to the 19th Centuries* (Ann Arbor: Michigan Slavic Publications, 1996), p. 93.

St. Clement of Ohrid calls "Dragvica or Velika" and which was most likely located in the Vardar River valley and near the northern slopes of the Rhodope Mountains, south of present-day Sofia. Clement remained Bishop of Dragvica until his death in 916, but frequently visited his monastery in Ohrid.

A few years before Clement's appointment as bishop, Boris abdicated in favor of his eldest son Vladimir and retired to a monastery, perhaps in or near Pliska. But the new ruler had no sympathy for Christianity and a rebellion broke out that attempted to reestablish paganism. Large-scale massacres, to which fell victim the archbishop of Pliska himself, are illustrated by such archaeological assemblages as the mass burial at Kiulevcha, a few miles south from Pliska, which contains twenty-five skeletons, all of young males, many with clear evidence of fatal wounds by arrows. A similar interpretation has been advanced for yet another peculiar assemblage, the round burial in Devnia, near Varna, with the complete and incomplete skeletons of forty-three individuals, including a sixty-five-year-old man and an unborn foetus. A large number of the Devnia skeletons belong to females, many of whom died a violent death, as indicated by traces of blows by sharp-edged instruments on many bones. The violence of the revolt prompted Boris to return from his monastery to lead a coup that overthrew his son, whom he blinded. A council of all *boilades* was summoned in 893 at Preslav, as Pliska seems to have been utterly devastated. The Preslav council declared Vladimir deposed in favor of his younger brother, Symeon. Boris's younger son had spent some time in Constantinople, perhaps preparing to become a leading figure of the new Bulgarian church. His career course changed suddenly when he was proclaimed ruler. The Preslav council also declared Christianity a state religion, thus sanctioning the achievements of Boris's very long reign (852–889). On the other hand, the decisions of the council turned Old Church Slavonic into the official language of Church and State, an indication both of Clement's success in the southwestern and central regions of Bulgaria and of Boris's constant preoccupation with escaping the Byzantine tutelage. As the new ruler moved his residence to Preslav, away from the memories of the violent events that had marked the reign of Boris, the decisions of the 893 council also shifted the emphasis from Clement's achievements to the extraordinary activity of a group of scholars based in Preslav that would mark the "golden age" of medieval Bulgarian culture.

At the peak of the crisis created by Vladimir's rebellion, Bulgar forces attacked Svatopluk's Moravia. A year earlier, in 892, King Arnulf of Carinthia had dispatched an embassy to the Bulgars, asking "their kind Laodamir" to renew the peace and to stop the sales of salt to the Moravians.[162] Arnulf's demand confirms what is otherwise known from the *Life of St. Blaise of Amorion*, namely that during the second half of the ninth century the Bulgars engaged in trade along the newly opened Danube corridor to the west. As the salt in question could have only come from Transylvania via the Mureş River that flows westwards into the Tisza at Szeged (Hungary), this suggests a Bulgar control of the salt-mine district in southern Transylvania, an interpretation that is not contradicted by the existing archaeological evidence. The new Bulgar ruler does not seem to have changed the course of Frankish–Bulgar relations, and judging from the quick response to Arnulf's demands, the Bulgars continued to be involved in operations in the Middle Danube region. But Symeon's problems were elsewhere.

He had barely been in power for one year when a decision of Emperor Leo VI regarding the Bulgarian commerce sparked a new large-scale conflict with Byzantium. The exact reasons for Leo's measure are not known, but he seems to have separated the Bulgarian commerce from the "foreign markets" and abolished what might be viewed as a most-favored nation's status for Bulgarian merchants. As Symeon's protests were ignored, the Bulgarian armies raided Thrace. With his troops occupied in the East, Emperor Leo sent an embassy to the Magyars in the steppes north of the Danube Delta, asking them to attack Symeon from the north. The attack succeeded and the Magyars devastated northern Bulgaria, forcing Symeon to withdraw to Dristra (now Silistra) on the Danube. Once peace had been established with the Byzantines, Symeon attacked the Magyars, at the same time inciting against them their eastern neighbors, the Pechenegs, a group of people that had been itself driven out of its former lands on both sides of the river Volga by the Turkic tribe of the Oghuz, the formidable allies of the Khazars. The double attack on the Magyars put an end to their control of the steppes north of the Danube Delta. The destruction brought by the Pechenegs forced the remaining Magyars to embark on another migration, which took them into the Carpathian Basin. The events of 894/5 are thus of

[162] *Annals of Fulda*, s.a. 892, pp. 121–122; English translation by Reuter, p. 124.

crucial importance for the beginnings of medieval Hungary. The arrival of the Pechenegs in the lands formerly controlled by the Magyars had also a considerable influence on the Balkan polities, Bulgaria and the Byzantine Empire, as well as on the rising state of the Rus' of Kiev. A new page was thus opening in the history of Southeastern Europe.

4

IRON CENTURY OR GOLDEN AGE (900–1000)?

The events taking place in the steppes north of the Danube Delta and the Black Sea in the late ninth century opened a two-and-a-half-century period of turbulence marking a sharp contrast between West and East, to which some historians refer as the "last migrations."[1] The news of the disastrous defeat that had forced the Magyars to move to Central Europe reverberated well after AD 900, at a time when the Magyar raids had already brought destruction to most areas in the West. Writing in his Lotharingian abbey in 908, Regino of Prüm noted that the victors were the "Pecenaci." This is the first mention of the Pechenegs in Europe,[2] but the main source for their European history is Emperor Constantine Porphyrogenitus' *De administrando imperio*, which was written some forty years later. The richness of detail in this account is so extraordinary that very little could be said on the Pechenegs without it. As a consequence, Constantine's work has rightly been compared to Herodotus' account of the Scythians. Indeed, no other ancient or medieval source written in Greek describes in such detail the social and political organization in the steppe. The Turkic names of the Pecheneg clans, which

[1] V. Spinei, *Ultimele valuri migratoare la nordul Mării Negre şi al Dunării de Jos* [The Last Migrations to the Region North of the Black Sea and the Lower Danube] (Iaşi: Helios, 1996).

[2] Regino of Prüm, *Chronicon*, s.a. 889, ed. by F. Kurze (Hanover: Hahnsche Buchhandlung, 1890; reprint 1989), MGH SS 50:131–2. For Regino as the first European to mention the Pechenegs, see O. Pritsak, "The Pechenegs: a case of social and economic transformation," *AEMA*, vol. 1 (1975), p. 217.

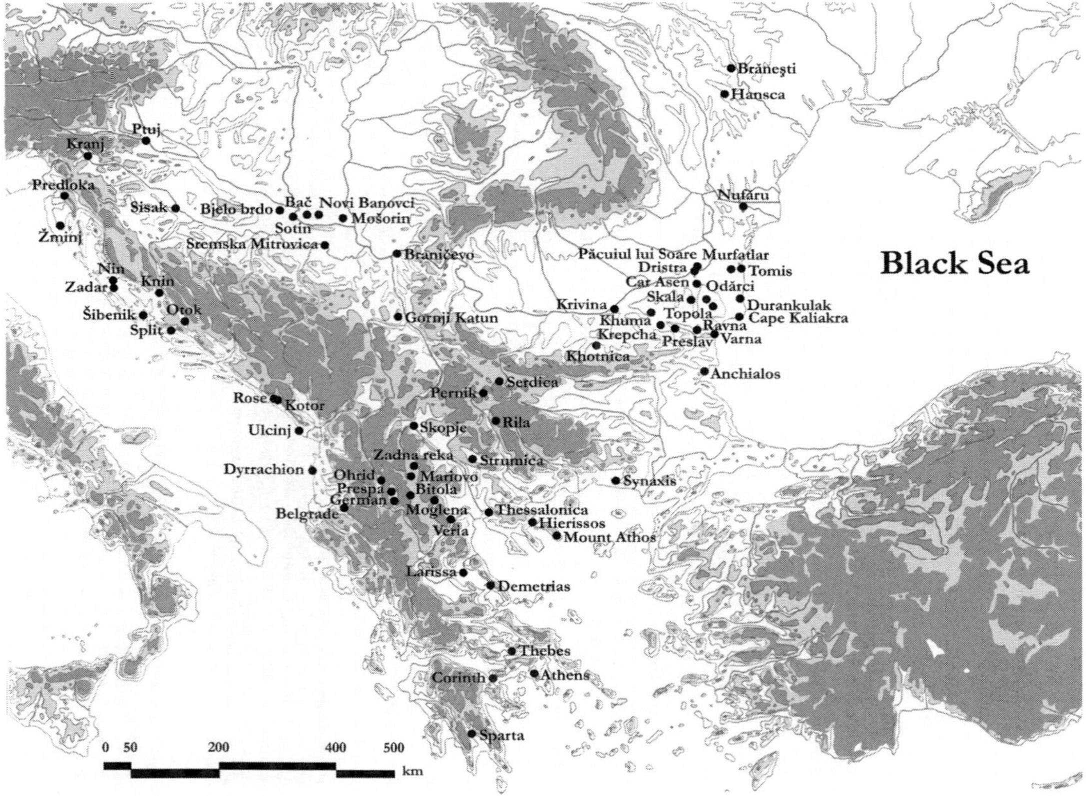

Map 4 Southeastern Europe in the tenth century.

were rendered in Greek without any attempt to translate them or even understand their meaning, as well as the precise location of the Pecheneg "provinces" (*themata*) betray Constantine's source of information, which must have been of Pecheneg origin, perhaps collected in the Crimean city of Chersonesus, where the nomads were bringing their hides and wax and received in exchange "purple cloth, ribbons, loosely woven cloths, gold brocade, pepper, scarlet or 'Parthian' leather, and other commodities which they require."[3] According to Constantine, "Patzinakia," the land of the Pechenegs, was divided into eight "provinces," each with five districts. Constantine's "provinces" were most likely the territories of the leading clans. Three of them – Chabouxingyla, Iabdiertim, and Kouartzitzour – were ranked higher than the remaining five and were called Kangar, meaning "more valiant and noble than the rest."[4] Of the eight "provinces," four were located west of the Dnieper River, with Iabdiertim, the highest in rank, on the border of three Slavic tribes – the Ulichians, the Derevlianians, and the Polianians – south of Kiev, to the Rus' rulers of which they had been forced to pay tribute. It is in this region that the political center of Patzinakia was located, the "city of tents" that the mission of St. Bruno of Querfurt reached in 1007, after four days of traveling by foot from the southernmost border of Rus'.[5] Further to the west, between the Bug and the Dniester, was Charaboi. Chabouxingyla is said to have bordered "Tourkia," by which Constantine meant the territory that was occupied at that time (*c.* 950) by the Magyars. This "province" must therefore have stretched across the

[3] Constantine Porphyrogenitus, *De administrando imperio* 6, pp. 52–53. Constantine also knew that the Pechenegs were trading with the Rus', who bought their cattle, sheep, and horses (*De administrando imperio*, pp. 50–51). Equally informative must have been several Byzantine embassies sent to the Pechenegs during the first half of the tenth century. See E. Malamut, "L'image byzantine des Petchénègues," *BZ*, vol. 88 (1995), pp. 109–112.

[4] Constantine Porphyrogenitus, *De administrando imperio* 37, pp. 170–171. For the meaning of Kangar, see Pritsak, "The Pechenegs," pp. 212–214. It is important to note that the accuracy of Constantine's Pecheneg account can be checked against that of al-Mas'udi, writing some twenty years earlier. According to the Arab polymath, there were eight Pecheneg clans and their names perfectly match those supplied by Constantine. See J. Marquart, *Osteuropäische und ostasiatische Streifzüge. Ethnologische und historisch-topographische Studien zur Geschichte des 9. und 10. Jahrhunderts (ca. 840–940)* (Leipzig: Dieterich'sche Verlagsbuchhandlung, 1903; reprint Hildesheim: Georg Olm, 1961), p. 65.

[5] Bruno of Querfurt, *Letter to King Henry*, ed. by A. Bielowski, in *Monumenta Poloniae historica*, vol. 1 (Cracow: Naklad Akademii Umejetności, 1864; reprint Warsaw: Państwowe Wydawnictwo Naukowe, 1960), pp. 224–225.

upper courses of the Siret, Prut, and Dniester Rivers, all of which are mentioned as flowing through Patzinakia. Finally, Giazichopon was separated from Bulgaria by the river Danube and must therefore be located in the Walachian Plain. The entire steppe corridor between the Danube and the Dnieper Rivers was thus under Pecheneg control.

De administrando imperio describes a system of social organization based on the principle of genealogical seniority, with rank inherited by the eldest male member of each clan. The emperor noted with some surprise the existence of certain forms of "democracy" within the clan aristocracy, which undoubtedly served to stabilize authority. Marriage alliances allowed new clans to emerge and claim access to power and territory. By the mid-eleventh century, there were already thirteen, instead of just eight, clans, and competition between chieftains made it necessary to organize a general council, with delegates from each clan. It has been shown that the Turkic names of the Pecheneg "provinces" in *De administrando imperio* are all compounds in which the first part designates a color, while the second is the name of the dignity associated with the chief of the "province." Iabdiertim, for example, was "glittering white," while Chabouxingyla and Charaboi were "bark-" and "black-colored", respectively. The terms in question may have referred to the color of the horsetails attached to spears in order to distinguish different units in battle.[6] What Constantine described as "provinces," therefore, may have initially been a form of military organization.

The Pecheneg economy was predominantly pastoral. The distribution north of the Black Sea of archaeological sites attributed to the nomads suggests that the Pechenegs practiced a form of seasonal migration from the lowlands near the Danube and the Black Sea (in winter) to the middle and upper courses of the Danube's northern tributaries or of the rivers flowing into the Black Sea (in summer). No temporary camps have so far been found in either region, as the archaeology of pastoralism in Southeastern Europe is only in its incipient phase. Graves of nomadic horsemen were often dug into prehistoric barrows that were more prominent in the tenth-century steppe landscape than they are now. Such "secondary burials" have been found in the Walachian Plain, in the region of the Kahul, Ialpukh, and Katlabukh Lakes just north of the Danube Delta, as well as in

[6] K. H. Menges, "Etymological notes on some Păčänäg names," *Byzantion* 7 (1944–1945), pp. 256–280. The second element in the name Chabouxingyla may be the title *gyula* attested among the Magyars.

the Black Sea lowlands between the delta and the mouth of the Dniester River.[7] Most typical for these burials is the presence of horse bones indicating that during the funeral feast a horse was sacrificed. The stripped hide with the skull and lower limbs was placed in the grave pit, together with the harness, often on the left side of the human body. The associated grave goods are most typical of life in the saddle and show a number of innovations that the tenth-century nomads introduced to the region. In order to have a more efficient control of the horse in combat, the Pechenegs used unjointed snaffles with rigid mouthpieces, either straight or curved, of which several have been found in the Walachian Plain (especially on the territory of the present-day city of Bucharest and its hinterland), Romanian Moldavia, the Republic of Moldova, and southern Ukraine. Equally new in the early 900s were the round stirrups that were easier to use with soft-soled boots. One such pair of stirrups from a tenth-century burial in the Walachian Plain was decorated with damascened ornamentation very similar to contemporary stirrups found in burial assemblages from Hungary.[8] That these were burials of warriors, and not just horsemen, is confirmed by finds of such weapons as battle-axes, sabers, as well as spear- and arrowheads. No burial in the steppe corridor north of the Danube Delta and the Black Sea could rival the extraordinary richness and variety of grave goods of Pecheneg burial assemblages in Left Bank Ukraine. However, there are some signs of wealth, perhaps also of rank, differentiation, such as golden ear- and finger-rings, as well as remains of gold brocade.[9] Some graves

[7] Most rivers in this steppe corridor have names ending in *–ui* (Bahlui, Covurlui, Derehlui, Vaslui, Călmăţui), which are all of Turkic, possibly Pecheneg origin. See I. Conea and I. Donat, "Contributions à la toponymie petchénègue-coumane de la Plaine Roumaine du Bas-Danube," in *Contributions onomastiques publiées à l'occasion du VIe Congrès international des sciences onomastiques à Munich du 24 au 28 août 1958*, ed. by E. Petrovici (Bucharest: Académie de la République Populaire Roumaine, 1958), pp. 139–169.

[8] V. Leahu and G. Trohani, "Două morminte de călăreţi nomazi din Cîmpia Teleormanului [Two nomadic horseman burials in the Teleorman Plain]," *SCIVA*, vol. 29 (1978), pp. 529–539.

[9] The only burials producing such artifacts are those of the Black Sea lowlands between the Danube Delta and the mouth of the Dniester River. A few Byzantine gold and silver coins minted for the joint rule of Constantine VII Porphyrogenitus and Romanus II have been found in the same region. See E. S. Stoliarik, *Essays on Monetary Circulation in the North-Western Black Sea Region in the Late Roman and Byzantine Periods (Late 3rd Century–Early 13th Century AD)* (Odessa: Polis, 1992), pp. 143–144.

were apparently double burials, often with one male and one female skeleton. More often than not, the same prehistoric barrow was used for more than one burial, but no site produced more than ten burials, an indication that these may have been family cemeteries used over one or two generations or only during seasonal migrations.

Unlike the situation in Left Bank Ukraine, where most sites of the sedentary population in the forest-steppe belt were abandoned in the early 900s as a consequence of the Pecheneg raids, most settlements in the region between the Danube and the Dniester continued to be occupied after *c.* 900 and no significant changes in material culture have been noted that could be attributed to the defeat of the Magyars and the subsequent Pecheneg migration. To be sure, the strongholds in the Middle Dniester region that were erected during the 800s (Alcedar, Echimăuţi, Rudi) were all destroyed at some point during the tenth or early eleventh century. Some of them have been linked to the Tivercians, a Slavic tribe which, according to the twelfth-century *Russian Primary Chronicle*, "lived by the Dniester and extended as far as the Danube."[10] If so, then responsible for the destruction of these forts were the Rus', not the Pechenegs. The *Chronicle* mentions that Prince Oleg of Kiev attacked in 885 the Tivercians, who were subsequently forced to send troops for the Rus' expeditions against Byzantium in 907 and 944.[11] In any case, the strongholds in the Middle Dniester region were apparently the southernmost link in the trade network spreading over a vast area in Eastern Europe. During the Viking Age, enormous quantities of silver in the form of Arab dirhams began to move across this area from south to north. Both Alcedar and Echimăuţi produced dirhams of tenth-century Samanid rulers, while earlier dirhams of eighth-century Abbasid caliphs have been found in association with silver jewelry in a tenth-century hoard from Răducăneni near Iaşi (Romania).[12] There is otherwise no

[10] *Povest' vremennykh let*, ed. by D. S. Likhachev and V. P. Adrianova-Perec (Moscow and Leningrad: Izdatel'stvo Akademii Nauk SSSR, 1950), p. 14; English translation by Cross and Sherbowitz-Wetzor, p. 56. See also A. V. Boldur, "The enigma of the Ulichy-Tivertsy people," *BS*, vol. 9 (1968), pp. 55–90.

[11] *Povest' vremennykh let*, pp. 23 and 33; English translation by Cross and Sherbowitz-Wetzor, pp. 64 and 72.

[12] For the Alcedar and Echimăuţi dirhams, see A. A. Nudel'man, *Topografiia kladov i nakhodok edinichnykh monet* [The Distribution of Hoard and Individual Coin Finds] (Kishinew: Shtiinca, 1976), pp. 89–90. For the Răducăneni hoard, see D. Gh. Teodor, "Tezaurul de la Răducaneni-Iaşi [The Răducăneni hoard]," *SCIVA*, vol. 31 (1980), pp. 403–423. See also R. K. Kovalev, "Dirham mint output of

evidence of any influence that the trade routes between Scandinavia and the Muslim world may have had on the region. The communication established during the Viking Age between Scandinavia and Eastern Europe has left no mark on Southeastern Europe.

By contrast, some 400 settlement sites have been found so far in the region between the eastern Carpathian Mountains and the river Dniester. Occupation on many of them had begun in the ninth and continued into the eleventh century. Other settlements appeared during the 900s and were abandoned only in the mid-eleventh century. Tenth-century settlement sites have been excavated primarily in the Moldavian and Bessarabian Uplands on both sides of the Lower Prut River, immediately north of the steppe corridor. They cluster around the Kahul, Ialpukh, and Katlabukh Lakes as well, one of the areas that also produced large numbers of burials attributed to the nomads, which suggests some form of peaceful coexistence between pastoralists and native communities. In permanent need of agricultural produce, much like all pastoralists, the Pechenegs had no reason to destroy the local network of rural settlements that had flourished in the 800s under the protection of neighboring Bulgaria. Moreover, the coexistence of pastoralists and agriculturists is indicated by the occasional presence on settlement sites of typically Pecheneg dress accessories or horse gear. Some influence of nomadic burial customs can also be detected in cemeteries excavated further to the north, in the Bessarabian Uplands. To be sure, the region seems to have been well synchronized with changes taking place in Bulgaria. At Brăneşti near Orhei (Republic of Moldova), a cemetery dated to the tenth and early eleventh century produced ninety-eight burials, only three of which were cremations, the latest of their kind in the whole of Southeastern Europe. As in ninth-century Bulgaria, gender differences were particularly evident in the greater quantity of dress accessories associated with female burials.[13] With the exception of ceramic pots, grave goods completely disappeared from tenth-century

Samanid Samarqand and its connection to the beginnings of trade with northern Europe," *H&M*, vol. 17 (2002), pp. 197–216. No dirhams have been found in the steppe belt, which suggests that the Pechenegs were neither participants in this trade network, nor very successful in tapping its resources.

[13] G. B. Fedorov, G. F. Chebotarenko, and M. S. Velikanova, *Braneshtskii mogil'nik. X–XI vv.* [The Tenth- to Eleventh-Century Cemetery in Brăneşti] (Kishinew: Shtiinca, 1984). For the associated settlement, see R. A. Rabinovich and V. D. Gukin, "Rezul'taty razkopok na poselenii Braneshti XIII i nekotorye spornye voprosy izucheniia pamiatnikov tipa Petrukha-Lukashevka [The results of

burial assemblages in Hansca–Căprăria near Chişinău (Republic of Moldova). Two thirds of all graves excavated there had no grave goods. But besides grave pits, archaeologists found three pits with animal, but not human, bones, including the whole skeleton of a young cow.[14] The same is true for the even larger cemetery excavated nearby, at Hansca–Limbari, which began only after AD 1000. Besides human burials, this cemetery produced pits containing whole skeletons of domestic animals (but no human bones) – a sheep, a pig, and two horses (see chapter 5).

The Pechenegs relied heavily on trade with, as well as raids against, neighboring states, particularly Rus' and Byzantium. There is no evidence of Pecheneg trade with Bulgaria, and the closest Byzantine port of trade was Chersonesus in Crimea, against which the Pechenegs never conducted raids. Instead, the main targets of their attacks were to the north. According to the *Russian Primary Chronicle*, the Pechenegs first attacked "the land of Rus'" in 915, but they laid siege to Kiev only in 968. However, in the mid-tenth century, Constantine Porphyrogenitus knew that the Rus' could not reach Constantinople "either for war or for peace" without peaceful relations with the Pechenegs. The reason, he explained, was that, when the Rus' came with their ships to the barrages (rapids) of the river (Dnieper), and could not pass through them unless they lifted their ships off the river and carried them past by porting them on their shoulders, they were extremely vulnerable to Pecheneg attacks.[15] In 972, it was precisely in that region that Sviatoslav, the prince of Kiev, was ambushed and killed by the Pechenegs upon his return from the Balkan campaign. In the words of the twelfth-century Rus' chronicler, "the nomads took his head, and made a cup out of his skull, overlaying it with gold, and they drank from it."[16] Less than two decades later, Sviatoslav's son Vladimir began building a number of forts on the tributaries of

excavations on the Brăneşti 13 settlement site and some issues concerning the study of sites of the Petruha-Lukashovka type]," in *Drevnosti Iugo-Zapada SSSR*, ed. by P. P. Byrnia, V. A. Dergachev, R. A. Rabinovich, et al. (Kishinew: Shtiinca, 1991), pp. 205–224.

14 I. G. Hâncu, *Kapraria – pamiatniki kul'tury X–XII vv.* [Căprăria. Monuments of the Tenth- to Twelfth-Century Culture] (Kishinew: Shtiinca, 1972).

15 Constantine Porphyrogenitus, *De administrando imperio* 2, pp. 50–51. For the importance of the Dnieper portages for the Rus' trade, see J. Martin, *Medieval Russia, 980–1584* (Cambridge: Cambridge Unviversity Press, 1995), pp. 17–19.

16 *Povest' vremennykh let*, s.a. 6423 (915), 6467 (968), and 6480 (972); English translation by Cross and Sherbowitz-Wetzor, pp. 71, 85–86, and 90.

the Dnieper near, and south of, Kiev, in order to protect the southern frontier of Rus' against the nomads.[17] The Pechenegs reacted by repeatedly attacking the Rus' territories (992, 995, and 997), while Vladimir barely escaped alive from one of his encounters with the nomads. Hostilities between the Rus' and the Pechenegs continued well into the eleventh century.

By contrast, relations with Byzantium were, with some exceptions, peaceful. After attacking the Magyars in alliance with Symeon, the Pechenegs switched sides several times in the early 900s. In 917, they accepted the demand of the Byzantine *drungarios* Romanus Lecapenus (the future emperor Romanus I) to attack Symeon, but the Byzantine attempt to transport the Pecheneg warriors across the Danube on ships of the imperial fleet was thwarted by conflicts between the Byzantine commanders. No raids against either Byzantium or Bulgaria are known from Byzantine sources. Only Mas'udi reports that the Pechenegs participated in 934 in a Magyar raid across Bulgaria and into Byzantine territories.[18] On the other hand, when the Byzantines tried to incite the Magyars against the Pechenegs, the memories of the events of 893 seem to have been much stronger than any possible gains the Magyar chieftains could hope to obtain from such expeditions.[19]

The Magyars had moved into the Middle Danube region via the mountain passes of the eastern Beskides (Dukla or Ushko) on the present-day border between Poland, Slovakia, and Ukraine. No evidence exists of Magyars crossing the eastern Carpathian Mountains into Transylvania, or even moving westwards from the Middle Danube region into Transylvania before the middle of the tenth century. Nor did they occupy the entire territory of the Carpathian Basin. Large parts of Transdanubia (western Hungary) remained under Frankish rule throughout the reign of Arnulf, while Moravia

[17] *Povest' vremennykh let*, s.a. 6496 (988); English translation by Cross and Sherbowitz-Wetzor, p. 119. See also J. Shepard, "The Russian steppe-frontier and the Black Sea zone," *Archeion Pontou*, vol. 35 (1978), pp. 218–237. Although the most important fortifications were in Left Bank Ukraine, the building project also included territories on the right bank of the Dnieper, especially the valley of the Stuhna River.

[18] Al-Mas'udi, *Kitāb al-Tanbīh wa'l-išrāf (Le livre de l'avertissement et de la revision)*, translated by B. Carra de Vaux (Paris: Imprimerie nationale, 1896; reprint Frankfurt am Main: Institut für Geschichte der arabisch-islamischen Wissenschaften an der Johann Wolfgang Goethe-Universität, 1986), p. 245.

[19] Constantine Porphyrogenitus, *De administrando imperio* 8, pp. 56–57.

only fell after 900. Initially, at least, buffer zones of uninhabited land must have separated the conquered territory from the northern, western, and southern neighbors of the Magyars. Most early raids were directed against neighboring territories to the west. In 898 and 899, the Magyars attacked Berengar's march of Friuli, and even spent the winter of 899/900 in the Po valley. Both raids must have reached Italy along the Drava valley, the route of the ninth-century Bulgar and Roman envoys traveling back and forth between Rome and Pliska. In 901, Carantania was devastated by the Magyar raids, and in 907 the nomads crushed a Bavarian army at Bratislava. Magyar raids into Byzantium started comparatively later and had a considerably smaller impact. Raids are mentioned in the *Life of St. Basil the Younger* and the *Life of St. Luke the Younger*, in the latter in connection with some unspecified region in Greece. Another raid through Thrace reaching as far as Constantinople is mentioned in the continuation of the chronicle of George the Monk, as well as in the works of Theophanes Continuatus and John Skylitzes. All three authors mention a fourth raid taking place in 943, which ended in a victory for the Byzantines, who demanded hostages from among the Magyar nobility as a warranty for peace. Two more raids took place in 959 and 961, respectively, and both ended in defeats for the Magyars. With the exception of the raid mentioned in the *Life of St. Luke the Younger*, no raid seems to have gone farther than Thrace, and all were relatively easy to spot and stop, an indication, perhaps, of the relatively small number of Magyar troops.

Shortly after 900, major changes took place in the organization of power of the Magyar confederacy. Until then, and before moving into the Middle Danube region, the Magyars were ruled by a *kende*, a chieftain that had initially been appointed to them by the Khazars, under whose authority the Magyars had been throughout much of the ninth century. By 900, however, the *kende* was just a nominal ruler, for power was in fact in the hands of two military commanders, the *gyula* and the *harka*. Moreover, the *kende* died in 902 in an ambush, and leadership passed onto the *gyula*, a man named Arpad. Much like with contemporary Pechenegs, succession was governed by the principle of seniority: one of Arpad's kinsmen became *gyula*, and the man's son, Bulcsu, became *harka*. Bulcsu is mentioned in 948 among visitors to the imperial court in Constantinople. He received baptism with Emperor Constantine Porphyrogenitus as sponsor at his baptismal font. A few years later, the *gyula* also visited Constantinople and was baptized. Unlike Bulcsu, however, he was also given a bishop named Hierotheos who accompanied him back to "Tourkia." Several seals of eleventh-century bishops of "Tourkia" are known and their see was located in what is today Bačka, the northernmost region of Serbia, on the border with Hungary.[20]

It is not known what chieftains controlled what territories, but it is possible that both *gyula* and *harka* ruled over the southern region of the Carpathian Basin. It is also possible that the raids into Byzantine territories had been launched from that same region. While very vague about the geography of the central and northern regions occupied by the Magyars, Constantine Porphyrogenitus was well-informed about the territories they had under control near, as well as south of, the Danube River. He specifically mentions that the Magyars occupied lands "between the Danube and the Sava River."[21] Apparently his source of information were the visitors of the mid-tenth century who had accepted baptism in Constantinople. If so, they must have told the emperor what they knew best, namely the extent of the territories assigned to them and to their fellow tribesmen. This conclusion is substantiated by the archaeological evidence pertaining to the presence of the tenth-century nomads. Most finds of tenth-century artifacts of Byzantine origin found in Hungary cluster at the confluence of the Tisza and Mureş Rivers, which is also the region that produced the largest number of tenth- and eleventh-century Byzantine coins found in Hungary. The majority of pectoral crosses, many of which are of Byzantine origin, have also been found on sites in the Tisza Plain and in Banat near the present-day border between Romania, Serbia, and Hungary. Their distribution strikingly coincides with the territory of ecclesiastical jurisdiction of the

20 John Skylitzes, *Synopsis historiarum*, p. 239. For *gyula* as a title, not a name, see L. Varady, "Revision der Ungarn-Image von Konstantinos Porphyrogenetos," *BZ*, vol. 82 (1989), pp. 36–38. For the bishopric of "Tourkia," see I. Baán, "The metropolitanate of Tourkia. The organization of the Byzantine church in Hungary in the Middle Ages," in *Byzanz und Ostmitteleuropa, 50–1453. Beiträge zu einer table-ronde des XIX Internationalen Congress of Byzantine Studies, Copenhagen 1996*, ed. by G. Prinzing and M. Salamon (Wiesbaden: Otto Harrassowitz, 1999), pp. 45–53.

21 Constantine Porphyrogenitus, *De administrando imperio* 42, pp. 182–183. See L. S. Tóth, "The territories of the Hungarian tribal federation around 950 (some observations on Constantine VII's 'Tourkia')," in *Byzanz und Ostmitteleuropa, 950–1453. Beiträge zu einer table-ronde des XIX Internationalen Congress of Byzantine Studies, Copenhagen 1996*, ed. by G. Prinzing and M. Salamon (Wiesbaden: Otto Harrassowitz, 1999), pp. 23–33.

eleventh-century bishopric of Bač. But Bačka properly speaking – the region between the Lower Tisza and the Danube – has so far produced only limited evidence of a tenth-century settlement network. Many sites in the region seem to have begun in earnest only after AD 1000. The only exception is Mošorin, near the confluence of the Tisza and Danube Rivers, a village that appeared in the late 900s, with an associated cemetery nearby.[22] Other cemeteries dated to the tenth and eleventh century have been found on the banks of the Lower Tisza, as well as along the Danube, both north and south of its confluence with the Drava River. As for the region between the two rivers, just north of Novi Sad, it was a large swamp sparsely inhabited before AD 1000. Moreover, only a few horseman burials have been found on the left bank of the Danube, which suggests that the area of the Great Roman Ditch erected in the ninth century in the region now served as a buffer zone. To the north of that zone, especially around the confluence of the Tisza and Mureş Rivers, the cluster of finds dated to the tenth century may be associated with the areas under the control of the *gyula* and the *harka*, two of the most important political figures of the Magyar confederacy. South of the buffer zone and of the Danube River, no horseman burials have been found so far, but the archaeological evidence suggests the presence of a relatively numerous population.

CROATIA AND CROATIAN KINGS

To date, no burial assemblages in Slavonia, the region of Croatia south of the Lower Drava River, can be dated earlier than the mid-tenth century. After that date, a number of very large cemeteries appear in eastern Slavonia, between the confluence of the Danube with the Drava and Sava Rivers, respectively, as well as along the Drava, just south of the present-day border between Croatia and Hungary. All these cemeteries contain only inhumations and

[22] For the settlement, see R. L. Veselinović, "Starosrpsko naselie na Bostanishtu kod Moshorina u Bachkoj (Prilog istoriji materijalne kulture Juzhnikh Slovena X–XII veka) [The Old Serbian population of Bostanište near Mošorin in Bačka (Contribution to the material culture history of the South Slavs during the tenth to twelfth centuries)]," *RVM*, vol. 2 (1953), 5–58. For the cemetery: P. Wellenreiter, "Starosrpsko groblje iz X–XII veka kod Bostanishta vlizu Moshorina u Bachkoj [Old Serbian tenth- to twelfth-century cemetery in Bostanište near Mošorin in Bačka]," *RVM*, vol. 2 (1953), pp. 148–151.

continued well into the eleventh, sometimes even the twelfth, century. This explosion of population is hard to explain, particularly because unlike neighboring Bačka, no tenth-century settlement sites have so far been identified in Slavonia. In the absence of settlement features, the tenth- to twelfth-century burial assemblages provide the only source of information for one of the most important periods in the medieval history of the region. Grave goods consist of a variety of artifacts, but especially numerous are female dress accessories, such as ear- and finger-rings, bracelets, torcs, beads, and pendants, so typical that the name of one of the largest cemeteries excavated near Osijek, Bjelo Brdo, was given to the entire archaeological culture of tenth- to twelfth-century Croatia. It has become increasingly clear that, far from being a phenomenon restricted to Slavonia, the demographic explosion indicated by cemeteries of the "Bjelo Brdo culture" must be associated with the beginnings of the medieval state of Hungary, for such archaeological evidence has also been found in other regions of the Carpathian Basin. Hoop earrings with S-shaped ends, the hallmark of the "Bjelo Brdo culture," have been found in large numbers in such distant areas as Slovakia and Transylvania. On the other hand, recent research on the beginnings and history of this archaeological phenomenon has identified a number of regional varieties. For example, south of the Sava River, assemblages attributed to the "Bjelo Brdo culture" are easily recognizable by specific female dress accessories, especially "beaded" earrings with grape-like pendants evidently imitating granulated ornaments of ninth-century specimens. Such earrings were certainly produced locally in large numbers, as attested by molds found in Sisak and by miscasts found in Sisak, Sotin, Novi Banovci, and Sremska Mitrovica.

There are many questions of historical relevance raised by burial assemblages of the "Bjelo Brdo culture." First, its established chronology seems to point to a decisive beginning in the mid-tenth century, which coincides with the radical political changes within the Hungarian confederacy that took place after the disaster at Lechfeld. Second, the rarity of weapons and the conspicuous marking of female burials with multiple sets of dress accessories suggest that this was a population very different from that which buried its deceased in horseman burials. The exact identity of the population using the cemeteries of the "Bjelo Brdo culture" has been the subject of much debate. Croatian archaeologists and historians often stress the importance of a late source, the *Chronicle of the Priest of Dioclea*, written in Bar shortly before 1200, but preserved only in sixteenth- or seventeenth-century redactions (see chapter 6 below). The *Chronicle* maintains that a Croatian king named Tomislav defeated in battle the Hungarian king Attila.[23] From this, some have concluded that during the first third of the tenth century, Slavonia must have been incorporated into the Croatian medieval state. Others, rightly doubting the veracity of the twelfth-century account, believed instead that in the history of Slavonia, the 900s were a period of complete anarchy. The archaeological record is at variance with both interpretations. If Tomislav defeated the Magyars in battle and included Slavonia into the Croatian state, he must have moved large numbers of people into a previously sparsely populated area, given the size and continuity noted on all sites of the "Bjelo Brdo culture". Moreover, he must have been also responsible for very similar assemblages found in the central areas of Hungary or as far north as Slovakia. However, there is absolutely no support in the historical sources for this interpretation. On the contrary, Constantine Porphyrogenitus clearly indicates that in the mid-900s the Magyars occupied the lands between the Sava and the Danube, no doubt including Slavonia. On the other hand, there are many analogies between the ninth-century material culture of Croatian sites on the Adriatic shore, on the one hand, and the "Bjelo Brdo culture," on the other. But the cemeteries excavated in Slavonia have also produced a remarkable quantity of artifacts similar to those in the northern areas of Hungary, Slovenia, northern Serbia, and Macedonia. The impression one gets from an attentive examination of the archaeological evidence is that a population of new settlers may indeed have been responsible for the inception of the "Bjelo Brdo culture" in Slavonia, but the exact circumstances in which such a transfer of population may have taken place remain unclear. The conclusion that political changes need not have a direct reflection in the archaeological record springs from comparison with another region bordering Croatia, namely Istria. Beginning with the 930s, the rulers of Istria changed frequently, as the region came under the direct influence and control of the patriarch of Grado, himself under Venetian patronage. However, together with the patriarchate

[23] *Chronicle of the Priest of Dioclea* 12, ed. by V. Mošin (Zagreb: Matica hrvatska, 1950), p. 58. See also E. Peričić, *Sclavorum Regnum Grgura Barskog. Ljetopis Popa Dukljanina* [The *Sclavorum Regnum* by Gregory of Bar. The Chronicle of the Priest of Dioclea] (Zagreb: Kršćanska sadašnjost, 1991), p. 258.

of Aquileia and the Friulan march, the duchy of Istria was placed in 952 under the direct authority of the Bavarian archduke Henry, King Otto's brother. When Otto II separated Carinthia from Bavaria in 976, Istria became a march under the direct rule of the Carinthian duke, but after 995 it passed to the powerful Eppenstein family of Carinthia, when Duke Henry II briefly reincorporated Carinthia into Bavaria. Yet, despite so many changes in political leadership, the great number of estates owned by the patriarchate of Aquileia, as well as an increasing number of Germanic names among the inhabitants of coastal cities, there are absolutely no changes in material culture throughout the tenth century. On the contrary, two of the largest cemeteries found in Istria, Žminj and Predloka, which began in the ninth century, continued well after AD 1000.

The shifts in the administration of tenth-century Istria were part of a drastic rearrangement taking place on the southeastern frontier of Bavaria in the aftermath of the battle at Bratislava (907) and the defeat inflicted upon the Bavarian duke by the Magyars. To cope with the presence of the nomadic horsemen in Pannonia, but also in order to prepare for a possible expansion in the future, the southeastern territories turned into marches, each focused on the upper course of one of the major rivers in the region: Carinthia along the Mur River; Pettau/Ptuj on the Drava; Souna on the Savinja, and Carniola on the Sava. Count Rechwin, who is mentioned in two charters of 980 and 985, ruled over the march of Pettau from his castle at Ptuj in what is now northeastern Slovenia. Excavations in and around the church on the Castle Hill in Ptuj have revealed a large cemetery, the last phase of which may be dated to the second half of the tenth and to the eleventh century. Attributed to the second phase of the so-called Köttlach culture of contemporary Carinthia, the Ptuj cemetery is in fact not much different from burial assemblages of the "Bjelo Brdo culture" in neighboring Croatia.[24] South of the land of Count

[24] P. Korošec, *La nécropole de Ptujski grad, Ptuj* (Ljubljana: Société archéologique de Yougoslavie, 1971). The Ptuj cemetery has even produced artifacts with good analogies in horseman burials in Hungary. See P. Korošec, "Ungarische Elemente aus der Nekropole auf der Burg zu Ptuj," *Arheološki vestnik*, vol. 36 (1985), pp. 337–350. Although not yet confirmed archaeologically, the earliest occupation on the Castle Hill in Ptuj can be dated back to the ninth century on the basis of the written evidence. See P. Korošec, "Development of the early mediaeval Ptuj settlement," in *Istoriia i kul'tura drevnikh i srednevekovykh slavian*, ed. by V. V. Sedov (Moscow: Editorial URSS, 1999), pp. 15–19.

Rechwin was Carniola (Krain), mentioned as a march in 973. The center of the march must have been in Kranj, at the confluence of the Sava and Kokra Rivers, where Slovenian archaeologists have recently identified an early medieval cemetery.[25] In 973, Emperor Otto II made a large land donation to the archbishop of Freising in the region to the southwest of Kranj, near Škofja Loka, and added more territories to it in a second charter issued in the same year. The donation was subsequently confirmed by Otto III in 989 and by Henry II in 1002.

A strip of sparsely inhabited territory north of the Kupa River separated the southeastern Bavarian marches from what Constantine Porphyrogenitus called "baptized Croatia." The emperor was also aware of the "great power and multitude of men" of early tenth-century Croatia. According to him, "baptized Croatia" mustered as many as 100,000 foot soldiers, 60,000 horsemen, 60 galleys, and 100 cutters. He also knew that the country had eleven districts under the authority of local *zhupans* and three separate regions under the rule of *bans*. Much had changed since the ninth century in the administrative structure of the polity ruled by the Croatian dukes. The *ban* now wielded considerable power. Constantine mentions a certain *ban* Pribounias, who had "made away" with Prince Miroslav, thus opening a period of "quarrels and numerous dissensions."[26] The district prefects mentioned in charters and inscriptions during the ninth century had by now multiplied, especially in the regions in the interior, such as Pset, Pliva, and Livno (all in western Bosnia),[27] which had recently fallen under the rule of the Croatian dukes. A later source, the thirteenth-century *History of Salona* written by Thomas of Spalato, lists as "counties" some of the regions mentioned by Emperor Constantine, but the *zhupanias* were more or less autonomous, not administrative units of a fully integrated polity.[28] However, the power of the

25 M. Sagadin, *Kranj. Križišče Iskra. Nekropola iz časa preseljevanja ljudstev in staroslovanskega obdobja* [Kranj, the Iskra Crossroads. A Cemetery of the Great Migration Period and the Early Middle Ages] (Ljubljana: Narodni Muzej, 1987). A castle at Kranj is mentioned only in the late eleventh century. See also T. Knific, "Carniola in the early Middle Ages," *Balcanoslavica*, vol. 5 (1976), pp. 111–121.

26 Constantine Porphyrogenitus, *De administrando imperio* 31, pp. 150–151.

27 The *Chronicle of the Priest of Dioclea* 29, p. 73, attributes the conquest of Bosnia to one of Tomislav's successors, Michael Krešimir II. See also Peričić, *Sclavorum Regnum*, p. 262.

28 Thomas of Spalato, *Historia Salonitana*, ed. by F. Rački (Zagreb: Ex officina Societatis Typographicae, 1894), p. 45.

Croatian ruler appeared, at least to outsiders, as substantially different from that of his ninth-century predecessors. A letter of Pope John X calls Tomislav a "king" ruling "in the province of the Croats and in the Dalmatian regions."[29] There are no inscriptions of Tomislav to confirm the title, but a later inscription confirms that his tenth-century successors called themselves "kings." Moreover, the mention of Dalmatia has been interpreted as an indication that by 920 Tomislav was granted some form of control over the coastal cities in the Byzantine theme. Given that at that time he was certainly in conflict with Symeon of Bulgaria, it is indeed possible that he had been rewarded by the imperial government with some share of the tribute collected from the Dalmatian cities, much like other Slavic rulers (*archontes*) in the days of Emperor Basil I. In any case, in 927 Pope John X sent his legates, Bishop Madalbert and a certain John, who bore the title of *dux Cumas*, to mediate between Croats and Bulgarians. The papal legates were also to attend the synod of the Dalmatian bishops gathered in Split in 928. This was the second meeting of the bishops in that city, and everything we know about both synods comes from the letters Pope John X wrote to the archbishop of Split and to his suffragans, as well as to Tomislav, King of the Croats, and to Prince Michael of Zahumlje. The letters were preserved in a version of Archdeacon Thomas of Spalato's *History of Salona* copied at a later time to include a number of documents that the author may have apparently used as sources for his narrative. As a consequence, the authenticity of the letters included in the "longer" version of the *History* (known as *Historia Salonitana maior*) has come under suspicion, but there can be little doubt about the synods themselves, the decisions of which were confirmed at later councils.

What caused the first synod of Split that took place in 925 was apparently a quarrel over diocesan borders between the archbishop of Split and the bishop of Nin. At stake were the Dalmatian sees, some of which, according to John X, were now under Tomislav's authority. The early history of the bishopric of Nin is obscure, but the see seems to have expanded shortly after its creation in the ninth

[29] *Documenta historiae Chroaticae periodum antiquam illustrantia*, ed. by F. Rački (Zagreb: Sumptibus Academiae Scientiarum et Artium, 1877), p. 187. For the interpretation of this passage, see L. Margetić, "The Croatian state during the era of rulers from the Croatian national dynasty," in *Croatia in the Early Middle Ages. A Cultural Survey*, ed. by I. Supičić (London: Philip Wilson Publishers and Zagreb: AGM, 1999), p. 204.

century, mainly at the expense of Split. A bishop of Nin even became Archbishop of Split in the late ninth century, albeit at the risk of the pope's irritation over his seeking ordination from Aquileia, not Rome. The incident is not mentioned in any one of Pope John X's letters, but it must have been on the minds of those who attended the synod of 925. That synod decided in favor of the archbishop of Split, but following the protests of the bishop of Nin, a second synod was summoned in 928. This time, the gathering of bishops decided to abolish the see of Nin, while the jurisdiction of the archbishop of Split was now extended over Croatia. The political implications of this church affair can hardly be ignored. Without being in any sense the "capital" of the dukes of the Croats, Nin had nevertheless been the first bishopric established in the country after conversion. Tomislav attended the synods, and the pope apparently counted on his support for Archbishop John of Split. Sacrificing the bishopric of Nin was apparently the price demanded from him for the political expansion of the Croatian polity in southern Dalmatia.

But the letters of Pope John X indicate that there was a second, equally troubling issue on his mind in relation to the church affairs in Dalmatia. In his letter to the archbishop of Split and the other Dalmatian bishops, the pope scolded them for embracing "Methodius' teaching" (*Methodii doctrina*), "which is nowhere to be found in the teaching of the Holy Fathers," and urged everybody to follow the advice of his legates and use only Latin in the liturgy. The pope further called Methodius' teaching a "bad root" and described the Slavic language as "barbarous."[30] The tenth canon of the synod of 925 promptly prohibited the use of the Slavic language in liturgy and banned the elevation into higher orders of priests who did not have proper knowledge of Latin. Historians have long seen these decisions as the first indication of the influence of the Moravian mission in Dalmatia and the beginning of a peculiar cultural phenomenon of medieval Croatia known as "Glagolism." More recently, however, it has been noted that the decisions of the 925 synod pertaining to the use of Slavic in the liturgy are in fact repeated verbatim in the documents of another council of Split that took place in 1060. It is therefore possible that the text preserved in the "longer" version of Thomas of Spalato's *History of Salona* contains later interpolations. Besides Pope John X's letters, no shred of evidence exists

[30] *Documenta*, p. 192.

that the Slavic liturgy was in use in Croatia during the tenth century and everything points to Glagolism being an eleventh-, not tenth-century phenomenon. The earliest manuscript written in Glagolitic script, known as the *Glagolita Clozianus*, cannot be dated earlier than AD 1000. Vatroslav Jagić has suggested that the so-called *Vienna Leaflets* (two leaves of parchment containing a fragment of the liturgy of the Mass), the oldest liturgical Croatian document in Old Church Slavonic, may be associated with the activity of Methodius' disciples in Croatia shortly before and after AD 900.[31] But the fact that the text of the *Leaflets* is a translation of a Gregorian sacramentary suggests a date in the late eleventh century, and the manuscript itself cannot be dated earlier than 1100.

Judging from the existing evidence, the tenth-century religious life in Croatia was dominated by the Benedictine monks. The abbot of the Benedictine monastery of Sv. Krševan (St. Chrysogonus) in Zadar is first mentioned in 918, but the monastery had a new beginning in 986, when a monk from Monte Cassino was appointed abbot. The Benedictine abbey of St. Bartholomew was established in the tenth century on the Kapitul Hill near Knin. Although the abbey appears in documents only after AD 1000, recent archaeological excavations have revealed the tenth-century church and a number of sculptural elements from the earliest building phase.[32] The tenth-century also witnessed the foundation of the Benedictine abbey of St. Stephen Under the Pines near Split. The Benedictine influence was likewise responsible for the fact that the oldest Latin manuscripts produced in Dalmatia were written in Beneventan, the script most typical for the Benedictine monastery of Monte Cassino (Italy). An episcopal book of ritual now in the library of the Russian Academy in St. Petersburg and known as the Kotor Cathedral Pontifical can be dated to the tenth century on the basis of such features of the Beneventan script as "a" written as "cc" or tall "i" at the beginning of a word or in a semiconsonantal position. To the same period may be dated a fragment of a text containing the epistle of St. Paul to the Philippians

31 V. Jagić, *Entstehungsgeschichte der kirchenslavischen Sprache* (Berlin: Weidmann, 1913), p. 246.

32 F. Smiljanić, "Kapitul kod Knina [Kapitul near Knin]," *Radovi Filozofskog fakulteta u Zadru*, vol. 38 (1986–1987), pp. 53–95. For tenth-century sculptural elements from the Monastery of St. Bartholomew, see T. Burić, "Ranosrednjovjekovna skulptura s Kapitula kod Knina [Early medieval sculpture from Kapitul near Knin]," *Izdanja Hrvatskog arheološkog društva*, vol. 15 (1992), pp. 97–121.

which was found in Split. The same is true for the earliest manuscript in Caroline script written in Croatia, a codex from the Franciscan monastery in Šibenik containing a collection of books of the liturgy in the form in existence before the reform movement of the late eleventh century collapsed them into the Missal.

Latin, and not Old Church Slavonic, is the language of tenth-century inscriptions found in Croatia. A duke named Držislav (*Dirzisclu ducem magnum*) is mentioned in an inscription on two stone panels, perhaps from the pulpit of the first church of the St. Bartholomew Abbey in Knin. The fragmentary inscription also mentions that somebody else, whose name was not preserved, was the "duke of the Croats" during Držislav's reign.[33] The inscription contains no date, but the identity of Duke Držislav was established on the basis of a later charter of King Peter Krešimir IV, dated to 1066, which confirmed a donation of an estate named Diklo that had been made to the Monastery of Sv. Krševan in Zadar by the king's predecessor, Krešimir II. The charter also mentions the names of the four sons of Krešimir's successor, King Držislav. But the succession to power and the genealogy of the Croatian kings was reconstructed primarily on the basis of perhaps the most famous inscription in Latin from tenth-century Croatia. The inscription was found broken in several fragments in Otok near Solin. It is an epitaph for Helena, the wife of a certain king Michael and the mother of a certain king Stephen.[34] The exact date of her death is given (October 8, 976) and from that a Croatian historian has reconstructed the genealogy and the years of the long reigns of the kings now known as Michael Krešimir II (949–969) and Stjepan Držislav (969–997).[35] The Otok inscription is important for a number of other reasons as well. First, it clearly shows that Tomislav's successors during the second half of the tenth century retained the title of "king," even though on another inscription Držislav appears as "Grand Duke." Together with the 1066 charter of King Peter Krešimir IV, the evidence of the inscription shows that

[33] Matijević-Sokol, "Latin inscriptions," 243.

[34] *Namentragende Steininschriften*, pp. 53–54 (for the English translation, see Matijević-Sokol, "Latin inscriptions," p. 245). For the most recent commentary, see M. Suić, "Prilog tumačenju natpisa kraljice Jelene [Contribution to the interpretation of Queen Helena's inscription]," *SP*, vol. 14 (1984), pp. 15–39.

[35] F. Šišić, "Genealoški prilozi o hrvatskoj narodnoj dinastiji [Genealogical contribution to the history of the Croat dynasty]," *Vjesnik Hrvatskoga arheološkoga društva*, vol. 13 (1913–1914), pp. 1–93.

a dynastic principle was set in Croatia, which is also evident in the use of one and the same church as royal mausoleum. Second, and perhaps more importantly, the inscription shows that Helena, who is called "famous" (*famosa*), ruled the kingdom (*habenas tenuit regni*), a quality the anonymous author of the text associates with her protection of orphans and widows described in the words of the *Psalms* (67.6). Certainly Helena was in power after the death of her husband. She must therefore have ruled alone or in her son's name for no less than seven years. Unfortunately, nothing else is known about Helena or her reign. Her position of power, not just as the spouse of one king and the mother of another, but also as a queen in her own right, is in sharp contrast with her contemporaries, Maria Lekapena, who married Peter of Bulgaria, and Anna, the bride of Vladimir of Kiev, neither of whom exercised any significant political power or influence.

According to Constantine Porphyrogenitus, writing in the mid-tenth century, Pagania was a political entity separate from Croatia and located on both sides of the Neretva River, including also the islands of Hvar, Korčula, Mljet, and Brač. The Paganians, also known as Narentans from other sources, were in almost permanent conflict with Venice, because of their naval capabilities that threatened Venetian convoys sailing south along the Dalmatian coast. By 930, the Venetians had already established their control over some urban centers in Istria, and in 972 the Doge Peter Candiano IV obtained Isola from Emperor Otto I.[36] Emperor Basil II's privilege of 992 secured a preferential treatment of Venetian merchants within Byzantine borders, and a few years later a Venetian fleet defeated the Narentans, while at the same time defending the theme of Dalmatia against the attacks of the Bulgarian emperor Samuel. Around AD 1000, Venice thus laid the foundations of a long-term control of the coastal cities in Dalmatia. Neighboring polities were quickly drawn into the orbit

36 G. de Vergottini, "Venezia, e l'Istria nell'Alto Medioevo," in *Storia della civiltà Veneziana*, ed. by V. Branca (Florence: Sansori, 1979), p. 80. In 932, Venice imposed on the inhabitants of Koper an annual tribute of 100 amphorae of wine. See John the Deacon, *Venetian Chronicle*, ed. by G. Monticolo (Rome: Forzani, 1890), p. 156. A year later, when, with the margrave of Istria on their side, several Istrian cities seized Venetian properties within their territory, the doge ordered the blockade of the entire peninsula, which quickly led to a peace, whereby the Venetians recuperated all their assets. See P. Štih, "Der ostadriatische Raum um das Jahr 1000," in *Europe around the Year 1000*, ed. by P. Urbańczyk (Warsaw: Wydawnictwo DiG, 2001), pp. 205–208.

of the emerging power. In recognition of the Venetian overlordship over Dalmatia, but also in order to seal an alliance with Croatia, the daughter of the Venetian doge Peter II Orseolo (1008–1026) married Stjepan, Držislav's grandson and the father of King Peter Krešimir IV.

BYZANTINE PROVINCES AND BYZANTINE CLIENTS

There was a visible growth in the number of Byzantine themes in the Balkans during the tenth century. Emperor Leo VI created the themes of Strymon in eastern Macedonia and Nikopolis in northwestern Greece. All of the subsequently created themes were small and tended to cluster in the northern region of Greece. The theme of Veroia, west of Thessalonica, may be dated to the 970s, while Larisa, in northern Thessaly, appeared at an unknown date before Emperor Basil II's death in 1025. Basil also created the theme of Philippopolis in present-day Bulgaria in the 990s during his war against Bulgaria. The role of the new themes was thus primarily to protect the Byzantine provinces in Greece and Thrace from Bulgarian raids, such as those ordered in 917 by Symeon, which reached as far south as the Gulf of Corinth, and in 976 by Samuel, who removed a substantial number of inhabitants and the relics of St. Achilleus from Larisa in Thessaly. However, the themes offered no protection against attacks by sea. In 901, a Syrian fleet under a Christian renegade named Damian of Tarsus sacked the port of Demetrias, on the northern shore of the Pagasic Bay in Thessaly. Three years later, an Arab fleet under the command of another Christian renegade named Leo of Tripoli appeared in the Sea of Marmara. After having been chased off by the imperial fleet, the Arabs sacked the custom station at Abydos and then attacked Thessalonica. The imperial fleet could not intervene and an appeal of the local military governor to the neighboring Slavs produced only a few volunteers. As a consequence, after a brief siege, the Arabs stormed the sea walls and conquered and plundered the city, killing or capturing almost half of its inhabitants.[37] Many captives were later

[37] The authenticity of John Kameniates' account of the sack of Thessalonica has been disputed by Al. H. Kazhdan, "Some questions addressed to the scholars who believe in the authenticity of Kaminiates' 'Capture of Thessalonica'," *BZ*, vol. 71 (1978), pp. 301–314. However, the Arab conquest of the city is confirmed by both Byzantine and Arab sources. See J. D. C. Frendo, "The 'Miracles of St. Demetrius' and the capture of Thessaloniki. An examination of the purpose,

sent to Tarsus in Cilicia, in order to be exchanged against Muslims captured by the Byzantines. One of the first visitors to Thessalonica after the sack of 904 was St. Elias the Younger, who died in that city less than a week after the withdrawal of the Arab fleet. Elias was on his way to Constantinople, where he had been invited by Emperor Leo VI, and his impression of Thessalonica was one of sheer misery.[38] The same was true of St. Nikon the Metanoiete's impression of Salamis, which he found devastated when coming to Greece in 968. All the inhabitants of the island had fled to the mainland, and Athens was surrounded by a wall built around the base of the Acropolis, behind which the population could take refuge.

The Byzantine provinces were also confronted with internal revolts. According to Constantine Porphyrogenitus, during the reign of Romanus I (920–944) the Milings and the Ezerites of Peloponnesus constantly refused to accept the ruler imposed on them by the military governor of the province, John Protevon. Their dissatisfaction seems to have been fueled by increasing demands for troops for the military expeditions to Italy. In 921, the Milings and the Ezerites arose against the new military governor of the province, Krinitis Arotras, who began campaigning against them "in March and burned the crops and plundered the lands of the Slavs until November."[39] As a consequence, the rebels quickly sued for peace and agreed to pay an increased tribute directly to the imperial treasury. However, soon after that, Krinitis was transferred to the neighboring province of Hellas and replaced with Bardas Platypodis. Bardas's term as military governor of Peloponnesus was marked by "disorder and strife," apparently caused by conflicts with members of the local nobility led by a certain

significance and authenticity of John Kaminiates' 'De Expugnatione Thessalonicae'," *Byzantinoslavica*, vol. 58 (1997), pp. 205–224; R. K. Odetallah, "Leo Tripolites–Ghulam Zurafa and the sack of Thessaloniki in 904," *Byzantinoslavica*, vol. 56 (1995), pp. 97–102. See also W. A. Farag, "Some remarks on Leo of Tripoli's attack on Thessaloniki in 904 AD," *BZ*, vol. 82 (1989), pp. 133–139.

38 *Life of St. Elias the Younger*, p. 110. See also Yannopoulos, "La Grèce dans la *Vie de S. Elie le Jeune*," pp. 215–216.

39 Constantine Porphyrogenitus, *De administrando imperio* 50, pp. 234–235. The fact that in order to quell the revolt, Krinitis Arotras had to burn the crops is an indication that the Milings and the Ezerites had by now moved into the lowlands on both sides of Mount Taigetos. For the date of the revolt, see R. J. H. Jenkins, "The date of the Slav revolt in Peloponnese under Romanus I," in *Late Classical and Mediaeval Studies in Honor of Albert Mathias Friend, Jr.*, ed. by Kurt Weitzmann (Princeton: Princeton University Press, 1955), pp. 204–211.

protospatharios named Leo Angelastos, who was eventually expelled from the province. These events are most likely the same as those in which Arethas of Caesarea found himself entangled in 921 or 922. Arethas, by then a resident of Constantinople, had visited his native province in the early 900s, mainly to participate in the reconsecration of devastated churches. However, he later wrote a tract to defend himself against accusations that he had tried to convince a certain notable of Patras named Symbatios to declare himself emperor. Symbatios had declined the offer and promptly denounced the plot, while sending two conspirators to Constantinople under imperial guard. The "disorder and strife" must therefore have had political ramifications, the most destructive outcome of which was the subsequent rebellion of those whom Constantine Porphyrogenitus calls "Slavesians." These were Byzantine troops recruited from among Slavs in Asia Minor and stationed in Peloponnesus, as reinforcements for the local thematic army, along with the Mardaite sailors.[40] It is interesting to note that, "fearing (that the Slavesians) might join forces with the Slavs [the Milings and the Ezerites] and bring about a total destruction of this same province," Emperor Romanus I agreed to reduce the tribute of the Peloponnesian Slavs to the amount paid before the campaign of Krinitis Arotras. At the same time, and perhaps to alleviate the pleas of the local population, the emperor allowed the soldiers of the theme of Peloponnesus to redeem their military obligation to go on a campaign to Italy at the rate of five gold coins apiece, or half of that if they were poor.[41]

Despite so much turbulence, tenth-century Peloponnesus seems to have been a land of opportunities. The very fact that involved in the events of 921 were not just rebels in the mountains, but also some of the most important members of the local nobility, men bearing such

[40] Constantine Porphyrogenitus, *De administrando imperio* 50, pp. 234–235. The Slavesians are also mentioned in the emperor's *De cerimoniis*, p. 651, as troops recruited for the 911 expedition to Crete. The Slavesians also participated in the siege and subsequent conquest of the Cretan fort of Candia in 961. They were most likely recruited from the theme of Opsikion. See Ditten, *Ethnische Verschiebungen*, pp. 265–267. For the Mardaites of Peloponnesus, Nikopolis, and Cephalonia, see Constantine Porphyrogenitus, *De ceremoniis*, pp. 655, 656, and 665. Elsewhere in the Balkan provinces, settlers were either of Armenian or Byzantine origin. In 989, after Bardas Skleros submitted to him, Emperor Basil II moved his former enemy, together with his family, from Anatolia to Adrianople, where he expected them to help fight the Bulgarians.

[41] Constantine Porphyrogenitus, *De administrando imperio* 51, pp. 256–257.

lofty titles as that of *protospatharios* and equal in rank with the military governor of the province, is an indication of relative prosperity. The *Life* and *Testament of St. Nikon the Metanoiete*, written during the first half of the eleventh century, mention that when Nikon arrived in Lacedaemona (Sparta) in *c.* 970, the local "leading men" (*archontes*) requested his assistance against a particularly destructive outbreak of plague. Patrons of the monastery Nikon eventually built in the middle of the market place in Lacedaemona were not only the military governor of Peloponnesus, but also a certain "lord Basil Apokaukos," a Byzantine general whom Nikon reassured of victory over Samuel of Bulgaria and his troops that were threatening Corinth. While the military governor donated to the monastery an entire village, Perissos, together with its inhabitants, local noblemen opposed Nikon's decisions to expel the Jews from Lacedaemona and to build his church in the marketplace, on the very spot where they used to entertain themselves by playing polo.[42]

Contemporary villages in the Byzantine provinces in eastern Macedonia were relatively small, with no more than 100 inhabitants each, and coexisted with isolated farms and large estates owned by the emperor, imperial officials, officers of the Byzantine army, or the Church. Peasants were organized in village communities collectively responsible for the payment of taxes, but also acting collectively on such matters as the management of village property, land sales, and purchases. Some villages even had archives, as indicated by the fact that a copy of a judge's verdict in a case of 995 was given to the village of Siderokausia. During the tenth century, a significant number of lands were abandoned, reclaimed by the state, and subsequently sold to rich landowners. Why did people abandon the land? In many cases it was because of invasions or raids of foreign enemies. For example, in 996, peasants from three villages – Restnika, Mousdolokon, and Batonia (all in the hinterland of Thessaloniki) – fled to a monastic estate because their villages had been destroyed by the Bulgarians.

[42] *Testament of Nikon the Metanoiete for the Church and Monastery of the Savior, the Mother of God, and St. Kyriake in Lakedaimon*, English translation by A. Bandy in *Byzantine Monastic Foundation Documents. A Complete Translation of the Surviving Founders'* Typika *and Testaments*, ed. by J. Thomas and A. C. Hero (Washington: Dumbarton Oaks Research Library and Collection, 2000), p. 317. For the *Life of St. Nikon*, see Ch. Stavrakos, "Die Vita des hl. Nikon Metanoeite als Quelle zur Prosopographie der Peloponnes im späten 10. Jahrhundert," *Südost-Forschungen*, vol. 58 (1999), pp. 1–7.

However, fiscal pressure should not be discounted as an important reason for land abandonment. During the years of bad harvests and famine, many peasants sold their land for just a little food or money. Others preferred the monastic estates because they were sheltered from taxes by exemptions granted to the monks. In 974 and 975, the fiscal agents identified a great number of peasants who had moved to monastic estates, and forced them to return to their lands and pay taxes. However, when lands were abandoned for more than thirty years, they were usually resold to local landowners, many of whom were officers of the Byzantine troops stationed in nearby forts.

Local noblemen were also prominent in Dyrrachion in the 970s. According to John Skylitzes, who wrote in the late eleventh century, the most prominent among them was a certain John Chryselios, whose daughter married Samuel of Bulgaria. He later married another of his daughters to the Byzantine renegade Ashot, who had joined Samuel and was subsequently appointed governor of Dyrrachion. In exchange for imperial recognition for himself and the title of *patrikios* for his two sons, John eventually turned the city back to the Byzantine authorities after the defeat of Samuel.[43] John may have also been responsible for the remarkable building activity taking place in Dyrrachion shortly before and after AD 1000. The city walls were repaired and a church was erected on the site of what is now the Fatih Mosque. Further to the north, at Shurdhah on the river Drin, Albanian archaeologists have identified a large stronghold with several buildings and a number of churches, some of which were probably built in the tenth century. Shurdhah may well have been a fort on the northeastern frontier of the theme of Dyrrachion, but the presence of tenth- and eleventh-century coins and Byzantine fine quality pottery indicates that this was not an isolated settlement in the middle of the mountains.

An image of relative prosperity is also confirmed by finds of hoards and isolated Byzantine coins in Greece. In Corinth, Athens, and Thebes, the tenth century witnessed an increased number of coins, in itself an indication of an accelerated economic development. Moreover, seven coin hoards from Peloponnesus that were buried during

[43] John Skylitzes, *Synopsis historiarum*, pp. 342–343 and 349. See J. Ferluga, *Byzantium on the Balkans. Studies on the Byzantine Administration and the Southern Slavs from the VIIth to the XIIth Centuries* (Amsterdam: Adolf Hakkert, 1976), pp. 227 and 231–232.

the reign of Constantine VII Porphyrogenitus contain mostly coins of that emperor and of his co-rulers, which shows an active monetary economy with a continuous flow of fresh money into the region. In the early tenth century, Thessalonica had two permanent markets, one apparently serving trade with the neighboring Slavs. Both markets were full of native and foreign goods and merchants. Thessalonica had its own manufacture in the form of glass-making workshops.[44] In the early 900s, there were just a few settlements in the hinterland of Thessalonica. By 950, the situation had changed dramatically. By 942, the abbot of a monastery "of Athos" is referred to in an agreement made with the inhabitants of Hierissos. Athanasius, the founder of the Great Lavra, arrived at Athos in 958 and immediately began promoting large-scale agriculture and viticulture, much to the dissatisfaction of older monks. The first imperial document concerning the organization of the monastic communities was issued by Emperor John Tzimikes at some point between 970 and 972. The document, known as the Tragos ("billy goat," from the parchment on which it was written), was based on a thorough investigation of the situation at Athos by a committee sent at the special order of the emperor. A summary of the report that the committee later gave to the emperor is included in the document. Some of the committee's conclusions are particularly relevant for the economic and social situation in northern Greece in the late 900s. At that time, apparently, there were many monks at Athos "who possessed fields and sold them, then purchased others in turn, and sold them again for the sake of profit and shameful gain."[45] Estates were also owned collectively by various monasteries, which designated stewards to manage the monastic property. They

[44] John Kameniates, *De expugnatione Thessalonicae*, ed. by G. Böhlig (Berlin and New York: De Gruyter, 1973), pp. 26–27, 491–494, 500, 561–562, 567–569, and 578–580. See also R. A. Nasledova, "Remeslo i torgovlia Fessaloniki konca IX–nachala X v. po dannym Ioanna Kameniaty [Crafts and trade in Thessalonica in the late ninth and early tenth century, according to John Kameniates]," *VV*, vol. 8 (1956), pp. 61–84.

[45] Typikon *of Emperor John Tzimiskes* 13, English translation by G. Dennis in *Byzantine Monastic Foundation Documents. A Complete Translation of the Surviving Founders'* Typika *and Testaments*, ed. by J. Thomas and A. C. Hero (Washington: Dumbarton Oaks Research Library and Collection, 2000), p. 238. Some monks are said to have worked under contract for some of the superiors (abbots) and they were paid in cash. By contrast, "forced labor" imposed upon monks by some of these superiors was viewed as an indication of "worldly, not monastic life" (Typikon *of Emperor John Tzimiskes* 19, p. 239).

often resided in farmhouses, which were easy to distinguish from other rural settlements by the presence of church buildings. In addition, many monasteries purchased land from the fisc, onto which they brought new settlers from neighboring villages with impoverished peasant population or even from neighboring Bulgaria. At some point before 960, forty "Bulgarian Slavs" were settled on the estates of the Monastery of Kolobos.[46] The amount of rent the monasteries received on a regular basis from their tenants was often stipulated in a written contract. Monks also sold significant quantities of wine to "laymen from the Zygos river in towards the Mountain."[47] That the monks were not alone in engaging in such activities is shown by other documents surviving in the archives of the Great Lavra, which point to peasants buying land from the fisc, which they cleared and turned into cultivated fields. The prosperity of tenth-century Macedonia also explains the rapid growth of the Athonite monasteries. In 956, an imperial decree granted land to the Monastery of St. Nicephorus of Xeropotamou. The Monastery of Iviron established by Georgian monks in 979 swallowed the Monastery of Kolobos, which was located at the northern end of the peninsula. Kolobos had previously absorbed other monasteries and their possessions, one of which was Leontia near Thessalonica. As a result of such developments, the size of the estates the Monastery of Iviron owned in Macedonia shortly before AD 1000 grew to an estimated total of 20,000 acres.[48]

The remarkable growth of the Athonite monasteries that began during the last few decades of the tenth century and continued into

[46] F. Dölger, *Ein Fall slavischer Einsiedlung im Hinterland von Thessalonike im 10. Jahrhundert* (Munich: Verlag der Bayerischen Akademie der Wissenschaften, 1952), pp. 7 and 10–13. See also G. C. Soulis, "On the Slavic settlement in Hierissos in the tenth century," *Byzantion*, vol. 23 (1953), pp. 67–72. The monastery was founded in 866 on the territory of the village of Siderokausia. See J. Lefort, "Population et peuplement en Macédoine orientale, IXe–XVe siècle," in *Hommes et richesses dans l'Empire byzantin*, ed. by V. Kravari, J. Lefort, and C. Morrisson, vol. II (Paris: Pierre Lethielleux, 1991), p. 69.

[47] Typikon *of Emperor John Tzimiskes* 15, p. 238.

[48] A. Harvey, "The monastic economy and imperial patronage from the tenth to the twelfth century," in *Mount Athos and Byzantine Monasticism. Papers from the Twenty-Eighth Spring Symposium of Byzantine Studies, Birmingham, March 1994*, ed. by A. Bryer and M. Cunningham (Aldershot and Brookfield: Variorum, 1996), p. 91. In addition to land, the Athonite monks benefited from other forms of imperial munificence. Emperor Romanus I (920–944) began sending to Athos yearly cash payments which amounted to one gold coin per monk.

the eleventh century had been also made possible by changes taking place at Athos in the aftermath of Athanasius' foundation of the Great Lavra. In the mid-900s, the Athonite monks already had a collective representation in the eyes of the law, in the form of a leader of all monastic communities known as *protos*, and a council of abbots (*hegoumenoi*) that met twice a year. But after 963, the favored form of monastic life was not that of isolated anchorites coming together to celebrate the liturgy only on Sundays and on feast days, but a more advanced form of common, "cenobitic" life. The rule that Athanasius drew for the occasion of his foundation stressed common life within the walls of the monastery, obedience to the abbot, and manual work. The total number of monks for his foundation was set at eighty, no more than five of whom were allowed to leave the monastery and live as hermits, if they had proved themselves worthy of being granted that privilege. Monks at the Great Lavra ate together "two cooked dishes – garden vegetables and legumes," which they seasoned "both with three litrai of olive oil." On feast days, they also ate fish, cheese, and eggs and were allowed to drink three measures of wine.[49] More importantly, the architecture of the new foundation was a clear illustration of the cenobitic ideals. The Great Lavra has a courtyard plan with a free-standing church in the middle, surrounded on all sides by inward-facing cells and dependencies that back on to the enclosure walls guarded by a tower. Both the rule and the architecture of Athanasius' foundation were immediately imitated, so much so that by 1100, half of the monasteries now in existence on the peninsula had already been founded. Moreover, the new emphasis on cenobitism changed the pattern of imperial support for the Athonites. Instead of yearly payments for all monks (those in cenobitic communities, as well as hermits), emperors now preferred to grant land or privileges to their favorite houses, especially to the Great Lavra and to Iviron. For example, Emperor Basil II's decree of 978 increased the level of financial assistance for the Great Lavra to a level where over

[49] *Rule of Athanasius the Athonite for the Lavra Monastery 22*, English translation by G. Dennis in *Byzantine Monastic Foundation Documents. A Complete Translation of the Surviving Founders'* Typika *and Testaments*, ed. by J. Thomas and A. C. Hero (Washington: Dumbarton Oaks Research Library and Collection, 2000), p. 226. For Athanasius, see K. Ware, "St. Athanasios the Athonite: traditionalist or innovator?," in *Mount Athos and Byzantine Monasticism. Papers from the Twenty-Eighth Spring Symposium of Byzantine Studies, Birmingham, March 1994*, ed. by A. Bryer and M. Cunningham (Aldershot and Brookfield: Variorum, 1996), pp. 4–16.

six times more monks could be supported than initially stipulated by Athanasius. The trend continued into the eleventh and twelfth centuries, with new monasteries temporarily rivaling the Great Lavra in terms of the imperial munificence they enjoyed.

Mount Athos was neither an exclusively Byzantine, nor the only monastic center in the Balkan provinces of the Empire. In 979, three Iberian noblemen established the monastery of Iviron with the support of the Iberian prince David of Upper Tao, soon followed by Bulgarian monks who founded the Monastery of St. Zographos. Other monasteries existed in tenth-century Macedonia, such as Kolobos or the one excavated near Maroneia, at Synaxis. The latter reused materials from a sixth- or early seventh-century basilica in ruins to create a courtyard arrangement similar to that of the Great Lavra. Two marble slabs from the chancel of the free-standing church of the monastery were carved with decorative patterns of linked quatrefoils, most typical for the ninth- and tenth-century Byzantine art. Ashes on a fireplace found in one of the rooms in the monastery's northern wing contained oyster shells and fish-bones, the remains of a monastic diet not very different from that prescribed by Athanasius for the monks of the Great Lavra. However, the fine quality pottery found in the earthfill of the courtyard may indicate that life in the Synaxis Monastery was not devoid of some refinement.

It is from the Byzantine provinces of northern Greece that the church architecture associated with the forts and monastic centers in Macedonia began to spread into the central regions of the Balkans. The church dedicated to St. Achilleus excavated on an island compound in the middle of Lake Prespa was most likely built in the late tenth century by Samuel, who may have been buried within its atrium. A church recently excavated in Rose, in the Bay of Kotor, may be of the same date. Two tenth-century churches in northeastern Montenegro and southwestern Serbia, respectively, are replicas of Byzantine churches, such as those found in the strongholds of Macedonia and Albania.[50] During the tenth century, the valleys of

[50] Church of St. Peter near Bijelo Polje (Montenegro): Radivoje Ljubinković, "Iskopavanja na crkvi Svetog Petra u Bijelom Polju [Archaeological research in the Church of St. Peter near Bijelo Polje]," in *Referati i koreferati sa VII kongresa arheologa Jugoslavije. Herceg-Novi, 1966*, ed. by N. Tašić (Belgrade: Arheološko Društvo Jugoslavije, 1967), pp. 103–111. Petrovo near Novi Pazar (Serbia): G. Milošević, "Ostaci kasnosrednjovjekovne crkve i profane gradjevine u selu Petrovi kod Novog Pazara [Remains of an early medieval church and secular buildings in Petrovo near

the upper courses of the rivers Lim and Ibar were beyond the reach of the Byzantine garrisons stationed in such strongholds. Instead, the two churches testify to the influence of Byzantine Christianity and architecture among the elites of the Byzantine clients in the central and western regions of the Balkans.

According to Constantine Porphyrogenitus, the Slavs of the Dalmatian *zhupanias* of Pagania, Zahumlje, Travounia, and Konavli all "descended from the unbaptized Serbs."[51] This has been rightly interpreted as an indication that in the mid-tenth century the coastal *zhupanias* were under the control of the Serbian *zhupan* Časlav, who ruled over the regions in the interior and extended his power westwards across the mountains to the coast. Before AD 1000, the southernmost *zhupania* of Duklja (in present-day Montenegro) must have been under Byzantine control, despite the later attempts of the author of the *Chronicle of the Priest of Dioclea* to construct a half-legendary genealogy for the twelfth-century princes of Duklja. In the mid-tenth century, Constantine Porphyrogenitus had nothing to say about the rulers of Duklja, but insisted that the country had been "under the emperor of the Romans."[52] In 997, during the war with Basil II, Samuel of Bulgaria attacked Ulcinj, south of Lake Skadar, and from Duklja he began devastating the entire Dalmatian coast as far as Zadar. Samuel only withdrew when the Venetian fleet stabilized the region and reestablished nominally the Byzantine control over the coastal cities. Similarly, the early tenth-century ruler of Hum (Zahumlje), a neighbor of Croatia, bore the lofty titles of proconsul and *patrikios*. Michael of Zahumlje, who is mentioned together with Tomislav of Croatia in Pope John X's letter of 925 and who participated in that same year in the first synod of Split, was nevertheless an independent ruler, whose genealogy is specifically mentioned by Constantine Porphyrogenitus as having been different from that of all other Slavs in Dalmatia who were descendants of the "unbaptized Serbs." Michael was on good terms with Bulgaria during Symeon's

Novo Pazar]," *Novopazarski zbornik*, vol. 11 (1987), pp. 47–62. For an example of a fort church in the neighboring area of the theme of Dyrrachion, see G. Karaiskaj, "Qyteti shqiptar i Sardës. Origjina dhe zhvillimi i qyteti mesjetar në Shqipërinë e Veriut [The Albanian city of Sarda. The origins of the medieval city in northern Albania]," *Monumentet*, vol. 33 (1987), pp. 73–83.

51 Constantine Porphyrogenitus, *De administrando imperio* 34, pp. 162–163; 33, pp. 160–161; 36, pp. 164–165.

52 Constantine Porphyrogenitus, *De administrando imperio* 35, pp. 162–163.

war with Byzantium, for he warned Symeon against possible attacks from Serbia.[53] Equally independent from both Byzantium and Croatia was the region on both sides of the Neretva River. According to Constantine Porphyrogenitus, its inhabitants were called Pagani "because they did not accept baptism at the time when all the Serbs were baptized," the implication being that like the Terbuniotes and the Kanalites, the Narentans too were "descended from the unbaptized Serbs."[54] He knew that at the time Michael ruled over Hum, "Pagania" was "under the control of the prince of Serbia."[55] Similarly, he claims that "the princes of Terbounia have always been at the command of the prince of Serbia."[56] It is not altogether clear where exactly was Constantine's Serbia, but the Serbian prince in question is undoubtedly Časlav (Tzeeslav), born in Bulgaria, the son of Mutimir's nephew Klonimir and his Bulgarian wife. Everything we know about tenth-century Serbian princes comes from chapter 32 of the *De administrando imperio*, and without it there would be very little to say, for the archaeology of tenth-century Serbia is notoriously underdeveloped. Although the basic historical narrative can be reconstructed on the basis of Constantine's text, almost nothing is known about social relations or the representation of political power.

A former protégé of Boris of Bulgaria, Klonimir had died in 897 or 898 in a failed attempt to recuperate the power usurped by his cousin Peter, the son of Gojnik. In the course of his action against Peter, Klonimir had briefly occupied a stronghold in eastern Serbia named Destinikon. The exact location of this fort, as well as of five other strongholds mentioned by Constantine Porphyrogenitus, remains unknown. However, judging from the developments described by Constantine, with various claimants to rule in Serbia fleeing to either Croatia or Bulgaria, the territory attacked by Klonimir must have been in what is now central-eastern Bosnia. At an unknown date in the early 900s, Klonimir's rival Peter had expanded across Bosnia into the valley of the Neretva River and the region known to Constantine Porphyrogenitus as "Pagania." Although he had defeated a rival presumably supported by Bulgarian troops, during the Byzantine–Bulgarian war Peter was seeking the alliance of the

[53] Constantine Porphyrogenitus, *De administrando imperio* 32, pp. 156–157.
[54] Constantine Porphyrogenitus, *De administrando imperio* 36, pp. 164–165.
[55] Constantine Porphyrogenitus, *De administrando imperio* 32, pp. 156–157.
[56] Constantine Porphyrogenitus, *De administrando imperio* 34, pp. 162–163.

powerful ruler of Bulgaria, Symeon. Nevertheless, from his newly acquired territories at the mouth of the Neretva River he also established contact with the military governor of Dyrrachion. According to Constantine Porphyrogenitus, the governor bribed Peter in 917 to attack Symeon together with the Magyars,[57] which suggests that the power of the Serbian prince may have reached as far north as the Sava River. Forewarned by his loyal ally, Michael of Zahumlje, Symeon reacted accordingly. Besides Klonimir, there must have been many other Serbian political refugees in Bulgaria, for Symeon now sent an army with one of Mutimir's grandsons to replace Peter, who was captured and taken to Bulgaria, where he died in prison. Another grandson of Mutimir, Zacharias, had meanwhile been in Constantinople. He was soon dispatched to his homeland with Byzantine military support, in an attempt to regain power. He was defeated, captured, and sent to Bulgaria by Symeon's newly installed protégé. But in 921, Zacharias returned to Serbia, now with Bulgarian instead of Byzantine support, and eventually defeated his rival. Once in power, he switched sides and allied himself with Byzantium. He managed to defeat a Bulgarian army and eagerly sent the heads and weapons of the Bulgarian generals to Constantinople, "as tokens of his victory." A second Bulgarian campaign against him brought Klonimir's son, Časlav, to replace Zacharias, who fled to Croatia. Apparently, the Bulgarians were concerned with eliminating any possibility of future resistance. They rounded up all the Serbian *zhupans* and displaced a great number of people, "both old and young," whom they carried with them to Bulgaria. The campaign continued into Croatia, but Tomislav defeated the Bulgarians. As for Serbia, Constantine maintains that following the Bulgarian expedition and the deportation of the Serbian population, "the country was left deserted,"[58] and as a consequence, Časlav had to return to Bulgaria. However, in 931 he was back to Serbia, which he found devastated by the Bulgarian expedition.[59] Časlav brought back in Serbia many of the political refugees who had escaped to Croatia, Bulgaria, and Constantinople. He became a client of Romanus I and recognized himself in

[57] Constantine Porphyrogenitus, *De administrando imperio* 32, pp. 156–157. See also Ćirković, *Serbs*, p. 18.

[58] Constantine Porphyrogenitus, *De administrando imperio* 32, pp. 158–159.

[59] According to Constantine Porphyrogenitus, he found "no more than fifty men, without wives or children, who supported themselves by hunting" (*De administrando imperio* 32, p. 159).

the emperor's "servitude and subjection." Romanus showered him with gifts, and with Byzantine assistance Časlav was able to restore his country, expanding into Pagania and establishing control over Terbouniotes and Kanalites. Next to nothing is known about his polity during the second half of the tenth century, but what little is known indicates that the Serbs remained loyal Byzantine clients. A document from the Great Lavra at Mount Athos refers to Serbian envoys to Constantinople, who were captured in 993 by Arab pirates on the island of Lemnos in the Aegean Sea. Because of the war with Samuel, the Serbs had been forced to go by sea, no doubt from one of the Dalmatian ports in Duklja, Travounia, or Pagania. Possibly in response to this alliance, Samuel attacked Duklja in 997 and gained control over all Serbian territories. Whether the Serbs of 993 were coming from the interior or from one of the coastal regions that had been under Peter or Časlav's control during the first half of the tenth century, Samuel's domination of Duklja and the Slavs in southern Dalmatia seems to have contributed to a shift of the power center from the interior to the coast. During the eleventh century, most political developments are associated with Duklja, while the region in which Vlastimir, Mutimir, Peter, and Časlav had ruled in the 900s disappears from the radar of the historical sources for almost a century.

THE GOLDEN AGE OF BULGARIA

Before returning to Bulgaria in *c.* 888 and long before he was chosen to be ruler by his father, Symeon had spent some ten years in Constantinople, most likely in preparation for what Boris may have planned for him, namely to become the head of the Bulgarian church. It is not known what exactly and with whom did Symeon study, but according to the Italian bishop Liutprand of Cremona, who visited Constantinople almost a century later, Symeon was "half a Greek, and in his boyhood was taught at Byzantium the rhetoric of Demosthenes and the logic of Aristotle."[60] He certainly brought with him

[60] Liutprand of Cremona, *Antapodosis* III.29, ed. by J. Becker (Hanover and Leipzig: Hahnsche Buchhandlung, 1915; reprint 1993), MGH SS 41:87; English translation from J. Shepard, "The ruler as instructor, pastor, and wise: Leo VI of Byzantium and Symeon of Bulgaria," in *Alfred the Great. Papers from the Eleventh-Centenary Conferences*, ed. by T. Reuter (Aldershot: Ashgate, 2003), p. 347.

from Constantinople a great number of books. In a panegyric written shortly after AD 900, a contemporary author described Symeon's collection of "all the most reverend sacred books," and called him a "new Ptolemy" for having established a library in the new capital at Preslav. Symeon also took his religious vocation very seriously, as indicated by his commitment to maintaining and promoting Orthodoxy in Bulgaria. Christ and the Holy Virgin appear on his personal seals as frequently as on his father's. Symeon truly believed he was a "ruler from God" (*ek theou archon*). He often compared himself with Moses, and viewed his task as carrying out God's will and guiding his people towards the Promised Land.[61] He continued to support his father's protégé Clement and his mission to Macedonia. In 893, shortly after his rise to power, Symeon appointed Clement Bishop of Velika north of the Rhodope Mountains. To replace Clement in Ohrid, he sent Naum, who until then had been active in Preslav. Naum built a second monastery, which he dedicated to the Holy Archangels. Until his death in 910, he continued Clement's missionary work, and turned Ohrid into a major center of Old Church Slavonic culture, deeply influenced by the tradition of the Moravian mission of Constantine-Cyril and Methodius. The earliest Glagolitic manuscript of the Gospel, known as *Codex Zographensis*, was certainly written in this milieu, although its exact date remains a matter of dispute.[62] At Naum's death, Clement initiated the process of canonization, whereby his friend became the first "native" saint of Bulgaria and the only personality of the tenth-century "Golden Age" to have a biography.

[61] Nicholas Mystikos, *Letters*, ed. by R. J. H. Jenkins and L. G. Westerink (Washington: Dumbarton Oaks Center for Byzantine Studies, 1973), pp. 176–167. Symeon's title of "ruler from God" appears in the inscription of Narash dated to 904. See Beshevliev, *Die protobulgarischen Inschriften*, pp. 215–219.

[62] *Codex Zographensis* was dated to the tenth or eleventh century, but the archaic features of some of its parts are strong arguments in favor of an early date. The manuscript was found in 1834 in the library of the Monastery of St. Zographos on Mount Athos. This manuscript is different from, and earlier than, the so-called Zographos Fragments, two folios of parchment found in the same library in 1906 that contain the oldest Old Church Slavonic translation of the monastic rule of St. Basil the Great. For Codex Zographensis, see *Quattuor evangeliorum codex glagoliticus olim Zographensis nunc Petropolitanus*, ed. by V. Jagić (Berlin: Weidmann, 1879). For the Zographus Fragments, see P. A. Lavrov, "Les Feuillets de Zograph," *RES*, vol. 6 (1926), pp. 5–23.

Symeon's collection of books was not just a luxury to be used as a symbol of power and prestige. It served a well-defined purpose, namely to contribute to a vast program of translations, which he initiated at about the same time as offering his support to Ohrid. A group of gifted churchmen, some of whom may have been his classmates in Constantinople, undertook the formidable task of establishing solid foundations for the Christian religion and the Old Church Slavonic culture in Bulgaria. With no precedent in the history of Southeastern Europe, this cultural project came to be associated primarily with Preslav and with Symeon's court established there in 893. Unlike the churchmen in Ohrid, the Preslav scholars were much more dependent upon Greek models and quickly abandoned the Glagolitic script in favor of an adaptation of the Greek uncial to the needs of Slavic, which is now known as the Cyrillic alphabet.[63] The innovation did certainly not go without some resistance, especially from the conservative scholars from Ohrid. Around AD 900, a certain monk Khrabr ("the brave"), perhaps a disciple of Clement or of Naum, composed a treatise entitled *On the Letters* to defend the Glagolitic letters as better suited for rendering the sounds of Slavonic. Since Khrabr's polemical edge is turned against Cyrillic under the guise of Greek, his work has long been perceived as a reaction to the strong Byzantine influence associated with Preslav.[64] Soon after Khrabr wrote his treatise, Preslav and Ohrid grew increasingly different in terms not just of scriptorial

[63] "Cyrillic" may have initially designated what is now known as Glagolitic, a name most certainly created in the early modern period perhaps in the Catholic milieu of Dalmatia. Some Cyrillic manuscripts contain letters, words, or sentences in Glagolitic, an indication that the two alphabets coexisted for a while. However, while several palimpsests exist of Cyrillic over Glagolitic, there is none of Glagolitic over Cyrillic. See A. M. Schenker, *The Dawn of Slavic. An Introduction to Slavic Philology* (New Haven and London: Yale University Press, 1995), p. 177.

[64] The treatise enjoyed great popularity during the Middle Ages, as indicated by no less than eighty manuscripts from Bulgaria, Serbia, Russia, and Moldavia. See Chernorizec Khrabăr, *O pismenekh* [Khrabr the Monk, *On Letters*], ed. by A. Giambelluca-Kossova (Sofia: Izdatelstvo na Bălgarskata Akademiia na Naukite, 1980); English translation in I. Duichev, *Kiril and Methodius, Founders of Slavonic Writing. A Collection of Sources and Critical Studies* (Boulder and New York: Columbia University Press, 1985), pp. 157–160. *On the Letters* has been compared with Hrabanus Maur's *On the Invention of Letters*. See B. Peytscheff, "Das Werk 'De inventione litterarum' des Hrabanus Maurus und die altbulgarische Schrift 'O pismenech cranoristza Hrabra'," *Archiv für mittelrheinischen Kirchengeschichte*, vol. 34 (1982), pp. 37–41.

practice, but also of the Slavic lexicon in use. The divergence was most evident in the choice of different words for concepts such as "house" (*khramina* vs. *khlěvina*), "large" (*velii* vs *velik*), or "near" (*iskr'nii* vs. *blizh'nii*), a choice now used to separate manuscripts associated with one or the other tradition.

But it would be a mistake to view Khrabr's treatise as evidence of rivalry between Ohrid and Preslav. In fact, one of the most important figures of the latter milieu, Constantine of Preslav, was a disciple of Methodius like Clement and Naum and may have spent some time in Ohrid. He began his career in Bulgaria as priest in Pliska and Preslav and became Bishop of Preslav when Naum had to move to Ohrid. Constantine is the author of some skillful translations and adaptations from Greek, the most famous of which is the *Homiliary Gospel*, for which he wrote an introduction and the 42nd homily.[65] The introduction is a poem celebrating in much the same way as Khrabr's treatise the creation of the Slavic letters: "Therefore harken, all ye Slavs! For this gift is given by God, a divine gift from God's right hand, a gift to men that never perishes."[66] Constantine also wrote hymns: a canon for the Archangel Michael; a hymn for the Lent triodion (the liturgical book in use during Lent); and a long canon in honor of Methodius. The latter is a particularly good example of his sophisticated approach to poetry. A canon consists of nine odes of several stanzas, each associated with biblical canticles. Constantine's canon contained an acrostic spread over the first, third, fourth, and fifth odes, which in translation reads "Well, Methodius, do I praise you. Constantine." The same poetic device was applied in the *Alphabet Prayer*, a poem in which each line begins with a letter of the Glagolitic alphabet in a consecutive order.[67] Because of that, the poem may predate the reform of the script associated with the introduction of the Cyrillic alphabet. Constantine translated the catechesis of Cyril of Jerusalem, which suggests that in Preslav, unlike Ohrid, there was a demand for fundamental works of Christian edification. Much more controversial is the reason for Constantine's translation of four homilies written by Athanasius of Alexandria against the heretics.

65 A. Vaillant, "Une homélie de Constantin le Prêtre," *Byzantinoslavica*, vol. 28 (1967), pp. 68–81.

66 English translation from Schenker, *Dawn of Slavic*, p. 218. See also R. Jakobson, "St. Constantine's *Prologue to the Gospel*," *St. Vladimir's Seminary Quarterly*, vol. 7 (1963), pp. 14–19.

67 For an English translation, see Duichev, *Kiril and Methodius*, pp. 143–146.

Apparently, in the early 900s there was some concern in Preslav with the rectitude of faith.

Orthodoxy was also on the minds of the tenth-century translators. In order to avoid accusations of heresy, they made serious efforts to stay as close as possible to the Greek original text, while still capturing and rendering elegantly some grammatical and stylistic complexities:

> We have attempted to use precise terms, fearful of adding to the Gospel . . . Wherever there was agreement between Greek and Slavic, we translated by the same word. But where an expression was longer or was losing its meaning, then, not forsaking the meaning, we rendered it with another word . . . For it is impossible to retain everywhere a Greek word, but it is necessary to preserve the meaning.[68]

These were certainly the principles that inspired the *Heavens* (*Nebesa*), an abridged translation of *On the Orthodox Faith*, itself a part of John of Damascus' theological treatise *The Fount of Knowledge*. Its author was a member of the high clergy in Preslav known as John the Exarch. Unlike Constantine, John was of Bulgar noble origin, a fact to which he often referred with pride. Judging by the extraordinary breadth of knowledge in his writings, he may have received his education in Constantinople, perhaps as a classmate of Symeon. In fact, John is the only tenth-century Bulgarian author whose name is directly associated with that of his ruler. Besides *Heavens*, he wrote several sermons and eulogies. One of them is *In Praise of Tsar Symeon*, in which John singled out Symeon's education and love for books. John's literary reputation rests on a compilation modeled on similar Greek works, entitled *Six Days* (*Shestodnev*), in which he blended the biblical account of the six days of Creation with excerpts from scientific and philosophical works. Woven into the text are also John's observations on the world surrounding him, including a remark about the system of succession to the throne among the Bulgars, according to which, much like with the Khazars, the deceased ruler was followed either by his son or by his brother. Much more famous is John's comment on the awe-inspiring wonders of human anatomy in a passage influenced by Aristotle's *History of Animals*. In order to bring his point a little closer to home, John imagined a visit to the royal court in Preslav:

[68] *Macedonian Folio*, in A. Vaillant, "La préface de l'Evangéliaire vieux slave," *RES*, vol. 24 (1948), pp. 7–10; English translation from Schenker, *Dawn of Slavic*, p. 195. Vaillant thought that the text was written by Constantine-Cyril and used as a model for John the Exarch's preface to his translation of John of Damascus.

Like a humble and poor man and a stranger, having come from afar to the portals of a prince's court and having seen them is amazed; and having come close to the gates marvels asking to be let in; and having come inside sees on both sides houses standing, embellished with stone and wood, painted all over; and further when having entered the courtyard and seeing tall palaces and churches decorated richly with stone and wood and paint, and on the inside with marble and copper, silver, and gold, then he does not know with what to compare them because he had not seen in his own land such things, only a poor hut covered with straw. And, as if he had lost his mind, he marvels at them there.[69]

The excavations carried out since 1905 in Preslav have confirmed the magnitude and complexity of the building program that so much impressed John the Exarch's contemporaries. Like Pliska, the city was based on a concentric plan, with an Inner and Outer Town, but the total area enclosed by stone walls was only 865 acres, more than six times smaller than Pliska. The Inner Town was built on a high terrace on the right bank of the Ticha River, and thus served as citadel. Before becoming Symeon's capital, Preslav may have been a military and administrative center, most likely the headquarters of the *ichirgu boilas*.[70] The northern wall of the ninth-century fortification was dismantled, in order to make room for a much larger palatial compound. In addition, the Inner Town received a sophisticated water supply and drainage system. The Outer Town was built on rough, broken terrain, but a number of manors were discovered on its eastern side, between the Inner and the Outer Town enclosures, which most likely belonged to the members of the court aristocracy. Each had a small church usually placed in the middle of the compound, and some have produced evidence of multistory houses. All manors had dependencies, either storage facilities or workshops. Other manors have been

[69] *Das Hexaemeron des Exarchen Johannes*, ed. by R. Aitzetmüller (Graz: Akademische Druck- und Verlagsanstalt, 1971), pp. 1–3; English translation from Schenker, *Dawn of Slavic*, p. 226. See also R. Panova, "Dvorec, chovek, bog v 'Shestodnev' na Ioan Ekzarkh [Courtier, man, and God in John the Exarch's *Shestodnev*]," in *1100 godini Veliki Preslav*, ed. by T. Totev, I. Iordanov, R. Rashev, et al., vol. 1 (Shumen: Izdatelstvo na VPI "Konstantin Preslavski," 1995), pp. 136–139.

[70] That Preslav existed as an important political center before Symeon is demonstrated, among other things, by the discovery of a leaden seal of Emperor Theophilus (dated between 830 and 835) next to the southern gate of the Outer Town. See I. Iordanov, "Pechati na chuzhdi vladeteli, namereni v Preslav [The seals of foreign rulers found in Preslav]," in *1100 godini Veliki Preslav*, ed. by T. Totev, I. Iordanov, R. Rashev, et al., vol. 1 (Shumen: Izdatelstvo na VPI "Konstantin Preslavski," 1995), pp. 140–141.

found in satellite settlements around Preslav. The northern area of the Outer Town is separated from the rest by the Rumska Creek and served as the quarter of the artisans. In the southern section, next to the gate controlling access on the road to Constantinople, there were eighteen premises equal in size directly attached to the rampart. A great number of amphorae found in these buildings, perhaps carrying wine or oil to or from Constantinople, bespeak the commercial character of the quarter. Preslav has produced vast quantities of Byzantine pottery and small objects of white porcelain, in addition to occasional fragments of tenth-century pottery from the Near East. Some 200 coins minted for tenth-century emperors, in addition to 1 dirham, indicate that in the 900s trade with Byzantium consisted not just of barter, but of monetary exchanges as well. On the other hand, Preslav also appears as an important center of production. Workshops in the southern section of the Outer Town produced fine-quality ceramics, kaolin ware with red paint and glazed ware, both of which were found in significant quantities all over northeastern Bulgaria. Close to the southern gate of the Outer Town were also workshops producing ceramic tiles, but the main center for the production of glazed architectural ceramic decorations was located at a short distance from Preslav, in Tuzlalăka, where Bulgarian archaeologists have excavated a large compound with a church in the middle, quickly interpreted as a monastery.[71] Another compound excavated in the early twentieth century in Patleina, about a mile and a quarter southwest of Preslav, has produced an incredible amount of glazed ceramic icons, the most famous of which is that of St. Theodore, Bulgaria's oldest monumental icon. To be sure, no less than eight compounds identified as monasteries have so far been excavated in or around Preslav, all built during the early 900s. But a recent analysis of tenth-century monasteries excavated in Bulgaria suggests that some of them were not different from the manors also excavated on

[71] T. Totev, *Manastirăt v "Tuzlalăka" – centăr na risuvana keramika v Preslav IX–X v.* [The Tuzlalăka, a Ninth- to Tenth-Century Center for the Production of Painted Ceramics near Preslav] (Sofia: Izdatelstvo na Bălgarskata Akademiia na Naukite, 1982). For the workshops near the southern gate of the Outer Town, see T. Totev, "L'atelier de céramique peinte du monastère royal de Preslav," *CA*, vol. 35 (1987), pp. 65–80. For Bulgarian ceramic decoration, see I. Akrabova-Zhandova, "Preslav inlaid ceramics," in *Studies in Memory of David Talbot Rice*, ed. by G. Robertson and G. Henderson (Edinburgh: Edinburgh University Press, 1975), pp. 25–33; E. C. Schwartz, "Medieval ceramic decoration in Bulgaria," *Byzantinoslavica*, vol. 43 (1982), 45–50.

the eastern side of the Outer Town.[72] Four of the eight "monasteries" had workshops specializing in the production of fine-quality kaolin ware, ceramic icons, marble sculptural elements, mosaic, glass, and bone artifacts. These luxuries were not meant for trade, but for highly localized consumption within the region of Preslav. In one of the manors in the Outer Town, archaeologists found an icon certainly produced in the workshops built next to the southern gate, as well as fragments of another produced outside Preslav, in Patleina. The buildings too hastily interpreted as monastery churches may have in fact been family chapels. This is certainly the case with the church excavated in Patleina, the crypt of which contained three skeletons, a male, a female, and a child. On the other hand, neither Patleina nor Tuzlalăka produced inscriptions and graffiti on the scale of other archaeological assemblages clearly identified as monasteries, such as that of Ravna built probably during the reign of Boris or the first years of Symeon's reign. Most prominent among the datable artifacts found there are the seals of Symeon and his son Michael, both indicating that Ravna was a royal monastery. Most Greek inscriptions found at Ravna are in late ninth- or tenth-century minuscules, and some of them contain liturgical texts carved on the outside wall of a room identified as the monastery *scriptorium* on the basis of the wax tablets and writing instruments found within its perimeter. Nothing comparable has been found in either Tuzlalăka or Patleina.

Twenty-five churches built in the 900s have so far been found in Preslav, but the most famous monument of all is the Golden Church, so called because of its identification with the church referred to in a colophon to the four homilies against Arians written by Athanasius of Alexandria and translated by Constantine of Preslav: "And the monk Theodore Doksov copied them, at the command of the same prince [Symeon], in the year 6415, in the eleventh indiction [AD 907], at the mouth of the Ticha River, where a sacred and revered golden church has been newly built by that same prince."[73] Whether or not this

[72] R. Kostova, "Bulgarian monasteries, ninth to tenth centuries: interpreting the archaeological evidence," *Pliska–Preslav*, vol. 8 (2000), pp. 190–202; and "Imalo li e manastiri-ergasterii v Bălgariia prez X vek? [Were there monastery workshops in tenth-century Bulgaria?]," in *Civitas divino-humana. V chest na profesor Georgi Bakalov*, ed. by C. Stepanov and V. Vachkova (Sofia: Centăr za izsledvaniia na bălgarite "Tangra" TanNakRa IK, 2004), pp. 457–469.

[73] Theodore Doksov's colophon, in Butler, *Monumenta Bulgarica*, p. 137. Theodore Doksov was a cousin of Symeon. See P. Georgiev, "Koi e Tudor chernorizec

identification is correct, the Preslav church, also known as the Round Church, is a remarkable monument, without any parallel in contemporary Byzantine architecture. It consists of a rectangular courtyard lined with columns, a two-story forechurch with corner turrets, and a rotunda (thirty-four feet in diameter) with wall niches and two tiers of columns around the dome. A Carolingian source of inspiration has been proposed for this building, but its models were more likely rotundas of the Justinianic age, such as the Octagon in Philippi or the Church of St. George in Thessalonica. The Round Church produced a great number of inscriptions in Glagolitic, including the so-called Preslav Abecedarium, containing the first thirteen letters of the Glagolitic alphabet. However, Preslav was the center from which the scriptorial innovation associated with the introduction of Cyrillic spread to other regions of Bulgaria. One of the earliest documents in Cyrillic is a bilingual (Slavic and Greek) inscription on a ceramic jug dated to 931.[74] Another late tenth-century Cyrillic inscription on a slab covered the tomb of the *ichirgu boilas* Mostich, who served under both Symeon and his son Peter, before taking monastic vows and entering a monastery near Preslav, where he eventually died.[75] These two inscriptions, as well as others, demonstrate that in Preslav the Cyrillic alphabet was introduced relatively early in the tenth century to replace Glagolitic. Since no Cyrillic manuscripts of the tenth century are known to date, the inscriptions also show how the scriptorial innovation presumably created for writing on parchment could be used for messages carved in stone because of the uniform shape and size of the new letters.

But use of Cyrillic was not restricted to the capital. Tenth-century Cyrillic inscriptions have been found in Ravna and in a cave monastery near the village of Krepcha, not far from Târgovishte,[76]

Doksov? (Kăm văprosa za bălgarskata patronimiia prez srednovekovieoto) [Who was Theodore, the monk Doksov? On the question of Bulgarian patronymics in the Middle Ages]," *SL*, vol. 20 (1987), pp. 87–94.

[74] D. Ovcharov, "A Cyrillic inscription of 931 in Preslav," *BHR*, vol. 4 (1976), pp. 71–75.

[75] K. Popkonstantinov and O. Kronsteiner, *Starobălgarski nadpisi*, vol. 1 (Salzburg: Institut für Slawistik der Universität Salzburg, 1994), p. 185. For an English translation of the inscription of Mostich, see Schenker, *Dawn of Slavic*, p. 279. For Mostich, see I. Duichev, "Mostič, un haut dignitaire bulgare du Xe siècle," *Byzantinoslavica*, vol. 29 (1968), pp. 281–289.

[76] Popkonstantinov and Kronsteiner, *Starobălgarski nadpisi*, pp. 47–59 and 215–233. One of the Krepcha inscriptions contains the date 6430. If correct, this would

not only in the hinterland of the capital city, but also in locations as distant from Preslav and from each other as Murfatlar in Dobrudja (Romania), Hagios Germanos, a village on the shore of Lake Prespa (Greece), and Gornji Katun near Varvarin (Serbia).[77] Perhaps the most impressive body of Cyrillic inscriptions outside Preslav is a number of leaden pendants bearing apocryphal prayers and used as amulets against fever or demons. Such pendants have been found in several tenth-century strongholds: Pet Mogili, Ruino, and Odărci, all three in northeastern Bulgaria; Krăn near Stara Zagora, in central Bulgaria; Oreshak near Varna, on the Black Sea coast; Pernik in western Bulgaria; Păcuiul lui Soare, an island on the Danube River, now in Romania; as well as north of the Danube River, in Călăraşi (Romania). The standard form of both leaden amulets and prayers suggests that the vehicle for the spread of Cyrillic was the religious literature for which Preslav served as the most important center of production. On the other hand, the apocryphal prayers indicate the degree of Christianization in the hinterland of the capital city, dotted with strongholds erected at some point during the tenth century. Some of these strongholds were erected on top of ruins of early Byzantine forts on high cliffs or along the Danube's tributaries on the right bank. Others were built anew in areas without any occupation dated to the early Byzantine period. All such forts were equipped with walls

make the inscription a decade earlier than that of Preslav, for 6430 is AD 921. Another inscription found in the Ossuary Church of the Krepcha monastery is a curse against desecrators and it is also Cyrillic. Several other inscriptions were written by visitors (or pilgrims). Among them was a certain George "from the village of Mashtovica."

77 For Murfatlar, see K. Popkonstantinov and V. Popkonstantinova, "Die Inschriften des Felsklosters Murfatlar," in *Paleobalkanistika i starobălgaristika. Părvi esenni nacionalni cheteniia "Profesor Ivan Gălăbov,"* ed. by E. Dogramadzhieva and K. Popkonstantinov (Veliko Tărnovo: Universitetsko izdatelstvo "Sv. sv. Kiril i Metodii," 1995), pp. 111–134. Another Cyrillic inscription referring to events taking place in 6451 (AD 943) was found near Murfatlar, in Mircea Vodă. See I. Bozhilov, "L'inscription du jupan Dimitre de l'an 943 (théories et faits)," *Etudes Historiques*, vol. 6 (1973), pp. 11–28. For the Hagios Germanos inscription, see Ph. Malingoudis, *Die mittelalterlichen kyrillischen Inschriften der Hämus-Halbinsel. I. Die bulgarischen Inschriften* (Thessaloniki: Association hellénique d'études slaves, 1979), pp. 39–42. For the Gornji Katun inscription, see S. Radojčić, "Temnički natpis. Sujeverice srednjovekovnih graditelja o čudotvornoj moci imena i likova sevastijskih mučenika [The Temnic inscription. A medieval builder's superstitious beliefs in the powers of the name and glory of the holy martyrs]," *ZLU*, vol. 5 (1969), pp. 1–11.

made of stone bonded with clay and towers of massive stonework, with no parallel in contemporary Byzantine fortifications. The process of fortification can be followed with some degree of detail in the case of Car Asen, a ninth-century open settlement in the vicinity of Silistra, which at some point in the tenth century received massive protective walls with powerful gates, as well as three single-naved churches. One of the stronghold's areas had extra walls, most likely serving as an inner enclosure. Inside the fort, archaeologists identified forty-eight habitation units, mostly sunken-floored houses with stone ovens or hearths, all of which were dated to the tenth and eleventh century. At Durankulak, on the Black Sea coast, a settlement was established shortly before 900 on an offshore island. During the tenth century, over 200 houses were built on the island, mostly sunken-floored buildings, one of which produced a large quantity of charred seeds of wheat and millet that bespeak the agricultural occupation of the fort's inhabitants. Despite its peripheral location, Durankulak maintained relations with Preslav, as indicated by fragments of kaolin ware with red paint that were produced in the capital. Similar forts excavated in northeastern Bulgaria at Skala near Tervel and Khuma near Razgrad confirm the conclusions drawn on the basis of the evidence from Car Asen and Durankulak: these were fortified, but not military, sites. It remains unclear what exactly caused the fortification, but there is no doubt that these were civilian sites. Only houses have been found within the area enclosed by ramparts, and no barracks or other indications of a military presence have so far been identified. Moreover, remains of large, open settlements immediately adjacent to the forts indicate the presence of a considerably numerous civilian population. Judging from the existing evidence, the forts at Car Asen, Skala, and Khuma may have operated as regional centers with economic and perhaps religious, but no military functions. It is thus possible that the fortification of such sites was a local initiative, perhaps related to the rise of local elites whose power resided in control of land rather than state offices or ranks granted by the ruler. Except the ramparts, there is nothing in the strongholds in Car Asen, Skala, and Khuma that is different from contemporary open settlements in Bulgaria. Clay cauldrons, so typical of tenth-century rural settlements in Bulgaria, have been found both on the Black Sea coast, at Durankulak and Cape Kaliakra, and on sites in the interior, such as Krivina near Ruse or Pernik near Sofia. Kilns for mass production of wheel-made pottery, including clay cauldrons, were in existence in northeastern (Topola near Dobrich) as well as central Bulgaria (Khotnica near Veliko Tărnovo). Moreover, judging from the evidence of hoards of Byzantine gold coins found in tenth-century settlement assemblages, some inhabitants of open settlements of northern Bulgaria were apparently as wealthy as owners of manors erected in the early tenth century inside the Outer Town at Pliska. Rural cemeteries, such as that from Batin near Ruse, have produced exquisite dress accessories, especially pectoral crosses and silver finger-rings and torcs, a favorite female dress accessory.[78] The exact origin of that wealth remains unknown, but there is little doubt that many of those who lived at a great distance from Preslav had access to and took profit from the trade with Byzantium that was going through that city and was responsible for the modest monetization of exchanges. Byzantine copper coins, whose presence could hardly be explained in terms of either booty or gifts, have turned up in some numbers on several rural sites in northwestern and northeastern Bulgaria. Links with Preslav were also responsible for the relatively quick adoption of Christian burial customs, such as the absence of grave goods. Occasionally, as in a large cemetery excavated in Varna, commoners were buried in cists imitating sarcophagi not unlike the one found in the modern cemetery of Preslav, which was associated with a silver cup with an inscription mentioning a certain *zhupan* named Sivin.[79]

The rapid adaptation of Byzantine cultural models taking place in Preslav and other centers of northeastern Bulgaria can most likely be dated to the first decades of the tenth century, when relations between Bulgaria and Byzantium improved considerably. Following the defeat of the Magyars at the hands of his allies, the Pechenegs, Symeon once again invaded the theme of Macedonia (eastern Thrace). In the spring of 896, he inflicted a serious defeat upon a Byzantine army at Bulgarophygon and devastated the countryside in the whole of

78 D. Stanchev, "Rannosrednovekoven nekropol do s. Batin, Rusenski okrăg [An early medieval cemetery from Batin near Ruse]," *Godishnik na Muzeite ot Severna Bălgariia*, vol. 11 (1985), pp. 45–54. For torcs as a favorite aristocratic fashion of the early 900s, see T. Mikhailova, "Metalni grivni ot Preslav (kraia na X–XIV v.) [Late tenth- to fourteenth-century metal torcs from Preslav]," in *Prinosi kăm bălgarskata arkheologiia. Dekemvriiski dni na bălgarskata arkheologiia "Prof. dr. Stancho Vaklinov,"* ed. by D. Ovcharov and I. Shtereva, vol. II (Sofia: Arges, 1993), pp. 114–126.

79 T. Totev, "Srebărna chasha s nadpis ot Preslav [A silver bowl with inscription from Preslav]," *IAI*, vol. 27 (1964), pp. 5–15; and "Za edin paralel na chashata na Sivin zhupan ot Preslav [On an analogy for the bowl of *zhupan* Sivin from Preslav]," *Arkheologiia*, vol. 8 (1966), pp. 31–37.

Thrace. At the peace, he agreed to release a great number of prisoners, both military and civilian, in exchange for an annual tribute. Despite a number of changes taking place in the Byzantine provinces on the border with Bulgaria (such as the creation of the themes of Strymon and Nikopolis mentioned above), the peace established in 897 was interrupted in the subsequent years only episodically by raids. Symeon did not take advantage of the sack of Thessalonica by the Arab pirate Leo of Tripoli and he is not known to have tried to push the frontier with Byzantium closer to that great city of Macedonia. The only period of open, full-scale warfare in the history of the next thirty years of his reign was that between 913 and 924.

In August 913, as the Byzantine emperor Alexander refused to pay the tribute established through the peace of 897, Symeon suddenly appeared with an army before the walls of Constantinople demanding to meet with the emperor and with Patriarch Nicholas Mystikos. This was the first time since Krum that a ruler of Bulgaria had marched against Constantinople. Patriarch Nicholas met with Symeon in the Hebdomon palace compound outside the city walls, and under circumstances that are not very clear Symeon received a crown, while a marriage was arranged between his daughter and the minor emperor Constantine VII. There has been much dispute as to what kind of crown was bestowed upon Symeon at Hebdomon, but whatever Patriarch Nicholas's intentions may have been and whatever the spin the imperial propaganda put on these events in the subsequent decades, Symeon had barely returned to Bulgaria when he began striking seals whose legends included the terms "Symeon the emperor (*basileus*)." This must have referred, at least initially, to his position as ruler of Bulgaria, for there is no evidence to support the idea that Symeon had any intentions to usurp the Byzantine imperial title. However, an emperor of Bulgaria was the equal of the Byzantine rulers, of which there was none in 913 to match Symeon. When Patriarch Nicholas was toppled in a coup led by Constantine VII's mother, Zoe, she immediately cancelled the marriage arrangements made in 913. Symeon sent his troops to raid Thrace and the environs of Dyrrachion. At the peace, the 913 agreement was confirmed and Symeon regained his position of power over the regime established in Constantinople. When Zoe tried to persuade the Pechenegs to attack Bulgaria, the Byzantine fleet sent to the Lower Danube failed to transport the horsemen of the steppe across the river. Later attempts to bribe the Serbs to attack Bulgaria together with the Magyars were equally abortive. Symeon invaded Serbia, deposed Peter, and replaced him with a ruler loyal to him. A surprise attack by a Byzantine army marching up the Black Sea coast ended in disaster. On August 20, 917, at Anchialos, Symeon inflicted upon the Byzantine troops the most devastating defeat since the days of Emperor Nicephorus' campaign against Krum. Again, he marched on Constantinople and defeated once more the remains of the army he had crushed at Anchialos. Patriarch Nicholas Mystikos wrote a number of letters to Symeon trying to persuade him to spare Constantinople and capitalizing upon the sincere faith of Symeon, who, in 913, was apparently still doing penance for the sins he had committed when attacking fellow Christians in the 890s. Instead of storming the walls of Constantinople, Symeon invaded Greece, which he raided as far south as Corinth. When an Armenian officer in the Byzantine army, Romanus Lecapenus, married his daughter to Constantine VII in 919, and was soon proclaimed co-emperor, Symeon's response was to send his troops to ravage everything up to the walls of Constantinople. He may have had greater things in mind, as he established contact with the Muslim rulers of North Africa and Tarsus, whom he needed as allies for an attack on the city on both land and sea. As Symeon's embassy was intercepted, the Byzantines bribed the Arabs into abandoning him. In the meantime, the Serbs obtained a major victory against Symeon's troops led by two generals, Marmaim and Sigritzis Theodore, whose heads Zacharias, the prince of Serbia, sent to Constantinople.[80] However, soon after that, as we have seen, Symeon rounded up the Serbian *zhupans*, whom he transported to Bulgaria, as a punitive measure against his western neighbor. In the summer of 924, he reappeared under the walls of Constantinople demanding an interview with Emperor Romanus I. This time, the war was one of political symbols as well. At the carefully arranged meeting that took place on a specially constructed jetty built on the Golden Horn, Symeon appeared surrounded by soldiers hailing him in Greek as emperor. Romanus accepted the reinstation of the tribute to Bulgaria, but seems to have had more problems with the title of the Bulgarian ruler. In the meantime, Symeon began styling himself not just emperor (of the Bulgarians), but, more importantly, "Emperor

[80] Constantine Porphyrogenitus, *De administrando imperio* 32, pp. 158–159.

of the Romans."[81] However, it is unlikely that this title represented any claim to Constantinople. Instead, Symeon may have intended to represent his quality of ruler over "Romans" inside Bulgaria, at the same time pushing the imperial agenda in an attempt to stress that he was equal to the emperor in Constantinople. In the end, by 927, Symeon obtained the raise of status for his senior churchman (most likely the archbishop of Bulgaria residing in Preslav) to that of patriarch. He may have intended to create by such means the legal basis for the proclamation of the Bulgarian emperors by their own means and through the leaders of their own church.

When he died in 927, Symeon was succeeded by Peter, the eldest son from his second marriage to the sister of a powerful *boila* named George Sursuvul. Peter and his uncle acting as regent continued Symeon's aggressively anti-Byzantine policies. The Bulgarian troops raided the theme of Macedonia, and the Thracian towns that had been under Bulgarian occupation for several years were deserted and razed to the ground.[82] However, faced with problems at home, including an invasion of locusts, Peter was forced to negotiate. The peace of 927 was based on a compromise: Peter's title was shortened to just "Emperor of the Bulgarians," while Romanus I agreed to restart the payment of the Byzantine tribute, albeit at a much-reduced rate. In addition, Peter married the daughter of Romanus' eldest daughter, Maria, whose name, according to Liutprand of Cremona, was appropriately changed for the occasion to Irene ("peace" in Greek).[83] Maria appears as co-emperor of Bulgaria on Peter's seals, on which she is sometimes represented holding the cross above Peter's hand, as a symbol of seniority. This and a few other details gleaned from contemporary Byzantine sources have led some historians to the conclusion that with the marriage between Peter and Maria the Byzantine influence in Bulgaria increased considerably. But there is very little evidence of that in the material culture of Bulgaria until Maria's death in the early 960s and of Peter in 969.

Before he could establish himself firmly in power, Peter was confronted first with the brief and unsuccessful opposition from some

[81] For Symeon's seal as "Emperor of the Romans," see Beshevliev, *Die protobulgarischen Inschriften*, pp. 330–331, comparing Symeon with Otto II, proclaimed emperor of the Romans in 982.

[82] Theophanes Continuatus, p. 412. Hostilities continued until right before the marriage between Peter and Maria.

[83] Liutprand of Cremona, *Antapodosis* III.38, p. 92.

members of the aristocracy headed by Symeon's two other sons, John and Michael. For the remaining forty years of his long reign, nothing is reported about Peter's regime being challenged from either *boilas* or other members of the royal family. Instead, the picture to be drawn from the disappointingly little evidence that we have on Bulgaria during Peter's reign is one of economic and institutional growth. Such developments had their roots in the long period of peace and prosperity at the beginning of Symeon's reign. An inscription found in Narash near Thessaloniki mentions one of Symeon's dignitaries named Theodore who was Count of Dristra (Silistra),[84] and an important official at Symeon's court, named Gregory, "the *magistros* of the Bulgars," is mentioned on four of his known seals.[85] He may have been the head of the royal chancery. In the 960s, a Jewish traveler from Spain, Ibrahim ibn-Ya'kub, compared Peter with the great monarchs of his day and noted that he enjoyed great authority, had secretaries, heads of offices, and senior functionaries.[86] Indeed, there are more seals of Peter than of any other ruler of Bulgaria.

The economic growth during Peter's reign is visible in the continuation of the building programs of his father, in Preslav as well as elsewhere. Next to nothing is known about court life in Preslav, but a hoard of gold and silver found in 1975 in Kastana, near Preslav, may serve as an illustration of the degree of sophistication of some members of the Bulgarian aristocracy. The find includes some 150 pieces of gold and enamel furnishings, silver objects, ancient gems,

[84] Beshevliev, *Die protobulgarischen Inschriften*, pp. 215–219. See also I. Andreev, "Naryshskaia nadpis' kniazia Simeona i administrativnoe ustroistvo bolgarskogo gosudarstva v konce IX i nachale X v. [The Narash inscription of Prince Symeon and the administrative structure of late ninth- and early tenth-century Bulgaria]," *EB*, vol. 14 (1978), pp. 121–131.

[85] I. Iordanov, "Pechati na Grigorii Magistăr na bălgarite prez X vek [The seals of Gregory, the tenth-century *magistros* of the Bulgars]," in *Civitas divino-humana. V chest na profesor Georgi Bakalov*, ed. by C. Stepanov and V. Vachkova (Sofia: Centăr za izsledvaniia na bălgarite "Tangra" TanNakRa IK, 2004), pp. 507–511.

[86] *Relacja Ibrahima ibn Ja'kūba z podróży do krajów słowiańskich w przekazie al–Bekrīego* [The account of Ibrahim ibn-Ya'kub's travel to the Slavic lands preserved in the redaction of al-Bakri], ed. by T. Kowalski (Cracow: Gebethner i Wolff, 1946), pp. 51 and 148. For Ibrahim ibn-Ya'kub, see P. Engels, "Der Reisebericht des Ibrahim ibn Ya'qub (961–966)," in *Kaiserin Theophanu. Begegnung des Ostens und Westens in die Wende des ersten Jahrtausends*, ed. by A. von Euw and P. Schreiner (Cologne: Böhlau, 1991), pp. 413–420; Dmitrii Mishin, "Ibrahim ibn-Ya'qub at-Turtushi's account of the Slavs from the middle of the tenth century," *AMS* (1994–1995), pp. 184–199.

and 15 silver coins struck in 959 for Emperors Constantine VII and Romanus II. The exquisite necklace with medallions is clearly a Byzantine work. The same is true of the diadem plates representing scenes from the life of Alexander the Great, which were clearly associated with the Macedonian dynasty in power in Constantinople since the late ninth century. The diadem was certainly meant for a member of the royal family in Preslav, and the spherical pendants of gold with enamel ornamentation may have been part of a long, gem-studded scarf worn only by members of the imperial family in Constantinople. It has been suggested that the hoard belonged to one of Peter's two daughters, who may have acquired the furnishings during a visit to Constantinople in 940 in the company of her mother Maria. If true, this would indicate how close the position of power of the ruler in Preslav had come to the means of representation until then reserved only for the emperors in Constantinople.

We have seen that several Magyar and Pecheneg raids directed at Byzantium crossed Bulgaria during Peter's long reign. The Stone Dike in Dobrudja, the largest work of fortification in tenth-century Bulgaria, may well have been associated with these raids. Running from the Danube to the Black Sea, the frontier covered by this dike is thirty-seven miles long, twice as large as Danevirke, the complex of fortifications on the southern frontier of early medieval Denmark. The Stone Dike is the biggest medieval monument in Southeastern Europe. The earthwork consists of a ditch to the north about six feet deep and a rampart rising up to six feet above it to the south, surmounted by a stone wall about five feet tall. Archaeological excavations have shown that, in addition to materials from ruins of ancient buildings in the Roman city of Tomis (present-day Constanţa), the wall was built with stone from several neighboring quarries, one of which was at Murfatlar, some ten miles west of the Black Sea shore and twenty miles east of the Danube River. Associated with the dike is a series of twenty-six forts built against the rampart, one every two or three miles. One of them, fort no. 20, which was located just eighteen miles west of the Murfatlar quarry, produced a fragmentary Cyrillic inscription referring to the attack of an unknown enemy against the "Greeks" in the year 6451 (AD 943), "as Demetrius was *zhupan*." Scholars argued at length over who exactly was the enemy, whether Magyars or Pechenegs. In both cases, the raid against Byzantium must have crossed Bulgaria, which suggests that the inscription commemorated a victory of *zhupan* Demetrius against the invading armies. It is very likely that Demetrius was in charge of the military administration of, at least, one portion of this barrier erected on the northern frontier of tenth-century Bulgaria.[87] Some forts also produced evidence of buildings and rooms, others were associated with clusters of extramural houses built in stone. That the Stone Dike is the most recent of all three dikes running across Dobrudja results from the fact that one of its forts was built on top of the Large Dike, and another on top of the Small Dike. The date of the Large Dike is much disputed, although it may have been erected during Symeon's reign as suggested by pottery remains of the late ninth or early tenth century found during its excavation. In any case, the relation between the Stone and the Large dike, as well as the inscription of *zhupan* Demetrius, indicate that the Stone Dike is a later construction, perhaps erected during the last years of Symeon's reign or, more likely, during Peter's reign.

What makes the Stone Dike unique is the presence in its immediate vicinity of a monastic site consisting of several churches, galleries, and cells, all cut into the northern slope of a solitary crag near Murfatlar. The archaeological evidence suggests that occupation of the site began only after work had ceased in the limestone quarry. The best-preserved church is a single-naved, well-cut construction with longitudinally barrel-vaulted narthex and a small nave. There are runic and Cyrillic inscriptions and graffiti on all walls. A second, partially destroyed church was found about six feet beneath the first one. Its narthex was separated from the nave by three arcades with rock-cut pillars covered with Cyrillic inscriptions and graffiti, especially images of elongated horses, horsemen, and crosses. A rock-cut gallery connected this church with another one underneath. The gallery produced grave pits carved in rock with few skeletal remains. The walls of the gallery are all covered with graffiti, mostly images of ships. A few sherds of ceramic-glazed ware were found on the gallery's floor. Fragments of limestone rock bearing traces of red paint, which were found inside the church, suggest the existence of a different kind of decoration. The most spectacular church was cut on the lowest

[87] D. P. Bogdan, "Dobrudzhanskaia nadpis' 943 goda. Paleograficheskii i lingvisticheskii ocherk [The Dobrudja inscription of 943. A paleographical and linguistic contribution]," *Romanoslavica*, vol. 1 (1958), pp. 88–104; V. Giuzelev, "Dobrudzhanskiiat nadpis i săbitiiata v Bălgariia prez 943 g. [The Dobrudja inscription and the events in Bulgaria in 943]," *Istoricheski pregled*, vol. 24 (1968), pp. 46–48.

level of the monastic complex. Unlike the other three, this is a large, three-aisled construction, with the narthex separated from the nave by three arcades with rock-cut pillars covered with inscriptions and graffiti. One of them bears the image of a bird, presumably an eagle, and a Cyrillic inscription, perhaps an invocation on behalf of a donor named Tăngai. Across the inscription, a different hand carved four Glagolitic letters rendering the name Iliia. Another Cyrillic inscription on the western wall of the narthex is a biblical citation: "For it is written: I will smite the shepherd, and the sheep will be scattered" (Mark 14.27). The most remarkable feature of this church is a crypt with skeletal remains, on the western side of the nave. Above the entrance to the crypt, there is a large, labyrinth-like graffito, and on its left the image of a saint identified as St. John the Baptist by the accompanying inscription in runes. A second inscription, presumably in Greek, was initially interpreted as a date (982), but this reading proved to be wrong. On the eastern wall of the nave, there are images of horses and tendril patterns very similar to those decorating the folios of the *Codex Zographensis*. The altar, separated from the nave by three arcades with arches painted with red lines, contains two other Cyrillic inscriptions. One refers to a traveler, an unknown priest, who visited the church; the other mentions a certain Dimian. A military saint, identified as St. Theodore by the accompanying Greek inscription, is depicted with his lance in hand on the eastern arcade separating the apse from the nave. Outside the cave complex, archaeologists found an above-ground, small house very similar to those in clusters around the forts of the Stone Dike. The ceramic assemblage from the house also included the pottery categories represented in the forts, especially amphorae with glazed decoration. Finally, a small cemetery with nine burials in rock-cut grave pits was found north of the cave complex. One of these burials produced a cross carved in limestone.

Although the chronology of the site is still a matter of dispute, it is quite clear that at least three of the five churches were in use at the same time. The graffiti found in Murfatlar are very similar to explicitly Christian images, such as church plans or images of saints and prophets, crosses, ships, trees, ladders, dragons, or plows, all of which were carved on blocks of city walls, churches, or civilian buildings in Preslav and Pliska. To judge from the great variety of inscriptions – runic, Glagolitic, Cyrillic, and Greek – several languages were in use at the same time on the site. The community living in the caves of

Murfatlar seems to have been visited by many pilgrims. Scholars studying the inscriptions have been able to identify the name of a patron, Tăngai. The first part of the inscription referring to him contains the name of a certain *zhupan* George, who was probably a colleague or successor of *zhupan* Demetrius mentioned in the inscription found in the neighboring fort no. 20 of the Stone Dike. This suggests that the monastic community at Murfatlar was in the middle of a military district on the northern frontier of Bulgaria. During the tenth century, the association of military sites and cave monasteries was by no means unique. The most remarkable parallel is that of Byzantine churches, chapels, monasteries, and hermitages that were cut into the soft volcanic tufa of Cappadocia (Turkey). Occupation of many Cappadocian sites began in the late tenth century, and there is plenty of evidence that, like Murfatlar, Cappadocian cave monasteries had strong associations with families of powerful borderlords. Recently, similar sites have been identified in great numbers in northeastern Bulgaria, where the ridges and canyons resulting from the erosion of stratified limestone provided suitable sites for the excavation of caves, as well as in northern Greece, Macedonia, and Moldova. The unusual combination of images and languages displayed on the walls of cave churches, but especially the emphasis the Murfatlar inscriptions place upon the values of ascetic life, points to a widespread monastic phenomenon of mid-tenth-century Bulgaria. Several works regarding the monastic life were available in Old Church Slavonic translation in the 900s. The most popular among them, especially during the reign of Peter, was the *Ladder of Divine Ascent* written in the 500s by the abbot of the Monastery of Saint Catherine on Mount Sinai, John Climacus. To judge by the number of manuscripts, equally popular was a collection of tales from the lives of monks and hermits known as the *Sayings of the Fathers*. The same is true of the earliest Old Church Slavonic translation of another collection of tales about famous monks known as the *Roman Paterik*, originally composed in Latin by Pope Gregory the Great, then translated into Greek. With such works of edification available in translation, one would have expected in Bulgaria a monastic movement not very different from that epitomized in the late tenth century by Mount Athos. However, to judge from the evidence of actual monastic practice, monasticism in Bulgaria was gradually moving in a different direction.

The prime figure of Bulgarian monasticism in the tenth century was St. John of Rila. He was born in 880 in a village near Sofia, not far from the region to which Symeon would later assign Clement of Ohrid as Bishop of Dragvica (Velika). John became monk and joined an established monastery dedicated to St. Demetrius somewhere in his native region. After spending some time in the community, he felt himself called to the ascetic life. John was given the blessing of the abbot and he removed himself to a place of solitude, a forest cave. Disciples flocked to join him and a little community grew up, which would become in 930 or 931 the monastery of Rila. As soon as he found a disciple to whom to entrust the leadership of that community, John left his growing monastery for a mountain retreat. He died in 946 and was canonized shortly thereafter. His life and activity are known from nine different biographies, seven in Old Church Slavonic and two in Greek, in itself an indication of the popularity his teachings and role model enjoyed in later centuries. The earliest Life, commonly known as *Zavet*, was written by an unknown author sometime after the saint's death and before 1183. John's only surviving work is his Testament issued on March 25, 941, when he decided to leave Rila for his mountain retreat. The Testament is a unique document, for unlike slightly later developments at Mount Athos, John encourages monks to establish relations with and support neighboring solitaries, while still endorsing cenobitic values. He even goes as far as to recommend that one of the fundamental readings be the Life of St. Anthony, the archetype of anchoritic life.[88] John stressed the importance of ascetic retirement in order to escape the snares of the world. True, he urged his monks to "establish the newly enlightened" from their own "race" in the faith and to instruct them to abandon the "indecent pagan rites and the evil customs" which they kept even after receiving baptism,[89] a remark that brings back to memory Clement of Ohrid's problems in Macedonia and his list of priorities. On the other hand, when offered a royal donation by Emperor Peter – perhaps an annuity like those attested for Mount Athos in the late 900s – the saint promptly rejected it and, according to the *Zavet*, even prophesied that Peter would need all that gold for hiring soldiers to battle his enemies. Stressing the value of manual labor, John urged monks to have no desire for riches or power and to have

[88] *Testament of John of Rila* 16, English translation by I. Iliev in *Byzantine Monastic Foundation Documents. A Complete Translation of the Surviving Founders'* Typika *and Testaments*, ed. by J. Thomas and A. C. Hero (Washington: Dumbarton Oaks Research Library and Collection, 2000), p. 133.

[89] *Testament of John of Rila* 18, p. 133.

nothing to do with the princes of this world. John's recommendation was instead humility, obedience, sexual continence, anonymity, and silence, in short strict ascetism. A symbol of his peculiar form of monasticism, the cave is a central theme in the *Zavet*. Two of John's disciples, St. Prohor Pshinskii and St. Joachim Ostrogovski, followed in their spiritual father's footsteps and lived in caves.

John's teaching was in sharp contrast with other aspects of contemporary monastic life in Bulgaria, in particular with the creation of large royal monasteries in the hinterland of Preslav, such as Ravna or Kalugerica. Under Symeon and his son Peter, such cenobitic communities were planted in the middle of densely populated areas and benefited from royal (later, imperial) munificence. In criticizing the kind of monasticism that relied almost exclusively on the generosity of the ruler, John of Rila was certainly not alone. In the mid-tenth century, similar opinions were expressed in the ascetic works of Peter the Monk[90] and in those of one of his contemporaries, a priest known as Cosmas. Like John of Rila, Cosmas had harsh words for some monks. To be sure, he rejected neither monasticism, nor eremitism per se, but resented those who, instead of remaining in their monasteries, suddenly decided to go to Jerusalem or to Rome.[91] According to him, a monk was supposed to leave his cell only in case of enemy invasion, perhaps an allusion to Magyar and Pecheneg raids that may have reached the rich monastic communities around Preslav. However, there are substantial differences between John of Rila's and Cosmas's attitude towards mainstream monastic life in Bulgaria. Citing the same Life of St. Anthony that John of Rila recommended to his disciples, Cosmas used it to emphasize the advantages of cenobitic life over eremitism. He disliked those who left their families to join monasteries and strongly believed that going into the wilderness without struggling against one's passions was of no use. Cosmas specifically attacked hermits who, followed by their

[90] For Peter the Monk, see R. Pavlova, *Petăr Chernorizec, starobălgarski pisatel ot X vek* [Peter the Monk, an Old Bulgarian Author of the Tenth Century] (Sofia: Izdatelstvo na Bălgarskata Akademiia na Naukite, 1994). For his comments on contemporary monasticism, see D. Petkanova, *Starobălgarska literatura IX–XVIII vek* (Sofia: Universitetsko izdatelstvo "Kliment Okhridski," 1992), p. 295.

[91] *Le traité contre les Bogomiles de Cosmas le prêtre*, ed. and transl. into French by A. Vaillant (Paris: Librairie Droz, 1945), pp. 93 and 104. Cosmas acknowledged the existence of "excellent monks," who fully observed the rules of cenobitic life. He also praised those of whom the world was not worthy and who "wandered in deserts and in mountains, and in dens and caves of the earth (*Hebrews* 11.39)."

disciples, lived in small communities in which the only rule was the example given by the elder, his behavior and habits, a direct criticism of precisely the form of monasticism that John of Rila favored. Cosmas was outraged that some of these elders even attracted female disciples.[92] What upset Cosmas was especially the wealth and influence these hermits wielded, which in his eyes was against the ideals of prayer and ascetism. As a consequence, he saw only hypocrisy in their claims to sainthood. Much like John of Rila, Cosmas condemned the involvement of monks in worldly affairs, buying and selling land, exchanging letters with powerful patrons, some even from foreign countries (perhaps Byzantium).

Cosmas's point was to blame the degradation of monastic ideals for the rise of the heresy of a certain priest named Bogomil. In fact he went as far as to point to heretics behaving "so as not to be distinguished from orthodox Christians" and as a consequence being approached by many with questions about salvation. Cosmas was probably writing at the time the state authorities were already taking drastic measures against the heretics, for he mentions some of Bogomil's disciples thinking of themselves "as people suffering for truth, who will receive some reward from God for their chains and prison."[93] In about 940, Peter had written to Theophylact, the patriarch of Constantinople, asking for background information and advice about punishment. Theophylact's answer does not refer explicitly to Bogomil, but points to dualism as the basic tenet of the heresy. Much of what is known about the heresy of Bogomil comes from the work of Cosmas, to whom Bogomil was no "beloved of God."[94]

92 *Le traité contre les Bogomiles*, pp. 101 and 104.

93 Cosmas the Priest, *Sermon Regarding the Newly Appeared Bogomil Heresy*, English translation from Butler, *Monumenta Bulgarica*, pp. 161 and 165.

94 Cosmas the Priest, *Sermon*, p. 161. Bogomil in Slavonic means "beloved of God." For Cosmas's treatise and its date, see also I. Duichev, "Zur Datierung der Homilie des Kosmas," *Welt der Slawen*, vol. 8 (1963), pp. 1–4; F. J. Thomson, "Cosmas of Bulgaria and his discourse against the heresy of Bogomil," *SEER*, vol. 54 (1976), pp. 263–269. The date is substantiated by a tenth-century Cyrillic inscription from Gigen (northern Bulgaria) which refers to heretical ideas, no doubt those of Bogomil. See A. Margos, "Niakoi belezhki po cheteneto na protivobogomilskiia nadpis ot srednovekovnata cărkva pri s. Gigen [Some remarks on the reading of the anti-Bogomilic inscription from the medieval church of Gigen]," *SL*, vol. 15 (1984), pp. 119–125. However, others have advanced a much later date in the 1200s. See M. Dando, "Peut-on avance de 240 ans la date de composition du traité de Cosmas le Prêtre contre les Bogomiles?," *Cahiers d'études cathares*, vol. 100 (1983), pp. 3–25.

According to him, the Bogomils believed that the creator of the world was not God, but his son Satan, and as a consequence rejected the Old Testament. Apparently, Bogomil's teaching was that the soul was imprisoned in the body, itself a creation of Satan. The Bogomils believed that Christ had been sent to deliver a message for the imprisoned human souls as to how to escape from the world and return to the spiritual kingdom. That was also the message contained in the Gospels. Christ himself was viewed as a purely spiritual being, and as a consequence the followers of Bogomil denied all of His earthly experiences, from His birth from the Virgin Mary to the Crucifixion. They also rejected baptism with water and any material objects used in the liturgical service, such as crosses, icons, or church buildings. Since sexual reproduction perpetuated the prison of the soul, ascetic life was viewed as a key to salvation. The Bogomils had leaders who dedicated themselves to the ascetic life and to administering spiritual initiation to others. There was apparently a tendency for the Bogomils to separate themselves from society, although Cosmas insists on their ability to blend in with the crowd. According to him, Bogomil's followers "teach their people not to submit to their rulers; they malign the rich; they hate the emperor; they mock their local chiefs; they blame the nobility; they consider those who work for the emperor hateful to God; and they command every servant not to serve his master."[95] This description has often been interpreted as an indication of social unrest in tenth-century Bulgaria. However, Cosmas clearly states that those among Bogomil's followers who led ascetic lives did no manual labor and were fed by others. The message of disobedience was a direct result of what Bogomil preached, namely a radical rejection of social hierarchy as part of the idea of forswearing all material ends and embracing total spirituality. On the other hand, Cosmas's account of Bogomil's ideas about society is a clear indication that the "Golden Age" of Bulgaria witnessed and may have produced considerable social differentiation. *Boilas* had made their appearance during the events of the mid-eighth century; mid-tenth century Bulgaria already had an emperor, court nobility, and "local chiefs."

[95] Cosmas the Priest, *Sermon*, p. 161. For Bogomilism as a form of social dissent, see G. Semkov, "Der sozial-ökonomische Hintergrund der Bogomilen in Bulgarien und Byzanz wie auch der Patarener in Bosnien," *Heresis*, vol. 4 (1985), pp. 37–62.

THE FALL OF BULGARIA

Not much changed in relations between Bulgaria and Byzantium after the peace of 927. However, when Bulgarian envoys came to Constantinople in 966 to collect the annual tribute, they were met with an angry rejection from Emperor Nicephorus II Phokas, who had just returned from a victorious campaign against the Arabs. He had only contempt for Peter, who, in the words attributed to him by Leo the Deacon, was nothing but a princeling clad in leather skins ruling over a Scythian people, poor and unclean.[96] The Byzantine emperor accused Peter of allowing Magyar raids to cross Bulgaria on their way to Byzantine-held territories, an accusation that may refer to an event narrated by Liutprand of Cremona, who arrived at Constantinople three years later. According to Liutprand, at some point after Nicephorus' rise to imperial power in 963, a party of 300 Magyars had taken captive 500 imperial subjects living near Thessalonica and had transported them to Pannonia.[97] Whatever the reason for Emperor Nicephorus' anger, he moved his troops to the frontier with Bulgaria, where the Byzantines destroyed a number of forts in a show of military might, before returning to the eastern front. In an attempt to appease Nicephorus and to offer a warranty of his good intentions, Peter sent his two sons, Boris and Romanus, to Constantinople as hostages. However, he also dispatched envoys to Emperor Otto I in Magdeburg, perhaps in an attempt to rally support against Byzantium.[98] For his part, Nicephorus decided to apply to Bulgaria the same kind of pressure that Leo VI had chosen in his conflict with Symeon in 893. In the absence of reliable Pecheneg allies in the steppe, he chose Prince Sviatoslav of Kiev, whom he bribed into attacking Bulgaria.[99] What the emperor had in mind was most

[96] Leo the Deacon, *History*, ed. by C. B. Hase (Bonn: E. Weber, 1828), pp. 61–62.

[97] Liutprand of Cremona, *Report on an Embassy to Constantinople* 45, ed. by J. Becker (Hannover and Leipzig: Hahnsche Buchhandlung, 1915; reprint 1993), MGH SS 41:199.

[98] *Relacja Ibrahima ibn Ja'kūba*, pp. 148–149. See V. Giuzelev, "Bălgarskite pratenichestva pri germanskiia imperator Oton I v Magdeburg (965 g.) i v Quedlinburg (973 g.) [Bulgarian embassies to the German Emperor Otto I in Magdeburg (965) and Quedlinburg (973)]," in *Civitas divino-humana. V chest na profesor Georgi Bakalov*, ed. by C. Stepanov and V. Vachkova (Sofia: Centăr za izsledvaniia na bălgarite "Tangra" TanNakRa IK, 2004), pp. 385–396.

[99] Leo the Deacon, *History*, p. 65.

likely a number of punitive raids that would bring Peter to heel. But things did not exactly go according to plan.

The Rus' arrived at the Danube in the summer of 968, crushed the Bulgarian army, and blockaded the remaining troops in Dristra (Silistra). According to the *Russian Primary Chronicle*, the Rus' prince "took up his residence" in Bulgaria and began ruling from "Pereiaslavec."[100] The location of Pereiaslavec or Preslavica ("Little Preslav") is a matter of much dispute, but from the description of Sviatoslav's movements in the *Chronicle* and of the Byzantine armies in Byzantine sources it is quite clear that the town was located on the Lower Danube, most likely in northern Dobrudja. Several scholars have tentatively located Preslavica at Nufăru near Tulcea, on the southern bank of the St. George arm of the Danube Delta, but according to the most recent archaeological research, a fortification was erected there only after AD 1000. In any case, the Rus' do not seem to have entered the vital region of Bulgaria south of the Stone Dike and were satisfied with controlling the southern shore of the Danube and the Delta region. This was sufficient to convince Peter to dispatch envoys to Constantinople and ask for peace. This time, Nicephorus had harsh conditions, not just words. He demanded the deposition of Peter and his replacement with his son Boris, who was promptly sent back to Bulgaria for the occasion. Like his grandfather Boris, Peter retired to a monastery near Preslav, where he died soon after on January 30, 969. A special service was created for him by his fellow monks, who first used the epithet "saint" in relation to the former emperor. Peter's portrait would appear on icons of later centuries.

Boris II's reign began under good auspices, as the Rus' withdrew from Bulgaria upon receiving the news of the Pecheneg siege of Kiev.[101] However, as soon as Sviatoslav "drove the Pechenegs out into the steppes," he decided to return to Bulgaria, this time in the company of his Pecheneg and Magyar allies. He must have been impressed with the wealth and sophistication of his previous residence in Pereiaslavec, for he reputedly wrote to his mother Ol'ga in Kiev: "I do

[100] *Povest' vremennykh let*, s.a. 6475 (967), p. 85. The chronicler also mentions the tribute Sviatoslav received from the "Greeks," no doubt the "gifts and honors in abundance," which Nicephorus' embassy had promised in 967. See John Skylitzes, *Synopsis historiarum*, p. 277.

[101] *Povest' vremennykh let*, s.a. 6476 (968), p. 85. Besieged within Kiev was Sviatoslav's mother Ol'ga, together with her grandsons Iaropolk, Oleg, and Vladimir.

not care to remain in Kiev, but should prefer to live in Pereiaslavec on the Danube, since that is the center of my realm, where all riches are concentrated: gold, silks, wine and various fruits from Greece, silver and horses from Hungary and Bohemia, and from Rus' furs, wax, honey, and slaves."[102] However, in 969, the Bulgarians, who had meanwhile retaken the fort, put up a strong resistance against the Rus' siege. Only after much carnage was Pereiaslavec stormed and eventually taken. The Rus' moved swiftly across the Stone Dike, probably left without any defense, and took Preslav and Dristra, before crossing the Stara Planina range in an attack against Philippopolis (present-day Plovdiv) in Thrace. Despite so much destruction brought by Sviatoslav's invasion, the presence of the Rus' in northern Bulgaria is only sporadically attested in the archaeological record by such artifacts as the quillon of a Viking-age sword found in Păcuiul lui Soare near Silistra. In Preslav, Sviatoslav left Boris in power, apparently in an attempt to rally Bulgarian support for his now openly anti-Byzantine presence in Bulgaria. Nicephorus unsuccessfully attempted to entice Boris to come over to his side by offering the grandsons of Constantine VII, Basil (the future emperor Basil II) and Constantine (the future emperor Constantine VIII), in marriage to two Bulgarian princesses, no doubt members of the imperial family still ruling in Preslav.[103] The new emperor, John Tzimiskes, had a much more aggressive approach. First, he sent to Thrace the domestic of the East, Bardas Skleros, who obtained a major victory against the Rus' near Philippopolis. Then, in the spring of 971, the emperor himself led an army of 40,000 across the Stara Planina range, while a Byzantine fleet of some 300 ships entered the Danube through the Delta to attack the Rus' from the north.[104] Taking advantage of the fact that no mountain pass seemed to have been guarded, Emperor John quickly reached Preslav, where he defeated the Rus' and surrounded the city. The Byzantine troops stormed the Inner Town killing more Rus' and capturing Boris and his family. Preslav was immediately renamed

[102] *Povest' vremennykh let*, s.a. 6477 (969), p. 86. See A. D. Stokes, "The background and chronology of the Balkan campaigns of Sviatoslav Igorevich," *SEER*, vol. 40 (1961–1962), pp. 44–57.

[103] Leo the Deacon, *History*, p. 79.

[104] Leo the Deacon, *History*, pp. 129 and 132. For the total number of troops, see W. Treadgold, *A History of the Byzantine State and Society* (Stanford: Stanford University Press, 1997), pp. 509 and 949 n. 18.

Ioannopolis after the emperor himself, and a certain Katakalon was named military governor there, as attested by his seal.[105]

In Dristra, fearing a local uprising, Sviatoslav had ordered the execution of 300 *boilas* when the Byzantine troops appeared under the city's strong walls. Emperor John put Dristra under siege for three months, before defeating the Rus' in a fierce battle that forced Sviatoslav to sue for peace.[106] The emperor agreed to let the Rus' prince withdraw to Kiev with a supply of grain, but on his way back home, Sviatoslav was attacked and killed by the Pechenegs. The Byzantines occupied Dristra, which they renamed Theodoropolis, after St. Theodore the Stratelate, who is said to have appeared in full military array on his white horse in the middle of the final battle with the Rus'. Leo Sarakenopoulos, the former commander of the Hikanatoi, one of the leading regiments of the standing army, was appointed military governor of Dristra.

John Tzimiskes' triumphal return to Constantinople was carefully staged to symbolize the end of Bulgaria. According to Leo the Deacon, following the emperor on a white horse was a wagon with an icon of the Holy Virgin and the Bulgarian imperial regalia captured in Preslav, in particular two crowns, one a simple diadem, the other a crested crown similar to those Byzantine emperors wore when celebrating victories. Boris followed Emperor John on his own horse. In the Forum of Constantine, he was symbolically stripped of the symbols of his imperial authority. Emperor John dedicated Boris's crown to God in the Hagia Sophia church, and Boris, now a simple aristocrat of Bulgarian origin, received in exchange the dignity of *magistros*. The patriarch of Bulgaria was replaced with a metropolitan of Ioannopolis subject to the patriarch in Constantinople. Another bishop was established in Dristra, whose church was restored at some point before AD 1000, and an episcopal see may have also been established at about the same time in Tomis (Constanţa), on the Black Sea coast.

[105] I. Iordanov, *Pechatite ot strategiiata v Preslav (971–1088)* [Leaden seals of the military province of Preslav (971–1088)] (Sofia: Universitetsko izdatelstvo "Sv. Kliment Okhridski," 1993), pp. 134–135.

[106] Leo the Deacon, *History*, pp. 153–154; John Skylitzes, *Synopsis historiarum*, p. 301. See also S. McGrath, "The battles of Dorostolon (971): rhetoric and reality," in *Peace and War in Byzantium. Essays in Honor of George T. Dennis, S. J.*, ed. by T. S. Miller and J. Nesbitt (Washington: Catholic University of America, 1995), pp. 152–164.

For the first time since the seventh century, the northern frontier of the Byzantine Empire was established on the Danube River. Fearing the return of the Rus' warriors, the Byzantines restored and augmented all fortresses in northern Bulgaria, and added harbor installations to the powerful fortress previously erected on a Danube island not far from Silistra, at Păcuiul lui Soare. The annexed territory was divided into military provinces. A province called "Mesopotamia of the West" was created in northern Dobrudja. A certain Peter replaced as military governor of Dristra Leo Sarakenopoulos, who at some point before 975 became governor of both Dristra and Ioannopolis (Preslav).[107] Some time after that a new province, Thrace and Ioannopoulis, was created with the same Leo at its command. This change may have been caused by raids from western Bulgaria, where Byzantine control was lost to local rebels shortly after John Tzimiskes' death in 976. The leaders of the rebellion were the four sons of a regional commander in Macedonia known as Count Nicholas. He may have been of Armenian origin, but his rank was certainly similar to that of a count of Dristra named Theodore, who appears together with his king Symeon in the Narash inscription. Because of his title, Nicholas's sons came to be known as Kometopouloi, the "sons of the count." By 973, they had already established contact with the German Emperor Otto I to build an anti-Byzantine alliance.[108] Two of the four brothers died before 976; the other two conquered Preslav from the Byzantines in 986, before one of them died in 987 or 988. By that time the rebellion had already expanded into central Bulgaria and eastern Thrace, and the only surviving son, Samuel, had become its uncontested leader. Boris and his brother Romanus managed to escape from Constantinople in order to join the rebels. A Bulgarian sentry accidentally killed Boris, but Romanus eventually reached Macedonia, where he was soon crowned emperor. By 980, there was apparently a new Bulgarian patriarch whose see was initially in Serdica (Sofia) before moving to Ohrid in about 990. It was at Serdica that the new Byzantine emperor, Basil II, directed his first attack against the rebels in 986, but the campaign ended in disaster

[107] Eighteen seals are known of Leo Sarakenopoulos in his capacity of military governor of Dristra and Ioannopolis, all found in Preslav. See Iordanov, *Pechatite*, pp. 136–137.

[108] Thietmar of Merseburg, *Chronicon* II.31, ed. by R. Holtzmann (Berlin: Weidmann, 1935; reprint 1996), MGH SS rer. Germ. 9:76.

and the emperor barely escaped capture.[109] The campaign seems to have been a response to Samuel's bold attack on Thessaly, where he took Larisa in 985, after the military governor of Hellas residing in that city acknowledged his authority. Samuel transferred the relics of St. Achilleus to Prespa, where he had meanwhile moved his headquarters. Another Byzantine raid into Macedonia took place in 991, but nothing is known about its outcome. The raid signals the transfer of the center of power from Serdica to Prespa, closer to the Byzantine regions that Samuel's troops would raid almost every year during the subsequent decade. In 996, the emperor moved together with some of his troops to the eastern front, leaving behind Gregory of Taron, the duke of Thessalonica, as commander of the Balkan armies. Gregory's son was captured by Samuel a year later in a raid into the region of Thessalonica, and Gregory himself was ambushed and killed when trying to rescue his son. The Bulgarians raided northern and central Greece reaching as far south as Peloponnesus, where St. Nikon the Metanoiete was prophesying Samuel's downfall.[110] However, on their way back, the Bulgarians were ambushed in the Spercheios valley in Thessaly by the Byzantine forces reorganized by Nicephorus Ouranos, the new duke of Thessalonica to whom Emperor Basil II had given the command of the Balkan armies. Samuel and his son, Gabriel Radomir, escaped alive only after hiding among the corpses of the slain, and managed to return to Prespa with few survivors.

But the defeat on the Spercheios River did not diminish Samuel's determination. By 997, Romanus, who had meanwhile been captured by the Byzantines, died in captivity in Constantinople, and Samuel proclaimed himself Emperor of the Bulgarians in his stead. Judging from the little evidence there is on the organization of his empire, Samuel's power was based on a network of large forts operating as central places of the surrounding regions, each under the rule of a fort governor who often had as subordinates commanders of smaller forts. Many of the ranks and titles in existence during Symeon's and Peter's reign remained in use under Samuel, and like the Bulgarian court aristocrats who owned manors in the Outer Town of Preslav, some fort governors owned estates in the surrounding districts. Finally, the two most important towns in Samuel's

[109] Leo the Deacon, *History*, pp. 171–173. The battle took place in one of the major passes through the central region of the Stara Planina, the Traianova vrata.

[110] *Life of St. Nikon*, pp. 148–149. See P. Stephenson, *The Legend of Basil the Bulgar-Slayer* (Cambridge and New York: Cambridge University Press, 2003), pp. 16–17.

Bulgaria – Ohrid and the settlement on the St. Achilleus Island in the middle of Lake Prespa – also functioned as the nodal points within a network of bishoprics, especially after the patriarch moved to Ohrid in about 990. Samuel's power extended over a large portion of Dalmatia after his 997 campaign against the Byzantine clients on the Adriatic coast, between Dyrrachion and Zadar. He captured the prince of Duklja, John Vladimir, who was brought to Macedonia, married to Samuel's daughter Theodora, and later appointed governor of Dyrrachion. As in the case of his other campaign into Thessaly, Samuel transferred the relics of St. Tryphon from Kotor to Ohrid in an attempt to turn the two centers of his empire – Prespa and Ohrid – into the religious capitals of the central region of the Balkans. Besides the Church of St. Achilleus in Prespa, several other churches are known in Ohrid (St. Sophia) and Strumica (the Church of the Fifteen Martyrs of Tiberiopolis), the basilical plan of which follows the models of early Byzantine architecture that were the source of inspiration for the tenth-century churches of Bulgaria. The strong influence of the fashions of mid-tenth-century Bulgaria is also visible in the large number of dress accessories, especially bronze earrings and glass bracelets, associated with female burials, such as those that have been found in Zadna Reka and Mariovo near Prilep. Cave monasticism and the graffiti phenomenon so strongly associated with tenth-century Bulgaria are both attested in Macedonia and western Bulgaria in the late 900s.

The only source for the Balkan war between Basil and Samuel is the *History* of John Skylitzes, which was written between 1079 and 1096, almost a century after the events narrated. Skylitzes' account is sometimes confused, with considerable gaps in the narrative, but it is still clear that the conflict cannot be described either as Basil's methodical conquest of Bulgaria or as a series of razzias without any overall strategy. Judging by the order of events in Skylitzes' narrative, Basil's tactics were very flexible, always ready for a last-minute change of plans and for shifts in operations from central or northeastern Bulgaria to the southern front in Thessaly. The emperor's return to the Balkans in 1001 resulted in the conquest of Serdica and some of the neighboring forts. Byzantine troops also reoccupied Preslav, Pliska, and Preslavica in northeastern Bulgaria. New military governors of Preslav, Dristra, and Preslavica appear on leaden seals, and finds of Byzantine coins indicate that garrisons were stationed in the main fortresses along the Lower Danube. A brief campaign into northern Greece led to the capture of several other fortresses, including Servia and Vodena (now Edessa), both of which fell after the surrender of their respective governors, duly rewarded with high-ranking dignities for their prompt submission. In 1002, the target area of the Byzantine attack shifted to northern Bulgaria, as Basil took Vidin after a prolonged siege.[111] The land troops were greatly assisted by the intervention of the Byzantine fleet moving swiftly up the Danube River and by its expert use of the "Greek fire" against the besieged. Elsewhere, Basil was not so successful. Krakras, the governor of Pernik (near Sofia), stubbornly refused any offers from Basil when the emperor brought his troops under the walls of that fortress and succesfully defended its strong ramparts against Byzantine attacks.

Samuel's strategy was not much different from that of Emperor Basil, for his response to the Byzantine operations in northwestern Bulgaria was a surprise attack on Adrianople in the summer of 1002. However, the raid had little effect on the movements of the Byzantine armies in the northern Balkans. As in northeastern Bulgaria, garrisons were stationed at such key points as Sirmium (Sremska Mitrovica) or Braničevo. A year later, Basil moved his theater of operations to Macedonia. Samuel was defeated in 1003 near Skopje, and the fortified town was sacked by the Byzantine troops. Other forts fell without much fighting, as in the case of Veroia (south of Edessa, in northern Greece). Dobromir, the governor of that fort, was related by marriage to Samuel, but decided to turn the fort over to Basil in exchange for a military command over Byzantine troops stationed in Thrace and the Mesopotamia of the West. This new position is attested by his leaden seals found in Preslav. But besides attacking key points around the heartland of Samuel's empire, Basil was not interested in conquering any large tracts of land. Moreover, no further campaigns were organized during the subsequent decade and both sides seem to have accepted the status quo. Skylitzes has nothing to report about further developments in the Balkans until 1014.

In that year, Samuel barricaded the Kleidion ("Key") mountain pass on the Strumica River between the Vardar and the Strymon valleys (near the present-day Bulgarian–Macedonian–Greek border) and sent troops against Thessalonica under the command of a general named Nestorica. The Bulgarians were defeated by the duke of Thessalonica, Theophylact Botaneiates, and on July 29, 1014, the

[111] John Skylitzes, *Synopsis historiarum*, p. 346.

troops led by Emperor Basil himself managed to get through the barricade in the Kleidion pass and to eliminate the Bulgarian forces defending it. But Kleidion was neither the great battle imagined by John Skylitzes, who wrote much later,[112] nor a decisive victory for the Byzantines. Before he could reach the main army led by the emperor, the duke of Thessalonica was ambushed in the mountains and killed together with most of his troops. Instead of pushing the raid further into Macedonia, Basil decided to return to Thessalonica, "destroying nothing in the vicinity except an imperial foundation" in Bitola (Bitolj, Macedonia), the base of Samuel's son, Gabriel Radomir.[113]

Samuel died in October 1014, allegedly after an apoplectic attack caused by the news of Basil's victory at Kleidion. He was buried in the Church of St. Achilleus in Prespa and his may be one of the four graves excavated inside the basilica and associated with a gilded bronze-chain mail and a vestment of silk woven with gold thread. His son proclaimed himself emperor under the name of Romanus Symeon, a coronation apparently opposed by his cousin John Vladislav. The process of disintegration of the Bulgarian Empire, which had already begun under Samuel, continued during Romanus Symeon's brief reign (1015–1016). In 1016, sapping operations under the walls of Moglena (near Edessa) led to the surrender of the fort by its Bulgarian governor Ilica and the *kavkhan* Dometian, one of Romanus Symeon's high-ranking dignitaries residing there. The fort was demolished and a Byzantine garrison stationed nearby at Enotia.[114] The Bulgarian emperor was assassinated in that same year by John Vladislav, the son of Samuel's brother Aaron, who seems to have been initially inclined to cooperate with Basil.[115] Disgruntled, perhaps, at the lack of imperial generosity towards him, John Vladislav later turned against Basil, who raided the lands around Lake Ostrovo and took Ohrid,

[112] John Skylitzes, *Synopsis historiarum*, pp. 348–349. For a detailed dicussion of the battle at Kleidion, see P. Stephenson, *Byzantium's Balkan Frontier. A Political Study of the Northern Balkans, 900–1204* (Cambridge: Cambridge University Press, 2000), pp. 71–74.

[113] John Skylitzes, *Synopsis historiarum*, pp. 350–351; English translation from Stephenson, *Legend*, p. 26.

[114] John Skylitzes, *Synopsis historiarum*, p. 352. For Moglena, see D. Evgenidou, "Servia and Moglena, two Byzantine cities of Macedonia," *Istorikogeographika*, vol. 2 (1987–1988), 15–22.

[115] John Skylitzes, *Synopsis historiarum*, p. 357. John Vladislav's defection is also mentioned in the *Chronicle of the Priest of Dioclea* 36, pp. 81–82. For a comparison of these two sources and their interpretation, see Stephenson, *Legend*, pp. 26–28.

where he devastated the imperial palace. Barricaded in Bitola, John Vladislav proclaimed himself Emperor of the Bulgarians, a title mentioned in an inscription dated to 6522 (AD 1014/5), which commemorates the construction of the fort as "a haven for the salvation of the Bulgarians."[116] He gathered some support from powerful magnates, such as Krakras, the lord of Pernik, who was again besieged unsuccessfully by Basil in 1015. Krakras was on John Vladislav's side in 1017, together with his Pecheneg allies. But John Vladislav was killed during an attack on Dyrrachion in February 1018 and the Byzantines were able to bribe the Pechenegs into deserting the Bulgarians.[117] Many of Samuel's magnates who may have resented John Vladislav's assassination of Romanus Symeon quickly surrendered to Emperor Basil, in exchange for Byzantine titles. Among the first was John Vladislav's *ichirgu boilas* named Bogdan, who surrendered near Serrai (Strumica, in Macedonia). He was followed by the governor of that fort, Dragomouzos, as well as other fort commanders, such as Nikolitzas, the governor of Skopje; Krakras, the lord of Pernik, together with the commanders of thirty-five other forts; and Elemag (or Elinag Frantzes), the governor of Belgrade (now Berat, in Albania), together with his "co-governors." However, none of these men was allowed to remain in the lands they owned in the Balkans, and several were transferred either to Constantinople or to the Byzantine provinces in Anatolia. Some, like Bogdan or Nikolitzas, the governor of Servia captured in 1001, were later involved in acts of rebellion against the Byzantine emperor. Others were capable of blending in and were successfully assimilated into the Byzantine aristocracy. Elemag, for example, was sent to Thessalonica after being granted the title of *patrikios* and he may be the same as a certain Frantzes who was a donor of the St. Panteleimon monastery on Mount Athos. One of the daughters of Samuel's old general Demetrius, who surrendered to Basil in 1018, is the mother of the Byzantine writer Kekaumenos, the eleventh-century author of a memoir addressed to

[116] I. Zaimov and V. Tăpkova-Zaimova, *Bitolski nadpis na Ivan Vladislav, samodărzhec bălgarski. Starobălgarski pametnik ot 1015–1016 godina* [The Bitola Inscription of John Vladislav, the Bulgarian Autocrat. An Old Bulgarian Monument of 1015–1016] (Sofia: Izdatelstvo na Bălgarskata Akademiia na Naukite, 1970), pp. 33–34; English translation from Stephenson, *Legend*, p. 29. See also I. Zaimov, "Eindeutige und umstrittene Stellen in der Bitolja-Inschrift des bulgarischen Selbstherrschers Ivan Vladislav (11. Jh.)," *Zeitschrift für Balkanologie*, vol. 13 (1978), pp. 194–204.

[117] John Skylitzes, *Synopsis historiarum*, p. 356.

his sons known as the *Strategikon*. Christopher, who was perhaps the son of Boris II, served in the Byzantine army in Italy between 1028 and 1029.[118] In Ohrid, Basil also received the wives and children of Samuel, Romanus Symeon, and John Vladislav. The latter's surviving sons, Presian, Alusian, and Aaron, submitted to Basil in Prespa.[119] The Bulgarian Empire had ceased to exist. In the words of Yahya ibn-Sa'id of Antioch, the emperor "married Roman sons to Bulgarian daughters, and Bulgarian sons to Roman daughters; in uniting one with the other he brought to an end the ancient animosity which had existed between them."[120]

[118] I. Bozhilov, *Bălgarite văv Vizantiiskata imperiia* [Bulgarians in Byzantium] (Sofia: Akademichno izdatelstvo "Prof. Marin Drinov," 1995), pp. 273–275.

[119] John Skylitzes, *Synopsis historiarum*, pp. 360–363.

[120] Yahya ibn-Sa'id, *History*, ed. by I. Kratchkovsky and transl. by F. Micheau and G. Tropeau (Turnhout: Brepols, 1997), p. 407. See also Stephenson, *Legend*, p. 36. Ekaterina, the daughter of John Vladislav, married the future emperor Isaac I Comnenus. See P. D. Angelov, "The Bulgarians through the eyes of the Byzantines," *BHR*, vol. 22 (1994), p. 21.

5

THE FIRST BYZANTINE CENTURY (1000–1100)

Even before his final victory over Samuel and his followers Gabriel Radomir and John Vladislav, Emperor Basil's war against Bulgaria had a considerable influence upon political and military developments in the neighboring regions. The so-called *Long Life of Saint Gerald*, an early fourteenth-century compilation of different sources, contains a much earlier and extraordinary account, perhaps written by an eyewitness, of a chieftain ruling over the region of western Romania and southwestern Hungary now known as Banat.[1] Named Achtum, he was a powerful pagan "king" who "had taken his power from the Greeks" and had been baptized in the Orthodox faith in Vidin, an event that must have postdated the Byzantine conquest of that city in 1002. His base of power was in Morisena (now Cenad, on the Romanian–Hungarian border), a stronghold on the Lower Mureş River, close to its confluence with the Tisza. Shortly after his baptism in Vidin, Achtum established a monastery dedicated to St. John the Baptist in Morisena, which he populated with Greek monks, no doubt coming from Byzantium. Achtum's power was based on considerable resources, mainly cattle and horses, but given the

[1] *Vita Maior Sancti Gerardi*, ed. by I. Szentpétery, in *Scriptores rerum Hungaricarum*, vol. II (Budapest: Academia litteraria Hungarica, 1938; reprint Budapest: Nap kiadó, 1999), pp. 480–560. Achtum's story appears in chapter 10. For the date and purpose of the compilation, see C. A. Macartney, "Studies of the earliest Hungarian historical sources. I: The Lives of St. Gerard," *Archivum Europae Centro-Orientalis*, vol. 18 (1938), 1–35. The author of Achtum's story was probably associated with the family of Chanadinus (Csanád).

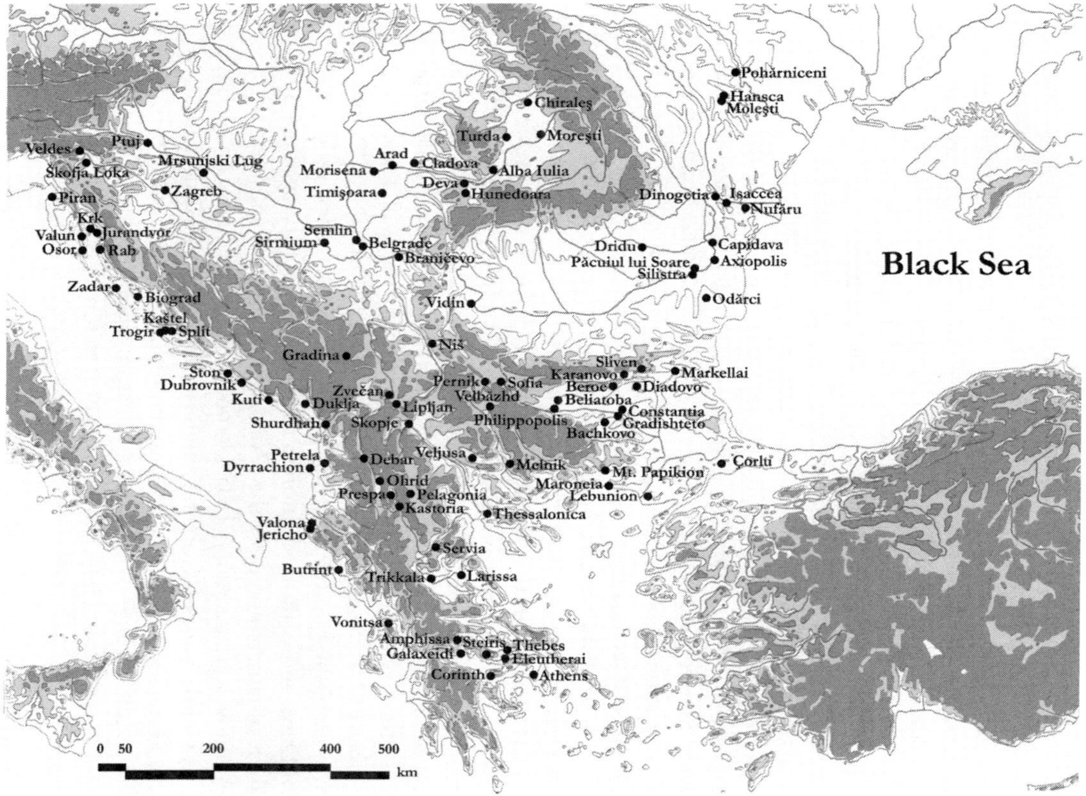

Map 5 Southeastern Europe in the eleventh century.

position of his stronghold at Morisena, he also controlled traffic along the Mureş River and taxed transports of salt from Transylvania to the heartland of Pannonia. It is in relation to salt that he found himself in conflict with Stephen, the newly proclaimed king of Hungary. One of Achtum's retainers named Chanadinus fled to the Hungarian king, only to return at the head of a large army, with which he eventually defeated and killed Achtum in Stephen's name. Chanadinus was granted large estates in Achtum's "kingdom," and with his help a Venetian monk named Gerald began a mission of Christianization of the entire region. Gerald established a new monastery dedicated to St. George near Morisena, now conveniently renamed Cenad (Csanád) after its conqueror Chanadinus, and became Bishop of Cenad in 1030, as well as tutor to the heir apparent, Prince Emeric. He was killed together with two other Hungarian bishops during the pagan revolt of 1046, and officially declared a saint in 1083, together with King Stephen and his son Emeric. Gerald had been a suffragan of the archbishop of Kalocsa, together with the bishop of Transylvania, whose see had been in Alba Iulia since 1009. The first episcopal church in that city may have been the single-naved church found underneath the late medieval cathedral and most likely built in the early eleventh century.[2] In addition to burials found near the church, three cemeteries have been excavated in Alba Iulia, which produced artifacts very similar to those from burial assemblages in Slavonia and the Hungarian Plain that have been attributed to the "Bjelo Brdo culture."[3] One of the earliest Bjelo Brdo cemeteries in Transylvania is that of Deva, on the middle course of the Mureş River. Another was established shortly after AD 1000 in Hunedoara, a few miles south of Deva, and continued through the eleventh century, as attested by finds of coins minted for the Hungarian kings Stephen (997–1038), Andrew I (1046–1060), Béla I (1060–1063), and Solomon (1063–1074). Like some Slavonian cemeteries of the "Bjelo Brdo culture," the Hunedoara cemetery does not continue into the twelfth century, no doubt because of the drastic measures taken by Kings Ladislas I (1077–1095) and Coloman (1095–1116) to force people to bury their dead next to the newly founded parish churches. As a consequence,

[2] E. Benkö, "Alba Iulia (Gyulafehérvár)," in *Europe's Centre around AD 1000*, ed. by A. Wieczorek and H.-M. Hinz (Stuttgart: Theiss, 2000), pp. 389–391.

[3] R. R. Heitel, "Die Archäologie der ersten und zweiten Phase des Eindringens der Ungarn in das innerkarpatische Transilvanien," *Dacia*, vols. 38–39 (1994–1995), pp. 417 and 423.

burial in most pre-Christian cemeteries ceased by AD 1100, while church graveyards were first established by that same time. On the other hand, the proximity of some of the Bjelo Brdo cemeteries of Transylvania to the valley of the Mureş suggests that in the aftermath of Chanadinus' victory over Achtum, the Hungarian conquest of and settlement in Transylvania moved mainly along the axis of that river, with its most important political and religious center in Alba Iulia. Eleventh-century earth-and-timber strongholds protecting the Mureş artery have been found in Cladova (near Lipova, in Romania) and Arad, not far from the confluence of the Mureş and Tisza Rivers. Only one settlement has so far been fully excavated in Transylvania that could be dated to the eleventh century. The first occupation phase at Moreşti (near Târgu Mureş) had no sunken-floored huts, only above-ground buildings associated with ceramic assemblages marked by the omnipresent clay cauldrons.[4] No coins were found in Moreşti, but the number of coin finds from Transylvania increases suddenly with specimens minted for King Ladislas I and his successors. Judging from the presence of such coins in both settlements and cemeteries, Transylvania experienced some economic growth in the late eleventh century, no doubt based on the salt trade. The first written document pertaining to Transylvania is in fact a royal charter of 1075 referring to taxes on that trade levied at *castrum Turda*, north of Alba Iulia. It was most likely the relative prosperity of the province that attracted the Pecheneg raid of 1068 across the eastern Carpathian Mountains.[5] The combined armies of King Solomon and Géza, the duke of the eastern regions of Hungary, inflicted a serious defeat upon the marauders near a mountain called Kyrieleys (perhaps Chiraleş, near Bistriţa).[6] In 1091, a Cuman army

[4] K. Horedt, *Moreşti. Grabungen in einer vor- und frühgeschichtlichen Siedlung in Siebenbürgen* (Bonn: Rudolf Habelt, 1984). Similar finds are known from other, not fully excavated sites in Alba Iulia and its environs.

[5] Simon de Keza, *Chronicle*, ed. by I. Szentpétery, in *Scriptores rerum Hungaricarum*, vol. II (Budapest: Academia litteraria Hungarica, 1938; reprint Budapest: Nap Kiadó, 1999), p. 182; *Annals of Bratislava*, ed. by I. Madzsar, *Scriptores rerum Hungaricarum*, vol. I (Budapest: Academia litteraria Hungarica, 1937; reprint Budapest: Nap kiadó, 1999), p. 126. Another raid is mentioned during the reign of King Stephen. See V. Spinei, *Moldavia in the 11th–14th centuries* (Bucharest: Editura Academiei Republicii Socialiste România, 1986), pp. 86–87.

[6] Solomon, dethroned and later imprisoned by King Ladislas, was released in 1083 and fled to the Pechenegs, with whose help he unsuccessfully attempted to invade Hungary, no doubt crossing Transylvania.

crossed the mountain passes into Transylvania, laying waste the entire region. The Cumans followed the Mureş River to the Hungarian Plain but were routed by King Ladislas in Banat, near Timişoara.[7]

By that time, Vojvodina had been fully incorporated into the Hungarian kingdom, following King Solomon's attack on Byzantine Belgrade in 1071. According to the fourteenth-century *Hungarian Chronicle*, the Byzantines not only used the "Greek fire" against the ships the Hungarians used to storm the fortress, but also incited the Pechenegs against them.[8] Belgrade fell to the Hungarians after a long siege, but was later recuperated by the Byzantines. Sirmium may also have fallen into Hungarian hands at the same time, for King Solomon transferred to the church of that city a relic, namely the arm of St. Procopius, which had been captured by the Hungarians during the 1071 raid along the Morava valley that reached as far south as Niš. Much like Samuel before him, Solomon's intention was to attach to Sirmium not just the spoils of his successful campaign against Byzantium, but also a religious significance, which could have been appealing to the Christian population in the hinterland of the city. Indeed, unlike Belgrade, Sirmium remained under Hungarian control until 1165, and the entire district north of the city now known as Fruška Gora was organized as a march. The Hungarian conquest had little consequence for the local population. There is in fact no sign of discontinuity on any one of the sites located in the hinterland of Sirmium, either at Mošorin or at Bač. An Orthodox metropolitan continued to reside in Bač, while another was established across the river Sava from Sirmium, at Mačvanska Mitrovica, a site that remained

[7] *Hungarian Chronicle*, ed. by A. Domanovszky, in *Scriptores rerum Hungaricarum*, vol. 1, pp. 412–414. See also A. Páloczi-Horváth, *Pechenegs, Cumans, Iasians: Steppe Peoples in Medieval Hungary* (Wellingborough: Corvina, 1990), p. 44. The Cuman raid has been associated with the burial of three hoards of denars minted for King Ladislas found in Turda, Frata, and Sântandrei. See I. Bóna, "From Dacia to Erdöelve: Transylvania in the period of the Great Migrations (271–896)," in *History of Transylvania*, ed. by L. Makkai and A. Mócsy, vol. 1 (New York: Columbia University Press, 2001), p. 319.

[8] *Hungarian Chronicle*, pp. 369–377. No evidence exists that the Pechenegs who invaded Transylvania in 1068 were bribed by the Byzantines, which would then justify Solomon's attack on Belgrade as a punitive expedition. It is however possible that the fourteenth-century chronicler attributed the attack of 1068 to the course of events that led to the conquest of Belgrade in 1071. See V. Spinei, *The Great Migrations in the East and South East of Europe from the Ninth to the Thirteenth Century* (Cluj-Napoca: Center for Transylvanian Studies and Brăila: Istros, 2003), p. 131.

in Byzantine hands throughout the eleventh century.[9] Together with his Byzantine homologue in Belgrade, the Hungarian governor of Semlin (now Zemun, Serbia) opposed the first crusaders led by Walter "the Penniless," who appeared on the Danube in 1096.[10]

To judge from the relatively large number of cemeteries excavated so far, Slavonia, the region of present-day Croatia between the Drava and the Sava Rivers, had a numerous population during the eleventh century. The largest number of burial assemblages of the "Bjelo Brdo culture" were dated to this period, and most cemeteries opened in the tenth century continued after AD 1000. Typical dress accessories of the "Bjelo Brdo culture," such as earrings of the so-called Volin class, with their exquisite filigree decoration; finger-rings of plaited silver wire or with perforated bezels bearing the Latin inscription PAX ("Peace"); and necklaces of glass, rock crystal, and colored stone beads – all made their appearance during the eleventh century. Like contemporary cemeteries in Hungary and Transylvania, burial assemblages in Slavonia produced coins minted for the Hungarian kings of that century: Stephen I (997–1038), Samuel and Peter (1038–1046), Andrew I (1046–1060), Béla I (1060–1063), Solomon (1063–1074), Ladislas I (1077–1095), and Coloman (1095–1116). In addition to cemeteries, the archaeological record of Slavonia includes rural settlements. The earliest habitation phase at Mrsunjski Lug (near Bjelovar, not far from the Croatian–Hungarian border), the only fully excavated settlement in the region, was dated to the late eleventh century. The site consists of several above-ground buildings similar to those found in Moreşti and placed together within an area surrounded by circular, massive earthworks.[11] An archaeological field

[9] D. Minić, *Le site d'habitation médiéval* [sic] *de Mačvanska Mitrovica* (Belgrade: Arheološki Institut, 1980), pp. 58–59.

[10] Albert of Aachen, *Historia Hierosolymitana*, in *Recueil des historiens des Croisades*, vol. IV (Paris: Imprimerie Nationale, 1879), p. 276. See J. Kalić, "Podaci Alberta Ahenskog u ugarsko-vizantijskom odnosima krajem XI veka [Albert of Aachen on the Hungarian–Byzantine relations in the late eleventh century]," *ZFF*, vol. 10 (1968), pp. 183–192; Stephenson, *Byzantium's Balkan Frontier*, pp. 177 and 191–192. For Zemun under Hungarian rule, see also M. Janković, "Slovensko naselje kod Zemuna [A Slavic settlement near Zemun]," *RVM*, vols. 37–38 (1996), pp. 123–137.

[11] V. Sokol, "The archaeological heritage of the early Croats," in *Croatia in the Early Middle Ages. A Cultural Survey*, ed. by I. Supičić (London: Philip Wilson Publishers and Zagreb: AGM, 1999), pp. 141–142. Like Moreşti, Mrsunjski Lug produced a considerable quantity of iron artifacts, mainly tools, nails, wedges, locks, and chains, many of which are associated with the second habitation phase dated to the twelfth century.

survey in central and southern Slavonia has revealed a number of other villages with similar fortifications whose existence coincided in time with that of Mrsunjski Lug.[12]

Such villages indicate a growth in population, but they also bespeak the quasi-military organization of the region, which was located on the southwestern border of Hungary. It remains unclear who exactly was the enemy against whom the inhabitants of the Slavonian villages tried to defend themselves by erecting massive fortifications of earth and timber. Until the last decade of the century, there is no evidence of military conflicts between Croatia and Hungary, the two neighboring kingdoms. Moreover, the fact that many fortified villages have been found in the central and southern sections of Slavonia suggests that the perceived danger was not neighboring Croatia, but most likely the marches on the southeastern frontier of the Holy Roman Empire. The eleventh-century history of Hungary is marked by repeated invasions from the Empire, but all known attacks came from the northwest, not from the marches on the upper Drava and Sava Rivers. However, the region of the present-day border between Croatia and Slovenia was certainly a military frontier in the late eleventh century. Shortly after 1100, the archbishop of Salzburg ordered the building of forts at Ptuj and several other key points to defend his estates against Hungarian attacks.[13]

During the eleventh century, Carniola became a march independent from Carinthia, first attested as such in 1040 in a charter of Emperor Henry III. At that time, the ruler of the march was Eberhard of Sempt-Ebersberger, from a family of Bavarian origin with large estates and considerable power in Bavaria and Carinthia.[14] After the death in 1036 of William II, the margrave of Souna, Carniola incorporated a strip of land south of the upper course of the Sava River, and in his charter of 1040 Emperor Henry referred to the enlarged

[12] Ž Tomičić, "Rezultati ranosrednjevjekovnih arheoloških istraživanja u Međimurju i varaždinskoj regiji [The results of research on the early medieval sites in the Mura valley and the Varaždin region]," *Izdanja Hrvatskog arheološkog društva*, vol. 2 (1978), pp. 209–222.

[13] *Vita Chunradi archiepiscopi Salisburgensis* 20, ed. by W. Wattenbach (Hanover: Hahnsche Buchhandlung 1854; reprint 1994), MGH SS 11:75.

[14] A member of the Eppensteiner-Ebersberger family that controlled Carinthia was also duke of Istria in the early eleventh century. After AD 1000, most dukes of Istria were of Bavarian origin. See Štih, "Der ostadriatische Raum," p. 207.

march as "Carniola and the Wendish march." By 1058, Carniola had another margrave in the person of Ulrich, a member of the Weimar-Orlamünde family from northern Germany that owned large estates in Istria. A few years later, he is also mentioned as Margrave of Istria, which may have been attached to Carniola by means of a personal union. Both marches were at the forefront of the political struggles surrounding the Investiture Controversy. In 1077, Emperor Henry IV granted Carniola, together with Istria and Friuli, to Sigehard, the patriarch of Aquileia, no doubt in an attempt to secure imperial access to and from Italy through German-controlled territories with no ties to papal allies. But Sigehard's follower had pro-papal views, and as a consequence Carniola and Istria were taken from Aquileia and given to Henry, the brother of Liutpold of Eppenstein, who was at that time the duke of Carinthia. When, at his brother's death, Henry became the new duke of Carinthia, the emperor retroceded Carniola to Aquileia, while Istria was given a new margrave in the person of Poppo of Weimar-Orlamünde, the son of the Carniolan margrave Ulrich. Despite its independence, Carniola was thus part of a large web of family connections across the Karawanken to the north and the Kapela Mountains to the south. During the eleventh century, the march was also the target of some large imperial donations to two suffragans of the archbishop of Salzburg. The bishop of Freising had already acquired from Otto II the large estate near Škofja Loka (see chapter 4). During the the eleventh century, the bishops of Freising introduced new agricultural techniques and divided the land into hides that were distributed to settlers of Carinthian and Bavarian origin.[15] Settlements with precisely defined land boundaries clustered in administrative units which eleventh- and twelfth-century documents call *officia*, but which appear to have continued local traditions, since the command of each was in the hands of a *zhupan* (*suppanus*). Demesnes were also introduced into the region; as many as three were in existence by 1100, but they controlled less than a tenth of the entire area under cultivation, an indication that free hides (*manses*) must have been the rule in the Freising domains of present-day Slovenia. By 1100, these domains covered over 120,000 acres and comprised more than 300 farmsteads, with perhaps as many

[15] W. Baum, "Die Kirchen von Freising und Brixen, die Grafen von Görz und die Entstehung der deutschen Sprachinseln in Friaul und Slowenien," *Der Schlern. Zeitschrift für Südtiroler Landeskunde*, vol. 54 (1980), pp. 428–440.

as 2,000 people.[16] Otto II's land grant of 973 appears to have created a sudden demographic growth in a region that had until then been sparsely populated. But the Freising domains were not unique. In 1004, Emperor Henry II granted the estate of Veldes (Bled on the upper Sava River, near Jesenice) to the bishop of Brixen (now Bressanone, Italy). Seven years later, the Carinthian bishop also received the neighboring castle of Veldes, together with thirty royal hides at the foot of the Triglav Mountain. Emperor Henry III's charter of 1040, while recapitulating the previous grants, refers to a demesne of Veldes, which was at that time in the hands of Altwin, Bishop of Brixen. It is to this demesne that a cemetery excavated at Bled-Pristava most likely belonged. The careful phasing of its 203 burials shows that between 25 and 35 individuals were buried at any one time, which further suggests that the Veldes demesne had between four and six farmsteads and was thus considerably smaller than that of Freising near Škofja Loka. Nevertheless, much like in the case of Škofja Loka, the administrative structure of the Brixen estates appears to have relied on a local *zhupa*.[17]

For most of the eleventh century, a "no-man's-land" remained in existence north of the Kupa River separating the marches on the southeastern frontier of the Holy Roman Empire from Croatia. Direct communication was possible around 1100 between Ptuj on the Drava River and Piran in the hinterland of Koper, on the Bay of Trieste. A parallel road came into existence south of the Kupa River at about the same time, from Zagreb on the Sava River to Sinj on the Dalmatian coast. But very little evidence exists of communication between these marches and the kingdom of Croatia. It is unlikely that the southeastern marches played any role in the transmission of Ottonian influences upon the pre-Romanesque architecture of Croatia so salient in the belfry and the two-story atrium of the Church of the St. Savior near the source of the Cetina

[16] S. Vilfan, "Zur Struktur der freisingischen Herrschaften südlich der Tauern im Frühmittelalter," in *Karantanien und der Alpen-Adria-Raum im Frühmittelalter*, ed. by G. Hödl and J. Grabmeyer (Vienna, Cologne, and Weimar: Böhlau, 1993), p. 216.

[17] A. Pleterski, *Župa Bled. Nastanek, razvoj in prezitki* [The Bled *zhupa*. Its Origins, Development, and Surviving Elements] (Ljubljana: Slovenska Akademija Znanosti in Umetnosti, 1986); J. Giesler, *Der Ostalpenraum vom 8. bis 11. Jahrhundert. Studien zu archäologischen und schriftlichen Zeugnissen* (Rahden: Marie Leidorf, 1997), pp. 413 and 418.

River.[18] For the most part, eleventh-century Croatia appears to have been influenced more by developments on the Dalmatian coast than by those in Central Europe.

Little is known about the first three Croatian kings of the eleventh century, Krešimir III, Gojslav, and Stjepan I. In 1066, Peter Krešimir IV styled himself "King of Croatia and Dalmatia," although it is doubtful that Croatian kings exercised any effective authority over the Dalmatian cities. At some point during the early regnal years of the Byzantine emperor Romanus III Argyros (1028–1034), the governor of Zadar and Split, a man called Dobronas, traveled to Constantinople "to prostrate himself in front of the blessed emperor," who showered him with gifts and honors "and sent him back to his homeland with great wealth." He returned a few years later and "was honored again, although not as abundantly as the first time."[19] Dobronas took the name Gregory, and he is most likely the military governor of Dalmatia mentioned in several charters drawn in the 1030s in Zadar as having the rank of *protospatharios*. It has been suggested that the wealth he brought to Zadar after his first visit to Constantinople helped finance the monumental building projects in Zadar. The dating of the sculptural decoration associated with these projects is in fact based on a large *ciborium* found in the belfry of the cathedral of Zadar, which bears an inscription in verse referring to a "a humble proconsul" named Gregory.[20] The same carvers may have been responsible for the rich decoration of the Churches of St. Thomas and Sv. Nediljica (Domenica) in Zadar. The Zadar sculptures are remarkably similar to and slightly later than those of the Church of St. Génis-des-Fontaines

[18] M. Jurković, "Sv. Spas na vrelu Cetine i problem westwerka u hrvatskoj predromanici [The Church of the Holy Savior at the headwaters of the Cetina River and the problem of the *westwerk* in the pre-Romanesque architecture of Croatia]," *SP*, vol. 22 (1995), pp. 55–80. In the northern Adriatic region, the strongest connections with the Ottonian art are those of Istria, as illustrated by the early Romanesque frescoes in the southern aisle of the Basilica of Euphrasius in Poreč. See I. Fisković, "Painting," in *Croatia in the Early Middle Ages. A Cultural Survey*, ed. by I. Supičić (London: Philip Wilson Publishers and Zagreb: AGM, 1999), pp. 493–509.

[19] Kekaumenos, *Strategikon* XVI.2, ed. by G. G. Litavrin (Moscow: Nauka, 1972), p. 300; Spanish translation by J. Signes Codoñer (Madrid: Alianza Editorial, 2000), p. 141.

[20] Matijević-Sokol, "Latin inscriptions," p. 246. The *ciborium* is richly decorated with interlace ornaments and has been dated to 1035/6. See Ž. Rapanić, *Predromaničko doba u Dalmaciji* [Pre-Romanesque Art in Dalmatia] (Split: Logos, 1987), p. 148.

(*c.* 1020) in southwestern France, which are generally viewed as the earliest example of Romanesque sculpture in Europe. In both cases, the scenes are divided by means of the "person-under-arcade" motif deriving from the sculpted decoration of late antique sarcophagi. However, unlike the French reliefs, the tablets of the altar screen from Sv. Nediljica in Zadar are of monumental proportions.

In or soon after 1036, Dobronas made a third trip to Constantinople, during which he was imprisoned at the order of Emperor Michael IV. He died in jail during the reign of Constantine IX (1042–1055).[21] Dobronas' death coincides in time with the emperor's decision to impose direct Byzantine rule over Zadar, perhaps in connection with the revolt of Peter Delian, which reached as far as Dyrrachion. Despite his title of "King of Croatia and Dalmatia" displayed in a charter of 1066 which is often interpreted as an indication of his control of the Dalmatian cities, now supposedly freed of any Byzantine control, the date in Peter Krešimir IV's charter granting land to the convent of St. Mary in Zadar is given in reference to the reign of the Byzantine emperor Constantine X. Among those who witnessed the transaction were also people with offices imitating Byzantine court ranks, such as *risarius* (vestry clerk), the equivalent of the Byzantine protovestiary.[22] In fact, an imperial *protospatharios* and *katepan* of Dalmatia named Leo appears as witness in another charter of King Peter Krešimir IV for the Abbey of St. Chrysogonus in Zadar. The idea of a Byzantine presence in the eleventh-century waters of the eastern Adriatic has been substantiated by the discovery at the entrance into the harbor of Nin of two shipwrecks with cargoes of Byzantine amphorae.

However, it is equally true that by the late eleventh century the Byzantine power in Dalmatia was waning, and many of the major cities on the coast (Split, Zadar, Trogir) became independent, ruled only by their own priors and bishops, who often cooperated with the Croatian kings. John Orsini, the bishop of Trogir, served as counsellor to both Peter IV Krešimir and his successor, Zvonimir. When confirming the decision of a provincial council in Split, Pope Alexander II wrote to both King Peter IV Krešimir and the Dalmatian bishops. The council had taken place in 1060 in the presence of Pope

[21] Kekaumenos, *Strategikon* XVI.2, p. 302; Spanish translation by Signes Codoñer, p. 142.

[22] J. Stipišić, "Hrvatski dvorski dignitar 'risarius' [The *risarius*, a Croatian court dignitary]," *Zbornik Historijskog Zavoda Jugoslavenske Akademije Znanosti i Umjetnosti*, vol. 12 (1982), pp. 1–7.

Nicholas II's legate and was the first major attempt to implement the Church Reform in Croatia. Issues such as celibacy, simony, the sporting of priestly beards, as well as the ordination of Slavs who did not speak and read Latin figured prominently on the council's agenda. The participating bishops forbade under threat of excommunication any ordination of priests who did not have a thorough command of Latin, an indication that Slavic may have been used in the liturgy. The reform was further supported by an increasing number of monastic communities. Under the diligent rule of Abbess Cika, the Convent of St. Mary in Zadar became the spearhead of the reform. The eleventh century witnessed the foundation of many other Benedictine abbeys, particularly around the newly founded city of Biograd: St. John of Rogovo (before 1060); the Convent of St. Thomas; and the Vrana Abbey (before 1075). Many more abbeys appeared on the Dalmatian coast: St. Benedict on the island of Lokrum near Dubrovnik (1023); St. Peter in Osor (1044); St. Peter in Supetarska Draga on the island of Rab (1059); St. John the Baptist in Trogir (1064); and St. Peter In the Village near Split (1069). One of the most important consequences of the growing monastic movement was a considerable increase in the activity of *scriptoria*, especially that of St. Chrysogonus in Zadar, which produced many of the surviving manuscripts dated to the eleventh century, some of them richly illuminated. The Zadar Evangeliary, now in the State Library in Berlin, and the *Breviary* that belonged to Abbess Cika of the Convent of St. Mary, now in the library of the Hungarian Academy of Sciences, were both written in that *scriptorium*. But its most famous product is the so-called Vekenega Evangeliary (named after the daughter of Abbess Cika), now in the Bodleian Library in Oxford.[23] Another renowned product is a richly illuminated Psalter now in the Metropolitan Library in Zagreb, which was written in Beneventan script in *c.* 1020 by a deacon named Maio for Archbishop Paul of Split (1015–1030). A luxury Evangeliary, also written in Beneventan script and now in the Vatican Library, was finished in 1081 in the Abbey of St. Nicholas in Osor, on the island of Cres. It contains prayers for the Byzantine emperor and for

[23] V. Novak and B. Talebaković-Pecarski, "Večenegin evanđelistar [The Vekenega Evangeliary]," *Starine Jugoslavenske Akademije Znanosti i Umjetnosti*, vol. 51 (1962), pp. 5–60. Two other manuscripts containing services and prayers, one in the Bodleian Library, the other in the library of the Hungarian Academy of Sciences in Budapest, were also produced in the St. Chrysogonus *scriptorium* during the second half of the eleventh century.

King Peter Krešimir IV incorporated into a melodically developed *Exultet*. There are several manuscripts with musical notation (neumes) from this period, all with church music of the Gregorian repertoire. Moreover, Adam of Paris, a French visitor to Split, is known to have composed hymns dedicated to St. Domnius, the patron saint of that city, at the request of Archbishop Lawrence (1059–1099).[24]

The eleventh century also witnessed the production of the first cartularies, collections of charters that were important enough for various monastic foundations to be compiled for future reference. Such collections contain unique information about donations, donors, and the considerable wealth accumulated by eleventh-century monastic communities in Croatia. One of the earliest is the cartulary of the Abbey of St. Peter In the Village (also known as the Sumpetar cartulary), a private foundation of a wealthy citizen of Split named Petar Crni of Gumaj. The cartulary contains many documents pertaining to the slaves working for the abbey. The founder had bought a great number of them under various conditions, often at a price of three to four gold coins for each of them. On one occasion, Petar exchanged a horse for a slave; on another, he bought a son from his father, in order to have him receive the appropriate education for becoming priest. The cartulary also contains a list of books that Petar Crni donated to his foundation, including a Psalter said to have been written in "the French script" (*cum litteris Francigenis*), most likely a reference to the Caroline minuscule. Whether or not the book truly originated in France remains unknown, for none of the books on the list actually survived. But Petar certainly had access to products of French workshops, as indicated by another list of liturgical vessels and robes that he had bought for the abbey, which includes a copper crucifix, said to have been produced in Limoges. A hoard of eleventh-century French denars found in Novi Vinodolski, in the Velebit Canal, demonstrates that such long-distance links were not exceptional.[25]

The cartulary of the Convent of St. Mary in Zadar was written in a variety of scripts (Caroline, Beneventan, and early Gothic) in the

[24] S. Tuksar, "The first centuries of Croatian music," in *Croatia in the Early Middle Ages. A Cultural Survey*, ed. by I. Supičić (London: Philip Wilson Publishers and Zagreb: AGM, 1999), pp. 562 and 564.

[25] I. Mirnik, "Nalaz francuskog novca 11. st. iz Novog Vinodolskog [A hoard of eleventh-century French coins from Novi Vinodolski]," *Numismatičke vijesti*, vol. 33 (1991), pp. 43–47.

early thirteenth century. It contains documents from a long period between 1066 and 1236. Among them are items such as a charter from Archbishop Lawrence of Split granting a part of the whitebait catch owed by fishermen in the Split area, as well as a detailed list of all the landed property purchased by Cika during her term as abbess of the St. Mary Convent. At the end of the cartulary, there is also a *Sanctus* in two parts, with tropes, one of the earliest examples of polyphonic singing in Southeastern Europe.[26]

The considerable output of monastic *scriptoria* was only matched by that of the royal chancery. It is no accident that a larger number of charters survived from the reign of King Peter Krešimir IV than from any other Croatian ruler. Many of them were issued on behalf of monastic communities benefiting from royal munificence, and thus indicate the strong ties between Benedictine houses and the king. However, they are equally significant for the information they provide on the multiplication of court offices and titles in eleventh-century Croatia. For example, one of the first charters of Peter Krešimir IV was issued in February 1060 for the Abbey of St. John of Rogovo, to which the king donated an island and a manor near Biograd. The generous donation is said to have been made in the presence of the papal legate and the bishop of Biograd. In addition, there is a long list of witnesses, including such important dignitaries as *ban* Gojzo and all the *zhupans* of the kingdom. One of the court dignitaries listed along with these men is Boleslav, who is called both *tepchi* and count palatine, most likely one and the same title. Another court dignitary named Jurana was *vratar*, "door-keeper." King Peter's charter thus contains the earliest mention of court offices by their Croatian names. Judging by contemporary evidence, some of these men were remarkably powerful. In the early eleventh century, a church was built in Kaštel, between Trogir and Split, and its founder mentioned in the dedicatory inscription was also a *tepchi* named Ljubimir.[27] During the last quarter of the eleventh century, the *zhupans* had their own private armies, such as the retinue of Strezinja, the governor of Bribir. The *ban* had also a considerable influence, as indicated by the events

[26] V. Novak, *Zadarski kartular samostana svete Marije* [The Cartulary of the Convent of St. Mary in Zadar] (Zagreb: Jugoslavenska Akademija Znanosti i Umjetnosti, 1959).

[27] Matijević-Sokol, "Latin inscriptions," pp. 245–246. For *tepchi* as the equivalent of a Byzantine court title, see L. Margetić, "Toparque, *tepči* (*topotèrètes*) et *dad* en Croatie au 11e siècle," *REB*, vol. 44 (1986), pp. 257–262.

that took place at the end of Peter Krešimir IV's reign. In 1074, a Norman lord from Italy named Amico of Giovinazzo invaded Dalmatia and occupied many of the maritime cities, as far south as Split. A letter of 1075 which the papal legate sent to Stephen, Bishop of Zadar, mentions the capture of the Croatian king by Amico, and no mention exists of Peter Krešimir IV after that date.[28] Only the intervention of the Venetian fleet drove the Normans out of the northern Adriatic waters. In Croatia, the *ban* who had been in office under Peter Krešimir IV was now crowned by the papal legate as King Zvonimir. In return, the king took an oath of allegiance to Pope Gregory VII, by which he promised his full support for the implementation of the Church Reform in Croatia. Zvonimir pledged that he would "take heed of the way the bishops, the priests, the deacons and archdeacons live to make sure that they lead a pure life in accordance with the rules" and promised to oppose incestuous marriages and the "selling of people into slavery."[29] He also committed himself to paying an annual fee of 200 Byzantine gold coins to Rome, in addition to the donation of the Abbey of St. Gregory in Vrana, together with all its riches, to serve as accommodation for papal legates coming to Croatia. The detailed description of Zvonimir's coronation in Split has no parallel in contemporary sources in Southeastern Europe. One of the slabs used to form the baptismal font in the Split Baptistery shows a king on the throne, with a man standing by his side and another prostrated below him. The scene may have nothing to do with either Peter Krešimir IV or Zvonimir, and may well be a representation of Christ's parable of the unmerciful servant. However, the relief still alludes to contemporary images of royal power. This is substantiated by the fact that the slab in question was initially part of an altar screen in the Church of St. Peter and Moses in Solin, the very building in which Zvonimir's coronation was apparently performed. Much like the banner, the sword, the scepter, and the crown bestowed upon him

[28] *Documenta*, p. 99. See also J. Stipišić, "Croatia in diplomatic sources up to the end of the 11th century," in *Croatia in the Early Middle Ages. A Cultural Survey*, ed. by I. Supičić (London: Philip Wilson Publishers and Zagreb: AGM, 1999), pp. 294 and 297. For the Norman raid on the Dalmatian coast, see also V. Košćak, "Gregorio VII e la Croazia. Presupposti politico-sociali," *SG*, vol. 14 (1991), pp. 258–259.

[29] An English translation of the oath preserved in a late twelfth-century copy is available in Stipišić, "Croatia in diplomatic sources," pp. 316–317. For the implementation of the Reform under King Zvonimir, see F. Šanjek, "La réforme grégorienne en Croatie sous le règne de Demetrius Zvonimir (1075–1089)," *SG*, vol. 14 (1991), pp. 245–251.

by the papal legate, the image of a king sitting on a throne displayed on the altar screen slab may have pointed to the subtle association between the heavenly kingdom and the realm of Zvonimir, king "by the grace of God and by the bestowal of the Apostolic see." This insistence upon the symbolism of objects and postures is remarkably similar, though on a different level, to the attitude of Zvonimir's brother-in-law, the new king of Hungary, Géza I (1074–1077). Having rejected papal overlordship, Géza turned instead to Byzantium in order to obtain a crown and the political recognition needed for his regime. The enameled plaques on the crown he received from Emperor Michael VII Dukas associate the divine and the earthly ruler and explicitly compare the position of the Hungarian king vis-à-vis the emperor to that of the archangels Michael and Gabriel vis-à-vis Christ. The parallel between Zvonimir and Géza is no accident. The marriage of Zvonimir and Helena, Géza's sister, may be seen as an attempt to build an alliance against Emperor Henry IV, who had backed both Géza's rival Solomon and attacks from the marches of Istria or Carniola against Croatia.[30]

Following King Zvonimir's coronation, the papal legates summoned another church council in Split, which reiterated the ban on the use of Slavic in the liturgy and the condemnation of Methodius' invention of the "Gothic letters," which the council of 1060 had branded as heresy. Three years later, the issue had developed into a serious schism. In the conflict between Gregory VII's predecessor, Alexander II (1061–1073), and his rival, Honorius II (anti-pope in 1061–1062), the bishops of Osor and Krk sided with the latter, for Honorius appears to have been quite tolerant of the use of Slavic in the liturgy. A rebellion thus broke against the decisions of the church council of 1060 to condemn the use of Slavic in the liturgy. The movement was led by a bishop of Krk named Cededa, who had newly arrived on the island as Honorius' legate. At the instigation of a certain priest named Ulfus, Cededa sided with a local abbot named Poteba in opposing the decisions of the council of Split. As the previous bishop of Krk had been expelled from the island, Cededa began consecrating churches and ordaining priests. He was still on

[30] In a letter of October 4, 1079, Pope Gregory VII threatened the addressee, a knight from Istria or Carniola named Wezelin, that he would be struck by the "sword of St. Peter" if planning to attack the king "who was instituted by the Apostolic see to rule Dalmatia." See *Codex diplomaticus*, p. 171; Košćak, "Gregorio VII e la Croazia," p. 263.

the island in 1075, when another council was summoned in Split by the papal legate Gerald, Bishop of Siponto, to solve a conflict between the Dalmatian bishops generated by the re-creation of the see of Nin.[31] At that time, Pope Gregory VII was so worried about the rebellious bishop and his followers that he approached King Sven II Estridsson of Denmark with proposals for a military expedition against the "heretics."[32] On the island of Krk at least two Benedictine monasteries existed in the last quarter of the eleventh century, in which Slavic written in the Glagolitic alphabet was permitted. A Glagolitic inscription from Krk refers to an abbot named Maj, who was responsible, together with three other individuals, for the building of a church.[33] A second inscription dated to *c.* 1100 was found in Jurandvor near Baška and mentions two abbots of the monastery, one of whom was the founder of the abbey church of St. Lucia.[34] Moreover, the archipelago in the Kvarner Bay produced evidence of bilingualism. This is illustrated, among other things, by one of the earliest Glagolitic inscriptions found in Croatia. The eleventh-century Valun tablet from the island of Cres is a tombstone over a family grave containing the remains of three generations, namely grandmother Teha, her son Bratohna, and her grandson Junna. The line referring to Teha is in Slavonic written with Glagolitic letters, while those referring to Bratohna and Junna are in Latin.[35]

But it would be a gross mistake to treat the Benedictine abbeys using Glagolitic and, presumably, Slavic for the liturgical service as isolated communities of rebels. The Baška inscription mentions a

[31] The council also decided to free the priest Ulfus, who had been arrested in 1063 and thrown into jail. The papal legate took Ulfus with him to Rome, after he obtained from him the abjuration of heresy. Forminius, the bishop of the newly restored see of Nin, participated in the council, together with the bishops of two other new sees, those of Biograd and Knin. All three were suffragans of the archbishop of Split.

[32] *Gregorii VII registrum*, ed. by E. Caspar (Hanover: Hahnsche Buchhandlung, 1920), MGH Epist. selectae 2:194. See Košćak, "Gregorio VII e la Croazia," p. 260.

[33] B. Fučić, "The Croatian Glagolitic and Cyrillic epigraphs," in *Croatia in the Early Middle Ages. A Cultural Survey*, ed. by I. Supičić (London: Philip Wilson Publishers and Zagreb: AGM, 1999), p. 265.

[34] Fučić, "Croatian Glagolitic and Cyrillic epigraphs," pp. 266–268. The Baška tablet mixes Glagolitic and Cyrillic letters, as well as Old Church Slavonic and the Čakavian dialect of Serbo-Croatian.

[35] Fučić, "Croatian Glagolitic and Cyrillic epigraphs," pp. 264–265. See also C. Simpson, "The Croats and the Glagolitic alphabet," *Medieval World*, vol. 7 (1992), pp. 17–23.

grant of a meadow by King Zvonimir (the first mention of a king in Croatian), an indication that the abbey in Jurandvor benefited from the royal munificence in much the same way as the "traditional" Benedictine abbeys in which Latin, and not Slavic, was the language of service. Moreover, among witnesses the inscription mentions a certain Desimira, the *zhupan* of Krbava, as well as the king's officials from Vinodol and the island of Krk.[36] Clearly, Glagolitic was not the "secret alphabet" of a group of renegades on the island of Krk, and the use of Slavic was not restricted to the Benedictine monks of Jurandvor. In fact, the earliest evidence of Glagolitic letters on parchment, as opposed to stone, is to be dated to the same period. According to Marija Pantelić, the fragment of a Western-rite sacramentary of the late tenth or early eleventh century known as the Kiev Missal (since it is now in the library of the Ukrainian Academy of Sciences in Kiev) may have been in use somewhere in southern Croatia.[37] Two folios of a Life of St. Symeon the Stylite written in Glagolitic, known as the Budapest Fragments and dated to *c.* 1100, are certainly of Croatian origin.[38]

Following Zvonimir's death in 1089, Ladislas I – Helena's brother and the new king of Hungary (1077–1095) – laid claim to the Croatian throne. Following a campaign that swept through Slavonia, the Hungarian king occupied most of Croatia, except the region of the Kapela Mountains in the north, where a Croatian king named Peter resisted until 1097. In a letter of 1091 to Oderizius, the abbot of Monte Cassino in Italy, King Ladislas announced the "acquisition" of "Sclavonia," which was now open for land grants to the Benedictine monks, much like in his native Hungary.[39] The newly conquered territory was bestowed upon Ladislas's nephew Almos, the son of the former king Géza I. Facing the ire of Pope Urban II, who,

[36] Fučić, "Croatian Glagolitic and Cyrillic epigraphs," p. 268.

[37] M. Pantelić, "O Kijevskim i Sinajskim listicima [On the Kiev and Sinai Fragments]," *Slovo*, vol. 35 (1985), pp. 5–56. However, according to others, the Missal is most likely of Bohemian or Moravian, but not Croatian, origin. See J. Hamm, *Das glagolitische Missale von Kiev* (Vienna: Verlag der Österreichischen Akademie der Wissenschaftern, 1979); J. Schaeken, *Die Kiever Blätter* (Amsterdam: Rodopi, 1987).

[38] J. Reinhart and A. A. Turilov, "Budapeshtskii glagolicheskii otryvok: drevneishi slavianski spisok Zhitiia Simeona Stolpnika [The Budapest Glagolitic Fragments: the earliest Slavic manuscript of the Life of St. Symeon the Stylite]," *Slovo*, vols. 39–40 (1990), pp. 37–44.

[39] *Codex diplomaticus*, p. 197.

as Gregory VII's successor, was the overlord of the kingdom once ruled by Zvonimir, Ladislas joined the anti-papal camp of Urban's rival, Emperor Henry IV. Shortly after the conquest of Croatia, King Ladislas founded the bishopric of Zagreb under the authority of the archbishop of Esztergom, and it quickly became the religious center of Slavonia and the neighboring regions to the west and south. The first bishop of Zagreb was Duch, who, although of Bohemian origin, was an active promoter of the French influence that was very strong at that time in Hungary. Many of the books brought to Zagreb for the liturgical service in the cathedral had been produced in Hungary: the Sacramentary of St. Margaret; the Pontifical, the Evangeliary, and the Benedictional, all three written in Caroline minuscule. Others were manuscripts produced in France and Italy, as well as in *scriptoria* on the Dalmatian coast.

However, a complete conquest of Croatia took place only under King Coloman (1095–1116), who in 1097 defeated Peter, the last Croatian ruler, in the Kapela Mountains. Coloman was crowned King of Croatia in Biograd in 1102. After scrupulous preparations, he also invaded Dalmatia in 1105, forcing Zadar to surrender after a brief siege and demanding two-thirds of the custom revenues from every maritime city.[40] In fact, Coloman granted privileges to most maritime cities in exchange for their submission.[41] The most important ones were the right for every city to elect its own bishop and prior, whom the Hungarian king only confirmed, and the prohibition on any Hungarian settling in that city. No city was forced to pay tribute, while royal agents established in some cities supervised the collection of the custom duties without interfering in local politics. The only garrison left behind after the king returned to Hungary was that of Split, under the command of a Hungarian duke who was responsible for the collection of the tribute from Croatian territories inland. Following the Hungarian invasion, the Venetian doge sailed to both Trogir and Split, where he attempted to extract oaths of loyalty from the leading citizens. The inhabitants of Split even promised to provide 2 galleys or 1,000 gold coins for the Venetian military expeditions.

40 A fleet under the command of a *ban* named Ugra attacked the islands in the Kvarner Bay. Ugra remained on the island of Krk for an entire year after the invasion. Split was also besieged but eventually spared destruction through negotiations.

41 N. Klaić, "Jos jednom o tzv. privilegijama trogirskog tipa [Once again on the so-called privileges of the Trogir type]," *Istorijski časopis*, vol. 20 (1973), pp. 15–87.

But the maritime cities remained firmly attached to the Hungarian crown and Venice continued to recognize the Hungarian occupation of Croatia first acknowledged through the so-called *Conventio amicitiae* (The Friendship Convention) of 1098, whereby Hungary and Venice had formed an alliance against the Normans. Coloman's royal title ("King of Hungary, Slavonia, Croatia, and Dalmatia"), first attested in 1108, marked both the end of an independent kingdom of Croatia and the absorption, albeit incomplete, of the conquered territories into the kingdom of Hungary. During the following century, Croatia, although nominally under Hungarian authority and ruled in the name of the king by a *ban*, remained separate from the administrative organization of the kingdom. The basis of that preferential treatment has long been thought to be the so-called *Pacta conventa*, the arrangements allegedly made by twelve leading Croatian magnates with King Coloman before his coronation in Biograd in 1102. However, the earliest manuscript attestation of that document is of the late fourteenth century. The *Pacta conventa* is most likely a late medieval forgery, not a twelfth-century source. Nevertheless, its source of inspiration must have been the political and social developments that had taken place over a 300-year period following the conquests of Ladislas I and Coloman. The Croatian nobility had retained its laws and privileges, including the restriction of the military service that they owed to the king within the boundaries of Croatia, and not of the entire kingdom of Hungary. Despite occasional royal grants in Croatia, very few Hungarian noblemen moved permanently south of the Sava and Kupa Rivers. But it is equally true that the conquest of Croatia marked the beginning of a long period of Hungarian expansion into Southeastern Europe, which transformed Hungary into a major power in the region, rivaling and at times surpassing that of Byzantium.

BYZANTIUM AND ITS CLIENTS

As a reaction to Samuel's campaign in Dalmatia in 997, and perhaps in anticipation of his planned expedition to Sicily, Emperor Basil II created a new theme based in Dubrovnik (Raousion/Ragusa), an event that must be dated at some point during the last decades of his reign. The correlate of this measure may have been the expansion on the Dalmatian coast of the episcopal sees subordinated to the archbishop of Dyrrachion, a reconfiguration that is reflected in one of the lists of episcopal sees subject to the patriarch of Constantinople.[42] Until *c.* 1000, there were just four suffragan bishops in the archdiocese of Dyrrachion. By 1020, the metropolitan of that city had under his authority no less than fifteen sees. Some were located in the interior (Glavinica, Pulcheropolis/Berat – both in Albania), but the majority were on a long segment of the Adriatic coast between Valona (now Vlorë in Albania) to the south and Bar to the north. The northernmost see was Duklja, on the Morača River in present-day Montenegro.

Not long after the expansion of the archbishopric of Dyrrachion to the north, Dubrovnik was also granted metropolitan status, with jurisdiction over the neighboring client polities of Travounia and Zahumlje. The creation of the new metropolitan see appears to have taken all the bishoprics in southern Dalmatia away from the authority of the archbishop of Split. However, the new arrangement did not isolate either Dubrovnik or the episcopal sees in the south from developments in northern Dalmatia or Italy. By the time the metropolitan see of Dubrovnik was created, a group of Italian monks established a monastery dedicated to St. Benedict not far from the city walls, on the island of Lokrum. Another monastery was later founded in the Travounian hinterland of Dubrovnik, in present-day Trebinje.[43] The fresco with the procession of the Church Fathers in the ruined apse of the basilica underneath the Cathedral in Dubrovnik is a remarkable example of early Romanesque art most typical of Istria and the northern Dalmatian coast. Examples of early Romanesque sculpture are also known from sites in southern Dalmatia, such as the Church of St. Sergius on the island of Koločep and the Church of St. Thomas in Kuti near Herceg-Novi, on the Bay of Kotor.

During the 1030s, the military governor of Dubrovnik could count on the loyalty of most of the imperial clients in the neighboring regions. The ruler of Duklja, Stefan Vojislav, recognized his authority in exchange for gifts, and the governor even agreed to be the

[42] *Notitiae episcopatuum ecclesiae Constantinopolitanae*, ed. by J. Darrouzès (Paris: Institut français d'études byzantines, 1981). For the *notitia* 10 showing the early eleventh-century expansion of the archbishopric of Dyrrachion, see Stephenson, *Legend*, pp. 22 and 24.

[43] M. Popović, "Monastère St. Pierre de Campo près de Trebinje," *WMBHL*, vol. 6 (1979), pp. 271–287. The southernmost Benedictine abbey was that of St. Michael in Prevlaka, in the hinterland of Kotor. See also I. Bagarić, "Die Rolle der Benediktiner in der kroatischen Geschichte," *Mariastein*, vol. 28 (1982), pp. 62–68.

sponsor at the baptismal font of Vojislav's son.[44] An imperial charter dated to 1039, now in Dubrovnik, bestowed imperial ranks and titles onto Ljutovid, the ruler of Zahumlje. Ljutovid's loyalty appears to have been put to the test during the rebellion of Stefan Vojislav, who managed to ambush and capture the military governor of Dubrovnik, whom he took to Ston, on the island of Pelješac. Vojislav further seized a large amount of gold from an imperial ship wrecked on the Dukljan coast. When Emperor Constantine IX ordered the military governor of Dyrrachion to move against the Dukljan ruler together with Ljutovid and other local rulers, Vojislav ambushed the allied forces in the mountains of southern Serbia. He then invaded Travounia, as well as Ljutovid's Zahumlje, and incorporated them into his own polity. At Vojislav's death in 1043, his sons rose against each other in a bitter struggle for power, the only account of which is that of the *Chronicle of the Priest of Dioclea*, written more than a century later. According to the *Chronicle*, two brothers, Gojislav and Predimir, took Travounia, while two others were given *zhupanias* in the mountains and on the coast. The lands east and northeast of the Bay of Kotor belonged to Vojislav's fifth son, Michael. During the subsequent decade, the two brothers from Travounia were murdered and the others invaded their domain. Michael took advantage of the interest one of his surviving brothers had in Travounia and in his absence occupied his *zhupania*, which he then gave to his eldest son Vladimir.[45] Another son, Bodin, invaded Raška, in the region of the upper courses of the Lim, Ibar, and Western Morava Rivers now divided between Serbia and Bosnia. After 1053, Michael took the title of king and appears to have married a relative of Emperor Constantine IX.[46] His growing prestige in the western and central Balkans may explain the fact that he was approached by the leaders of a Bulgarian rebellion that broke in Macedonia at the time of the bold

[44] Kekaumenos, *Strategikon* VII.11.1, Spanish translation by Signes Codoñer, p. 63.

[45] He may have done so with the assistance of local chieftains, such as *zhupan* Grd mentioned in a Cyrillic inscription on his tombstone found in the ruins of the village church in Police near Trebinje (southeastern Bosnia). See Fučić, "Croatian Glagolitic and Cyrillic epigraphs," p. 276, who wrongly dated the inscription to the twelfth century. The inscription refers to the "days of the Great Prince Mihajlo" who can only be the eleventh-century Michael, son of Vojislav. No ruler by that name is known for the twelfth century in either Duklja or Travounia.

[46] *Chronicle of the Priest of Dioclea* 40, p. 94. See Stephenson, *Byzantium's Balkan Frontier*, pp. 139–140. According to John Skylitzes, *Synopsis historiarum*, p. 475, Michael also received the rank of *protospatharios*.

attacks of the Hungarian king Solomon on Sirmium and Niš. The rebels apparently asked for Michael's son to become their emperor. Bodin was thus sent with a small troop to Prizren in the southwestern area of present-day Kosovo, where he was promptly proclaimed emperor as Peter, no doubt in commemoration of Symeon's son, the first emperor of the Bulgarians recognized as such by the Byzantines. Bodin-Peter further managed to defeat a Byzantine army, then marched on to Niš, but was captured and exiled to Antioch. The Norse mercenaries in the imperial troops that defeated Bodin were plundering the lands around Lake Prespa, when in Duklja, Bodin's brothers rose against each other. Michael appears to have survived many of his sons who either were assassinated or died in battle against their own brothers. Perhaps in an attempt to emulate Zvonimir of Croatia, he approached Pope Gregory VII in the context of the dispute between the archbishops of Split and Dubrovnik over jurisdiction in southern Dalmatia. But unlike Zvonimir, Michael did not need a crown, for he was already a king. According to the letter he received from the pope in 1078, he had demanded from Gregory the banner of St. Peter, as a sign of papal patronage.[47] Very little is known about Michael's seat of power, but he is most likely the crowned ruler depicted in an eleventh-century fresco in Ston as dedicating to God the Church of St. Michael.

The papal–Dukljan rapprochement bore fruit. Shortly after Michael received the banner of St. Peter from Rome, his son Bodin returned from his Byzantine exile on a Venetian ship and married the daughter of the Norman governor of Bari. The alliance between Duklja and the Normans, most certainly brokered by Pope Gregory VII, appears to have been directed against the Byzantine control of the south Dalmatian coast. As a consequence, Bodin was promptly approached by the military governor of Dyrrachion with gifts, in an attempt to bring him back to the Byzantine side. Bodin was indeed in the Byzantine camp during the battle under the walls of Dyrrachion

[47] *Gregorii VII registrum*, p. 365. The point was often misunderstood in the recent literature on this topic. See Stephenson, *Byzantium's Balkan Frontier*, p. 144. Pope Gregory VII's letter calls Michael "King of the Slavs" (*Sclavorum rex*), a title he presumably already had, and makes no reference to any crown being dispatched to the Dukljan ruler. Michael may be the ruler mentioned in a fragmentary inscription found in Ston. See I. Ostojić, "O Mihajlovu natpisu u Stonu [On the inscription of Michael from Ston]," *Prilozi povijesti umjetnosti u Dalmaciji*, vol. 14 (1962), pp. 34–39.

that opposed the Norman army led by Robert Guiscard to Emperor Alexios I Comnenus (1081). But instead of participating in the fighting, he waited cautiously on the side, and when victory was clearly in the hands of the Normans, quickly returned to Duklja. His attitude had little to do with the influence of Bodin's Norman wife and more to do with his father's death in that same year, probably shortly after the defeat of Emperor Alexios at the hands of the Normans. At any rate, though perhaps the designated successor, Bodin's power did not go unchallenged. The conflict that opposed Bodin to some of his relatives appears to have been so serious that the bishop of Bar had to intervene and mediate a settlement. Perhaps in an attempt to improve his image as a ruler, Bodin invaded Raška and Bosnia, where he now installed Dukljan *zhupans*. According to Anna Comnena, the biographer of Emperor Alexios I, Bodin was a constant threat to the Byzantine cities in the themes of Dyrrachion and Dubrovnik.[48] His control of Dubrovnik indicates that in the late eleventh century the Byzantine theme had ceased to exist as a significant power structure in the region. Moreover, the authority of the archbishop of Dubrovnik over sees in southern Dalmatia was now challenged not just from Split, but also from Bar. In 1089, the anti-pope Clement III (Guibert of Ravenna) issued a bull raising the bishop of Antibari (Bar) to the status of Archbishop of Dioclea, with jurisdiction over all cities south of Dubrovnik and in the region of Lake Skadar, which had previously been under the authority of the metropolitan of Dyrrachion. Bodin appears to have supported the idea, particularly because he was now in open conflict with the military governor of Dyrrachion, John Dukas. To judge from two letters Theophylact, the archbishop of Ohrid, wrote to the governor, John was at war with the Dukljan ruler, whom he defeated and even captured at some point between 1085 and 1090, before restoring him to power as a Byzantine client.[49] Bodin appears to have coordinated his attacks on John Dukas with

[48] Anna Comnena, *Alexiad*, ed. by B. Leib, vol. II (Paris: Les Belles Lettres, 1940), p. 115; English translation by E. R. A. Sewter (Harmondsworth: Penguin, 1969; reprint London: Penguin, 2004), p. 237. For Bodin's conflict with his relatives and the subsequent invasion of Raška, see also the *Chronicle of the Priest of Dioclea* 42, pp. 96–97; Stephenson, *Byzantium's Balkan Frontier*, p. 147.

[49] Theophylact of Ohrid, *Letters*, ed. by P. Gautier (Thessaloniki: Association de Recherches Byzantines, 1986), pp. 152–155 and 186–189. See also M. Mullett, *Theophylact of Ochrid. Reading the Letters of a Byzantine Archbishop* (Aldershot and Brooksfield: Variorum, 1997), p. 360.

those of Bolkan, his *zhupan* of Raška, on the neighboring Byzantine lands, where Bolkan seized several border fortresses located between Skopje and Niš. Like Bodin, Bolkan was defeated by John Dukas. Bodin and his *zhupan* were again raiding the Byzantine territories in 1092 and according to Anna Comnena, Bolkan even managed to get as far as Lipljan in present-day Kosovo. However, as soon as Emperor Alexios led an army against him, Bolkan "left for Zvečan, a tiny fortress" on the Ibar River, before suing for peace as soon as Alexios occupied Skopje.[50] The archaeological evidence suggests that following his submission, Alexios briefly occupied a number of forts in the Ibar valley, including Zvečan. A similar situation has been revealed by systematic excavations at Gradina near Pazarište, a site identified with Ras, which is known from earlier and later sources to have been located on the western border of Bulgaria. Except specimens struck for Emperors Nicephorus III Botaneiates (1078–1081) and Alexios I Comnenus (1081–1118), no other eleventh-century coins have been found on the site. Most likely during Alexios' reign, the fort abandoned in the late tenth century was extensively renovated and new drystone and earthwork-palisade ramparts were built, which can be dated to the years after Bolkan's submission. As for Bodin, he is last mentioned in 1096. His successor may have been a certain George Bodin mentioned on a leaden seal found in Bulgaria. Around 1100, Duklja disappears from the radar of the written sources, which instead devote a great deal of attention to the rulers of Raška.

On the southern border of Duklja, a number of forts were repaired and enlarged in what appears to have been the most extensive effort of fortification in the history of the Byzantine theme of Dyrrachion. Dyrrachion itself received new towers of circular plan, all built in stone with irregular bands of brickwork, as well as curtain walls extending to the southwest from the ancient city. According to Anna Comnena, the ramparts rose up to eleven feet and were so thick that "more than four horsemen could ride abreast in safety."[51] Hoards of

[50] Anna Comnena, *Alexiad*, vol. II p. 167; English translation by Sewter, p. 276. For the Byzantine fort of Zvečan and the associated church dedicated to St. George, see M. Popović, "Les forteresses du système défensif byzantin en Serbie aux XIe–XIIe siècles," *Starinar*, vol. 42 (1991), pp. 177–178.

[51] Anna Comnena, *Alexiad*, vol. III, p. 97; English translation by Sewter, p. 403. For the eleventh-century fortification of Dyrrachion, see G. Karaiskaj, "Kalaja Durrësit në msjetë [The citadel of Durrës during the Middle Ages]," *Monumentet*, vol. 13 (1977), pp. 29–53.

coins minted for Emperor Alexios I Comnenus (1081–1118) suggest that the fortification project is to be dated to the last quarter of the eleventh and the first decades of the twelfth century. The same is true for other forts, both north and south of Dyrrachion. At Shurdhah, the lower circuit of walls was rebuilt in the late eleventh or early twelfth century, and several buildings within the enclosed area have been dated by means of coins struck for Emperor Alexios I or his successors. At Petrela, just north of present-day Tirana, the fort was repaired in the late eleventh and early twelfth century, when a second circular tower and a gate complex were added. Pectoral crosses found in eleventh-century forts in Albania, some with Greek inscriptions, indicate the presence of Byzantine garrisons stationed at key points on the coast and around the main passes across the mountains.

The interpretation of such efforts to improve the defense lines around Dyrrachion must take into account that during the eleventh century the city and its hinterland witnessed serious military confrontations. In 1043, George Maniakes, the general appointed to lead the Byzantine troops in Sicily, proclaimed himself emperor and sailed to Dyrrachion, which his forces briefly occupied, before moving quickly along the old imperial road to Thessalonica (Via Egnatia) and defeating the imperial troops at Ostrovo. In 1078, another rebel, the very governor of Dyrrachion, Nicephorus Basilakes, followed the same route with an army of Bulgarians and Albanians, before being defeated and killed by the troops of the commander-in-chief of the western armies, Alexios Comnenus.[52] Three years later, Dyrrachion faced a very different kind of threat. Norman warriors under Robert Guiscard crossed the Strait of Otranto and conquered the island of Kerkyra. Soon after that, the invaders took several fortified sites on the coast of Epirus, among them Vonitsa on the Ambracian Bay, Butrint, and Valona. However, their ultimate goal was Dyrrachion.[53]

[52] Michael Attaleiates, *History*, ed. by I. Bekker (Bonn: E. Weber, 1853), p. 297. Attaleiates also mentions Albanians among soldiers participating in Maniakes' revolt. See A. Ducellier, "Les Albanais dans l'Empire byzantin: de la communauté à l'expansion," in *Hoi Albanoi sto mesaiona*, ed. by Ch. Gasparis (Athens: Institouto Byzantinon Ereunon, 1998), pp. 38–40.

[53] William of Apulia, *The Deeds of Robert Guiscard*, ed. by M. Mathieu (Palermo: Istituto Siciliano di Studi Bizantini e Neoellenici, 1961), p. 302. The attack on Kerkyra is to be dated to the spring of 1081, shortly after Alexios I Comnenus' coronation. The Normans had crossed on ships provided by the citizens of Dubrovnik and other maritime cities in Dalmatia. See W. B. McQueen, "Relations between the Normans and Byzantium, 1071–1112," *Byzantion*, vol. 56 (1986), pp. 427–476.

Robert Guiscard had brought with him a man said to be the deposed emperor Michael VII Dukas, whom he paraded before the walls of the city. In a first encounter with the Normans, the duke of Dyrrachion, George Paleologus, was defeated and wounded. Many local leaders in the theme had already joined the Normans, when Emperor Alexios dispatched under the commander-in-chief Gregory Pakourianos an army consisting of the so-called Varangian Guard (including Englishmen that had come to Byzantium as refugees after the conquest of their country by William the Conqueror), regiments of "Franks" (Western mercenaries), Turks (possibly Hungarians) that had been settled in the Vardar valley, and Paulicians from Thrace. When the army arrived near Dyrrachion, Robert Guiscard promised to call off the siege in exchange for Norman control of the entire Dalmatian coast. Emperor Alexios rejected the offer, but on October 18, 1081, his army suffered a defeat more damaging militarily than the debacle at Mantzikert in 1071. The Varangian Guard was completely wiped out and many Byzantine officers were either killed or taken prisoner. So great was the disaster that during subsequent decades Alexios had to improvise in order to recruit a sufficient number of mercenaries to sustain what, in 1081, may have appeared a lost cause. In the desperate situation created by the Norman victory at Dyrrachion, the citadel within the city walls was entrusted to Alexios' Venetian allies, while the rest of the city was put under the command of a certain "Comiscortes from Albania."[54] This is one of the first historical references to Albanians, the local population in the theme of Dyrrachion and its surrounding regions, which was fully integrated into the political and military structures of the Byzantine province.

Shortly after the military debacle under the walls of the city, the Venetians received further concessions: the titles of *protosebastos* and Duke of Dalmatia and Croatia for the doge; trade and property rights in Dyrrachion, including the Church of St. Andrew with all appurtenances; several warehouses in Constantinople and three quays in Galata, from which to trade throughout the Empire free of any sales tax or port duty. In the meantime, Robert Guiscard had returned to Italy, but his son Bohemond continued the conquest of

[54] Anna Comnena, *Alexiad*, vol. 1, p. 168; English translation by Sewter, p. 153. "Comiscortes" is a corruption of a Byzantine title, *komes tes kortes*, "count of the tent." Since it is unlikely that Anna Comnena was unaware of the significance of that title, the name of the Albanian leader must have been derived from a title previously bestowed either on him or on one of his ancestors.

the western Balkans and took Ioannina and Glavinica on the border between the themes of Dyrrachion and Nikopolis. Bohemond twice defeated Alexios in pitched battles and managed to occupy Skopje, but could not take either the citadel of Ohrid, staunchly defended by the city's governor, or several other fortresses in Bulgaria. Moreover, the Byzantines were able to destroy all the fortresses the Normans had hastily erected, such as that of Moglena near Edessa. However, they could not prevent Bohemond from expanding in 1082 into northern Greece, where he conquered Pelagonia (Bitolj, near the Greek–Macedonian border), Trikkala and Kastoria (both in northern Greece), and laid siege to Larisa. After being defeated so many times in pitched battles, Emperor Alexios began employing stratagems reminiscent of tactics used by steppe horsemen to lure the Norman cavalry away from the main concentration of forces, only to return in full force and attack their camp. Defeated, Bohemond withdrew to Valona and in 1083 moved to Italy, while Alexios quickly recovered Kastoria. The emperor's Venetian allies retook the island of Cephalonia from the Normans. But Robert Guiscard returned to the Balkans in 1084. While the Venetian fleet blockaded the Norman troops that had managed to cross over the Strait of Otranto, the Byzantine forces ambushed some of Robert Guiscard's men in the mountains. Guiscard himself was trapped for two months in Jericho (Orikurn, near Vlorë) with no food supplies, before withdrawing his forces to conquer Cephalonia, where he eventually died on July 17, 1085. In the meantime, the Byzantines recovered Dyrrachion, which the emperor placed under the command of his brother-in-law, John Dukas. Another of the emperor's relatives, John Comnenus, replaced John Dukas in 1092 or 1093, followed by his brother, Alexios Comnenus, in 1107. Alexios began rebuilding and expanding the circuit walls in preparation for another Norman attack. The emperor closed the mountain passes on the eastern border of the theme of Dyrrachion by means of barricades of felled timber,[55] and a fleet was dispatched to Dyrrachion to prevent the Normans from crossing the sea. Bohemond succeeded in conquering Valona and a number of other forts on the southern border of the theme of Dyrrachion. He also won over to his side a number of Albanian leaders who were "thoroughly acquainted with the mountain passes." The Albanians were instrumental in the Norman conquest of Debar, a fort at the

[55] Anna Comnena, *Alexiad*, vol. III, p. 104; English translation by Sewter, p. 408.

confluence between the Radika and Drin Rivers, on the present-day Albanian–Macedonian border. To cope with this new invasion, Emperor Alexios adopted a guerrilla-type warfare, ambushing foraging Norman parties and strengthening the naval blockade of Dyrrachion to cut the Norman supply lines from Italy. The strategy worked, for Bohemond quickly sued for peace and eventually agreed to the Treaty of Devol (September 1108). In exchange for an oath of allegiance and obeisance, Bohemond received the title of *sebastos* and an annual stipend of 200 gold coins. In fact, the treaty was never implemented and with the Norman threat removed, the western Balkans experienced a long period of peace and relative prosperity.

The same is true for the eleventh-century Byzantine provinces in the southern Balkans. Greece, particularly its northern part, was affected by the Oghuz invasion of 1064 (see below).[56] Piraeus near Athens was plundered in 1034, perhaps by Harald Hardrada and his fellow Norsemen in the Varangian Guard. Six years later, Bulgarian troops reached as far south as Demetrias, where Delian appointed as governor an "old soldier with experience in battle," named Lutoboes (Litovoi), who began repairing the crumbling walls of the city.[57] In Boeotia, both Galaxeidi (modern Galaxidhion), on the Bay of Corinth, and Amphissa (modern Amfissa), west of Mount Parnassos, were plundered. Demetrias was sacked in 1070 by Arab pirates.[58] However, twelve years later, Demetrias was among the flourishing coastal centers in which Emperor Alexios I Comnenus granted rights and privileges to the Venetians. Neither Bulgarians nor pirates had any impact on the remarkable economic growth that Byzantine Greece experienced during the eleventh century. The prosperity of the region attracted the interest of the imperial family as well. Among the first *pronoiai* (temporary grants) that Emperor Alexios awarded to members of his family were the revenues of Thessalonica and Chalkidiki. By 1037, Hellas supplied Constantinople with large quantities of corn,[59] and the wealth of many Byzantine cities in Greece was largely agricultural in origin, as eleventh-century landowners appear to have made considerable investments in agriculture. A fiscal

[56] Attaleiates, *History* , pp. 83–87. The Oghuz invasion of Hellas is also mentioned in the continuation of the chronicle of Skylitzes, *Synopsis historiarum*, p. 114.

[57] Kekaumenos, *Strategikon* VII.12, Spanish translation by Signes Codoñer, p. 64.

[58] Kekaumenos, *Strategikon* VII.20.1–2, Spanish translation by Signes Codoñer, pp. 71–72.

[59] Skylitzes, *Synopsis historiarum*, p. 411.

document known as the Cadaster of Thebes mentions several water-mills in villages near Thebes, jointly owned by landlords in that area. Most of the lands around Thebes were owned by rich families residing in the city or in neighboring Athens, Chalki, and Euripos. The Cadaster shows that out of fourteen landowners in the village of Tache, just outside Thebes, only two were local residents. One lived in Thebes and three others were Athenians.[60] In Athens, the cultivated fields were located inside, not outside the city walls. Another eleventh- or twelfth-century fiscal document reveals that, while Athens was organized into a number of neighborhoods, a good portion of the area covered by the Byzantine city consisted of crop fields, some of which were immediately "below the neighborhood of the purple dye makers."[61] Athens produced purple dye from murex shells, which was sold to producers of silk in nearby Thebes. Production of silk textiles began in the mid-eleventh century and it was entirely carried out in privately owned workshops, many of which were in the hands of Jews who had fled from the Fatimid Caliphate. It was the silk industry that attracted the Venetians to Thebes. Emperor Alexios' privilege of 1082 gave them the right to own factories and to trade in the city at greatly reduced tariff rates. The prosperity of Byzantine Boeotia also attracted imperial patronage. Two years after his privilege for the Venetian merchants, Emperor Alexios granted 422 gold coins from revenues in the region of Athens to the Monastery of St. Meletios near Eleutherai, south of Thebes.

A confraternity was established in Thebes in 1048, which was devoted to an icon of the Holy Virgin kept in a convent in Naupaktos. Every month, the icon was taken out in a procession to another church in the confraternity.[62] Many participants were members of aristocratic families owning land in the environs of Thebes. For example, Gregory Kalandos had a wealthy relative named Theodore

[60] N. Svoronos, "Recherches sur le cadastre byzantin et la fiscalité aux XIe et XIIe siècles: le cadastre de Thèbes," *Bulletin de Correspondance Hellénique*, vol. 83 (1959), 1–166; L. A. Neville, *Authority in Byzantine Provincial Society, 950–1100* (Cambridge: Cambridge University Press, 2004), pp. 171–172. For the absentee tax payers in Tache, see L. A. Neville, "Local provincial elites in eleventh-century Hellas and Peloponnese," Ph.D. dissertation (Princeton University, 1998), p. 226.

[61] E. Granstrem, I. Medvedev, and D. Papachryssanthou, "Fragment d'un *praktikon* de la région d'Athènes (avant 1204)," *REB*, vol. 34 (1976), pp. 5–43.

[62] J. Nesbitt and J. Wiita, "A confraternity of the Comnenian era," *BZ*, vol. 68 (1975), pp. 360–384.

who appears in the Cadaster of Thebes as owning land in the village of Tache. A female member of the confraternity, Maria Kamateros, was married to a member of one of the most prominent families in eleventh- and twelfth-century Hellas. Christopher Kopsinos was a prominent and powerful fiscal official in charge of the bookkeeping for taxes collected on the island of Kos. The name of a fourth person, Theodore Leobachos, appears on a list of people to be commemorated by the confraternity. He had been the abbot of the Monastery of St. Luke at Steiris, mentioned as such together with several other high-ranking titles in a funerary inscription found on that site. Theodore was a member of a powerful aristocratic family in tenth- and eleventh-century Hellas and he is most likely the individual responsible for the lavish mosaic decoration of the monastery church of St. Luke in *c.* 1020.

In eleventh-century Greece there is plenty of archaeological evidence for urban expansion. The extensive domestic, workshop, and shop quarter that archaeological excavations revealed in the area of the ancient Roman forum of Corinth came into existence during that century. Houses were separated by narrow alleys and had one, two, or three rooms that may have served as shops, each with less than six square feet of retail and storage area. A workshop for the production of gold and bronze artifacts was found at the southwestern end of the forum area, which suggests that eleventh-century Corinth was a production center of some importance. But the archaeological evidence is overwhelmingly in favor of interpreting the growth of Corinth as based on trade. Two coin hoards found in the city point to long-distance contacts, perhaps of pilgrims en route to or from the Holy Land. Besides coins minted for the Byzantine emperors of the eleventh century, they also contain Western (French deniers of Clermont and Le Puy), as well as Eastern coins (bronze coins issued for the Seljuk rulers of Syria). Extensive excavations in Corinth also produced fragments of cylindrical glass flasks decorated with animal and geometrical designs arranged in bands, very similar to the Byzantine glassware found in Constantinople. A recent analysis of the ceramic assemblages of Corinth revealed significant changes taking place in the late eleventh century, as glazed wares from Constantinople were introduced together with a "democratization" of luxury ceramics that had previously been available only to the rich.[63]

[63] G. D. R. Sanders, "New relative and absolute chronologies for 9th to 13th century glazed wares at Corinth: methodology and social conclusions," in *Byzanz*

Numerous churches were built in Athens during the eleventh and twelfth centuries, mostly by members of the local aristocracy of landowners and state officials. All surviving examples (Holy Apostles in the Agora, Panagia Lykodemou, Kapnikarea, the Church of the Two Saints Theodore, the Little Metropolitan Church) have a dome resting on four columns placed within a square ground plan. When adding apses at the ends of the cross arms, the resulting roseate plan allowed for a sophisticated manipulation of volume and light, as in the case of the Church of the Holy Apostles. An even more elegant variation is the cubical nave of the monastery church of St. Luke's in Steiris, crowned with eight arches on which was placed a broad twenty-eight-foot dome. The church received a rich mosaic decoration in the 1020s, similar in many respects to that of the monastery at Daphni near Athens dated to the 1080s. By contrast, the walls of the crypt under the monastery church of St. Luke's were covered with frescoes. The bright color palette, the linear drapery, and the expressive faces link these frescoes to those of the Church of Panagia ton Chalkeon in Thessalonica (dated to 1028) and to those of the Church of the Dormition in Episkopi (Evritania, to the southeast of Arta). Elsewhere, archaeological excavations have shown that patrons in Greece and Macedonia had access to craftsmen and artists from Constantinople. For example, excavations on Mount Papikion near Komotini, on the slopes of the Rhodopes near the Greek–Bulgarian border, revealed a monastic compound with a church decorated with superb frescoes in the style of the Constantinopolitan foundations of the Comnenian period. The same is true for the fresco decoration in what is now the Metropolitan Church in Servia.

The growth of cities brought to the forefront of political life local rulers, who were often members of the leading families in the region and who appear as "dynasts" in contemporary sources. According to Kekaumenos, at the time of the Arab attack on Demetrias in *c.* 1070, the city had one such "dynast" in the person of a certain Noah, whose business acumen secured his position of lord or patron of the city.[64] The power that Noah wielded was different from that associated with

als Raum. Zu Methoden und Inhalten der historischen Geographie des östlichen Mittelmeerraumes, ed. by K. Belke, F. Hild, J. Koder, and P. Soustal (Vienna: Verlag der Österreichischen Akademie der Wissenschaften, 2000), pp. 153–173. Similar conclusions have been drawn on the basis of ceramic assemblages from Thebes. See P. Armstrong, "Byzantine Thebes: excavations on the Kadmeia, 1980," *ABSA*, vol. 88 (1993), pp. 331–332.

[64] Kekaumenos, *Strategikon* VII.20.2, Spanish translation by Signes Codoñer, p. 72.

the position of city governors appointed by the emperor, even if they too were often members of the local aristocracy. Such was the position of Nikulitzas Delphinas, Kekaumenos' father-in-law, who, although governor of Larisa, found himself – apparently unwillingly – at the head of a revolt against a tax surcharge imposed by Emperor Constantine X (1059–1067). Nikulitzas belonged to a prominent family in the city. In 980, Emperor Basil II had appointed his grandfather as leader (*archon*) of the Vlachs, a local ethnic group that was also at the center of the rebellion of 1066–1067. The leaders of that rebellion were all prominent men of Larisa, two of whom are specifically mentioned by Kekaumenos as being Vlachs: Slavota Karmalakis and a certain Beriboes (Berivoi), in whose house the conspirators used to gather to discuss their plans.[65] In addition, the rebellion appears to have drawn large numbers of Vlachs living in the hinterland of Larisa, on both sides of the river Bliuris. In anticipation of serious military turbulence, the Vlachs had sent their wives and children to the "mountains of Bulgaria," which may suggest that they had more or less permanent settlements there and were possibly involved in transhumant pastoralism.[66] Among the rebels of 1066–1067, Kekaumenos also mentions "Trikkalites" (inhabitants of neighboring Trikkala) and Bulgarians.[67] When Nikulitzas discovered the conspiracy, he promptly warned the emperor about it, but without much success. The governor of Larisa thus found himself in the embarrassing position of being placed at the head of the rebellion that quickly spread to the neighboring Thessalian city of Servia, which controlled the main road from Thessaly to Macedonia. Shortly after the conquest of Servia, the emperor opened negotiations with the rebels and promised to remit the taxes, only to capture Nikulitzas whom he imprisoned in Amaseia, on the Black Sea coast of Asia Minor. In an effort to defend the political legacy of his relative, Kekaumenos placed the blame entirely on the Vlachs. His is the first mention of that ethnic group in Southeastern Europe.

65 Kekaumenos, *Strategikon* XII.3.4, Spanish translation by Signes Codoñer, p. 114. Nikulitzas ordered the arrest of Slavota after the conquest of Servia. Besides the Vlach leaders in the city, other Vlachs, perhaps herdsmen in the city hinterland, are said to have joined the rebels. For the revolt of 1066–1067, see also N. Djuvara, "Sur un passage controversé de Kekaumenos," *RRH*, vol. 30 (1991), pp. 23–66.

66 Kekaumenos, *Strategikon* XII.3.4 and 5, Spanish translation by Signes Codoñer, pp. 115 and 116. For the Vlachs of Larisa, see also A. Risos, "The Vlachs of Larissa in the 10th century," *Byzantinoslavica*, vol. 51 (1990), pp. 202–207.

67 Kekaumenos, *Strategikon* XII.3.3 and 4, Spanish translation by Signes Codoñer, pp. 113 and 115.

While depicting them as an "extremely unfaithful and depraved people," Kekaumenos traced back their lack of loyalty to antiquity and identified the Vlachs with the "so-called Dacians and Bessi, who used to live near the Danube and Sava rivers, where now the Serbs live, in inaccessible and inhospitable places."[68] Infuriated by their repeated raids, the Romans had crushed them in battle and forced them to abandon their homeland. The Vlachs had thus spread into Epirus and Macedonia, "although the majority of them settled in Hellas." Kekaumenos' account of the Vlachs is thus different from that of the *Chronicle of the Priest of Dioclea*, according to which after the Bulgar invasion of the Balkans, local inhabitants known as Romans became Morovlachs ("that is black Latins").[69] However, both Kekaumenos and the *Chronicle* depict the Vlachs as rebels, always ready to join any attempts to undermine the imperial authority in the Balkans. Their concerns were justified. The Vlachs showed the Cumans the way through the passes of the Stara Planina during the invasion of 1092.[70]

In the territories annexed in 1018, Emperor Basil II levied taxes in kind, not in cash, while at the same time securing key points in the defense of the newly conquered territories by means of fortified towns and fortresses. The duke of Thessalonica was designated in 1018 commander of Sirmium and the surrounding territories known as Serbia, and a new theme by that name came into being during the first half of the century. In Sirmium, the eleventh-century occupation phase appears to have been restricted to a small area near the southern ramparts. Extensive restoration work is also attested at Belgrade, as well as on numerous sites in the Iron Gates region of the Danube, where several early Byzantine forts were restored or repaired. A new fortress was built in Braničevo at the confluence of the Danube and Mlava Rivers. Eleventh-century Byzantine coins and seals found on

68 Kekaumenos, *Strategikon* XII.4.2, Spanish translation by Signes Codoñer, p. 122. According to Kekaumenos, it was the Vlachs that Emperor Trajan attacked and defeated in the early second century AD. It was "their" king Decebalos that the emperor killed and whose head he then exposed in the Roman forum. For Kekaumenos' sources on Dacian history, see A. Armbruster, *Romanitatea românilor. Istoria unei idei* [Romanians as Descendants of the Romans. The History of an Idea], 2nd edn. (Bucharest: Editura Enciclopedică, 1993), p. 27.

69 *Chronicle of the Priest of Dioclea* 5, p. 45. For a survey of the abundant literature on the origin of the Vlachs, see E. Scărlătoiu, "La romanité balkanique. Origines et diffusion," *RESEE*, vol. 29 (1991), pp. 191–202; and vol. 30 (1992), pp. 11–17.

70 Anna Comnena, *Alexiad*, vol. II, p. 194; English translation by Sewter, p. 299.

those sites indicate the presence of garrison troops and imperial officers. Sirmium, Belgrade, and Braničevo were the most important episcopal sees on the northern frontier of the Empire, with authority over several fort and parish churches. Six parishes are known to have been under the jurisdiction of the bishop of Braničevo. Emperor Basil II's edict of 1020, which outlined the rights and possessions pertaining to the autocephalous archbishop of Ohrid, gave to his suffragan, the bishop of Vidin, the right to have forty clergymen under his orders, in addition to forty tenant farmers (*paroikoi*) working on the see's estates.[71]

A significant correlate of the presence of Byzantine troops in the forts and fortified towns is the relatively large number of reliquary crosses, some made of steatite (soapstone), that were found in northern Serbia, many of which seem to be replicas of the first specimens introduced into the region in the early eleventh century. But the archaeological record also suggests that some, at least, of the soldiers in the garrison of Belgrade were Pechenegs, perhaps recruited from among the prisoners taken after the defeat inflicted upon the nomads by the former commander of Sirmium, Constantine Diogenes, in 1027.

Soon after that, all Byzantine troops were withdrawn from the region and moved on a new line of defense between Niš and Skopje. Sirmium and its hinterland appear to have been left in the hands of local rulers acting as clients of the Byzantine emperor. However, the withdrawal of the Byzantine armies may have been perceived as a sign of weakness and appears to have encouraged separatism. In 1040, Peter Delian, a local ruler in the region of Belgrade who claimed to be the grandson of Samuel, was proclaimed Emperor of the Bulgarians by his followers. It is not clear what caused Peter Delian to attack the Byzantine line of defense between Niš and Skopje, but John Skylitzes

[71] H. K. G. Gelzer, "Ungedruckte und wenig bekannte Bistümerverzeichnisse der orientalischen Kirche," *BZ*, vol. 2 (1893), pp. 42–46. Basil issued three successive imperial decrees on this matter. One of them confirmed the suffragan status of many sees in Macedonia, Bulgaria, and the region of Sirmium. Another added to the list of suffragans the bishop of Vidin, together with those of Dristra (Silistra), Ras, Butrint, and other sees, while extending the jurisdiction of the archbishop of Ohrid over the Vlachs of Thessaly. See also A. Madgearu, "The church organization at the Lower Danube between 971 and 1020," *EBPB*, vol. 4 (2001), pp. 82–85.

insists on Peter's claims to be a legitimate successor of the Bulgarian emperors.[72] In 1037, on the death of John of Debăr, the last Bulgarian archbishop of Ohrid, a Greek-speaking archbishop was appointed in the person of Leo, a former archivist of the patriarch in Hagia Sophia. Whether or not this change of religious policy vis-à-vis Bulgaria had any influence on Peter's movement, he seems to have left a lasting impression on monastic circles in northern Bulgaria, as evidenced by the apocrypha produced in that area in the mid-eleventh century. John Skylitzes' insistence upon Peter's claims to Bulgarian imperial lineage is only matched by the *Vision of Isaiah*, an anonymous apocryphal text written in Old Church Slavonic and extolling Peter Delian as "Emperor Gagan [qagan] Odelian."[73] Delian has long been depicted as the head of a rebellion caused by the decision taken under Emperor Michael IV (1034–1041) to change the tax collection in the Bulgarian lands from in-kind to cash payments. However, the movement began in the region of Belgrade, from which no taxes were collected at the time, as Byzantine troops had withdrawn some ten years before the proclamation of Peter as emperor. According to Michael Psellos, what generated support for the movement was a desire for "freedom" among certain notables and a wider sense of their own ethnic identity.[74] That at stake were political, not social or economic issues is also apparent from the way in which the movement developed after Delian was able to seize Niš and Skopje. Although the governor of Dyrrachion promptly marched against the Bulgarians, he was soon arrested on charges of treason and replaced by one of his subordinates, who managed to antagonize the soldiers, many of whom were also of Bulgarian origin. Disgruntled, they chose from among themselves a "wise and brave man" named Tihomir and proclaimed *him* Emperor of the Bulgarians, in a move no doubt replicating Peter Delian's bid for imperial power. Peter proposed an alliance

[72] Skylitzes, *Synopsis historiarum*, pp. 409–411. See Stephenson, *Byzantium's Balkan Frontier*, pp. 130–132.

[73] A. Miltenova and M. Kaimakamova, "The uprising of Peter Delian (1040–1041) in a new Old Bulgarian source," *Byzantinobulgarica*, vol. 8 (1986), pp. 227–240. The other ruler of Bulgaria mentioned as qagan in the mid-eleventh-century apocrypha is Boris-Michael. See I. Venedikov, "Legendata za Mikhail Kagan [The legend of Michael Qagan]," *Preslav. Sbornik*, vol. 2 (1976), pp. 179–208.

[74] M. Psellos, *Chronographia*, ed. by E. Renauld, vol. 1 (Paris: Les Belles Lettres, 1926), pp. 76–77; English translation from E. R. A. Sewter, *Fourteen Byzantine Rulers* (Harmondsworth: Penguin, 1968), pp. 109–110.

to Tihomir, but quickly gained control over the allied forces and ordered his rival to be stoned, before proclaiming himself emperor for a second time in Skopje. By 1041, Peter Delian had control over Dyrrachion, Prespa, and parts of northern Greece, while allying himself with the rebels in Epirus, who had initially risen against a corrupt tax collector in the theme of Nikopolis. Delian's rapid success and apparently great popularity convinced Emperor Michael IV to seek a radical solution to the crisis. Although seriously ill, he personally led his army against Delian, who had meanwhile marched against Thessalonica. Despite some initial success in taking forts in the vicinity of Serdica,[75] the imperial troops were eventually defeated by the Bulgarians. They pursued the emperor fleeing to Constantinople, ambushed, and eventually captured his baggage train. It is most likely during this period that Delian appointed Lutoboes (Litovoi) as governor of Demetrias, before the duke of Thessalonica managed to capture him. By that time, there was already another challenge to Peter Delian's project of restoring the Bulgarian Empire. Alusian, the son of John Vladislav, came to Bulgaria. He had spent several years in Byzantine service, both in Constantinople and as governor of Theodosiopoulos in Asia Minor. Using his ascendancy, he began building a network of loyal supporters, in an attempt to hijack Delian's movement, as "the majority of the Bulgarians transferred their allegiance to him, the real heir."[76] Delian was forced to recognize Alusian as a legitimate ruler and appeared to cooperate with him, although both were now treating each other with great suspicion. At the head of a large force, Alusian marched on Thessalonica, which he besieged. In a sally, Constantine, the duke of Thessalonica, inflicted a crushing defeat upon the attackers, and Alusian used the opportunity to blame Delian, whom he ordered arrested and blinded. After another defeat at the hands of the imperial troops, Alusian opened negotiations with the emperor. In exchange for high honors, he submitted to him and with that the movement that Delian had started in 1040 was over.

75 Kekaumenos, *Strategikon* VII.6.2, Spanish translation by Signes Codoñer, p. 69.

76 Michael Psellos, *Chronographia*, vol. 1, p. 82; English translation by Sewter, p. 115. According to J. V. A. Fine, *The Early Medieval Balkans. A Critical Survey from the Sixth to the Late Twelfth Century* (Ann Arbor: University of Michigan Press, 1983), p. 206, Alusian was a Byzantine agent, whose only goal was to destroy Delian's movement.

The changes taking place in the tax system in Bulgaria were fully implemented only after *c.* 1050. The state now relied on tax farmers who often advanced large amounts of cash, which the government needed for the payments to the military and to the clients on the fringes of the Byzantine provinces in the Balkans. By 1060 the fiscalization and privatization of taxation in Bulgaria was complete. Accompanying this gradual change was the separation of military and civilian administration. The 1060s witnessed the introduction of a civilian administrator known as *praitor*, who often held the same rank as, and operated side by side with, the duke of Skopje, the supreme military commander of all troops stationed in Bulgaria. One of the most remarkable signs of the alignment of Bulgaria to the policies, aspirations, and tastes of Constantinople is the remodeling of the cathedral church in Ohrid by Archbishop Leo (1037–1056). A reminder of Hagia Sophia in Constantinople, the new domed basilica erected in *c.* 1050 was equally dedicated to the Holy Wisdom and decorated with frescoes which were executed by painters brought from Constantinople. Elsewhere, close links established by art historians between the painted decorations of churches in Thessalonica and its hinterland suggest that local bishops may have relied on painters from that city, as in the case of frescoes in the Church of St. George in Sofia, as well as those, closely related, of the monastery church of the Mother of God of Mercy in Veljusa (near Strumica, in Macedonia). When establishing that monastery in 1080, Manuel, the bishop of Strumica, secured an imperial decree from Emperor Alexios I Comnenus granting exemption from all public charges and independence from both civil and religious authorities. In all its details, the monastery church was inspired by the architecture of Constantinople and the surrounding region in northwestern Anatolia. The frescoes of the choir, the naos, the narthex, and the small south chapel bespeak the artistic and political ambitions of the founder.

Unlike his predecessor, John of Debăr, Archbishop Leo does not appear to have promoted the rich traditions of Old Church Slavonic literature developed in Ohrid. To be sure, two out of the four most famous Old Church Slavonic manuscripts produced in the eleventh century are certainly of Macedonian origin. Although one of them was found in the Monastery of the Holy Mother of God on Mount Athos (hence its name, *Codex Marianus*), both were written in Glagolitic either in Ohrid or in one of the monastic centers in the region. A Cyrillic evangeliary known as Sava's Book was transcribed from a lost Glagolitic text, perhaps in one of the same centers.[77] All three manuscripts have been dated to the early eleventh century and most likely antedate Leo's appointment as Archbishop of Ohrid.

The most frequently cited example of the condescending attitude the Greek-speaking clergy had towards Bulgarians and Bulgaria is the rich correspondence of one of Leo's successors, Theophylact Hephaistos (Archbishop of Ohrid from *c.* 1090). In his letters, Theophylact often complained in good rhetorical tradition about the "bumpkin lifestyle" that had become his "daily companion," after many years spent in Ohrid.[78] But he also viewed himself as "a Constantinopolitan, and strange to tell, a Bulgarian."[79] In over 130 letters that he wrote to various officials or friends in Constantinople and in the Balkans, Theophylact painted a bleak picture of his life in Ohrid. But this was much more rhetorical affectation than an accurate eyewitness account for the consumption of later

[77] For *Codex Marianus*, see V. Jagić, *Mariinskoe chetveroevangelie s primechaniiami i prilozheniiami* [The Tetraevangeliary from the Monastery of the Holy Mother of God, together with Introduction and Commentary] (St. Petersburg: Imperatorskaia Akademiia Nauk, Otdelenie russkogo iazyka i slovesnosti, 1883). For Sava's Book, see V. N. Shchepkin, *Savvina kniga* [Sava's Book] (St. Petersburg: Imperatorskaia Akademiia Nauk, Otdelenie russkogo iazyka i slovesnosti, 1903). Two other manuscripts are most likely of the same date. One of them, known as *Codex Assemanianus*, is a Glagolitic evangeliary handsomely illuminated, now in the Vatican Library. See V. Ivanova-Mavrodinova and A. Dzhurova, *Asemanievoto evangelie. Starobălgarski glagolicheski pametnik ot X vek* [The *Codex Assemanianus*. An Old Bulgarian Glagolitic Monument of the Tenth Century] (Sofia: Nauka i izkustvo, 1981). *Codex Suprasliensis*, the largest Old Church Slavonic manuscript known to date, is a Bulgarian collection of saint lives and homilies written in Cyrillic. See I. Zaimov and M. Capaldo, *Suprasălski ili Retkov sbornik* [The Supraśl Collection] (Sofia: Izdatelstvo na Bălgarskata Akademiia na Naukite, 1982). For illuminations of eleventh-century Bulgarian manuscripts, see M. Harisiadis, "L'enluminure des manuscrits glagolitiques des XIe et XIIe siècles," in *Actes du XVe Congrès international d'études byzantines. Athènes, septembre 1976*, ed. by P. Zepos, vol. II (Athens: Association internationale des études byzantines, 1981), pp. 193–204; A. Dzhurova, "L'ornement des manuscrits vieux-bulgares glagolitiques et leurs rapports avec l'art de Byzance, des provinces grecques d'Orient et de l'Italie du sud (sur l'ornement de l'Evangéliaire d'Assemani)," *Byzantiaka*, vol. 8 (1988), pp. 23–39.

[78] Theophylact of Ohrid, *ep.* 34, p. 243. The "bumpkin lifestyle" is a paraphrase of line 485 from Euripides' *Orestes*. See Mullett, *Theophylact of Ochrid*, pp. 275–276.

[79] Theophylact of Ohrid, *ep.* 4, p. 141. To Theophylact, Bulgaria was a *barbaros oikoumene*, "the barbarian (part of the) civilized world." See *ep.* 13, p. 171.

historians.[80] True, he often used ethnic stereotypes to vent his frustration at Bulgarians slandering him in Constantinople. To Theophylact, "the Bulgarian nature nourishes all kinds of evils" and the complaints were just "bewailing and making a big fuss by other methods [which are] common for the Bulgarians."[81] But the archbishop also protested against the abuses of the tax collectors in the region of Ohrid, called for the assistance of the duke of Dyrrachion against the taxation of monks and of the bishopric of Devol, and against the rounding-up of Bulgarian peasants to serve in the army. He boldly criticized the patriarch himself for having allowed a certain monk to establish a "house of prayer" in Macedonia, that is within the area under the jurisdiction of the archbishop of Ohrid to whom Emperor Basil II had granted independence from the patriarch of Constantinople and for whom he had established the diocesan boundaries in 1019/20: "What rights has the patriarch in the land of Bulgaria, he who has no authority to ordain anyone here, nor any other privilege in this land, which had acquired an autocephalous archbishop?"[82] Theophylact also defended the abbot of a monastery in the diocese of Serdica against the bishop, whom he eventually placed under interdict in order to curb his abuses.[83] He may have been responsible for the idea that the archbishop of Ohrid was a legitimate successor of the sixth-century archbishopric established by Justinian's novel of 535 in Iustiniana Prima (see chapter 1), an idea of considerable importance for the medieval history of the see of Ohrid. Perhaps more important for his attitude towards the ecclesiastical history of Ohrid is Theophylact's writing of the so-called *Long Life of St. Clement of Ohrid*, in which he did not hesitate to describe his hero as "a new Paul to the new Corinthians, the Bulgarians."[84] He also used "Bulgarian"

[80] There is absolutely no evidence to substantiate the idea of Theophylact's "systematic destruction of Slavic manuscripts" or closing of Slavic schools (Fine, *Early Medieval Balkans*, p. 220).

[81] Theophylact of Ohrid, *epp.* 80 and 98, pp. 425 and 501. For the image of the Bulgarians in Theophylact's letters, see also M. Mullett, "Byzantium and the Slavs: the views of Theophylact of Ochrid," *GSU*, vol. 87 (1994), pp. 55–70.

[82] Theophylact of Ohrid, *ep.* 82, p. 437.

[83] Theophylact of Ohrid, *epp.* 58 and 59, pp. 327–335 and 337–341.

[84] Theophylact of Ohrid, *Life of St. Clement of Ohrid* 22, p. 126; English translation from Obolensky, *Six Portraits*, p. 69. See also G. Podskalsky, "Two archbishops of Achrida (Ohrid) and their significance for Macedonia's secular and church history: Theophylaktos and Demetrios Chomatenos," in *Byzantine Macedonia: Identity, Image, and History. Papers from the Melbourne Conference, July 1995*, ed. by J. Burke and R. Scott (Melbourne: Australian Association for Byzantine Studies, 2000), pp. 139–148.

to refer to what is otherwise known as Old Church Slavonic, and attributed the baptism of Boris to Methodius.[85] Such ideas could hardly have been his and it has rightly been argued that he must have found them in the Old Church Slavonic sources on the basis of which he wrote his biography of Clement. However, these ideas are foreign to all known sources associated with the Cyrillo-Methodian tradition in tenth-century Bulgaria. In fact, the first examples of Bulgarian "nationalism" predate the beginning of Theophylact's term as Archbishop of Ohrid by a few decades. Anonymous aprocrypha written in Old Church Slavonic in the mid-eleventh century propagated not only an eschatological view of the future, but also a bright vision of the Bulgarian past, portraying the reigns of Boris, Symeon, and Peter as the glorious days long gone. Much of this literature about Doomsday may be interpreted as a reaction to the expected end of the world in the seventh millennium of its creation, more exactly in AM 6600 (AD 1092). Many apocrypha insist on the Bulgarian origin of both Cyril and Methodius and describe them as Bulgarian, not Slavic enlighteners. The *Interpretation of Daniel*, which unlike other apocrypha is an original Bulgarian work based on several historical and apocalyptic sources, attributes the foundation of the Bulgarian kingdom to "Michael Qagan" (Boris-Michael). Even more powerful is the account in the *Vision of Isaiah*, an adaptation of a Greek apocryphal text about Isaiah's visit to heaven. To that an anonymous Bulgarian author writing in the 1070s added a long account of how, after his return from heaven, Isaiah founded the Bulgarian nation, followed by what is now known as the *Bulgarian Apocryphal Chronicle*.[86] While the explosion of apocrypha extolling the Bulgarian past, many of which are of west Bulgarian origin, may well have been related to millennialist fears, recent studies point to the remarkable coincidence in time of both apocrypha and key political events that brought the

[85] Theophylact of Ohrid, *Life of St. Clement* 2, 4, and 22; pp. 70, 80, and 124–126. See Obolensky, *Six Portraits*, pp. 64–65.

[86] The *Vision of Isaiah*, which has long been misinterpreted as a Bogomil text, was published by I. Ivanov, *Bogomilski knigi i legendi* (Sofia: Pridvorna Pechatnica, 1925). An important fragment of the *Vision* containing the account of Isaiah's visit to heaven is available in English translation in Butler, *Monumenta Bulgarica*, pp. 173–184. For a reassessment of this important source, see M. Kaimakamova, "Istoriografskata stoinost na *Bălgarski apokrifen letopis* [The historiographic value of the *Bulgarian Apocryphal Chronicle*]," in *Civitas divino-humana. V chest na profesor Georgi Bakalov*, ed. by C. Stepanov and V. Vachkova (Sofia: Centăr za izsledvaniia na bălgarite "Tangra" TanNakRa IK, 2004), pp. 417–441.

issues of imperial power and Bulgarian past glory to the forefront. In 1073, a rebellion broke in Skopje under the leadership of a certain George Vojteh. According to John Skylitzes, what caused the uprising was the oppression and the exactions of the Byzantine administration. But the Bulgarian noblemen who followed Vojteh had other goals in mind. We have seen that they sent an embassy to Michael of Duklja, requesting his son Bodin to accompany them on their way back in order to be proclaimed Emperor of Bulgaria. Bodin was proclaimed emperor in Prizren, not in Skopje, where the Byzantine power had been meanwhile reestablished. An army of Bulgarians recruited in the region, which the duke of Skopje sent against the rebels, was quickly routed. Bodin delegated command to a certain Petrilus, who moved to Ohrid via Kastoria. While Ohrid quickly fell, the governor of Kastoria, himself perhaps of Bulgarian origin, inflicted a serious defeat upon Petrilus, forcing him to withdraw to the mountains. George Vojteh surrendered to another army marching on Skopje, which also managed to defeat and capture Bodin.

Five years later, the Byzantine administration in the Balkans was confronted with another rebellion in the environs of Serdica. This time, the rebels were Paulicians, descendants of the settlers brought from Asia Minor on several occasions from the mid-eighth to the late tenth century. Despite imperial hopes that once removed from their strongholds in eastern Anatolia the Paulicians would rapidly assimilate, a strong sense of a separate Paulician identity appeared during the eleventh century. That sense of identity did not derive from an imperial past, but from radical religious views, branded as heretical in Constantinople and persecuted at various moments in time by the ecclesiastical establishment. The Paulicians were dualist, and they believed that the god of the Old Testament was evil, which placed them squarely in opposition to the orthodox views of most members of the Byzantine establishment. The largest cluster of Paulician population in the Balkans was in western Thrace around Philippopolis (Plovdiv), but there were also numerous Paulician communities in the hinterland of Serdica. It is not clear what caused their rebellion of 1078, led by a man named Lekas, who seized the important fortress of Beliatoba near Philippopolis, which controlled access to the mountain passes. He was able to consolidate his position of power by marrying the daughter of a Pecheneg chieftain, and allied himself with Dobromir, another rebel from Mesembria, on the Black Sea coast. Their combined armies sacked Niš and Serdica, where Lekas ordered the local bishop to be executed. The swift intervention of the Byzantine troops crushed the rebellion before it could develop further. However, no large-scale reprisals are known to have followed victory. Lekas and Dobromir were captured, but soon released and given rich presents and lofty titles. Since the Paulicians were renowned for their martial qualities, they were drafted for the military units of the Byzantine army operating in the Balkans. A force of some 3,000 Paulicians participated in the battle of Dyrrachion (1081), in which Emperor Alexios was utterly defeated by the Normans. The leaders of the Paulician communities seem to have promised more military assistance during the following years, but never fulfilled their promises. Alexios ordered them to be arrested and their property to be confiscated, no doubt in an attempt to break the extraordinary solidarity of the Paulician community. Many Paulician leaders were exiled, others were forced to convert. The situation began to deteriorate rapidly when, in 1083, the survivors of Alexios' purges were gathered together by a converted Paulician named Travlos, who had served in the emperor's household. Like Lekas before him, Travlos seized Beliatoba and began raiding the surrounding countryside. He established contacts with the Pecheneg chieftains in control of important cities and forts in northeastern Bulgaria and, like Lekas, married the daughter of one of them. Two Byzantine expeditions were necessary to crush the uprising and to bring the Paulicians to heel. The first army Emperor Alexios dispatched against the rebels was under the command of the Grand Domestic (commander-in-chief of the armies in the Balkans) Gregory Pakourianos, who had been granted large estates in the region of Philippopolis by the emperors Nicephorus III Botaneiates and Alexios Comnenus. Pakourianos was of Iberian (Georgian) origin and shortly before the campaign he had established a monastery of Georgian monks, mostly former soldiers, on his land at Petritzonitissa, near the present-day village of Bachkovo, south of Plovdiv. In the *typikon* (rule) he wrote for the occasion, Gregory explains that his intention was to build a church "among the unsettled people living in the theme of Philippopolis in its more northerly parts."[87] But he was also worried about the possibility that his foundation might fall under bad influence. This concern seems to

[87] Typikon *of Gregory Pakourianos for the Monastery of the Mother of God Petritzonitissa in Bačkovo* 1, English translation by R. Jordan in *Byzantine Monastic Foundation Documents. A Complete Translation of the Surviving Founders'* Typika *and Testaments*, ed. by J. Thomas and A. C. Hero (Washington: Dumbarton Oaks Research Library and

have prompted the general to stipulate his monastery's independence from "any harassment at harmful hands, whether imperial or patriarchal, or of any of the metropolitans [. . .] or of archbishops, or of any other persons of any kind whether ecclesiastic or governmental." He seems to have had in mind the all too powerful archbishop of Philippopolis.[88] Pakourianos wanted his monastery to have no more and no less than fifty monks, but he specifically ordered that no "Greek should ever be appointed a priest or a monk in this holy monastery of mine, except only as a notary." Again, he seems to have been concerned with attempts by outsiders, perhaps from Constantinople, to seize his foundation: "I give this instruction and insist upon it for the following reason, lest [the Greeks], being violent, devious, or grasping, should create some deficiency or cause harm to the monastery or lest they appoint someone opposed to the place and eager to gain control over it or gain for himself the office of superior or appropriate the monastery on some abominable pretext."[89] In order to secure the economic independence of his monastery, a handsome endowment was made from Pakourianos' estates that had been granted to him "with an inalienable right of family possession, complete ownership and true authority."[90] The revenue from these properties was expected to defer expenses involved in maintaining a school for six boys until they have "attained the proper age for the rank of priest."[91] A detailed list of "sacred treasures and revered holy icons and the rest of the offerings of all kinds assigned, consecrated, and handed over to our aforesaid holy monastery" may be

Collection, 2000), p. 523. A similar concern with heretical neighbors is expressed by Manuel, Bishop of Tiberiopolis (Strumica), in his *Rule* for the Monastery of the Mother of God *Eleousa* in Veljusa (Macedonia). According to Manuel, not only did he "turn away from the inventors of such propositions and tenets as well, and stigmatize them as heretics," but he also subjected "to a curse the newly appearing teachings and tenets that are introduced by them". See *The* Rule *of Manuel, Bishop of Strumitza, for the Monastery of the Mother of God* Eleousa 2, English translation by A. Bandy in *Byzantine Monastic Foundation Documents. A Complete Translation of the Surviving Founders'* Typika *and Testaments*, ed. by J. Thomas and A. C. Hero (Washington: Dumbarton Oaks Research Library and Collection, 2000), p. 174.

[88] Typikon *of Gregory Pakourianos* 3, English translation by R. Jordan p. 527.

[89] Typikon *of Gregory Pakourianos* 24, English translation by R. Jordan p. 547.

[90] Typikon *of Gregory Pakourianos* 2, English translation by R. Jordan p. 524. The most important gift to his foundation was "the fort situated in the same theme of Philippopolis, that is, the village named Petritzos (generally called Basilikis by the common people) together with the hamlets below it."

[91] Typikon *of Gregory Pakourianos* 31, English translation by R. Jordan p. 551.

compared to the list drawn at about the same time by Peter Crni of Gumaj for his monastery of St. Peter In the Village. Pakourianos' list includes such items as a "Greek Gospel lectionary," "a copy of the four Gospels in Georgian," "a book of St. Gregory the Theologian," "two copies of *The Heavenly Ladder* by John Klimakos," and "a book by Theodore the Studite."[92] In addition, Pakourianos provided for the distribution of annual allowances on Easter Sunday for every member of the monastic community. In order for the monks not to go "out of the monastery for such necessities, whether to buy something or to procure sandals, and be at the doors of leather-workers or other people and with this excuse incur harm," the founder also instituted an annual fair "beside the most holy monastery, so that all of them may purchase their necessity."[93]

Pakourianos' monastery in Bachkovo was neither the only, nor the largest one in the region. But his *typikon* suggests that eleventh-century Thrace was a prosperous region and the archaeological evidence confirms this impression. At Constantia, near Simeonovgrad, a suburb developed outside the city walls, soon followed by another non-fortified settlement on the opposite bank of the Marica River, at Gradishteto. On the other side of the Rhodopes, an eleventh- and early twelfth-century neighborhood came into existence in Maroneia along a street that cut through the ruined atrium of an early Byzantine basilica. In the outer corners of the city ramparts, there were wine-presses, attesting the wine production and trade that supported the economic growth of Maroneia during this period. Several large villages have been excavated in the region. Diadovo, near Nova Zagora, was established in the mid-eleventh century, as indicated by coins minted for Emperor Constantine X (1059–1067), the earliest found on the site. The village consisted of 75 sunken-featured buildings and 23 farm premises, and had a cemetery with 266 graves and 2 chronological phases. The neighboring village of Karanovo, on the southern slopes of the Stara Planina mountains, was built on top of an earlier, late ninth- and tenth-century settlement. During the eleventh and early twelfth century, the village had eighteen sunken-featured

[92] Typikon *of Gregory Pakourianos* 33, English translation by R. Jordan p. 552–553. Some books mentioned in the list had silver-gilded covers with rich enamel and precious stone decoration.

[93] Typikon *of Gregory Pakourianos* 9, English translation by R. Jordan pp. 534–535. For the abbot, Pakourianos set aside thirty-six gold coins annually, while common monks received ten coins each.

buildings and four farm premises in addition to a small, single-naved church surrounded by graves of the local cemetery. Most villages in Thrace were relatively close to each other and seem to have come into existence in the late 1040s or early 1050s, perhaps as a consequence of the immigration of the population from the northern Balkans devastated by the Pecheneg raids. But the presence on many sites of a peculiar kind of slip-coated pottery suggests another explanation. This pottery is unique to Bulgaria, for it has no local traditions of either fabric or shapes. The coating consists of a micaceous slip, which gives pots a golden or silver glimmer, no doubt intended to imitate gold or silver vessels. Slip-coated pots were found in large quantities in urban centers (Philippopolis, Sliven, Melnik, Pernik), but also on rural sites, such as Diadovo. Their production in the region cannot be dated earlier than *c.* 1000 and may have been associated with the growth of communities of Armenian and Paulician settlers.

Eleventh-century Thrace, Macedonia, and the southernmost Balkan provinces of the Empire are in sharp contrast to the situation on the Danube frontier. During the last years of Basil II's reign and under his successors Constantine VIII (1025–1028), Romanus III (1028–1034), and especially Michael IV (1034–1041), Pecheneg marauders crossed the river several times and raided deep into the interior of the Balkan provinces. In 1017, Basil II dispatched a Georgian officer named Tzotzikios to Dristra for negotiations with a group of Pechenegs that had recently arrived on the left (northern) bank of the Danube.[94] Ten years later, the Pechenegs crossed the Danube and massacred a great number of Byzantine troops, before being driven back across the river by the swift intervention of the duke of Thessalonica, Constantine Diogenes. However, his victory did not put an end to the raids. Those taking place between 1032 and 1036 crossed the region between the Danube and the Balkans, the Stara Planina range of mountains, and devastated Thrace, reaching as far south as Thessalonica. Those raids utterly destroyed a number of forts erected on the Lower Danube in the aftermath of John Tzimiskes' victory of 971 or shortly after the recovery of the northeastern territories in 1018. At Dinogetia (Garvăn, across the Danube from Galaţi), the civilian settlement that had grown outside the fort was destroyed in the spring of 1036. The catastrophe appears to have taken the inhabitants by surprise. One of the houses dated by means of a coin

[94] John Skylitzes, *Synopsis historiarum*, p. 356.

struck for Emperor Constantine VIII (1025–1028) produced yarns of raw silk, linen, and flax, all left behind as the owner hurried outside to take cover. An even grislier picture is that of seven skeletons found in a sunken-featured building together with a coin struck for Emperor Michael IV (1034–1041). These were most likely the victims of the attack. Following the devastating Pecheneg raid, the site was abandoned for a while. When it was reoccupied, perhaps in the late 1060s, there were no sunken-featured buildings any more, only above-ground houses that must have been very similar to those in existence at the same time at Păcuiul lui Soare, near Călăraşi, a Byzantine fort on an island in the middle of the Danube that had been used as a harbor for the Danube fleet, but was now a simple bridgehead land fortification. The episcopal church in Silistra was also seriously damaged during the raids of 1035/6 and not restored until the reign of Constantine IX (1042–1055), as attested by a dedicatory inscription.[95] At Odărci near Dobrich, the Byzantine fort built in the late tenth or early eleventh century was destroyed and abandoned in the 1030s or 1040s. A few decades later, a community of Christianized Pechenegs settled on the site. No new buildings were erected, but a number of open-air fireplaces, as well as a large quantity of pottery remains (especially clay cauldrons), indicate the presence of a human group inhabiting the abandoned ruins of the Byzantine fort. A cemetery found at the foot of the hill on which the fort once stood produced rich evidence of how far the Byzantine (or rather Balkan Byzantine) material culture had been adopted by the newcomers: bracelets with serpent-shaped ends, rings with engraved eagles or five-cornered stars, as well as pectoral crosses, bespeak the rapid assimilation of the Pechenegs. On the other hand, bronze bridle-bosses employed for the ornamentation of the headband or the cheek strap of the horse gear were deposited ritually in burials with female skeletons. As no parallels to the burial customs attested in Odărci are known from the Pecheneg "homeland" north of the Danube River, it has been suggested that such customs may be cultural responses to the new political circumstances in which the first Pecheneg settlers found themselves shortly before and after the middle of the eleventh century.

[95] V. Beshevliev, "Novi otkăsleci ot părvobălgarski i drugi srednovekovni nadpisi ot Pliska i Silistra [New fragments of Bulgar and other medieval inscriptions from Pliska and Silistra]," *IAI*, vol. 20 (1955), pp. 288–290.

In spite of clear evidence of widespread destruction, other forts in Dobrudja seem to have been continously occupied throughout the eleventh century. Moreover, there is clear indication that these forts received constant supplies of food and ammunition from Constantinople, some of which may have been brought on commercial ships, such as that on which St. Cyril the Phileote used to work as a sailor.[96] Amphorae carrying olive oil or wine have been found in Dinogetia, Silistra, and Păcuiul lui Soare, and are remarkably similar to those dated to the eleventh century and found in excavations in Constantinople. Even glazed wares produced in Constantinople appear in small quantities on military sites in the Lower Danube region. On the other hand, pottery was also produced locally. In Nufăru, a group of kilns existed inside the fort, another outside the walls near one of the fort's cemeteries. The operation of a kiln found in Păcuiul lui Soare has been coin-dated to the reign of Romanus III (1028–1034).[97] But trade connections reached even farther. Several artifacts have been found in Dinogetia that are clearly of Rus' origin, while others may have come from as far as Volga Bulgharia. More importantly, the signs of a prosperous trade in the region coincide with a massive injection of coins, many of which were minted between 1025 and 1055. The largest quantity of coins appears to have been introduced into the region at the same time as the process of monetization and fiscalization of taxation in Bulgaria entered its final phase.

In the early 1040s, the number of Byzantine troops stationed in the Lower Danube region appears to have been large enough for handling small-scale invasions. In 1043, the survivors of the failed expedition sent by Grand Prince Iaroslav of Kiev against Constantinople attempted to return by land along the western coast of the Black Sea. They were intercepted and defeated at Varna by the Byzantine army.[98] Two years later, a very large group of Pechenegs approached

[96] *Life of St. Cyril the Phileote*, ed. by E. Sargologos (Brussels: Subsidia Hagiographica, 1964), p. 63. See also P. Diaconu and E. Stănescu, "Le commerce fluvial et maritime dans la région comprise entre le Danube et la Mer Noire aux IVe–XIIe siècles," in *Etudes d'histoire maritime, présentées au XIIIe Congrès international des sciences historiques par la Commission internationale d'histoire maritime à l'occasion de son XIIe colloque, Moscou, 16–23 août* (Moscow: n. p., 1970), pp. 290–293.

[97] S. Baraschi, "Un cuptor de ars oale de la Păcuiul lui Soare (sec. al XI-lea) [An eleventh-century kiln in Păcuiul lui Soare]," *SCIVA*, vol. 25 (1974), pp. 461–472.

[98] George Kedrenos, *Chronicle*, ed. by I. Bekker, vol. II (Bonn: E. Weber, 1839), p. 555.

the Danube frontier under the leadership of a chieftain named Kegen. John Skylitzes relates that the Pecheneg leader contacted the military commander responsible for the defense of the frontier, who promptly dispatched him to Constantinople, where Kegen was baptized and given the rank of *patrikios* and the command of three forts on the Danube frontier, most likely in the region of the present-day Balta Ialomiţei, a large island between the Danube and its western arm known as Borcea.[99] Many of his followers were allowed to settle within that region, while others moved further south to Odărci, the fort destroyed during the raids of the 1030s. Throughout the eleventh century, most soldiers in the fort garrisons in the Lower Danube region appear to have been of Pecheneg origin, as attested archaeologically in Garvăn (Dinogetia) and Nufăru by such artifacts as bone arrow tips, plates of reflex bows, or bone quiver mounts, all of which are typical for nomadic warriors in the steppe. Kegen appears to have sufficiently trusted his new position of power to harass the Pechenegs on the other side of the Danube, which provoked a large-scale invasion across the frozen river in the winter of 1046. It is perhaps in such circumstances that the main gate of the Byzantine fort of Păcuiul lui Soare was hastily blocked with architectural and sculptural remains of early Byzantine and medieval monuments on the site. The last occupation phase in Capidava (south of Hârşova) ended at the same time. That the Pechenegs may have been responsible for the destruction of Capidava is indicated by a pit of dismembered bodies and burnt debris found on the site, which can be dated to its last phase of occupation. Only the outbreak of a deadly epidemic (perhaps plague) forced the invading Pechenegs to surrender. Tyrach, the paramount chief, as well as other leaders under his command were taken to Constantinople, where, much like Kegen, they were baptized and granted high ranks. However, the other Pecheneg captives were not allowed to settle alongside Kegen's men, but instead moved to the province of Bulgaria, in order to serve as guards on both sides of the imperial road between Niš and Serdica. Nonetheless, an attempt to draft them for a campaign against the Seljuks on the eastern frontier of the Empire sparked a rebellion in 1048, during

[99] John Skylitzes, *Synopsis historiarum*, p. 433. For Kegen's seal, see I. Iordanov, "Pechati na Ioan Kegen, magistăr i arkhont na Pechenegiia (1050–1051) [Seals of John Kegen, *magistros* and *archon* of Pechenegia (1050–1051)]," *Numizmatika i sfragistika*, no. 1 (1998), pp. 96–101.

which those who had been taken with the Byzantine troops into Asia Minor returned to the Balkans and settled in the vicinity of Preslav, not far from Kegen's Pechenegs, with whom they now joined hands. The allied forces crushed a Byzantine army sent against them and won a victory over another in the vicinity of Adrianople. To cope with the formidable force of the steppe horsemen and with the lack of military forces available for a massive intervention, Emperor Constantine IX broke the troops remaining in the eastern Balkans into smaller units stationed in forts, from which they were now to launch surprise attacks on the Pechenegs. The guerrilla tactics appear to have worked to the emperor's advantage, as the Byzantines were able to drive the nomads back to the Danube, as far as the Iron Gates near Vidin. However, the conflict between the newly appointed military commanders of Bulgaria and of the northeastern region led to a complete failure of Constantine's plans to annihilate the Pechenegs. Now beaten at their own game, the Byzantine troops barely managed to barricade themselves in Preslav, which they had previously conquered from the Pechenegs. An attempt to escape from the Pecheneg blockade ended in disaster, with most Byzantine troops being massacred. In the end, Constantine IX was forced to allow a group of Pechenegs to settle between the Danube and the Stara Planina range of mountains, in a region called the "Hundred Hills." At the peace agreed upon in 1053, the Pecheneg leaders received many gifts and titles, much like the inhabitants of the cities in the Lower Danube region, whose loyalty and support for the Byzantine troops had meanwhile become a key element for maintaining control on the Danube frontier. However, the peace had come at a great price. A number of other forts in the region were abandoned and life seems to have completely ceased on such sites as Krivina near Ruse or Car Asen near Dobrich. Further south, the monastic compound in the old Bulgarian capital at Pliska was abandoned in the mid-eleventh century, a couple of decades after the manors in the Outer Town.

An independent command in the northeastern region appeared during these years, as attested by several leaden seals of *katepans* (commanders) of Paradounavon ("the lands by the Danube"). One of the first commanders of the new province was Demetrius Katakalon, known from several seals found in Silistra.[100] In addition to *katepans*,

[100] Iordanov, *Pechatite*, pp. 143–144.

the numerous seals found in northeastern Bulgaria and in Dobrudja bespeak the presence of army officers and churchmen. Conspicuously rare, if not altogether absent, are civilian, especially fiscal officials. Unlike Bulgaria, no *praitor* was ever appointed for Paradounavon.

Constantine's peace provided only a temporary solution to the Pecheneg problem. A joint Pecheneg–Hungarian attack in 1059 was met with military resistance from Emperor Isaac, who defeated them near Serdica and forced the marauders to demand peace. Five years later, the Oghuz invasion crossed the northern Balkans in an attempt to reach as quickly as possible the southern regions near Thessalonica and in northern Greece. The new invaders were members of a tribal confederation related to the Seljuks who had meanwhile attacked the eastern regions of Asia Minor. The Oghuz had been allies of the Khazars in the 900s, but by the mid-eleventh century they are mentioned as raiding the southern frontier of Rus'. At about the same time, they began threatening the lands of their western neighbors, the Pechenegs. In 1064, the Oghuz invasion left a trail of destruction throughout Paradounavon, most visible archaeologically in Dinogetia and in Tulcea. The invasion may have also been responsible for the end of the small civilian settlement near the present-day city of Constanţa. The Oghuz wiped out all military resistance and captured the *katepan* of Paradounavon and future emperor Nicephorus Botaneiates, together with Basil Apokapes, the commander of the imperial reinforcements sent to the northern frontier. However, another outbreak of epidemic soon began decimating the marauders. The survivors were quickly recruited into the Byzantine army, while others returned to the lands north of the Danube River. The devastation in the northeastern region of the Balkans does not seem to have been very serious, although the Byzantine authorities certainly lost control of the area. St. Cyril the Phileote sent a friend to Anchialos, on the Black Sea coast, to purchase wheat, an indication that the local market had a constant supply from the interior. However, an Armenian merchant traveling by land between Derkos in Thrace and Varna on the Black Sea coast was ambushed in the mountains and killed by brigands.[101]

In order to bring the rebellious Pechenegs into the fold, Emperor Constantine X (1059–1067) dispatched a mission of evangelization, which began performing mass baptisms in the waters of the Danube

[101] *Life of St. Cyril the Phileote*, pp. 117, 126–127, 343, and 352–353. See also Stephenson, *Byzantium's Balkan Frontier*, p. 96.

River. It was perhaps during these years that an archbishop was established in Dristra (Silistra), with five suffragan bishops under his jurisdiction, one of whom may have been that of Axiopolis (Hinog, near Cernavodă). The fresco decoration of the episcopal church in Dristra may also be dated to this period. The small fort church of square plan with an apsed side that was found in Dinogetia, as well as the triconch church found in 1954 in Niculiţel during salvage excavations, may be of a late eleventh-century date. The relatively large number of pectoral crosses, leaden or steatite icons, and medallions with images of saints that have been found on all military sites bespeak the presence of Christians in the region.

But the Pechenegs were not the only problem the Byzantine administration faced in Paradounavon. Shortly after the Oghuz invasion, a group of Pechenegs crossed the Danube and joined ranks with Tatous (also known as Khales), Sesthlav, and Satzas, the Pecheneg chieftains who controlled the cities and forts on the Lower Danube. Tatous was the lord of Dristra, where a rebellion broke in 1072 against the decision taken by Emperor Michael VII's chief minister, Nikephoritzas, to cut all stipends to the troops of "mixed barbarians" stationed on the Danube frontier, as well as the gifts for the Pecheneg leaders. Nestor, the man the emperor sent to settle the conflict, was a native of the northern Balkans, but while on mission to Paradounavon, he joined the rebels led by the Pecheneg chieftain Tatous, the lord of Dristra. Nestor brought the combined armies to the walls of Constantinople, threatening to besiege the city unless Nikephoritzas was removed. However, at odds with his Pecheneg allies, Nestor soon withdrew north of the Stara Planina. Despite his rebellion, there is no indication that contacts between Constantinople and the cities on the Lower Danube were interrupted. On the contrary, coin series continued without any break on many sites in northern Dobrudja, in sharp contrast to the decline of coin series on sites in the south, which seem to have been sacked by the rebels. Moreover, recent numismatic studies have revealed the existence of a mint in Isaccea, which produced cast imitations of coins struck for Emperors Michael VII Dukas (1067–1078) and Nicephorus III Botaneiates (1078–1081).[102]

[102] E. Oberländer-Târnoveanu, "Un atelier monétaire byzantin inconnu de la deuxième moitié du XIe siècle dans le thème de Paristrion," *RESEE*, vol. 21 (1983), pp. 261–270.

The Pechenegs raided Thrace again in 1077, while offering their support to the duke of Dyrrachion, Nicephorus Basilakes, in his bid for the imperial throne, only ten years after the duke of Serdica (and future emperor Romanus IV Diogenes) had also asked for their assistance against Emperor Constantine X. In the 1070s and 1080s, all major contenders for the Imperial power in the Balkans sought the Pecheneg alliance. We have seen that both leaders of the Paulician rebellions, Lekas and Travlos, secured their alliance with the steppe horsemen by marrying Pecheneg princesses. It was in battle against the Pechenegs allied with Lekas that the founder of the Bachkovo monastery, the Grand Domestic Gregory Pakourianos, was killed and his army dispersed. In 1087, the Pechenegs north of the Danube organized another invasion, this time in association with Cumans and Hungarians under the command of the former king of Hungary, Solomon. The Pechenegs crossed into Bulgaria but were ambushed in the mountains by a Byzantine army under general Nicholas Mavrokatakalon. The coordination of the Byzantine troops may have had something to do with the intense correspondence between military commanders in the Lower Danube region and Emperor Alexios, as attested by his seals found on various sites in northeastern Bulgaria and Dobrudja. Although the marauders were badly mauled and their chieftain, Tzelgu, killed, the survivors did not return north of the Danube, but decided to remain on the right bank.[103] Emperor Alexios Comnenus was forced to make peace with them in an attempt to secure temporarily Thrace and Macedonia. Soon thereafter, he began a series of energetic campaigns against the Pechenegs. In June 1087, he sent a fleet to Dristra, and decided to cross the Stara Planina and battle the Pechenegs on their own ground. On August 1, he met with an embassy of 150 Pechenegs demanding peace in exchange for military assistance for the emperor's wars elsewhere. Alexios took advantage of a solar eclipse announced by court astronomers to predict the dimming light and thus terrify the envoys. He then ordered all of them arrested and dispatched them as hostages to Constantinople. However, on their way to the capital, the Pechenegs massacred their guards and escaped back to their abodes. This did not deter Alexios from marching upon Dristra, via Pliska, with a Pecheneg named Argyros Karatzas as commander of the foreign

[103] Anna Comnena, *Alexiad*, vol. II, pp. 87–89; English translation by Sewter, pp. 217–218.

auxiliaries in the Byzantine army. The siege of Dristra failed, as the emperor found himself surrounded by the Pechenegs. As he called off the siege, the lord of Dristra, Tatous, fled north of the Danube, in an attempt to gather Cuman assistance against Alexios. The emperor engaged the enemy force, but the Pechenegs, moving behind their wagons, which they employed as mobile fortresses, inflicted a disastrous defeat on the Byzantines. The Veil of the Virgin, which Alexios had used as his standard, fell into their hands, and the emperor himself withdrew in a hurry, leaving a great number of prisoners in the hands of his enemies. In the meantime, the Cuman reinforcements that Tatous was able to secure began attacking the Pechenegs, who refused to share any of the spoils obtained after the defeat of Alexios' troops. In the end, the Pechenegs were beaten, but Alexios, who had meanwhile reached Beroe (Stara Zagora, Bulgaria), did not intervene to take advantage of the changing situation. Instead, he tried to ransom the captives the Pechenegs still had and appealed to Robert, Count of Flanders, for military assistance. During the winter of 1087/8, the Pechenegs crossed the mountains into Thrace and established their camp near Markellai, not far from present-day Karnobat, on the Black Sea coast. Fearing a Cuman–Pecheneg alliance, Alexios immediately sued for peace and the Pechenegs agreed to a truce, which they immediately broke in order to take advantage of Alexios' notorious lack of troops and invade Thrace. The emperor offered peace one more time, hoping that he could keep the barbarians as far away from Constantinople as possible. In reply, the Pechenegs massacred the elite of the Byzantine army in a surprise attack. Desperate, the emperor began recruiting the locals, even peasants with their wagons, but his troops were besieged by the Pechenegs at Çorlu, in the hinterland of Constantinople. By February 1091, the Pechenegs were under the walls of the capital, although permanently harassed by Alexios' troops in a guerrilla-type warfare. To make things worse, the Seljuk emir Tzachas, who had meanwhile conquered Chios and Mitylene in the Aegean Sea, established contact with the Pechenegs in order to coordinate attacks for a final assault on Constantinople. However, by May of that same year, the Pechenegs had been utterly defeated and their numbers seriously diminished. On April 29, 1091, with the assistance of 40,000 Cuman horsemen, Alexios obtained a major victory against them at Levunion, not far from Ainos, and in the aftermath of the battle most prisoners, men, women, and children, were killed in a large-scale massacre. Those who did survive were immediately recruited for the Byzantine units that Alexios later employed against the crusaders, while others were settled around Moglena in Macedonia. Following the battle of Levunion, the situation in Paradounavon appears to have been temporarily stabilized as the emperor appointed a new military commander in the person of Leo Nikerites. But Paradounavon and the Balkan provinces of the Empire now faced a new threat, the Cumans. In 1092, the marauders moved swiftly across the Stara Planina with the support of the local population. Emperor Alexios, who had established his headquarters in Anchialos, attacked the main group of marauders under the command of a chieftain named Kitzes, and his victory brought the other Cumans to submission. The emperor sealed the mountain passes and either massacred or captured the Cuman forces who had refused to submit.[104]

Around 1100, a number of new forts appeared in Paradounavon, while others disappeared. When a double-curtain wall was built at Isaccea shortly before 1100, the site had already become the most important military and political center on the Lower Danube. By contrast, Dinogetia was utterly destroyed by the Cumans and remained deserted for some twenty-five years. The occupation of the Byzantine site at Nufăru was also interrupted for a few decades, but both Păcuiul lui Soare and Preslav were abandoned for good.

PECHENEGS AND CUMANS

Despite their obsessive preoccupation with the Pechenegs, eleventh-century Byzantine sources rarely inform us about developments north of the Danube, as their focus was almost exclusively on the Pecheneg groups established on Byzantine territory. Nothing is known from these sources about either the Oghuz or the Cumans, prior to their invasions of 1064 and 1078, respectively. Similarly, to the author of the *Russian Primary Chronicle* writing in the early twelfth century, the most important event in the eleventh-century history of the Pechenegs was the major victory Iaroslav the Wise obtained against them near Kiev in 1036. The victory put an end to the Pecheneg raids against Rus' and was memorialized, among other things, by

[104] Anna Comnena, *Alexiad*, vol. II, p. 203; English translation by Sewter, p. 306.

the Cathedral of St. Sophia erected on the battlefield site.[105] Prior to the battle of Kiev, Iaroslav had extended the line of fortifications on the southern border, along the river Ros, to which he moved the captives taken during his campaigns into Poland. It is therefore possible that the strong force of Pechenegs that besieged Kiev in 1036 had come from the steppe lands in Right Bank Ukraine. At any rate, it is most likely from that region that Iaroslav's brother, Sviatopolk, recruited allies during the power struggle that erupted in 1018, at the death of Vladimir, between his many sons.[106] That the Pechenegs were Sviatopolk's allies is also confirmed by an early thirteenth-century biography of St. Olaf of Norway, which is preserved in a late fourteenth-century Icelandic manuscript known as Flateyjarbók.[107] The unknown author of the biography mentions Vlachs (*Blókumenn*) among Sviatopolk's allies, which suggests that the Pechenegs in question were those in the steppe lands north of the Lower Danube. The existence of Vlachs in that region is also confirmed by an eleventh-century rune-stone from the Sjonhem cemetery on the island of Gotland in the Baltic Sea.The inscription commemorates a merchant named Rodfos who was traveling to Constantinople through the land of the Vlachs (*Blakumen*), where he was robbed of his belongings and killed.[108] In both cases, the Vlachs in question are clearly north, not south of the river Danube,

[105] *Russian Primary Chronicle* AM 6542–6544, English translation by Hazzard Cross and Sherbowitz-Wetzor, pp. 136–137. See Martin, *Medieval Russia*, p. 48.

[106] Sviatopolk had fled to the Pechenegs, when attacked by Iaroslav in 1018. See *Russian Primary Chronicle* AM 6542–6544, English translation by Hazzard Cross and Sherbowitz-Wetzor, p. 132.

[107] *Flateyjarbók*, ed. by V. Guðbrandur and C. R. Unger, vol. II (Christiania: P. T. Malling, 1862), p. 126.

[108] S. B. F. Jansson and E. Wessén, *Gotlands runinskrifter*, vol. I (Stockholm: Almqvist and Wiksell, 1962), pp. 263–268. For an English translation of the inscription and a brief commentary, see E. Piltz, "Varangian companies for long distance trade: aspects of interchange between Scandinavia, Rus' and Byzantium in the 11th–12th centuries," in *Byzantium and Islam in Scandinavia. Acts of a Symposium at Uppsala University, June 15–16 1996*, ed. by E. Piltz (Jonsered: P. Astroms Forlag, 1998), pp. 88–89. See also B. Sawyer, *The Viking Age Rune-Stones. Custom and Commemoration in Early Medieval Scandinavia* (Oxford and New York: Oxford University Press, 2000), p. 56. For Vlachs north of the Danube mentioned in Norse sources, see A. Armbruster, *Der Donau-Karpatenraum in den mittel- und westeuropäischen Quellen des 10.–16. Jahrhunderts. Eine historiographische Imagologie.* (Cologne and Vienna: Böhlau, 1990), pp. 34–36.

although the exact region in which Rodfos encountered them cannot be established with any precision.

It is perhaps during this period of time that most, albeit not all, sites south and east of the Carpathian Mountains were deserted. By 1050, the sites that had flourished during the tenth century in the region of the Kahul, Ialpukh, and Katlabukh Lakes had already been abandoned. At the opposite end of the Danube frontier of the Byzantine Empire, a recent analysis of the ceramic remains found during excavations in Orşova, in the Iron Gates region, has revealed the possibility of a brief occupation of the site in the early eleventh century, perhaps in association with the Byzantine presence on the opposite bank of the Danube, between Braničevo and Vidin. No evidence exists, however, that the occupation continued into the second half of the eleventh century.[109]

The region north of the Lower Danube was probably the main area of confrontation between Kegen and Tyrach, the two Pecheneg chieftains responsible for the massive migration of the Pechenegs to the Balkans. The fact that the intention of Tyrach, who led the Pecheneg invasion of 1046/7, was to settle in the Balkans together with his warriors has led to speculations about the possibility that shortly before the middle of the century the Oghuz had already made their presence felt in the steppe lands between the Dnieper and the Danube. In fact, according to John Skylitzes, it is Kegen's military achievements in confrontations with the Oghuz that elevated his status among his fellow Pechenegs. By contrast, although having at his disposal a much greater number of warriors, Tyrach does not seem to have been terribly successful against the Oghuz. Fearing that Kegen's military prowess would eventually undermine his own position of power, Tyrach made an attempt to assassinate his rival, who managed to flee into the marshy region on the right bank of the Dnieper.[110] From there he mobilized the Pecheneg warriors of two clans (Belermanis and Pagumanis) and attacked Tyrach. Defeated in the first encounter, Kegen decided to cross the Danube into the Byzantine Empire together with his followers. That Kegen had on his

[109] C. Cosma, "Ceramica prefeudală şi feudală timpurie de la Orşova [Early medieval and medieval pottery from Orşova]," *Ephemeris Napocensis*, vol. 2 (1992), pp. 231–235.

[110] John Skylitzes, *Synopsis historiarum*, pp. 455–456; Kedrenos, *Chronicle*, vol. II, p. 582. For Skylitzes' account as a Byzantine interpretation of a Pecheneg source, see Malamut, "L'image byzantine des Petchénègues," p. 118.

side two clans, while Tyrach ruled over eleven other rival clans, speaks volumes about the dramatic political transformations taking place among the steppe nomads since the days of Emperor Constantine VII Porphyrogenitus (see chapter 4). It is hard, if not impossible, to locate the main concentration of Pecheneg forces under Tyrach's control, but all sources pertaining to the eleventh-century history of the Pechenegs appear to support the idea that after *c.* 1000, the Pecheneg power center shifted to the Lower Danube region. Tyrach may not have ruled over all Pechenegs, but in the 1040s he seems to have come very close to establishing a unified polity stretching from the Lower Danube into the steppes north of the Black Sea. It is notoriously difficult to assign precise dates to eleventh-century horseman burials found in the region. However, those that have been dated with some degree of certainty to the first half of that century appear to cluster in the region of the Lower Dniester River around Tiraspol (Republic of Moldova). A second cluster has been identified in the Lower Danube region and may represent the power-center shift taking place during the confrontation between Tyrach and Kegen. However, it would be a mistake to imagine the former's position as anything similar to a form of centralized power, for not all Pechenegs hostile to Kegen eventually followed Tyrach in his campaign south of the Danube River.

While Kegen and Tyrach were fighting over power within the Pecheneg polity, the Oghuz had already begun raiding the southern regions of Rus' that are now in Right Bank Ukraine.[111] According to the *Russian Primary Chronicle*, in 1060 the sons of Iaroslav the Wise who ruled in Kiev, Chernigov, and Pereiaslavl', respectively, together with the prince of Polock, organized a massive expedition "by horse and ship" against the "Torks." The chronicler relates how, fearing the approach of the Rus', the nomads fled "and are fleeing even to this day."[112] Shortly after 1060, the Oghuz moved into the steppe north of the Danube River and then burst into the Empire in 1064. It has been suggested that the Rus' expedition had caused the Oghuz migration westwards, but equally significant must have

[111] They were most likely the "Torks" that Vsevolod, one of Iaroslav the Wise's sons ruling in Pereiaslavl', is said to have attacked in the winter of 1055. See *Russian Primary Chronicle*, AM 6562, English translation by Hazzard Cross and Sherbowitz-Wetzor, p. 143.

[112] *Russian Primary Chronicle*, AM 6568, English translation by Hazzard Cross and Sherbowitz-Wetzor, p. 143.

been the approach of the Cumans from the east. The twelfth-century Armenian chronicler Matthew of Edessa describes how in 1050 or 1051 the "snake-people" marched into the land of the "Yellow men" (the Armenian name for Cumans) smashing and forcing them to move against the Oghuz and the Pechenegs.[113] In the mid-eleventh century, the Cumans made their first appearance on the southern frontier of Rus', but seem to have reached the Lower Danube only after the departure of the Oghuz and their failed invasion of 1064. However, by 1070 the Cumans certainly controlled the entire steppe corridor north of the Black and Caspian Seas, a region hence known as "the steppe of the Cumans."

An effective presence of the Cumans on the Danube frontier of the Byzantine Empire can thus be dated shortly before 1078, the date of their first known raid into the Balkans. The oldest Turkish chronicle, the *Oghuz-name*, which is preserved in a copy incorporated into a seventeenth-century text, relates that Kipchak, the eponymous hero of the Cumans, had defeated many nations, including the Vlachs (*Ulâq*), no doubt those previously mentioned in Norse sources.[114] During the relatively short period between the failed expedition of the Oghuz and the arrival of the Cumans, the region north of the Lower Danube seems to have remained under the control of those Pechenegs who did not accompany Tyrach in 1046/7. That Tyrach's migration southwards across the Danube still left a considerable military force behind may explain the Pecheneg raid of 1068 into Transylvania. The steppe warriors were led by a chieftain named Osul, whom King Solomon and Duke Géza eventually defeated in battle at Chiraleş. Less than twenty years later, the main threat on the eastern frontier of the Hungarian kingdom were the Cumans.[115] In 1085/6

113 Matthew of Edessa, *Chronicle*, ed. by E. Dulaurier (Paris: A. Durand, 1858), p. 89; English translation from Páloczi-Horváth, *Pechenegs, Cumans, Iasians*, p. 39. The identity of the "snake-people" has been much debated, without any satisfactory solution being offered. It is clear, however, that Matthew had in mind a chain reaction, which is the favorite historiographic metaphor for describing the "last wave of migrations" in Eastern Europe.

114 Ebülgâzi Bahadir Han, *Histoire des Mogols et des Tatares*, ed. by D. Desmaisons, vol. II (St. Petersburg: Imprimerie de l'Académie Impériale des Sciences, 1874), p. 19. That the mention of the Vlachs can be dated to the time of the first recension of the *Oghuz-name* has been disputed. See N. Beldiceanu, "Sunt Valahii amintiţi în Oguzname? [Are the Vlachs mentioned in the *Oghuz-name*?]," *Buletinul Bibliotecii Române*, vol. 12 (1985), pp. 287–292.

115 Spinei, *Ultimele valuri migratoare*, pp. 134–135.

and again in 1091/2, the Cumans invaded Hungary, reaching as far as Timişoara before being defeated by King Ladislas. By 1090, the power of the Cumans was well established in the Lower Danube region and important enough for the Pecheneg lord of Dristra, Tatous, to ask for Cuman military assistance against Emperor Alexios I Comnenus. It has been suggested that the Cumans may have intended to expand into Dobrudja and northeastern Bulgaria, which may explain the emperor's circumspection vis-à-vis Cumans during the following few years, despite the growing hostility of the Cumans against the Pechenegs. On the other hand, the Cumans who invaded Paradounavon in 1094 were certainly not those recently established on the northern bank of the river Danube, but followers of Tugorkan, a man mentioned several times in the *Russian Primary Chronicle* as one of the Cuman chieftains in the Lower Dnieper region. Together with Tugorkan, another Cuman chieftain named Boniak offered his assistance to Emperor Alexios I Comnenus against the Pechenegs. Both participated in the battle at Levunion, and led a raid through Hungary and Transylvania on their way back to the steppe north of the Lower Danube.

A number of dramatic changes in the material culture of local communities took place within a relatively short period of time between *c.* 1050 and *c.* 1080. These changes are believed to be responsible for what has been dubbed the "Răducăneni culture." When compared to sites of the previous period (ninth to early eleventh century), the distribution of eleventh- to thirteenth-century settlements in Moldavia and the Republic of Moldova shows that in the late eleventh century there was a significant shift in population away from the steppe corridor in the vicinity of the Danube and into the densely forested area of the Central Moldavian Plateau, on both sides of the middle course of the river Prut. These were villages of agriculturists, not temporary camp sites of nomadic pastoralists. Many of them were occupied for almost a century and some have produced agricultural implements. To the same conclusion point the charred seeds of spelt, rye, and wheat that were found in Pohărniceni-Petruha, or of millet found in Hansca and Moleşti (all three sites in the Republic of Moldova).[116] None of the sites in Moldavia was

[116] I. Tentiuc, *Populaţia din Moldova centrală în secolele XI–XIII* [The Eleventh- to Thirteenth-Century Population of Central Moldavia] (Iaşi: Helios, 1996), p. 66. For the Răducăneni culture, see Spinei, *Moldavia*, pp. 63–64.

fortified. However, recent archaeological excavations in Dridu, a site in the steppe-like lowlands of southern Romania known as the Bărăgan, have brought to light the existence of earthworks not different in layout and size from those surrounding the contemporary village of Mrsunjski Lug in Slavonia. Only a few cemeteries have been excavated within the area of the "Răducăneni culture," the largest of which is Hansca–Limbari (Republic of Moldova) with 108 burials dated to the eleventh and twelfth centuries. Much like in Hansca–Căprăria, at Limbari archaeologists found several pits without human remains, but with complete skeletons of domestic animals (a sheep, a pig, and two horses). Grave goods were rare (82 out of 108 burials had no grave goods at all), mostly ceramic pots and spindle whorls, as well as knives, belt buckles and mounts, buttons, and earrings. Five burials contained skeletons with an orientation conspicuously different from that of all other graves within the cemetery. They produced the only weapons and stirrups found on site, an indication of a later date (twelfth or early thirteenth century), but also of the influence of nomadic lifestyles. Further conclusions about links to the culture of the nomads have been drawn on the basis of the forensic examination of several skulls of skeletons found in the cemetery, both male and female. Several of them appear to have been ritually trepanned after death, a practice also attested on tenth-century burial sites in Hungary.[117]

That the population of eleventh-century Moldavia did not live in isolation is also shown by finds of Byzantine glazed ware produced in Constantinople. At Hansca, for example, the ceramic assemblage of practically every sunken-featured building in the eleventh- to thirteenth-century settlement included a few fragments of glazed ware. But clay cauldrons represent the most frequent class of ceramic vessels found on Răducăneni sites and one that was certainly produced locally. On the other hand, contacts with the Byzantine provinces in the Balkans are documented by finds of pectoral crosses, very similar to those identified on military sites in Dobrudja, as well as of amphorae that may have carried wine or olive oil. Equally significant is the relatively large number of eleventh-century

[117] I. G. Hâncu, *Limbar'. Srednevekovyi mogil'nik XII–XIV vekov v Moldavii* [Limbari. A Twelfth- to Fourteenth-Century Cemetery in Moldova] (Kishinew: Shtiinca, 1970).

Byzantine coins, both copper and gold, that have been found in the Lower Danube region. It has been noted that the coin finds in the steppe basically follow the fluctuations of the monetary market in Dobrudja, but a careful examination of their distribution indicates a contrast between coins struck before and after *c.* 1050. Specimens of the first half of the eleventh century appear in Oltenia, on both sides of the river Olt, while very few coins minted after *c.* 1050 have been found in that region. By contrast, late eleventh-century coins have been found in some quantity in the Bărăgan, a region from which no coins of the first half of the century are known. Nonetheless, coins from both periods appear in two clusters of finds in the Central Moldavian Plateau and around the lakes Kahul, Katlabukh, and Ialpukh. The absence from the latter region of any settlement sites that could be safely dated to the second half of the eleventh century suggests that responsible for the presence of at least some of the Byzantine coins found north of the Lower Danube were the nomads. However, no burial assemblage in the region has so far produced any eleventh-century Byzantine coins. It is therefore notoriously difficult to separate early from late eleventh-century assemblages. Archaeologists tend to date relatively earlier male burials with a west–east orientation, which contain horse body parts, and view as comparatively later those burials that display a typical east–west orientation and include whole horse skeletons. Others have noted significant differences in weaponry, with straight short blades for the earlier, and long curved sabers for the later group, respectively. Many burials of the later group have been found in those lowland areas from which the native population seems to have been removed after the middle of the eleventh century. However, it is important to note that there are no significant differences in grave goods either between the two groups or between burials of the same group. There is a sharp contrast between the rich grave goods deposited with both male and female skeletons in the Pecheneg cemetery in Odărci and the modest means of the steppe horsemen buried north of the Lower Danube during the eleventh century. It has been suggested that the large amounts of low value coinage injected into Dobrudja and the neighboring regions of the Empire were meant to facilitate the access of the nomads to commodities of Byzantine origin that may have been available on local markets, and that the Pechenegs were ultimately "bought" before being defeated in battle.[118] In fact, the existing evidence indicates that, while some of Kegen and Tyrach's Pechenegs may have succeeded in accumulating considerable power and wealth, very little, if anything, was redistributed among the nomads remaining north of the Lower Danube.

[118] Stephenson, *Byzantium's Balkan Frontier*, pp. 114–116. See also P. Stephenson, "The Byzantine frontier at the Lower Danube in the late tenth and eleventh centuries," in *Frontiers in Question. Eurasian Borderlands, 700–1700*, ed. by D. Power and N. Standen (New York: St. Martin's Press, 1999), pp. 80–104.

6

THE SECOND BYZANTINE CENTURY (1100–1200)

Throughout the twelfth century, the steppe corridor between the Dnieper and the Danube remained under the control of the Cumans, as part of what Arab and Persian sources called Desht-i Kipchak, the "Cuman Desert."[1] Given the absence of any twelfth-century source for the history of the medieval steppe lands similar to Constantine VII Porphyrogenitus' *De administrando imperio*, the exact disposition and names of the Cuman tribes remain unknown. However, judging from the many references to Polovcians (Russian term for Cumans) in the *Russian Primary Chronicle*, by 1100 or shortly after that, the power in the "Cuman Desert" was in the hands of Cuman chieftains in Right Bank Ukraine. Two of them, Boniak and Togorkan, had offered their military assistance to Emperor Alexios I Comnenus in the war against the Pechenegs. Boniak also led a raid against Hungary, which destroyed in 1099 a Hungarian army under King Coloman near Przemyśl, at that time in the western lands of the Rus' principality of Galicia. However, during the twelfth century, the Cuman tribes in Right and Left Bank Ukraine, respectively, ceased to be under a single leadership and, as a consequence, the Rus' princes of Kiev were capable of driving a wedge at the line of the Dnieper River. Writing

[1] Coined in the eleventh century by the Persian poet Nasir Khusraw, the phrase remained in use in the Islamic world long after the Cumans had been conquered by the Mongols and completely disappeared from written sources. See Abd-Allah ibn-Rizvan, *La chronique des steppes Kiptchak* Tevarih-i Dešt-i Qipčak *du XVIIe siècle (mss. Istanbul, Topkapi Sarayi B. 289)*, ed. by A. Zajaczkowski (Warsaw: Panstwowe Wydawnictwo Naukowe, 1966), p. 13.

in the mid-1100s at the court of the Norman king of Sicily, the Arab geographer al-Idrisi knew that the Dnieper separated the "Black Cumans" from the "White Cumans," but that division illustrates less the true political fragmentation of Cuman power than Idrisi's scholarly approach.[2]

Shortly after Boniak's raid against Hungary, the Cumans made their presence visible in the Lower Danube region. In 1114, they crossed the Danube and devastated the hinterland of Vidin, before being defeated by Emperor Alexios, and pursued through the region north of the Danube River. Niketas Choniates mentions an invasion of the "Scythians" into Thrace, but according to Michael the Syrian, the marauders were Cumans.[3] Emperor John II Comnenus opened negotiations with some of the chiefs, only to make the marauders believe that he was ready to make concessions. The Byzantine troops attacked the "Scythians" by surprise near Stara Zagora (Bulgaria), but the nomads circled their wagons to fight behind them "as though they were walls." However, the Varangian Guard broke through the rampart and "the wagon folk fell by the thousands." Following the defeat, many "Scythians" were settled "in the villages along the western borders of the Roman empire," most likely along the Byzantine frontier with Hungary.[4] Others were recruited as soldiers for the auxiliary troops in Byzantine service. It is possible that the invasion of 1122 was the result of the 1121 expulsion from Rus' of the remnants of the Oghuz and the Pechenegs.[5] This would certainly explain why following his success against the invaders, Emperor John II Comnenus

[2] *Géographie d'Edrisi*, ed. by P.-A. Jaubert, vol. II (Paris: Imprimerie royale, 1840), pp. 400–401. Hungarian chronicles appear to place the Black Cumans in the steppes north of the Black Sea and east of the Carpathian Mountains. These may also be the abodes of the so-called "savage Cumans" mentioned in the Russian chronicles. See Spinei, *Ultimele valuri migratoare*, pp. 125–126; P. B. Golden, "The *Polovcii Dikii*," *Harvard Ukrainian Studies*, vols. 3–4 (1979–1980), 296–309.

[3] According to Choniates' *History*, the invasion took place "in the fifth year of John [II Comnenus'] reign," that is in either 1122 or 1123. See Niketas Choniates, *Historia*, ed. by J. L. van Dieten (Berlin and New York: De Gruyter, 1975), pp. 20–23; English translation by H. J. Magoulias (Detroit: Wayne State University Press, 1984), p. 10. For the marauders as Cumans, see Michael the Syrian, *Chronicon*, ed. by J. B. Chabot (Paris: Ernest Leroux, 1899; reprint Brussels: Culture et Civilisation, 1963), p. 206.

[4] Choniates, *Historia*, English translation by Magoulias, pp. 10–11.

[5] *Ipat'evskaia letopis'*, ed. by A. A. Shakhmatov (St. Petersburg: Tipografiia M. A. Aleksandrova, 1908), p. 8; English translation in L. L. Heinrich, "The Kievan Chronicle: a translation and commentary," Ph.D. dissertation, Vanderbilt University (Nashville, 1978), p. 3.

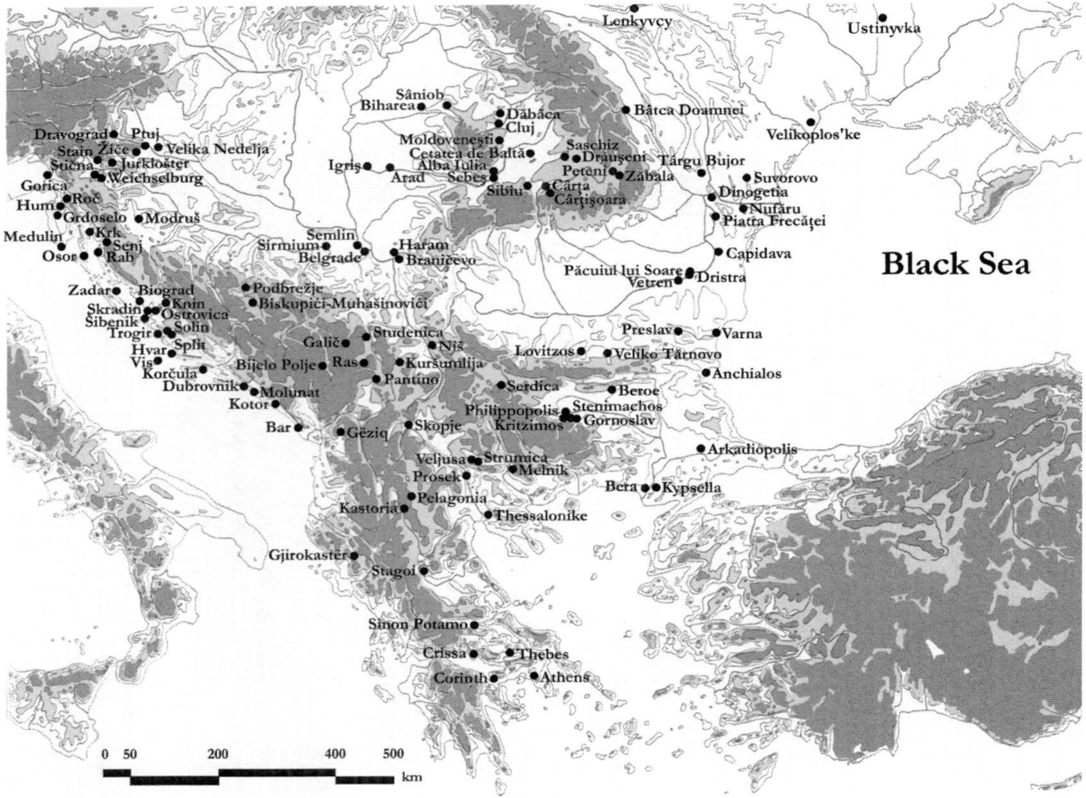

Map 6 Southeastern Europe in the twelfth century.

is said to have instituted a new feast in Constantinople known as the "festival of the Patzinaks" (Pechenegs). If there were indeed Pechenegs among the marauders of 1122 or 1123, then that was their last notable action, for the Pechenegs disappear from the radar of written sources during the second half of the twelfth century. They were mentioned for the last time in relation to events in Rus' in 1169 and appear only episodically in the Balkans as auxiliary troops in Byzantine service attacking or escorting the crusading armies from the West.

The Byzantines seem to have kept the Danube line under firm control, as indicated by the use of ships entering from the Black Sea through the Delta in both 1127 and 1156, during the conflicts with the Hungarians. However, in both cases, the mission of the imperial fleet was to support the land troops engaged in specific campaign operations, not to patrol the Danube in order to prevent its crossing by enemies coming from the other side. No fleet prevented the Cumans returning to the Lower Danube in 1148, although the emperor "directed ships to be brought from Byzantium to the Danube through Anchialos."[6] Like his grandfather Alexios before him, Emperor Manuel Comnenus led a bold counter-attack across the river. John Kinnamos describes the swift progress of the Byzantine cavalry troops moving against the nomads, as the Byzantines reached the camp of the nomad warriors in the vicinity of a mountain called Tenu Ormon, "which extends to the boundaries of Russia."[7] In the ensuing battle, the Byzantines had the upper hand and managed to capture a Cuman chieftain named Lazarus, "a man who had attained the highest degree of valor and was respected by the chiefs among them."[8] Given that while chasing the Cumans across what is

[6] John Kinnamos, *The Deeds of John and Manuel Comnenus*, ed. by A. Meinecke (Bonn: E. Weber, 1836), p. 95; English translation by Ch. M. Brand (New York: Columbia University Press, 1976), p. 76.

[7] John Kinnamos, *Deeds*, English translation by Brand, p. 78. "Tenu Ormon" is a place name of undoubtedly Turkic origin. In an attempt to locate the area in which the Byzantine troops operated in 1148, some have compared Tenu Ormon with Teleorman, the name of equally Turkic origin ("wild woodland") of an administrative district in southern Romania on the left bank of the Danube. See P. Şt. Năsturel, "A propos du Tenou Ormon (Teleorman) de Kinnamos," in *Geographica Byzantina*, ed. by H. Ahrweiller (Paris: Centre de Recherches d'Histoire et Civilisation Byzantines, 1981), pp. 81–91. However, there are no mountains in Teleorman, and no large navigable rivers in that region of Romania.

[8] John Kinnamos, *Deeds*, English translation by Brand, p. 79. Lazarus may have been a paramount chief of all Cuman warriors, but his position was that of a *primus inter pares*, for Kinnamos explicitly refers to several chieftains participating in the raid who were defeated by Manuel's counter-strike.

now southern Romania, the Byzantines had to cross two navigable rivers by rafts, Manuel's counter-attack must have targeted a region in southern Moldavia or eastern Walachia, in which case the two rivers in question may be the Ialomiţa and the Siret. If so, then this was the first time since the days of Emperor Maurice (582–602) that a Byzantine army had moved so deeply into the territory north of the Danube River. It remains unclear whether or not the reason for this attack was to strike at the heart of the Cuman settlement area in the vicinity of the Lower Danube. No settlements are mentioned in Kinnamos' account, which refers exclusively to warriors who had apparently come from afar. How far from the Danube was the Cuman settlement area remains equally unclear. In any case, the main concentration of forces may not have been too far, given that just two years after Manuel's raid into the region north of the river, the Cumans returned and attacked the forts in the Lower Danube region. This time, they managed to defeat the army sent against them, but once again the emperor dispatched troops on the other side of the river. He must have learned by now that the main Cuman forces were far from the Danube, for he sent a fleet into the region north of the Sea of Azov to attack the nomads in their own homeland. It is perhaps from this region that the Cumans launched another raid at some point after 1150, only to withdraw as soon as Manuel moved against them. In 1159, a candidate to the Galician throne, Ivan Rostislavich, "went to the steppe to the Polovcians (Cumans) and, having gone with the Polovcians, halted in the cities around the area of the Danube river." Before his attack on Galicia was repelled by Iaroslav Osmomysl', Ivan is said to have attacked "two ships and taken many goods in them, and did harm to the Galician fishermen," a detail suggesting that the Galician influence may have extended as far as southern Moldavia.[9] On the other hand, the 1100s witnessed a sudden increase in the number of strongholds in Bukovina, which suggests that the military frontier of Galicia was on the upper courses of the Dniester and Prut

[9] *Ipat'evskaia letopis'*, p. 497; English translation by Heinrich, pp. 235–236. The issue of the southern frontiers of Galicia is a controversial one. The old idea of a Galician control of Moldavia and Moldova during the twelfth century, all the way to the Lower Danube, has by now been rejected. See E. Frances, "Les relations russo-byzantines au XIIe siècle et la domination de Galicie au Bas-Danube," *Byzantinoslavica*, vol. 20 (1959), pp. 50–62; N. F. Kotliar, "Galician–Volhynian Rus' and Byzantium in the twelfth–thirteenth centuries: real and imaginary relations," in *Acts. XVIIIth International Congress of Byzantine Studies. Selected Papers*, ed. by I. Ševčenko, G. G. Litavrin, and W. K. Hanak, vol. 1 (Shepherdstown: Byzantine Studies Press, 1996), pp. 319–326.

Rivers. However, many of the strongholds excavated in Bukovina were not just military outposts, but also centers of production for a variety of artifacts, ranging from pottery to weapons, horse gear, and even pectoral crosses. Such crosses, some with Cyrillic inscriptions, began to appear in relatively large numbers on sites in the region of the Central Moldavian Plateau, on both sides of the river Prut, during the last decades of the twelfth century.

There is no mention of Cumans during the 1160s, when both Andronicus, the emperor's rebellious cousin, and Manuel's troops are known to have moved at ease in the region north of the Danube. In 1164, Andronicus had just escaped from prison and was on his way to the court of the Rus' prince of Galicia, Iaroslav Osmomysl' (1153–1187). However, after crossing the Danube, he was intercepted not by Cumans, but by Vlachs, who "had heard rumors of his escape." As Andronicus is specifically said to have reached the borders of Galicia, the Vlachs in question may have been located somewhere in present-day Moldavia.[10] Two years later, Emperor Manuel launched a combined attack on Hungary, with an expeditionary corps crossing the Danube from "the regions near the so-called Euxine Sea" (Dobrudja) in order to reach Transylvania through the passes across the Transylvanian Alps. The corps led by Leo Vatatzes is said to have included a large number of Vlach recruits, most likely from the eastern regions of the Balkans.[11] But the Byzantine forces encountered no Cuman warriors on their way to and from Transylvania. A second expedition led by John Dukas attacked from "someplace higher up the Hungarians who live near Russia." Unlike Leo Vatatzes, who seems to have moved from Dobrudja across the mountains into Transylvania (perhaps along the Buzău valley and through the Buzău pass), Dukas' troops first marched along one of the main rivers in

[10] Choniates, *Historia*, p. 171; English translation by Magoulias, p. 74. The Vlachs returned Andronicus to the emperor, perhaps in exchange for a handsome retribution for their services. For this episode, see Spinei, *Moldavia*, p. 56.

[11] John Kinnamos, *Deeds*, p. 260; English translation by Brand, p. 195. See P. Şt. Năsturel, "Valaques, Coumans et Byzantins sous le règne de Manuel Comnène," *Byzantina*, vol. 1 (1969), pp. 167–186. It may be that one reason for the noticeable number of Vlach recruits was the need to rely on their ability to communicate with other Vlachs that may have lived within the region north of the Danube River or in Transylvania. See G. G. Litavrin, "Vlakhi vizantiiskikh istochnikov X–XIII vv. [The Vlachs of the Byzantine sources, tenth to thirteenth century]," in *Iugo-Vostochnaia Evropa v srednie veka. Sbornik statei*, ed. by I. S. Grosul, vol. 1 (Kishinew: Shtiinca, 1972), p. 102.

Moldavia (perhaps Siret), before crossing the Carpathians through some other, more northerly pass, possibly Oituz. Before entering Transylvania, the Byzantine troops "passed through some wearisome and rugged regions," "a land entirely bereft of men."[12] Again, there is no mention of a Cuman presence in the region.

Nevertheless, there were many Cumans north of the Danube during the last two decades of the century, as when attacked by Emperor Isaac in 1186, the two Vlach rebels, Peter and Asen, fled across the Danube into Walachia, only to return with Cuman military assistance. In 1199, both Vlachs and Cumans are mentioned crossing the Danube from north to south in order to plunder Thrace.[13] In 1200, another Cuman raid led to the destruction of Dinogetia. Against the Cumans, emperor Alexios III asked for assistance from Roman Mstislavich of Volhynia. The Volhynian prince had meanwhile incorporated Galicia into his realm and was eager to respond to Alexios' request. He attacked the Cumans twice, first in 1201/2 and then in 1203/4, before being himself attacked by the deposed Kievan prince Riurik Rostislavich and his Cuman allies, the chieftains Köten and Somogur.[14] When Roman died while campaigning in Poland, his successors were unable to maintain a Volhynian hold on the south-western part of Galicia, which was occupied by Andrew II of Hungary in 1205, when he assumed the title of "King of Galicia and Lodomeria." Although initially no more than assistance for one of the candidates to the Galician throne, the Hungarian king's action in fact opened the first phase of the thirteenth-century Hungarian expansion across the Carpathian Mountains. To control access to Transylvania from the lands neighboring the southernmost Galician territories, the Hungarians built a fort at Bâtca Doamnei (near Piatra Neamţ, Romania) on the Bistriţa River. Coins struck for the late twelfth-century Hungarian kings have been found on that site, as well as within the more northerly stronghold at Lenkyvcy (near Chernyvcy, Ukraine) on the Upper Prut River, where a Hungarian garrison may have been established shortly after 1205.

[12] John Kinnamos, *Deeds*, p. 261; English translation by Brand, p. 196.

[13] Choniates, *Historia*, p. 663; English translation by Magoulias, p. 275. The Vlachs in question were certainly from the region north of the river, not Balkan Vlachs.

[14] Choniates, *Historia*, p. 691; English translation by Magoulias, p. 287. Roman had occupied Kiev in 1199 and had battled the Cumans both as allies of Riurik Rostislavich and as traditional enemies of Kiev. See Martin, *Medieval Russia*, p. 119.

On the other hand, the archaeological evidence suggests that in the 1100s many settlements in what is now southern and eastern Romania, as well as Moldova, diminished in size or altogether disappeared. At Hansca, out of fifty-five huts excavated, only fifteen have been dated on the basis of the associated artifacts to the twelfth or early thirteenth century.[15] No twelfth-century settlements have so far been found in the steppe lands in eastern Walachia and north of the Danube Delta. Moreover, it has been suggested that the presence of the Cumans in the steppe corridor may have caused the abandonment of some of the settlements that had previously existed on the border between the steppe and the forest-steppe belts in the Central Moldavian Plateau. Among settlements beyond that border, none was totally excavated to permit any conclusions as to changes possibly taking place during the twelfth century in local communities as a result of the presence of the Cuman warriors in the steppe. Twelfth-century horseman burials cluster in the steppe north of the Danube Delta or in the hilly region in southern Moldavia in close proximity to the river. In their appearance and associated grave goods, they are remarkably different from those in Left Bank Ukraine. There is to date nothing comparable to the extraordinarily rich chieftain burial excavated in 1981 in Chingul near Zaporizhzhia, with its exquisitely decorated artifacts of Middle Eastern, Rus', and Western origin.[16] The only possible analogy is between the helmet of the Chingul chieftain and that from a horseman burial accidentally found in a suburb of Târgu Bujor (near Galaţi, in Romania), which also produced fragments of a mail coat similar to that from Chingul.[17] But in all other aspects, the Târgu Bujor burial assemblage is only a pale imitation of lavishly furnished graves in the Lower Dnieper region. The closest one can come to a rich horseman burial in the steppes north of the Black Sea is the grave found in the 1970s in a prehistoric mound in Suvorovo, near Izmail (Ukraine), which produced thirteen coins struck for the Byzantine emperors Manuel Comnenus, Andronicus I, and Isaac II Angelos. Coins of Isaac II Angelos have also been found in burial mounds excavated in Velikoploskoe near Odessa and Ustinovka near

[15] Tentiuc, *Populaţia din Moldova*, p. 35.

[16] V. V. Otroshchenko and I. I. Rassamakin, "Der Polovzer-Khan aus dem Čingul'-Kurgan," in *Gold der Steppe. Archäologie der Ukraine*, ed. by R. Rolle, M. Müller-Wille, and K. Schietzel (Neumünster: Karl Wachholtz, 1991), pp. 269–271.

[17] Spinei, *Realităţi etnice*, p. 114. Another parallel may be established between the sabers found with both burial assemblages.

Kirovohrad (Ukraine). In addition, the Lower Danube region produced a number of hoards of twelfth-century Byzantine coins, with closing coins struck for Manuel, Isaac II Angelos, and Alexios III Angelos. No twelfth-century hoards and no Byzantine coins have so far been found beyond the Inhulec and Lower Dnieper Rivers. As for the steppe north and northwest of the Black Sea, contacts with the Byzantine world seem to have been established not only across the Danube frontier of the Empire, but also via Crimea. During the first half of the century, there is a noticeable increase in imports from Crimea, best illustrated, among other things, by amphorae produced in Crimea and cast coins issued by one or several mints in Chersonesus.

TWELFTH-CENTURY BYZANTIUM IN THE BALKANS

The absence of any clear indication of links between the territories north of the Lower Danube and the Byzantine provinces adjacent to that river may be explained in terms of the considerable contraction of the Byzantine military sites. This is particularly true of Dobrudja. Capidava and Beroe (Piatra Frecăţei near Brăila) had already been abandoned by the mid-eleventh century. Păcuiul lui Soare was abandoned a little later and the site remained unoccupied throughout the entire twelfth century. Dinogetia and Nufăru were destroyed at some point in the early twelfth century, perhaps during the Cuman invasions of 1114 or 1122. But the fort at Dinogetia was restored and reoccupied, as indicated by finds of Fine Sgraffito ware as well as the seal of a metropolitan Michael of Rus' who seems to have been in contact with some Byzantine authority in Dinogetia. Dinogetia was again destroyed around 1200, subsequently lost entirely its military significance, and was eventually abandoned. Nufăru seems to have been rebuilt during the first years of Emperor Manuel's reign (1143–1180), a period for which there is a substantial increase in the number of coins found on that site. However, the new settlement was much smaller than the previous one and seems to have existed only for a short while. Isaccea was also devastated by the Cuman attacks of the mid-twelfth century, and like Nufăru was restored from ground up. During the second half of the twelfth century, Isaccea seems to have become the most important military base in the region, as suggested by a number of seals found on that site: a seal of Emperor Isaac II Angelos (1185–1195) and another of John Vatatzes, the commander of the imperial guard under Manuel (1143–1180). By contrast, the twelfth-century site at Nufăru produced no seals of military or political leaders. It has been suggested that the rapid decline of Nufăru and the parallel rise of Vicina (a town mentioned in several written sources, beginning with Anna Comnena and Idrisi, but not yet identified[18]) may have something to do with the gradual abandoning of the St. George arm of the Danube Delta in favor of the Kilia arm, which became the most important axis of trade in the Lower Danube and Black Sea area after *c.* 1200. But similar phenomena of contraction and site abandonment have also been noticed elsewhere.

Not much is known about twelfth-century Dristra (Silistra), except that the episcopal church continued to be used. Dristra seems to have retained some military importance in the region and maintained contact with the capital, as suggested, among other things, by the discovery of a seal of Alexander, Count of Gravina, a Norman exile at Emperor Manuel's court in Constantinople. However, major forts in the vicinity, such as Vetren (some twelve miles west of Dristra), were completely abandoned during the twelfth century. At Preslav, there are very few coins dated to the first half of the twelfth century, and only a slight increase has been noticed for the second half of that century. It has been suggested that Preslav served as the first capital to Peter, one the two Vlach rebels of the late twelfth century (see below).[19] If so, this may well explain the fact that by 1200, the political center of the new empire moved westwards to the Carevec Hill in present-day Veliko Tărnovo, as Preslav had very little to offer to an expanding court and a growing state apparatus. By contrast, the growth of the settlement on the Carevec Hill began during the reign of Manuel I, when a number of large churches were erected, one of which was rebuilt in the 1200s and incorporated into a large palatial compound. By that time, a monastery dedicated to the Forty Holy Martyrs had already been established on the Yantra River not far from the residential core on the Carevec Hill. During the second

[18] Vicina has been identified with the Byzantine site at Nufăru, but the chronology of that site's occupation does not match the evidence of the written sources mentioning Vicina, according to which the site grew in importance as soon as the Kilia branch of the Danube Delta became the most important trade artery in the Lower Danube region. See G. Atanasov, "La Vicina médiévale et la forteresse de Nufăru," *EB*, vol. 30 (1994), pp. 109–128.

[19] Zh. Zhekova, "Za Preslav sled văstanieto na Asenevci [Preslav after the Assenid uprising]," *Preslav. Sbornik*, vol. 6 (2004), pp. 344–349.

half of the twelfth century, Tărnovo became an important industrial center, with a number of smithies, shops of stone-cutting, production of lead and copper artifacts, and kilns. Some of these facilities seem to have produced for the army at a time of intense military engagement in the central and northern regions of the Balkans, during Manuel's wars with Hungary. However, the production of other workshops was clearly geared towards local demand. Moreover, the center for copper manufacturing found in the southeastern section of the Carevec Hill produced a number of copper flans ready to be sent to a local or neighboring mint, which is still to be identified. The settlement grew rapidly, with a new residential district established at the foot of the Momina Krepost Hill, which also included smithies and kilns for the production of domestic wares. That all this building activity must be dated to the second half of the century is indicated by the large number of coins found on the site that had been struck for Emperor Manuel (1143–1180).

There are more signs of prosperity and growth on the other side of the Stara Planina range of mountains, in Thrace. With few exceptions, most twelfth-century hoards of Byzantine gold have been found in that region. While their small size suggests that some may be nothing more than personal savings of officers in the Byzantine army, Thrace also produced the largest twelfth-century hoard of gold coins known so far for the entire Empire. The 786 *hyperpera nomismata*, the standard, highest-quality and highest-value coins accidentally found in a copper jug in Gornoslav near Plovdiv, have been interpreted as the amount collected for annual payments of the neighboring monastery of Petritzonitissa (Bachkovo) established in the late eleventh century by Gregory Pakourianos (see chapter 5).[20] Ever since the late eleventh century, Philippopolis had become the metropolis of the central Balkans, a city that grew considerably during the twelfth century, as indicated by recent archaeological excavations in present-day Plovdiv. In 1097, the army of Godfrey of Bouillon, the duke of Lower Lorraine and one of the most important leaders of the First Crusade, remained in the city for eight days, in itself an indication that Philippopolis had the appropriate resources to meet the demands

[20] M. F. Hendy, "The Gornoslav hoard, the emperor Frederick I and the monastery of Bachkovo," in *Studies in Numismatical Method Presented to Philip Grierson*, ed. by C. N. L. Brooke, I. Stewart, J. G. Pollard, and T. R. Volk (Cambridge: Cambridge University Press, 1983), pp. 179–191.

of the crusading army. According to Albert of Aachen, Bohemond of Taranto had even advised Godfrey to establish himself in Philippopolis in preparation for a combined attack against Emperor Alexios I.[21] Philippopolis was also an important marketplace in the region. In February 1100, the crusaders from Lombardy were allowed to purchase food there. That they also engaged in plundering both houses and churches within the city further demonstrates that there was considerable wealth within the city walls. In 1147, Emperor Conrad's army camped just outside Philippopolis. The residential quarter outside the city walls is also mentioned by Odo of Deuil, the chronicler of King Louis VII's expedition, as the "Latin quarter (*burgus*)," an indication that it was perhaps fortified. The Latin quarter appears to have come into existence shortly after the passing of the First Crusade through the Balkans, as a consequence of the growing importance of the marketplace in Philippopolis. At any rate, the Latin quarter outside the city served as a temporary camp to Conrad's army and it is certainly there that King Louis VII was later met by the clergy and the inhabitants of the city.[22] Although not mentioned by name, responsible for the warm reception of the French king must have been the bishop of Philippopolis, Michael Italikos, who had already befriended Emperor Conrad.[23] The Latin quarter in Philippopolis acquired a special significance for the French crusaders, as Alvis, Bishop of Artois, died in that city and was buried in front of the altar of a certain Church of St. George, which seems to have been the most important outside the city walls.[24] The Latin quarter was

21 Albert of Aachen, *Historia Hierosolymitana*, p. 309.

22 Odo of Deuil, *Liber de via sancti sepulchri*, ed. by G. Waitz (Hanover: Hahnsche Buchhandlung, 1882; reprint 1975), MGH SS 26:65.

23 Choniates, *Historia*, pp. 62–63; English translation by Magoulias, pp. 36–37.

24 The Church of St. George was located on the site of the present-day Armenian Church of Surp Kevork, on the northwestern slope of the Nebet tepe Hill in Plovdiv. See A. Dancheva-Vasileva, "Plovdiv à l'époque des premières Croisades (1097, 1147, 1189)," *BHR*, vol. 26 (1998), pp. 20–23. In 1185, the person chosen to lead the embassy that the *katholikos* of the Armenian Church, Gregory IV Dega (1173–1193), sent to Rome was Gregory, the Armenian bishop of Philippopolis. For the archaeology of twelfth-century Philippopolis, see I. Dzhambov, Zh. Tankova, and Kh. Dzhambov, "Srednovekovniiat Plovdiv i prinosăt mu v kulturno-istoricheskoto nasledstvo na Vizantiia i Bălgariia XI–XIV v. [Medieval Plovdiv and its contribution in the cultural–historical heritage of Byzantium and Bulgaria between the eleventh and the fourteenth century]," in *Mezhdunarodna konferenciia "Vizantiiskoto kulturno nasledstvo i Balkanite". Plovdiv, 6–8 septemvri 2001. Sbornik dokladi*, ed. by G. Bakalov and I. Dzhambov (Plovdiv: Iuri Gagarin BT, 2001), pp. 32–42.

also used by the crusading army of Emperor Frederick I Barbarossa, who arrived in Philippopolis on August 24, 1189. Niketas Choniates, who was the governor of the city at that time, had received orders from Emperor Isaac II Angelos to repair the city walls, but was soon instructed to demolish them, in order to prevent the crusaders from using the defenses against the Byzantines.[25] Indeed, unlike Conrad and Louis VII, Frederick I quickly moved into the city, which had meanwhile been abandoned by its inhabitants. While the crusaders remained in Philippopolis for twelve weeks, they took a number of neighboring forts, including Beroe (Stara Zagora), and systematically pillaged the surrounding countryside. There was an abundance of animals that the crusaders found in the hinterland of Philippopolis, an indication of the relative prosperity of the region.[26] It is therefore no surprise that following the 1204 conquest of Constantinople by participants in the Fourth Crusade, that region became one of the first fiefs carved out of the former Byzantine provinces in the Balkans and granted to Renier de Trith, Duke of Philippopolis.

Throughout the twelfth century, Macedonia appears to have been equally prosperous. Much like in Thrace, the origin of this relative wealth was primarily agricultural. Although twelfth-century documents are particularly rare in the archives at Mount Athos, the evidence that exists suggests that by 1100 all free village communities in existence in the region during the tenth and eleventh centuries had disappeared, as they were replaced by estates, first of the fisc, later ceded either to monasteries or to laypersons. Some of the landowners in the region were members of the imperial family. Such was the case of Alexios Comnenus, son of Theodora Comnena, Emperor Alexios I's daughter, who founded the Church of St. Panteleimon at Nerezi near Skopje, which contains some of the finest frescoes of twelfth-century Byzantine art.

Alexios' foundation in Nerezi may be compared to the Monastery of the Mother of God *Kosmosoteira* near Vera (now Ferrai near Alexandroupolis, on the Greek–Turkish border), which was founded by Isaac Comnenus, the brother of Emperor John II (1118–1143). Like Alexios, Isaac owned large estates in the region, which he listed in the foundation charter for his monastery: Neokastron "with its dependent peasants settled both inside and outside"; "the two

[25] Choniates, *Historia*, p. 402; English translation by Magoulias, p. 221.

[26] *Historia peregrinorum*, ed. by A. Chroust (Hanover: Hahnsche Buchhandlung, 1928; reprint 1989), MGH SS rer. Germ. 5:41.

military villages Tou Dilianou and Dragavasta"; "the market Sagoudaous, with the dependent peasants and residents settled in it, with its ships [. . .] and its warehouses"; as well as farms "outside Traianoupolis."[27] In good rhetorical tradition, the region in which Isaac placed his monastery is said to have been "devoid of men and houses, [the haunt] only of snakes and scorpions," and "formerly nothing but thickets." However, elsewhere in the charter Isaac describes the surrounding region as an "immense plain," and talks of "the panoramic view, especially in summertime, of corn in flower and in ear, which impresses great gladness on those who direct their gaze there."[28] In other words, Isaac's foundation was placed in a middle of a prosperous agricultural region of southern Thrace. Most of the estates enumerated were Isaac's "immovable properties" that had come to him "from family inheritance through imperial decrees and commands"; others had been bought at various moments in time.

But foundation of churches was not restricted to members of the high aristocracy. In Macedonia, as well as elsewhere in the Empire, smaller churches were erected by members of prominent families in the region. Near Kastoria (south of Florina, in Greek Macedonia), local potentates erected family chapels, such as the famous St. Nicholas tou Kasnitze built in the mid-twelfth century by a certain Nicholas Kasnitzes sporting the court title of *magistros*. Local elites may have also paid for the building and the decoration of small churches in the environs of present-day Gjirokastër (Albania). Despite the presence of the Byzantine governor of the city, twelfth-century Dyrrachion was in fact under the control of local powerful families, some members of which were *archontes* with apparently more power than the governor himself. One of them, named Romanus, alienated his fellow citizens to the point of causing the surrender of the city to the Normans in 1185.[29] Local potentates were also visible in the hinterland of the city. An *archon* named Progon appears together with

[27] Typikon *of the* Sebastokrator *Isaac Komnenos for the Monastery of the Mother of God* Kosmosoteira *near Vera* 69, English translation by N. P. Ševčenko in *Byzantine Monastic Foundation Documents. A Complete Translation of the Surviving Founders'* Typika *and Testaments*, ed. by J. Thomas and A. C. Hero (Washington: Dumbarton Oaks Research Library and Collection, 2000), pp. 828–829.

[28] Typikon *of the* Sebastokrator *Isaac Komnenos* 1, 2, and 74, pp. 798, 799, and 833.

[29] Eustathios of Thessalonike, *The Capture of Thessalonike*, ed. and transl. by J. R. Melville Jones (Canberra: Australian Association for Byzantine Studies, 1988), pp. 65 and 194.

his sons Demetrius and Gjin in an inscription from the Monastery of St. Mary in Trifandina in Gëziq (near Gjegjan, northern Albania).[30] On the other hand, the evidence suggests the existence of a growing class of peasants who had been settled on state or church land. By the mid-twelfth century, the twelve landless peasants that had been allowed by imperial decree to settle on the property of the Monastery of the Mother of God of Mercy in Veljusa had become *zeugaratoi*, that is peasants holding each a piece of land that could be cultivated with a pair of oxen. All were otherwise dependent peasants owing dues and services to the monastery. Equally well endowed were some of the bishoprics in Greece. An imperial decree of 1163 established the assets of the bishop of Stagoi (modern Kalavaka, in Thessaly) to 1,000 *modioi* of land and 46 peasant families settled there, in addition to mills on the neighboring river Salavria.

The agricultural growth taking place in the central and southern Balkan provinces of the Empire was responsible for a remarkable urban growth. When visiting the city in 1165, Benjamin of Tudela, a Jewish traveler from Spain, described Thessalonica as "a very large city, with about 500 Jews," who "lived by silk-weaving."[31] The city had a six-day long fair on St. Demetrius' feast day in October, which was attended by Italian merchants. The cult of the saint was controlled by a confraternity of local potentates, many of whom owned estates in the environs, as well as dwellings, shops, and workshops in the city, which they often rented out. The land register of Thebes also testifies to the existence of a powerful land aristocracy owning estates around a very prosperous city. Although the silk and the silk producers had been removed by the Normans in 1147, the raid had little, if any, impact on production. Less than twenty years later, Benjamin of Tudela visited Thebes and described the city as large, with a considerable community of Jews, many of whom were prominent manufacturers of silk and purple cloth. But he also knew of Jews who cultivated their own fields, such as the 200-strong community in Crissa, on the southern slope of Mount Parnassos, near

[30] D. S. Shuteriqi, "Një mbishkrim i Arbërit (1190–1216) [Inscriptions from Albania (1190–1216)]," *Studime Historike*, vol. 3 (1967), p. 155.

[31] *The Itinerary of Benjamin of Tudela. Travels in the Middle Ages*, translated by M. N. Adler (Malibu: J. Simon, 1987), p. 69. Thessalonica also appears as a large city on Idrisi's map of 1154. See *Géographie d'Edrisi*, p. 296.

modern-day Dhestina.[32] In Thebes, the Jews had their own residential quarter on the northwestern side, in modern Evraika. No silk-production workshops have so far been identified by archaeological means, but a workshop was found not far from the Jewish quarter, near the Dirke stream, and may have been connected with the production of silk. Within the same area, dye shops were found which utilized a sophisticated system of underground pipes hewn from the limestone to bring water into the manufactory. During the twelfth century, Thebes had "exceedingly fine water" due to the efforts of the city's metropolitan, John Kaloktenes, who paid for the building of an aqueduct to bring water from the hills on the southern side of the city.[33]

Like Thebes, Corinth was sacked by the Normans in 1147, but it survived and continued to flourish during the second half of the century, as attested by Idrisi's description of 1154.[34] By that time, the city may have had between 15,000 and 20,000 inhabitants. The Corinthian market was abundant in low-cost goods, such as foodstuffs, as indicated by the remarkably large number of twelfth-century low denomination coins found on the site, and the rarity of gold or silver coins either in hoard or in stray finds. According to Niketas Choniates, the city had two harbors and a marketplace below the citadel on the Acrocorinth. Corinth was visited by many Westerners, both before and after the Norman attack of 1147. One of them must have been the pilgrim en route to the Holy Land who lost a purse containing nine coins from Valence and five from Lucca. During the reign of John II (1118–1143), the number of Westerners in Greece increased considerably, as more and more Venetians became involved in local trade. Initially, the Venetians

[32] *Itinerary of Benjamin of Tudela*, p. 68. Benjamin had certainly met the Jews of Crissa, for he mentions the names of three rabbis at the head of the local community. For the land-ownership register of Thebes, see N. Svoronos, "Recherches sur le cadastre byzantin et la fiscalité aux XIe et XIIe siècles: le cadastre de Thèbes," *Bulletin de Correspondance Hellénique*, vol. 83 (1959), pp. 1–166.

[33] V. Th. Delvenakiotes, *Ho metropolites Ioannes ho Kaloktenes kai hai Thebai, 12 m. Ch. aion* [The Metropolitan John Kaloktenes and Thebes during the Twelfth Century] (Athens: n.p., 1970), pp. 72–73. See also A. Louvi-Kizi, "Thebes," in *The Economic History of Byzantium from the Seventh through the Fifteenth Century*, ed. by A. E. Laiou (Washington: Dumbarton Oaks Research Library and Collection, 2002), pp. 634 and 637.

[34] *Géographie d'Edrisi*, pp. 122–126.

worked through middlemen, but after the middle of the century they seem to have increased their direct participation. Between 1165 and 1171, an agent of the Venetian merchant Romano Mairano almost monopolized the Venetian share of the oil market in Corinth. The city may have also been a production center for Fine Sgraffito ware, which is found in significant quantities on most twelfth-century sites in the Balkans, as well as in Italy. Wasters of Fine Sgraffito ware have been found in Corinth, and a kiln underneath the Monastery of St. John produced twelfth-century glazed and unglazed wares.

Like Thebes and Corinth, Athens was a prosperous city during the first half of the twelfth century. It was during this period of time that densely built residential quarters appeared on the site of the ancient Agora, on the southern slopes of the Areopagus, on the southern side of the Acropolis, and north of the ruined Temple of Zeus. Since houses built in stone bonded with clay, with storage jars in the basement, seem to have belonged to low- and middle-class inhabitants of the city, it remains unknown where the Athenian aristocrats lived in the 1100s. But the *archontes* of Athens were undoubtedly present and powerful in the late twelfth century, when the city's metropolitan, Michael Choniates, asked for the emperor's intervention to prevent them from acquiring peasant lands. Heavy taxation and corruption, as well as a certain willingness to connive at local power were responsible for a rapid decline of Athens during that period. Choniates, the last Orthodox bishop before the Latin conquest, described Athens as a small, impoverished town at the mercy of tax collectors and Saracen pirates, in which many previously inhabited areas had been turned into farmland. However, the description must not be taken at face value. Under Emperor Alexios III Angelos (1195–1203), the *praitor* of the theme of Hellas could still descend upon Athens, demanding to be entertained together with his train. His staff raised ship money along with the Grand Duke's agents and the local *archontes*. Shortly before the Latin conquest, the power of the local rulers increased considerably, as illustrated by the case of Leo Sgouros. He had inherited from his father the control over Nauplion and he took advantage of the rapid decline of the local administration during the reign of Isaac II and Alexios III Angelos to extend his authority over Corinth and Argos, most likely with local backing.

THE BYZANTINE–HUNGARIAN WARS AND THE RISE OF SERBIA

The gradual evanescence of the Byzantine power in the northeastern region of the Balkans is in sharp contrast with its increasing presence at the opposite end of the Danube frontier, in the northern part of present-day Serbia. Throughout much of the twelfth century, this was the area of almost permanent military confrontation between the Empire and the Hungarian kingdom. South of the river Danube, the Serbs were the most important allies of the Hungarian king. Shortly after his victory over the Pechenegs in 1122, Emperor John II organized a punitive expedition against them. The exact reason for that is unknown, but it is most likely at this time that the Byzantine border fort at Ras (Gradina), which had been erected during Alexios I's reign, was burned. The heavy destruction layer identified by archaeologists within the ramparts and inside the four log-houses excavated there has been coin-dated to the reign of John II.[35] Despite the fact that the Byzantine army devastated the region around Ras and took a great number of prisoners that would later be settled in Asia Minor, the ties between the Serbian *zhupans* and Hungary were not weakened. The appearance of the name Uroš among the Serbian elite during this period is attributed to Hungarian influence. The daughter of the first *zhupan* named Uroš became Queen of Hungary in 1131, when the crown passed to her husband, Béla II.[36]

According to Niketas Choniates, Béla's father Álmos "had fled to the emperor (John II) and had been warmly received."[37] In response, the ruling Hungarian king, Stephen II (1116–1131), launched a punitive expedition against the Byzantine garrisons on the Danube. At Braničevo, the Hungarians are said to have torn down the walls, the stones of which they transported to the neighboring Hungarian fort at Semlin (now Zemun, west of Belgrade). But the Hungarian raids pushed deep into the Balkans, as far south as Serdica. Emperor John II took some time to organize an efficient reaction. He first ordered a fleet to move from the Black Sea into the Danube Delta and upstream

[35] Popović, *Tvrđava Ras*, p. 404. Following the victory over both Serbs and Hungarians, the fort was rebuilt with five log-houses and a rectangular building with walls coated with water-resistant plaster, most likely a granary.

[36] Ćirković, *Serbs*, p. 30. For Uroš I (*c.* 1113–*c.* 1131), see the *Chronicle of the Priest of Dioclea* 45, p. 102.

[37] Choniates, *Historia*, p. 17; English translation by Magoulias, p. 11.

to the confluence of the river with the Morava. The Byzantine troops took back Braničevo, in which the emperor left a strong garrison. Then the emperor crossed the Danube into Hungarian territory and the Byzantine cavalry obtained a great victory against the Hungarians in the region north of Sirmium known as Frangochorion (now Fruška Gora). Two Hungarian fortresses, Semlin/Zemun and Haram (Nova Palanka, across the Danube from Braničevo), were also stormed and sacked. No source mentions the reconstruction of the fort at Braničevo, but the archaeological evidence points to an expansion outside the ramparts of the twelfth-century settlement. Seven houses attributed to this phase show that the fort was manned by soldiers who lived together with their families, as indicated by the accompanying artifacts, such as bracelets with widened ends and earrings with filigree decoration. To the same phase belongs a pectoral cross with a Greek inscription, as well as ceramic material brought from the south, such as Fine Sgraffito wares.

Despite Emperor John II's force demonstration, the Hungarian presence in the central Balkans, perhaps mediated by the Serbian *zhupan* Uroš I, became even more visible. Under the joint rule of King Béla II and Helena, Uroš's daughter, a Hungarian army first entered Bosnia in 1137. Béla's son, Géza II (1141–1162), allied himself with Uroš II and attacked the Byzantine forts on the eastern border of what was increasingly known in the twelfth century as Raška, "the province of Ras."[38] It is during this period that the newly restored fort at Ras (Gradina) was again destroyed. Emperor Manuel's punitive expedition reached and took Galič, one of the most important strongholds in the heartland of the Serbian territory. The prisoners the Byzantines took during this expedition were later resettled near Serdica and elsewhere in the Empire. However, the expedition of 1149 does not seem to have removed Uroš from the Hungarian alliance. In 1150 the Byzantines intercepted the Hungarian troops King Géza II had sent to assist Uroš, and those who escaped moved south along the Morava River to reach their Serbian allies. After pitching his camp at Sečanica, not far from Niš, Emperor Manuel defeated the Serbs and some of their Hungarian allies on the Tara River in western Serbia. At the peace, the *zhupan* was forced to promise he would send 500 warriors for Manuel's wars in Asia Minor and 2,000 for his wars in

[38] Theodore Prodromos, *Historical Poems*, ed. by W. Hörandner (Vienna: Verlag der Österreichischen Akademie der Wissenschaften, 1974), p. 354.

Europe. The emperor returned to the Danube region to attack Sirmium and to punish King Géza for his alliance with Uroš.[39] For a second time within a relatively short period of time, the Byzantine troops crossed the Danube and devastated Frangochorion, a region from which they took a great number of prisoners. Once the Byzantine troops withdrew south of the Danube, Géza began preparing a counter-attack, but Manuel's swift move to the north thwarted him from proceeding to attack the Byzantine territory. Moreover, Manuel dispatched troops under the command of a Hungarian claimant to the throne, Boris, the son of Coloman, to raid repeatedly the Hungarian territory in order to provoke the Hungarian king to engage in a pitched battle. In April 1151, King Géza sued for peace and some 10,000 of the prisoners taken by Manuel's troops from Frangochorion returned home.[40] But two years later, most likely at the instigation of the Norman king Roger II, Géza reopened the conflict by attacking the Byzantine forts on the Danube. However, before Manuel could move to the frontier, King Géza dispatched envoys to Serdica and sued for peace, an indication that the entire operation may have been nothing more than a diversion to release some of the pressure Roger II was feeling at that time in Italy.

While in Pelagonia (Bitolj, in Macedonia) in 1153, the emperor appointed his cousin, Andronicus, as Duke of Niš and Braničevo. Andronicus immediately allied himself with Géza, to whom he promised he would cede the entire region under his authority, provided that the Hungarian king would assist him in overthrowing Manuel. But Andronicus failed to assassinate the emperor during a hunting party near Pelagonia, in the fall of 1154. He was captured and thrown into prison.[41] In the meantime, Géza began besieging Braničevo with Czech and Saxon troops on his side, but at the news

[39] For the chronology of these events from Kinnamos' narrative (*Deeds of John and Manuel Comnenus*, pp. 100, 105, 113–114, 118–121, 124, 130–131, and 133–134), see P. Stephenson, "Manuel I Comnenus and Geza II: a revised context and chronology for Hungaro-Byzantine relations, 1148–1155," *Byzantinoslavica*, vol. 55 (1994), pp. 257–263. For Sečanica and Tara, a small river near present-day Valjevo, see M. Blagojević, "Sečenica (Setzenica), Strymon (Strymon) i Tara (Tara) u delu Jovana Kinama [Sečenica (Setzenica), Strymon (Strymon) and Tara (Tara) in John Kinnamos' work]," *ZRVI*, vol. 17 (1974), pp. 65–76; R. Novaković, "Još nešto povodom bitke na Tari 1150. godine [One more time on the battle of the Tara River, 1150]," *Istorijski časopis*, vols. 25–26 (1978–1979), pp. 5–28.

[40] John Kinnamos, *Deeds of John and Manuel Comnenus*, p. 120; Stephenson, "Manuel I Comnenus and Geza II," p. 264.

[41] John Kinnamos, *Deeds of John and Manuel Comnenus*, p. 127.

of Manuel's arrival, his forces withdrew immediately. A number of Byzantine troops under Basil Tzintziloukes attacked the withdrawing Hungarians, but were defeated in the process. Neither Géza, nor Manuel, who remained in Beroe (Stara Zagora), had any intention of pursuing the limited successes they had obtained. Meanwhile, the emperor intervened in the dynastic affairs in Raška, where he restored to power Uroš II, who had been deposed by his brother Desa, perhaps with Hungarian assistance. Desa was the ruler of "the region of Dendra, a prosperous and populous area near Niš,"[42] but following the arbitration, he was granted Zeta and Travounia on the Dalmatian coast, most likely in an attempt to keep in check Radoslav, the ruler of the Byzantine client state of Duklja.[43] Manuel also established the border between the territories controlled by Uroš II and his brother Desa.

Following the war with Hungary and the intervention in Raška, Manuel began to restore and rebuild many of the Byzantine strongholds on the Danube frontier. In the late 1150s, a new fortress was built in Belgrade in the northwestern corner of the steep hill above the Danube. Outside its ramparts and at the foot of the cliff, on the river bank, Serbian archaeologists identified a civilian settlement which produced large quantities of locally manufactured pottery, in addition to imported wares, such as Fine Sgraffito. The fort itself was built of drystone with double layers of brick to reinforce the structure, a technique most typical of Byzantine military architecture of the Comnenian age. This is further substantiated by a coin struck for Manuel in or shortly after 1143, which was found within the fabric of the western section of the precinct. Perhaps more interesting is the presence of fragments of carved stonework included within that section which was clearly visible from the opposite bank of the river, where the Hungarian fort at Semlin (Zemun) was located. It has been suggested that the use of decorative stonework on the western façade of the fort may have been intended as a propaganda effect, which is otherwise attested for other Byzantine fortresses built elsewhere within the Empire during Manuel's reign.[44] Impressive fortification

[42] John Kinnamos, *Deeds of John and Manuel Comnenus*, p. 204; English translation by Brand, pp. 155–156. According to Kinnamos, the name of the Serbian ruler overthrown by Desa was Primislav, not Uroš.

[43] *Chronicle of the Priest of Dioclea* 47, p. 104.

[44] Stephenson, "Manuel I Comnenus and Geza II," p. 270. For the twelfth-century stronghold at Belgrade, see Popović, *Beogradska tvrđava*, pp. 42–56. For imported slip-coated wares in Belgrade, see V. Bikić, "Vizantijska grnčarija sa zlatnim i

works have also been attested on the neighboring site at Braničevo, where a new rampart was built on the peak of the rocky plateau near the confluence of the Morava and Danube Rivers. Known as Veliki Grad, the new rampart substantially enlarged the fortified area, but does not seem to have been used for anything other than mustering the imperial troops, when they were needed in the region. As coin and seal finds come almost exclusively from the area within the repaired walls of the previously existing fortress, it has been suggested that the administrative center remained Mali Grad, separated from the newly built extension by a fortified gate.[45] The presence of Byzantine garrisons is also attested on sites in the Iron Gates segment of the Danube frontier, in both fortifications and the neighboring cemeteries.

At King Géza's death in 1162, Emperor Manuel intervened in the dynastic affairs of Hungary. He supported Stephen IV, brother of the deceased king, against Géza's son, Stephen III. Manuel seems to have bribed a number of Hungarian supporters of Stephen IV in the southern region of Hungary, which was under the direct influence of the Orthodox metropolitan of Bač or of the Catholic archbishop of Kalocsa. It was over that region that Stephen IV eventually ruled during the brief reign of his brother Ladislas II (1162–1163), before becoming king on January 27, 1163. Less than three months later, ousted by Stephen III, Stephen IV sought assistance from Manuel, but the emperor negotiated a compromise with the Hungarian ruler: in exchange for Manuel abandoning Stephen IV, Stephen III agreed to let his brother Béla go to Constantinople, where he was rebaptized Alexios and was betrothed to Manuel's daughter, Maria, under the expectation that he would succeed to the imperial throne. Since Béla had been the Hungarian duke of Dalmatia and Croatia, Stephen III was forced to cede Frangochorion to the Byzantines, as the region was theoretically part of Béla's domain.[46] When Stephen IV came

srebrnim premazom sa Beogradske tvrđave [Gold and silver slip-coated Byzantine pottery from the Belgrade fortress]," *Godišnjak grada Beograda*, vol. 37 (1990), pp. 63–67.

[45] Most prominent among seal finds from Braničevo is that of John Kamateros, the archbishop of Ohrid. The seal was most likely attached to a letter addressed to the bishop of Braničevo. See L. Maksimović and M. Popović, "Les sceaux byzantins de la région danubienne en Serbie," *Studies in Byzantine Sigillography*, vol. 2 (1990), pp. 224–225.

[46] John Kinnamos, *Deeds of John and Manuel Comnenus*, p. 215; English translation by Brand, p. 163.

to Sirmium in 1164, he managed to secure the support of many inhabitants, which prompted Stephen III to march on the city. The emperor also moved to the Danube to defend Béla's rights to Frangochorion, rightly perceiving the growing hostilities as a Hungarian attempt to remove not only Stephen IV, but also the Byzantine presence from the region. Manuel's swift response seems to have been instrumental in bringing Stephen III, now deprived of his Czech allies, to the bargaining table. During negotiations that took place in Bač, the most important Orthodox center in the region, the Hungarian king acquiesced to the settlement whereby Stephen IV remained in Sirmium and Frangochorion in the company of a considerable Byzantine force. But Stephen III attacked Sirmium again in 1165. In Semlin (Zemun), a faction favorable to him managed to assassinate Stephen IV, and the Hungarian king reoccupied Frangochorion, thus removing all Byzantine military presence from the most important strongholds. In retaliation, Manuel allied himself with the Venetians, who attacked the Hungarian positions in Dalmatia. The Byzantine army moved against Sirmium and Semlin, where many inhabitants were massacred, and regained Frangochorion. Strong Byzantine garrisons were placed at key points under the orders of the generals Constantine Angelos and Basil Tripsychos, who began rebuilding the fortifications at Belgrade, Semlin, and Niš.[47]

Stephen III launched another attack on Sirmium in 1166, when he obtained a great victory against the Byzantine troops led by the generals Michael Gabras and Michael Branas. In retaliation, troops under the command of Béla-Alexios raided the Hungarian territory across the Danube, while others under the command of Leo Vatatzes and John Dukas attacked Transylvania from the southeast through the passes across the Carpathians. Meanwhile, Manuel had again intervened in the dynastic affairs of Raška, where Desa was tried before the emperor in 1165 on charges of allying himself with the Hungarian king. He was arrested and sent to Constantinople and in his stead the emperor appointed Tihomir, son of Zavid, a relative of previous Serbian *zhupans*. Tihomir ruled jointly with his brothers Sracimir, Miroslav, and Nemanja, each one of them being assigned to a specific region of Raška, just like Manuel had forced Desa and Uroš to rule jointly. Nemanja ruled in eastern Serbia, most likely in the region of the river Toplica, thus closer to territories under direct

[47] Choniates, *Historia*, p. 136; English translation by Magoulias, p. 77.

Byzantine control. He nevertheless aspired to lands farthest from his domain, as during the Byzantine–Hungarian war of 1166–1167 "he subjugated Croatia and took possession" of Kotor on the Dalmatian coast.[48] Soon after that, Nemanja attacked the domain of his brother Tihomir, whom he managed to kill in battle at Pantino, not far from Zvečan (near Kosovska Mitrovica, in northern Kosovo). His other brothers quickly acknowledged Nemanja as grand *zhupan*. He allied himself with Venice, a move that Emperor Manuel interpreted as hostile, for in 1171 he had ordered the arrest of all Venetians in the Empire and the expropriation of their properties. At the death of the Hungarian king Stephen III in 1172, after establishing Béla-Alexios as the new king, the emperor therefore decided to take action against Nemanja. He led a swift raid "through steep and precipitous regions," pressing forward "to engage the grand *zhupan*."[49] According to Niketas Choniates, without any serious resistance, Nemanja "prostrated himself at Manuel's feet."[50] John Kinnamos gives an even more powerful description of Nemanja's submission: "he came and approached the tribunal [on which the emperor was sitting], with head uncovered and arms bare to the elbow, his feet unshod; a rope haltered his neck and a sword was in his hand. He offered himself to the emperor for whatever treatment he desired."[51] The Serbian ruler was taken prisoner and paraded as such in the triumphal procession that the emperor organized on his return to Constantinople. Nevertheless, after pledging his allegiance to Manuel, he was released and returned to Raška. His possessions on the Dalmatian coast, especially Kotor, must have meanwhile reverted to Byzantine control.

At Manuel's death in 1180, Nemanja openly declared his allegiance to King Béla III of Hungary, who immediately took advantage of the political crisis to recuperate Sirmium and Frangochorion. The news of Andronicus' accession seems to have encouraged Béla to raid deeply into the theme of Niš-Braničevo. One of the two generals in charge of the troops in that theme rebelled against the new

[48] Choniates, *Historia*, p. 159; English translation by Magoulias, p. 90.

[49] John Kinnamos, *Deeds of John and Manuel Comnenus*, p. 287; English translation by Brand, p. 215.

[50] Choniates, *Historia*, p. 159; English translation by Magoulias, p. 90.

[51] John Kinnamos, *Deeds of John and Manuel Comnenus*, p. 287; English translation by Brand, p. 215. Nemanja was clearly acting as the "slave" of the emperor. For the interpretation of this political ritual, see Stephenson, *Byzantium's Balkan Frontier*, p. 268.

emperor, but was captured and mutilated before reaching his supporters in Asia Minor. In the meantime, Béla's troops reached Serdica, captured the body of St. John of Rila, and removed it to Esztergom, much like the arm of St. Procopius had been transferred in 1071 from Niš to Sirmium at the order of King Solomon. The relics of St. John of Rila returned to Serdica when the Hungarian troops withdrew from the entire region of Niš–Braničevo, following the peace treaty whereby Emperor Isaac II Angelos married the daughter of King Béla III. In Raška, Nemanja had already taken advantage of the new balance of powers to declare openly his alliance with Hungary. Serbian warriors had participated in Béla's attack on Serdica. In 1181, Nemanja again attacked Kotor and then Bar, the stronghold of Mihajlo, the grand *zhupan* of Duklja, who was his nephew. Threatening Dubrovnik and Korčula, Nemanja's intrusion on the coast directly challenged Norman and Venetian rule. At the peace of 1186, Dubrovnik was forced to acknowledge Raškan control of the surrounding countryside, especially in Hum (Zahumlje), now under the rule of Nemanja's brother Miroslav. His eldest son, Vukan, was appointed ruler of Zeta (Duklja), while Nemanja kept for himself Raška and the surrounding territories. By the time he offered his military assistance to Emperor Frederick I Barbarossa and his crusading army against Byzantium, Nemanja had "occupied by sword and bow the city of Niš and surrounding lands as far as Serdica."[52] A subsequent attack on Skopje led to Emperor Isaac II's punitive expedition of 1191 or 1192, during which Nemanja was defeated in battle "at the Morava River."[53] Nevertheless, his control over Raška, Hum, Travounia, and Duklja remained unchallenged. Moreover, the peace following Isaac II's campaign was sealed by the marriage of Emperor Isaac's niece Evdokia to Nemanja's son Stefan. Since Evdokia was the daughter of Alexios III Angelos, who in 1195 overthrew his brother Isaac to assume the crown, Nemanja's son, now an imperial son-in-law, was bestowed the title of *sebastokrator*. To smooth his son's accession to power in Raška, Nemanja abdicated and designated him as successor at the assembly of Ras in 1196. He then withdrew to the monastery of Studenica (near Ušće, in the Middle Ibar region of

[52] Ansbert, *Historia de expeditione Friderici imperatoris*, ed. by A. Chroust (Hanover: Hahnsche Buchhandlung, 1928; reprint 1989), MGH SS rer. Germ. 5:30. For the English translation, see Stephenson, *Byzantium's Balkan Frontier*, p. 295.

[53] Choniates, *Historia*, p. 434; English translation by Magoulias, p. 239.

central Serbia), his own foundation of *c.* 1183. The Church of the Holy Virgin at Studenica is a unique combination of a dome with an elongated nave with Romanesque decoration on the façade, a sign of the Western influences that had by then reached Raška, perhaps via Kotor or another city on the Dalmatian coast.[54] Most striking in this context is the tympanum over the west portal with its representation of the enthroned Virgin with Child, flanked by the Archangels Michael and Gabriel, identified as such by the accompanying Cyrillic inscription. A similarly striking combination of Western influences and Byzantine traditions may also be identified in the Miroslav Evangeliary, written in 1180 for the Church of St. Peter in Bijelo Polje (near Berane, Montenegro), the foundation of Nemanja's brother Miroslav. The evangeliary is a Cyrillic manuscript in Old Church Slavonic exhibiting features of a Serbian recension, with rich illuminations reminiscent of Romanesque book illustrations, but also of the decorative patterns employed at Studenica.[55]

Having taken the monastic vows, Nemanja (now rebaptized Simeon) moved to Mount Athos in 1198 together with his younger son Ratko. Ratko became a monk at the Vatopedi Monastery under the name Sava. While on Mount Athos, the son and the father founded the Hilandar Monastery. Sava traveled to Constantinople to obtain permission from his imperial relatives, and his brother Stefan, the grand *zhupan* of Raška, provided the necessary funds for the new foundation. Simeon died on February 3, 1199 within the precinct of his foundation at Hilandar. He was canonized soon after that and became the first "national" saint of Serbia and the only Balkan example in a thirteenth-century series of royal saints.

Studenica was not Nemanja's only foundation. He is the founder of three other churches: St. Nicholas near Kuršumlija (on the Toplica

[54] S. M. Ćirković, *La Serbie au Moyen Age* (Paris: Zodiaque, 1992), pp. 145–146. See also S. M. Ćirković, V. Korać, and G. Babić, *Studenica Monastery* (Belgrade: Jugoslavenska revija, 1986).

[55] N. Rodić and G. Jovanović, *Miroslavljevo jevanđelje. Kritičko izdanje* [The Miroslav Evangeliary. A Critical Edition] (Belgrade: Srpska Akademija Nauka i Umetnosti, 1986); V. Radosavljević, *Miroslavljevo jevanđelje. Studie i vezi sa technologijom izrade, stanjem izaštitom* [The Miroslav Evangeliary. Studies Regarding the Technology of its Production, its Condition and Preservation] (Belgrade: Narodna biblioteka Srbije, 1994). For the parallels between the illuminations of the Miroslav Evangeliary and the sculptural decoration in Studenica, see J. Maksimović, *Srpske srednovjekovne minijature* [Serbian Medieval Book Illuminations] (Belgrade: Prosveta, 1983).

River, in central Serbia); St. George (Đurđevi Stupovi) in Ras; and St. Panteleimon in Niš. The former was built at some point before 1168, perhaps incorporating an earlier structure. Like Studenica, St. Nicholas near Kuršumlija betrays the influence of Western art, particularly through its western exonarthex with a twin-tower façade, whose immediate source of inspiration is the cathedral Church of St. Tryphon in Kotor, the building of which ended in 1166. It was also during this period of time that the stronghold at Gradina near Pazarište (Ras) was rebuilt and considerably enlarged. New buildings were added within the ramparts that suggest a dramatic change of function. To be sure, much like earlier occupation phases associated with the presence of Byzantine garrisons, late twelfth-century Ras had log-houses and a granary. But the twelfth-century occupation phase included a palatial compound in the northern part of the fort, with large cellars (one of which is the largest granary known in the Balkans) and a residential area of some 300 square meters divided into 2 interconnected buildings. In addition, a tower was incorporated into the compound and turned into residential quarters, a feature strikingly reminiscent of contemporary Western fashions. Below the fortress, a cave monastery was established at some point between 1160 and 1200. On top of a conical rock structure, a large cave known as Orlova pecina ("The Eagle's Cave") may have served for some communal gatherings or perhaps as *scriptorium*.[56] A single-naved church was built in the late 1100s inside the fort as a funerary chapel for the fort's cemetery. The fort and the monastery form an ensemble that is clearly associated with the presence on the site of more than just a garrison of soldiers. The special nature of the late twelfth-century occupation at Ras is betrayed by the presence of exquisite pottery imports, such as early thirteenth-century protomaiolica or a bowl of south Baltic origin with an engraved image of Mercury. An ampulla for holy oil and a small pectoral icon of lead point to contacts with pilgrimage sites in the region (Thessalonica) or elsewhere in Byzantium. But a mold for medallions with the image of the Holy Virgin with Child demonstrates that there was also a local production of Christian artifacts. In short, Ras has rightly been viewed as a royal residence, first built by Nemanja and then used by his son Stefan. But it was certainly not the permanent residence of the grand *zhupans*, for Nemanja is known to have had "palaces" in various other parts of his

[56] Popović, *Tvrđava Ras*, p. 406.

realm, including Kotor. Nevertheless, through its impressive palatial compound, the luxurious objects of daily use found on the site, and its religious components, Ras reflects a process of dramatic transformations announcing the political prominence of Serbia during the 1200s.

DALMATIA AND THE NORTHWESTERN REGION

The signs of prosperity so evident in Thrace and Greece are also visible in the twelfth century in the hinterland of Dyrrachion. That prosperity was primarily based on agriculture, especially in the plain around Valona, which had supported the Norman invaders of the late eleventh century. The estates in the region were primarily ecclesiastical, such as those of the archbishop of Dyrrachion. Lay landowners must be recognized behind the *archontes* often mentioned in contemporary documents as founders of new churches or political brokers. On the other hand, much like in Greece, local prosperity attracted the investments of the Italian merchants, especially of the Venetians, who had already established themselves in Dyrrachion. Despite a brief interruption in 1171, when all Venetians in the Empire were arrested and their property confiscated, Venetian commercial activities in present-day Albania expanded during the last few decades of the twelfth century. By 1200, the Venetian presence is attested not only in Dyrrachion, but also in Valona, Jericho, and Kanina. When, in 1190, two Venetians joined their efforts in a commercial contract (*colleganza*) for a trip to Dyrrachion, Kerkyra, and Thessalonica, the ports on the Albanian coast had already become key points along the trade routes linking Venice to the major commercial centers in the eastern Mediterranean and the Aegean Sea.

No early twelfth-century Byzantine governors of Dyrrachion are known, except a certain Pirogordus mentioned in the *Chronicle of the Priest of Dioclea*.[57] The next governor of Dyrrachion, Alexios Kontostephanos, intervened in the dynastic conflicts in neighboring Duklja opposing "king" George to his brother Gradihna. The Byzantine troops led by the governor of Dyrrachion devastated the country and managed to capture George who was sent in chains to

[57] *Chronicle of the Priest of Dioclea* 45, p. 103. Judging from the chronology of events in the *Chronicle*, Pirogordus must have been in office during Emperor John II's reign (1118–1143).

Constantinople.[58] According to the author of the *Chronicle of the Priest of Dioclea*, under the rule of Gradihna, many Dukljans who had fled to neighboring regions or across the sea to Apulia returned home, and Duklja remained a client state during the term of the third governor of Dyrrachion known for the twelfth century, Alexios Dukas. However, during the early regnal years of Emperor Manuel (1143–1180), Duklja and Travounia became the target of Raškan expansion. The emperor granted Zeta and Travounia to Desa, Uroš II's brother, while Radoslav, Gradihna's son, was left only with a narrow strip of land on the coast from Kotor to Ulcinj.[59] By that time, the authority of the governor of Dyrrachion had been restricted to the hinterland of the city, for a Byzantine duke of Valona is mentioned in 1155. The Raškan presence in the region was felt again in the late 1160s, when Nemanja seized Kotor. However, the communal regime established there in the meantime was not abolished. It was during those years that the Cathedral of St. Tryphon was erected, one of the most remarkable Romanesque churches on the Dalmatian coast, whose architecture had immediate effects on churches built inside Raška. A few years later, during the Hungarian–Byzantine war, a duke of the entire Dalmatian coast was appointed in the person of Constantine Dukas, who certainly exercised authority over Dukljan territories, as well as over Dyrrachion.[60] Following Manuel's death, Nemanja attacked Kotor again in 1181, when he also seized Bar, and soon installed his brother Miroslav in Hum (Zahumlje) and his son Vukan in Zeta (Duklja). In the meantime, Bosnia appears to have gained its independence under *ban* Kulin, mentioned in a Cyrillic inscription from Biskupići–Muhašinovići (near Viskoko, to the northwest from Sarajevo). The inscription is dated to 1194 and refers to Kulin's conquest of the region. A second inscription found in Podbrežje near Zenica mentions one of Kulin's judges named Gradeša, who may have been appointed after that conquest.[61]

[58] *Chronicle of the Priest of Dioclea* 45, p. 103. For Alexios Kontostephanos, see Stephenson, *Byzantium's Balkan Frontier*, p. 184.

[59] *Chronicle of the Priest of Dioclea* 45, p. 104.

[60] Stephenson, *Byzantium's Balkan Frontier*, p. 184.

[61] Fučić, "Croatian Glagolitic and Cyrillic epigraphs," pp. 277 and 279. Both inscriptions mention the donors' wives. That of Podbrežje also contains the name of the carver, Prodan. A third Cyrillic inscription from Bosnia, which was found in Blagaj, mentions a contemporary *zhupan* who had built a church "in the days of the celebrated Nemanja." See Fučić, "Croatian Glagolitic and Cyrillic epigraphs," p. 279.

The political developments taking place during the second half of the twelfth century in the southern region of the Adriatic Sea are also paralleled by significant shifts in the ecclesiastical administration of the area. By 1180, the archbishop of Dyrrachion had lost most of his suffragans in the neighboring region of Duklja. Orthodox and Catholics lived side by side in the region, often with parallel church hierarchies. However, shortly before 1200 the influence of the Church of Constantinople began to diminish in favor of that of Rome. In 1187, Pope Alexander III congratulated the bishop of Kruje for having removed the last remnants of Orthodox influence from his diocese. In the late 1190s, Vukan, the ruler of Zeta, wrote to the pope in Rome asking for religious guidance. In response, Innocent III called Vukan "the illustrious king of Dalmatia and Dioclea," and dispatched two legates, while at the same time announcing the (re-)elevation of the bishop of Bar to the status of archbishop.[62] But the major concerns of the prelates gathered for the synod convened in Bar in 1199 were priestly celibacy and priestly beards, which shows that Orthodox practices were still prevalent. Nine years later, Demetrius, a local potentate in northern Albania, followed Vukan's example in asking for religious guidance from Pope Innocent III.[63]

During the first half of the twelfth century, the middle and northern sections of the Dalmatian coast were the object of bitter disputes between Hungary, on the one side, and Venice and Byzantium, on the other. In 1111, a charter of King Coloman for Bishop Paul of Rab listed as witnesses all the most important bishops of Dalmatia under Hungarian control: Crescentius of Split, Anastasius of Knin, John of Trogir, Bonus of Biograd, Mark of Zadar, Domin(i)cus of Krk, and Peter of Osor.[64] Four years later, a naval expedition restored Venetian control over Krk and the other islands of the Kvarner Archipelago, which had been conquered by the Hungarians in 1105. The expedition sent by the doge Ordelaffo Falier (1102–1118) failed to take

[62] Although the status of archbishop had already been recognized in 1089, the bishop of Bar during the twelfth century seems to have been a suffragan of the archbishop of Dubrovnik. See L. Waldmüller, *Die Synoden in Dalmatien, Kroatien und Ungarn. Von der Völkerwanderung bis zum Ende der Arpaden (1311)* (Paderborn, Munich, Vienna, and Zürich: F. Schöningh, 1987), p. 160.

[63] A. Ducellier, *La façade maritime de l'Albanie au Moyen Age. Durazzo et Valona du XIème au XVème siècle* (Thessaloniki: Institute for Balkan Studies, 1981), p. 139. Demetrius was the son of Progon, the *archon* mentioned in the Gëziq inscription.

[64] Waldmüller, *Die Synoden*, p. 143.

either Zadar, on the coast, or Biograd, in the interior, but another expedition managed to defeat the Hungarian garrison of Zadar and to seize the city in 1116. In Split, the Hungarian garrison secured the support of the archbishop, but the prior led an attack of the citizens of Split against the Hungarian positions, and the city eventually went over to the Venetians.[65] At Emperor Alexios I's death in 1118, all cities in the northern section of the Dalmatian coast were under Venetian control.

The Hungarian reply came in 1124, when Stephen II sent an army to recuperate the positions lost to Venice. Since the king is known to have granted privileges to the citizens of Trogir and Split, the conclusion has been drawn that Hungarian control was established in at least those two cities.[66] Both were retaken by the Venetian retaliatory expedition, which also destroyed Biograd, where the Hungarians had taken refuge. Venice had again firm control over the entire northern region of the Adriatic Sea. The prior of Zadar appears in a charter of 1134 as Venetian "count" of that city.[67] Eight years later, the Hungarians reclaimed authority over the Dalmatian city. While troops under the command of the *ban* of Bosnia, himself in Hungarian service, attacked Dubrovnik in 1142, King Géza II renewed the oaths of allegiance previously taken by King Coloman from the citizens of Split, in exchange for renewing their privileges and freedoms. In response, the Venetian Doge Pietro Polani (1130–1148) secured papal support for establishing a new bishopric of Hvar and Brač, two islands in front of Split, in order to diminish the power of that city's bishop who had been appointed by the Hungarian king.[68] Lampradius, the new bishop of Hvar and Brač, was transferred in 1154 to Zadar, which was then elevated to the status of archbishopric, with suffragan bishops in Osor, Krk, Rab, and Hvar, all under Venetian control. Pope Anastasius IV's bull *Licet universalis Ecclesiae pastor* issued in that same year acknowledged Venice's control over the most important islands of the Kvarner Bay and the Dalmatian coast. One year later, Pope

[65] *Annales Venetici breves*, ed. by H. Simonsfeld (Hanover: Hahnsche Buchhandlung, 1883; reprint 1988), MGH SS 14:71.

[66] *Codex diplomaticus regni Croatiae, Dalmatiae et Slavoniae*, ed. by T. Smičiklas, vol. II (Zagreb: Ex officina Societatis Typograficae, 1904), pp. 37–38. See Stephenson, *Byzantium's Balkan Frontier*, p. 204.

[67] *Codex diplomaticus*, vol. II, pp. 44–5.

[68] Thomas of Spalato, *Historia Salonitana*, p. 64. See Waldmüller, *Die Synoden*, pp. 143–144.

Hadrian IV decreed that the archbishop of Zadar be subject to the jurisdiction of the patriarch of Grado, thus strengthening even more the ties between Venice and the Dalmatian city. Zadar offered shelter to Pope Alexander III fleeing Rome after the invasion of Frederick Barbarossa, and a contemporary account mentions that the pontiff was acclaimed by the local populace "with endless songs and chants of praise about him in their Slavonic tongue."[69] By that time, Venice had already secured her domination over the north Adriatic region by means of the 1145 treaties with the Istrian cities of Koper and Pula. In 1150, when the Istrian cities tried to move away from Venetian control, the doge Domenico Morosini (1148–1156) forced them to take an oath of allegiance and to pay tribute, thus turning them into Venetian subjects.[70] His successor, Vitale II Michiel (1156–1172), appointed the first agents of Venetian power in the persons of his sons Nicholas, as prior of Rab, and Leonardo, as count of Osor. Domenico Morosini's son, who was also the commander of the Venetian fleet, became Count of Zadar in 1159. But in 1165, when King Stephen III of Hungary incited a rebellion in Zadar against Venetian control, the count was expelled and a Hungarian garrison moved into the city.

Coordinating their actions with the war Emperor Manuel was waging on Hungary, the Venetians launched an expedition on Dalmatia, which recovered Zadar, while the Byzantine general John Dukas moved swiftly from Raška across Bosnia and retook most of the Dalmatian cities: "Then Trogir and Šibenik came under the Romans, and in addition Split and the nation of the Kačićes, Klis [. . .] and Skradin and Ostrovica and Solin, and whatever other [cities] are situated in Dalmatia, fifty-seven in all."[71] John Kinnamos' mention of Skradin and Ostrovica suggests that the Byzantine conquest of Dalmatia moved north of the Krka River, thus approaching the hinterland of

69 *Liber Pontificalis*, ed. by L. Duchesne, vol. II (Paris: E. Thorin, 1892), p. 437; English translation from Boso, *Life of Alexander III*, transl. by G. M. Ellis (Oxford: Blackwell, 1973), p. 103. For Pope Alexander III's visit to Zadar, see A. M. Strgačić, "Papa Aleksandar III u Zadru [Pope Alexander III in Zadar]," *Radovi Zavoda za povijesne znanosti HAZU u Zadra*, vol. I (1954), pp. 153–187.

70 *Codex diplomaticus*, vol. II, pp. 64–67.

71 John Kinnamos, *Deeds of John and Manuel Comnenus*, pp. 248–249; English translation by Brand, p. 187. See I. Goldstein, "Byzantine rule in Dalmatia in the 12th century," in *Byzanz und Ostmitteleuropa, 950–1453. Beiträge zu einer table-ronde des XIX Internationalen Congress of Byzantine Studies, Copenhagen 1996*, ed. by G. Prinzing and M. Salamon (Wiesbaden: Otto Harrassowitz, 1999), pp. 107–109.

Zadar which was at that time under Venetian control. The "nation of the Kačićes" was the territory between Split and the Neretva River, which was at that time under the rule of the independent dukes of Omiš, all members of the powerful Kačić family of pirates. In 1167, Duke Nicholas Kačić signed a treaty with Kotor, promising not to attack any ship sailing to Kotor "up to Molunat" (a point on the coast between Kotor and Dubrovnik), an indication of the power that the "nation of the Kačićes" had over a significant portion of the Dalmatian coast. Similarly, Ostrovica must have been under the direct control of the local Šubić family, the dukes of Bribir, who controlled the entire area between Zadar and Šibenik. Much like in the valley of the Neretva, the Byzantine power relied on the allegiance of local potentates, whom the Byzantine dukes of Dalmatia rewarded with membership of their retinue. For example, Duke Miroslav Šubić, the son of Bogdanac, is said to have been appointed escort to the last Byzantine governor of Dalmatia, Roger Sclavonus, a Norman exile in Byzantine service. Roger's overlordship was recognized in a charter of 1180 by several ecclesiastical and secular lords in Dalmatia, including six *zhupans* (one of whom was Duke Miroslav) and the bishops of Senj and Knin.[72]

During the Hungarian–Byzantine war of 1166–1167, a Hungarian army invaded Dalmatia and managed to capture the first Byzantine duke of Dalmatia, Nicephorus Chalouphes.[73] Manuel's retaliatory expedition in the Danube region also caused the restoration of Byzantine power in Dalmatia. Moreover, when in December 1167, Stephen III's daughter married Nicholas, the former prior (now count) of Rab, Venice obtained formal recognition from the Hungarian king for her domination over the entire north Dalmatian coast and its cities, to which the doge had begun to appoint counts. Similarly, the Byzantines seem to have introduced "consuls" in Dalmatian cities, as representative of the local communes, such as the consul of Dubrovnik who in 1168 signed a peace treaty between his city, on the one hand, and Split and Pisa, on the other.[74] Meanwhile, the new Byzantine duke of Dalmatia, Constantine Dukas, presided over the general arrest of

[72] *Codex diplomaticus*, vol. II, pp. 113–114. See Goldstein, "Byzantine rule in Dalmatia," p. 117. The second duke of Dalmatia, Constantine Dukas, arbitrated in 1171 a conflict between Split and Klis. See *Codex diplomaticus*, vol. II, p. 130.

[73] John Kinnamos, *Deeds of John and Manuel Comnenus*, pp. 262–263; English translation by Brand, p. 197.

[74] *Codex diplomaticus*, vol. II, pp. 124–125.

the Venetians. He was still in office when the Venetians attacked and destroyed Trogir and Dubrovnik in retaliation. Although the Hungarians were allowed to establish themselves briefly in Zadar, the city was back in Venetian hands by 1174.[75]

The Byzantine conquest of Dalmatia does not seem to have caused in any way the alienation of the local clergy of Roman obedience. In 1167, the new archbishop of Split, now a Byzantine city, was appointed by the pope, but when the archbishop was asked to swear allegiance to Emperor Manuel, there was no papal protest. Eight years later, another archbishop of Split even visited the emperor in Constantinople, where he was lavishly entertained and showered with gifts.[76] Much like Dobronas in the early eleventh century, Raynerius of Split must have acted on behalf of the entire city when traveling to the capital of the Empire. Unlike him, the archbishop does not seem to have invested the gifts in a building program in Split. In fact, because of its brevity, the military and political presence of Byzantium in twelfth-century Dalmatia left only a few traces in material culture: some sculptural elements in Split and Dubrovnik; four reliquary crosses (*enkolpia*) accidentally found on various sites on the northern Dalmatian coast; and two hoards of Byzantine coins. The influence of Byzantine art is visible in decorative ensembles of otherwise Western figural composition, such as the frescoes in the side apses of the Church of St. Chrysogonus, most likely painted by masters from southern Italy commissioned by Archbishop Lampradius of Zadar in 1175. Much more surprising are the frescoes in Byzantine style decorating the walls of the small Church of St. Jerome in Hum (Istria), which had been erected in the early twelfth century on land belonging to the patriarchate of Aquileia.[77] The painter was clearly familiar with the techniques and themes of the painted ensembles in the central Balkans and may have come from the southern Dalmatian area. In the same direction points the presence of a Glagolitic graffito on the fresco inside the church mentioning a series of thirty masses to be celebrated for the soul of a deceased blacksmith named Martin. The graffito is by no means unique, as several other

[75] Stephenson, *Byzantium's Balkan Frontier*, p. 262.

[76] Thomas of Spalato, *Historia Salonitana*, pp. 72–73. The visit is also mentioned in the *Life of St. Raynerius*, in *Legende i kronike*, ed. by V. Gligo and H. Morović (Split: Čakavski sabor, 1977), p. 138.

[77] B. Fučić, "Hum, ciklus romanicko-bizantinskih zidnih slikarija [Hum, the cycle of Romanesque–Byzantine frescoes]," *Peristil*, vols. 6–7 (1963–1964), pp. 13–22.

Glagolitic inscriptions are known from twelfth-century Istria, some short (the Grdoselo and Supetar fragments), others relatively long (the Glagolitic Abecedarium carved on the dedicatory cross on the wall of the Church of St. Anthony the Hermit in Roč).[78] By contrast, no such inscription is known from the islands of the Kvarner Bay, which had produced eleventh-century Glagolitic epigraphs. The only twelfth-century inscriptions known from the northern Adriatic are Latin and refer to donors. This is the case of the dukes Bartul and Vid from the island of Krk, who appear together with a priest named Bonus on late twelfth-century dedicatory inscriptions, or of the archdeacon Kuzma, who in 1181 built a bell tower in Rab.[79] Both abbeys and cathedrals operated as centers of writing and learning, as indicated by the fact that the first public notaries that appeared in the Dalmatian cities in the mid-1100s were members of the local chapters. But the twelfth century also witnessed a broadening of the audience of the written text. Besides liturgical codices, such as the Roman Missal in Caroline script from the Cathedral in Split or the one in Beneventan script written in Dubrovnik and now in the Bodleian Library in Oxford, a list of twelfth-century Latin manuscripts produced in Croatia must include the Korčula Codex, written in Zadar or at the Abbey of St. Chrysogonus shortly after 1131. This manuscript is a compilation of texts including such diverse items as a Latin translation of Flavius Josephus' *Jewish War*, lists of popes, archbishops of Ravenna, and patriarchs of Aquileia, as well as excerpts from Paul the Deacon's *History of the Lombards*, the *Liber pontificalis*, and Eusebius'

[78] Fučić, "Croatian Glagolitic and Cyrillic epigraphs," pp. 273–275. The Grdoselo fragment is from a dedicatory inscription. The Supetar inscription consists of the word "Amen" in Cyrillic and the name Jacob in Glagolitic. See also B. Fučić, "Supetarski ulomak [The Supetar fragment]," *Slovo*, vol. 38 (1988), pp. 55–62. That the Glagolitic alphabet was in use during the twelfth century in the southern region of the Dalmatian coast is indicated by the so-called Gršković and Mihanović fragments of two different apostols (collections of readings from the Acts and the Epistles of the Apostles) that were certainly written in Duklja.

[79] *Namentragende Steininschriften*, p. 9; I. Ostojić, *Benediktinci u Hrvatskoj* [The Benedictine Order in Croatia] (Split: Benediktinski priorat Tkon, 1963), pp. 355–356. For the role of the local potentates in the spread of Romanesque architecture on the Krk island, see M. Jurković, "Uloga Zadra, Clunya i kneževa Frankopana u promociji romanike na otoku Krku [The role of Zadar, Cluny, and the Frankopan princes in the promotion of the Romanesque style on the island of Krk]," in *Umjetnost na istočnoj obali Jadrana u kontekstu europeske tradicije. Zbornik radova za znanstevnog skupa u Opatiji u svibnju 1992. posvečenog djelu Prof. Dr. Radmile Matejčić*, ed. by N. Kudiš and M. Vicelja (Rijeka: Pedagoski fakultet, 1993), pp. 176–189.

Ecclesiastical History.[80] The compilation certainly reflects a genuine interest in history, and the notes regarding Dalmatia and Croatia added to the *Liber pontificalis* demonstrate a concern with local events. The Korčula Codex is thus very similar in its intent to the work of Gregory, the late twelfth-century archbishop of Bar, who is believed to be the author of the *Chronicle of the Priest of Dioclea*. The material packed in the Latin version of this historical work, the first of its kind in Southeastern Europe, is as diverse and at times as incongruent as that of the Korčula compilation. Its purpose was propagandistic, namely to demonstrate the superiority of the archbishopric of Bar over that of Split, perhaps in the context of the reelevation of the status of Bar and the Dukljan–papal contacts of the late 1100s. Condemned by modern historians for its inconsistencies, obscurities, or downright fictional character, the *Chronicle* is in fact a remarkable indicator of both high levels of literacy and the political implications of literary production in twelfth-century Dalmatia. When compared with the Korčula Codex and with Thomas of Spalato's *History of Salona*, which was written less than a century later, the *Chronicle* thus appears as a historical witness to shifting mentalities in a region of shifting borders.

At Manuel's death in 1180, a Hungarian army under Duke Maurus invaded Dalmatia and occupied Zadar. A Hungarian named Peter was appointed Archbishop of Split, and by 1182 Maurus himself had become Count of Dalmatia, a position no doubt aping the Byzantine duke of Dalmatia.[81] At about the same time, the islands of Korčula and Vis were attacked by Nemanja, but most of what constituted Byzantine Dalmatia during Emperor Manuel's reign was taken by Hungary. In the aftermath of the Byzantine victories over the Norman invaders of 1185, William II seems to have retained some control over the Dalmatian coast, as in 1186, when making peace with Dubrovnik, Nemanja and his brothers Miroslav and Sracimir acknowledged that the city was "in the hands of the most glorious king William."[82] But during the last two decades of the twelfth century the Hungarian hold

[80] Katičić, "Language and literacy," pp. 363–364.

[81] Thomas of Spalato, *Historia Salonitana*, p. 75. Peter left Split in 1187 to become Archbishop of Kalocsa. His successor was another Hungarian named Peter (Archbishop of Split between 1188 and 1196), who had until then been abbot of the Abbey of St. Martin in Pannonhalma. See Waldmüller, *Die Synoden*, p. 154.

[82] *Codex diplomaticus*, vol. II, pp. 201–202; English translation from Stephenson, *Byzantium's Balkan Frontier*, p. 288.

on Dalmatia and Croatia went uncontested. When at King Béla III's death, his two sons began to struggle for power, Andrew (the future king Andrew II) declared Croatia and Dalmatia an independent principality, a status it preserved until 1205, when Andrew became king. In doing so, the Hungarian prince undoubtedly relied on the support of the local aristocracy, whose privileges he was quick to confirm and expand. For example, in 1193, he granted to Bartholomew of Krk the office of Count of Modruš (near Karlovac, Croatia) as a hereditary dignity. Most likely through donation of royal land, the Babonići family in Slavonia began building some of the largest estates in the region, and through control of the roads linking the Dalmatian coast to Hungary, they increased their revenues from the extraction of tolls. Prince Andrew also built alliances with the powerful lords on the other side of the frontier separating his principality from the southeastern marches of the Holy Roman Empire. Most prominent among them were the counts of Andechs from Bavaria, whose ministerials (knights born into servitude who were granted fiefs by their liege-lords) in Carinthia are first mentioned in 1197. Two members of the Andechs family, Berthold IV and Berthold V, are mentioned in 1143 or 1147 and 1154 or 1161, respectively, as counts of Stein (Kamnik, north of Ljubljana), a town founded by their family in the middle of perhaps their largest domain in the area. Berthold VI, who was in the retinue of Emperor Frederick I Barbarossa and led one of the four detachments of the army that crossed the Balkans in the summer of 1189, was the first duke of Merania, the region around the Bay of Trieste. His son, Henry II of Andechs, became Margrave of Istria, and after the death in 1209 of his father-in-law, Count Albert of Weichselburg (Višnja Gora, near Ljubljana), he inherited large estates in Lower Carniola at the Croatian border, thus becoming the most powerful lord in the southeastern marches of the Empire, with over thirty ministerials.[83] The Andechs thus became Prince Andrew's most important ally in the region. The alliance was sealed in 1204

[83] M. Kosi, "The age of the Crusades in the South-East of the Empire (between the Alps and the Adriatic)," in *The Crusades and the Military Orders. Expanding Frontiers of Medieval Latin Christianity*, ed. by Zs. Hunyadi and J. Laszlovszky (Budapest: Department of Medieval Studies, Central European University, 2001), pp. 129–130 and 156. The rise to power of the Andechs family in the southeastern marches coincides with Emperor Frederick I's conflict with Byzantium and his preparations for the Third Crusade, an indication that the Andechs were agents of imperial power on the frontier.

when he married Henry II's daughter, Gertrud, while her young brother, Berthold, was appointed *ban* of Croatia and Archbishop of Kalocsa. Another brother, Otto, accompanied his father in the Third Crusade and succeeded him as the second duke of Merania in 1205. It is important to note that shortly before and after 1200, the Andechs had secured their control of the southeastern marches and yielded considerable influence in neighboring Croatia and Hungary.

But the situation elsewhere on the western frontier of Hungary was not so favorable to the future king Andrew II. To be sure, King Béla II had signed in 1131 a peace treaty with Archbishop Conrad I of Salzburg, an event that opened a long period of peace and stability.[84] It was during the subsequent decades that trade between Hungary and Italy intensified along the routes crossing the southeastern marches of the Empire. As a consequence, the Friesach penny, first minted in Carinthia in 1125, was later struck at several other mints in Styria and Carniola, and became the most common coin in use in the northwestern region of the Balkans, on both sides of the frontier between Hungary and the Holy Roman Empire. But in the late 1100s, the burggraves of Ptuj, who were ministerials of the archbishop of Salzburg, took advantage of the struggle for power between Emeric and Andrew, the two sons of the deceased king of Hungary. The burggraves seized a strip of land, nineteen miles wide, on the southeastern border of Styria, inside Hungary. In the middle of the newly conquered territory, at Velika Nedelja (near Čakovec, in Croatia), Frederick III, the burggrave of Ptuj, granted a large estate to the Teutonic Knights, who immediately began to attract settlers in order to populate a region that had been left deserted to mark the "no-man's-land" between Hungary and Styria.

During the long reign of Leopold VI of Babenberg (Duke of Austria between 1198 and 1230, but of Styria since 1194), the southeastern marches, especially Carniola, were more firmly attached to the cultural development of Western Europe. To be sure, by that time the Cistercians were already a familiar presence in the region. Their abbey at Stična (near Višnja Gora), founded in 1135 by the counts of Weichselburg, is the most significant monument of Romanesque art in present-day Slovenia. The three-aisled abbey church reminds one of the conservative architecture of the Cluniac order rather than of contemporary Cistercian buildings. The Carthusian monks

[84] *Vita Chunradi archiepiscopi Salisburgensis*, pp. 73–75.

established the first house within the Holy Roman Empire at Žiče (near Slovenska Bistrica, in northeastern Slovenia) in 1160. The church of the Upper Abbey (*domus superior*), as well as the church in Špitalič, the site of the Lower Abbey, betray the work of French stoneworkers. The builders of Žiče introduced the ribbed vault to the region, an innovation that found no imitators. It was only the ribbed vaults of the second Carthusian abbey established by Duke Leopold VI in Jurklošter near Laško in 1208 that were imitated, first and foremost in the parish church in Laško, which is also a foundation of Duke Leopold. The Romanesque churches of present-day Slovenia that may be dated to the reign of Leopold VI, shortly before and after 1200, are characterized by the presence of a tower erected on the side end of the church. The best known example is the Church of St. Vitus in Dravograd (near the present-day Austrian–Slovenian border), a foundation of Otto I of Trixen-Unterdrauburg, the powerful ministerial of the Spanheim ducal family of Carinthia.

During the first half of the twelfth century, members of the Spanheim family ruling in Carinthia also controlled the neighboring marches. Engelbert II and Engelbert III of Spanheim were Margraves of Istria between 1103 and 1171. Their neighbors across the Bay of Trieste were the powerful Meinhardines, counts of Gorica. Meinhard II (*c.* 1160–1231) accompanied the bishop of Halberstadt on his way back from Acre in the Holy Land, after the bishop had landed in Istria in 1198.[85] The Meinhardines held Gorica, formally within the duchy of Friuli, in vassalage from the see of Aquileia. The counts owned land in the karst region behind Gorica, while their ministerials controlled land on their behalf in Friuli, Carinthia, and, just before 1200, in Istria. Very few of these lands were allodial property; many were in fact held in vassalage from the Church, especially from the see of Aquileia and its suffragan bishops. But following the military conflicts that opposed the patriarch of Aquileia to the counts of Gorica, especially Engelbert II (1132–*c.* 1191) and his son Meinhard II, many of these fiefs were turned into grants in perpetuity. They also increased their power in the region by means of matrimonial alliances. Meinhard II's brother, Engelbert III, married the sister of the duke of neighboring Merania, Berthold VI of Andechs. The counts of Gorica had regalian rights over tolls, roads,

[85] *Gesta episcoporum Halberstadensium*, ed. by L. Weiland (Hanover: Hahnsche Buchhandlung, 1874; reprint 1986), MGH SS 23:112–113.

and coinage in the area. In the early 1200s, when they began minting their own coinage, they had already made their appearance in the imperial entourage.[86] Involved in the events surrounding the capture of King Richard I of England in the course of his return from Acre in 1192, Meinhard II also participated in Emperor Henry VI's crusade of 1195.

But unlike the counts of Andechs, neither the Spanheims nor the Meinhardines became involved in the domestic affairs of the neighboring countries to the south of their possessions in the southeastern marches of the Empire. Besides Venice, no other power based in the lands to the north and northeast of the Adriatic Sea had any interest in Dalmatia or Croatia. Despite the growing trade between northeastern Italy and Hungary during the twelfth century, there was little economic and cultural interaction across the no-man's-land separating the southeastern marches of the Empire from Hungary and Croatia.

TRANSYLVANIA, THE OTHER BORDERLAND

A much wider no-man's-land seems to have separated the eastern and southeastern frontier of the Hungarian kingdom from its Cuman neighbors in the steppe corridor north of the Lower Danube and the Black Sea. The first mention of Transylvania (*terra Ultrasilvana*) within the borders of Hungary is in the *Deeds of the Hungarians* (*Gesta Hungarorum*), the earliest surviving chronicle of Hungary, which was written at some point after the reign of Béla III (1172–1196).[87] Its author described the land as rich, particularly in gold and salt, but

[86] P. Štih, *Studien zur Geschichte der Grafen von Görz. Die Ministerialen und Milites der Grafen von Görz in Istrien und Krain* (Vienna: Oldenbourg, 1996), p. 32. After *c.* 1200, the Meinhardines added *Dei gratia* to the formulaic introduction of their charters, as a sign of their increasing power.

[87] *Die "Gesta Hungarorum" des anonymen Notars. Die älteste Darstellung der ungarischen Geschichte*, ed. by G. Silagi (Sigmaringen: Jan Thorbecke, 1991). The date of the *Gesta* is one of the most controversial issues of Hungarian historiography. At stake is the identity of its author, a former notary of a Hungarian king named Béla, who called himself, somewhat mysteriously, Master P. Most Hungarian historians now accept the idea that the king in question is Béla III. See see K. Szovák, "Wer war der anonyme Notar? Zur Bestimmung des Verfassers der *Gesta Hungarorum*," *Ungarn-Jahrbuch*, vol. 19 (1991), pp. 1–17; G. Győrffy, "Anonymus Gesta Hungaroruma [*Gesta Hungarorum*]," in *A Honfoglaláskor írott forrásai*, ed. by L. Kovács and L. Veszprémy (Budapest: Balassi kiadó, 1996), pp. 193–213.

did not know much else about its geography beyond the northwestern area around Dăbâca. There is no mention of Alba Iulia, which at the time the *Deeds of the Hungarians* was written had become the residence of a powerful governor called *voevode*, as well as of the bishop of Transylvania. On the basis of little more than place names of Hungarian origin, scholars have reconstructed a system of fortified frontiers (*indagines*) consisting of entrance points blocked with palisades and wooden or stone barriers separating Hungarian Transylvania from the "deserted lands" beyond it. According to such views, the frontier was guarded by foreign groups of eastern origin, mainly Pechenegs and Szeklers, the latter being a group that the author of the *Deeds* viewed as "the people of King Attila"[88] allied to the Hungarians since times immemorial. There is in fact no direct evidence for the existence during the twelfth century of a fortified frontier in Transylvania, and the presence of the Pechenegs and the Szeklers inside the region, which has been predicated upon the expansion of that frontier, still remains a matter of debate. Moreover, the "desert" on the other side of the frontier does not seem to have been in any way different from the narrow strip of land deliberately evacuated to form a "no-man's-land" on the western frontier of the kingdom.

Nevertheless, the archaeological evidence does support the idea of a settlement area expanding from northwest and west to south and east, respectively, during the twelfth century. At some point in the early 1100s, strongholds erected in the eleventh century in the northwest (Biharea, Dăbâca, Cluj-Mănăştur, Moldoveneşti) had their ramparts repaired and heightened. Churches were built inside each one of them, and around those churches grew the twelfth-century cemeteries that Romanian archaeologists group together in what they call the "Citfalău phase" following the disappearance of the "Bjelo Brdo culture."[89] These are often large cemeteries, sometimes with hundreds of graves, often devoid of any grave goods except dress accessories (torcs, earrings, and ball-headed pins) normally found with female skeletons. Some such cemeteries have burials clustering around an empty space in the middle, which has been interpreted as

88 *Gesta Hungarorum* 50, p. 116.

89 K. Horedt, *Siebenbürgen im Frühmittelalter* (Bonn: Rudolf Habelt, 1986), pp. 116–117. The name is that of a cemetery excavated near an eleventh- and twelfth-century settlement found in Moreşti (near Târgu Mureş). See Horedt, *Moreşti*, vol. II, pp. 51–64.

the mark of a wooden church. The distribution of churches of either stone or wood overlaps that of the increasing number of finds of coins struck for the twelfth-century kings of Hungary. Almost all such finds are from burials, as the deposition of a coin either in the hand or in the mouth of the deceased became a widespread funerary practice in twelfth-century Central Europe. Outside Transylvania proper, for example, most twelfth-century finds from Arad come from burials around the Church of St. Martin, some with coins minted for King Stephen III (1162–1172). Inside Transylvania, such cemeteries were in existence during the second half of the twelfth century next to the present-day cathedrals in Alba Iulia and Cluj. One of the easternmost cemeteries of the Citfalău phase was found at Zăbala near Covasna, on the edge of the Carpathian Mountains. The earliest of its 218 burials have been coin-dated to the reign of Géza II (1141–1162), while the latest cannot be dated after *c.* 1200. A second, equally large cemetery was found in the neighboring village of Peteni, which besides coins struck for Géza II, Stephen III, and Béla III, produced uncommonly rich artifacts, mainly golden dress accessories. Outliers within the Citfalău-phase group of cemeteries, Zăbala and Peteni may thus be viewed as evidence for an expansion of the eastern frontier of the kingdom during the second half of the twelfth century antedating by just a few decades the establishment of Hungarian garrisons on the other side of the Carpathians, at Bâtca Doamnei and Lenkyvcy. On the other hand, Peteni clearly shows that those pushing the frontier eastwards were not mere auxiliary troops in Hungarian service, but communities with affluent and, most likely, high status individuals. Whether or not caused by the Hungarian–Byzantine conflicts in the 1150s and 1160s, the expansion signaled by both cemeteries bears testimony to the fact, otherwise not clearly attested in written sources, that by 1200 the Hungarian kingdom had established its frontiers firmly on the Carpathians. The expansion to the Transylvanian Alps is indicated, among other things, by the sudden appearance *c.* 1150 of the first "guest" settlers brought from the West by King Géza II. Although later claimed for the history of the local Saxons (German-speaking population of Transylvania), the earliest settlers may have instead been Flemings or Walloons. Probably no larger than some 500 families, the first group of "guests" settled in the environs of present-day Sibiu and Sebeş, just south of Alba Iulia. This was by no means a homogeneous group, and there are indications that some of the earliest settlers may have come from regions as far from each other as the Lower Rhine and the Wetterau area north of present-day Frankfurt am Main.[90] The most important settlements established by the newcomers were named after *locatores*, who were responsible for the recruitment of the colonists and the division of land granted to them by the Hungarian king. For example, the German name of the present-day city of Sibiu is Hermannstadt, a name derived from that of the entrepreneur who may have acted as middleman at the time of the first settlement. The settlers had economic and judicial privileges, including that of having their own church independent of the jurisdiction of the bishop of Alba Iulia. The "church of the Germans" is first mentioned in documents in 1191, while the "priors of the Flemings" appear in charters dated between 1192 and 1198. "Saxons" as a generic name for the "guests" was not established before 1206. Although the colonists are said in documents to have been settled on wasteland on the southern frontier, there is clear archaeological evidence that in fact their settlements were not the first ones in the region. For example, in Sebeş, burials of the Citfalău group of Transylvanian cemeteries have been found under the present-day Evangelical Church, itself incorporating an older church built around 1200. The same is true for Drăuşeni, a little village between Rupea and Odorheiu Secuiesc in eastern Transylvania. Here a cemetery has been found next to the church in the middle of the fortress erected in the early fifteenth century. Coin finds indicate that the cemetery was in use during the second half of the twelfth century, between the reigns of Géza II and Stephen III. A pectoral cross (*enkolpion*) of Byzantine origin accidentally found in Saschiz near Sighişoara suggests that an earlier settlement may have existed on the site before the arrival of the first Saxon settlers at some point after 1200. On the other hand, the arrival of the settlers is signaled archaeologically by such novelties as high-quality wheeled-made pottery (Gray Ware) with no analogies in the neighboring regions, but similar to that produced in a number of kilns in the Hildesheim region of Thuringia.

[90] H. Zimmermann, "Die deutsche Südostsiedlung im Mittelalter," in *Deutsche Geschichte im Osten Europas. Land an der Donau*, ed. by G. Schödl (Berlin: Siedler, 1995), p. 32. The dialect spoken by Transylvanian Saxons resembles that of Luxemburg, but a number of linguistic links have been established with the so-called "Letzelburger Platt" spoken in the Meuse region and in Franconia. See Misch Orend, "Die Entstehung der Märchen von der Luxemburger Herkunft der Siebenbürger Sachsen," *Orbis*, vol. 20 (1971), pp. 370–383.

The "guests" were not the only agents of the twelfth-century expansion in Transylvania. Present in the borderlands were also the Cistercian monks, who first arrived in Transylvania during the reign of Béla III. To be sure, the number of monasteries in Transylvania increased considerably during the 1100s, with four new Benedictine abbeys established in Meseş (1165), Sâniob near Oradea (1169), and two other unidentified locations on the Someş and Criş Rivers (1189 and 1199, respectively).[91] The abbey at Cârţa near Victoria was a daughter house of one of the first Cistercian abbeys established by King Béla III at Igriş near Nădlac (close to the present-day Hungarian–Romanian border). At Igriş, archaeological excavations revealed a three-aisled brick basilica with three apses very similar to the Romanesque cathedral in Pécs or to the Benedictine abbey church in Somogyvár, both in western Hungary. Only Romanesque sculptural elements were found at Igriş, and it is known that the abbey was enlarged and refurbished by Andrew II who intended to turn it into a royal burial ground. Igriş was founded on royal land. By contrast, when its daughter house at Cârţa was established, the monastic estates were carved out of the "land of the Vlachs." An early thirteenth-century property register mentions King Andrew II's order that estates previously in Vlach hands be transferred to the Cistercian abbey (see chapter 7). A Vlach presence on the southern frontier of Transylvania clearly antedates the arrival of the Cistercians. This is substantiated by the hoard of silver found in Cârţişoara, not far from the site of the abbey and within the boundaries of the estates the monks managed to snatch with royal support from the local Vlachs. Besides a silver chain from a headgear and 900 grams of hacksilver, the hoard also contained a Byzantine gold coin struck for Emperor John II (1118–1143).[92] Although no remains of settlements or cemeteries have so far been found in the "land of the Vlachs" in southern Transylvania, that was most certainly the area in which the "guests" settled on royal land beginning with the reign of Géza II first came to know the Vlachs. And it is apparently through the

[91] Most important among them is the Sâniob Abbey, because of the precious relic of St. Stephen's right hand housed between its walls. For early monasticism in Transylvania, see L. Makkai, "Transylvania in the medieval Hungarian kingdom (896–1526)," in *History of Transylvania*, ed. by L. Makkai and A. Mócsy, vol. 1 (New York: Columbia University Press, 2001), pp. 533–539.

[92] Horedt, *Siebenbürgen*, pp. 150–152, who calculates that the amount of precious metal in the hoard was sufficient for buying some fifty acres of arable land, two large grazing fields, two vineyards, and three farmsteads.

settlers that the audience of some of the earliest epics in German learned about them as well. The Nibelungenlied composed in the Vienna–Passau region shortly after 1200 contains the first mention not only of the "land of the Vlachs" (*Vlâchen lant*), but also of a certain duke Ramunc, said to have been present at the court of Etzel, the king of the Huns.[93] Attempts to identify the duke with a historical figure must be regarded with great suspicion, for it is most likely that the name the Vlachs gave to themselves (*român*) served as a basis for the creation of the fictional character Ramunc.[94] The author of the *Deeds of the Hungarians*, who had no knowledge of the "guests," nevertheless knew that Transylvania was inhabited by Slavs and Vlachs.[95] However, before King Andrew II's grant to the Cârţa Abbey, there is no mention of Vlachs in the royal charters.

Out of twenty-six known charters dated to the twelfth century and pertaining to Transylvania, half mention royal officers as witnesses, an indication of the special character of the region as the kingdom's borderland. Two charters of 1111 and 1113 refer to a certain Mercurius said to have been *princeps Ultrasilvanus*. This is commonly interpreted as an attempt to turn the region into an administrative unit modeled after principalities within the Holy Roman Empire. In reality, Mercurius may have been just the most important lord in the region, with no specially designed office. It has in fact been suggested that he was one and the same person as a count of Alba Iulia mentioned in a charter of 1097. A specially appointed *voevode* named Leustachius is only attested in 1176. By that time there was still a separate office of Count of Alba Iulia. However, shortly after 1200, the *voevode* was also Count of Alba Iulia, a cumulation of administrative tasks that points to the increasing importance of the central and southern regions of Transylvania. By contrast, most other counts mentioned in documents before 1200 are those of the northwestern area of Transylvania: Saul, count of Biharea (1111); John, count of Crasna (1164); Leustachius,

93 *Der Nibelungen Noth und die Klage*, ed. by K. Lachmann (Berlin: G. Reimer, 1878), pp. 173–174, 240, and 310. In the sequel known as the *Klage* there is a second ruler of the Vlachs named Sigehêr. Ramunc also appears in another medieval German epic, the *Biterolf*, composed in the mid-thirteenth century, and his native country is again the "land of the Vlachs." See *Biterolf und Dietleib*, ed. by O. Jänicke (Berlin: Weidmann, 1867; reprint 1963), pp. 18, 51, and 55–56. In Rudolf of Ems' rhymed chronicle, written in the early 1200s, the Vlachs appear in association with the Cumans and with the snow-covered mountains (*Weltchronik*, ed. by G. Ehrismann [Berlin: Weidmann, 1915], p. 36).

94 Armbruster, *Der Donau-Karpatenraum*, pp. 54–59.

95 *Gesta Hungarorum* 26, p. 76.

count of Dăbâca (1164); Thomas, count of Cluj (1177); Nicholas, count of Satu Mare (1181).[96] Outside Transylvania proper, the counts of Timişoara, Cenad, and Caraş were first mentioned in documents of the last quarter of the twelfth century.[97] However, other counts may have been in office though they do not appear in contemporary documents. For example, the castle at Turda is mentioned in 1075 in relation to the salt trade, the monitoring and royal taxation of which must have been in the hands of the local count.[98] *Castrum Cuculiensis* (Küküllő, now Cetatea de Baltă near Târnăveni) is first mentioned in 1177, but the count appears only in 1214.[99] The multiplication of Transylvanian counts in charters of the second half of the twelfth century suggests drastic administrative changes taking place under King Géza II and his successors, especially Béla III. Key to this reorganization was the division of the initial county in the middle of the region, which had been centered upon Alba Iulia, into smaller administrative units, such as Cluj or Cetatea de Baltă. The rearrangements of the late twelfth century were clearly accompanied by demographic growth. Over fifty new settlements are mentioned in charters dated between 1150 and 1200, more than half of which are still existing villages or towns. Many of them can be located in the northwestern region, around the old county seats at Biharea, Dăbâca, and Cluj, where royal estates were most numerous. It is in this region that in 1176 King Béla III granted estates to a certain Lob in recognition of his military service during the Hungarian–Byzantine wars.[100] Internal migration may have been responsible for the multiplication of settlements,[101] but archaeological excavations in Moreşti, near Târgu Mureş, have unearthed a twelfth- to early thirteenth-century

[96] *Documente privind istoria României. C. Transilvania* [Documents regarding the History of Romania. Series C: Transylvania], ed. by M. Roller, vol. 1 (Bucharest: Editura Academiei Republicii Populare România, 1951), pp. 2–3, 6, and 8.

[97] *Documente*, pp. 6, 13, and 19.

[98] *Documente*, p. 1. For the eleventh- and twelfth-century salt trade on the Mureş River, see G. Kovach, "Date cu privire la transportul sării pe Mureş în secolele X–XIII [Data regarding the transportation of salt on the Mureş River during the tenth to thirteenth century]," *Ziridava*, vol. 12 (1980), 193–200.

[99] *Documente*, pp. 21 and 66.

[100] *Documente*, pp. 242–243.

[101] Two villages named Devecher (*superior* and *inferior*) are mentioned in the Cluj region during the last quarter of the twelfth century. The latter was clearly a foundation of immigrants from the former. See *Documente*, p. 242. The same is true of several other villages near Biharea and Alba Iulia mentioned in the early 1200s.

small village located next to an older royal fort whose earthen ramparts received a stone reinforcement at some point after 1100.[102] The sunken-featured buildings found on the site produced wheel-made pottery (the so-called "Moreşti C Ware"), but also clay pans reminiscent of early medieval food-preparation traditions.[103] Given the short distance between village and fort, Moreşti may have been a settlement of specialized workers (peasants and craftsmen) serving the exclusive needs of the neighboring fortress's ruler, possibly the local count. As such, the village is an indication of the measures taken by the Hungarian kings during the second half of the twelfth century, which prepared the way for the dramatic transformations of the eastern and southern frontier of the kingdom after 1200 and the beginning of the Hungarian expansion beyond the Carpathian Mountains.

THE VLACH REVOLT

While the author of the *Deeds of the Hungarians* made the Vlachs the inhabitants of the rich lowlands of Transylvania, his Jewish contemporary from Tudela described them as mountain people in Boeotia. Traveling through Greece in 1165, Benjamin of Tudela learned about the Vlachs living in the mountain region in the hinterland of Sinon Potamo (near Lamia, in Phtiotis), a region he called "Vlachia." To Benjamin the traveler, the Vlachs were as lawless as the Druses of the Sidon region of Lebanon: "No man can go up and do battle against them, and no king can rule over them."[104] Like the Jews in the mountainous country near the Strait of Aden, they were also "swift as hinds" as they swept "down from the mountains to despoil and ravage the land of Greece."[105] Both Jews and Vlachs hated Christians. To Benjamin the rabbi, the parallel was too strong to be ignored: the Vlachs were not true Christians, since they gave themselves Jewish names. "Some people say that they are Jews and, in fact, they call the Jews their brethren, and when they meet with them, though they rob them, they refrain from killing them as they kill the Greeks."[106]

[102] Horedt, *Moreşti*, vol. II, pp. 11–34. For a brief description of the fort, see Horedt, *Siebenbürgen im Frühmittelalter*, pp. 133–134.

[103] K. Horedt, "Backteller und Tonkessel in Moreşti," *Slovenská Archeológia*, vol. 26 (1978), pp. 59–68.

[104] *Itinerary of Benjamin of Tudela*, pp. 68 (Vlachs) and 78 (Druses).

[105] *Itinerary of Benjamin of Tudela*, pp. 68 (Vlachs) and 125 (Jews of Aden).

[106] *Itinerary of Benjamin of Tudela*, p. 68.

Given his concern with a typology of alterity, Benjamin's account of the Vlachs is difficult to assess in terms of historical value. But it is equally clear that to him, the Vlachs were an element of instability and disturbance within the Byzantine society of twelfth-century Greece. We have seen that the Vlachs already appear as rebellious in Kekaumenos' *Strategikon*. They had taken a leading part in the revolt against imperial taxation in Thessaly, the region of Greece next to that where Benjamin placed his Vlachs. But twenty years after his visit, the revolt of the Vlachs in the northeastern Balkans triggered changes of a political magnitude that was beyond the reach of either the Vlachs who followed Nikulitzas Delphinas in 1066 or the brigands described a century later by Benjamin of Tudela. That Peter and Asen, the two brothers who led the revolt of 1186, were Vlachs is spelled out clearly by sources dealing with this event. With the exception of Ansbert's brief references to the diplomatic contacts between the rebels and Emperor Frederick I Barbarossa during the passage of the Third Crusade through the Balkans (see below and chapter 7), the only source for the revolt itself is Niketas Choniates' *History* of the Empire from the reign of Alexios I Comnenus to the fall of Constantinople in 1204. The lack of alternative sources is only partially compensated by the fact that Choniates was a participant in the Byzantine campaigns against the Vlach rebels in the late 1180s and the 1190s. His attitude towards Vlachs is ambiguous, his coverage of events patchy.

According to Choniates, what sparked the revolt was a tax that Emperor Isaac II Angelos decided to levy in order to cover the expenses for his wedding to the daughter of the Hungarian king Béla III. Since the Vlachs are often depicted in historical studies as transhumant pastoralists, it is presumed that the tax must have been on the flocks of the Vlachs, although Choniates has nothing to say about Vlach transhumance. What he does say, though, is that the pretext that led to the uprising was "like that alleged on behalf of Patroklos," namely the rustling of the cattle belonging to the Vlachs and their own ill-treatment.[107] At no point are Peter and Asen described as owning cattle, but instead they appear as interested in acquiring land,

[107] Choniates, *Historia*, p. 368; English translation by Magoulias, p. 204. The reference to Patroklos is from *Iliad* 19.302, where Patroklos' death is attributed by Achilles to his quarrel with Agamemnon over a female captive, Briseis. If Choniates' parallel is to be followed with any consistency, the meaning of this passage is that the conflict between Peter and Asen, on the one hand, and Emperor Isaac II Angelos,

for during a visit to Kypsella (Ipsala, near Keşan, close to the Turkish–Greek border) they asked the emperor to grant them an estate near the mountains, "which would provide them with a little revenue."[108] Rebuffed and insulted (Asen was "struck across the face" at the order of John Dukas as a punishment for his insolence), the two brothers returned to their abodes, which must have been in the eastern Stara Planina range, although no geographical precision may be obtained from Choniates' account. According to him, shortly after their return, the two brothers built a "house of prayer" dedicated to St. Demetrius, the patron saint of the city of Thessalonica.[109] Choniates explains that prophets and prophetesses "of both races" (i.e., both Vlachs and Bulgarians), whom he calls "demoniacs" and "soothsayers," gathered in the church to predict that "the God of the race of the Bulgars and Vlachs had consented to their freedom and assented that they should shake off after so long a time the yoke from their neck."[110] Since elsewhere we are told that Peter and Asen were striving to "unite the

on the other, was the division of spoils. If true, then the rustling of cattle may refer not to the herds of the Vlachs, but to cattle they may have captured by violent means from someone else. Choniates reports that after their first attacks on the Byzantine towns in the lowlands of Thrace, the rebels took many prisoners, but also cattle, draft animals, sheep, and goats (*Historia*, p. 372; English translation by Magoulias, p. 205). Although it is hard to envisage the rustling of Vlachs' cattle as tax-levying for the emperor's wedding, it is nevertheless clear that Choniates had in mind some kind of administrative abuse verging on despoliation.

108 Choniates, *Historia*, p. 369; English translation by Magoulias, p. 204. Taken at face value, Choniates' account would imply that what Peter and Asen wanted was a *pronoia* (revenue derived from an estate that remained in imperial hands). In addition, they requested from Isaac to be recruited in the Roman army, most likely as officers.

109 It is commonly assumed that this is the Church of St. Demetrius in Veliko Tărnovo, which seems to have been rebuilt at some point during the last two decades of the twelfth century. See T. Teofilov, "Izsledvaniia vărkhu problema za stilovata rekonstrukciia na cărkvata Sv. Dimităr Solunski văv Veliko Tărnovo [Research on the style of the reconstruction of the Church of St. Demetrius of Thessalonica in Veliko Tărnovo]," *Godishnik na muzeite ot Severna Bălgariia*, vol. 17 (1991), pp. 67–87. If indeed this is the case, then the beginning of the revolt may be associated with the feast of the saint celebrated on October 26, 1185. See G. Prinzing, "Demetrios-Kirche und Aseniden-Aufstand. Zur chronologischen Präzisierung der Frühphase des Aseniden-Aufstandes," *ZRVI*, vol. 38 (1999–2000), pp. 262–264.

110 Choniates, *Historia*, pp. 369 and 371; English translation by Magoulias, pp. 204–205. Despite the shamanistic aura of Choniates' description of such prophesying practices, the use of prophets was not exclusively Vlach. In 1194, while in Rhaidestos (Tekirdağ, in Turkey), Isaac himself consulted a "holy man" named

political power of Mysia and Bulgaria into one empire as of old," what started as a revolt of the Vlachs alone seems to have quickly gained popularity among all those inhabiting the Bulgarian lands still under Byzantine control in the late 1100s. On the other hand, Choniates' account suggests that already by 1186 the revolt had taken a different turn. Peter and Asen showed a remarkable political sense by claiming that St. Demetrius had abandoned his city (Thessalonica, which had just been sacked by the Normans in 1185) to come on their side. Their own talents as prophets may have played an important role in building their reputation and prestige.[111] More importantly, Peter began sporting a gold chaplet on his head and scarlet buskins in his feet, in this way fundamentally replacing the initial claims that had led to his and his brother's rebellion with claims to the imperial title. Moreover, the first city the rebels attacked was Preslav, the old capital of Symeon's Bulgaria. Peter eventually moved to that city, which he seems to have preferred to Tărnovo, the stronghold which his brother chose for his residence and which Choniates describes as "the best fortified and most excellent of all cities along the Haemus [Stara Planina], encompassed by mighty walls, divided by a river, and built on a mountain ridge."[112]

The attacks of the rebels on cities and villages in Thrace were repelled by a Byzantine offensive that forced Peter and Asen to flee across the Danube, where they found trustworthy allies among the Cumans, with whom they may have already been in contact. It is important to note that after taking many Vlach strongholds in the mountains, where he left Byzantine garrisons, Emperor Isaac found "crops gathered in heaps," to which he set fire, an indication that the population supporting the rebels was not one of transhumant shepherds.[113] It was on this occasion that the emperor took an icon of St. Demetrius from Peter's house, thus symbollically reappropriating the saint for the Byzantines. During the following years, Vlach–Cuman forces raided Thrace and defeated a number of armies sent

Basilakios and his "Greek women," who behaved in a way suspiciously similar to that of the Vlach and Bulgarian prophets gathered in the church of Peter and Asen. See Choniates, *Historia*, pp. 448–450; English translation by Magoulias, pp. 246–247.

[111] For Peter and Asen engaging in prophesying, see Choniates, *Historia*, p. 437; English translation by Magoulias, p. 240.

[112] Choniates, *Historia*, p. 470; English translation by Magoulias, p. 258.

[113] Choniates, *Historia*, p. 373; English translation by Magoulias, p. 206.

against them. Choniates attributes their successes to Asen's ability to employ tactics that made the Byzantine efforts worthless, as the Vlachs attacked at one point and withdrew immediately after Isaac's troops approached, only to attack some place else. In October 1187, near Beroe (Stara Zagora in Bulgaria), the Byzantine army was routed by the Cumans, who used steppe warfare stratagems, especially the feigned retreat, to lure their pursuers into breaking ranks. Choniates' testimony of the military role the Cumans already played in the rebellion is very important, for he participated in the battle as Emperor Isaac's secretary. During the following year, the theater of operations shifted even farther to the west, as Isaac unsuccessfully besieged Lovitzos (Lovech, near Pleven, in northern Bulgaria). But the emperor "seized Asen's wife and received his brother John as a hostage," perhaps as a consequence of some negotiations about which nothing else is known.[114] When the army of Frederick I Barbarossa made its appearance in the region, Peter (but not Asen) sent envoys who reached the Roman emperor in Adrianople with offers of military support in exchange for "the imperial crown of the realm of Greece."[115] Peter's goals seem to have been different from those of Asen, who is not mentioned at any point as aspiring to the imperial title. The growing difference between the political views of the two brothers led to a conflict between them in the spring of 1193, at which point Asen began expanding his territory by taking over strongholds and lands along the Strymon River and in the vicinity of Serres. The conflict may have encouraged Emperor Isaac to gain one of the brothers on his side and incite him against the other. But in 1191, both rebels were viewed as equally dangerous. Isaac seems to have changed tactics again, as he attacked Peter and Asen from the east, across the low-altitude passes in the eastern Stara Planina. Quickly entering the enemy territory, he noticed that "fortresses and citadels were more strongly fortified than before with newly built walls marked off at intervals by crowned towers."[116] This may be viewed as an indication both of the growing military potential of the rebellion and of the remarkable mobilization of material and human

[114] Choniates, *Historia*, p. 399; English translation by Magoulias, p. 219. For Asen's wife, Elena, see I. Bozhilov, *Familiiata na Asenevci (1186–1460): genealogiia i prosopografiia* (Sofia: Izdatelstvo na Bălgarskata Akademiia na Naukite, 1994), p. 35.

[115] Ansbert, *History of Frederick's Expedition*, p. 58.

[116] Choniates, *Historia*, p. 428; English translation by Magoulias, p. 236.

resources that the two brothers had at their disposal. But the support Peter and Asen enjoyed among local warlords was by no means unanimous. On its way back to Thrace from his campaign north of Stara Planina, Isaac's army was ambushed in a mountain defile, most likely the Shipka pass, and the emperor escaped only by removing his helmet so that he would not be recognized. The imperial life and safety were entrusted to John Dukas (who had ordered in 1185 that Asen be struck in the face), himself relying on a Vlach officer in the imperial troops, who knew an alternative route.[117] Emboldened by their success, the Vlach rebels and their Cuman allies took Anchialos and Varna, destroyed Serdica, and removed inhabitants and cattle from Niš. The range of their activities suggests that the entire region of the northern Balkans was at that time under their control. Although both Nemanja and Peter had established contacts with Emperor Frederick Barbarossa in 1189, nothing is known about relations between them. The Vlach and Cuman raids did not cross the Morava, while no Serbian intervention in the region east of that river is known to have taken place before *c.* 1200. By 1195, Asen took Serdica and transferred to Tărnovo the relics of St. John of Rila.

To Niketas Choniates the region north of the Stara Planina was a separate political entity, which he called Zagora[118] and carefully distinguished from territories under Byzantine control south of that mountain range. In the late 1190s, Byzantine troops moving against the rebels were reluctant to cross the mountains into Zagora and demanded that they be brought back to their "own land."[119] By contrast, the range of the Vlach and Cuman attacks expanded considerably across the mountains. In 1194, a raiding party reached as far south as Arkadiopolis (Lüleburgaz, in Turkish Thrace). To cope with the growing threat, Emperor Isaac solicited the assistance of Béla III, who promised to send troops from Vidin on the Danube to attack the rebels in Zagora.[120]

In the mid-1190s, Peter and Asen began using personal seals and striking their own coins modeled after those minted for Emperors Manuel I, Isaac II, and Alexios III. Known as "Bulgarian Imitative" trachea (debased billon cup-shaped coins), this was the first coinage

[117] Choniates, *Historia*, p. 430; English translation by Magoulias, p. 237.
[118] Choniates, *Historia*, p. 398; English translation by Magoulias, p. 219.
[119] Choniates, *Historia*, p. 471; English translation by Magoulias, p. 258.
[120] Choniates, *Historia*, p. 437; English translation by Magoulias, p. 245.

struck for local rulers in Bulgaria during the Middle Ages. It has been suggested that one of the mints was in Beroe, which would in turn suggest that the decision to use such coins, perhaps for the payment of his Cuman allies, was Asen's.[121] But his ruthless rule in Zagora does not seem to have gone without challenge. Asen was murdered in 1196 by a nobleman named Ivanko, who seized Tărnovo and immediately called upon the assistance of the Byzantine armies to help him against Asen's brother Peter moving against him from Preslav. However, the troops sent to his rescue from Philippopolis rebelled before crossing the mountains and Ivanko had no other solution than to flee to Constantinople, where he offered his services to Emperor Alexios III. During the subsequent years, Ivanko distinguished himself fighting against his fellow Vlachs. A year later, Dobromir Chrysos, another Vlach warlord who had been on the Byzantine side, was arrested for "leaning towards his fellow Vlachs," before being released and appointed to the defense of Strumica in Macedonia.[122] Soon after that Chrysos declared himself independent in Strumica and began expanding his power over Prosek (Gradek near Gevgelija, in Macedonia), a powerful stronghold on a cliff above the river Vardar. Chrysos ordered the repair and enlargement of Prosek by building an advanced fortification to protect the gates. He had already gathered stone-throwing machines, weapons, and food supplies within the citadel,

[121] For seals, see I. Iordanov, "Pechat na părviia Asenevec [The seal of the first Assenid]," *Izvestiia na istoricheskiia muzei – Veliko Tărnovo*, vols. 15–16 (2000–2001), pp. 192–200. For the "Bulgarian Imitative" trachea and the mint in Beroe, see I. Iordanov, "Ranni formi na monetno proizvodstvo (XI–XIII v.) v bălgarskite zemi [The first attempts at striking coins in the Bulgarian lands (eleventh to thirteenth century)]," *Numizmatika*, vol. 14 (1980), pp. 4–15. The attribution of these coins to Peter and Asen is still a matter of dispute, with some scholars regarding them as expediency coinage struck by the Byzantines in late twelfth-century Thrace. See D. M. Metcalf, "Byzantinobulgarica: the Second Bulgarian Empire and the problem of 'Bulgarian imitative' trachea before and after 1204," *Numismatic Circular*, vol. 81 (1973), pp. 418–421. "Bulgarian Imitative" trachea also appear in Dobrudja, which was presumably under the control of Peter in the 1190s, but the number of finds is considerably smaller than that from hoards south of the Stara Planina range. See E. Oberländer-Târnoveanu, "Moneda Asăneştilor în contextul circulaţiei monetare din zona gurilor Dunării [The coinage struck by the Assenids in the context of the coin circulation in the Danube Delta region]," in *Răscoala şi statul Asăneştilor*, ed. by E. Stănescu (Bucharest: Editura Ştiinţifică şi Enciclopedică, 1989), pp. 114–152.

[122] Choniates, *Historia*, p. 487; English translation by Magoulias, p. 267. According to Choniates, Chrysos was "a Vlach by birth and short in stature."

when an army of Seljuk mercenaries in Byzantine service stormed the advanced fortification taking many Vlach prisoners without, however, conquering the citadel.[123] Emperor Alexios was forced to allow Chrysos to retain Prosek and Strumica, as well as the surrounding territory. East of the river Strymon, at the foot of the Pirin Mountains, another warlord barricaded himself in Melnik (near Sandanski, in southwestern Bulgaria). Alexios Slav was a nephew of Peter and Asen, and he turned the fort into a quasi-urban center. The building of the residential quarter Chatala in Melnik as a parallel center to the core of the city on the St. Nicholas Hill is to be attributed to this period. The most remarkable monument in the Chatala district is the so-called Boyar's House, an aristocratic house erected during Alexios Slav's rule over Melnik and its hinterland. The still-standing building has two stories and a powerful tower in the southeastern corner, in addition to a large hall, a cistern, and a private chapel.[124]

After forcing Ivanko to flee and occupying Tărnovo, Peter entrusted the city to his younger brother Ioannitsa (John), who had just returned from Constantinople, where he had been retained as hostage for many years. Soon after that, Peter was assassinated by his own men,[125] and John became sole ruler. Although quite young, he was a charismatic figure immediately acknowledged as such by the independent warlords near Philippopolis and in Macedonia. In 1198 or 1199, both Dobromir Chrysos and Ivanko recognized Ioannitsa's overlordship. Ensconced in Philippopolis, where he had been appointed by the emperor as a trustworthy ally against Ioannitsa's Vlachs, Ivanko had consolidated his power by building a number of strongholds around the city, the most important of which was

[123] Choniates, *Historia*, pp. 503–504; English translation by Magoulias, pp. 277–278. Chrysos had also hired a Byzantine renegade as the engineer in charge of the machines. It is at this juncture that Choniates mentions that there were problems with allowing the Seljuks to take Vlach prisoners. Unlike Benjamin of Tudela, Choniates knew that the Vlachs were "people who worship the same God we profess," and as a consequence they could not be left in Muslim hands.

[124] V. Nesheva, D. Serafimova, G. Stoianov, et al., "Arkhitektura [The architecture]," in *Melnik. Gradăt v podnozhieto na Slavova krepost*, ed. by S. Georgieva and V. Nesheva, vol. 1 (Sofia: Izdatelstvo na Bălgarskata Akademiia na Naukite, 1989), pp. 41–63. The Boyar's House and other buildings in the town produced large quantities of Fine Sgraffito wares. See B. Cvetkov, "Keramika [The pottery]," in *Melnik*, vol. 1, pp. 120–159.

[125] Choniates, *Historia*, p. 472; English translation by Magoulias, p. 259.

Kritzimos (Krichim).[126] He ambushed a Byzantine army sent against him under the command of the general Manuel Kamytzes, whom Ivanko's men managed to capture alive. A new Byzantine campaign in 1200/1 began with the siege and eventual conquest of Stenimachos (Asenovgrad, near Plovdiv, in Bulgaria), another important stronghold in the vicinity of Philippopolis. The emperor invited Ivanko at a conference to negotiate a settlement, but the warlord was captured and thrown into prison. Soon after that, Alexios' troops retook all the forts Ivanko had controlled in the region and "put to flight his brother Mitos."[127]

By that time, however, Ioannitsa had become a major player in the politics of the region. When his Vlach and Cuman troops reached the outskirts of Constantinople in 1200/1, Ioannitsa had already entered negotiations with Pope Innocent III in order to secure a crown and the recognition of the imperial title for himself. The Vlach revolt had turned into the Second Bulgarian Empire.

[126] Choniates, *Historia*, p. 512; English translation by Magoulias, p. 282. For Krichim, see D. Conchev, "Krichim prez srednovekovieto [Krichim during the Middle Ages]," *Godishnik na narodniia arkheologicheski muzei Plovdiv*, vol. 1 (1948), pp. 75–87.

[127] Choniates, *Historia*, p. 519; English translation by Magoulias, p. 285.

7

BETWEEN THE CRUSADE AND THE MONGOL INVASION (1200–1250)

The passage of the first three crusades through the Balkans produced both destruction and opportunities for the local leaders to assert their independence, especially in Bulgarian and Serbian territories under direct Byzantine control. In 1096, the pilgrims led by Walter the Penniless plundered the countryside around Belgrade, and they were in turn attacked by the locals. The pilgrims sacked a little town near Semlin, while bands of "infidel" Pechenegs, perhaps auxiliaries in Byzantine service, harassed the pilgrims and forced them to hide in the "Bulgarian forest."[1] The pilgrims of Peter the Hermit followed the same route from the Hungarian–Byzantine border at Semlin to Niš, with a number of bloody skirmishes with the locals on their way.[2] Skirmishes with the locals are also mentioned in relation to the crusaders who in 1098 followed a land route from Aquileia through northern Istria into Croatia under the leadership of Raymond of St. Gilles, Count of Toulouse. Under permanent attack by bands of locals emerging from the mountains of "Sclavonia," Raymond stayed with his rearguard and ordered the mutilation of prisoners in

[1] Albert of Aachen, *Historia Hierosolymitana*, p. 277.

[2] Albert of Aachen, *Historia Hierosolymitana*, p. 283. A third group of pilgrims under Godescalc followed the same route and encountered similar problems. See Albert of Aachen, *Historia Hierosolymitana*, pp. 289–290. For the military road from Niš to Adrianople on which the movements of the pilgrims were directed, see S. Runciman, "The first crusaders' journey across the Balkan Peninsula," *Byzantion* 19 (1949), 207–221; K. Gagova, "Părviiat krăstonosen pokhod po *Via militaris* [The First Crusade invasion along the *Via militaris*]," *Minalo* 3 (1996), 56–61.

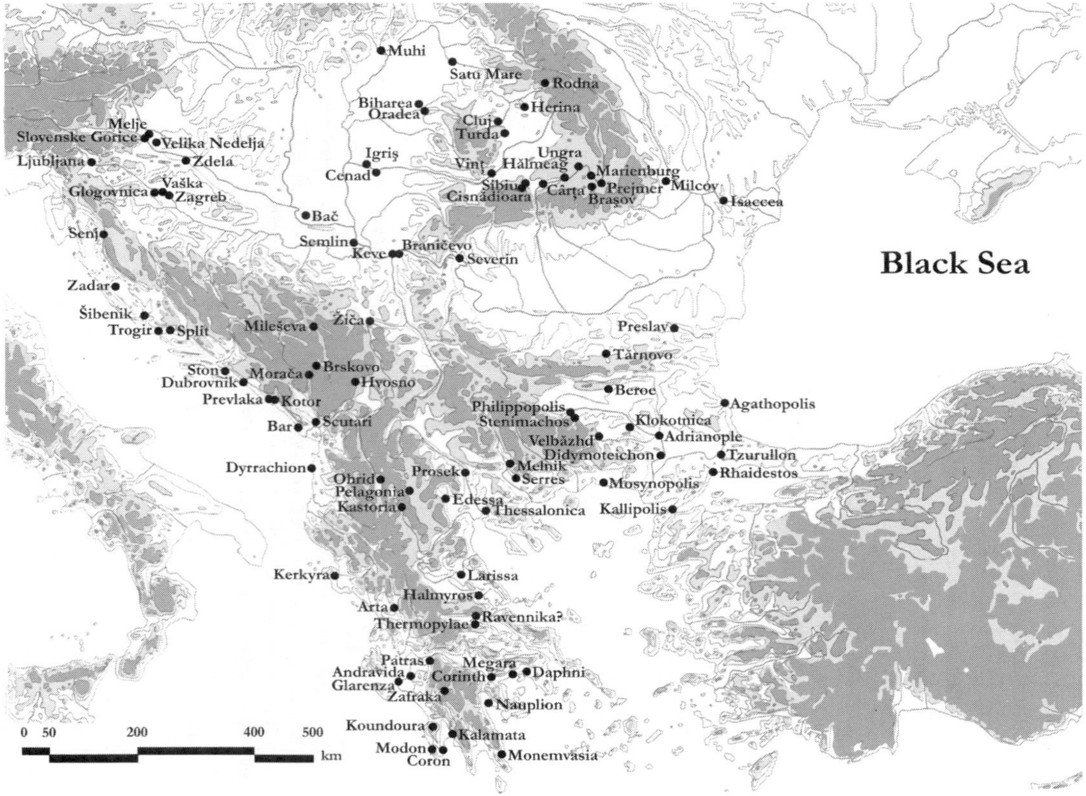

Map 7 Southeastern Europe between 1200 and 1250.

order to deter further attacks.[3] Raymond of Aguilers, the chronicler of the count of Toulouse, describes the local population as "aggressive and primitive," a "wild people" with no knowledge of God. He further distinguished between the inhabitants of the local towns, who apparently spoke a Latin idiom recognized as such by the crusaders, and natives living inland who "employ the Slavonic tongue and have the habits of barbarians." William of Tyre, the only source to describe the trip in some detail, mentions Zara (Zadar), Salona (also called Spalato), Antivari (Bar) and Ragusa (Dubrovnik). However, there is no mention of any of these cities opening its gates to welcome the crusaders. Nor did the crusaders have access to local markets in order to replace their rapidly diminishing supplies. It was first in Duklja that they were given permission by the local ruler, Bodin, to purchase provisions. In Dyrrachion, St. Gilles was greeted by the local governor, John Comnenus, who provided him with more supplies and a Pecheneg escort on his way to Constantinople along the Via Egnatia.[4] Bohemond of Taranto and his army also landed at Dyrrachion, but instead of following the Via Egnatia, they moved to Pelagonia (Bitolj, in Macedonia) and then along the valley of the river Vardar to Thessalonica. The army of Godfrey of Bouillon, the duke of Lower Lorraine, moved from Semlin to Philippopolis, along the military road across the Balkans, but unlike the pilgrims of Walter the Penniless and Peter the Hermit, they had no violent encounter with the local

[3] Raymond of Aguilers, *The History of the Franks who Conquered Jerusalem*, ed. by J. H. Hill and L. L. Hill (Paris: P. Geuthner, 1969), pp. 36–37; English translation by J. H. Hill and L. L. Hill (Philadelphia: American Philosophical Society, 1968), p. 17. This was a very unusual route, as no pilgrims to the Holy Land are known to have followed the coast. See I. Duichev, "The Balkan Slavs and the West during the period of the Crusades," in *The Meeting of Two Worlds. Cultural Exchange between East and West during the Period of the Crusades*, ed. by V. P. Goss (Kalamazoo: Medieval Institute Publications, 1986), pp. 411–412. For "Sclavonia" and the image of Croatia in Raymond of Aguilers, see A. Ilieva and M. Delev, "Sclavonia and beyond: the gate to a different world in the perception of crusaders (c. 1104–c. 1208)," in *From Clermont to Jerusalem. The Crusades and Crusader Societies 1095–1500. Selected Proceedings of the International Medieval Congress, University of Leeds, 10–13 July 1995*, ed. by A. V. Murray (Turnhout: Brepols, 1998), pp. 153–171.

[4] John Comnenus also assisted Hugh of Vermandois and his men who in August 1096 made their appearance on the coast just north of Dyrrachion. Unlike St. Gilles, Hugh of Vermandois was escorted to Constantinople via Philippopolis. See Anna Comnena, *Alexiad*, vol. II, p. 214; English translation by Sewter, p. 314. The pilgrims of Walter the Penniless were also escorted to Constantinople through Serdica and Philippopolis, after first encountering the Byzantine authorities in Niš.

population. The discipline of an army, as opposed to that of several bands of armed pilgrims, may explain the fact that Godfrey's troops were allowed to remain for eight days in Philippopolis, where the leaders of the crusaders were richly supplied by Emperor Alexios I.[5] This is in sharp contrast with the army of crusaders from Lombardy, who arrived in the Balkans in late September 1100. Although allowed to purchase food in several cities, while in Philippopolis the crusaders plundered houses and churches and killed many people.[6]

Minor incidents in Philippopolis and Adrianople are also reported in reference to the 1147 passage of the German contingent of the Second Crusade under Emperor Conrad III. According to John Kinnamos, before entering the Byzantine territory the crusaders were specifically asked to take an oath in front of Emperor Manuel's envoys that they would not harm the emperor's subjects.[7] There were indeed no incidents until the crusaders reached Thrace, when they began pillaging and killing those who opposed them. According to Niketas Choniates, more violence was prevented in Philippopolis by the local bishop, Michael Italikos, who befriended Emperor Conrad. However, in Adrianople, Duke Frederick (the future emperor Barbarossa) burned to the ground a local monastery together with the monks inside it, in order to revenge the death of several crusaders at the hands of "certain ruthless Romans."[8] Niketas accused his fellow citizens of taking advantage of the desperate need the crusaders constantly had to replenish their provisions. He even mentioned the order given by Emperor Manuel to "set up ambushes in strategic places and along the defiles of mountain passes."[9] In contrast to Emperor Conrad's army,

[5] The good relations established with the Byzantine authorities may also explain Godfrey's rejection of Bohemond's proposal of an alliance against Emperor Alexios. According to Albert of Aachen (*Historia Hierosolymitana*, p. 309), Bohemond had asked Godfrey to occupy the "Bulgarian cities" of Philippopolis and Adrianople.

[6] Albert of Aachen, *Historia Hierosolymitana*, p. 560. The crusaders were under the leadership of Archbishop Anselm of Milan and had traveled from Aquileia over the karst passes of Carniola. They moved from northern Croatia along the Sava River to Belgrade, and then followed the military road to Philippopolis.

[7] John Kinnamos, *Deeds*, p. 95; English translation by Brand, p. 63. One of the two envoys was Alexander, Count of Gravina, whose seal was found in Dristra (see chapter 6).

[8] Choniates, *Historia*, pp. 62–64; English translation by Magoulias, pp. 36–37. For the German crusaders in Philippopolis, see Dancheva-Vasileva, "Plovdiv à l'époque des premières Croisades," pp. 19–20.

[9] Choniates, *Historia*, p. 66; English translation by Magoulias, pp. 38–39.

the passage of the French crusaders led by King Louis VII does not seem to have caused any comparable disruption.[10] Like the Germans before them, the French camped outside Philippopolis, but there were no incidents of violence, despite the apparently widely known fact that Emperor Manuel had struck coins of debased silver to be used in transactions with the crusaders.[11] Much more destructive were the attacks of the Norman fleet of King Roger II. While the German and French crusaders were crossing the Balkans, the Normans managed to take Kerkyra and to sack Thebes and Corinth.[12]

A much more lasting effect of the Second Crusade on Southeastern Europe was the appearance of the military orders in Croatia. The Templars are mentioned in Zdela in 1154 and 1163, in Vrana near Biograd at some point before 1169, and in Zagreb shortly after that. By that time, the Hospitallers had already been established in St. Martin near Vaška.[13] The arrival of the military orders coincides in time with the Byzantine–Hungarian wars of the 1150s and 1160s. However, the initial grants in favor of the Knights were not from the king. The first one came from Borić, the *ban* of Bosnia who also had large estates in Slavonia. The most important papal donation was the Vrana Abbey. Prodanus, the bishop of Zagreb (1170–1175), gave the Templars land in that city, while the bishop of Nin donated a village in his diocese. A Croatian nobleman named Volkiša is known to have donated another village in northern Croatia. Royal donations followed soon after that, with King Béla III granting to the Templars the town of Senj. During Prince Andrew's rule in Croatia and Slavonia (1197–1202), a third order, the Canons of the Holy Sepulchre, was established in Glogovnica near Zagreb, in close proximity to the estates of the Templars. The estates of the Canons further increased by donations from a local nobleman named Gyula Kean.

[10] Odo of Deuil, *Liber*, p. 64.

[11] Choniates, *Historia*, p. 67; English translation by Magoulias, p. 39.

[12] Choniates, *Historia*, p. 75; English translation by Magoulias, p. 45. Choniates reports the rumor that the Normans had acted "in compact with the king of Germany" (*Historia*, p. 72; English translation by Magoulias, p. 43). However, Kerkyra was taken back in 1149 by Byzantine troops with German assistance.

[13] L. Dobronić, "The military orders in Croatia," in *The Meeting of Two Worlds. Cultural Exchange between East and West during the Period of the Crusades*, ed. by V. P. Goss (Kalamazoo: Medieval Institute Publications, 1986), p. 432. For the military orders in Croatia, see also B. Grgin, "The impact of the Crusades on medieval Croatia," in *The Crusades and the Military Orders. Expanding Frontiers of Medieval Latin Christianity*, ed. by Zs. Hunyadi and J. Laszlovszky (Budapest: Department of Medieval Studies, Central European University, 2001), pp. 167–171.

Both Templars and Canons benefited from grants of King Andrew II. In preparation for his crusade of 1217, Andrew gave the Templars Gačka and the castle of Šibenik.[14] By that time, the military orders had already been established in the neighboring marches of the Holy Roman Empire. For example, the Hospitallers had estates in Melje, near Maribor, where their interests clashed with those of Frederick, the burggrave of Ptuj. Frederick favored the Teutonic Knights, previously established in Velika Nedelja (near Čakovec, Croatia), Ljubljana, and Slovenske Gorice (near Maribor, Slovenia).[15] However, neither Hospitallers nor Teutonic Knights played any significant political role in the region until their involvement in the expansion of the Hungarian kingdom beyond the Carpathians.

Indeed, neither the Second Crusade nor the arrival of the military orders had any immediate effect on Southeastern Europe. The first such impact was made by the Third Crusade, which coincided in time with some of the most important political developments in the late twelfth-century Balkans. Like the armed pilgrims of the First Crusade, the army of Emperor Frederick Barbarossa met with much hostility after crossing the Danube from Hungary from both Byzantine officials (such as the duke of Braničevo) and the local population. Like Manuel before him, Emperor Isaac II had ordered the restoration of forts in the mountain passes and of city fortifications by which the crusaders were expected to pass. Moreover, instead of following the military road across the Balkans, the crusading army was shown a second, much rougher tract, which had been previously blocked at key points in preparation for possible ambushes. On its way to Niš, the army was indeed ambushed several times by Greeks, Bulgarians, Serbs, and "semi-barbarian Vlachs."[16] Much like with the first two crusades, the Germans began plundering the countryside in search for provisions. They were often harassed by auxiliary troops in Byzantine service, who carefully avoided any direct confrontation with the entire army.[17] The crusaders managed to put to flight the troops sent against them and even seized several forts in Thrace, including

[14] Dobronić, "Military orders in Croatia," pp. 433–444.

[15] Kosi, "The age of the Crusades," p. 143. A crusader himself, Frederick of Ptuj accompanied Duke Leopold VI of Austria to Syria in 1217.

[16] Ansbert, *History of Frederick's Expedition*, p. 28. See G. Cankova-Petkova, "Friedrich I. Barbarossa und die sozial-politischen Verhältnisse auf dem Balkan zur Zeit der III. Kreuzzuges," *Palaeobulgarica*, vol. 6 (1982), pp. 69–74.

[17] Choniates, *Historia*, p. 403; English translation by Magoulias, p. 221. See also Ansbert, *History of Frederick's Expedition*, pp. 37 and 41.

Beroe (Stara Zagora) and Adrianople. After leaving Philippopolis at the end of a twelve-week sojourn, Frederick left a garrison in the city and returned briefly from Adrianople to check on its assignments.

In 1189 and 1190, the crusaders remained in the Balkans longer than in any of the previous crusades. This may also explain the presence of occasional artifacts of clearly Western origin, such as spurs, which were found on several sites in the central Balkans.[18] But the Third Crusade also offered many more political opportunities to local rulers. In Niš, Nemanja and his brothers approached Emperor Frederick with an offer of military assistance against the Byzantines. The envoys of the Vlach rebel Peter reached the crusading army in Adrianople and promised a force of 40,000 Vlach and Cuman archers for an assault on Constantinople, provided that the emperor would recognize Peter as "King of Greece."[19] Even higher aspirations were made possible by the acute political and religious polarization brought by the Fourth Crusade. The conquest of Constantinople by the crusaders "turned the opposition between the two centers of medieval Christian spirituality into a great political and ideological confrontation, which involved the entire Eastern Christendom."[20]

The crusaders had already conquered Zadar in 1202 on behalf of the Venetian doge Enrico Dandolo. Although the event is often presented as a turning point in the history of the Fourth Crusade, it had no immediate impact on the region. The conquest of Zadar must in fact be viewed as another episode in the long series of twelfth-century confrontations between Venice and Hungary (see chapter 6). Compared to the destruction brought by the Norman raids to Dyrrachion and northern Greece in the late eleventh century, to Thebes and Corinth in 1147, and to Thessalonica in 1185, the 1202 attack on

18 L. Dzhidrova, "Crusaders in the central Balkans," in *The Crusades and the Military Orders. Expanding Frontiers of Medieval Latin Christianity*, ed. by Zs. Hunyadi and J. Laszlovszky (Budapest: Department of Medieval Studies, Central European University, 2001), pp. 189 and 197, with examples from Macedonia, Bulgaria, and Serbia. See also E. Koicheva, "Everyday life of the crusaders on the Balkan," in *Centre, Region, Periphery. Medieval Europe Basel 2002*, ed. by G. Helmig, B. Scholkmann, and M. Untermann, vol. II (Basel: Dr. G. Wesselkamp, 2002), pp. 352–353.

19 Ansbert, *History of Frederick's Expedition*, p. 58. See S. Lishev, "Tretiiat krăstonosen pokhod i bălgarite [The invasion of the Third Crusade and the Bulgarians]," *IIBI*, vol. 7 (1957), pp. 205–221.

20 Ş. Papacostea, *Between the Crusade and the Mongol Empire. The Romanians in the 13th Century* (Cluj-Napoca: Center for Transylvanian Studies, Romanian Cultural Foundation, 1998), p. 22.

Zadar was not particularly shocking. Both King Emeric of Hungary and Pope Innocent III vehemently protested the sack of Zadar, but both were concerned as much with the diversion of the Fourth Crusade as with the effusion of Christian blood caused by the crusaders.[21] It is equally doubtful that the pope, who condemned the attack on Zadar before it actually took place, later supported it as a means of eradicating the Bogomil heresy from the city. In reality, there is little evidence that the heretics the pope had encouraged King Emeric to crush were at all Bogomils, and even less that they all resided in Zadar.[22]

Only the conquest of Constantinople (April 13, 1204) drastically altered the balance of power in the entire Southeast European region and had long-term consequences. Even before the fall of the city, the Vlach ruler Ioannitsa, who had meanwhile assumed the title of Emperor of Bulgaria (see chapter 6), hastened to make overtures of peace to the crusaders, only to be rebuffed in the strongest terms possible.[23] When Boniface of Montferrat began the conquest of Greece in October 1204, a fief had already been carved out of the European territory of the Empire around the city of Philippopolis, next to the lands under Ioannitsa's control. Renier de Trith and his relatives occupied the city and began repairing or even expanding some of the satellite forts, especially Stenimachos. However, as the conquest of Peloponnesus was making progress, Renier was abandoned by most

[21] King Emeric of Hungary had himself taken the crusading vows in 1201. See D. E. Queller and T. F. Madden, "Some further arguments in defense of the Venetians on the Fourth Crusade," *Byzantion*, vol. 62 (1992), pp. 448–449; and *The Fourth Crusade. The Conquest of Constantinople*, 2nd ed. (Philadelphia: University of Pennsylvania Press, 1997), p. 80.

[22] Queller and Madden, *The Fourth Crusade*, p. 65. For Innocent III and the conquest of Zadar, see A. J. Andrea and I. Motsiff, "Pope Innocent III and the diversion of the Fourth Crusade army to Zara," *Byzantinoslavica*, vol. 33 (1972), pp. 6–25; O. Hageneder, "Innocenz III. und die Eroberung Zadars (1202). Eine Neuinterpretation des Br. V 160 (161)," *Mitteilungen des Instituts für Österreichische Geschichtsforschung*, vol. 100 (1992), pp. 197–213. The heresy may have come to Zadar from Italy, not from neighboring Bosnia. In Split, the Patarene heresy was a problem sufficiently serious in the late twelfth century for Archbishop Bernard to take drastic measures against it. See Thomas of Spalato, *Historia Salonitana*, p. 80, and F. Šanjek, *Les chrétiens bosniaques et le mouvement cathare, XIIe–XVe siècles* (Brussels, Paris, and Louvain: Nauwelaerts, 1976), pp. 50–51.

[23] Robert de Clari, *The Conquest of Constantinople*, ed. by J. Longnon (Paris: J. Tallandier, 1981), p. 228; English translation by E. H. McNeal (New York: Columbia University Press, 1936), pp. 86–88.

of his relatives. Under constant attack by Vlachs, he was forced to leave Philippopolis in February 1205 with a force of no more than fifteen knights.

Following the conquest of Constantinople, "not even the northern regions [in the Balkans] were exempted from the casting of lots," as the territories under direct or only nominal rule of Byzantium were allocated as fiefs by a partition committee of twelve Venetians and twelve Franks.[24] It is unlikely that the "northern regions" to be apportioned included anything beyond southern Thrace and the hinterland of Constantinople.[25] The Latin emperor got the region closest to the city stretching to the west up to a line from Agathopolis (Akhtopol, just north of the present-day Bulgarian–Turkish border) on the Black Sea coast, to Rhaidestos (Tekirdağ, in Turkey), on the northern coast of the Sea of Marmara. Beyond that line were the Venetian lands, which included such important centers as Adrianople, Tzurullon (Çorlu, Turkey), and Kallipolis (Gallipoli, now Gelibolu, in Turkey). From the Venetian lands up to Mosynopolis (near Komotini, in Greece) were the lands of the crusaders and beyond that no territory was assigned to anyone. Greece was divided along the Pindos Mountains between crusader lands to the east and Venetian lands to the west, which also included Peloponnesus. With the exception of Philippopolis, granted to Renier de Trith, no lands in the valley of the Marica River were apportioned. Moreover, the actual conquest followed the partition only in very general lines. To be sure, the political and military circumstances following the conquest made changes to the initial partition necessary, and at the same time became a source of conflict. When Emperor Baldwin marched on Thessalonica in the summer of 1204 and began to seize territory beyond the crusader lands by Mosynopolis, Boniface of Montferrat responded by attacking Adrianople, where, in the absence of any Venetian garrison, the emperor had established his own men.

In Greece proper, Boniface alone organized the conquest. Niketas Choniates noted with disgust how the inhabitants of the Thermopylae region "submitted to the marquis [Boniface of Montferrat]

[24] Choniates, *Historia*, p. 595; English translation by Magoulias, p. 327. For the *partitio Romaniae*, see P. Lock, *The Franks in the Aegean, 1204–1500* (London and New York: Longman, 1995), pp. 45–51.

[25] Robert de Clari knew that Ioannitsa's "Vlachia" (*Blaquie*) was "a land which belongs to the emperor." See his *Conquest of Constantinople*, p. 228; English translation by McNeal, p. 87.

readily in the base and despicable spirit which is ever disposed to side with the more powerful."[26] Leo Sgouros and his private army were forced to withdraw into Peloponnesus, where the resistance concentrated on Corinth and Nauplion. At the siege of Nauplion, Boniface passed the command to Geoffrey of Villehardouin and to his fellow Champagnard, William de Champlitte. Both had a force of no more than 500 men, only 100 of whom were knights. In the spring of 1205, moving from Nauplion on the Argolid Bay to Corinth (which fell only in 1210, two years after Sgouros' death), and then to Patras, Champlitte and Villehardouin followed the western coast of Peloponnesus to the southern end of the Bay of Kiparissia, without encountering any Venetian presence. Their goal must have been to secure the supply and communication lines by sea. In May, their small corps defeated at Koundoura (near Kiparissia, in northwestern Messenia) an army of 4,000 local recruits and mercenaries sent from Epirus. However, not all Greeks offered resistance. In Modon (Methoni), one of the most powerful *archontes* in central Peloponnesus, Leo Chamaretos, met with Geoffrey of Villehardouin with an offer of cooperation, while other Greek aristocrats fled to Epirus.[27] Some additional fighting took place in Patras, as well as in Coron (Koroni) and Kalamata, where Byzantine fortifications seem to have been in operation. Before the end of 1205, William of Champlitte was proclaimed Prince of Achaia, while the Venetian fleet occupied Modon and Coron. After William's return to France in 1208, Geoffrey of Villehardouin became Prince of Achaia in his stead. He agreed to recognize Venetian suzerainty over Morea and the boundaries between the Latin and the Venetian territory around Modon and Coron. Despite its initially rapid progress, the conquest of Peloponnesus was in fact a long-drawn process, which ended in 1249 with the surrender of Monemvasia to Prince William II. Sporadic resistance is documented even after *c.* 1250. Slavic rebels in the region of Mount Taigetos prompted the construction of a number of castles, the archaeological investigation of which has only begun.

The conquest brought no fundamental changes to the economic profile of the region. The second generation of Latins established in

[26] Choniates, *Historia*, p. 609; English translation by Magoulias, p. 334.

[27] Geoffrey of Villehardouin, *The Conquest of Constantinople*, ed. by E. Faral (Paris, 1939), pp. 134–136. For Leo Chamaretos, see A. Bon, *Le Péloponnèse byzantin jusqu'en 1204* (Paris: Presses Universitaires de France, 1951), pp. 123, 172–173, and 204–205.

Greece saw a substantial growth of the agriculture that had sustained economic growth since the eleventh century. Very little is known about the organization of estates during the first half of the thirteenth century, and virtually nothing about the relations between conquerors and local farmers. Later sources, such as the fourteenth-century inventories of the lands of the Acciaioli family, suggest that the customary dues paid to the lord by his peasants were in fact not much different from the taxes paid to the Byzantine state in the eleventh and twelfth centuries. While continuity may also be noticed in the urban environment, a few new towns came into being as a consequence of the conquest. The Venetians rebuilt from ground up the abandoned town of Modon, while erecting new ramparts and an aqueduct to bring water from the neighboring hills. Geoffrey of Villehardouin built Glarenza (Killini, near Gastouni), where the first mint of Frankish Greece would later be established. Excavations in Corinth have produced significant quantities of Aegean Ware, which made its appearance in the early 1200s to become one of the most popular ceramic wares in the Eastern Mediterranean. The lack of a local Frankish coinage during the first half of the thirteenth century was mitigated by the continuing use of Byzantine coins, some as old as Emperor Manuel's first issues. Moreover, following the conquest a significant number of debased deniers tournois from France and of sterlings from England were imported into the circulating medium in Greece under circumstances that are not yet fully understood.

Perhaps most indicative of the prosperity of early thirteenth-century Greece is the number of grants to monastic and military orders. The first duke of Athens, Otho de la Roche (1205–1225), granted in 1207 the monastery of Daphni to the Cistercian Abbey of Bellevaux in Burgundy. Geoffrey of Villehardouin, Prince of Achaia, established Cistercian monks in his foundation at Zaraka (near Langhadia, in Arcadia), the only Gothic building in Greece to be dated before 1250. As they had taken an active role in the conquest of Greece, the Templars acquired much land in Thessaly and central Greece, soon followed by Hospitallers and the Teutonic Knights. At Patras, the local cathedral chapter was handed over to the regular canons from St. Ruff (near Avignon). In all other cases in Greece, cathedral chapters remained secular. The first appointments of Latin bishops and archbishops took place immediately after the conquerors began apportioning the territory under their control. For example, the first Latin archbishop of Athens was appointed in 1206 with the support of Otho de la Roche, who one year later promoted his candidate to the see of Thebes. At the same time, Nivelon de Cherissy became the first Latin archbishop of Thessalonica with the backing of Boniface of Montferrat. On the other hand, Pope Innocent III had already proposed the confirmation of the Greek archbishops provided that they acknowledged papal primacy. There were at least four such archbishops in 1210, while a group of Orthodox priests in Thessalonica demanded confirmation of their privileges and income of their churches in exchange for canonical obedience. Where no Orthodox bishopric had existed before, as in Thermopylae, Megara, or Andravida, new sees were created, but the general tendency seems to have been to consolidate existing bishoprics that were regarded as either too small or too poor. No parish structure developed in Latin Greece and many formerly Orthodox churches were simply reused, with little structural alteration to the buildings in addition to occasional rededication.

Power relations in Latin Greece were confirmed by the Parliament in Ravennika (unknown location, perhaps near Lamia), which was summoned by Henry, the new emperor of Constantinople, in 1209. Henry had previously marched on Thessalonica to dislodge a regency council formed at the death of Boniface of Montferrat in 1207. Demetrius, Boniface's son by his wife Margaret of Hungary, was still a child, and the regents wanted to replace him with Boniface's eldest son, William IV, the marquis of Montferrat. But Henry crowned Demetrius on January 6, 1209 as King of Thessalonica, a title later recognized by the pope as well. Moving from Thessalonica into Greece, Henry summoned the parliament in Ravennika where he confirmed most of the lordships already in existence in the region, in exchange for recognition of his imperial overlordship. He campaigned briefly in Greece and moved against Michael Angelos Dukas of Epirus (1204–1215), a former ally of Boniface who had withdrawn into the mountain region around Arta to organize the resistance against the Latins. Michael agreed to marry his daughter to Henry's brother Eustace, who had been appointed regent to Demetrius, King of Thessalonica. Henry had requested from Michael a formal submission, but he seems to have renounced such claims when the marriage alliance was sealed. However, as soon as Henry's army withdrew from the region, Michael swore allegiance to Peter Ziani, the doge of Venice. Allied with Strez, the Bulgarian lord of Prosek, Michael's troops of Latin mercenaries attacked the kingdom of Thessalonica. The campaign took on a particularly religious note, as Michael began decapitating Latin priests and ordered that Amédée de Pofoy, the constable of Thessalonica, be crucified together with three of his companions.[28] Although eventually unable to take Thessalonica, Michael occupied Larisa, Halmyros, and a number of other, smaller towns in Thessaly. During the subsequent decade, Thessaly became the arena of military confrontation between the Epirote troops and the Latins of Greece. But Michael's power also expanded to the north in the direction of Dyrrachion, which fell to his mercenaries in 1213, and Kerkyra, which Michael took from the Venetians a year later. When Michael was replaced by his half-brother Theodore Dukas (1215–1230), Ohrid and Pelagonia came under Epirote rule. Theodore defeated Emperor Henry's successor, Peter of Courtenay, who was captured and killed by the Epirotes in 1217. Pushing into Macedonia, Theodore took Serres in 1221, completely surrounding Thessalonica by the following year. William IV, the marquis of Montferrat, gathered military assistance for the besieged Latins, but in 1224 the garrison in Thessalonica surrendered to the Epirotes. Theodore, who had refused to acknowledge the title of Emperor bestowed upon his rival, John Vatatzes of Nicaea, was crowned emperor in 1227 by the archbishop of Ohrid. He had become the ruler of one of the most important powers in Southeastern Europe. When his troops arrived in 1225 under the walls of Adrianople, the Nicaean garrison John Vatatzes had previously left there surrendered without a fight. By the end of the year, almost all of Thrace was in Epirote hands. The conquest of Thrace contributed to the increasing Bulgarian–Epirote rivalry of the late 1220s, which ultimately led to the invasion of Bulgaria in 1230. The Epirote troops were mauled at Klokotnica (near Haskovo, in southern Bulgaria), where Theodore himself was captured. The Bulgarians then occupied Thrace and Macedonia. Michael II Dukas (*c.* 1232–1271), Theodore's successor in Epirus, ruled over a much diminished state. Theodore's brother Manuel escaped from Bulgarian captivity and managed to seize power in Thessalonica. When in 1237 the Bulgarians released Theodore, whom they had previously blinded, he incited a coalition of aristocrats in Thessalonica to depose and exile

[28] The incidents are reported in a letter of Pope Innocent III dated December 7, 1210 (PL 216:353–354). It is in this context that the pope allowed the archbishop of Larisa to move to a neighboring and safer location. See Lock, *Franks in the Aegean*, p. 211.

Manuel and to proclaim instead Theodore's son John as Emperor of Thessalonica. John Vatatzes managed to capture Theodore, but his 1242 expedition against Thessalonica did not dislodge John and his supporters, although it did force him to recognize Nicaean overlordship. When Vatatzes returned to attack Bulgaria in 1246, Michael II Dukas took advantage of the situation thus created and seized Ohrid. A conspiracy in Thessalonica turned the city to Vatatzes, who thus annexed the kingdom of Thessalonica to the Nicaean domains, but left Theodore Dukas as lord of Edessa. By 1248, Michael II Dukas acknowledged Vatatzes' overlordship and married his son Nicephorus to Vatatzes' granddaughter Maria. After an unsuccessful rebellion against Vatatzes in 1251, Michael was forced to acknowledge the Nicaean occupation of much of his Epirote lands, from Kastoria and Ohrid to the outskirts of Dyrrachion. By the mid-thirteenth century, Nicaea had established a firm control over most of the Balkan lands, which had been under Byzantine rule before 1204. Vatatzes had completely surrounded the Latin Empire of Constantinople, now reduced to little more than the city. More importantly, he had no rival in the Balkans, as the power of the Bulgarian emperor had begun to wane.

THE SECOND BULGARIAN EMPIRE

After Niketas Choniates, the most important source for the history of the Vlach rebellion is a series of four letters written by Pope Innocent III (1198–1216) to Ioannitsa, the young brother of Asen and Peter. In his first letter of early December 1199, the pope addressed him as "the noble man Ioannitsa" and responded to his unspecified proposals by sending his envoy, the archpresbyter "of the Greeks at Brindisi." Innocent claimed to have learned, perhaps from Ioannitsa's envoys to Rome, that his ancestors had come "from the nobility of the City of Rome" and that Ioannitsa "had received from them the generous blood and feelings of sincere devotion," which, according to the pope, explained Ioannitsa's devotion to the Apostolic see.[29] If Innocent's intention was to flatter Ioannitsa by pointing out his

[29] *Acta Innocentii PP III (1198–1216)*, ed. by T. Halushchyns'kyi (Rome: Typis Polyglottis Vaticanis, 1944), p. 207; English translation from Butler, *Monumenta Bulgarica*, p. 219. The comments about Ioannitsa's Roman ancestry are repeated in the letter of November 27, 1202 (*Acta Innocentii*, pp. 226 and 228). See R. L. Wolff, "The 'Second Bulgarian empire'. Its origin and history to 1204," *Speculum*, vol. 24 (1949), pp. 190–191 and 193–194.

Vlach origins, his strategy worked. In his second letter of November 27, 1202, the pope mentions Ioannitsa's response written in "the Bulgarian language" (*Bulgaricum*, i.e., Old Church Slavonic), which was translated in Rome into Greek and then into Latin. In his letter, Ioannitsa, who called himself "Emperor of the Bulgarians and the Vlachs," acknowledged the Roman ancestry attributed to him by Innocent, while at the same time claiming lineal descent from the Bulgarian kings. He demanded a crown as well as privileges, "just as our emperors had in days gone by." Ioannitsa had apparently been able to find "written in our books" that both Peter (927–970) and Samuel (997–1014) had received crowns from Rome.[30] It remains unknown what particular "books" contained such information, but it is possible that Ioannitsa had access either to late eleventh-century apocrypha, which extolled the Bulgarian past, or to some other works inspired by that body of literature. In any case, Ioannitsa presented himself as continuing the imperial traditions of Bulgaria, while at the same time acknowledging Rome as the source for his legitimate crown. If the unspecified proposal to which Innocent alluded in his letter of December 1199 had anything to do with Ioannitsa's request to have a crown sent from Rome, then his efforts must be regarded as a continuation of his older brother's imperial aspirations (see chapter 6). In other words, although encouraging Innocent to believe in his Roman ancestry, Ioannitsa's true concern was to obtain the recognition of the political claims his brother Peter had been unable to obtain for himself.

In his response, Innocent cautiously called him "Kaloiannis, ruler of the Bulgarians and Vlachs," thus recognizing Ioannitsa's right to rule over Symeon's and Peter's Bulgaria, but not his imperial title.[31] To make his reply palatable to Ioannitsa, the pope acknowledged the Vlach ruler's request of a crown to match "Peter, Samuel, and others among your ancestors, according to your books." He also mentioned the correspondence and relations between Nicholas I and Hadrian IV,

[30] *Acta Innocentii*, p. 563; English translation from Butler, *Monumenta Bulgarica*, p. 223.

[31] The name Kaloiannis ("John the Fair" or "the Good") may have been the Greek translation of a Bulgarian title emphasizing Ioannitsa's lofty aspirations. As such it appears in an Old Church Slavonic dedicatory inscription from Karydochorion (near Sidhirokastron, in the Strymon valley near the present-day Bulgarian–Greek border). The inscription refers to a "grand duke" named Vrana who built a fort for "Emperor Kaloiannis." See Popkonstantinov and Kronsteiner, *Starobălgarski nadpisi*, vol. II, p. 81.

on the one hand, and Boris, on the other, as well as the latter's eventual turn to Constantinople. Fearing that Ioannitsa may do the same, Innocent dispatched his chaplain, John of Casmari, to Bulgaria, with the mission to confirm Basil, the metropolitan of Beroe (Stara Zagora), and to consecrate other bishops in Ioannitsa's land.[32] The chaplain was also to look into Ioannitsa's "books" and investigate the problem of the Bulgarian crown.

Innocent's reply was not to Ioannitsa's satisfaction. In his response summarized in Innocent's third letter of August 1203, Ioannitsa dropped the Vlachs from his imperial title, calling himself "Emperor of the Bulgarians." He urged the pope to fulfill his requests, as the "Greeks" had apparently learned about his contacts with Rome and had decided to send him a patriarch, while Emperor Alexios III had promised that he would recognize Ioannitsa's imperial claims. As a proof of his good intentions towards Rome, Ioannitsa sent Archbishop Basil of Beroe to Rome with a large train, cattle, silken clothes, wax, silver, horses, and mules, all as gifts for the pope and his close associates. In exchange, he asked for cardinals empowered to crown him emperor.[33] That Archbishop Basil could travel safely from Beroe (or Tărnovo) to Dyrrachion is an indication that on the eve of the crusaders' conquest of Constantinople, Ioannitsa's power extended over the entire northern and central section of the Balkans, the area that a few years later Gervaise of Tilbury would call "the land of the Vlachs."[34]

[32] John of Casmari had distinguished himself in Bosnia, where he had been commissioned to investigate reports about heresy. He was in Bosnia in the spring of 1203 and in Hungary in June of that same year, on his way to Tărnovo. See J. R. Sweeney, "Innocent III, Hungary and the Bulgarian coronation: a study in medieval papal diplomacy," *Church History*, vol. 42 (1973), pp. 321–322.

[33] *Acta Innocentii*, pp. 226–227; English translation from Butler, *Monumenta Bulgarica*, p. 227. In a separate letter to Innocent, Archbishop Basil explained that he had been prevented from crossing over to Italy from Dyrrachion by the local duke and the local Latin clergy. Ioannitsa's letter (but not gifts) eventually arrived in Rome with his constable, Sergius, and a priest named Constantine who traveled on Basil's behalf.

[34] Gervaise of Tilbury, *Otia imperialia*, ed. by R. Pauli and F. Liebermann (Hanover, 1885; reprinted 1975), MGH SS 27:371. See S. Brezeanu, "'Blachi' and 'Getae' on the Lower Danube in the early thirteenth century," *RESEE* 19 (1981), pp. 595–604. For Ioannitsa's control of the roads through the central Balkan region at the time of Archbishop Basil's trip to Dyrrachion, see J. R. Sweeney, "Basil of Trnovo's journey to Durazzo: a note on Balkan travel at the beginning of the 13th century," *SEER*, vol. 51 (1973), pp. 118–120.

How can we explain Ioannitsa's imperial claims? In his dealings with the pope and request for a crown, he went far beyond his older brother's aspirations. His negotiations with Rome coincide in time with the political ascendancy of Nemanja's son Stefan. Stefan was clearly a step ahead of Ioannitsa, for he had married Eudokia, thus becoming a member of the imperial family in Constantinople, once his father-in-law was proclaimed Emperor Alexios III Angelos. Ioannitsa certainly had more practical reasons for insisting on being called emperor in the tradition of the tenth-century rulers of Bulgaria, a title that may have appealed to some aristocrats in the central and northern regions of the Balkans. Finally, an imperial title was the only possibility to counteract Hungarian claims to previously Byzantine territories over which Ioannitsa now ruled. His suddenly impatient demands to Pope Innocent may thus have been caused by recent events. In the summer of 1203, Ioannitsa had sent an expedition to Raška in support of Stefan, at the end of which he occupied Niš and established as bishop in that city a suffragan of Basil of Beroe. This action was most certainly directed against the Hungarian king Emeric, whose protégé, Vukan, was Stefan's brother and rival. The region of the former theme of Niš–Braničevo had been evacuated by Hungarian troops in 1185, when Emperor Isaac II Angelos married Margaret, the daughter of King Béla III of Hungary. Margaret's brother, King Emeric, now claimed that region as part of his sister's dowry and as rightfully his after the deposition of his brother-in-law. Nothing is known about the history of the region between 1185 and 1203, but given the reaction of King Emeric in the aftermath of Ioannitsa's invasion, the former theme of Niš–Braničevo may have become for all practical purposes a no-man's-land, if not actually a Hungarian march. Both Serbs and Vlach rebels raided the region in the late 1180s and early 1190s (see chapter 6). That Ioannitsa had control over Braničevo is shown by the fact that one of his letters to Innocent III was taken to Rome by Blasius, Bishop of Braničevo.[35] Moreover, in another letter to the pope, Ioannitsa complained that the king of Hungary had invaded and occupied five dioceses on the border, and had destroyed many churches in the area. He asked for the arbitration of the pope in the conflict over the Bulgarian–Hungarian border.

Innocent eventually sent to Bulgaria the cardinal priest Leo Brancaleoni. The papal legate brought a scepter and a crown for Ioannitsa,

[35] *Acta Innocentii*, p. 227 (*episcopus Brandizuberensis Blasius*).

as well as episcopal insignia for the archbishop of Veroia and the bishops of Preslav and Velbăzhd (Kyustendil). In the accompanying letter of February 1204, the pope formally appointed Ioannitsa as King of the Bulgarians and the Vlachs "who have been separated from the breasts of their mother for a long time."[36] The papal legate was supposed to enter Bulgaria from Hungary, no doubt because he had instructions regarding the border dispute between Emeric and Ioannitsa. He seems to have initially been successful, as the Hungarian king disbanded the army he had gathered to invade Ioannitsa's lands. However, the papal legate was not allowed to cross over the Danube into Bulgaria, but was instead put under arrest by the local count of Keve (Kovin, near Smederevo, Serbia). He was released only in late September or early October 1204. Meanwhile, perhaps in an attempt to gain allies against Emeric, Ioannitsa approached the crusaders gathered under the walls of Constantinople. According to Robert de Clari, he had "sent word to the high barons that if they would crown him king so that he would be lord of his land of Vlachia (*Blaquie*), he would hold his land and kingdom from them and would come to their aid to help them take Constantinople with all of a hundred thousand men."[37] Rebuffed by the crusaders, Ioannitsa had to wait until November 8, when the papal legate finally arrived in Tărnovo and crowned him king. In his letter of response to Pope Innocent III, Ioannitsa referred to himself as "King of Bulgaria and Vlachia," but to the territory under his authority as his "empire" and to Basil as "patriarch."[38] Innocent's letter had granted Ioannitsa the "unrestricted right to strike state coinage inscribed" with his image.[39] None of these coins, if they were ever struck, survived, and only Ioannitsa's ring and seal may serve to illustrate his imperial aspirations.[40]

[36] *Acta Innocentii*, pp. 251–253; English translation from Butler, *Monumenta Bulgarica*, pp. 229 and 231. The "mother" in question is, of course, Rome.

[37] Robert de Clari, *The Conquest of Constantinople*, p. 228; English translation by McNeal, pp. 86–87.

[38] *Acta Innocentii*, p. 251. For "Vlachia" in Ioannitsa's title, see S. Brezeanu, "*Imperator Bulgariae et Vlachiae*. În jurul genezei şi semnificaţiei termenului Vlachia din titulatura lui Ioniţă Asan [*Imperator Bulgariae et Vlachiae*. On the appearance and significance of the term Vlachia in Ioannitsa's titulature]," *Revista de istorie*, vol. 33 (1980), pp. 651–674.

[39] *Acta Innocentii*, p. 253; English translation from Butler, *Monumenta Bulgarica*, p. 231.

[40] I. Duichev, "La bague-sceau du roi bulgare Kalojan," *Byzantinoslavica*, vol. 35 (1975), pp. 173–183; N. A. Mushmov, "Un sceau en plomb du tsar Kaloyan (1196–1207)," *Byzantinoslavica*, vol. 4 (1932), pp. 135–138.

Ioannitsa's coronation did nothing to remove the grudges he had against the crusaders. Nor was Pope Innocent capable of persuading either Ioannitsa or the crusaders to work towards a common good. Ioannitsa had meanwhile married a Cuman princess and, as a consequence, had large numbers of Cuman warriors at his disposal. In February 1205, he led his combined troops in a devastating raid against the crusader lands in Thrace in support of the Greek rebels in the cities conquered after the fall of Constantinople. He crushed the Latin army near Adrianople on April 14, 1205, and captured Emperor Baldwin himself. Ioannitsa "gave over for plunder to the Cumans those towns near Byzantion which were tributary to the Latins."[41] Soon after that, he moved against Thessalonica, where, just before the battle at Adrianople, power had been briefly in the hands of a "Vlach named Etzyismenos, who kept watch over Prosek and the neighboring territories subject to Ioannitsa."[42] On their way to Thessalonica, Ioannitsa's troops defeated the Latin garrison at Serres and took the city.[43] Then they suddenly marched on Philippopolis to crush the revolt of the local Greeks. In 1206 and 1207, the Vlachs and the Cumans again raided Thrace, attacking Adrianople and Didymoteichon. Ioannitsa also allied himself with Theodore Laskaris, the emperor of Nicaea, thus forcing the Latins to fight on two fronts, one in Asia Minor, the other in Thrace. Finally, a Vlach–Cuman raiding party ambushed and killed Boniface of Montferrat in the environs of Mosynopolis (September 1207). A month later, Ioannitsa was murdered, most likely by his own men, while laying siege to Thessalonica.

At Ioannitsa's death, a conflict erupted between the partisans of John Asen, Asen's underage son, and those of a relative named Boril.[44] Fearing for the life of the child, John Asen's supporters took him out of the country, first to the Cumans, then – after Boril married Ioannitsa's widow – to Galicia. Boril began his rule by leading a raid into Thrace, most likely in an attempt to show that he had no intentions

41 Choniates, *Historia*, p. 618; English translation by Magoulias, p. 338. According to Geoffrey de Villehardouin, Ioannitsa had come to Adrianople with 13,000 Cuman warriors. See Villehardouin, *The Conquest of Constantinople*, p. 198.

42 Choniates, *Historia*, p. 619; English translation by Magoulias, p. 339.

43 The shifting campaign may have been caused by the hot weather, to which the Cumans were not accustomed. See Papacostea, *Between the Crusade and the Mongol Empire*, p. 26.

44 Boril's mother was a sister of Peter, Asen, and Ioannitsa. See Bozhilov, *Familiiata na Asenevci*, pp. 69–77.

of changing his predecessor's policies. But he seems to have faced some serious opposition. A rebellious aristocrat named Alexios Slav declared himself independent in his stronghold at Melnik and established contacts with Henry, the Latin emperor of Constantinople. Another rebel, Strez, took refuge in Raška and obtained the protection of the grand *zhupan* Stefan against Boril. In 1208, Strez invaded western Bulgaria with Serbian assistance and established himself in Prosek, a stronghold from which he began expanding into neighboring Macedonia. Meanwhile, on July 8, 1208, Emperor Henry had obtained a great victory against Boril at Philippopolis, which marked the beginning of a more aggressive Latin policy in Thrace. Philippopolis was occupied by Latin troops and immediately enfeoffed to Gerard de Stroem.

Strez seems to have made peace with Boril, for he was present at a church synod that, in an attempt to distract attention from his military and political failures, Boril summoned in 1211 for the condemnation of Bogomilism. The final document of that synod condemned "the priest Bogomil, who in the time of the Bulgarian king Peter adopted the Manichean heresy, and disseminated it in the Bulgarian land." But the show trial of those who, according to article 93 of the document, were "sowers of impiety" did not bring any substantive measures and no changes are known to have taken place in the organization of the Bulgarian church as a consequence of the 1211 synod.[45] Nor was there any improvement of Boril's political situation. Following Ioannitsa's death, the Hungarians had occupied the valley of the Morava River, from Niš all the way up to Braničevo. Boril is not known to have made any attempts to recuperate the lost territories. Moreover, in either 1211 or 1213, a rebellion broke against him in Vidin, on the border with Hungary. The exact reasons for that rebellion are unknown, but its leaders were three Cuman chieftains. Unable to quell the revolt, Boril had no choice but to ask for assistance from the Hungarian king Andrew II. An army of Saxons, Vlachs, Szeklers, and Pechenegs, all under the command of Joachim, Count of Sibiu, crossed the Carpathians from Transylvania and defeated a number of troops from "Cumania" before storming and conquering Vidin.[46]

[45] Butler, *Monumenta Bulgarica*, pp. 207 and 213.

[46] *Documente*, pp. 338–339. See Papacostea, *Between the Crusade and the Mongol Empire*, p. 47; N. Iliev, "Otnosno vremeto na potushavane bunta sreshtu car Boril văv Vidin [On the exact date of the rebellion in Vidin against Boril]," *Izvestiia na Muzeite v Severozapadna Bălgariia*, vol. 9 (1984), pp. 83–96.

The events of 1211 or 1213 show that less than thirty years after the beginning of the Vlach revolt many Cumans had settled more or less permanently in Bulgaria, where some of them may have obtained high-ranking positions in the administration of the emerging state. The Hungarian–Bulgarian rapprochement caused by the events of Vidin was soon followed by a peace between Boril and Emperor Henry, which a papal legate negotiated in 1213. To seal the agreement, Henry married Boril's stepdaughter (born to his Cuman wife from her previous marriage with Ioannitsa), while Boril married the daughter of Henry's sister. Henry's death in 1216 deprived Boril of an important ally, and his position in Bulgaria further weakened when his other ally, King Andrew II of Hungary, departed for the Fifth Crusade. The political situation was thus ripe for John Asen's return from Galicia. The inhabitants of Tărnovo opened the city gates to him, and in 1218, John Asen captured and blinded Boril. Almost nothing is known about the first twelve years of his reign, except that shortly after coming to power, John Asen captured Andrew II on his return from the Fifth Crusade and did not release him until the king agreed to the marriage of his daughter Maria to John Asen. Maria's dowry was the region of Belgrade and Braničevo, which John Asen promptly occupied. His position was further strengthened by the victory he obtained in April 1230 at Klokotnica over Theodore Dukas, Emperor of Thessalonica. This extraordinary military success allowed John Asen to occupy much of the territory under Epirote rule, a feat described in some detail in a Cyrillic inscription on a column in the Church of the Forty Holy Martyrs in Tărnovo. In the text of that inscription, John Asen speaks of himself as autocrat (*samodr'zhec'*) and of his occupation of the entire "land of the Greeks" from Odrina (Adrianople) to Dyrrachion, as well as to the Albanian and Serbian lands, leaving only Constantinople and the land around it to the "Franks."[47] A similar list of territories appears in a charter John Asen issued for the merchants of Dubrovnik, to whom he granted free access to the cities of Bulgaria, of which he mentioned four by name: Vidin, Braničevo, Belgrade, and Tărnovo. Traders from Dubrovnik were also free to travel to Preslav, the "Karvunas region" (most likely southern Dobrudja), Odrin (Adrianople), the region of Skopje, Prilep, Devol, the "Albanian land," and Thessalonica.[48]

47 Popkonstantinov and Kronsteiner, *Starobălgarski nadpisi*, vol. II, pp. 166–168.

48 English translation from Butler, *Monumenta Bulgarica*, p. 237. Neither inscription nor charter referred to Thracian cities such as Philippopolis, the surrounding

Trade was undoubtedly the reason for the relatively abundant coinage struck for John Asen in the subsequent years. The economic prosperity of Bulgaria during John Asen's reign is well illustrated by his building program in Tărnovo, dominated by the large Church of the Forty Holy Martyrs with its façades decorated with ceramic tiles and frescoes that established the fame of the so-called Tărnovo School.[49] Shortly after the inauguration of the church following the battle at Klokotnica, the monastery of the Great Lavra was established in the vicinity, which like that in contemporary Ras soon became a center of writing.

The victory at Klokotnica turned Bulgaria into the greatest power in the early thirteenth-century Balkans and a great threat to the Latin Empire in Constantinople. One by one, the Thracian cities controlled by the Latins opened their gates to John Asen's troops. In each one of them, the Bulgarian emperor replaced bishops or priests appointed by the Latin patriarch in Constantinople with suffragans of the metropolitan of Tărnovo. This is most likely the context in which Pope Gregory IX called crusaders in Hungary to support the new emperor of Constantinople, Jean de Brienne, in his efforts to defend the Empire against its enemies. If the pope had in mind John Asen, the call did not go unanswered. In 1231, a Hungarian army attacked Belgrade and Braničevo. In his letter of March 21, 1232 to the bishop of Cenad, the pope established a deadline for bringing back the bishops of both towns to the practices of the Roman church, an indication that by that time the ties between Rome and the Bulgarian church had been severed.[50] An attack on Vidin failed in 1232, but the Hungarian pressure on the Danube frontier with Bulgaria did not recede.

forts of which were certainly occupied and repaired under John Asen. A Cyrillic inscription of 1231 refers to the restoration of Stenimachos. See Popkonstantinov and Kronsteiner, *Starobălgarski nadpisi*, vol. II, p. 15.

49 K. Totev, I. Chokoev, and E. Dermendzhiev, "Cărkvata 'Sv. chetirideset măchenici' văv Veliko Tărnovo spored poslednite arkheologicheski razkopki [The Church of the Forty Holy Martyrs in Veliko Tărnovo according to the most recent archaeological excavations]," in *Obshchestvo, ekonomika, kul'tura i isskusstvo slavian*, ed. by V. V. Sedov (Moscow: Institut Arkheologii, Rossiiskaia Akademiia Nauk, 1998), pp. 104–115. It is in this church that the body of St. Sava was first laid to rest in 1236, before being transferred to Serbia. For the frescoes, see D. Koseva, "Novootkrit stenopis v diakonikona na cărkvata 'Sv. 40 măchenici' văv Veliko Tărnovo [A newly discovered fresco in the *diakonikon* of the Church of the Forty Holy Martyrs in Veliko Tărnovo]," *Palaeobulgarica*, vol. 23 (1999), pp. 30–40.

50 *Acta Honorii III (1216–1227) et Gregorii IX (1227–1241)*, ed. by A. L. Tăutu (Vatican: Typis polyglottis Vaticanis, 1950), p. 231.

King Andrew II created a new march across the Danube from Vidin, in western Walachia, which he placed in 1233 under the authority of the *ban* of Severin (Drobeta Turnu-Severin). Papal registers mention the Dominicans and their missionary activity in that region. In response to such measures, John Asen established contacts with Germanus II, the patriarch of Nicaea, and soon entered an alliance with the Nicaean emperor John Vatatzes. The alliance was based on Vatatzes' recognition of the archbishop of Tărnovo as Patriarch of Bulgaria and John Asen's concomitant recognition of the patriarch of Nicaea as Ecumenical Patriarch. The Bulgarian emperor also renounced any claims over Thessalonica and Mount Athos. He sealed the alliance by marrying his daughter Helen to Theodore II Laskaris, the heir to the Nicaean throne. In 1236, his troops and those of the Nicaean emperor laid siege to Constantinople. Although threatened with excommunication by the pope, John Asen did not completely sever his ties with Rome, for he is known to have received the visit of a papal legate in 1237. In fact, by that time, he had renounced his alliance with Vatatzes, as he attacked the Nicaean garrison in Tzurullon with his Cuman allies. However, when the plague broke in Tărnovo in 1237, killing his wife Maria, his eldest son and heir, and the patriarch, John Asen is said to have interpreted the tragedy as God's wrath over his betrayal of Vatatzes. He immediately called off the siege of Tzurullon and made peace with the Nicaeans. By December 1237, he was back in the alliance against the Latin Empire of Constantinople. Pope Gregory IX condemned him as "faithless" and "protector of heretics." Against John Asen, the pope called for a crusade, which he entrusted to King Béla IV of Hungary. Bulgaria was declared a land unjustly possessed by the heretics and, as a punishment, the pope allowed its conquest and devastation by those upon whom he had called to eradicate the evil. The threat seems to have been considerable, as John Asen again left his alliance with Vatatzes and in 1239 allowed the crusaders gathered by Baldwin II to cross over from Hungary en route to Constantinople. The anti-Bulgarian crusade never took place and a Bulgarian–Hungarian rapprochement is visible in 1240, no doubt prompted by the alarming news about the Mongol onslaught in the East. But John Asen's faltering policies caused much dissatisfaction among Bulgarian aristocrats. He died in June 1241, only a few months after the Mongols invaded Hungary and shortly before their devastation of Bulgaria (see below). Several aristocratic factions, including the regents of John Asen's minor son

Coloman, immediately began quarreling, while some local lords seized the opportunity to declare themselves independent from Tărnovo. Little is known about the political situation in Bulgaria during Coloman's brief rule, but his half-brother Michael II Asen (1246–1257) was forced to recognize Mongol overlordship and paid tribute to the Golden Horde. The Mongol influence in Bulgarian affairs increased considerably during the last decades of the century, especially after Nogai asserted his independence in the western lands against Möngke Temür, the khan of the Golden Horde.

SERBIA AND DALMATIA

The canonization of Nemanja following his death in February 1199 was the result of a complicated political process. In 1202, his younger son Vukan attacked Stefan, whom Nemanja had designated his successor at the Ras assembly in 1196. While his father was still alive, Vukan had adopted the royal title displayed in an inscription from the Church of St. Luke in Kotor, in which Nemanja is mentioned only as grand *zhupan*. This may well be Vukan's distorted version of the events of 1196. At any rate, he did not hesitate to ask in 1199 for a crown from Pope Innocent III and for the elevation of the bishop of Bar to the rank of archbishop. While the status of archbishopric was indeed granted to the see of Bar, Vukan never received any crown. Nevertheless, it is clear that shortly before and after 1200 Rome was perceived by both Vlach and Serbian rulers as the only legitimate source of royal power. This is further substantiated by Stefan's own attempt to obtain a crown from Innocent in 1201 or 1202, shortly before his conflict with Vukan. His request was turned down immediately because of the intervention of Emeric, the king of Hungary, who had meanwhile thrown his support on Vukan's side. Vukan was initially successful. For a while he ruled as grand *zhupan*, and it is most likely in that capacity that he commissioned one of the most beautiful Old Church Slavonic lectionaries produced in Serbia, the so-called Vukan Gospel.[51] Not long after assuming power, Vukan was confronted by his brother who had returned with the support of Ioannitsa's expedition of 1203. The internecine strife continued for another year or so, until Stefan was restored to power, while Vukan remained a ruler in Zeta. To ease the tensions between his brothers,

[51] J. Vrana, *Vukanovo jevanđelje* [The Vukan Gospel] (Belgrade: Naučno delo, 1967).

Sava returned from Mount Athos, where Nemanja-Simeon's remains had miraculously begun to produce myrrh. The relics were transferred to Nemanja's foundation at Studenica and with that the cult of St. Simeon the "myrrh-bearer" was established, a major component of Stefan's political agenda for his second reign. Stefan himself promoted the cult of his father, for he is the author of one of several Lives of St. Simeon. Based on Nemanja's proclamation of abdication at the Ras assembly of 1196, as well as on oral sources, Stefan's Life insisted on his father's faith and his persecution of heretics. Stefan's Nemanja appears as an "isapostolic" ruler, second only to Constantine the Great. On the other hand, the Life is also a detailed description of Nemanja's military achievements in his role of protector of the country. By the time Stefan wrote his Life, there was more than one biography of Nemanja. Sava had written a liturgy dedicated to his father and then, in 1208, the *Life of Lord Simeon*. But instead of depicting a saint, Sava described Nemanja as "our lord and autocrat, and ruler of the whole Serbian land."[52] Like his brother Stefan, Sava viewed his father as a Christian ruler consecrating churches, building monasteries, sustaining the poor, feeding the orphans, and protecting the widows. To him, Nemanja was "a second Abraham, a hospitable man, an angel on earth, and a man from heaven."[53] But unlike his brother, Sava's Life has no room for the warrior-king. At the center of his narrative is the Ras assembly of 1196 and Nemanja's decision to pass power to his son Stefan. What follows is a "prince's mirror," as Nemanja gives instructions to both Stefan and Vukan as to how to

[52] Sava, *Life of Lord Simeon*, Prologue, English translation from Kantor, *Medieval Lives*, p. 257. For the circumstances in which Sava wrote his Life, see R. Marinković, "Istorija nastanka Života gospodina Simeona od svetoga Save [The genesis of St. Sava's *Life of Lord Simeon*]," in *Meždunarodni naučni skup "Sava Nemanjić-Sveti Sava. Istorija i predanje". Decembar 1976*, ed. by V. Djurić (Belgrade: Srpska Akademija Nauka i Umetnosti, 1979), pp. 201–214. A third Life of St. Simeon was written in 1264 by Domentian, a Serbian monk from Hilandar, who seems to have used Stefan's, not Sava's, work, in addition to material from a eulogy of Prince Vladimir of Kiev written by Metropolitan Ilarion in 1049. It is Domentian's, not Sava's, Life that eventually turned Nemanja into St. Simeon. For a textual comparison between the three texts, see J. Reinhart, "Sintaksa žitija Simeona Nemanje od sv. Save, Stefana Prvovenčanoga i Domentijana [The syntax of the Lives of Simeon Nemanja by St. Sava, Stefan the First Crowned, and Domentian]," in *Meždunarodni naučni skup "Stefan Nemanja-Sveti Simeon Mirotočivi. Istorija i predanje", Septembar 1996*, ed. by J. Kalić (Belgrade: Srpska Akademija Nauka i Umetnosti, 2000), pp. 137–154.

[53] Sava, *Life of Lord Simeon* 1, p. 259.

behave as good rulers. The remaining part of Sava's Life deals with Nemanja as a monk under his new name of Simeon. The counterpart of the "prince's mirror" is the advice he gave to his son Sava regarding his duties as a man of the Church. The last part of Sava's Life is an account of how the remains of the "venerable and blessed father and founder" Simeon were translated from Hilandar to Studenica.

The two Lives of Nemanja-Simeon laid the foundation stones for the cult of the Serbian ruler, now viewed as the founder of a "dynasty of sacred roots." Icons with his portrait appeared in the late 1200s, the first such representation being mentioned in an inventory that a certain *zhupan* Desa deposited in Dubrovnik in 1281. That the cult had turned Stefan's rule into something very different from that of previous grand *zhupans* results from the absence, beginning with his reign, of any partitioning of the country between members of the ruling dynasty. In Hum, the widow of Miroslav (Nemanja's brother) and her son Andrew faced a rebellion of a relative named Peter. Stefan intervened and in the process only the coastal area and the hinterland of Trebinje remained in the hands of Andrew, the other parts being incorporated into Serbia. Stefan also established good relations with the Albanian lords in the region of the upper course of the river Fani i Madh. He gave his daughter in marriage to Demetrius, the *archon* who, like Stefan, had asked in 1208 for Pope Innocent III's guidance. But the alliance with Stefan did not protect Demetrius from the aggressive policies of Michael Dukas of Epirus. Having taken Dyrrachion in 1213, Michael moved against the Albanian lords and then against Zeta. In 1214 he took Scutari (Shkodër) before being murdered by one of his servants. Meanwhile, Stefan managed to avoid an invasion of the combined armies of Boril of Bulgaria, Emperor Henry of Constantinople, and Strez of Prosek. Michael Dukas' half-brother Theodore agreed to make peace with Stefan, to whom he returned Scutari in exchange for the hand of his sister. But Stefan did not support Theodore in his war with Venice. Instead, in 1216 he married Anna, the granddaughter of the Venetian doge Enrico Dandolo. The Catholic influence in Serbia increased considerably as a result of this marriage and a papal legate even came in 1217 to crown Stefan, now proclaimed king. The developments following Stefan's second marriage (he had repudiated his first wife, Evdokia, the daughter of Emperor Alexios III Angelos) provoked strong opposition from the church hierarchy and it is under such circumstances that Sava returned to Mount Athos, while Stefan wrote his Life of Nemanja in an attempt to vouch for the continuity of St. Simeon's cult and for that of his own regime. Since he referred to himself as "the first-crowned" (Prvovenčani), Stefan is traditionally viewed as the first king of Serbia. However, his official title was autocrat (*samodržac*), which is the word later used in the inscription from the Church of the Forty Holy Martyrs in Tărnovo in reference to John Asen.

Like John Asen, Stefan was in need of a patriarch or, at least, of a self-governing church. The opportunity was seized when the conflict between Nicaea and Epirus began taking increasingly ecclesiastic overtones in the late 1210s. Against the patriarch of Nicaea, Manuel I Sarantenos, the Epirote churchmen, and especially the newly appointed archbishop of Ohrid, Demetrius Chomatenos, argued for ecclesiastical autonomy. Besides disputing the legality of the synod of 1208 that had elected Manuel's predecessor, Michael IV Autorianus, as Ecumenical Patriarch, Demetrius claimed that the church of Epirus had the right to make appointments for vacant sees without seeking the approval of the patriarch of Nicaea. A key argument for Archbishop Demetrius was the idea, first expressed by his predecessor, Theophylact Hephaistos, that Ohrid was the successor of the archbishopric of Iustiniana Prima founded by Emperor Justinian in the sixth century. As a consequence, Ohrid was ranked higher than Nicaea, a see that had never been elevated to the status of archbishopric.[54] Serbia was within the area of jurisdiction claimed by the archbishop of Ohrid, but the monk Sava on Mount Athos did not share Chomatenos' anti-Nicaean opinions. In 1219, he traveled to Nicaea and obtained permission to create an autonomous archbishopric of Serbia. With the approval came his nomination and consecration as the first archbishop of Serbia (December 6, 1219).

[54] D. Dragojlović, "Archevêché d'Ohrid dans la hiérarchie des grandes églises chrétiennes," *Balcanica*, vol. 22 (1991), pp. 43–54. For a detailed history of the conflict, see A. D. Karpozilos, *The Ecclesiastical Controversy between the Kingdom of Nicaea and the Principality of Epiros (1217–1233)* (Thessaloniki: Kentron Byzantinon Ereunon, 1973). For the parallel between Demetrius Chomatenos and Theophylact of Ohrid, see Podskalsky, "Two archbishops of Achrida (Ohrid)," pp. 139–148. Like Theophylact, Chomatenos wrote a Life of St. Clement of Ohrid (known as the "Short Life"), for which see I. Duichev, "Kratkoto Klimentovo zhitie ot Dimitrii Khomatian [Demetrius Chomatenos' Short Life of Clement]," in *Kliment Okhridski. Sbornik ot statii po sluchai 1050 godini ot smărtta*, ed. by B. S. Angelov, B. Angelov, P. Dinekov, et al. (Sofia: Izdatelstvo na Bălgarskata Akademiia na Naukite, 1966), pp. 161–171.

Sava then returned to his homeland accompanied by monks and pupils from Hilandar, whom he appointed to important offices in the newly created church.

In the absence of any major cities, the archbishop established his see at Žiča (near Kraljevo, on the Western Morava River), the monastery that Stefan had begun building in 1208 in a typical combination of stone and brick courses imitating the architecture of Mount Athos.[55] To the three sees in Serbia that had previously been under the jurisdiction of Ohrid, Sava added seven new ones. Some he planted in western Serbia (Dabar, the region between the upper course of the Western Morava and the lower course of the Lim River; Budimlje on the middle course of the Lim River), between Ras and Niš (Toplica) and between Ras and Prizren (Hvosno, near Peć). Two other sees were established on the coast, at Prevlaka in the Bay of Kotor, and at Ston. In both cases, the local Catholic bishops chose to leave at the moment the Serbian Orthodox bishops appeared, only to return a few years later. In fact, no evidence exists of a Catholic opposition to Sava's measures. Much stronger was the reaction of Demetrius Chomatenos, the archbishop of Ohrid, who condemned Sava's appointment by Patriarch Manuel I Saratenos as non-canonical. He also questioned the probity of Sava's life, contrasting his earlier life as a monk at Hilandar to his later involvement in secular affairs, which Chomatenos deeply resented. However, and despite Chomatenos' vociferous protests, the ruler of Epirus, Theodore Dukas (whom Chomatenos would later crown Emperor of Thessalonica) chose to maintain good relations with Stefan.

Sava summoned a synod at Žiča in 1221, at which he delivered a sermon against heretics and discussed marital relations, apparently the two most important items on the archbishop's agenda at that time. In neighboring Bosnia, heretics of an unspecified kind are mentioned at that time in papal documents, as the pope called on the Hungarian king to move against them. Sava may have been concerned

[55] M. Kašanin, Đ. Bošković, and P. Mijović, *Žiča. Istorija, arhitektura, slikarstvo* [Žiča: History, Architecture, Paintings] (Belgrade: Knijževne novine, 1969). The Athonite inspiration betrays Sava's influence on this royal foundation. See M. Čanak-Medić, "Žička Spasova crkva – zamisao Svetog Save [The Church of Our Savior in Žiča: St. Sava's concept]," in *Sveti Sava u srpskoj istoriji i tradiciji*, ed. by S. Ćirković (Belgrade: Srpska Akademija Nauka i Umetnosti, 1998), pp. 173–187. The monastery was richly endowed by Stefan, which may explain its devastation by the Mongols in 1242.

with the same issue, although nothing betrays the exact nature of his concerns.[56] He presented his translation and adaptation of the *Nomokanon*, a seventh-century compilation of conciliar canons and imperial decrees, which was now to become the legal foundation of the Serbian Church. The explosion of literary activity that followed the synod had a great influence on the standardization of legal institutions and practices, on the training of the clergy, and on the uniformity of ceremonies, while Old Church Slavonic, often with strong influences from the Serbian vernacular, became the language of both the Church and the royal chanceries.

If Sava had intended his autocephalous archbishopric to be an attack on the claims of Ohrid to ecclesiastical preeminence, he certainly did not oppose the increasing Epirote infuence during the brief reign of Stefan's son and successor, Radoslav (1227–1234). Radoslav had married the daughter of Theodore Dukas, the Emperor of Thessalonica, but after the battle of Klokotnica his position had become precarious at best. In addition, the situation in neighboring Bosnia had deteriorated rapidly after the pope had accused the local bishop of protecting the heretics. With John Asen's star rising, Radoslav was removed from power by a conspiracy of disgruntled nobles. Their choice was Radoslav's brother Vladislav, who had meanwhile married the daughter of the victor at Klokotnica. It is under such circumstances that the stronghold at Ras that had been meanwhile restored was destroyed once again and eventually abandoned. Radoslav went first to Dubrovnik, where his name appears in charters dated after 1234, and then to Dyrrachion. Meanwhile, upset by the conflict between his nephews, Sava embarked on a pilgrimage to the Holy Land. He died in Bulgaria on his way back to Serbia, and was buried in Tărnovo, before his remains were transferred in 1237 to Mileševa (near Prijepolje, in western Serbia), the monastery built by Vladislav in 1234. It was an appropriate choice for Sava's tomb. The monastery church had just received magnificent frescoes, which

[56] The Bosnian heretics mentioned in the 1220s are often viewed as either Cathars or Bogomils. See R. Manselli, "Les 'chrétiens' de Bosnie: le catharisme en Europe orientale," *Revue d'histoire ecclésiastique*, vol. 2 (1977), pp. 600–614; S. Rakova, "Le bogomilisme et l'église bosniaque," *Heresis*, vol. 19 (1992), pp. 19–29. Both interpretations have been dismissed as not grounded in the existing evidence. See J. V. A. Fine, *The Bosnian Church: A New Interpretation. A Study of the Bosnian Church and Its Place in State and Society from the 13th to the 15th Century* (Boulder and New York: Columbia University Press, 1975).

represent the first illustration of the ideological developments brought about by the implementation of the cult of Nemanja-Simeon in the early 1200s. In Mileševa, Nemanja appears as monk Simeon, his son Stefan as the incarnation of the ideal king, and Archbishop Sava as a saint.[57] In fact, soon after his death, Sava became the subject of a cult similar to that of his father.[58]

In 1242, Serbia was devastated by the Mongols returning from their campaign in Dalmatia (see below). Following the Mongol invasion, King Béla IV revived his predecessors' aggressive policies towards Serbia. Matthew Ninoslav, the *ban* of Bosnia, had reasserted his independence in the aftermath of the Mongol invasion. In the 1240s, he issued a number of charters for the merchants of Dubrovnik, an indication that he was controlling some of the most important market towns in the region. Between 1246 and 1252, King Béla wrote several letters to Pope Innocent IV requesting that ecclesiastical jurisdiction over Bosnia be transferred to the archbishop of Kalocsa. Two expeditions in 1244 and 1253 reinforced the Hungarian influence in that region. In addition, King Béla created two new marches on the southern frontier of Hungary. One of them was Braničevo, directed against Bulgaria. By contrast, Mačva stretched between the Sava and the Ub river, in the environs of present-day Valjevo, and was clearly directed against Serbia. War between Hungary and Serbia broke in the 1260s, during the reign of Uroš I, who had replaced Vladislav in 1243.

King Uroš also intervened in the conflict between Bar and Dubrovnik. In 1247, at the death of the archbishop of Bar, the

[57] O. Kandić, S. Popović, and R. Zarić, *Manastir Mileševa* [The Mileševa Monastery] (Belgrade: Republički zavod za zaštitu spomenika kulture, 1995). For the frescoes, see D. Nagorni, "Bemerkungen zum Stil und zu den Meistern der Wandmalerei in der Klosterkirche Mileševa," in *XVI. internationaler Byzantinistenkongreß. Akten. II*, ed. by W. Hörandner, C. Cupane, and E. Kislinger, vol. v (Vienna: Verlag der Österreichischen Akademie der Wissenschaften, 1982), pp. 159–172. For Sava's tomb, see R. Nikolić, "O grobu svetog Save u Mileševi [On St. Sava's tomb in Mileševa]," *Saopštenja* , vol. 14 (1982), pp. 7–24.

[58] The earliest Life of St. Sava was written just seven years after Sava's death by Domentian, the author of the third (and latest) Life of St. Simeon. For Domentian's views of Sava, see S. Radojčić, "Lik svetoga Save u Domentijanovom Životu i podvizima arhiepiskopa sve srpske i pomorske zemlje prepodobnog i bogonosnog nastavnika Save [St. Sava in Domentian's Life]," in *Meždunarodni naučni skup "Sava Nemanjić-Sveti Sava. Istorija i predanje". Decembar 1976*, ed. by V. Djurić (Belgrade: Srpska Akademija Nauka i Umetnosti, 1979), pp. 215–222.

archbishop of Dubrovnik had sent an envoy to that city to state Dubrovnik's claims to preeminence. Disregarding such claims, Pope Innocent IV appointed a new archbishop of Bar in the person of John Plano Carpini, a Franciscan who had just returned from a trip to Karakorum on a mission to the Great Khan of the Mongols. Carpini tried to reach a compromise by proposing an arbitration of the conflict by the bishop of Kotor, the only Dalmatian suffragan of the archbishop of Bari in Italy. The bishop of Kotor had great influence in the Serbian lands, where all Catholics were under his jurisdiction. The conflict was brought in 1252 to the papal court, but without resolution. Upon Carpini's death, his vacant see faced an alliance between Dubrovnik and Michael Asen of Bulgaria, which was meant to expel Uroš from Serbia and to curb the claims to preeminence of his protégé, the archbishop of Bar. But Dubrovnik made peace with Uroš in 1255, as it became apparent that the conflict with Bar was detrimental to the economic interests of Dubrovnik in Serbia.

Such interests became apparent shortly before 1250, as a remarkable economic growth began in Serbia, which continued well into the fourteenth century. At its origin was the opening of the rich silver mines in the region of the Upper Lim River. The miners were "Saxon" settlers brought from Hungary, who were granted privileges very similar to those applying to the "guests" in that kingdom ever since the late twelfth century (see chapter 6). The first silver mine mentioned in documents was Brskovo (near Mojkovac, in northeastern Montenegro), where the output seems to have been sufficiently large to allow the creation of a mint at which Uroš struck the first silver coins of Serbia.[59] These were large groats imitating the Venetian *matapan* in terms of weight and type.[60] Since they seem to have been struck in relatively large quantities only to accommodate the needs of the foreign trade, especially with Dubrovnik, Uroš's *grossi* were appropriately marked with inscriptions in Latin. Due to their high

[59] Radoslav had previously struck copper coins imitating Epirote issues minted in Thessalonica, but these coins had only a limited circulation. See M. Popović, "La découverte d'un dépôt de monnaie du roi Stéphane Radoslav dans la forteresse de Ras," in *Kovanje i kovnice antičkog i srednjovekovnog novca*, ed. by V. Kondić (Belgrade: Arheološki Institut, 1976), pp. 115–119; V. Ivanišević, "Novac kralja Radoslava [The coins of King Radoslav]," *ZRVI*, vol. 37 (1998), pp. 87–95.

[60] S. Dušanić, "Jedan groš matapanskog tipa i pitanije početka kovanija srpskog novca u srednijem veku [A *matapan*-type of groat and the beginnings of the Serbian medieval coinage]," *Numizmatičar*, vol. 14 (1991), pp. 73–78. *Matapan* was the name given in Venice to the large silver coin commonly known as groat (*grosso*).

quality and specific use, these coins were circulated outside Serbia and are common in hoards found in Hungary, Romania, or Bulgaria, but also in those of northern Italy and Greece. The prosperity of the mountain region around Brskovo attracted the interest of both the Church and members of the royal family. Jurisdiction over the Saxon church in Brskovo in the 1250s was under dispute between the bishop of Kotor and the archbishop of Bar and at stake was the collection of tithes. In 1252, Vukan's son Stefan built a monastery at Morača (near Kolašin, to the southwest of Brskovo) which he endowed from his own estates and share of the silver mines.[61] However, Stefan was not the ruler of the region. Under Uroš, all traces of autonomy of the old family appanages, such as Zeta and Hum, disappeared. Much like Stefan, Andrew, the son of Miroslav (Nemanja's brother who had ruled over Hum), was only lord of a small region south of the Neretva River, at the foot of the Viduša Mountain in the hinterland of Trebinje. King Stefan's intervention on his behalf pushed Andrew's brother and rival Peter to the northern bank of the Neretva River. Peter continued to style himself "Prince of Hum" and seems to have had some political prominence, for in 1225 the citizens of Split designated him as their "prince." Toljen, a relative of Peter, is also mentioned as "Prince of Hum" a few years later. Like Peter, he was also involved in the political struggles in Split, where he unsuccessfully opposed the powerful Subić family and their Hungarian allies, a policy continued by his successor Andrew, who is last mentioned in 1249.

The choice of a member of Nemanja's family as "Prince of Split" may surprise, given that Bosnia separated the hinterland of Split from Serbia. But in the early 1200s, the citizens of Split were making desperate efforts to remove themselves from the growing influence of the Subić family in central Croatia. Formerly counts of Bribir, the Subići ruling from that fort began to style themselves "Princes of Bribir" and gradually expanded into the surrounding region, in an attempt to gain control over the entire coast. By 1221, a member of the Subić family was elected Prince of Split, followed by his uncle, Gregory. Ten years later, Gregory also controlled Šibenik, while his nephew Stjepko established himself in Trogir. The citizens of Split

[61] S. Petković, *Morača* (Belgrade: Srpska književna zadruga IRO "Prosveta," 1986). Fragments of the original paintings, especially scenes from the life of Prophet Elias, survive in the *diakonikon* of the monastery church.

tried to resist the Subić encroachment by electing as their prince Peter of Hum in 1225 and Matthew Ninoslav, the *ban* of Bosnia, in 1244. But the Subići were well connected and they managed to convince King Béla IV to bring a large army under the walls of the city. As a consequence, beginning in 1250, deputies of the *ban* of Croatia ruled in the name of the king in Split and Trogir. Both cities had flourished throughout the entire period, despite much political and military unrest. This is best illustrated by the remarkable monuments of Romanesque art associated with the names of two artists, Andrew Buvina and Radovan. Buvina is the author of the twenty-eight scenes from the Life of Jesus carved in walnut for the doors of the Cathedral in Split, a masterpiece he executed in 1214. Radovan is mentioned in an inscription of 1240 on the tympanum of the west portal of the Cathedral in Trogir. He carved half of the tympanum decoration, in addition to the inner archivolt reliefs and the jambs, all works betraying the influence of the contemporary sculptures in San Marco in Venice.[62]

The outcome of the conflict between Split and the Subić clan illustrates the degree to which throughout the thirteenth century Croatia had become a separate entity within the Hungarian kingdom. Power rested with its nobles rather than with the king's representatives, the *ban*s of Croatia and Slavonia. The noble families had been able to secure more grants, while their claims to specific territories were rarely contested and more often confirmed by the Hungarian kings. For example, in 1225 Vid of Krk (a member of the family later known as Frankapan) received in perpetuity from King Andrew II two major counties of northern Croatia, Modruš (already granted in 1193 to another member of the family, Bartholomew) and Vinodol, the coastal region in front of the Krk island. The privileged status of the nobles of Krk was further increased when Pope Innocent IV granted to the bishop of Senj, the most important see in Vinodol, permission to employ Glagolitic Slavonic in his diocese. The old debate surrounding the Slavic liturgy thus ended with a papal decision meant to accommodate the needs of the increasingly powerful family of Krk and of their even more powerful protector, the king

[62] V. Gvozdanović, "Master Radovan and the lunette of the Nativity at Trogir," *Studies in Medieval Culture*, vols. 8–9 (1976), pp. 85–98. The influence of the Venetian sculpture has often been interpreted as evidence that Radovan had been trained in Venice. See O. Demus, "Bemerkungen zu Meister Radovan in San Marco," *JOB*, vol. 38 (1989), pp. 389–393.

of Hungary. Equally illustrative is the rise of the Babonić family of Slavonia. In the late 1100s, members of that family already owned large estates along the Kupa River, but after 1200 they even moved across the frontier, into the marches of the Holy Roman Empire, and acquired land in Carniola (near Kranj) and in Friuli (near Gorica). Unlike the nobles of Krk, the Babonići came to challenge the power of the king and of his appointee, the *ban* of Slavonia, whom they managed to kill in open conflict during the last decade of the thirteenth century.

The situation in Carniola was not much different. Ever since the late twelfth century, a number of powerful families controlled the southeastern marches of the Holy Roman Empire. Most prominent among them were the Andechs, who after 1200 took over the entire region along the Croatian and Hungarian border in addition to building a strong alliance with King Andrew II of Hungary. Otto, the son of the first Andechs to become Duke of Merania, was the brother of Henry II, the margrave of Istria and Carniola between 1204 and 1228. Both were close relatives of Queen Gertrud of Hungary and of her brother, Berthold, the archbishop of Kalocsa and, for a short period in 1212, *voevode* of Transylvania. After his sister's assassination in 1213, Berthold left Hungary and was soon elected Patriarch of Aquileia. His term in that church office coincides with the maximum expansion of the lands under the jurisdiction of Aquilea, for in 1220 Berthold received from Emperor Frederick II Istria, Carniola, and Friuli. He retained those lands until his death in 1251. Meanwhile, his nephew, Otto II, ruled over Merania. His sister Agnes married the duke of Carinthia, Ulrich III, who thus became lord of almost the entire march of Carniola. Ulrich's father, Bernhard II of Spanheim, founded in 1234 the Cistercian Abbey of Kostanjevica (near Novo Mesto, on the Croatian–Slovenian border) next to the family castle at Landestrost on the Krka River. Together with the Cistercian Abbey at Topusko, which King Andrew II of Hungary had founded in 1233, Kostanjevica was among the first buildings in Gothic style in the northwestern region of the Balkans. Bernhard's son Ulrich continued his father's work in Carniola. He founded the city of Ljubljana and completed the construction of the Carthusian Abbey of Bistra, which his father had established in the vicinity.

Throughout the first half of the thirteenth century, the southeastern marches of the Holy Roman Empire were in the hands of the powerful Andechs clan. But their hold soon came to an end, for

Ulrich of Carinthia had no male heirs either from his first marriage with Agnes, or from his second marriage to a Babenberg. The heir he eventually designated was his cousin Ottokar II Přemysl, the king of Bohemia. When the Bohemian rule was established in 1269, it ended a relatively long period of Andechs and Spanheim preeminence in Carniola.

TRANSYLVANIA AND THE CUMANS

Unlike Croatia and Slavonia, there were no powerful clans in early thirteenth-century Transylvania. To be sure, several individuals are known to have yielded considerable power and at the same time to have received royal grants in Transylvania. The first immunity is documented in 1202, when the wife of Benedict, the *voevode* of Transylvania, was allowed to collect revenue from a royal estate located between Cluj and Turda.[63] A Walloon nobleman named John Latinus, who lived among the "Saxons" of Transylvania, was the recipient in 1204 and 1206 of two land grants, which King Andrew II's son, Béla, confirmed in 1231 to John's sons Corrardus and Daniel.[64] During his term between 1209 and 1212, *voevode* Michael was granted land in the eastern part of the Cluj County. He was a member of the Kacsics family based in northern Hungary. When appointed *ban* of Slavonia, he retained no connection with Transylvania, although he most certainly kept his estates in that region.[65] In 1228, the beneficiary of King Andrew II's munificence was Denys, the chief treasurer of the kingdom, who also served as *voevode* of Transylvania between 1233 and 1234. By 1230, a certain count named Nicholas had lands in eight counties of Transylvania, from Alba to Arad and Caraş.[66]

[63] *Documente*, p. 20.

[64] *Urkundenbuch zur Geschichte der Deutschen in Siebenbürgen*, vol. 1, ed. by F. Zimmermann and C. Werner (Hermannstadt: Hochmeister, 1892), pp. 8–9 and 54–55. To Béla, John's sons were already "Saxon knights of Transylvania." See T. Nägler, *Aşezarea saşilor în Transilvania* [The Saxon Settlement in Transylvania] (Bucharest: Kriterion, 1992), pp. 84–85.

[65] Makkai, "Transylvania in the medieval Hungarian kingdom," p. 411. Michael's brother Simon of Kacsics may have been among the first great landowners to move to Transylvania from his family estates in northern Hungary. But his sojourn in Transylvania was short, for all his properties were confiscated as punishment for his participation in the plot responsible for the assassination of Queen Gertrud and her entourage in 1213. From northern Hungary was also the Kökényes-Radnót family, members of which acquired the large estate of Teaca in the Cluj County.

[66] *Documente*, pp. 240–241.

But before the middle of the century, no particular family is known to have risen to prominence in Transylvania. Instead, the region was dominated by the king's men known to contemporary sources as "castle warriors" (*iobagiones castri*), a social group associated with the increasing number of royal castles, many of which were established as seats of new counties.[67] The Oradea Register, a collection of 389 minutes of ordeals held at the chapter of the Cathedral of Oradea between 1208 and 1235, contains many references to the "freemen of the Holy King" (St. Stephen), who enjoyed free status granted to them, together with land, by the king.[68] A castle warrior served under the count, but still received a land grant in return for his service. He was exempt from taxes and other obligations to the local count. As the king's bondsman, he could in theory appeal to the king against the count. In other words, unlike the ministerials in the southeastern marches of the Holy Roman Empire (see chapter 5), the castle warriors served no other lord than the king. In that particular respect, their status had to be distinguished legally from the "castle folk" (*castrenses*), who were peasants owing labor, taxes, and military service to the castle and to its lord, the count. Such a distinction was necessary, for both castle warriors and castle folk lived side by side in villages grouped into hundreds (*centurionatus*) and administratively attached to a specific castle.[69] The tendency to amalgamate such distinctions was particularly visible in attempts to impose obligations or taxes upon the "freemen of the Holy King."

[67] The new counties of the early thirteenth century were all outside Transylvania proper: Caraş (1200), Arad (1214), and Keve (1238). Older castles are frequently mentioned in thirteenth-century charters. With the exception of the forts built by the Teutonic Knights, no stone castles existed in Transylvania before the Mongol invasion. See Gh. Anghel, "Les premiers donjons en pierre de Transylvania (Roumanie)," in *Château Gaillard, 8. Etudes de castellologie médiévale. Actes du colloque international tenu à Bad Muenstereifel (R.F.A.), 30 août–4 septembre 1976* (Caen: Centre des recherches archéologiques médiévales de l'Université de Caen, 1977), pp. 7–20.

[68] *Documente*, pp. 37–147. For this important source for the history of thirteenth-century Transylvania, see I. Zajtay, "Le registre de Varad: un monument juridique du début du XIIIe siècle," *Revue historique du droit français et étranger*, vol. 32 (1954), pp. 527–562. The Latin term *iobagio* derives from the Hungarian word *jobb* ("better"). Entire villages of *iobagiones* named after them are attested near Timişoara and Oradea (*Documente*, pp. 63 and 135).

[69] Hundreds are mentioned in the Oradea Register for Cluj in 1213 and for Biharea in 1217 and, again, in 1222. The 1217 reference is to castle warriors of Szekler origin (*Documente*, p. 83).

For example, in 1213, the folk of the Biharea castle who lived in the village of Cornust sued the villagers of Sob for trying to avoid their obligations towards that castle. The men of Sob defended themselves in front of the chapter in Oradea by claiming that they were in fact "freemen of the Holy King" and thus exempt from any obligations to the castle.[70] Castle warriors had landed estates, which they could pass on to their heirs. By contrast, castle folk owned land collectively and, as a consequence, the services that they owed could be transferred from one lord to another. For example, in 1221, the castle folk of the village of Voda accused a certain count Andrew of having taken a portion of the land they collectively owned and incorporated it into the estate he had received in that village from King Andrew II. Seven years later, Andrew's son Béla granted to the archbishop of Esztergom four farmhouses in Vinţ (south of Alba Iulia) that belonged to the castle folk in that village. The grant was one of service, not land, which apparently remained in the hands of the other castle folk families in the village.[71]

Equally eager to defend themselves against the amalgamation of legal distinctions were people who claimed "guest" status. Foreign settlers of Rus', Bohemian, "Latin," and German origin pleaded in such terms in front of the Oradea chapter.[72] The ethnic diversity of early thirteenth-century Transylvania did not go unnoticed. Writing in 1236, the German poet Neidhart of Reuenthal knew of "Vlachs, Szeklers, Germans, and Hungarians."[73] Shortly after 1250,

[70] *Documente*, p. 54. Both villages have meanwhile disappeared. Similar cases were brought in front of the chapter in 1215 and 1229 by the castle warriors of Tiream (near Carei, close to the present-day Hungarian–Romanian border) and Leginer (a village that had meanwhile disappeared). See *Documente*, pp. 71–72 and 140–141.

[71] *Documente*, pp. 116 and 230. In 1219, the castle folk of the village of Naimon accused some free men from that same village of being foreigners who attempted to usurp the status of *castrensis*. The accused defended themselves by arguing that they were not foreigners, since their lands were among those collectively owned by the castle folk of that village (*Documente*, p. 98).

[72] *Documente*, pp. 49, 59–60, 73, and 124. Free status was often granted to entire communities of "guests," such as the villages of Ighiu, Cricău, Romos, and Vinţ, all in the hinterland of Alba Iulia (charters of 1206, 1238, and 1248). See N.-M. Simina, "Contribuţii la cunoaşterea feudalismului timpuriu pe teritoriul comunei Vinţu de Jos (jud. Alba) [Contributions to the study of the early Middle Ages in Vinţu de Jos, Alba district]," *Acta Musei Napocensis*, vol. 32 (1995), pp. 473–488.

[73] Neidhart of Reuenthal, *Songs*, ed. by M. Haupt (Leipzig: S. Hirzel, 1858; reprint Stuttgart: S. Hirzel, 1986), p. 102. See also Armbruster, *Der Donau-Karpatenraum*, pp. 61–62.

the Szeklers appear in three districts in the region of the Upper Olt River in eastern Transylvania, but Szekler communities were already established around the Biharea castle in the early 1200s. Ever since 1224, King Andrew II spelled out the privileges of the German "guests" in a charter later referred to as the *Andreanum*.[74] Legal status was now given to the "Saxons," all of whom were placed under a single authority, that of their own "judge," the count of Sibiu. The king promised to refrain from granting away any portion of the Saxon land, and gave the Saxons the right to exclusive jurisdiction within their territory. They were also given access to the "forest of the Vlachs and the Pechenegs," as well as to the salt mines, without payment of custom duties. Their merchants could travel, sell and buy freely throughout the entire kingdom. In exchange, the Saxons had to pay an annual tax to the king's treasury, provide troops for the royal army, as well as free lodging and meals to the king and the *voevode*. By 1250, the "guests" had already established a number of flourishing market towns. The prosperity of Rodna, Sibiu, and Corona (Brașov) is betrayed by the fact that all three were specifically targeted by the Mongols in 1241 (see below).

The church of the Saxons was placed under the archbishop of Esztergom, and thus removed from the authority of the bishop of Alba Iulia. The ecclesiastical independence of the Saxon church may have something to do with the stylistic choices for such early thirteenth-century churches as Herina near Bistrița or Cisnădioara near Sibiu. Unlike contemporary churches in the region, these were large three-aisled basilicas inspired by the Romanesque architecture of the lands along the Rhine. The first Gothic building of Transylvania is the three-aisled church with transept erected after the Mongol invasion for the Cistercian Abbey of Cârța. As with the Jurklošter Abbey founded by Duke Leopold of Austria near Laško (see chapter 6), the ribbed vaults and the decorative sculpture of the Cârța Abbey church quickly found local imitators. However, unlike Carniola, the first imitations were foundations not of powerful aristocrats, but of communities of "guests," such as those of Prejmer, Hălmeag, and Brașov.[75]

[74] *Documente*, pp. 208–210.

[75] V. Drăguț, *Arta gotică în România* [The Gothic Art of Romania] (Bucharest: Meridiane, 1979), pp. 11–25 and 268–271.

A borderland still open to colonization, early thirteenth-century Transylvania received special royal attention in the context of the Hungarian involvement in the Balkan developments that followed the Vlach revolt of 1185 and Ioannitsa's military victories over the Latin armies of Constantinople. A major component of those developments, the Cumans were in the early 1200s a "problem of the Crusade."[76] They were thus a target for military action and missionary activity from Hungary. The assault on the Cumans in the Lower Danube region began with the introduction in 1211 of the Teutonic Knights to the region of Braşov in the southeastern region of Transylvania. We have seen that the Knights had already been established by that time on the western frontier of Hungary (see chapter 6). During the following years they received ecclesiastical jurisdiction over that borderland, which was confirmed in 1236 by the archbishop of Salzburg with the specific purpose of "correcting the Slavic people" in the region. Something similar was expected from them in Transylvania, for their task was to defend the frontier and to convert the Cumans. They were given a large territory within the limits marked by the upper course of the river Olt, the Transylvanian Alps, and the royal castles of Hălmeag (near Făgăraş) and Ungra (near Rupea). The Knights were allowed to build wooden castles on the frontier with the Cumans, but as they began expanding beyond the mountains, they also started to build stone fortifications. King Andrew II acknowledged in 1212 the progress they had made against the Cumans by giving to the Knights the newly built castle of Crucpurg together with its surrounding territory.[77] One year later, the Knights were also granted the right to collect the tithe from the royal subjects in the

[76] Papacostea, *Between the Crusade and the Mongol Empire*, p. 28. Little is known about the pre-Christian religious beliefs of the Cumans, but the stone statues in Desht-i Kipchak have been usually dated to the thirteenth century. Each of them represents a woman or a man in a sitting position holding with both hands a chalice or a chalice-like jar. There are over 1,000 such statues so far identified, but only 2 were found west of the Inhul River, in the regions most exposed to the missionary activity from Hungary. See G. L. Evdokimov and N. M. Kuprii, "Steinfiguren und Heiligtümer," in *Gold der Steppe. Archäologie der Ukraine*, ed. by R. Rolle, M. Müller-Wille, and K. Schietzel (Neumünster: Karl Wachholtz, 1991), pp. 264–268; Spinei, *Great Migrations*, pp. 242–243.

[77] The location of Crucpurg (Kreuzburg) is a much-debated issue. See Spinei, *Moldavia*, p. 50. For the castles built by the Teutonic Knights in southeastern Transylvania, see A. A. Rusu, "Die Frage der vom Deutschen Orden im Südosten Siebenbürgens errichteten Burgen," *Castrum Bene*, vol. 5 (1996), 165–172; J. Laszlovszky and Z. Soós, "Historical monuments of the Teutonic Order in

region. By that time, they may have also established themselves firmly in northeastern Walachia and southwestern Moldavia. In a charter of 1222 confirming their privileges, King Andrew II described their new acquisitions as reaching the "borders of the Brodniks" to the east and the river Danube to the south.[78] The Knights were given the right to build more stone castles and towns and the privilege to choose their own judge. Exemption from royal taxes was granted to all inhabitants from their domain in Transylvania stretching from the "land of the Vlachs" to the west to the "land of the Szeklers" to the north and northeast. Judging by their request to Pope Honorius III that their domain on both sides of the Carpathian Mountains be placed under papal authority, the ultimate goal of the Knights seems to have been to create a state on the southeastern frontier of Hungary. Encouraged by their military success against the Cumans and the enthusiastic support from Rome, the Knights thus came in direct conflict with the Hungarian king. At his instigation, the bishop of Alba Iulia rescinded in 1223 the decision to allow the Knights the collection of the tithe in southeastern Transylvania, but the pope denied the bishop's request to have jurisdiction over the Teutonic lands. Finally, in 1225, at the head of a large army, King Andrew II attacked the Teutonic Knights and expelled them from Transylvania. All the castles the Knights had built during their brief sojourn in the region (1211–1225) reverted to royal authority, including their main center at Marienburg (Feldioara near Braşov). The villages established by the German settlers that the Knights had brought to populate their domain were added to the Saxon lands established in 1224 through the *Andreanum*. Moreover, the Hungarian kings continued the aggressive expansion across the Carpathians which had been initiated by the Teutonic Knights. Responsible for that expansion was now King Andrew II's son, Béla

Transylvania," in *The Crusades and the Military Orders. Expanding Frontiers of Medieval Latin Christianity*, ed. by Zs. Hunyadi and J. Laszlovszky (Budapest: Department of Medieval Studies, Central European University, 2001), pp. 319–336.

[78] *Urkundenbuch*, p. 19. The authenticity of this charter has been affirmed by H. Zimmermann, "Der deutsche Ritterorden in Siebenbürgen," in *Die geistlichen Ritterorden Europas*, ed. by J. Fleckenstein and M. Hellmann (Sigmaringen: Jan Thorbecke, 1980), pp. 267–298; and disputed by M. Holban, *Din cronica relaţiilor româno-ungare în secolele XIII–XIV* [From the History of the Thirteenth- and Fourteenth-Century Romanian–Hungarian Relations] (Bucharest: Editura Academiei Republicii Socialiste România, 1981), pp. 9–48. The eastern border of the Teutonic acquisitions in southern Moldavia must have been on the Siret River. For the Brodniks, see Spinei, *Moldavia*, pp. 106–108.

(the future king Béla IV), who was appointed Duke of Transylvania in 1226.

The victories obtained by the Teutonic Knights against the Cumans predate by just a few years the crushing defeat the Cuman chieftains in Left Bank Ukraine suffered at the hands of the Mongols in the battle at the Kalka River (May 31, 1223). As a consequence of that battle, the interests of Köten, one of the Cuman chieftains who escaped the debacle at Kalka, shifted to the west. He was raiding the Galician territories under Hungarian control when Robert, the archbishop of Esztergom, obtained papal permission for creating a Cuman bishopric in the lands previously conquered by the Teutonic Knights in southern Moldavia and northeastern Walachia. Together with Bartholomew, the bishop of Pécs, and Raynaldus, the bishop of Alba Iulia, Robert organized in 1227 a ceremonial meeting with another Cuman chieftain named Boricius, who had expressed the desire to convert together with his family and retinue.[79] Béla, the duke of Transylvania, visited Boricius' lands across the mountains and in 1228 the superior of the Dominicans in Hungary was appointed Bishop of Cumania with jurisdiction over the entire territory stretching eastwards to the river Siret.[80] Military, more than religious concerns must have been on the mind of Béla, who attacked Galicia in 1230 together with Cuman troops under the command of a chieftain named Begovars. Defeated in battle by Prince Daniil Romanovich of Volhynia, the Hungarian troops had to return through northern Moldavia to the mountain passes leading to Transylvania. This was also the route taken five years later by Prince Rostislav of Chernigov, who fled to Hungary through Transylvania, with a brief halt in Rodna. Köten himself must have followed the same route, when in 1239 he requested permission to enter Hungary. Fleeing the Mongols, he demanded the protection of the Hungarian king for his retinue

[79] Alberic of Troisfontaines, *Chronicle*, ed. by P. Scheffer-Boichorst (Hanover: Hahnsche Buchhandlung, 1874; reprint 1986), MGH SS 23:920. In 1253, William of Rubruck, the envoy of King Louis IX of France to the Mongols, encountered a Christian Cuman on the Volga, who told him he had been baptized in Hungary. See *The Mission of Friar William of Rubruck. His Journey to the Court of the Great Khan Möngke, 1253–1255*, translated by P. Jackson (London: Hakluyt Society, 1990), pp. 135–136.

[80] The see of the newly appointed bishop was in Milcov near Focşani. It is most likely from Milcov that four Dominicans left in the early 1230s to travel along the northern shore of the Black Sea to the Volga, in search for the "pagan Hungarians."

and subjects. Like Boricius, the Cuman chieftain began by accepting conversion, with Béla IV as sponsor at his baptismal font. Köten's Cumans were then settled as "guests" in the heartland of the kingdom between the Tisza and Danube Rivers. The experiment ended in disaster for both sides. As hostility against the Cuman "guests" grew from all corners, Köten and his family were assassinated in 1241 by a lynching mob of Pest. The Cumans left Hungary en masse precisely when King Béla IV was preparing the defense against the impending Mongol invasion.[81]

The creation of the bishopric of Cumania coincides in time with the introduction of the new march of Severin into western Walachia. In both areas, the missionary activities of the Dominicans are well documented for the years before the Mongol invasion. Following the invasion, as Mongol control had by now been established in Cumania, King Béla IV decided to bring another military order on the most exposed segment of his kingdom's frontier. The royal charter for the Hospitallers, dated June 2, 1247, granted to the Knights of St. John a number of territories in the "land of Severin."[82] The delineation of those territories brought about a detailed description of several Vlach polities in the region, some of which extended on the northern side of the mountains into Transylvania. The grant to the Hospitallers included lands from two principalities in western Walachia (west of the river Olt). Each is called *kenezatus* in the document, a word derived from the Slavic word *knez* meaning "prince," for they are said to have been under the rule of Vlach princes named John and Farkas, respectively. Excluded from the grant was a third polity under a local *voevode* named Litovoi. His rule apparently extended on the

[81] Roger of Torre Maggiore, *Carmen miserabile super destructione regni Hungarie per Tartaros*, ed. by L. Juhász, in *Scriptores rerum Hungaricarum tempore ducum regumque stirpis Arpadianae gestarum*, vol. II (Budapest: Academia litteraria Hungarica, 1938; reprint Budapest: Nap kiadó, 1999), pp. 559 and 567. See N. Berend, *At the Gate of Christendom. Jews, Muslims, and "Pagans" in Medieval Hungary, c. 1000–c. 1300* (Cambridge: Cambridge University Press, 2001), pp. 71 and 87–88.

[82] *Documenta Romaniae historica, D. Relații între Țările Române* [Relations between the Romanian Principalities], vol. I, ed. by M. Berza et al. (Bucharest: Editura Academiei Republicii Socialiste România, 1977), pp. 21–28. See Zs. Hunyadi, "The Hospitallers in the Kingdom of Hungary: commanderies, personnel, and a particular activity up to c. 1400," in *The Crusades and the Military Orders. Expanding Frontiers of Medieval Latin Christianity*, ed. by Zs. Hunyadi and J. Laszlovszky (Budapest: Department of Medieval Studies, Central European University, 2001), pp. 253–268.

northern side of the Transylvanian Alps into the Hunedoara region (*terra Harszoc*), which the king now removed from Litovoi's authority and placed under the authority of the *voevode* of Transylvania. John, Farkas, and Litovoi were Hungarian clients, and the Hospitallers were granted half of the royal taxes collected from Litovoi's land. Exempt from any taxes to the king, although still a client, was another *voevode* named Seneslav, who ruled over the lands east of the Olt River. The eastern neighbor of Seneslav's principality had probably been the Cuman bishopric, which the Mongol invasion had meanwhile destroyed. A significant presence of the Vlachs within that bishopric is documented in the correspondence between King Béla IV and Pope Gregory IX, as the pope complained about Orthodox prelates active among the local Vlachs:

> As I was informed, there are certain people within the Cuman bishopric named Vlachs (*Walati*), who although calling themselves Christians, gather various rites and customs in one religion and do things that are alien to this name. For disregarding the Roman Church, they receive all the sacraments not from our venerable brother, the Cuman bishop, who is the diocesan of that territory, but from some pseudo-bishops of the Greek rite.[83]

The missionary activity in Cumania resumed soon after the Mongol invasion and its success were mentioned with great satisfaction in the papal correspondence of the early 1250s. This suggests that the power configuration on the southeastern border of Hungary described in the 1247 charter for the Hospitallers may have in fact been a political rearrangement in preparation for a new Mongol assault. The Hospitallers were specifically asked to come to the "kingdom's assistance in defending the Christian faith." However, with the Mongol presence firmly established in the Lower Danube region from the 1260s onwards, the frontiers of the Hungarian kingdom began to recede and eventually moved back across the mountains. New Vlach polities subsequently emerged in the shadow of the Mongol threat from the East.

THE MONGOL INVASION

According to later sources based on oral information from members of Genghis Khan's family, a decision to launch a massive campaign in

[83] *Documenta*, p. 20; English translation from Papacostea, *Between the Crusade and the Mongol Empire*, p. 99.

Eastern Europe was first taken in 1235 at the great assembly of the Mongol chieftains (*quriltai*).[84] Genghis Khan's son Jochi had been designated ruler of the western lands of the empire. As a consequence, Jochi's son Batu (*c.* 1206–1255) was given the supreme command of the expedition, which included the contingents of an impressive group of Mongol princes.[85] Participants in the largest Mongol campaign ever organized were Batu's brothers Ordu, Berke, and Siban; two sons of Ögödai, Güyük and Kadan; Möngke, the son of Tului (Genghis Khan's youngest son); Baidar and Büri, the son and grandson, respectively, of Chaghadai (Genghis Khan's second son). The campaign lasted six years (1236–1242) and followed a very careful preparation of troops and a detailed collection of intelligence. During the first phase, the Mongols attacked the Volga Bulghars, and in 1237 some of the most important cities in the Rus' principalities (Riazan', Vladimir, Kolomna, Moscow, and Suzdal'). A direct attack on the "Cuman Desert" came only in 1238 and seems to have encountered serious resistance from various Cuman chieftains. At least one of them, Köten, fled to the west to find shelter within the borders of the Hungarian kingdom. Two years later, Kiev fell and in the winter of 1240/1, the Mongol troops gathered in Galicia in preparation for a simultaneous attack on Poland and Hungary. The first reconnaissance units reached Lublin and Sandomierz in February. By late April 1241, the Mongols had already occupied Cracow and had crushed the army of Duke Henry II of Silesia. However,

[84] Ata Malek Joveyni, *The History of the World-Conqueror*, translated by J. A. Boyle, vol. 1 (Cambridge, Mass.: Harvard University Press, 1958; reprint Seattle: University of Washington Press, 1997), pp. 196–200 and 268–269; Rashīd al-Dīn, *The Successors of Genghis-Khan*, translated by J. A. Boyle (New York: Columbia University Press, 1971), pp. 61 and 107–108. Joveyni was born nine years after the *quriltai* and wrote his *History* in 1260 as governor of Baghdad under Genghis Khan's grandson Hülegü, the founder of the Ilkhanid dynasty of Persia. Commissioned to write a history of the Mongols by the sixth member of that dynasty, Mahmud Ghazan Khan (1295–1304), Rashīd al-Dīn finished his work in 1307 or 1308.

[85] Jochi died in 1227, before the *quriltai*. Much of the preliminary information the Mongols had about Desht-i Kipchak had been obtained during Jochi and Sübödai's expedition that ended with the victory on the Kalka River. See H. Göckenjan, "Der Westfeldzug (1236–1242) aus mongolischer Sicht," in *Wahlstatt 1241. Beiträge zur Mongolenschlacht bei Liegnitz und zu ihren Nachwirkungen*, ed. by U. Schmilewski (Würzburg: Bergstadtverlag Korn, 1991), pp. 37–75.

the main target of the 1241 invasion was Hungary.[86] Batu and his most experienced general Sübödai led the main corps that entered Hungary from Galicia through the Voric'kil Pass across the northern Carpathians, which King Béla IV had just fortified. On March 12, 1241, the Mongols broke through, after special units had cleared the way. The Hungarians who manned the fortification were either massacred or dispersed. On April 11, 1241, Batu inflicted a crushing defeat upon King Béla IV's army at Muhi (near Tiszaújváros on the Sajó River). A great number of noblemen, magistrates, archbishops, and bishops died on the battlefield. The king barely escaped alive, while his brother Coloman later died from his wounds.

While Batu's main army made its way across the northern Carpathians and along the Tisza River, another corps under the command of Kadan and Büri moved from Galicia into northern Moldavia to reach the passes across the eastern Carpathians. Following the valley of the Bistriţa River, the Mongols entered Transylvania and sacked Rodna in late March 1241. Six hundred armed Saxons were forced to accompany Kadan, most likely as guides.[87] The Mongols took Oradea and massacred the city's population. Roger of Torre Maggiore, who left a dramatic description of the invasion in his *Song of Lamentation on the Destruction of the Kingdom of Hungary by the Tartars*,[88] was archdeacon at the chapter in that city and he fled to Cenad together with a few companions. He found Cenad in ruins and devastated by the attack of a third Mongol army under a commander whom he called "Bochetor." This is most certainly a corruption of some other name, but the exact identity of the

[86] M. Rady, "The Mongol invasion of Hungary," *Medieval World*, vol. 3 (1991), pp. 39–46. According to Juveyni, *History*, p. 199, the Mongols had a greater interest in Desht-i Kipchak and Hungary than in Poland or the Balkan lands.

[87] Roger of Torre Maggiore, *Carmen miserabile*, p. 564.

[88] Roger of Torre Maggiore, *Carmen miserabile*, pp. 545–588. A German translation of the text is available in *Der Mongolensturm. Berichte von Augenzeugen und Zeitgenossen 1235–1250*, ed. by H. Göckenjan and J. R. Sweeney (Graz: Styria, 1985), pp. 129–223. Roger had come to Hungary in 1233 from his native Naples, as a member of the papal embassy led by Jacob of Pecora. He later returned to become Archdeacon of Oradea. Following the Mongol invasion he was appointed Archdeacon of Sopron and later Archbishop of Split. See T. Almási, "Megjegyzések Rogerius magyarországi méltósávigseléséhez [Remarks concerning the office held by Roger in Hungary]," *Acta Universitatis Szegediensis de Attila Jozsef nominatae. Acta Historica*, vol. 86 (1988), pp. 9–14.

commander remains a matter of debate. Rashīd al-Dīn mentions Kadan's battles with the Saxons (*Sasan*), but according to him another participant in the expedition was Böček, the son of Tului (Genghis Khan's youngest son and Möngke's brother). Crossing the mountains of the "Black Vlachs" (*Kara Ulagh*), Böček defeated the Vlachs and one of their leaders named Mišlav.[89] If we are to trust Rashīd al-Dīn's much later account, then Böček must be Roger's "Bochetor," the Mongol commander who moved along the Siret River across Moldavia, attacked and destroyed the Cuman bishopric, and eventually entered the Braşov region of Transylvania. This must then be the army that, according to other sources, defeated and killed Pousa, the *voevode* of Transylvania.[90] The same Mongol army moved along the Olt River, and sacked the Cârţa Abbey and Sibiu on the same day that Batu defeated King Béla IV at Muhi. Soon after that the Mongols devastated Cenad, which Archdeacon Roger and his companions already found in ruins when fleeing from Oradea. The Mongol army operating in southern Transylvania is also responsible for the massacre of the local noblemen and their families, who had barricaded themselves inside the Igriş Abbey.[91] All three Mongol armies then joined forces in the Hungarian Great Plain, which the Mongols occupied during the last months of 1241.

Kadan was sent with an army to capture King Béla IV who had fled first to Zagreb, then to Dalmatia. According to Thomas of Spalato, the most important source for the Mongol invasion in the western and central Balkans, Kadan spent the winter of 1241/2 in Dalmatia. In Croatia, the population fled to the mountains and to the woods, but the Mongols pitched camp in the hinterland of Senj, where they massacred the prisoners they had brought with them from

[89] Rashīd al-Dīn, *Successors*, p. 70. The Vlachs defeated in battle by Böček may have been either those of Walachia or, more probably, those of the "land of the Vlachs" in southern Transylvania. See A. Decei, "L'invasion des Tatars de 1241/1242 dans nos régions selon la *Djami' ot-Tevarikh* de Fäzl ol-lah Räšid od-Din," *RRH*, vol. 12 (1973), pp. 101–121. For Western sources confirming Rashīd al-Dīn's account, see V. Spinei, "Cronicari italieni despre repercusiunile marii invazii mongole din 1241–1242 asupra românilor [Italian chronicles on the consequences of the great Mongol invasion of 1241–1242 for the Romanians]," *Studii şi materiale de istorie medie*, vol. 19 (2001), pp. 169–204.

[90] *Annals of Freisach*, ed. by L. Weiland (Hanover, 1879; reprint 1975), MGH SS 24:65.

[91] Roger of Torre Maggiore, *Carmen miserabile*, p. 583.

Hungary.[92] The Hungarian king first went to Split, but a disagreement with the townsmen forced him to seek a better refuge in Trogir. In March 1242, the Mongols appeared before the walls of Split, where, according to Thomas, the inhabitants mistook them for Croatians. Kadan ravaged the countryside, and a great number of people moved into the city, which was already crowded with refugees from Hungary. The neighboring fort at Klis resisted the first assault, and Kadan abandoned the siege as soon as he learned that King Béla was not there. Sending some of his troops against Split, he turned his own to Trogir. At the approach of the Mongols, fearing for his life, the Hungarian king boarded a ship to survey the Mongol attack from a distance. But the attack failed, mainly because of the mudflats along the channel separating Trogir from the mainland, which prevented the Mongol horsemen from approaching the walls. In an attempt to cause a rift among the defenders, Kadan sent a messenger to address the citizens of Trogir in Croatian, but to no avail. Failing to take Trogir, the Mongols withdrew, but not before raiding several times the settlements on the coast. By April, Kadan had moved his troops into Bosnia and Serbia, heading towards southern Dalmatia. The Mongols bypassed Dubrovnik, but set fire to Kotor, before moving back across Serbia to join forces with Batu in Bulgaria. According to Rashīd al-Dīn, Kadan destroyed two cities named Qirqin (Tărnovo) and Qila (Kilia in the Danube Delta) in a country named Ulaqut (Vlachia), which can only be the Second Bulgarian Empire.[93] The majority of the Mongol forces had withdrawn from Hungary through Transylvania, which was again plundered thoroughly. The exact reason for the general withdrawal of the Mongols is a matter of scholarly debate, although it still seems logical to attribute the decision to Batu's learning the news of Great Khan Ögödai's death. Whatever the reason, there is no evidence that the goal in 1242 was to keep the devastated territories, for the Mongols left no garrisons or military detachments

[92] Thomas of Spalato, *Historia Salonitana*, p. 174. Thomas's account of the Mongol invasion of Dalmatia is also available in German translation in *Der Mongolensturm*, pp. 227–270. For Thomas's view of the Mongols, see J. R. Sweeney, "Thomas of Spalato and the Mongols: a thirteenth-century Dalmatian view of Mongol customs," *Florilegium: Carleton University Annual Papers on Classical Antiquity and the Middle Ages*, vol. 4 (1982), pp. 156–183.

[93] Rashīd al-Dīn, *Successors*, p. 71. For the Mongol invasion of Bulgaria, see P. Pavlov and G. Atanasov, "Preminavaneto na tatarskata armiia prez Bălgariia (1241–1242) [The passage of the Mongol army through Bulgaria (1241–1242)]," *Voennoistoricheski sbornik*, vol. 63 (1994), pp. 5–20.

in the Lower Danube region and did not take direct political control of the region for a long while after 1242. Although theoretically part of the Golden Horde established by Batu Khan, who ruled from Sarai on the Volga, the steppe corridor between the Dnieper and the Lower Danube was only a "region of hegemony," not of direct control.

Nevertheless, the invasion of 1241/2 was a major watershed in the medieval history of Southeastern Europe. Contemporary sources depict the utter desolation and destruction inflicted by the Mongols. Many take this record of devastation at face value and portray the invasion as a major catastrophe that left the region crippled and devastated. György Győrffy, for example, maintains that as much as half of the entire population of the Hungarian kingdom may have perished in just two years, 1241 and 1242.[94] According to such views, the disaster may well be compared to the effects of the Black Death in Western Europe. Given that much of the devastation took place in the eastern part of the kingdom, where certain regions were raided twice within a single year, the disaster was particularly visible in Transylvania. Upon returning from his Mongol captivity, Roger of Torre Maggiore wandered through Transylvania from village to village "without meeting anyone." In Alba Iulia, he saw only "corpses and skulls of those slaughtered by the invaders."[95] Most other urban settlements in Transylvania were little more than "ghost towns." Many villages were deserted and not reestablished until decades after the Mongol invasion. Archaeological surveys and excavations in southeastern Hungary have revealed that out of forty-three villages in existence before 1241 in the Orosháza region, east of Szeged, thirty-one ceased to exist after the invasion.[96] Fields previously under cultivation to which contemporary sources refer as *praedia* were deserted to such a scale that by 1300 the word *praedium* became a synonym for abandoned or uninhabited estate with fixed boundaries but no tenants. The famine that

[94] G. Győrffy, "A honfoglalok száma és az Árpád-kor népessége [The number of conquering Hungarians and the size of Hungary's population during the rule of the Arpadian dynasty]," in *Magyarország történeti demogfráfiája I. A honfoglalás és az Árpád-kor népessége. Az 1995. február 16-én Budapesten megrendezett Népesedéstörténeti Konferencia eloadásai*, ed. by J. Kovacsics (Budapest: Központi Statisztikai Hivatal, 1995), pp. 37–41.

[95] Roger of Torre Maggiore, *Carmen miserabile*, p. 586.

[96] P. Engel, *The Realm of St. Stephen. A History of Medieval Hungary, 895–1526* (London and New York: I. B. Tauris, 2001), p. 102. No such study exists for Transylvania, where destruction seems to have been particularly thorough.

immediately followed the invasion increased the death toll and contributed to the disruption or even cessation of many settlements.[97] The 1240 destruction of Kiev also led to the rapid decline of the east European trade transiting Hungary. In the aftermath of the Mongol invasion Keve and Bač were reduced to the status of insignificant villages, while the trade axis moved eastwards to the Danube Delta region.

The Mongol invasion was also the main factor behind the political rearrangements in the Lower Danube region.[98] In a letter of *c.* 1250 for Pope Innocent IV, King Béla IV expressed hopes that the Catholic faith would be extended "along the length of the Danube and up to the Sea of Constantinople, and thus we shall be able to help the Empire of Romania and even the Holy Land." To the Hungarian king, the Danube was a "river of confrontations."[99] In spite of his optimism, the Mongol onslaught effectively stopped the Hungarian expansion across the Carpathians for several decades, for no Hungarian army is known to have crossed the mountains until 1280. By then, an ambitious general of the Golden Horde named Nogai had established himself on the Lower Danube at Isaccea, no doubt attracted by the lucrative commerce with the Genoese merchants who had meanwhile gained control over the entire Black Sea area. Ensconced in the Lower Danube region, Nogai led another Mongol invasion of Transylvania in 1285 and made the Bulgarian ruler George Terter (1279–1292) and the Serbian king Uroš II Milutin (1282–1321) recognize his overlordship. By 1292, when the Mongol troops entered Mačva, the marches on the southern border of the Hungarian kingdom, as well as the neighboring client states in Walachia, had disappeared. A product of the Mongol invasion of 1241/2, the Golden Horde fundamentally altered the course of the medieval history of Southeastern Europe.

[97] In the mountain refuge where he eventually found shelter on his way back from the Mongol captivity, Roger of Torre Maggiore and his companions found nothing else to eat but black bread made from flour mixed with acorn shells. See Roger of Torre Maggiore, *Carmen miserabile*, p. 588.

[98] Berend, *At the Gate of Christendom*, pp. 37–38.

[99] *Vetera monumenta historica Hungariam sacram illustrantia*, ed. by A. Theiner, vol. I (Rome: Typis Vaticanis, 1859), pp. 230–232. In his letter, Béla compared his wars with the Mongols to Emperor Heraclius' confrontation with Khusro II. See Berend, *At the Gates of Christendom*, pp. 165–167; Papacostea, *Between the Crusade and the Mongol Empire*, pp. 294–295.

8

CONCLUSIONS AND LINGERING QUESTIONS

The current concerns with the definition and limits of Europe may be traced back to Leopold von Ranke (1795–1886) and his idea that, as an appropriate unit of analysis, Europe was a product of Latin and Germanic peoples. There was no room for the Slavs in the concept of Europe that some of Ranke's contemporaries had in mind, and little understanding for eastern Latin nations, such as the Romanians, or for their non-Latin, non-Germanic, and non-Slavic neighbors – the Hungarians. To Georg W. F. Hegel (1770–1831), Ranke's older contemporary, the Slavs were by no means "an independent element in the series of phases that Reason has assumed in the World."[1] Excluding the folkloric East from history was a matter of drawing lines of contrast against which the European high culture could be better defined. As one author sagaciously observed, "the invention of Eastern Europe was a subtly self-promoting and sometimes overtly self-congratulatory event in intellectual history, whereby Western Europe also identified itself and affirmed its own precedence."[2] Hegel and Ranke's formulations were subsequently modified to fit local concerns, but their premise remained unaltered. Early twentieth-century historians in many East European countries reinforced, rather

[1] Georg W. F. Hegel, *Lecture on the Philosophy of History*, English translation by J. Sibree (London: G. Bell and Sons, 1902), p. 363. For Ranke's interest in the modern history of Southeastern Europe, see F. Valjavec, *Ausgewählte Aufsätze* (Munich: R. Oldenbourg, 1963), pp. 82–103.

[2] L. Wolff, *Inventing Eastern Europe. The Map of Civilization on the Mind of the Enlightenment* (Stanford: Stanford University Press, 1994), p. 360.

than challenged, that premise. Każimierz Tymieniecki included into Eastern Europe the regions east of the Elbe now in eastern Germany and Poland, but excluded both Scandinavia and the Balkans. He viewed Scandinavia as a part of the "West," while the Balkans, in his eyes, were not truly European.

Some of Tymieniecki's contemporaries had a different understanding of the issue. At the end of the Balkan Wars and on the eve of World War I, the Romanian historian Nicolae Iorga created in Bucharest an institute specifically and exclusively dedicated to the study of Southeastern Europe. Iorga's purpose was to move away from the derogatory meaning attached to the phrase "Balkans," but also to endorse his country's foreign policy at a time of growing Romanian influence in that region. The study of Southeastern Europe survived both the dramas unfolding during World War II in that region and its subsequent political transformation. Institutes and associations for the study of Southeast European history were created in several capital cities in the region, which have received one after the other the regular meetings of the International Association of Southeast European Studies. *Revue des études sud-est européennes*, the journal published by the institute Iorga had founded in Bucharest, is now one of the leading periodicals in the region.

But the medieval history of the region is rarely treated as a whole and still remains locked within several, mutually exclusive national(ist) paradigms. The preceding seven chapters suggest a different perspective. The narratives contained therein have described in some detail specific developments, while at the same time highlighting arguments for comparison. A synchronous perspective typically emphasizes the process of state formation and the shifting balance of regional power marked by such developments as the Carolingian encroachment of the early ninth century or the Byzantine *reconquista* of the late tenth and early eleventh century. Issues of economic convergence, social structure, and religious identities have also been outlined in the preceding narratives. This chapter will review those themes, while stressing commonalities and emphasizing areas of future research.

ECONOMY

Southeastern Europe during the Middle Ages is often described as a world of small farms owned by peasants specializing in cereal cultivation.[3] This picture is confirmed by archaeological excavations in Romania, Bulgaria, Serbia, and Bosnia.[4] Cereal cultivation was a major component of the regional economy since Roman times, and Southeastern Europe may have been responsible for the introduction of some advanced plowing and harvesting techniques. For example, the earliest asymmetrical plowshares indicating swing plows with fixed moldboards capable of turning the turf on one side or the other have been found on sites in Slovenia and Romania.[5] In early medieval hoards of iron implements and weapons, plowshares appear in combination with coulters, as a toolkit most typical for a type of plow otherwise known from graffiti on the walls of the royal palace in Pliska.[6] Both shares and coulters are typically short and may thus be

[3] I. A. Rafalovich, "Zemledelie u rannykh slavian v Moldavii (VI–IX vv.) [The agriculture of the early Slavs in Moldova (sixth to ninth century)]," in *Dalekoe proshloe Moldavii*, ed. by N. A. Ketraru, V. I. Markevich, L. L. Polevoi, and G. D. Smirnov (Kishinew: Redakcionno-izdatel'skii otdel Akademii Nauk Moldavskoi SSR, 1969), pp. 75–90; Ş. Olteanu, "Agricultura la est şi sud de Carpaţi în sec. IX–XIV [Agriculture in the lands east and south of the Carpathian Mountains during the ninth to fourteenth century]," *Muzeul Naţional*, vol. 1 (1974), pp. 35–55; J. Henning, "Bulgarien zwischen Antike und Mittelalter im Spiegel der Wirtschaftsarchäologie," *Das Altertum*, vol. 32 (1986), pp. 100–112.

[4] E. Zaharia, *Săpăturile de la Dridu. Contribuţii la arheologia şi istoria perioadei de formare a poporului român* [Excavations in Dridu. Contributions to the archaeology and history of the period of Romanian ethnogenesis] (Bucharest: Editura Academiei Republicii Socialiste România, 1967); B. Borisov, "Ikonomikata na srednovekovnoto selishte vărkhu selishtnata mogila do s. Diadovo, Burgasko [The economy of the medieval village on the tell excavated in Diadovo near Burgas]," *Izvestiia na muzeite ot Iugoiztochna Bălgariia*, vol. 4 (1991), pp. 68–88; G. Marjanović-Vujović, "Rural settlements in the 9th and 10th centuries in the Danube Valley in Serbia," in *From the Baltic to the Black Sea. Studies in Medieval Archaeology*, ed. by D. Austin and L. Alcock (London: Unwin Hyman, 1990), pp. 236–247; I. Čremošnik, "Die Untersuchungen in Mušići und Žabljak. Über den ersten Fund der ältesten slawischen Siedlung in Bosnien," *WMBHL*, vol. 5 (1975), pp. 91–176.

[5] S. Ciglenečki, "Die Eisenwerkzeugen aus den befestigten Höhensiedlungen Sloweniens aus der Völkerwanderungszeit," *Balcanoslavica*, vol. 10 (1983), pp. 45–54; Gh. Lazin, "Două piese de metal din secolele 8–9 descoperite în localitatea Lazuri–Satu Mare [Two eighth- to ninth-century metal artifacts from Lazuri near Satu Mare]," *Studii şi comunicări*, vols. 5–6 (1981–1982), pp. 137–142; Gh. Popilian and M. Nica, *Gropşani. Monografie arheologică* [Gropşani. An Archaeological Monograph] (Bucharest: Institutul Român de Tracologie, 1998), pp. 33 and 174 fig. 22/12.

[6] T. Balabanov, "Zemedelski orădiia ot Pliska (IX–XI v.) [Agricultural implements from ninth- to eleventh-century Pliska]," *Bălgarska etnografiia*, vol. 10 (1985), pp. 19–29.

viewed as components of ards with soles. The absence of plow chains from any hoard dated earlier than *c.* 1100 demonstrates that these were not wheeled heavy plows, but light implements most appropriate for small-scale cultivation on fields of relatively limited size. Neither written nor archaeological evidence exists of water mills, but many settlement sites in Greece, Bulgaria, and Romania have produced quernstones.[7] To small-scale cultivation also points the frequent hoard association of plowshares and ardshares with various types of hoes and bill-knives, which are an indication of vineyard cultivation otherwise abundantly attested in written sources. The cellars of the royal palace were stacked with barrels of wine, when Emperor Nicephorus' troops stormed and sacked Pliska in 811. Just before and after year 1000, the monks on Mount Athos were involved in a lucrative commerce with the mainland, much of which was in wine. Wine is also among the commodities mentioned by Sviatoslav in his letter from Pereiaslavec on the Danube to his mother Ol'ga in Kiev. Wine production and trade was the main source of economic growth for eleventh- and twelfth-century Maroneia. In many areas of Peloponnesos, but also as far north as the Chalkidike Peninsula, olive trees had gradually taken some portions of the arable land, without completely eliminating crop cultivation. Similarly, mulberry trees must have been common in Peloponnesos and Boeotia, where the silk industry flourished in the eleventh and twelfth centuries.

Most scholars agree that the agricultural techniques employed throughout the Middle Ages and, in some cases, the early modern period were typical for extensive, not intensive agriculture. Although the common opinion is that in the early Middle Ages slash-and-burn agriculture was the norm, neither written nor archaeological evidence seems to confirm such views. Only a few pollen studies have so far been published and only for limited areas. However, such studies already suggest that the system in place may have been a flexible form of fallow sequence in which arable lands were periodically allowed

[7] T. E. Gregory, "An Early Byzantine (dark-age) settlement at Isthmia: preliminary report," in *The Corinthia in the Roman Period Including the Papers Given at a Symposium Held at the Ohio State University on 7–9 March, 1991*, ed. by T. E. Gregory (Ann Arbor: Journal of Roman Archaeology, 1993), pp. 149–160; Zh. Văzharova, *Srednovekovnoto selishte s. Garvăn, Silistrenski okrăg (VI–XI v.)* [The medieval village of Garvăn near Silistra] (Sofia: Izdatelstvo na Bălgarskata Akademiia na Naukite, 1986); S. Dolinescu-Ferche, "Habitats du VIe et VIIe siècles de notre ère à Dulceanca IV," *Dacia*, vol. 36 (1992), pp. 125–177.

to lie fallow for a varying number of years, sometimes as long as was needed for old fields to become wasteland.[8] Long-term archaeological excavations in Dulceanca (southern Romania) have identified four sixth- to seventh-century settlements located at about two miles from each other on the left bank of a creek. This has been interpreted not as a string of contemporary sites, but as the shifting hamlets of one and the same community moving around within a distance of no more than ten miles from the previous settlement. The most likely explanation for this phenomenon is what has been described as "itinerant agriculture": as arable land lost its fertility after repeated cultivation without manuring, the fields were abandoned for a number of years, during which time other fields previously left fallow were brought under cultivation.[9] However, many more studies are needed for areas in Southeastern Europe with a different landscape profile (such as central Croatia, Greece, or Thrace) before drawing any firm conclusions. The model of "itinerant agriculture" may not be applicable either to the entire region or to the entire period under study in this book. Moreover, long-term continuity may have coexisted with substantial alterations of the economic patterns. For example, paleobotanic studies of charred seeds found on several early medieval sites in Romania, Moldova, and Bulgaria indicate a high incidence of millet as the preferred cereal. Millet was still the preferred cereal in the hinterland of Dyrrachion in the early twelfth century, but by then wheat had replaced millet in the large granaries feeding the population of Constantinople, which were located in or near Philippopolis. Wheat, but also spelt and rye have replaced millet in the

[8] E. I. Emandi, "Cultura plantelor în nordul Moldovei (sec. IX–XV) în lumina cercetărilor paleobotanice [Crop cultivation in northern Moldavia between the ninth and the fifteenth century in the light of paleobotanical research]," *Hierasus*, vol. 3 (1981), 51; E. Hajnalová, "Die archäobotanische Funde," in *Iatrus-Krivina. Spätantike Befestigung und frühmittelalterliche Siedlung an der unteren Donau*, ed. by G. von Bülow and D. Schieferdecker, vol. IV (Berlin: Akademie Verlag, 1991), pp. 261–298. For more general conclusions regarding the landscape of the early medieval communities of agriculturists, see L. Björkman, A. Feurdean, and B. Wohlfarth, "Late Glacial and Holocene forest dynamics at Steregoiu in Gutâiului Mountains, Northwest Romania," *Review of Palaeobotany and Palynology*, vol. 124 (2003), pp. 79–111.

[9] Curta, *Making the Slavs*, p. 276. For itinerant agriculture in more recent times, see H. H. Stahl, *Traditional Romanian Village Communities. The Transition from the Communal to the Capitalist Mode of Production in the Danube Region* (Cambridge: Cambridge University Press and Paris: Editions de la Maison des Sciences de l'Homme, 1980), p. 61.

diet of the eleventh-century inhabitants of the Pohărniceni-Petruha rural site excavated in Moldova. Crop rotation is attested for twelfth-century Thessaly, Macedonia, and Thrace, but in the absence of any data from pollen analysis or the archaeological study of fields nothing is known about comparable developments in Transylvania, Serbia, or northeastern Bulgaria. This is indeed one of the areas in which much more work is needed in order to elucidate fundamental questions regarding both soil-tilling techniques and social and economic change.

The analysis of animal bones found on various sites excavated in Southeastern Europe has shown that the proportion of cattle, some used as burden animals, was only slightly larger than that of sheep and goats, with pigs following at some distance.[10] On the other hand, there is no evidence, archaeological or otherwise, of an advanced combination of crop cultivation and animal husbandry, the hallmark of West European developments during the early Middle Ages. Most scythes found in settlements or hoards are short-handled, most suitable for clearings, stony soils, and all spots where grass grew in abundance and had a sufficient height. Combined with the complete absence of any remains of storage facilities or stables on early medieval sites in the region, the evidence of scythes thus suggests that although livestock breeding may have been of some significance, no farmstead economy developed from the combination of farming and cattle breeding.[11] On the other hand, even with a predominantly pastoral economy, as the case seems to have been for the Avar qaganate,

[10] Zooarchaeological studies are particularly advanced in Hungary and Romania, but less so in Bulgaria, Greece, Serbia, and Croatia. See S. Haimovici, "Studiul resturilor mamiferelor domestice descoperite în aşezări din sec. VIII–XII situate în sud-estul României [The study of the faunal remains found on eighth- to twelfth-century sites in southeastern Romania]," *SCIVA*, vol. 35 (1984), pp. 311–319; L. Bartosiewicz, "Early medieval faunal remains from Pontes (Iron Gates Gorge, Eastern Serbia)," *AAASH*, vol. 48 (1991), pp. 281–315. For a general European perspective, see S. Bökönyi, "The development of stockbreeding and herding in medieval Europe," in *Agriculture in the Middle Ages: Technology, Practice, and Representation*, ed. by D. Sweeney (Philadelphia: University of Pennsylvania Press, 1995), pp. 41–61.

[11] J. Henning, "Unterscheide und Gemeinsamkeiten zwischen slawischer und fränkischer Landwirtschaft in Gebieten frühmittelalterlicher Stadtentwicklung," in *Trudy V Mezhdunarodnogo Kongressa arkheologov-slavistov. Kiev 18–25 sentiabria 1985 g.*, ed. by P. P. Tolochko, I. E. Borovskii, A. A. Kozlovskii, and A. P. Mocia, vol. II (Kiev: Naukova Dumka, 1988), pp. 224–225. Short-handled scythes are known from such diverse sites in Southeastern Europe as Shurdhah in northern Albania, Mohács in southern Hungary, and Shumen in northeastern Bulgaria.

as well as for the Bulgar and early Hungarian polities, agricultural produce appears to have been in abundance. Walter Pohl has noted that unlike Germanic federates of previous centuries, the Avars never received supplies of food from the Romans, while everything indicates that they were capable of organizing a very successful economic infrastructure.[12] The same is true for eighth- and ninth-century Bulgaria, but the ways in which nomads and non-nomads interacted within the early medieval landscape is not simply an issue hinging on social organization, because pastoralism and crop cultivation were not mutually exclusive modes of production.

With the notable exception of Hungary, there is so far little understanding of medieval (nomadic) pastoralism in Southeastern Europe.[13] Pastoralism in the Balkans is invariably associated with the Vlachs, but the basis for such association is to be found more in twentieth-century ethnographic reports[14] than in medieval sources.[15] Transhumant

[12] W. Pohl, "Zur Dynamik barbarischer Gesellschaften: das Beispiel der Awaren," *Klio*, vol. 73 (1991), pp. 595–600.

[13] Most illustrative in that respect is the work of the Hungarian historian G. Győrffy, "Système des résidences d'hiver et d'été chez les nomades et les chefs hongrois au Xe siècle," *AEMA*, vol. 1 (1975), pp. 45–153; *Wirtschaft und Gesellschaft der Ungarn um die Jahrtausendwende* (Vienna, Cologne, Graz: Böhlau, 1983); and "Nomades et seminomades: la naissance de l'état hongrois," in *Popoli delle stepe: Unni, Avari, Ungari, 23–29 aprile 1987*, vol. II (Spoleto: Pressa del Centro, 1988), pp. 621–636. Research on nomads and pastoralism in the steppe corridor was very advanced in the Soviet Union. See, for example, A. O. Dobroliubskii, *Kochevniki Severo-Zapadnogo Prichernomor'ia v epokhu srednevekov'ia* [The nomads of the northwestern region of the Black Sea during the Middle Ages] (Kiev: Naukova Dumka, 1986). By contrast, only broad generalizations are available for Bulgaria, e.g., V. Giuzelev, "Economic development and forms of social and political organisation of the Proto-Bulgarians prior to the foundation of the Bulgarian state (4th-7th c.)," *Barukan Sho Ajia kenkyu*, vol. 6 (1980), pp. 95–103.

[14] Much progress has been made in recent decades in the anthropology of pastoralist communities in the Balkans. See, for example, C. Chang, *Pastoral Transhumance in the Southern Balkans as a Social Ideology. An Ethnoarchaeological Research in Northern Greece* (Washington: American Anthropological Association, 1993). For pastoralism in the Carpathian Mountains, see C. Constantinescu-Mirceşti, *Păstoritul transhumant şi implicaţiile lui în Transilvania şi Ţara Românească în secolele XVIII–XIX* [The Transhumant Pastoralism and its Implications for Eighteenth- to Nineteenth-Century Transylvania and Walachia] (Bucharest: Editura Academiei Republicii Socialiste România, 1976).

[15] However, see M. Gyóni, "Les Vlaques du Mont Athos au début du XIIe siècle," *Etudes slaves et roumaines*, vol. 1 (1948), pp. 30–42; and "La transhumance des Vlaques balkaniques au Moyen Age," *Byzantinoslavica*, vol. 12 (1952), pp. 29–42. Revision of this topic is urgently needed in the light of both new evidence and new anthropological approaches to pastoralist communities.

pastoralism was indeed an economic strategy associated with mountains, and old preconceptions about "primitive" or "backward" mountain communities of shepherds may be responsible for the current lack of historical and archaeological studies of medieval pastoralists. Transhumance practices in the Balkans, with their typical traffic between upland and the adjacent coastal plains, may have been very different from that of Transylvania and the neighboring regions.[16] Here, again, more work is needed in order to answer fundamental questions about the role of pastoralism in regional economies, the social structures associated with such economic specialization, or the impact of early medieval states on pastoral practices.

The development of crafts in Southeastern Europe was largely determined by the market and the available resources. The raw material commonly used for most tools and weapons was bog iron, which required much tempering. Most of the iron artifacts found on early medieval sites in Bulgaria have steel edges welded to iron bases by means of forging.[17] Hoards of iron implements and weapons found in Romania, Bulgaria, and Serbia include hammers, anvils, and tongs, as well as iron ingots. However, late eighth- and early ninth-century swords with high-carbon steel blades found in Croatia were imported from Carolingian Francia. Similar conclusions may be drawn from the examination of other crafts. The pottery production attested by kilns excavated in Dulceanca (sixth to seventh century), Topola and Khotnica (tenth century), or Veliko Tărnovo (late eleventh and early twelfth centuries) was geared to local demand, but some interregional trade took place. In the eleventh and early twelfth centuries, the Fine Sgraffito Ware found on sites in the northern Balkans and in Dobrudja seems to have been imported, at least partially, from

16 As suggested by I. Donat, "La vie pastorale chez les Roumains et ses problèmes," *Dacoromania*, vol. 1 (1973), pp. 78–83.

17 S. Vitlianov, "Das Schmiedehandwerk in Bulgarien vom VII.–XIV. Jh.," *Slavia Antiqua*, vol. 32 (1989–1990), pp. 145–170; J. Piaskowski, "Metallkundliche Untersuchungen antiker und frühmittelalterlicher Eisengegenstände," in *Iatrus-Krivina. Spätantike Befestigung und frühmittelalterliche Siedlung an der unteren Donau*, ed. by G. von Bülow and D. Schieferdecker, vol. IV (Berlin: Akademie Verlag, 1991), pp. 241–260. For smelting techniques associated with bog-iron sources, see Ş. Olteanu, "Procédés d'influence slave pour la reduction du fer à l'est des Carpathes, au VIe–VIIe siècles dans le contexte de la technologie traditionnelle des autochtones," in *Rapports du IIIe Congrès international d'archéologie slave, Bratislava 7–14 septembre 1975*, ed. by B. Chropovský, vol. I (Bratislava: VEDA, 1979), pp. 581–586.

the pottery workshops in Greece, such as that excavated in Corinth. Equally imported, perhaps from Thuringia, was the Gray Ware found on some of the sites associated with the first Saxon "guests" of Transylvania. In tenth-century Bulgaria, specialized kilns in Pliska and Preslav produced tiles, bricks, and pipe segments for water conduits.

There is good archaeological evidence that much of the craft production of the earlier period was household-based. Crucibles, molds, dies, and defective casts found in settlement assemblages indicate that many metal artifacts, such as brooches or buckles, were often produced within the same structure that was used as a dwelling.[18] Spindle whorls and loom weights occasionally found in such structures suggest that textile production was also a cottage industry. Silk was produced in specialized workshops in twelfth-century Thebes, but imported silk was also identified archaeologically on such a remote site as Dinogetia on the Lower Danube. On the other hand, professionals were without any doubt of high social status during the earlier period, as indicated by the Avar artisan graves from Felnac or Band.[19] It has been suggested that, far from being simple collections of iron tools and weapons with intrinsic value, hoards of iron implements and weapons may have been associated with the aristocratic group known in ninth- and tenth-century Bulgaria as *tarqans*.[20] Almost all such assemblages of iron artifacts were found in or near the royal centers at Pliska and Preslav, which begs the question of what relation may have existed between craft specialization and the rise of the medieval states. At Pliska in the ninth, at Preslav in the tenth, and at Tărnovo in the late eleventh and early twelfth centuries, entire residential quarters were transformed into craft production centers geared exclusively to the demand of the local elites. Glass production is attested in ninth-century Pliska, as well as in tenth-century Preslav. Each one of these sites had a belt of satellite settlements whose role was to supply food and services for the aristocracy residing in

18 B. Sz. Szmoniewski, "Production of early medieval ornaments made of non-ferrous metals: dies from archaeological finds in north-east Romania," *Acta Archaeologica Carpathica*, vol. 37 (2002), pp. 111–135.

19 H. Winter, "Die Buntmetallbearbeitung bei den Awaren," in *Reitervölker aus dem Osten. Hunnen + Awaren. Burgenländische Landesausstellung 1996. Schloß Halbturn, 26. April–31. Oktober 1996*, ed. by F. Daim, K. Kaus, and P. Tomka (Eisenstadt: Amt der Burgenländischen Landesregierung, 1996), pp. 355–358.

20 F. Curta, "Blacksmiths, warriors and tournaments of value: dating and interpreting early medieval hoards of iron implements in Eastern Europe," *Ephemeris Napocensis*, vol. 7 (1997), pp. 211–268.

the nearby palatial compound.[21] "Service villages" may have also existed in the environs of ninth-century Nin or eleventh-century Bribir; late eleventh- and early twelfth-century Ras; or late twelfth- and early thirteenth-century Melnik. However, without extensive archaeological research at a micro-regional level, the existence of such settlements remains hypothetical. By contrast, Moreşti in Transylvania was an eleventh- to thirteenth-century village of specialized workers, peasants, and craftsmen, who may have served the exclusive needs of the neighboring stronghold and the residence of the local count.

SOCIETY

The typical village in Southeastern Europe consisted of a number of sunken-floored huts of almost standard structure and size with one or two heating facilities, either stone or clay ovens. Such buildings are common on most sites in the region throughout the entire medieval period.[22] Some sixth- and eleventh-century settlements (Dulceanca, Moreşti, Mrsunjski Lug, Dinogetia) also produced evidence of above-ground buildings, but sunken-floored huts and above-ground houses seem to have been mutually exclusive, as they rarely coexisted within the same settlement. Sunken-floored buildings were often found in clusters separated by larger or smaller open areas. Since the living area within each one of those buildings could accommodate no more than five individuals, it has been suggested that the basic social unit on early medieval sites in Southeastern Europe was the minimal family. The average settlement in the earlier period may thus have had between fifty and seventy people, with relatively larger numbers during later times.[23]

[21] J. Henning, "Vom Herrschaftszentrum zur städtischen Großsiedlung mit agrarischer komponente. Archäologische Nachweise der Landwirtschaft aus dem frü hmittelalterlichen Pliska," *Pliska–Preslav*, vol. 8 (2000), pp. 74–86.

[22] M. Takács, "Der Hausbau in Ungarn vom 2. bis zum 13. Jahrhundert n. Chr. – ein Zeitalter einheitlicher Grubenhäuser?," in *The Rural House from the Migration Period to the Oldest Still Standing Buildings. Ruralia IV, 8.-13. September 2001, Bad Bederkesa, Lower Saxony, Germany*, ed. by J. Klápšte (Prague: Institute of Archaeology, Academy of Sciences of the Czech Republic, 2002), pp. 272–290.

[23] Curta, *Making the Slavs*, p. 283. For similar conclusions based on the analysis of early medieval cemeteries, see V. Ruseva, "Mortality patterns and life expectancy in medieval skeleton populations from Bulgaria (VIII–X c. AD)," *AB*, vol. 7 (2003), pp. 77–84.

Next to nothing is known about land tenure during the earlier period, for which scholars assume a predominantly communal economy at a village level. This is further viewed in contrast to a domanial (seigneurial) economy of later times, when large estates appear in the written evidence. The "itinerant agriculture" briefly described above could not possibly have allowed for the developments of a hierarchy of access rights to land, but it would be equally wrong to think of communities of free peasants in terms of an egalitarian society.[24] It has often been said that in such societies, responsible for the early emergence of wealth and status differentiation must have been the dissolution of the community of free peasants. In reality, the relatively early evidence of "service settlements" in Bulgaria suggests that entire communities may have been moved from one place to another according to the needs of the ruler. The origins of servitude in the medieval society of Southeastern Europe may have much more to do with such phenomena of "despotic" power than with the fading away of pristine freedom. On the other hand, during the eleventh and twelfth centuries there was a clear correlation between the organization of vast estates in the central, southern, and eastern Balkans, on the one hand, and the disappearance of communities of free peasants, on the other. Most scholars describe the phenomenon in terms of a fundamental distinction between proprietors and tenant farmers, but new regional studies show that the picture was much more complicated.[25] Isaac Comnenus granted to his monastery of the Mother of God *Kosmosoteira* near Vera the estate of Neokastron together "with its dependent peasants settled both inside and outside."[26] Some of the inhabitants of two other villages he donated to his monastery were soldiers, who are described as "disobedient when it comes to paying the taxes they owe," an indication, perhaps, that they wanted their status to be distinguished from that of all other

24 M. Comşa, "Considérations relatives à la communauté villageoise en territoire roumain aux VI–VIIe siècles," in *Actes du XIIe Congrès international des sciences préhistoriques et protohistoriques, Bratislava, 1–7 septembre 1991*, ed. by J. Pavuj, vol. IV (Bratislava: Institut archéologique de l'Académie Slovaque des Sciences à Nitra, 1993), pp. 15–17.

25 See, for example, V. Kravari, *Villes et villages de Macédoine occidentale* (Paris: Pierre Lethielleux, 1989).

26 Typikon *of the* Sebastokrator *Isaac Komnenos* 69, English translation by Ševčenko, p. 828. Equally "dependent" were the peasants and the residents of the "market Sagoudaous" (p. 829).

dependent peasants.[27] That distinction was certainly on the mind of the early thirteenth-century castle warriors appearing in front of the Cathedral chapter in Oradea to defend themselves against attempts to treat them as castle folk. But tenant status did not preclude access to land. By 1150, the descendants of the tenant farmers established in the eleventh century on the monastic estates in Veljusa already owned the land they farmed. Most families in the fourteen villages that the chapter of the Cathedral in Arad owned in the early thirteenth century tilled their own fields, although they had some sort of obligation to the chapter, either in labor or in kind.

Very little is known about the organization of estates in tenth-century Bulgaria, but contemporary sources, such as the *Court Law for the People* (*Zakon sudnyi liudem*), refer to wage laborers (*naimniki*), as well as peasants without any land who were exempt from taxes (*slobodniki*).[28] Both categories also appear in Byzantine sources of the eleventh and twelfth centuries. On monastic or lay estates in the Balkans, the amount of land farmed by tenants and short-term leaseholders was by far larger than that of the domanial farm. The demesne was also considerably smaller than the land distributed as free hides on the estates owned in eleventh-century Carniola by the bishop of Freising. Moreover, sources such as the Cadaster of Thebes show a tendency towards parcellization, which has been interpreted as a consequence of both demographic pressure and a more intensive exploitation of the soil. Tenants without any land of their own also appear on the mid-thirteenth-century estates of the episcopal see in Alba Iulia. On the other hand, some slaves may have still been at work around AD 600 on medium-sized estates in Istria.[29] In Greece,

[27] Typikon *of the* Sebastokrator *Isaac Komnenos* 69, English translation by Ševčenko, p. 846. In another paragraph of the *typikon*, the two settlements with soldiers are mentioned as "military villages," which may indicate that the entire population of each of them may have enjoyed freedom at some point in the past.

[28] D. Angelov, "Die bulgarischen Länder und das bulgarische Volk in den Grenzen des byzantinischen Reiches im XI. und XII. Jahrhundert (1018–1185) (Sozial-ökonomische Verhältnisse)," in *Proceedings of the XIIIth International Congress of Byzantine Studies, Oxford 5–10 September 1966*, ed. by J. M. Hussey (London and New York: Oxford University Press, 1967), p. 158. See also G. Cankova-Petkova, "La population agraire dans les terres bulgares sous la domination byzantine aux XI–XIIe siècles," *Byzantinobulgarica*, vol. 1 (1962), pp. 299–311.

[29] V. Girardi Jurkić, "La continuità edilizia delle ville rustiche romane in Istria durante la dominazione bizantina," in *XVI. internationaler Byzantinistenkongreß. Akten. II*, ed. by W. Hörandner, C. Cupane, and E. Kislinger, vol. IV (Vienna: Verlag der

large estates of the earlier period were certainly worked by slaves, such as those owned by the Peloponnesian widow Danelis. There were many slaves working on the lands of the Abbey of St. Peter In the Village founded in 1069 near Split by Peter Crni of Gumaj. As late as 1228, King Andrew II of Hungary granted to his chief treasurer Denys an estate near Cluj with all its freed and (still) enslaved inhabitants. Judging from the evidence of the Register of Oradea, in early thirteenth-century Transylvania crime and the inability to pay one's debts were punished with enslavement, but some slaves appeared in front of the chapter to defend themselves against attempts to turn them into castle folk (*castrenses*). This suggests that both enslavement and freedom were fluid categories of social classification. On the other hand, nothing indicates that slaves had a predominant role in the domanial economy of Southeastern Europe, despite the fact that both the written and the archaeological evidence suggest the existence of an active slave trade.[30]

"Service settlements" and other similar phenomena may have also been responsible, at least in part, for the rise of certain segments of the Southeast European nobility. By 1250, many castle warriors in Transylvania claimed noble status and were subsequently included into the legal definition of nobility. Noble families with well-established power and control of state offices sported high-ranking titles that appear in ninth-century Bulgar inscriptions, but no information exists

Österreichische Akademie der Wissenschaften, 1982), pp. 585–594; R. Matijašić, "La produzione agricole in Istria nel VI–VII secolo," in *Radovi XIII. Međunarodnog Kongresa za starokršćansku arheologiju. Split–Poreč (25.9.–1.10. 1994)*, ed. by N. Cambi and E. Marin, vol. II (Vatican: Pontificio Istituto di Archeologia Cristiana and Split: Arheološki Muzej, 1998), pp. 1107–1120.

30 H. Köpstein, "Einige Aspekte des byzantinischen und bulgarischen Sklavenhandels im X. Jahrhundert. Zur Novelle des Joannes Tzimiskes über Sklavenhandelszoll," in *Actes du premier Congrès international des études balkaniques et sud-est européennes*, ed. by V. Tăpkova-Zaimova, S. Dimitrov, and E. Sarafova, vol. III (Sofia: Editions de l'Académie Bulgare des Sciences, 1969), pp. 237–247; N. Budak, "Slavery in late medieval Dalmatia/Croatia: labour, legal status, integration," in *La servitude dans les pays de la Méditerranée occidentale chrétienne au XIIe siècle et au-delà: déclinante ou renouvelée? Actes de la table ronde de Rome (8e et 9e octobre 1999)* (Rome: Ecole Française de Rome, 2000), pp. 745–760. For the archaeological evidence, see J. Henning, "Gefangenenfesseln im slawischen Siedlungsraum und der europäischen Sklavenhandel im 6. bis 12. Jahrhundert. Archäologisches zum Bedeutungswandel von 'sklabos-sakaliba-slavus'," *Germania*, vol. 70 (1992), pp. 403–426.

about their survival into the late tenth or early eleventh century.[31] Noble clans dominate the political life of late twelfth- and early thirteenth-century Croatia and Greece. Bulgar inscriptions often mention the "men of the ruler," whose death the ruler wanted to commemorate by having an inscription carved in stone. Whether or not such aristocrats may be compared to the king's men in eleventh- to thirteenth-century Hungary remains an open question. Nothing is known about the relation between ranks and landed estates in tenth-century Bulgaria, but the existing evidence suggests that the relations between the ruler and the court aristocracy may have still involved personal rather than group loyalty, as many noblemen involved in the state apparatus had their permanent residences in the vicinity of the royal palace and were probably granted land in the region. By contrast, no evidence exists of substantial grants of royal land to the aristocracy of tenth- and eleventh-century Croatia, members of which may have already owned estates when appearing in inscriptions or charters with titles referring to state offices. The same is true of the native aristocracy of Bulgaria in the aftermath of the Byzantine conquest. Until the late twelfth century, there is no indication of land grants (or revenue from imperial estates, in the form of *pronoiai*) as a form of imperial reward for the services of local noblemen. Nor do we hear, before 1185, of any demands for such rewards from local noblemen. Large estates originating in imperial grants are only attested for "outsiders," such as the Grand Domestic Gregory Pakourianos or Isaac Comnenus, the brother of Emperor John II Comnenus.[32] Nothing is known about the organization of land tenure in the northern Balkans during the eleventh and twelfth centuries, especially about the estates

[31] A. Granberg, "Observations on Bulgarian clan names in the 7th–9th centuries," in *Civitas divino-humana. V chest na profesor Georgi Bakalov*, ed. by T. Stepanov and V. Vachkova (Sofia: Centăr za izsledvaniia na bălgarite "Tangra" TanNakRa IK, 2004), pp. 551–561; G. N. Nikolov, "The Bulgarian aristocracy in the war against the Byzantine Empire (971–1019)," in *Byzantium and East Central Europe*, ed. by M. Salamon, G. Prinzing, and P. Stephenson (Cracow: Secesja, 2001), pp. 141–158.

[32] P. Tivchev and G. Cankova-Petkova, "Au sujet des relations féodales dans les territoires bulgares sous la domination byzantine à la fin du XIe siècle et pendant la première moitié du XIIe siècle," *Byzantinobulgarica*, vol. 2 (1966), pp. 107–125. See also S. N. Lishev, "Nekotorye voprosy feodal'nykh otnoshenii v Bolgarii X v. i v epokhu vizantiiskogo gospodstva [Some questions regarding the feudal relations in Bulgaria during the tenth century and the period of Byzantine rule]," *VV*, vol. 41 (1980), pp. 21–45.

of "outsiders" of lesser rank, such as Pecheneg and Cuman chieftains established south of the Danube River. Equally obscure are the status and economic privileges of the Serbian nobility under rulers of the dynasty established by Nemanja in the late twelfth century. St. Sava's *Life of Lord Simeon* refers to Nemanja's "chosen boyars, both the high and low in rank," who participated in the Ras assembly of 1196.[33] But both the nature of such rank distinctions and the basis of power of Nemanja's boyars remain unknown. Particularly needed for twelfth-century Serbia, as well as for contemporary Croatia and tenth-century Bulgaria, is a study of noble residences, their structure and organization. The complexity of the alterations brought to the formerly Byzantine fort at Ras in the late twelfth century, when the site may have become one of Nemanja's "capitals," can serve as an example of how much archaeology can reveal about status representation. Equally illustrative are the excavations in Melnik, the only site of the later period that has so far produced evidence of an aristocratic house. Compared to Ras, the Boyar's House in Melnik is strikingly similar: both show a preoccupation with fortification, most notable in the addition of towers, but also a concern with representation of power in the form of large halls designed to receive fairly large gatherings of men, either in assemblies or in feasts.

The landed aristocracy may well be elusive in the central regions of the Balkans, but it certainly is prominent in the history of medieval Greece. The role of the *archontes* in the provincial administration has been described in detail by Leonora Neville, and the previous chapters have alluded to the power of "tyrants" such as Leo Sgouros on the eve of the Latin conquest. Less detailed is our knowledge of local potentates in the urban environment, particularly in Athens, Corinth, Thessalonica, or Dyrrachion. That they wielded considerable power is demonstrated by such characters in the history of Dyrrachion as John Chryselios in the 970s or Romanus in 1185. Prominent men of Larisa were among the conspirators who placed Nikulitzas at the head of the revolt of 1066–7. Bishops Eustathius of Thessalonica and Michael Choniates of Athens tried hard to curb the power of the local *archontes*, but without much success. In the Dalmatian cities in which communes were established in the 1100s, bishops were more often among than against the leading men.

33 Sava, *Life of Lord Simeon* 3, English translation by Kantor, p. 263.

Cities and towns were not easy to distinguish in medieval Southeastern Europe, and the confusion persists in modern historiography. One of the most urgent tasks of future research is a synthesis of local studies of individual settlements, from Corinth to Kamnik and from Mesembria to Dubrovnik. The urban phenomenon in medieval Southeastern Europe is of utmost importance for the history of the entire continent, because the region contains all examples of urban development lines, from direct continuity from the old Roman centers (Athens, Dyrrachion, Mesembria, Thessalonica, Zadar), to medieval foundations within Roman ruins (Dristra, Philippopolis) and completely new foundations by either kings (Preslav, Biograd) or noblemen (Kamnik). Economic and social criteria are given clear preference in defining urban centers, as non-agricultural functions and activities or the presence of "classes" extracting income from such activities have by now replaced freedom in the sense of an autonomous community of merchants and craftsmen. Many more comparative studies are needed before drawing conclusions about the complex social structure of the medieval cities in Southeastern Europe, although it is already clear that a certain mixture may have been a critical element of stability and continuity.[34] Poorly understood is the role of the Venetians in such centers as Dyrrachion or Halmyros, as well as that of the early thirteenth-century participation of Dubrovnik in the Balkan trade. Neither Sibiu nor Braşov may be viewed as a town properly speaking before *c.* 1250, but the growth of these two settlements during the second half of the thirteenth century and after 1300 must have had a longer history. Relations between urban centers and their rural hinterlands are not very well understood, particularly in such cases as Tărnovo and Thessalonica.[35]

[34] S. M. Ćirković, "Unfulfilled autonomy: urban society in Serbia and Bosnia," in *Urban Society of Eastern Europe in Premodern Times*, ed. by B. Krekić (Berkeley: University of California Press, 1987), pp. 158–184.

[35] The question is at least raised for the towns on the Black Sea coast by K. Gagova, "Selishta v hinterlanda na iuzhnochernomorskite gradove prez XII–XIV vek [Villages in the hinterland of the twelfth- to fourteenth-century towns in the southern region of the Black Sea coast]," in *Srednovekovna Bălgariia i Chernomorieto. Sbornik dokladi ot nauchnata konferenciia, Varna 1980*, ed. by A. Kuzev (Varna: Knigoizdatelstvo "Georgi Bakalov", 1982), pp. 130–136.

RELIGION

The most important cities and towns in Southeastern Europe were also episcopal centers. The process of conversion to Christianity was accompanied by the building of new churches, many of which were founded by noblemen. This is certainly the case of the churches erected by a certain Guzma in Ulcinj during the reign of Emperor Leo V (813–820); by *zhupan* Gastika near the headwaters of the Cetina River in Croatia; or by the officers in the thematic troops of Hellas who were responsible for the building of the Church of St. John the Baptist in Athens. These were all "private churches," and their founders may have retained substantial rights in their administration. This is also true for the twelfth-century foundations of Nicholas Kasnitzes in Kastoria and Otto of Trixen-Unterdrauburg in Dravograd. Imperial dignitaries and royal officers were also founders of churches that were neither within urban centers, nor associated with any monastery, and could thus have served only as parish churches. This is certainly the case of the Church of the Holy Virgin at Skripou (873 or 874). Very little is otherwise known about the organization of the parish network in Southeastern Europe, and no comparative study exists that could elucidate questions regarding the growth of established dioceses or assess the number of parishes within any one of them.[36] The existence of parish churches is certainly implied by the laws the Hungarian kings Ladislas I and Coloman implemented to force people to bury their dead away from the pre-Christian cemeteries and in church graveyards. But even in Transylvania, the process whereby parish churches were implemented in each county during the late eleventh to early thirteenth century remains obscure.

In Dalmatia, diocesan boundaries were often a matter of dispute, as attested by numerous church synods between the tenth and

[36] For an attempt to delineate diocesan boundaries in "Dark Age" Greece, see P. Yannopoulos, "Métropoles du Péloponnèse mésobyzantin: un souvenir des invasions avaro-slaves," *Byzantion*, vol. 63 (1993), pp. 388–400. In Bulgaria, such boundaries can be traced back to Late Antiquity. See A. Krăstev, "Bischofssitze in den bulgarischen Ländern bis zum IX. Jahrhundert," in *Das Christentum in Bulgarien und auf der übrigen Balkanhalbinsel in der Spätantike und im frühen Mittelalter*, ed. by V. Giuzelev and R. Pillinger (Vienna: Verein "Freunde des Hauses Wittgenstein," 1987), pp. 233–239; B. Nicolova, "Division ecclésiastique en Thrace, en Mésie et en Illyricum oriental du IVe au VIIIe siècle," *BHR*, vol. 21 (1993), pp. 26–33.

the twelfth century.[37] Conflicts between the Dalmatian cities also emerged from hierarchical relations between archbishops and their suffragans, as the latter naturally aspired to obtain the elevation of their status. The rise to metropolitan status of many neighboring sees is also attested in Greece and southern Thrace. In Transylvania, all existing bishoprics (Alba Iulia, Oradea, and Cenad) were suffragans of the archbishop of Kalocsa, to whom was also subordinated the early thirteenth-century bishop of Bosnia. However, both the "church of the Saxons" and the Teutonic Knights, during their brief sojourn in Transylvania, were independent from the bishop of Alba Iulia, being under the jurisdiction of the archbishop of Esztergom and the pope, respectively. As a sign of their autonomous status, the archbishops of Bulgaria, Ohrid, and Serbia maintained their privilege to pass judgment on any of their suffragan bishops, an issue of great concern to Theophylact Hephaistos in the late eleventh and to Demetrius Chomatenos in the early thirteenth century. Church synods were summoned in both Bulgaria (1211) and Serbia (1221) at the behest of local archbishops. Moreover, the jurisdiction of the Serbian church was regulated in detail in Sava's translation and adaptation of the Byzantine lawcode known as the *Nomokanon*, which he presented to the synod of Žiča in 1221. Next to nothing is known about the corresponding jurisdiction of the Bulgarian church, despite the fact that Methodius' Old Church Slavonic translation of the *Nomokanon* must have been among the books Clement, Naum, and the other disciples brought to Bulgaria in the late 880s.

Bulgarian, Serbian, and Croatian dioceses were much larger than those on the Dalmatian coast or in Greece. By far the largest was the diocese of Ohrid, although it had somewhat diminished in size by the time Theophylact Hephaistos was appointed its archbishop. Initially the diocese included all the territories occupied by Basil II in 1018, but the neighboring archbishops of Thessalonica, Larisa, and Dyrrachion often disputed, sometimes successfully, the jurisdiction of the archbishop of Ohrid over several suffragan sees. Dioceses in Dalmatia, which were already small, were further subdivided in the twelfth century into smaller administrative areas governed by archdeacons on behalf of the bishop. Archdeacons were sometimes promoted to the episcopal office, as was the case with Thomas of Spalato, the author of the thirteenth-century *History of Salona*. It remains unclear

[37] Waldmüller, *Die Synoden*.

how widespread was the practice of subdividing archdeaconries into deaneries or archpresbyteries.

Few were the events in the history of the Church in Southeastern Europe that had a greater influence than Cyril and Methodius' mission to Moravia. The most enduring outcome of that mission, the Old Church Slavonic liturgy, became the foundation of the Bulgarian church in the tenth century. No evidence exists of its elimination after the Byzantine occupation of Bulgaria in 1018, as several eleventh-century apocrypha are known that were written in Old Church Slavonic. It was not within the Byzantine territories that Old Church Slavonic caused the greatest turmoil, but in the Dalmatian dioceses under Roman jurisdiction. Banned several times in regional synods, the use of the Slavic liturgy was eventually authorized by Pope Innocent IV for that region of northern Croatia that has also produced the earliest Glagolitic inscriptions.

By the early thirteenth century the use of Slavic liturgy had been replaced on the papal agenda by the Bosnian heresy. As early as 1199, Vukan of Duklja had accused *ban* Kulin of heresy. Pope Innocent III knew that Kulin protected heretics, whom he called Cathars in a letter of 1202. Not enough is known, however, about the beliefs of the Bosnian Christians to decide whether Innocent's name-calling was anything more than just that. At any rate, the pope ordered an investigation and dispatched a legate to Bosnia.[38] A synod was summoned in 1203 in Kulin's presence, at which the leaders of the Bosnian church formally renounced the heresy of which they were accused and promised to uphold the teachings of the church of Rome. But the papal preoccupation with and concerns about Bosnia did not stop there. In 1221, Pope Honorius III warned the archbishop of Split against the spread of the heresy and asked him to take immediate action. Less than ten years later, Pope Gregory IX appointed a German Dominican to the see of Bosnia, while at the same time removing that see from the jurisdiction of the archbishop of Dubrovnik and placing it under his own. The Hungarian expeditions into Bosnia (1234, 1244, and 1253) were all justified in terms of anti-heretical campaigns, and at least one of them was proclaimed a crusade with papal approval. Without sufficient knowledge of the early thirteenth-century Bosnian Church, it is difficult to disentangle genuine concerns about the rectitude of faith from political and military

[38] Šanjek, *Les chrétiens bosniaques*, p. 40.

interests. The Bosnian "heresy" may have been no more than a religious movement, perhaps of monastic inspiration, directed towards reforming Christian life through a general return to the apostolic ideals of poverty and communal life. An early thirteenth-century treatise against heretics written in northern Italy distinguished between heresies of Bulgarian and "Slavic" origin, but had no knowledge of Bosnia.[39] Nor is it possible to associate the thirteenth-century Bosnian church with the Bogomils of tenth-century Bulgaria, despite the coincidence in time of the papal concerns with the Bosnian church and a synod of the Bulgarian church that was summoned specifically to condemn Bogomilism. Given that in 1211 ties between Rome and the Bulgarian church had not yet been severed, it is nevertheless possible that the interest in the Bogomils had been stirred by contemporary concerns with the Bosnian heresy and with the Italian and French Cathars.[40]

The earliest evidence of the medieval cult of relics in Southeastern Europe is that of Dalmatia, but holy men otherwise based in southern Italy came to Greece as early as the ninth century. The first "native" saints of the region are those of Greece and Bulgaria. Despite Boris's attempt to commemorate the victims of Malamir's persecution, and possibly to establish the cult of his uncle Enravotas, early Bulgarian saints were all men of the Church of otherwise obscure social background (Naum, Clement, and John of Rila). By contrast, the first Serbian saints were princes (St. Simeon) or monks of aristocratic origin (St. Sava). Saints were the focus of religious and political interest, as indicated by several attempts in the course of military campaigns to remove and relocate relics. St. Procopius' arm and the body of St. John of Rila traveled north to Hungary after the Hungarian occupation of Niš and Serdica, respectively. The remains of John of Rila returned to Serdica, only to be moved later to Tărnovo. Samuel moved the body of St. Achilleus from Larisa to Prespa, and that of St. Tryphon from Kotor to Ohrid. A symbolic appropriation of St. Demetrius of Thessalonica took place at the beginning of the 1185 revolt of the Vlach brothers Peter and Asen. Nothing is known about pilgrimage to any of these sites, and the role of local shrines remains equally

39 Šanjek, *Les chrétiens bosniaques*, pp. 135–136.

40 A bishop of the Cathars in Lombardy named Nazarius is known to have been taught in the 1190s by the very head of the Bulgarian church. This has been often interpreted as an indication that around 1200 the Bogomils of Bulgaria had established contacts with the Cathars. See Šanjek, *Les chrétiens bosniaques*, p. 137.

obscure. In the mid-900s, the presbyter Cosmas alluded to Bulgarian monks, who instead of remaining in their monasteries, suddenly decided to go to Jerusalem or to Rome.[41] He may have had pilgrims in mind, and both leaden ampullae carrying holy oil and graffiti on the walls of tenth-century Bulgarian monasteries substantiate such an interpretation.[42] One of the most important saints of Southeastern Europe, St. Sava, is known to have died on his way back from the Holy Land.

Monasticism in Southeastern Europe is another problem in need of a comparative approach. Especially needed is a comprehensive study of the Western forms of monasticism. By 1100, there were some fifty monasteries on the Dalmatian coast, mainly Benedictine. Carthusian houses were only established in Carniola. The arrival of the Cistercians in Carniola, Slavonia, and Transylvania, but not on the Dalmatian coast, suggests a contrast with the distribution of Benedictine houses, but the pattern is still far from clear. In Southeastern Europe, Cistercian monasteries were established near important commercial routes and were involved in several economic sectors, not just agriculture. This is demonstrated, among other things, by the privilege on salt trade that King Andrew II granted to the Abbey of Igriş in 1230. A similar conclusion may be drawn from the analysis of the evidence pertaining to monasteries established in Thrace in the late eleventh and twelfth centuries. The *typika* (rules) for the monasteries in Bachkovo and Vera allude to fairs, from which the monks were to procure their necessities and levy sale taxes. Moreover, the monastery in Vera was granted rights over a marketplace and twelve ships, a

[41] *Le traité contre les Bogomiles*, pp. 93 and 100.

[42] I. Barnea, "Menasampullen auf dem Gebiet Rumäniens," in *Akten des XII. internationalen Kongresses für christliche Archäologie. Bonn, 22–28. September 1991*, ed. by E. Dassmann, K. Thraede, and J. Engemann, vol. 1 (Münster: Aschendorfsche Verlagsbuchhandlung, 1995), pp. 509–514; V. Gerasimova-Tomova, "Überblick über die Ampullen in Bulgarien," in *Von der Scythia zur Dobrudža*, ed. by Kh. Kholiolchev, R. Pillinger, and R. Harreither (Vienna: Verein "Freunde des Hauses Wittgenstein," 1997), pp. 140–155. Leaden ampullae were also produced in Thessalonica during the thirteenth century for local use. They contained myrrh from either the *ciborium* of St. Demetrius or the tomb of St. Theodora, both in Thessalonica. See Ch. Bakirtzis, "Byzantine ampullae from Thessaloniki," in *The Blessings of Pilgrimage*, ed. by R. Ousterhout (Urbana: University of Illinois Press, 1990), pp. 140–149. For images of boots as symbols of pilgrimage, see R. Kostova, "Boot-graffiti from the monastery of Ravna, and early pilgrimage in Bulgaria," *AMS* (1994–1995), pp. 140–165.

clear indication of commercial activity. Particularly problematic is the participation in the economic networks of the royal monasteries in tenth-century Bulgaria, and very little is known in that respect about monasteries in thirteenth-century Serbia. A fascinating, but still underdeveloped line of research is the study of cave monasticism, which seems to have been particularly popular in Southeastern Europe, from Late Antiquity to the thirteenth century.[43] Relations between communities of anchorites and local lords have not been sufficiently explored, as research has typically focused on cenobitic houses with royal or aristocratic founders.

There is plenty of evidence for deep religious feelings among members of the Southeast European elites. Boris, although forced to accept baptism in defeat, abdicated in favor of Vladimir and withdrew to a monastery, from which he returned only to restore the establishment threatened by his son's policies. The same is true of Nemanja, who, following his abdication, took the monastic vows and died at Mount Athos. Military disasters or misfortunes came to be viewed as God's punishments for transgressions. Symeon viewed himself as another Moses carrying out God's will and guiding his people to the Promised Land. He did penance for almost fifteen years for the sins he thought he had committed when waging war against fellow Christians in the 890s. In 1237, John Asen interpreted the outbreak of plague in Tărnovo, which killed his wife and child, as God's punishment for his betrayal of John Vatatzes and support for the Latins of Constantinople.

One of the most important areas of current research is the study of relations between Catholics and Orthodox. The invisible line separating dioceses of Roman obedience from those under the jurisdiction of Constantinople ran through the western part of the region, but the details of the local interactions between Catholics and Orthodox have not yet received scholarly attention, except for thirteenth-century Greece. The turning point was certainly the sack of Constantinople in 1204, but the impact of the Fourth Crusade on the confessional

[43] P. Diaconu and N. Petre, "Quelques observations sur le complexe archéologique de Murfatlar (Basarabi)," *Dacia*, vol. 13 (1969), pp. 448–456; G. Atanasov and D. Cheshmedzhiev, "Srednovekovniiat skalen manastir do Varna (Aladzha manastir) [A medieval cave monastery near Varna (the Aladzha Monastery)]," *Izvestiia na Narodniia muzei Varna*, vol. 26 (1990), pp. 110–140; G. Atanasov, "Rannovizantiiski skalni cărkvi i manastiri v Iuzhna Dobrudzha [Early Byzantine cave churches and monasteries in Southern Dobrudja]," *Arkheologiia*, vol. 23 (1991), 33–43.

frontier in Serbia, southern Hungary, or Transylvania has not been studied comparatively. Equally missing is a comparison with the reaction to the events of 1204 on other confessional frontiers, such as those of Galicia and Lithuania. On the other hand, there is little, if any, evidence of confessional hostility in Southeastern Europe before *c.* 1200. In at least two areas (southern Hungary and Dalmatia), parallel church administrations were in place and flourished in a tolerant atmosphere. The mechanisms of that coexistence are still poorly understood, particularly in the light of the absence of any comprehensive study of parish structure and development.

The study of medieval Southeastern Europe represents a challenge for historians. The region cannot be easily written out of European history, but its bewildering variety is often taken for a form of exceptionalism, an approach that proves to be wrong at a closer analysis. But the alternative is also difficult to accept: adding the Southeast to the standard narrative of European history will raise more questions than it will answer. Straddling twenty meridians and twelve degrees of northern latitude, Southeastern Europe was also a bridge between worlds that historians had long treated separately. Neither "Western," nor Byzantine history can elucidate the problems posed by this European region. Nor can its treatment as a periphery either of the "West" or of Byzantium do justice to the highly original developments of its medieval history. For the Southeast is much more than the Balkans. Boundaries are hard to pinpoint on the map, but neither Transylvania, nor the steppe corridor north of the Lower Danube and the Black Sea can be easily excluded. Equally important is the region of the southeastern Alps in present-day Slovenia. The study of medieval Southeastern Europe requires an expansion of our understanding of the Middle Ages and of the definition of Europe.

SELECT BIBLIOGRAPHY

Akrabova-Zhandova, I. "Preslav inlaid ceramics." In *Studies in Memory of David Talbot Rice*, pp. 25–33. Ed. by G. Robertson and G. Henderson. Edinburgh: Edinburgh University Press, 1975.

Aleksiev, I. "Predstolichniiat Tărnov." In *Sbornik v chest na akad. Dimităr Angelov*, pp. 196–200. Ed. by V. Velkov, Zh. Aladzhov, G. Bakalov, et al. Sofia: Izdatelstvo na Bălgarskata Akademiia na Naukite, 1994.

Anamali, S. "L'état actuel des recherches sur l'origine des villes du Moyen Age en Albanie." In *Actes du XIe Congrès international d'archéologie chrétienne. Lyon, Vienne, Grenoble, Genève et Aoste (21–28 septembre 1986)*, pp. 2617–2635. Vol. III. Rome: Ecole Française de Rome, 1989.

Andrea, A. J. and I. Motsiff. "Pope Innocent III and the diversion of the Fourth Crusade army to Zara." *Byzantinoslavica*, vol. 33 (1972), pp. 6–25.

Andreev, I. "Naryshskaia nadpis' kniazia Simeona i administrativnoe ustroistvo bolgarskogo gosudarstva v konce IX i nachale X v." *EB*, vol. 14 (1978), pp. 121–131.

Angelov, P. D. "The Bulgarians through the eyes of the Byzantines." *BHR*, vol. 22 (1994), pp. 18–32.

Bălgariia i bălgarite v predstavite na vizantiicite (VII–XIV vek). Sofia: Lik, 1999.

Angelova, S. "Razkopkite na cărkva no. 2 (arkhiepiskopiiata na Drăstăr) prez 1993–1998 godina." In *Zwischen Byzanz und Abendland. Pliska, der östliche Balkanraum und Europa im Spiegel der Frühmittelalterarchäologie*, pp. 47–52. Ed. by J. Henning. Frankfurt am Main: Johann Wolfgang Goethe Universität, 1999.

Angelova, S. and R. Koleva. "Zur Chronologie frühmittelalterlicher Nekropolen in Südbulgarien." In *Karasura, I. Untersuchungen zur*

Geschichte und Kultur des alten Thrakien. 15 Jahre Ausgrabungen in Karasura. Internationales Symposium Cirpan/Bulgarien, 1996, pp. 263–270. Ed. by M. Wendel. Weissbach: Beier & Beran, 2001.

Anghel, Gh. "Les premiers donjons en pierre de Transylvania (Roumanie)." In *Château Gaillard, 8. Etudes de castellologie médiévale. Actes du colloque international tenu à Bad Muenstereifel (R.F.A.), 30 août–4 septembre 1976*, pp. 7–20. Caen: Centre de recherches archéologiques médiévales de l'Université de Caen, 1977.

Antonopoulos, P. T. "Byzantium, the Magyar raids and their consequences." *Byzantinoslavica*, vol. 4 (1993), pp. 254–267.

Armbruster, A. *Der Donau-Karpatenraum in den mittel- und westeuropäischen Quellen des 10.–16. Jahrhunderts. Eine historiographische Imagologie.* Cologne and Vienna: Böhlau, 1990.

Asdracha, C. "Inscriptions byzantines de la Thrace orientale et de l'île d'Imbros (XIIe–XVe siècles). Présentation et commentaire historique." *Arkhaiologikon Deltion*, vol. 43 (1988), pp. 219–291.

"Inscriptions byzantines de la Thrace orientale (VIIIe–XIe siècles). Présentation et commentaire historique." *Arkhaiologikon Deltion*, vols. 44–46 (1989–1991), pp. 239–334.

"Inscriptions chrétiennes et protobyzantines de la Thrace orientale et de l'île d'Imbros (IIIe–VIIe siècles)." *Arkhaiologikon Deltion*, vols. 49–50 (1994–1995), 279–356.

Atanasov, G. "Rannovizantiiski skalni cărkvi i manastiri v Iuzhna Dobrudzha." *Arkheologiia*, vol. 23 (1991), pp. 33–43.

"Khristiianski medalioni ot rannosrednovekovni kreposti v Iuzhna Dobrudzha." *Dobrudzha*, vol. 9 (1992), pp. 146–162.

"Za edin starobălgarski skalen manastir ot X–XI vek v centralna Moldova." In *Bălgarite v severnoto Prichernomorie. Izsledvaniia i materiali*, pp. 61–73. Ed. by P. Todorov. Vol. II. Veliko Tărnovo: Velikotărnovski universitet "Sv. Sv. Kiril i Metodii." Istoricheski fakultet, 1993.

"La Vicina médiévale et la forteresse de Nufăru." *EB*, vol. 30 (1994), pp. 109–128.

"Croix-encolpions proche-orientales de la région de la Dobroudja du Sud (Bulgarie)." In *Akten des XII. internationalen Kongresses für christliche Archäologie. Bonn, 22–28. September 1991*, pp. 483–501. Ed. by E. Dassmann, K. Thraede, and J. Engemann. Vol. I. Münster: Aschendorfsche Verlagsbuchhandlung, 1995.

"Influences ethno-culturelles dans l'ermitage rupestre près de Murfatlar." *Byzantinoslavica*, vol. 57 (1996), pp. 112–124.

"On the origin, function and the owner of the adornments of the Preslav treasure from the 10th century." *AB*, vol. 3 (1999), pp. 81–94.

"Bălgaro-khazarskata granica i bălgaro-khazarskata vrazhdebnost ot kraia na VII do sredata na IX vek." In *Bălgari i khazari prez rannoto srednovekovie*, pp. 92–113. Ed. by C. Stepanov. Sofia: Centăr za izsledvaniia na bălgarite "Tangra" TanNakRa IK, 2003.

Avenarius, A. "Die Konsolidierung des Awarenkaganates und Byzanz im 7. Jahrhundert." *Byzantina*, vol. 13 (1985), pp. 1019–1032.

Avramea, A. *Le Péloponnèse du IVe au VIIIe siècle. Changements et persistances.* Paris: Publications de la Sorbonne, 1997.

Baán, I. "The foundation of the archbishopric of Kalocsa: the Byzantine origin of the second archdiocese in Hungary." In *Early Christianity in Central and Eastern Europe*, pp. 67–73. Ed. by P. Urbańczyk. Warsaw: Semper, 1997.

Bagarić, I. "Die Rolle der Benediktiner in der kroatischen Geschichte." *Mariastein*, vol. 28 (1982), pp. 62–68.

Bakalov, G. *Srednovekovniiat bălgarski vladetel: titulatura i insignii.* Sofia: Izdatelstvo na Bălgarskata Akademiia na Naukite, 1985.

Bakalova, E. "The role and importance of monasteries in the cultural history of Bulgaria." In *Taseis tou orthodoxou monakhismou, 9os–20os aiones. Praktika tou Diethnous Symposiou pou diorganotheke sta plaisia tou Programmatos "Hoi dromoi tou orthodoxou monakhismou. Poreuthentes mathete". Thessalonike, 28 Septembriou–2 Oktobriou 1994*, pp. 115–124. Ed. by K. Nikolaou. Athens: Institouto Byzantinon Ereunon, 1996.

Bakirtzis, Ch. "Western Thrace in the early Christian and Byzantine periods: results of archaeological research and the prospects, 1973–1987." *BF*, vol. 14 (1989), pp. 41–58.

"Byzantine Thrace (AD 330–1453)." In *Thrace*, pp. 151–210. Ed. by V. Papoulia, M. Meraklis, Ch. Symeonidis, et al. Athens: General Secretariat of the Region of East Macedonia–Thrace, 1994.

"Byzantine monasteries in eastern Macedonia and Thrace (Synaxis, Mt. Papikion, St. John Prodromos Monastery)." In *Mount Athos and Byzantine Monasticism. Papers from the Twenty-Eighth Spring Symposium of Byzantine Studies, Birmingham, March 1994*, pp. 47–54. Ed. by A. Bryer and M. Cunningham. Aldershot and Brookfield: Variorum, 1996.

Bálint, Cs. *Die Archäologie der Steppe. Steppenvölker zwischen Volga und Donau vom 6. bis zum 10. Jahrhundert.* Vienna and Cologne: Böhlau, 1989.

Barnea, I. "Les monuments rupestres de Basarabi en Dobroudja." *CA*, vol. 13 (1962), pp. 187–208.

"Dinogetia – ville byzantine du Bas-Danube." *Byzantina*, vol. 10 (1980), pp. 239–287.

"La céramique byzantine de Dobroudja, Xe–XIIe siècles." In *Recherches sur la céramique byzantine*, pp. 131–142. Ed. by V. Déroche and J.-M. Spieser. Athens: Ecole Française d'Athènes and Paris: de Boccard, 1989.

Baum, W. "Die Kirchen von Freising und Brixen, die Grafen von Görz und die Entstehung der deutschen Sprachinseln in Friaul und Slowenien."

Der Schlern. Zeitschrift für Südtiroler Landeskunde, vol. 54 (1980), pp. 428–440.

Bazaiou-Barabas, Th. "Das Bild des "Anderen" im Werk von Niketas Choniates. Das Beispiel von Peter und Asen." *Symmeikta*, vol. 10 (1996), pp. 283–293.

Belošević, J. *Materijalna kultura Hrvata od VII do IX stoljeća*. Zagreb: Sveučilišna naklada Liber, 1980.

Benkö, E. "Alba Iulia (Gyulafehérvár)." In *Europe's Centre around* AD *1000*, pp. 389–391. Ed. by A. Wieczorek and H.-M. Hinz. Stuttgart: Theiss, 2000.

Berend, N. *At the Gate of Christendom. Jews, Muslims, and "Pagans" in Medieval Hungary, c. 1000–c. 1300*. Cambridge: Cambridge University Press, 2001.

Bertels, K. "Carantania. Beobachtungen zur politisch-geographischen Terminologie und zur Geschichte des Landes und seiner Bevölkerung im frühen Mittelalter." *Carinthia*, vol. 177 (1987), pp. 87–190.

Beshevliev, V. "Les inscriptions du relief de Madara (nouvelle lecture, compléments et interprétation)." *Byzantinoslavica*, vol. 16 (1955), pp. 212–254.

Die protobulgarischen Inschriften. Berlin: Akademie Verlag, 1963.

Die protobulgarische Periode der bulgarischen Geschichte. Amsterdam: Adolf M. Hakkert, 1981.

"Nachaloto na bălgarskata dărzhava spored Apokrifen letopis ot XI vek." In *Srednovekovna Bălgariia i Chernomorieto. Sbornik dokladi ot nauchnata konferenciia, Varna 1980*, pp. 39–45. Ed. by A. Kuzev. Varna: Knigoizdatelstvo "Georgi Bakalov," 1982.

Părvobălgarsi nadpisi. 2nd ed. Sofia: Izdatelstvo na Bălgarskata Akademiia na Naukite, 1992.

Birkfellner, G. "Methodius Archiepiscopus Superioris Moraviae oder Anmerkungen über die historisch-geographische Lage Altmährens (Vorläufige Stellungnahme zu jüngsten hyperkritischen Lokalisierungsversuchen)." In *Leben und Werk der byzantinischen Slavenapostel Methodios und Kyrillos. Beiträge eines Symposions der Griechisch-deutschen Initiative Würzburg im Wasserschloß Mitwitz vom 25.–27. Juli 1985 zum Gedenken an den 1100. Todestag des hl. Methodios*, pp. 33–38. Ed. by E. Konstantinou. Münsterschwarzach: Vier-Türme Verlag, 1991.

Birnbaum, H. "Noch einmal zu den slavischen Milingen auf der Peloponnes." In *Festschrift für Herbert Bräuer zum 65. Geburtstag am 14. April 1986*, pp. 15–26. Ed. by R. Olesch and H. Rothe. Cologne: Böhlau, 1986.

"Where was the centre of the Moravian state?" In *American Contributions to the Eleventh International Congress of Slavists. Bratislava, August–September*

1993. Literature, Linguistics, Poetics, pp. 11–24. Ed. by R. A. Maguire and A. Timberlake. Columbus, OH: Slavica, 1993.

Blagojević, M. "Sečenica (Setzenica), Strymon (Strymon) i Tara (Tara) u delu Jovana Kinama." *ZRVI*, vol. 17 (1974), pp. 65–76.

"Zakon svetoga Simeona i svetoga Save." In *Meždunarodni naučni skup "Sava Nemanjić-Sveti Sava. Istorija i predanje". Decembar 1976*, pp. 129–166. Ed. by V. Djurić. Belgrade: Srpska Akademija Nauka i Umetnosti, 1979.

Blaznik, P. *Zemljiska gospostva v območju freisinske dolenjske posesti*. Ljubljana: Slovenska Akademia Znanosti in Umetnosti, 1958.

Boba, I. *Moravia's History Reconsidered. A Reinterpretation of Medieval Sources*. The Hague: Martinus Nijhoff, 1971.

Bogdan, D. P. "Dobrudzhanskaia nadpis' 943 goda. Paleograficheskii i lingvisticheskii ocherk." *Romanoslavica*, vol. 1 (1958), pp. 88–104.

Boiadzhiev, S. "Arkhitekturata na Krăglata cărkva v Preslav." In *Izsledvaniia vărkhu arkhitekturata na bălgarskoto srednovekovie*, pp. 5–130. Ed. by S. Boiadzhiev, N. Chaneva-Dechevska, and L. Zakharieva. Sofia: Izdatelstvo na Bălgarskata Akademiia na Naukite, 1982.

"Arkhitekturata na prabălgarskite khramove." *Problemi na prabălgarskata istoriia i kultura*, vol. 1 (1989), pp. 314–327.

Boldur, A. V. "The enigma of the Ulichy-Tivertsy people." *BS*, vol. 9 (1968), pp. 55–90.

Bon, A. *Le Péloponnèse byzantin jusqu'en 1204*. Paris: Presses Universitaires de France, 1951.

Bóna, I. "From Dacia to Erdöelve: Transylvania in the period of the Great Migrations (271–896)." In *History of Transylvania*, pp. 139–329. Ed. by L. Makkai and A. Mócsy. Vol. 1. New York: Columbia University Press, 2001.

Borisov, B. *Djadovo I. Medieval settlement and necropolis (11th–12th century)*. Tokyo: University Press, 1989.

"Settlements of northeast Thrace: 11–12 centuries." *AB*, vol. 5 (2001), pp. 77–92.

Bowden, W. "The construction of identities in post-Roman Albania." In *Theory and Practice in Late Antique Archaeology*, pp. 57–78. Ed. by L. Lavan and W. Bowden. Leiden and Boston: Brill, 2003.

Epirus Vetus. The Archaeology of a Late Antique Province. London: Duckworth, 2003.

Bowlus, C. R. "Imre Boba's reconsiderations of Moravia's early history and Arnulf of Carinthia's Ostpolitik (887–892)." *Speculum*, vol. 62 (1987), pp. 552–574.

Franks, Moravians, and Magyars. The Struggle for the Middle Danube 788–907. Philadelphia: University of Pennsylvania Press, 1995.

Bozhilov, I. A. "L'inscription du jupan Dimitre de l'an 943 (théories et faits)." *Etudes Historiques*, vol. 6 (1973), pp. 11–28.

"One of Omurtag's memorial inscriptions." *BHR*, vol. 1 (1973), pp. 72–76.

"Kăm istoricheskata geografiia na severozapadnoto Chernomorie: Mesopotamia – Mesopotamia tes Dyseos." *INMV*, vol. 12 (1976), pp. 19–32.

"A propos des rapports bulgaro-byzantins sous le tsar Syméon (893–912)." *Byzantinobulgarica*, vol. 6 (1980), pp. 73–81.

Familiiata na Asenevci (1186–1460): genealogiia i prosopografiia. Sofia: Izdatelstvo na Bălgarskata Akademiia na Naukite, 1994.

Bălgarite văv Vizantiiskata imperiia. Sofia: Akademichno izdatelstvo "Prof. Marin Drinov," 1995.

Brandt, M. "Dubrovnik i heretička Bosna u prvoj polovini XIII stoljeća." *Anali Historijskog instituta u Dubrovniku*, vol. 12 (1970), pp. 27–57.

Bratož, R. "Aquileia und der Alpen-Adria-Raum (von der Mitte des 6. Jahrhunderts bis 811)." In *Karantanien und der Alpen-Adria-Raum im Frühmittelalter*, pp. 151–208. Ed. by G. Hödl and J. Grabmeyer. Vienna, Cologne, and Weimar: Böhlau, 1993.

Brezeanu, S. "*Romani* şi *Blachi* la Anonymus. Istorie şi ideologie politică." *Revista de istorie*, vol. 34 (1981), pp. 1313–1340.

"'La Bulgarie d'au-delà de l'Ister' à la lumière des sources écrites." *EB*, vol. 20 (1984), pp. 121–135.

"'Vlahi' şi 'misieni' în sursele bizantine relative la începuturile statului Asăneştilor. Terminologie etnică şi ideologie politică." In *Răscoala şi statul Asăneştilor*, pp. 37–69. Ed. by E. Stănescu. Bucharest: Editura Ştiinţifică şi Enciclopedică, 1989.

Browning, R. "Athens in the 'Dark Age'." In *Culture & History. Essays Presented to Jack Lindsay*, pp. 297–303. Ed. by B. Smith. Sydney: Hale and Iremonger, 1984.

Budak, N. "Die südslawischen Ethnogenesen an der östlichen Adriaküste im frühen Mittelalter." In *Typen der Ethnogenese unter besonderer Berücksichtigung der Bayern*, pp. 130–136. Ed. by H. Wolfram and W. Pohl. Vol. 1. Vienna: Verlag der Österreichischen Akademie der Wissenschaften, 1990.

"Frühes Christentum im Kroatien." In *Karantanien und der Alpen-Adria-Raum im Frühmittelalter*, pp. 223–234. Ed. by G. Hödl and J. Grabmayer. Vienna, Cologne, and Weimar: Böhlau, 1993.

Prva stoljeća Hrvatske. Zagreb: Hrvatska sveučališna naklada, 1994.

"Slavery in late medieval Dalmatia/Croatia: labour, legal status, integration." In *La servitude dans les pays de la Méditerranée occidentale chrétienne au XIIe siècle et au-delà: déclinante ou renouvelée? Actes de la table ronde de Rome (8e et 9e octobre 1999)*, pp. 745–760. Rome: Ecole Française de Rome, 2000.

Bury, J. B. "The Bulgarian treaty of AD 814 and the Great Fence of Thrace." *English Historical Review*, vol. 25 (1910), pp. 276–287.

Butler, T., ed. *Monumenta Bulgarica. A Bilingual Anthology of Bulgarian Texts from the 9th to the 19th Centuries.* Ann Arbor: Michigan Slavic Publications, 1996.

Campbell, S. D. "The Cistercian monastery of Zaraka." *Echos du Monde Classique*, vol. 41 (1997), pp. 177–196.

Čanak-Medić, M. "Katedrala Svetog Tripuna kao izraz umetničkikh u Kotoru sredinom." *ZRVI*, vol. 36 (1997), pp. 83–98.

"Žička Spasova crkva – zamisao Svetog Save." In *Sveti Sava u srpskoj istoriji i tradiciji*, pp. 173–187. Ed. by S. Ćirković. Belgrade: Srpska Akademija Nauka i Umetnosti, 1998.

Cankova-Petkova, G. *Bălgariia pri Asenevci.* Sofia: Izdatelstvo na Bălgarskata Akademiia na Naukite, 1978.

"Friedrich I. Barbarossa und die sozial-politischen Verhältnisse auf dem Balkan zur Zeit der III. Kreuzzuges." *Palaeobulgarica*, vol. 6 (1982), pp. 69–74.

Capkova, V. "The Freising monuments." In *Irland und die Christenheit. Bibelstudien und Mission*, pp. 461–470. Ed. by P. Ni Chathain and M. Richter. Stuttgart: Klett-Cotta, 1987.

Caramessini-Oeconomides, M. "Contribution à l'étude de la circulation des monnaies byzantines en Grèce au XIIIe siècle." In *Actes du XVe Congrès international d'études byzantines. Athènes, septembre 1976*, pp. 121–128. Ed. by P. Zepos. Vol. II. Athens: Association internationale des études byzantines, 1981.

Changova, I. "Tărgovski pomeshteniia krai iuzhnata krepostna stena v Preslav." *IAI*, vol. 21 (1957), pp. 233–290.

Chanidzé, A. "Le grand domestique de l'occident, Gregorii Bakurianis-Dzé, et le monastère géorgien fondé par lui en Bulgarie." *Bedi Kartlisa*, vol. 28 (1971), pp. 133–166.

Cheshmedzhiev, D. "On the question of the localization of the Slav tribe Smoljani." *BHR*, vol. 25 (1997), pp. 89–93.

Christophilopoulou, E. "Byzantine Makedonia. Skhediasma gia ten epokhi apo ta tele tou 6' mekhri ta mesa tou 9' aiona." *Byzantina*, vol. 12 (1983), pp. 9–63.

Chrysos, E. K. "Die 'Krönung' Symeons in Hebdomon." *Cyrillomethodianum*, vol. 3 (1975), pp. 169–173.

"Die Nordgrenze des byzantinischen Reiches im 6. bis 8. Jahrhundert." In *Die Völker Südosteuropas im 6. bis 8. Jahrhundert*, pp. 27–40. Ed. by B. Hänsel. Berlin: Südosteuropa Gesellschaft, 1987.

Ćirković, S. M. *La Serbie au Moyen Age.* La-Pierre-qui-Vire: Zodiaque, 1992.

The Serbs. Malden, Oxford, and Carlton: Blackwell, 2004.

Comşa, M. *Cultura materială veche românească (Aşezările din secolele VIII–X de la Bucov-Ploieşti)*. Bucharest: Editura Academiei Republicii Socialiste România, 1978.

"Considérations relatives à la communauté villageoise en territoire roumain aux VI–VIIe siècles." In *Actes du XIIe Congrès international des sciences préhistoriques et protohistoriques, Bratislava, 1–7 septembre 1991*, pp. 15–17. Ed. by J. Pavuj. Vol. IV. Bratislava: Institut archéologique de l'Académie Slovaque des Sciences à Nitra, 1993.

Condurachi, E., I. Barnea, and P. Diaconu. "Nouvelles recherches sur le Limes byzantin du Bas-Danube aux Xe–XIe siècles." In *Proceedings of the XIIIth International Congress of Byzantine Studies. Oxford, 5–10 September 1966*, pp. 179–193. Ed. by J. M. Hussey, D. Obolensky, and S. Runciman. London, New York, and Toronto: Oxford University Press, 1967.

Constantine Porphyrogenitus. *De administrando imperio*. Greek text ed. by Gy. Moravcsik with English translation by R. J. H. Jenkins. Washington, D.C.: Dumbarton Oaks Center for Byzantine Studies, 1967.

Conversio Bagoariorum et Carantanorum. Latin text ed. and transl. into German by F. Lošek. Hannover: Hahnsche Buchhandlung, 1997.

Čremošnik, I. "Die Untersuchungen in Mušići und Žabljak. Über den ersten Fund der ältesten slawischen Siedlung in Bosnien." *WMBHL*, vol. 5 (1975), pp. 91–176.

Cronaca di Monemvasia. Ed. by I. Duichev. Palermo: Istituto Siciliano di Studi Bizantini e Neoellenici, 1976.

Čuk, R. *Srbija i Venecija u XIII i XIV veku*. Belgrade: Prosveta, 1986.

Curta, F. "Invasion or inflation? Sixth- to seventh-century Byzantine coin hoards in Eastern and Southeastern Europe." *Annali dell'Istituto Italiano di Numismatica*, vol. 43 (1996), pp. 65–224.

"Blacksmiths, warriors and tournaments of value: dating and interpreting early medieval hoards of iron implements in Eastern Europe." *Ephemeris Napocensis*, vol. 7 (1997), pp. 211–268.

"The cave and the dyke: a rock monastery on the tenth-century frontier of Bulgaria." *Studia monastica*, vol. 41 (1999), pp. 129–149.

The Making of the Slavs. History and Archaeology of the Lower Danube Region, c. 500–700. Cambridge and New York: Cambridge University Press, 2001.

"Peasants as 'makeshift soldiers for the occasion': sixth-century settlement patterns in the Balkans." In *Urban Centers and Rural Contexts in Late Antiquity*, pp. 199–217. Ed. by T. S. Burns and J. W. Eadie. East Lansing: Michigan State University Press, 2001.

"Transylvania around AD 1000." In *Europe around the Year 1000*, pp. 141–165. Ed. by P. Urbańczyk. Warsaw: Wydawnictwo DiG, 2001.

Daim, F. "Byzantine belts and Avar birds. Diplomacy, trade, and cultural transfer in the eighth century." In *The Transformation of Frontiers. From Late Antiquity to the Carolingians*, pp. 143–188. Ed. by W. Pohl, I. Wood, and H. Reimitz. Leiden, Boston, and Cologne: Brill, 2001.

Daim, F. and P. Stadler. "Der Goldschatz von Sînnicolaul Mare (Nagyszentmiklós)." In *Reitervölker aus dem Osten. Hunnen + Awaren. Burgenländische Landesausstellung 1996. Schloâ Halbturn, 26. April–31. Oktober 1996*, pp. 439–445. Ed. by F. Daim, K. Kaus, and P. Tomka. Eisenstadt: Amt der Burgenländischen Landesregierung, 1996.

Dancheva-Vasileva, A. "Plovdiv à l'époque des premières Croisades (1097, 1147, 1189)." *BHR*, vol. 26 (1998), pp. 10–32.

Decei, A. "L'invasion des Tatars de 1241/1242 dans nos régions selon la Djamï ot-Tevarikh de Fäzl ol-lah Räshid od-Din." *RRH*, vol. 12 (1973), pp. 101–121.

Delonga, V. "Donatorski natpis župana Gostihe iz crkve Sv. Spasa u Cetini (Vrh Rici)." *SP*, vol. 22 (1995), pp. 117–140.

Inscriptions des souverains croates du IXe au XIe siècle. Split: Museum of Croatian Archaeological Monuments, 1997.

Diaconu, P. "Autour de la localisation de la Petite Preslav." *RESEE*, vol. 3 (1965), pp. 37–56.

Les Coumans au Bas-Danube aux XIe–XIIe siècles. Bucharest: Editura Academiei Republicii Socialiste România, 1978.

"Sur l'organisation ecclesiastique dans la région du Bas-Danube (dernier tiers du Xe siècle–XIIe siècle)." *EBPB*, vol. 2 (1991), pp. 73–89.

Diaconu, P. and E. Stănescu. "Le commerce fluvial et maritime dans la région comprise entre le Danube et la Mer Noire aux IVe–XIIe siècles." In *Etudes d'histoire maritime, présentées au XIIIe Congrès international des sciences historiques par la Commission internationale d'histoire maritime à l'occasion de son XIIe colloque, Moscou, 16–23 août*, pp. 281–293. Moscow: n.p., 1970.

Diaconu, P. and D. Vîlceanu. *Păcuiul lui Soare. Cetatea bizantină*. Bucharest: Editura Academiei Republicii Socialiste România, 1972.

Dimitrov, I. "Novi danni za arkheologicheskata karta na Pliska." In *Prinosi kăm bălgarskata arkheologiia. Dekemvriiski dni na bălgarskata arkheologiia "Prof. dr. Stancho Vaklinov,"* pp. 58–67. Ed. by D. Ovcharov and I. Shtereva. Vol. 1. Sofia: Arges, 1992.

Dimitrov, Kh. *Bălgaro-ungarskite otnosheniia prez srednovekovieto*. Sofia: Akademichno izdatelstvo "Prof. Marin Drinov," 1998.

Istoriia na Makedoniia prez srednovekovieto. Sofia: Gutenberg, 2001.

Ditten, H. *Ethnische Verschiebungen zwischen der Balkanhalbinsel und Kleinasien vom Ende des 6. bis zur zweiten Hälfte des 9. Jahrhunderts*. Berlin: Akademie Verlag, 1993.

Djuvara, N. "Sur un passage controversé de Kekaumenos." *RRH*, vol. 30 (1991), pp. 23–66.

Dobroliubskii, A. O. *Kochevniki Severo-Zapadnogo Prichernomor'ia v epokhu srednevekov'ia*. Kiev: Naukova Dumka, 1986.

Dobronić, L. "The military orders in Croatia." In *The Meeting of Two Worlds. Cultural Exchange between East and West during the Period of the Crusades*, pp. 431–438. Ed. by V. P. Goss. Kalamazoo: Medieval Institute Publications, 1986.

Dochev, K. "Turnovo, sixth–fourteenth centuries." In *The Economic History of Byzantium from the Seventh through the Fifteenth Century*, pp. 673–678. Ed. by A. E. Laiou. Washington: Dumbarton Oaks Research Library and Collection, 2002.

Dölger, F. *Ein Fall slavischer Einsiedlung im Hinterland von Thessalonike im 10. Jahrhundert*. Munich: Verlag der Bayerischen Akademie der Wissenschaften, 1952.

Donat, I. "La vie pastorale chez les Roumains et ses problèmes." *Dacoromania*, vol. 1 (1973), pp. 78–83.

Doncheva-Petkova, L. "Mittelalterliche Tonkessel aus Bulgarien." In *Die Keramik der Saltovo-Majaki Kultur und ihrer Varianten*, pp. 101–111. Ed. by Cs. Bálint. Budapest: Institut für Archäologie der Ungarischen Akademie der Wissenschaften, 1990.

"A 11th century Pecheneg's necropolis by Odărtsi village, Dobrich district." *AB*, vol. 6 (1998), pp. 126–137.

Dostál, B. *Břeclav–Pohansko. Velkomoravský velmožsky dvorec*. Brno: Univerzita J. E. Purkyne, 1975.

Dragojlović, D. "Dyrrachium et les évêchés de Docléa jusqu'à la fondation de l'archevêché de Bar." *Balcanica*, vol. 21 (1990), pp. 201–209.

"Archevêché d'Ohrid dans la hiérarchie des grandes églises chrétiennes." *Balcanica*, vol. 22 (1991), pp. 43–54.

Ducellier, A. "L'Arbanon et les Albanais au XIe siècle." *T&M*, vol. 2 (1968), pp. 353–368.

"L'Albanie entre Orient et Occident aux XIe et XIIe siècles. Aspects politiques et économiques." *CCM*, vol. 19 (1976), pp. 1–7.

La façade maritime de l'Albanie au Moyen Age. Durazzo et Valona du XIème au XVème siècle. Thessaloniki: Institute for Balkan Studies, 1981.

"Les Albanais dans l'Empire byzantin: de la communauté à l'expansion." In *Hoi Albanoi sto mesaiona*, pp. 17–45. Ed. by Ch. Gasparis. Athens: Institouto Byzantinon Ereunon, 1998.

Duichev, I. "Slaviano-bolgarskie drevnosti IX-go veka." *Byzantinoslavica*, vol. 11 (1950), pp. 6–31.

"Zur Datierung der Homilie des Kosmas." *Welt der Slawen*, vol. 8 (1963), pp. 1–4.

"La chronique byzantine de l'an 811." *T&M*, vol. 1 (1965), pp. 205–254.

"Kratkoto Klimentovo zhitie ot Dimitrii Khomatian." In *Kliment Okhridski. Sbornik ot statii po sluchai 1050 godini ot smărtta*, pp. 161–171. Ed. by B. S. Angelov, B. Angelov, P. Dinekov, et al. Sofia: Izdatelstvo na Bălgarskata Akademiia na Naukite, 1966.
"I Responsa di papa Nicolò I ai Bulgari neoconvertiti." *Aevum. Rassegna di scienze storiche, linguistiche e filologiche*, vol. 42 (1968), pp. 403–428.
"Il patriarcato bulgaro del secolo X." In *I patriarcati orientali nel primo millennio. Relazioni del congresso tenutosi al Pontificio Istituto Orientale nei giorni 27–30 dicembre 1967*, pp. 201–221. Rome: Pontificium Institutum Studiorum Orientalium, 1968.
"La réforme monastique en Bulgarie au Xe siècle." In *Etudes de civilisation médiévale (IXe–XIIe siècles). Mélanges offerts à Edmond-René Labande Professeur à l'Université de Poitiers, Directeur du Centre d'Etudes Supérieures de Civilisation Médiévale à l'occasion de son départ à la retraite et du XXe anniversaire du C.E.S.C.M. par ses amis, ses collègues, ses élèves*, pp. 255–264. Poitiers: C.E.S.C.M., 1974.
"Some remarks on the Chronicle of Monemvasia." In *Charanis Studies. Essays in Honor of Peter Charanis*, pp. 51–59. Ed. by A. E. Laiou-Thomadakis. New Brunswick: Rutgers University Press, 1980.
Kiril and Methodius, Founders of Slavonic Writing. A Collection of Sources and Critical Studies. Boulder and New York: Columbia University Press, 1985.
"The Balkan Slavs and the West during the period of the Crusades." In *The Meeting of Two Worlds. Cultural Exchange between East and West during the Period of the Crusades*, pp. 409–417. Ed. by V. P. Goss. Kalamazoo: Medieval Institute Publications, 1986.

Dunn, M. "Evangelism or repentance? The re-Christianisation of the Peloponnese in the ninth and tenth centuries." *Studies in Church History*, vol. 14 (1977), pp. 71–86.

Dvornik, F. *Les légendes de Constantin et de Méthode vues de Byzance.* Hattiesburg: Academic International, 1969.

Dzhambov, I. *Srednovekovnoto selishte nad antichniia grad pri Khisar.* Asenovgrad: Ekobelan, 2002.

Dzhambov, I., Zh. Tankova, and Kh. Dzhambov. "Srednovekovniiat Plovdiv i prinosăt mu v kulturno-istoricheskoto nasledstvo na Vizantiia i Bălgariia XI–XIV v." In *Mezhdunarodna konferenciia "Vizantiiskoto kulturno nasledstvo i Balkanite". Plovdiv, 6–8 septemvri 2001. Sbornik dokladi*, pp. 32–42. Ed. by G. Bakalov and I. Dzhambov. Plovdiv: Iuri Gagarin BT, 2001.

Dzhidrova, L. "Crusaders in the central Balkans." In *The Crusades and the Military Orders. Expanding Frontiers of Medieval Latin Christianity*, pp. 187–211. Ed. by Zs. Hunyadi and J. Laszlovszky. Budapest: Department of Medieval Studies, Central European University, 2001.

Dzhurova, A. "L'ornement des manuscrits vieux-bulgares glagolitiques et leurs rapports avec l'art de Byzance, des provinces grecques d'Orient et de l'Italie du sud (sur l'ornement de l'Evangéliaire d'Assemani)." *Byzantiaka*, vol. 8 (1988), pp. 23–39.

Ercegović-Pavlović, S. *Srednjovjekovna naselja i nekropole u Boljetinu i Hajdučkoj Vodenici*. Beograd: Arheološki Institut, 1986.

Evans, H. M. A. *The Early Medieval Archaeology of Croatia* AD *600–900*. Oxford: British Archaeological Reports, 1989.

Evgenidou, D. "Servia and Moglena, two Byzantine cities of Macedonia." *Istorikogeographika*, vol. 2 (1987–1988), pp. 15–22.

Falkenhausen, V. von. "Eine byzantinische Beamtenurkunde aus Dubrownik." *BZ*, vol. 63 (1970), pp. 10–23.

Fedorov, G. B., G. F. Chebotarenko, and M. S. Velikanova. *Braneshtskii mogil'nik X–XI vv*. Kishinew: Shtiinca, 1984.

Feissel, D. "L'architecte Viktôrinos et les fortifications de Justinien dans les provinces balkaniques." *Bulletin de la Société nationale des antiquaires de France* (1988), pp. 136–146.

Ferjančić, B. "Dolazak hrvata i srba na balkanskog poluostrvo (osvrt na nova tumačenja)." *ZRVI*, vol. 35 (1996), pp. 117–154.

"Stefan Nemanja u vizantijskoj politici druge polovine XII veka." In *Meždunarodni naučni skup "Stefan Nemanja-Sveti Simeon Mirotočivi. Istorija i predanje", Septembar 1996*, pp. 31–46. Ed. by J. Kalić. Belgrade: Srpska Akademija Nauka i Umetnosti, 2000.

Ferluga, J. "Le soulèvement des comitopoules." *ZRVI*, vol. 9 (1966), pp. 75–84.

Byzantium on the Balkans. Studies on the Byzantine Administration and the Southern Slavs from the VIIth to the XIIth Centuries. Amsterdam: Adolf M. Hakkert, 1976.

L'amministrazione bizantina in Dalmazia. Venice: Deputazione di storia patria per le Venezie, 1978.

"Archon. Ein Beitrag zur Untersuchung der südslawischen Herrschertitel im 9. und 10. Jh. in lichte der byzantinischen Quellen." In *Tradition als historische Kraft*, pp. 254–266. Ed. by N. Kamp and J. Wollasch. Berlin and New York: De Gruyter, 1982.

"Überlegungen zur Geschichte der byzantinischen Provinz Istrien." *Jahrbücher für Geschichte Osteuropas*, vol. 35 (1987), pp. 164–173.

"L'Istria tra Giustiniano e Carlo Magno." *Arheološki vestnik*, vol. 43 (1992), pp. 175–190.

Fiedler, U. "Zur Datierung der Langwälle an der mittleren und unteren Donau." *Archäologisches Korrespondenzblatt*, vol. 16 (1986), pp. 457–465.

Studien zu Gräberfeldern des 6. bis 9. Jahrhunderts an der unteren Donau. Bonn: Rudolf Habelt, 1992.

Fine, J. V. A. *The Bosnian Church: A New Interpretation. A Study of the Bosnian Church and Its Place in State and Society from the 13th to the 15th Century*. Boulder and New York: Columbia University Press, 1975.

"A fresh look at Bulgaria under Tsar Peter (927–969)." *Byzantine Studies*, vol. 5 (1978), pp. 88–95.

The Early Medieval Balkans. A Critical Survey from the Sixth to the Late Twelfth Century. Ann Arbor: University of Michigan Press, 1983.

The Late Medieval Balkans. A Critical Survey from the Late Twelfth Century to the Ottoman Conquest. Ann Arbor: University of Michigan Press, 1987.

"Croats and Slavs: theories about the historical circumstances of the Croats' appearance in the Balkans." *BF*, vol. 26 (2000), pp. 205–218.

Florescu, R. and R. Ciobanu. "Problema stăpînirii bizantine în nordul Dobrogei în sec. IX–XI." *Pontica*, vol. 5 (1972), pp. 381–400.

Follieri, E. and I. Duichev. "Un'acolutia inedita per i martiri di Bulgaria dell'anno 813." *Byzantion*, vol. 33 (1963), pp. 71–106.

Frances, E. "Les relations russo-byzantines au XIIe siècle et la domination de Galicie au Bas-Danube." *Byzantinoslavica*, vol. 20 (1959), pp. 50–62.

Frasheri, K. "Les Albanais et Byzance aux VIe–XIe siècles." In *Hoi Albanoi sto Mesaiona*, pp. 47–57. Ed. by Ch. Gasparis. Athens: Institouto Byzantinon Ereunon, 1998.

Frazee, C. A. "The Balkans between Rome and Constantinople in the early Middle Ages 600–900 AD." *BS*, vol. 2 (1993), pp. 213–228.

Fučić, B. "The Croatian Glagolitic and Cyrillic epigraphs." In *Croatia in the Early Middle Ages. A Cultural Survey*, pp. 259–282. Ed. by I. Supičić. London: Philip Wilson Publishers and Zagreb: AGM, 1999.

Gagova, K. "Selishta v hinterlanda na iuzhnochernomorskite gradove prez XII–XIV vek." In *Srednovekovna Bălgariia i Chernomorieto. Sbornik dokladi ot nauchnata konferenciia, Varna 1980*, pp. 130–136. Ed. by A. Kuzev. Varna: Knigoizdatelstvo "Georgi Bakalov," 1982.

"Părviiat krăstonosen pokhod po Via militaris." *Minalo*, vol. 3 (1996), pp. 56–61.

Gatev, P. *Srednovekovno selishte i nekropol ot XII v. krai s. Kovachevo, Pazardzhishki okrăg*. Sofia: Izdatelstvo na Bălgarskata Akademiia na Naukite, 1985.

Gautier, P. "Clément d'Ohrid, évêque de Dragvista." *REB*, vol. 22 (1964), pp. 199–214.

Georgiev, P. "Golemiiat ezicheski khram v Pliska." *Problemi na prabălgarskata istoriia i kultura*, vol. 1 (1989), pp. 338–354.

Martiriumăt v Pliska i nachaloto na khristiianstvoto v Bălgariia. Sofia: Izdatelstvo na Bălgarskata Akademiia na Naukite, 1993.

"Zlatnata cărkva v Preslav." *Preslav. Sbornik*, vol. 5 (1993), pp. 7–25.

"Periodizaciia i khronologiia na zhivota i stroitelstvoto v raiona na Goliamata Bazilika v Pliska." In *Zwischen Byzanz und Abendland. Pliska, der östliche Balkanraum und Europa im Spiegel der Frühmittelalterarchäologie*, pp. 57–60. Ed. by J. Henning. Frankfurt am Main: Johann Wolfgang Goethe Universität, 1999.

"Koronaciiata na Simeon prez 913 g." *Istoricheski pregled*, vol. 57 (2001), pp. 3–20.

"Nachaloto na Aboba-Pliska." In *Studia protobulgarica et mediaevalia europensia. V chest na profesor Veselin Beshevliev*, pp. 175–182. Ed. by V. Giuzelev, K. Popkonstantinov, G. Bakalov, and R. Kostova. Sofia: Centăr za izsledvaniia na bălgarite "Tangra" TanNakRa IK, 2003.

Georgievski, B. "Rannovizantiiski skalni obekti ot raiona na Kriva reka, Republika Makedoniia." *Arkheologiia*, vol. 38 (1996), pp. 73–79.

Giambelluca-Kossova, A. *Chernorizec Khrabăr. O pismenekh*. Sofia: Izdatelstvo na Bălgarskata Akademiia na Naukite, 1980.

Giesler, J. *Der Ostalpenraum vom 8. bis 11. Jahrhundert. Studien zu archäologischen und schriftlichen Zeugnissen*. Rahden: Marie Leidorf, 1997.

Giuzelev, V. "Bulgarisch-fränkische Beziehungen in der ersten Hälfte des IX. Jh." *Byzantinobulgarica*, vol. 2 (1966), pp. 15–39.

"Zhitieto na Vlasii Amoriiski kato izvor za bălgarskata istoriia." *GSU*, vol. 61 (1968), pp. 19–33.

"La Bulgarie, Venise et l'Empire latin de Constantinople au milieu du XIIIe siècle." *BHR*, vol. 2 (1975), pp. 38–49.

"Allgemeine Charakteristik und Etappen der Errichtung der militärischen und administrativen Verwaltung des Ersten bulgarischen Staates (VII. bis IX. Jh.)." *EB*, vol. 14 (1978), pp. 71–77.

"Economic development and forms of social and political organisation of the Proto-Bulgarians prior to the foundation of the Bulgarian state (4th–7th c.)." *Barukan Sho Ajia kenkyu*, vol. 6 (1980), pp. 95–103.

Glaser, F. "Das Münster in Molzbichl, das älteste Kloster Kärntens." *Carinthia*, vol. 179 (1989), pp. 99–124.

Glavinas, A. A. "Hoi Normandoi ste Thessalia kai he poliorkia tes Larisas (1082–1083)." *Byzantiaka*, vol. 4 (1984), pp. 33–45.

Göckenjan, H. "Der Westfeldzug (1236–1242) aus mongolischer Sicht." In *Wahlstatt 1241. Beiträge zur Mongolenschlacht bei Liegnitz und zu ihren Nachwirkungen*, pp. 35–75. Ed. by U. Schmilewski. Würzburg: Bergstadtverlag Korn, 1991.

Golden, P. B. "The Polovcii Dikii." *Harvard Ukrainian Studies*, vols. 3–4 (1979–1980), pp. 296–309.

"The peoples of the south Russian steppes." In *The Cambridge History of Early Inner Asia*, pp. 256–284. Ed. by D. Sinor. Cambridge and New York: Cambridge University Press, 1990.

Goldstein, I. "O Tomislavu i njegovu dobu." *Radovi Instituta za hrvatsku povijest*, vol. 18 (1985), pp. 23–55.

Hrvatski rani srednji vijek. Zagreb: Zavod za hrvatsku povijest Filozofskog fakulteta Sveučilišta u Zagrebu, 1995.

"Between Byzantium, the Adriatic and Central Europe." In *Croatia in the Early Middle Ages. A Cultural Survey*, pp. 169–178. Ed. by I. Supičić. London: Philip Wilson Publishers and Zagreb: AGM, 1999.

"Byzantine rule in Dalmatia in the 12th century." In *Byzanz und Ostmitteleuropa, 950–1453. Beiträge zu einer table-ronde des XIX Internationalen Congress of Byzantine Studies, Copenhagen 1996*, pp. 97–125. Ed. by G. Prinzing and M. Salamon. Wiesbaden: Otto Harrassowitz, 1999.

"The disappearance of Byzantine rule in Dalmatia in the 11th century." In *Byzantium and East Central Europe*, pp. 129–139. Ed. by M. Salamon, G. Prinzing, and P. Stephenson. Cracow: Secesja, 2001.

Gorsky, A. A. "On the origins of the institutions of zhupans among the Slavs." In *Acts. XVIIIth International Congress of Byzantine Studies. Selected Papers*, pp. 232–241. Ed. by I. Ševčenko, G. G. Litavrin, and W. K. Hanak. Vol. 1. Shepherdstown, W.Va.: Byzantine Studies Press, 1996.

Goshev, I. *Starobălgarski glagolicheski i kirilski nadpisi ot IX i X v*. Sofia: Izdatelstvo na Bălgarskata Akademiia na Naukite, 1961.

Goss, V. P. *Early Croatian Architecture. A Study of the Pre-Romanesque*. London: Duckworth, 1987.

Granberg, A. "Observations on Bulgarian clan names in the 7th–9th centuries." In *Civitas divino-humana. V chest na profesor Georgi Bakalov*, pp. 551–561. Ed. by C. Stepanov and V. Vachkova. Sofia: Centăr za izsledvaniia na bălgarite "Tangra" TanNakRa IK, 2004.

Granstrem, E., I. Medvedev, and D. Papachryssanthou. "Fragment d'un praktikon de la région d'Athènes (avant 1204)." *REB*, vol. 34 (1976), pp. 5–43.

Guillou, A. "La présence byzantine dans les pays du nord de l'Adriatique. Un champ des mutations socio-économiques." *Byzantina*, vol. 13 (1985), pp. 201–216.

Gvozdanović, V. "Two early Croatian royal mausolea." *Peristil*, vols. 18–19 (1975–1976), pp. 5–10.

"Master Radovan and the lunette of the Nativity at Trogir." *Studies in Medieval Culture*, vols. 8–9 (1976), pp. 85–98.

Győrffy, G. "Das Güterverzeichnis des Klosters zu Szávaszentdemeter (Sremska Mitrovica) aus dem 12. Jahrhundert." *Studia Slavica*, vol. 5 (1959), pp. 9–74.

"Système des résidences d'hiver et d'été chez les nomades et les chefs hongrois au Xe siècle." *AEMA*, vol. 1 (1975), pp. 45–153.

"Anonymus Gesta Hungaroruma." In *A Honfoglaláskor írott forrásai*, pp. 193–213. Ed. by L. Kovács and L. Veszprémy. Budapest: Balassi kiadó, 1996.

Hageneder, O. "Innocenz III. und die Eroberung Zadars (1202). Eine Neuinterpretation des Br. V 160 (161)." *Mitteilungen des Instituts für Österreichische Geschichtsforschung*, vol. 100 (1992), pp. 197–213.

Hamm, J. *Das glagolitische Missale von Kiev*. Vienna: Verlag der Österreichischen Akademie der Wissenschaften, 1979.

Hâncu, I. G. *Limbar'. Srednevekovyi mogil'nik XII–XIV vekov v Moldavii*. Kishinew: Shtiinca, 1970.

Kapraria – pamiatniki kul'tury X–XII vv. Kishinew: Shtiinca, 1972.

Harisiadis, M. "L'enluminure des manuscrits glagolitiques des XIe et XIIe siècles." In *Actes du XVe Congrès international d'études byzantines. Athènes, septembre 1976*, pp. 193–204. Ed. by P. Zepos. Vol. II. Athens: Association internationale des études byzantines, 1981.

Härtel, R. "Notariat und Romanisierung. Das Urkundenwesen in Venetien und Istrien im Rahmen der politischen und der Kulturgeschichte (11.–13. Jh.)." In *Notariado público i documento privado de los origines al siglo XIV. Actas de VII Congreso Internacional de Diplomática, Valencia 1986*, pp. 879–926. Vol. II. Valencia: Conselleria de Cultura, Educaciò i Ciéncia, 1989.

Harvey, A. "Economic expansion in central Greece in the eleventh century." *BMGS*, vol. 8 (1982–1983), pp. 21–29.

"The monastic economy and imperial patronage from the tenth to the twelfth century." In *Mount Athos and Byzantine Monasticism. Papers from the Twenty-Eighth Spring Symposium of Byzantine Studies, Birmingham, March 1994*, pp. 91–97. Ed. by A. Bryer and M. Cunningham. Aldershot and Brookfield: Variorum, 1996.

Heiser, L. *Die Responsa ad consulta Bulgarorum des Papstes Nikolaus I. (858–867). Ein Zeugnis päpstlicher Hirtensorge und ein Dokument unterschiedlicher Entwicklungen in den Kirchen von Rom und Konstantinopel*. Trier: Paulinus Verlag, 1979.

Heitel, R. "Die Archäologie der ersten und zweiten Phase des Eindringens der Ungarn in das innerkarpatische Transilvanien." *Dacia*, vols. 38–39 (1994–1995), pp. 389–439.

Hendy, M. F. "The Gornoslav hoard, the emperor Frederick I and the monastery of Bachkovo." In *Studies in Numismatical Method Presented to Philip Grierson*, pp. 179–191. Ed. by C. N. L. Brooke, I. Stewart, J. G. Pollard, and T. R. Volk. Cambridge: Cambridge University Press, 1983.

Henning, J. "Bulgarien zwischen Antike und Mittelalter im Spiegel der Wirtschaftsarchäologie." *Das Altertum*, vol. 32 (1986), pp. 100–112.

"Unterscheide und Gemeinsamkeiten zwischen slawischer und fränkischer Landwirtschaft in Gebieten frühmittelalterlicher Stadtentwicklung." In *Trudy V Mezhdunarodnogo Kongressa arkheologov-slavistov. Kiev 18–25 sentiabria 1985 g.*, pp. 221–227. Ed. by P. P. Tolochko,

I. E. Borovskii, A. A. Kozlovskii, and A. P. Mocia. Vol. II. Kiev: Naukova Dumka, 1988.

"Gefangenenfesseln im slawischen Siedlungsraum und der europäischen Sklavenhandel im 6. bis 12. Jahrhundert. Archäologisches zum Bedeutungswandel von 'sklabos-sakaliba-slavus'." *Germania*, vol. 70 (1992), pp. 403–426.

"Vom Herrschaftszentrum zur städtischen Großsiedlung mit agrarischer Komponente. Archäologische Nachweise der Landwirtschaft aus dem frühmittelalterlichen Pliska." *Pliska–Preslav*, vol. 8 (2000), pp. 74–86.

Hercigonja, E. "Glagolists and glagolism." In *Croatia in the Early Middle Ages. A Cultural Survey*, pp. 369–398. Ed. by I. Supičić. London: Philip Wilson Publishers and Zagreb: AGM, 1999.

Herrin, J. "Aspects of the process of hellenization in the early Middle Ages." *ABSA*, vol. 68 (1973), pp. 113–126.

"Realities of Byzantine provincial government: Hellas and Peloponnesos, 1180–1205." *Dumbarton Oaks Papers*, vol. 29 (1975), pp. 253–284.

Herrmann, J. "Bulgaren, Obodriten, Franken und der bayrische Geograph." In *Sbornik v chest na akad. Dimităr Angelov*, pp. 41–46. Ed. by V. Velkov, Zh. Aladzhov, G. Bakalov, et al. Sofia: Izdatelstvo na Bălgarskata Akademiia na Naukite, 1994.

Holban, M. *Din cronica relaţiilor româno-ungare în secolele XIII–XIV*. Bucharest: Editura Academiei Republicii Socialiste România, 1981.

Horedt, K. "Archäologische Beiträge zur Herkunft der Siebenburger Sachsen." In *Archäologie als Geschichtswissenschaft. Studien und Untersuchungen*, pp. 447–459. Ed. by J. Herrmann. Berlin: Akademie Verlag, 1977.

"Backteller und Tonkessel in Moreşti." *Slovenská Archeológia*, vol. 26 (1978), pp. 59–68.

Moreşti. Grabungen in einer vor- und frühgeschichtlichen Siedlung in Siebenbürgen. Bucharest: Kriterion, 1979.

Moreşti. Grabungen in einer vor- und frühgeschichtlichen Siedlung in Siebenbürgen. Bonn: Rudolf Habelt, 1984.

Siebenbürgen im Frühmittelalter. Bonn: Rudolf Habelt, 1986.

Howard-Johnston, J. D. "The siege of Constantinople in 626." In *Constantinople and its Hinterland. Papers from the Twenty-Seventh Spring Symposium of Byzantine Studies, Oxford, April 1993*, pp. 131–142. Ed. by C. Mango and G. Dagron. Aldershot: Variorum, 1995.

Huxley, G. L. "Steppe-peoples in Konstantinos Porphyrogennetos." *JOB*, vol. 34 (1984), pp. 77–89.

Monemvasia and the Slavs: A Lecture on Some Works of Historical Geography in the Gennadius Library of the American School of Classical Studies at Athens. Athens: G. Huxley, 1988.

Iambor, P. "Archaeological contributions to the study of the early medieval town of Cenad (Timiş County)." *Transylvanian Review*, vol. 10 (2001), pp. 98–111.

Ilieva, A. and M. Delev. "Sclavonia and beyond: the gate to a different world in the perception of crusaders (c. 1104–c. 1208)." In *From Clermont to Jerusalem. The Crusades and Crusader Societies 1095–1500. Selected Proceedings of the International Medieval Congress, University of Leeds, 10–13 July 1995*, pp. 153–171. Ed. by A. V. Murray. Turnhout: Brepols, 1998.

Iordanov, I. *Pechatite na preslavskite vladeteli*. Sofia: Izdatelstvo na Bălgarskata Akademiia na Naukite, 1993.

Pechatite ot strategiiata v Preslav (971–1088). Sofia: Universitetsko izdatelstvo "Sv. Kliment Okhridski," 1993.

Korpus na pechatite na srednovekovna Bălgariia. Sofia: Agató, 2001.

"Preslav." In *The Economic History of Byzantium from the Seventh through the Fifteenth Century*, pp. 669–671. Ed. by A. E. Laiou. Washington: Dumbarton Oaks Research Library and Collection, 2002.

Corpus of Byzantine Seals from Bulgaria. Part I. Sofia: Agató, 2003.

Ivanova, V. "La Grande Basilique de Pliska." *Izvestiia na Bălgarskiia arkheologicheski institut*, vol. 12 (1938), pp. 365–375.

Ivanova-Mavrodinova, V. and A. Dzhurova. *Asemanievoto evangelie. Starobălgarski glagolicheski pametnik ot X vek*. Sofia: Nauka i izkustvo, 1981.

Jacoby, D. "The encounter of two societies: Western conquerors and Byzantines in the Peloponnesus after the Fourth Crusade." *American Historical Review*, vol. 78 (1973), pp. 873–896.

Jakobson, R. "St. Constantine's Prologue to the Gospel." *St. Vladimir's Seminary Quarterly*, vol. 7 (1963), pp. 14–19.

Jakšić, N. "Constantine Porphyrogenetus as the source for destruction of Salona." *Vjesnik za arheologiju i historiju Dalmatinsku*, vol. 77 (1984), pp. 315–326.

"La survivance des édifices paléochrétiens dans les terres de la principauté croate." *Hortium Artium Medievalium*, vol. 1 (1995), pp. 36–45.

Jenkins, R. J. H. "The date of the Slav revolt in Peloponnese under Romanus I." In *Late Classical and Mediaeval Studies in Honor of Albert Mathias Friend, Jr.*, pp. 204–211. Ed. by K. Weitzmann. Princeton: Princeton University Press, 1955.

"The peace with Bulgaria (927) celebrated by Theodore Daphnopates." In *Polychronion. Festschrift Franz Dölger zum 75. Geburtstag*, pp. 287–303. Ed. by P. Wirth. Heidelberg: Carl Winter, 1966.

Jovanović, S. "Srednjovekovna naselja i nekropole od IX do XIII veka u knjaževackom kraju." *Glasnik Srpskog arheoloskog društva*, vol. 6 (1990), pp. 196–207.

Jurčić, H. "Die sogenannten 'Pacta conventa' in kroatischer Sicht." *Ungarn-Jahrbuch*, vol. 1 (1969), pp. 11–22.

Jurković, M. "Uloga Zadra, Clunya i kneževa Frankopana u promociji romanike na otoku Krku." In *Umjetnost na istočnoj obali Jadrana u kontekstu europeske tradicije. Zbornik radova za znanstevnog skupa u Opatiji u svibnju 1992. posvečenog djelu Prof. Dr. Radmile Matejčić*, pp. 176–189. Ed. by N. Kudiš and M. Vicelja. Rijeka: Pedagoski fakultet, 1993.

"La rotonde de Saint-Donat de Zadar et les hexaconques préromanes en Croatie." In *Guillaume de Volpiano et l'architecture des rotondes*, pp. 237–256. Ed. by M. Jannet and C. Sapin. Dijon: Université de Dijon, 1996.

Kahl, H.-D. "Das Fürstentum Karantanien und die Anfänge seiner Christianisierung." In *Karantanien und der Alpen-Adria-Raum im Frühmittelalter*, pp. 37–99. Ed. by G. Hödl and J. Grabmayer. Vienna, Cologne, and Weimar: Böhlau, 1993.

Kaimakamova, M. "Istoriografskata stoinost na *Bălgarski apokrifen letopis*." In *Civitas divino-humana. V chest na profesor Georgi Bakalov*, pp. 417–441. Ed. by C. Stepanov and V. Vachkova. Sofia: Centăr za izsledvaniia na bălgarite "Tangra" TanNakRa IK, 2004.

Kalić, J. "Podaci Alberta Ahenskog u ugarsko-vizantijskom odnosima krajem XI veka." *ZFF*, vol. 10 (1968), pp. 183–192.

"Srpski državni sabori u Rasu." *Saopštenja*, vol. 29 (1997), pp. 27–33.

Kalligas, H. *Byzantine Monemvasia. The Sources*. Monemvasia: Akroneon, 1990.

Kandić, O., S. Popović, and R. Zarić. *Manastir Mileševa*. Belgrade: Republički zavod za zaštitu spomenika kulture, 1995.

Kantor, M. *Medieval Slavic Lives of Saints and Princes*. Ann Arbor: University of Michigan, Department of Slavic Languages and Literatures, 1983.

Kašanin, M., Đ. Bošković, and P. Mijović. *Žiča. Istorija, arhitektura, slikarstvo*. Belgrade: Knijževne novine, 1969.

Katičić, R. "Methodii doctrina." *Slovo*, vol. 36 (1988), pp. 11–44.

"Dopuna clanku 'Methodii doctrina'." *Slovo*, vols. 39–40 (1990), pp. 23–25.

"Language and literacy." In *Croatia in the Early Middle Ages. A Cultural Survey*, pp. 339–367. Ed. by I. Supičić. London: Philip Wilson Publishers and Zagreb: AGM, 1999.

Kazanaki-Lappa, M. "Medieval Athens." In *The Economic History of Byzantium from the Seventh through the Fifteenth Century*, pp. 640–646. Ed. by A. E. Laiou. Washington: Dumbarton Oaks Research Library and Collection, 2002.

Kekaumenos. *Strategikon*. Greek text ed. by G. G. Litavrin. Moscow: Nauka, 1972; Spanish translation by J. Signes Codoñer. Madrid: Alianza Editorial, 2000.

Khandzhiiskii, A. *Rock Monasteries*. Sofia: Septemvri, 1985.

Kiourtzian, G. "Le Psaume 131 et son usage funéraire dans la Grèce, les Balkans et la Cappadoce à la haute époque byzantine." *CA*, vol. 45 (1997), pp. 31–39.

Kislinger, E. *Regionalgeschichte als Quellenproblem. Die Chronik von Monembasia und das sizilianische Demenna. Eine historisch-topographische Studie.* Vienna: Verlag der Österreichischen Akademie der Wissenschaften, 2001.

Kiss, A. "Zur Frage der Bijelo Brdo Kultur. Bemerkungen zu den ethnischen Verhältnissen des heutigen Slawonien und Syrmien im 10.–11. Jahrhundert." *AAASH*, vol. 25 (1973), pp. 327–340.

"Zur Frage der Kontinuität bzw. Diskontinuität des awarischen Khaganats (567–796). Wieviele Khaganate hat es gegeben?" In *Ethnische und kulturelle Verhältnisse an der mittleren Donau vom 6. bis zum 11. Jahrhundert. Symposium Nitra 6. bis 10. November 1994*, pp. 83–98. Ed. by D. Bialeková and J. Zábojník. Bratislava: VEDA, 1996.

"The treasure of a Byzantine gold belt from the Sirmium region." *AAASH*, vol. 50 (1998), pp. 251–258.

Kiss, G. "Diesseits und jenseits der Donau. Über etliche Bestattungsitten in W- und N-Awaria." In *Ethnische und kulturelle Verhältnisse an der mittleren Donau vom 6. bis zum 11. Jahrhundert. Symposium Nitra 6. bis 10. November 1994*, pp. 167–178. Ed. by D. Bialeková and J. Zábojník. Bratislava: VEDA, 1996.

Klaić, N. *Povijest Hrvata u ranom srednjem vijeku.* Zagreb: Školska knjiga, 1971.

Vinodol od antičkih vremena do knežova Krčkih i Vinodolskog zakona. Pazin and Rijeka: Historijski arhiv, 1988.

Klen, D. *Fratrija. Feud opatije sv. Mihovila nad Limom u Istri i njegova sela (XI–XVII st.).* Pazin and Rijeka: Historijski arhiv, 1969.

Kniazkii, I. O. "Polovcy v Nizhnem Podunav'e." *Voprosy istorii*, vol. 3 (2000), pp. 121–129.

Knific, T. "Horizontalna stratigrafija grobišča Bled-Pristava II." In *Opuscula Iosepho Kastelić sexagenario dedicata*, pp. 315–326. Ed. by A. Jeločnik. Ljubljana: Narodni Muzej, 1974.

"Carniola in the Early Middle Ages." *Balcanoslavica*, vol. 5 (1976), pp. 111–121.

Koco, D. "Crkvata Sv. Sofija vo Okhrid." *Godishen zbornik. Filosofski fakultet na Unverzitetot Skopje*, vol. 2 (1949), pp. 343–358.

Koder, J. "Anmerkungen zum Slawen-Namen in byzantinischen Quellen." *T&M*, vol. 14 (2002), pp. 333–346.

Koicheva, E. "Everyday life of the crusaders on the Balkan." In *Centre, Region, Periphery. Medieval Europe Basel 2002*, pp. 352–353. Ed. by G. Helmig, B. Scholkmann, and M. Untermann. Vol. II. Basel: Dr. G. Wesselkamp, 2002.

Komata, D. "La culture arbère de Koman." *Dossiers, histoire et archéologie*, vol. III (1986), pp. 82–85.

Köpstein, H. "Einige Aspekte des byzantinischen und bulgarischen Sklavenhandels im X. Jahrhundert. Zur Novelle des Joannes Tzimiskes über Sklavenhandelszoll." In *Actes du premier Congrès international des études balkaniques et sud-est européennes*, pp. 237–247. Ed. by V. Tăpkova-Zaimova, S. Dimitrov, and E. Sarafova. Vol. III. Sofia: Editions de l'Académie Bulgare des Sciences, 1969.

Korać, V. "Prvobitna arkhitektonska koncepcija kotorske katedrale XII veka (njeno poreklo i njen značaj za arkhitekturu u Zeti i Raškoj)." *ZLU*, vol. 3 (1967), pp. 1–30.

Korošec, P. *La nécropole de Ptujski grad, Ptuj*. Ljubljana: Société archéologique de Yougoslavie, 1971.

"Ungarische Elemente aus der Nekropole auf der Burg zu Ptuj." *Arheološki vestnik*, vol. 36 (1985), pp. 337–350.

"Development of the early mediaeval Ptuj settlement." In *Istoriia i kul'tura drevnikh i srednevekovykh slavian*, pp. 15–19. Ed. by V. V. Sedov. Moscow: Editorial URSS, 1999.

Korres, Th. "Some remarks on the first major attempts of the Avaroslavs to capture Thessaloniki (597 and 614)." *Byzantina*, vol. 19 (1998), pp. 171–185.

Koščak, V. "Gregorio VII e la Croazia. Presupposti politico-sociali." *SG*, vol. 14 (1991), pp. 253–264.

Kosi, M. "The age of the Crusades in the South-East of the Empire (between the Alps and the Adriatic)." In *The Crusades and the Military Orders. Expanding Frontiers of Medieval Latin Christianity*, pp. 123–165. Ed. by Zs. Hunyadi and J. Laszlovszky. Budapest: Department of Medieval Studies, Central European University, 2001.

Kostova, R. "Boot-graffiti from the monastery of Ravna, and early pilgrimage in Bulgaria." *AMS* (1994–1995), pp. 140–165.

"Topography of three early medieval monasteries in Bulgaria and the reasons for their foundation: a case of study." *AB*, vol. 6 (1998), pp. 108–125.

"Lust and piety: graffiti from Bulgarian medieval monasteries." In *Disziplinierung im Alltag des Mittelalters und der frühen Neuzeit. Internationaler Kongreß, Krems an der Donau, 8. bis 11. Oktober 1996*, pp. 233–254. Ed. by G. Jaritz. Vienna: Verlag der Österreichischen Akademie der Wissenschaften, 1999.

"Bulgarian monasteries, ninth to tenth centuries: interpreting the archaeological evidence." *Pliska–Preslav*, vol. 8 (2000), pp. 190–202.

"Imalo li e manastiri-ergasterii v Bălgariia prez X vek?" In *Civitas divino-humana. V chest na profesor Georgi Bakalov*, pp. 457–469. Ed. by

C. Stepanov and V. Vachkova. Sofia: Centăr za izsledvaniia na bălgarite "Tangra" TanNakRa IK, 2004.
Kovačević, J. "Aperçu historique et archéologique sur le rôle des villes de la Dalmatie méridionale dans l'expansion du christianisme parmi les Serbes." *AAASH*, vol. 17 (1965), pp. 65–71.
"Avari na Jadranu." In *Referati sa simpozijuma praistorijske i srednjevjekovne sekcije Arheološkog Društva Jugoslavije*, pp. 53–81. Ed. by N. Tašić. Belgrade: Arheološko Društvo Jugoslavije and Društvo Muzejskih Radnika Vojvodine, 1966.
Kozlov, V. "Zur Besiedlungsstruktur der Nordostprovinzen des ersten Bulgarenreiches." In *Zwischen Byzanz und Abendland. Pliska, der östliche Balkanraum und Europa im Spiegel der Frühmittelalterarchäologie*, pp. 71–75. Ed. by J. Henning. Frankfurt am Main: Johann Wolfgang Goethe Universität, 1999.
Krăstev, A. "Bischofssitze in den bulgarischen Ländern bis zum IX. Jahrhundert." In *Das Christentum in Bulgarien und auf der übrigen Balkanhalbinsel in der Spätantike und im frühen Mittelalter*, pp. 233–239. Ed. by V. Giuzelev and R. Pillinger. Vienna: Verein "Freunde des Hauses Wittgenstein," 1987.
Kravari, V. *Villes et villages de Macédoine occidentale*. Paris: Pierre Lethielleux, 1989.
Kristó, G. "Ajtony and Vidin." In *Turkic–Bulgarian–Hungarian Relations (VIth–XIth Centuries)*, pp. 129–135. Ed. by G. Káldy-Nagy. Budapest: n.p., 1981.
"Anonymus a 9. századi Kárpát-medence bolgár fejedelmeiről." *Acta Historica*, vol. 113 (2001), pp. 11–19.
Kuev, K. M. "Pochvalata na car Simeon. Rekonstrukciia i razbor." *Palaeobulgarica*, vol. 10 (1986), pp. 3–23.
Kuleff, I. and R. Dzhingova. "Glass production during Roman and medieval times on the territory of Bulgaria." *AB*, vol. 6 (2002), pp. 101–108.
Lampropoulou, A., I. Anagnostakis, V. Konti, and A. Panopoulou. "Symbole sten ermeneia ton arkhaiologikon tekmerion tes Peloponnesou kata tous 'skoteinous aiones'." In *Hoi skoteinoi aiones tou Byzantiou (7os–9os ai.)*, pp. 189–229. Ed. by E. Kountoura-Galaki. Athens: Ethniko Idryma Ereunon and Institouto Byzantinon Ereunon, 2001.
Lampropoulou, A., I. Anagnostakis, V. Konti, et al. "Ho monakhismos sten Peloponneso kata te mese byzantine periodo." In *Taseis tou orthodoxou monakhismou, 9os–20os aiones. Praktika tou Diethnous Symposiou pou diorganotheke sta plaisia tou Programmatos "Hoi dromoi tou orthodoxou monakhismou. Poreuthentes mathete". Thessalonike, 28 Septembriou–2 Oktobriou 1994*, pp. 77–103. Ed. by K. Nikolaou. Athens: Institouto Byzantinon Ereunon, 1996.

Lászlo, G. and I. Rácz. *Der Goldschatz von Nagyszentmiklós.* Vienna and Munich: Anton Schroll, 1983.

Laszlovszky, J. and Z. Soós. "Historical monuments of the Teutonic Order in Transylvania." In *The Crusades and the Military Orders. Expanding Frontiers of Medieval Latin Christianity*, pp. 319–336. Ed. by Zs. Hunyadi and J. Laszlovszky. Budapest: Department of Medieval Studies, Central European University, 2001.

Lauterbach, H. "Untersuchungen zur Vorgeschichte der Protobulgaren nach einem Bericht bei Teofanes." In *Die Araber in der alten Welt*, pp. 539–619. Ed. by F. Altheim and R. Stiehl. Vol. I. Berlin: De Gruyter, 1967.

Lavrov, P. A. "Les Feuillets de Zograph." *RES*, vol. 6 (1926), pp. 5–23.

Lefort, J. "En Macédoine orientale au Xe siècle: habitat rural, communes et domaines." In *Occident et Orient au Xe siècle. Actes du IXe Congrès de la Société des Historiens Médiévalistes de l'Enseignement Supérieur Public (Dijon, 2–4 juin 1978)*, pp. 251–279. Paris: Les Belles Lettres, 1979.

"Population et peuplement en Macédoine orientale, IXe–XVe siècle." In *Hommes et richesses dans l'Empire byzantin*, pp. 63–89. Ed. by V. Kravari, J. Lefort, and C. Morrisson. Vol. II. Paris: Pierre Lethielleux, 1991.

Leroy-Molinghen, A. "Les fils de Pierre de Bulgarie et les Cométopoules." *Byzantion*, vol. 42 (1972), pp. 405–419.

Lilie, R.-J. "'Thrakien' und 'Thrakesion'. Zur byzantinischen Provinzorganisation am Ende des 7. Jahrhunderts." *JOB*, vol. 26 (1977), pp. 7–47.

Lishev, S. "Tretiiat krăstonosen pokhod i bălgarite." *IIBI*, vol. 7 (1957), pp. 205–221.

"Nekotorye voprosy feodal'nykh otnoshenii v Bolgarii v X v. i v epokhu vizantiiskogo gospodstva." *VV*, vol. 41 (1980), pp. 21–45.

Litavrin, G. G. "Vlakhi vizantiiskikh istochnikov X–XIII vv." In *Iugo-Vostochnaia Evropa v srednie veka. Sbornik statei*, pp. 100–103. Ed. by I. S. Grosul. Vol. I. Kishinew: Shtiinca, 1972.

"Bulgarian culture in the eleventh and twelfth centuries: conditions and development." In *To Hellenikon. Studies in Honor of Speros Vryonis, Jr.*, pp. 65–76. Ed. by J. S. Allen, Ch. P. Ioannides, J. S. Langdon, and S. W. Reinert. Vol. II. New Rochelle: Aristide D. Caratzas, 1993.

Lončar, M. "Porfirogenetova seoba Hrvata pred sudom novije literature." *Diadora*, vol. 14 (1992), pp. 375–448.

Louvi-Kizi, A. "Thebes." In *The Economic History of Byzantium from the Seventh through the Fifteenth Century*, pp. 632–638. Ed. by A. E. Laiou. Washington: Dumbarton Oaks Research Library and Collection, 2002.

Lučić, J. "Quelques traits caractéristiques dans les rapports entre l'Eglise et l'Etat dans la Croatie du Xe siècle." In *Vita religiosa, morale e sociale ed i concili di Split (Spalato) dei secc. X–XI. Atti del Symposium internazionale di storia ecclesiastica. Split, 26–30 settembre 1978*, pp. 205–217. Ed. by A. G. Matanić. Padova: Antenore, 1982.

Lunt, H. G. "Slavs, Common Slavic, and Old Church Slavonic." In *Litterae Slavicae medii aevi. Francisco Venceslao Mareŝ sexagenario oblatae*, pp. 185–204. Ed. by J. Reinhart. Munich: Otto Sagner, 1985.

Macartney, C. A. "Studies of the earliest Hungarian historical sources. I: The Lives of St. Gerard." *Archivum Europae Centro-Orientalis*, vol. 18 (1938), pp. 1–35.

Macháček, J. "Břeclav–Pohansko." In *Europe's Centre around* AD *1000*, pp. 210–211. Ed. by A. Wieczorek and H.-M. Hienz. Stuttgart: Theiss, 2000.

"Pohansko bei Břeclav – ein bedeutendes Zentrum Grossmährens." In *Velká Morava meži východem a západem. Sborník příspevku z mežinárodní vedecke conference. Uherské Hradiŝte, Stare Město, 28.9.–1.10.1999*, pp. 275–290. Ed. by L. Galuška, P. Kouřil, and Z. Meřínský. Brno: Archeologický ústav Akadémie věd Česke Respubliky, 2001.

Madgearu, A. "The downfall of the lower Danubian Late Roman frontier." *RRH*, vol. 36 (1997), pp. 315–336.

"The military organization of Paradunavon." *Byzantinoslavica*, vol. 60 (1999), pp. 421–446.

"The church organization at the Lower Danube between 971 and 1020." *EBPB*, vol. 4 (2001), pp. 71–85.

Românii în opera Notarului Anonim. Cluj-Napoca: Centrul de Studii Transilvane – Fundaţia Culturală Română, 2001.

"Salt trade and warfare in early medieval Transylvania." *Ephemeris Napocensis*, vol. 11 (2001), pp. 271–284.

Makk, F. *The Arpads and the Comneni. Political Relations between Hungary and Byzantium in the 12th Century*. Budapest: Akadémiai kiadó, 1989.

Makkai, L. "Transylvania in the medieval Hungarian kingdom (896–1526)." In *History of Transylvania*, pp. 333–589. Ed. by L. Makkai and A. Mócsy. Vol. 1. New York: Columbia University Press, 2001.

Maksimović, L. "O vremenu pohoda bulgarskog kneza Borisa na Srbiju." *ZFF*, vol. 14 (1979), pp. 69–76.

"The Christianization of the Serbs and the Croats." In *The Legacy of Saints Cyril and Methodius to Kiev and Moscow. Proceedings of the International Congress on the Millennium of the Conversion of Rus' to Christianity, Thessaloniki, 26–28 November 1988*, pp. 167–184. Ed. by A. E. Tachiaos. Thessaloniki: Hellenic Association for Slavic Studies, 1992.

Maksimovich, K. A. "Drevneishii pamiatnik slavianskogo prava 'Zakon sudnyi liudem': kompoziciia, perevodcheskaia tekhnika, problema avtorstva." *VV*, vol. 61 (2002), pp. 24–37.

Malamut, E. "L'image byzantine des Petchénègues." *BZ*, vol. 88 (1995), pp. 105–147.

Malenko, V. "Ranosrednovekovnata materijalna kultura vo Okhrid i Okhridsko." In *Okhrid i Okhridsko niz istorijata*, pp. 269–315. Ed.

by M. Apostolski. Vol. I. Skopje: Sobranie na opshtina Okhrid, 1985.

Malingoudis, Ph. *Die mittelalterlichen kyrillischen Inschriften der Hämus-Halbinsel. I. Die bulgarischen Inschriften*. Thessaloniki: Association hellénique d'études slaves, 1979.

"Die Nachrichten des Niketas Choniates über die Entstehung des Zweiten Bulgarischen Staates." *Byzantina*, vol. 10 (1980), pp. 51–147.

Malmquist, T. *Byzantine 12th Century Frescoes in Kastoria. Agioi Anargyroi and Agios Nikolaos tou Kasnitzi*. Uppsala and Stockholm: Almqvist and Wiksell International, 1979.

Mandić, D. "Gregorio VII e l'occupazione veneta della Dalmazia nell'anno 1076." In *Venezia e il Levante fino al secolo XV. Atti del I Convegno internazionale di Storia della Civiltà Veneziana, Venezia, 1–5 giugno 1968*, pp. 453–471. Ed. by A. Pertusi. Vol. I. Florence: Olschki, 1973.

Maneva, E. "Le problème des bracelets médiévaux en Macédoine." In *Actes du XIIe Congrès international des sciences préhistoriques et protohistoriques, Bratislava, 1–7 septembre 1991*, pp. 237–245. Ed. by J. Pavuj. Vol. IV. Bratislava: Institut Archéologique de l'Académie Slovaque des Sciences, 1993.

"La survie des centres paléochrétiens de Macédoine au Haut Moyen Age." In *Radovi XIII. Me đunarodnog Kongresa za starokršćansku arheologiju. Split-Poreč, 25.9.–1.10. 1994*, pp. 843–858. Ed. by N. Cambi and E. Marin. Vol. II. Vatican: Pontificio Istituto di Archeologia Cristiana and Split: Arheološki Muzej, 1998.

Manselli, R. "Les 'chrétiens' de Bosnie: le catharisme en Europe orientale." *Revue d'histoire ecclésiastique*, vol. 72 (1977), pp. 600–614.

Mănucu-Adameşteanu, Gh. "Nufăru (jud. Tulcea) – oraş bizantin fortificat, la Dunărea de Jos (sec. X–XIII)." *Arheologia medievală*, vol. 2 (1998), pp. 79–86.

"Les invasions des Petchénègues au Bas-Danube, 1027–1048." *EBPB*, vol. 4 (2001), pp. 87–112.

Maretić, T. "Prvi spljetski sabor i glagolica." In *Zbornik kralja Tomislava u spomen tisućugodišnjice hrvatskogo kraljevstva*, pp. 385–390. Zagreb: Tisak nadbiskupske tiskare, 1925.

Margetić, L. "Toparque, tepči (*topotèrètes*) et *dad* en Croatie au 11e siècle." *REB*, vol. 44 (1986), pp. 257–262.

"The Croatian state during the era of rulers from the Croatian national dynasty." In *Croatia in the Early Middle Ages. A Cultural Survey*, pp. 197–214. Ed. by I. Supičić. London: Philip Wilson Publishers and Zagreb: AGM, 1999.

"L'Istria bizantina ed alcuni problemi del Placito di Risano." In *Slovenia in sosednje dezele med antiko in karolinsko dobo. Začetki slovenske etnogeneze*, pp. 81–95. Ed. by R. Bratož. Ljubljana: Narodni Muzej Slovenije, 2000.

Dolazak Hrvata. Split: Knijževni krug, 2001.

Margos, A. "Niakoi belezhki po cheteneto na protivobogomilskiia nadpis ot srednovekovnata cǎrkva pri s. Gigen." *SL*, vol. 15 (1984), pp. 119–125.

Marinković, R. "Istorija nastanka Života gospodina Simeona od svetoga Save." In *Meždunarodni naučni skup "Sava Nemanjić-Sveti Sava. Istorija i predanje". Decembar 1976*, pp. 201–214. Ed. by V. Djurić. Belgrade: Srpska Akademija Nauka i Umetnosti, 1979.

Marinović, A. "Le caractère juridique de la charte (diplôme) royale pendant l'époque de la dynastie nationale croate (vers 839 à 1102 a.)." *Folia diplomatica*, vol. 2 (1976), pp. 7–16.

Marjanović-Vujović, G. "Archaeological proving the presence of the Pechenegs in Beograd town." *Balcanoslavica*, vol. 3 (1974), pp. 183–188.

Trnjane, srpska nekropola (kraj 11–početak 13. veka). Belgrade: Arheološki Institut, 1984.

"Rural settlements in the 9th and 10th centuries in the Danube Valley in Serbia." In *From the Baltic to the Black Sea. Studies in Medieval Archaeology*, pp. 236–247. Ed. by D. Austin and L. Alcock. London: Unwin Hyman, 1990.

Marušić, B. "Istarska grupa spomenika sakralne arhitekture s upisanom apsidom." *Histria Archaeologica*, vol. 5 (1974), pp. 7–188.

Starohrvatska nekropola u Žminju. Pula: Arheološki Muzej Istre, 1987.

Istra i sjevernojadranski prostor u ranom srednjem vijeku (materijalna kultura od 7. do 11. stoljeća). Pula: Arheološki muzej Istre, 1995.

Matijević-Sokol, M. "Latin inscriptions." In *Croatia in the Early Middle Ages. A Cultural Survey*, pp. 239–256. Ed. by I. Supičić. London: Philip Wilson Publishers and Zagreb: AGM, 1999.

McGrath, S. "The battles of Dorostolon (971): rhetoric and reality." In *Peace and War in Byzantium. Essays in Honor of George S. Dennis, S. J.*, pp. 152–164. Ed. by T. S. Miller and J. Nesbitt. Washington, D.C.: Catholic University of America, 1995.

McNally, S. "Split in the Byzantine Empire: the archaeological evidence." In *Acts. XVIIIth International Congress of Byzantine Studies. Selected Papers, Moscow 1991*, pp. 250–264. Ed. by I. Ševčenko, G. G. Litavrin, and W. Hanak. Vol. II. Shepherdstown, W.Va.: Byzantine Studies Press, 1996.

Medynceva, A. and K. Popkonstantinov. "Ktitorskaia nadpis' iz Krugloi Cerkvi v Preslave." *Palaeobulgarica*, vol. 7 (1983), pp. 39–54.

Megaw, A. H. S. "An early thirteenth-century Aegean glazed ware." In *Studies in Memory of David Talbot Rice*, pp. 34–45. Ed. by G. Robertson and G. Henderson. Edinburgh: Edinburgh University Press, 1975.

Menander the Guardsman, *History*. Ed. and transl. by R. C. Blockley. Liverpool: F. Cairns, 1985.

Mesterházy, K. "Der byzantinisch-balkanische Handel nach Ungarn im 10.–11. Jahrhundert im Spiegel der Gräberfunden." In *Byzance et ses voisins:*

Mélanges à la mémoire de Gyula Moravcsik à l'occasion du centième anniversaire de sa naissance, pp. 117–128. Ed. by T. Olajos. Szeged: Generalia, 1994.

Metcalf, D. M. "The currency of deniers tournois in Frankish Greece." *ABSA*, vol. 55 (1960), pp. 38–59.

"The Aegean coastlands under threat: some coins and coin hoards from the reign of Heraclius." *ABSA*, vol. 57 (1962), pp. 14–23.

"Byzantinobulgarica: the Second Bulgarian Empire and the problem of 'Bulgarian imitative' trachea before and after 1204." *Numismatic Circular*, vol. 81 (1973), pp. 418–421.

"Corinth in the ninth century: the numismatic evidence." *Hesperia*, vol. 42 (1973), pp. 180–251.

"Coinage and coin finds associated with a military presence in the medieval Balkans." In *Kovanje i kovnice antičkog i srednjovekovnog novca*, pp. 88–97. Ed. by V. Kondić. Belgrade: Arheološki Institut, 1976.

"Avar and Slav invasions into the Balkan peninsula (c. 575–625): the nature of the numismatic evidence." *Journal of Roman Archaeology*, vol. 4 (1991), pp. 140–148.

Mihaljčić, R., L. Steindorff, and M. Hellmann, eds. *Namentragende Steininschriften in Jugoslawien vom Ende des 7. bis zur Mitte des 13. Jahrhunderts*. Wiesbaden: Franz Steiner, 1982.

Miiatev, K. "Madarskiiat konnik." *Izvestiia na Bălgarskiia arkheologicheski institut*, vol. 5 (1928–1929), pp. 90–126.

Mijović, P. "Bar (Antibaris), est-elle l'héritie direct de Duklja?" In *I. Międzynarodowy kongres archeologii słowiańskej. Warszawa, 14–18 IX 1965*, pp. 140–154. Ed. by W. Hensel. Vol. v. Wrocław, Warsaw, and Cracow: Wydawnictwo Polskiej Akademii Nauk, 1970.

Mikhailov, S. "La grande basilique de Pliska et la tradition paléobyzantine de bâtir dans la Péninsule balkanique." In *Actes du premier Congrès international des études balkaniques et sud-est européennes*, pp. 583–598. Ed. by D. Dimitrov, H. Danov, V. Velkov, et al. Vol. II. Sofia: Editions de l'Académie Bulgare des Sciences, 1969.

"Kamennite sarkofazi do Goliamata bazilika v Pliska." *Pliska–Preslav*, vol. 1 (1979), pp. 44–59.

Miletić, N. "Ranoslovenske nekropole u Bosni i Hercegovini – komparativna razmatranja." *Glasnik Zemaljskog Muzeja Bosne i Hercegovine u Sarajevu*, vol. 44 (1989), pp. 175–200.

Milev, A. *Grăckite zhitiia na Kliment Okhridski*. Sofia: Izdatelstvo na Bălgarskata Akademiia na Naukite, 1966.

Milinković, M. "Rose-Malo Rose, Boka Kotorska – antično/kasnoantično naselje i srednjovekovna crkva." *Glasnik Srpskog arheoloskog društva*, vol. 13 (1997), pp. 167–181.

Miljković-Pepek, P. *Veljusa. Manastir Sv. Bogorodica Milostiva vo seloto Veljusa kraj Strumica*. Skopje: Fakultet za filozofsko-istoriski nauki na univerzitetot "Kiril i Metodij," 1981.

Miltenova, A. and M. Kaimakamova. "The uprising of Peter Delian (1040–1041) in a new Old Bulgarian source." *Byzantinobulgarica*, vol. 8 (1986), pp. 227–240.

Minaeva, O. *From Paganism to Christianity. Formation of Medieval Bulgarian Art*. Frankfurt am Main, Berlin, and New York: Peter Lang, 1996.

"On some peculiarities of the shape and decoration of the vessels from the Vrap treasure, Albania." *Problemi na izkustvoto*, vol. 1 (2001), pp. 13–22.

Minić, D. *Le site d'habitation médiéval [sic] de Mačvanska Mitrovica*. Belgrade: Arheološki Institut, 1980.

Mirnik, I. "Numizmatički nalazi u Dubrovniku (prethodni izveštaj o bizantskom novcu)." In *Etnogeneza Hrvata*, pp. 169–177. Ed. by N. Budak. Zagreb: Nakladni zavod Matice Hrvatske and Zavod za hrvatsku povijest, 1996.

Mitrea, I. "L'habitat médiéval ancien de Davideni-Neamţ. Précisions chronologiques et considérations ethno-culturelles." *Studia antiqua et archaeologica*, vol. 7 (2000), pp. 439–454.

Morris, R. "The origins of Athos." In *Mount Athos and Byzantine Monasticism. Papers from the Twenty-Eighth Spring Symposium of Byzantine Studies, Birmingham, March 1994*, pp. 37–46. Ed. by A. Bryer and M. Cunningham. Aldershot and Brookfield: Variorum, 1996.

"The Athonites and their neighbors in Macedonia in the tenth and eleventh centuries." In *Byzantine Macedonia: Identity, Image, and History. Papers from the Melbourne Conference, July 1995*, pp. 157–167. Ed. by J. Burke and R. Scott. Melbourne: Australian Association for Byzantine Studies, 2000.

Moutsopoulos, N. "Le tombeau du Tsar Samuil dans la Basilique de Saint Achille à Prespa." *EB*, vol. 3 (1984), pp. 114–126.

He basilike to Hagiou Achilleiou sten Prespa. Symbole ste melete ton byzantinon mnemeion tes perioches. Thessaloniki: Aristoteleio Panepistemio Thessalonikes, Kentro Byzantinon Ereunon, 1989.

Mullett, M. "Byzantium and the Slavs: the views of Theophylact of Ochrid." *GSU*, vol. 87 (1994), pp. 55–70.

Theophylact of Ochrid. Reading the Letters of a Byzantine Archbishop. Aldershot and Brookfield: Variorum, 1997.

Nägler, T. *Aşezarea saşilor în Transilvania*. Bucharest: Kriterion, 1992.

Nagy, J. "Dévouement du roi croate Zvonimir au Saint-Siège et le bas-relief au baptistère à Split." In *Vita religiosa morale e sociale ed i concili di Split (Spalato) dei secoli X–XI. Atti del symposium internazionale di storia ecclesiastica, Split, 26–30 settembre 1978*, pp. 99–111. Ed. by A. G. Matanić. Padua: Editrice Antenore, 1982.

Nagy, S. "Tvrđava Bač." *Rad Vojvođanskih Muzeja*, vol. 10 (1961), pp. 89–115.

"Mečka – ein frühmittelalterliches Gräberfeld beim Dorfe Aradac." *Študijné zvesti*, vol. 16 (1968), pp. 165–174.

Nallbani, E. "Transformations et continuité dans l'ouest des Balkans: le cas de la civilisation de Komani (VIe–IXe siècles)." In *L'Illyrie méridionale et l'Epire dans l'Antiquité. IV. Actes du IVe colloque international de Grenoble, 10–12 octobre 2002*, pp. 481–490. Ed. by P. Cabanes and J.-L. Lamboley. Paris: De Boccard, 2004.

Nasledova, R. A. "Remeslo i torgovlia Fessaloniki konca IX–nachala X v. po dannym Ioanna Kameniaty." *VV*, vol. 8 (1956), pp. 61–84.

Năsturel, P. Ş. "Valaques, Coumans et Byzantins sous le règne de Manuel Comnène." *Byzantina*, vol. 1 (1969), pp. 167–186.

"A propos du Tenou Ormon (Teleorman) de Kinnamos." In *Geographica Byzantina*, pp. 81–91. Ed. by H. Ahrweiller. Paris: Centre de Recherches d'Histoire et Civilisation Byzantines, 1981.

Nesbitt, J. and J. Wiita. "A confraternity of the Comnenian era." *BZ*, vol. 68 (1975), pp. 360–384.

Nesheva, V., D. Serafimova, G. Stoianov, et al. "Arkhitektura." In *Melnik. Gradăt v podnozhieto na Slavova krepost*, pp. 40–119. Ed. by S. Georgieva and V. Nesheva. Vol. 1. Sofia: Izdatelstvo na Bălgarskata Akademiia na Naukite, 1989.

Neville, L. A. "Local provincial elites in eleventh-century Hellas and Peloponnese." Ph.D. Dissertation. Princeton University, 1998.

Authority in Byzantine Provincial Society, 950–1100. Cambridge: Cambridge University Press, 2004.

Niavi, P. E. "Leon Sgouros: patriotes e tyrannos." *Byzantinai Meletai. Diethnes Epistemonike Hepeteris Byzantines kai Metabyzantines Ereunes*, vol. 4 (1993), pp. 333–357.

Nicolova, B. "Division ecclésiastique en Thrace, en Mésie et en Illyricum oriental du IVe au VIIIe siècle." *BHR*, vol. 21 (1993), pp. 26–33.

Nikolov, A. "Nabliudeniia vărkhu cikăla starobălgarski istoriko-apokaliptichni tvorbi ot X–XI v." *Palaeobulgarica*, vol. 21 (1997), pp. 91–107.

Nikolov, G. N. "The Bulgarian aristocracy in the war against the Byzantine Empire (971–1019)." In *Byzantium and East Central Europe*, pp. 141–158. Ed. by M. Salamon, G. Prinzing, and P. Stephenson. Cracow: Secesja, 2001.

Nikolov, S. "The Magyar connection or Constantine and Methodius in the steppes." *BMGS*, vol. 21 (1997), pp. 79–92.

Noll, R. "Ein Ziegel als sprechendes Zeugnis einer historischen Katastrophe (Zum Untergang Sirmiums 582 n. Chr.)." *Anzeiger der Österreichischen Akademie der Wissenschaften*, vol. 126 (1989), pp. 139–154.

Novak, V. *Zadarski kartular Samostana Svete Marije*. Zagreb: Jugoslavenska Akademija Znanosti i Umjetnosti, 1959.

"Something new from the Dalmatian Beneventana." *Medievalia et Humanistica*, vol. 14 (1962), pp. 76–85.

Novak, V. and B. Talebaković-Pečarski. "Večenegin evan đelistar." *Starine Jugoslavenske Akademije Znanosti i Umjetnosti*, vol. 51 (1962), pp. 5–60.

Obelić, B. and A. Sliepčević. "Correction of radiocarbon age of wooden beams from St. Donat's church in Zadar by dendrochronological method." *Vjesnik Arheološkog Muzeja u Zagrebu*, vols. 32–33 (1999–2000), pp. 197–206.

Oberländer-Târnoveanu, E. "Un atelier monétaire byzantin inconnu de la deuxième moitié du XIe siècle dans le thème de Paristrion." *RESEE*, vol. 21 (1983), pp. 261–270.

"Moneda Asăneştilor în contextul circulaţiei monetare din zona gurilor Dunării." In *Răscoala şi statul Asăneştilor*, pp. 114–152. Ed. by E. Stănescu. Bucharest: Editura Ştiinţifică şi Enciclopedică, 1989.

"Numismatic and historical remarks on the Byzantine coin hoards from the 12th century at the Lower Danube." *RESEE*, vol. 30 (1992), pp. 41–60.

"La monnaie byzantine des VIe–VIIIe siècles au-delà de la frontière du Bas-Danube. Entre politique, économie et diffusion culturelle." *H&M*, vol. 17 (2002), pp. 155–196.

Obolensky, D. "Theophylaktos of Ochrid and the authorship of the Vita Clementis." In *Byzance. Hommage à André N. Stratos*, pp. 601–618. Ed. by N. A. Stratos. Vol. II. Athens: N. A. Stratou, 1986.

Six Byzantine Portraits. Oxford: Oxford University Press, 1988.

Odorico, P. "La lettre de Photius à Boris de Bulgarie." *Byzantinoslavica*, vol. 54 (1993), pp. 83–88.

Oikonomides, N. "Recherches sur l'histoire du Bas-Danube aux X–XIe siècles. La Mésopotamie de l'Occident." *RESEE*, vol. 3 (1965), pp. 50–82.

"A propos des relations ecclésiastiques entre Byzance et la Hongrie au XIe siècle: le métropolite de Turquie." *RESEE*, vol. 9 (1971), pp. 527–533.

"Presthlavitza, the Little Preslav." *Südost-Forschungen*, vol. 42 (1983), pp. 1–9.

"Tribute or trade? The Byzantine–Bulgarian treaty of 716." In *Issledovaniia po slaviano-vizantiiskomu i zapadnoevropeiskomu srednevekov'iu. Posviashchaetsia pamiati Ivana Duicheva*, pp. 29–31. Ed. by P. Dinekov, A. Dzhurova, G. Bakalov, et al. Sofia: Centr dlia slaviano-vizantiiskikh issledovanii imeni Ivana Duicheva and Gosudarstvennoe izdatel'stvo imeni D-ra Petra Berona, 1988.

"L'archonte slave de l'Hellade au VIIIe siècle." *VV*, vol. 55 (1994), pp. 111–118.

"The medieval Via Egnatia." In *The Via Egnatia under Ottoman Rule (1380-1699)*, pp. 9-16. Ed. by E. Zachariadou. Rethymnon: Crete University Press, 1996.

"St. Andrew, Joseph the Hymnographer, and the Slavs of Patras." In *ΛΕΙΜΩΝ. Studies Presented to Lennart Rydén on His Sixty-Fifth Birthday*, pp. 71–78. Ed. by J. O. Rosenqvist. Uppsala: Almqvist and Wiksell International, 1996.

"A note on the campaign of Staurakios in the Peloponnese (783/4)." *ZRVI*, vol. 38 (1999–2000), pp. 61–66.

Olajos, T. "Quelques remarques sur une peuplade slave en Hellade." *VV*, vol. 55 (1994), pp. 106–110.

Olteanu, Ş. "Agricultura la est şi sud de Carpaţi în sec. IX–XIV. I." *Muzeul Naţional*, vol. 1 (1974), pp. 35–55.

"Procédés d'influence slave pour la reduction du fer à l'est des Carpathes, aux VIe–VIIe siècles dans le contexte de la technologie traditionnelle des autochtones." In *Rapports du IIIe Congrès international d'archéologie slave, Bratislava 7–14 septembre 1975*, pp. 581–586. Ed. by B. Chropovský. Vol. 1. Bratislava: VEDA, 1979.

Ostrogorski, G. "Un ambassade serbe auprès de l'empereur Basile II." *Byzantion*, vol. 19 (1949), pp. 187–194.

"Postanak tema Khelada i Peloponez." *ZRVI*, vol. 1 (1952), pp. 64–77.

Ovcharov, D. "A Cyrillic inscription of 931 in Preslav." *BHR*, vol. 4 (1976), pp. 71–75.

"Ship graffiti from medieval Bulgaria." *International Journal of Nautical Archaeology and Underwater Exploration*, vol. 6 (1977), pp. 59–61.

Bălgarski srednovekovni risunki-grafiti. Sofia: Septemvri, 1982.

"Kăm văprosa za ukrepitelnata sistema na Veliki Preslav." In *Prinosi kăm bălgarskata arkheologiia. Dekemvriiski dni na bălgarskata arkheologiia "Prof. dr. Stancho Vaklinov"*, pp. 43–47. Ed. by D. Ovcharov and I. Shtereva. Vol. 1. Sofia: Arges, 1992.

Ovcharov, D. and M. Vaklinova. *Rannovizantiiski pametnici ot Bălgariia (IV–VII vek)*. Sofia: Septemvri, 1978.

Ovcharov, N. and D. Khadzhieva. *Srednovekovniiat manastir v gr. Kărdzhali, centăr na episkopiiata Akhridos (XI–XIV v.)*. Sofia: Izdatelstvo na Bălgarskata Akademiia na Naukite, 1992.

Páloczi-Horváth, A. *Pechenegs, Cumans, Iasians: Steppe Peoples in Medieval Hungary*. Wellingborough: Corvina, 1990.

Pandžić, M. "Godina osnutka zagrebacke biskupije (Godine 1094. ili 1090?)." *Arhivski vjesnik*, vol. 37 (1994), pp. 161–170.

Panova, R. "Dvorec, chovek, bog v *Shestodnev* na Ioan Ekzarkh." In *1100 godini Veliki Preslav*, pp. 136–139. Ed. by T. Totev, I. Iordanov, R. Rashev, et al. Vol. 1. Shumen: Izdatelstvo na VPI "Konstantin Preslavski," 1995.

Stolichniiat grad v kulturata na srednovekovna Bălgariia. Sofia: Universitetsko izdatelstvo "Sv. Kliment Okhridski," 1995.

"The capital city in the medieval Bulgarian culture." *JOB*, vol. 46 (1996), pp. 437–440.

Papacostea, Ş. *Between the Crusade and the Mongol Empire. The Romanians in the 13th Century*. Cluj-Napoca: Center for Transylvanian Studies, Romanian Cultural Foundation, 1998.

Pavlikianov, C. "The Bulgarian Athonite monastery of Zographou from 980 to 1051 according to the evidence of its archive." In *Civitas divino-humana. V chest na profesor Georgi Bakalov*, pp. 563–569. Ed. by C. Stepanov and V. Vachkova. Sofia: Centăr za izsledvaniia na bălgarite "Tangra" TanNakRa IK, 2004.

Pavlova, R. *Petăr Chernorizec, starobălgarski pisatel ot X vek*. Sofia: Izdatelstvo na Bălgarskata Akademiia na Naukite, 1994.

Penna, V. "He zoe stis byzantines poleis tes Peloponnesou: he nomismatike martyria (80s–120s ai. m. Kh.)." In *Mneme Martin J. Price*, pp. 195–288. Ed. by A. P. Tzamalis. Athens: Hellenic Numismatic Society, 1996.

Peri, V. "Velika (Dragvista) e il primo vescovo della Chiesa bulgara." *Bolletino della Badia Greca di Grottaferrata*, vol. 46 (1992), pp. 159–187.

Peričić, E. *Sclavorum Regnum Grgura Barskog. Ljetopis Popa Dukljanina*. Zagreb: Krščanska sadašnjost, 1991.

Perkhavko, V. B. "Gde zhe nakhodilsia dunaiskii grad Pereiaslavec?" *Byzantinoslavica*, vol. 55 (1994), pp. 278–290.

Petkanova, D. *Starobălgarska literatura IX–XVIII vek*. Sofia: Universitetsko izdatelstvo "Kliment Okhridski," 1992.

Petković, S. *Morača*. Belgrade: Srpska književna zadruga IRO "Prosveta," 1986.

Petranović, A. and A. Margetić. "Il Placito del Risano." *Atti. Centro di ricerche storiche – Rovigno*, vol. 14 (1983–1984), pp. 55–75.

Petricioli, I. "Sculpture from the 8th to the 11th century." In *Croatia in the Early Middle Ages. A Cultural Survey*, pp. 475–491. Ed. by I. Supičić. London: Philip Wilson Publishers and Zagreb: AGM, 1999.

Petrova, G. *Cărkva i cărkovno pravo v srednovekovna Bălgariia*. Sofia: Sibi, 2005.

Peytscheff, B. "Das Werk 'De inventione litterarum' des Hrabanus Maurus und die altbulgarische Schrift 'O pismenech cranoristza Hrabra'." *Archiv für mittelrheinischen Kirchengeschichte*, vol. 34 (1982), pp. 37–41.

Pillon, M. "Sémantique et histoire de l'habitat: le *fosatum* proto-byzantin, le *fshat* albanais et le *sat* roumain." *Erytheia*, vol. 14 (1993), pp. 9–41.

Pivčević, E., ed. *The Cartulary of the Benedictine Abbey of St. Peter of Gumay (Croatia), 1080–1187*. Bristol: D. Arthur and Sons, 1984.

Pleterski, A. *Župa Bled. Nastanek, razvoj in prezitki*. Ljubljana: Slovenska Akademija Znanosti in Umetnosti, 1986.

Pliakov, Z. "La région de la Moyenne Struma aux VIIe–IXe siècles." *Palaeobulgarica*, vol. 13 (1989), pp. 100–115.

Podskalsky, G. "Die Organisation der bulgarischen Kirche nach der Taufe des Fürsten Boris-Michael." *EB*, vol. 26 (1990), pp. 54–58.

"Two archbishops of Achrida (Ochrid) and their significance for Macedonia's secular and church history: Theophylaktos and Demetrios Chomatenos." In *Byzantine Macedonia: Identity, Image, and History. Papers from the Melbourne Conference, July 1995*, pp. 139–148. Ed. by J. Burke and R. Scott. Melbourne: Australian Association for Byzantine Studies, 2000.

Pohl, W. "Das Awarenreich und die 'kroatischen' Ethnogenesen." In *Die Bayern und ihre Nachbarn. Berichte des Symposiums der Kommission fur Fruhmittelalterforschung 25. bis 28. Oktober 1982, Stift Zwettl, Niederosterreich*, pp. 293–298. Ed. by H. Wolfram and A. Schwarcz. Vol. 1. Vienna: Verlag der Österreichischen Akademie der Wissenschaften, 1985.

Die Awaren. Ein Steppenvolk im Mitteleuropa 567–822 n. Chr. Munich: C. H. Beck, 1988.

"Zur Dynamik barbarischer Gesellschaften: das Beispiel der Awaren." *Klio*, vol. 73 (1991), pp. 595–600.

"Die Beziehungen der Awaren zu den Slawen." In *Slovenija in sosednje dežele med antiko in karolinsko dobo. Začetki slovenske etnogeneze*, pp. 341–354. Ed. by R. Bratož. Ljubljana: Narodni Muzej Slovenije, 2000.

Popa, R. "Structures socio-politiques roumaines au sud de la Transylvanie aux commencements du Moyen Age." *RRH*, vol. 14 (1975), pp. 291–314.

"Knaufkrone eines wikingerzeitlichen Prachtschwertes von Păcuiul lui Soare." *Germania*, vol. 62 (1984), pp. 425–431.

La începuturile Evului Mediu românesc. Ţara Haţegului. Bucharest: Editura Academiei Republicii Socialiste România, 1988.

Popescu, E. "Die spätgriechische Inschriften aus Klein-Skythien." *Dacia*, vol. 11 (1967), pp. 163–176.

Inscripţiile greceşti şi latine din secolele IV–XIII descoperite în România. Bucharest: Editura Academiei Republicii Socialiste România, 1976.

"Notes on the history of Dobrudja in the 11th century: the bishopric of Axiopolis." *Byzantina*, vol. 15 (1989), pp. 237–262.

Popkonstantinov, K. "Les inscriptions du monastère rupestre près du village Murfatlar (Basarab)(Etats, théories et faits)." In *Dobrudža. Etudes ethno-culturelles. Recueil d'articles*, pp. 115–145. Ed. by D. Angelov. Sofia: Izdatelstvo na Bălgarskata Akademiia na Naukite, 1987.

"Das altbulgarische Kloster bei Ravna – das Schrifttums- und Kulturzentrum." In *La vie quotidienne des moines et chanoines réguliers au Moyen Age et temps modernes. Actes du Premier Colloque International du L.A.R.H.C.O.R. Wrocław-Książ, 30 nov. – 4 dec. 1994*, pp. 691–699. Ed. by M. Derwich. Wrocław: Institut d'histoire de l'Université de Wroclaw, 1995.

Popkonstantinov, K. and O. Kronsteiner. *Starobălgarski nadpisi. Altbulgarische Inschriften*. 2vols. Salzburg: Institut für Slawistik der Universität Salzburg, 1994 and 1997.

Popkonstantinov, K. and V. Popkonstantinova. "Die Inschriften des Felsklosters Murfatlar." In *Paleobalkanistika i starobălgaristika. Părvi esenni nacionalni cheteniia "Profesor Ivan Gălăbov"*, pp. 111–134. Ed. by E. Dogramadzhieva and K. Popkonstantinov. Veliko Tărnovo: Universitetsko izdatelstvo "Sv. sv. Kiril i Metodii," 1995.

Popov, A. "Tărnovskata 'Velika Lavra'." *Izvestiia na Bălgarskoto istorichesko druzhestvo*, vol. 37 (1980), pp. 83–98.

"Metalurgichnoto proizvodstvo v Tărnvograd (XII–XIV v.)." In *Sbornik v pamet na prof. Stancho Vaklinov*, pp. 204–207. Ed. by V. Giuzelev. Sofia: Izdatelstvo na Bălgarskata Akademiia na Naukite, 1984.

"Tărnovo à la lumière des études archéologiques." In *Harmos. Timetikos tomos ston kathegete N. K. Moutsopoulo gia ta 25 khronia pneumatikes tou prosphoras sto panepistemio*, pp. 1537–1541. Vol. III. Thessaloniki: Aristotelio Panepistemio Thessalonikes, 1991.

Popović, I. "Les particularités de l'outillage protobyzantin dans les Balkans du Nord." *Starinar*, vols. 45–46 (1994–1995), pp. 67–75.

Zlatni avarski poias iz okoline Sirmiuma. Belgrade: Narodni Muzej and Arheološki Institut, 1997.

Popović, M. "Monastère St. Pierre de Campo près de Trebinje." *WMBHL*, vol. 6 (1979), pp. 271–287.

Beogradska tvrđava. Belgrade: Arheološki Institut, 1982.

"Les forteresses du système défensif byzantin en Serbie aux XIe–XIIe siècles." *Starinar*, vol. 42 (1991), pp. 169–185.

"Vojvodina u okvirima ugarske srednjovekovne države (896–1526)." In *Muzej Vojvodine. Stalna postavka*, pp. 111–122. Ed. by L. Čerović. Novi Sad: Muzej Vojvodine, 1997.

"Zemaljano-palisadne i suhozidne fortifikacije u srpsko-vizantijskim sukobima krajem 11. veka." *ZRVI*, vol. 36 (1997), pp. 119–138.

"La céramique importée dans les forteresses byzantines des Serbie au XIIe siècle." In *Balkania kai Anatolike Mesogeios, 12os–17os aiones. Praktika tou Diethnous Symposiou ste Mneme D. A. Zakythinou. Athena, 14–15 Ianouariou 1994*, pp. 185–198. Ed. by L. Mavrommates. Athens: Institouto Byzantinon Ereunon, 1998.

Tvrđava Ras. Belgrade: Arheološki Institut, 1999.

"Vladarsko boravište Stefana Nemanje u Rasu." In *Meždunarodni naučni skup "Stefan Nemanja-Sveti Simeon Mirotočivi. Istorija i predanje", Septembar 1996*, pp. 233–248. Ed. by J. Kalić. Belgrade: Srpska Akademija Nauka i Umetnosti, 2000.

Popović, M. and V. Ivanišević. "Grad Braničevo u sredniem veku." *Starinar*, vol. 39 (1988), pp. 125–179.

Popović, S. "Prolegomena to early monasticism in the Balkans as documented in architecture." *Starinar*, vol. 49 (1998), pp. 131–144.

Popović, V. "L'évêché de Sirmium et l'église médiévale dans les Balkans." In *Le site d'habitation médiéval de Mačvanska Mitrovica*, pp. i–ix. Ed. by D. Minić. Belgrade: Institut archéologique, 1980.

"Byzantins, Slaves et autochtones dans les provinces de Prévalitane et Nouvelle Epire." In *Villes et peuplement dans l'Illyricum protobyzantin. Actes du colloque organisé par l'Ecole Française de Rome, Rome 12–14 mai 1982*, pp. 181–243. Rome: Ecole Française de Rome, 1984.

Poulos, P. D. *Sv. Ivan Rilski. Vechen nebesen pokrovitel na bălgarskiia narod*. Sofia: Universitetsko izdatelstvo "Sv. Kliment Okhridski," 1992.

Poulter, A. G. *Nicopolis ad Istrum: A Roman, Late Roman, and Early Byzantine City*. London: Society for the Promotion of Roman Studies, 1995.

Preshlenov, Kh. "A late antique pattern of fortification in the eastern Stara Planina mountain (the pass of Djulino)." *AB*, vol. 5 (2001), pp. 33–43.

Primov, B. "Bulgaria in the eighth century. A general outline." *Byzantinobulgarica*, vol. 5 (1978), pp. 7–40.

Prinzing, G. "Demetrios-Kirche und Aseniden-Aufstand. Zur chronologischen Präzisierung der Frühphase des Aseniden-Aufstandes." *ZRVI*, vol. 38 (1999–2000), pp. 257–265.

Pritsak, O. *Die bulgarische Fürstenliste und die Sprache der Protobulgaren*. Wiesbaden: Otto Harrassowitz, 1955.

"The Pechenegs: a case of social and economic transformation." *AEMA*, vol. 1 (1975), pp. 211–235.

"The initial formula ΚΑΝΑϹΥΒΗΓΗ in the proto-Bulgarian inscriptions." In *Studia slavica mediaevalia et humanistica Riccardo Picchio dicata*, pp. 595–601. Ed. by M. Colucci, G. dell' Agata, and H. Goldblat. Vol. II. Rome: Edizioni dell'Ateneo, 1986.

Radić, R. "Sveti Sava i smrt oblasnog gospodara Streza." In *Sveti Sava u srpskoj istoriji i tradiciji*, pp. 51–62. Ed. by S. Ćirković. Belgrade: Srpska Akademija Nauka i Umetnosti, 1998.

Radojčić, S. "Temnički natpis. Sujeverice srednjovekovnih graditelja o čudotvornoj moci imena i likova sevastijskih mučenika." *ZLU*, vol. 5 (1969), pp. 1–11.

"Lik svetoga Save u Domentijanovom Životu i podvizima arkhiepiskopa sve srpske i pomorske zemlje prepodobnog i bogonosnog nastavnika Save." In *Meždunarodni naučni skup "Sava Nemanjić-Sveti Sava. Istorija i predanje". Decembar 1976*, pp. 215–222. Ed. by V. Djurić. Belgrade: Srpska Akademija Nauka i Umetnosti, 1979.

Radosavljević, V. *Miroslavljevo jevan đelje. Studie u vezi sa tehnologijom izrade, stanjem i zaštitom*. Belgrade: Narodna Biblioteka Srbije, 1994.

Radosavljević-Krunić, S. "Une necropole médiévale à Ljubičevac." *Đerdapske sveske*, vol. 3 (1986), pp. 329–341.

Rădulescu, A. and V. Lungu. "Le christianisme en Scythie Mineure à la lumière des dernières découvertes archéologiques." In *Actes du XIe Congrès international d'archéologie chrétienne, Lyon, Vienne, Grenoble, Genève et Aoste, 21–28 septembre 1986*, pp. 2561–2615. Vol. III. Rome: Ecole Française de Rome, 1989.

Rady, M. "The Mongol invasion of Hungary." *Medieval World*, vol. 3 (1991), pp. 39–46.

Rafalovich, I. A. "Zemledelie u rannykh slavian v Moldavii (VI–IX vv.)." In *Dalekoe proshloe Moldavii*, pp. 75–90. Ed. by N. A. Ketraru, V. I. Markevich, L. L. Polevoi, and G. D. Smirnov. Kishinew: Redakcionno-izdatel'skii otdel Akademii Nauk Moldavskoi SSR, 1969.

Rakova, S. "Le bogomilisme et l'église bosniaque." *Heresis*, vol. 19 (1992), pp. 19–29.

Rapanić, Ž. *Predromaničko doba u Dalmaciji*. Split: Logos, 1987.

Rashev, R. "L'Onglos – témoignages écrits et faits archéologiques." *BHR*, vol. 10 (1982), pp. 68–79.

Starobălgarski ukrepleniia na Dolniia Dunav (VII–XI v.). Varna: Knigoizdatelstvo "Georgi Bakalov," 1982.

"Pliska – the first capital of Bulgaria." In *Ancient Bulgaria. Papers presented to the International Symposium on the Ancient History and Archaeology of Bulgaria, University of Nottingham 1981*, pp. 255–267. Ed. by A. G. Poulter. Nottingham: Department of Classical and Archaeological Studies, University of Nottingham, 1983.

"Les vallums de Dobrudža dans le développement de la fortification ancienne bulgare." In *Dobrudža. Etudes ethno-culturelles. Recueil d'articles*, pp. 48–56. Ed. by D. Angelov. Sofia: Izdatelstvo na Bălgarskata Akademiia na Naukite, 1987.

"K rannei istorii prabolgar na Nizhnem Dunae." In *Novoe v srednevekovoi arkheologii Evrazii*, pp. 184–191. Ed. by V. B. Kovalevskaia. Samara: Istoriko-kul'turnaia associaciia "Artefakt," 1993.

"La plus ancienne période de l'état bulgare." In *Von der Scythia zur Dobrudža*, pp. 49–54. Ed. by Kh. Kholiolchev, R. Pillinger, and R. Harreither. Vienna: Verein "Freunde des Hauses Wittgenstein," 1997.

"Madarskiiat konnik – stari i novi văprosi." *Istoricheski pregled*, vol. 54 (1998), pp. 192–204.

Rashev, R. and I. Dimitrov. *Pliska. 100 godini arkheologicheski razkopki*. Shumen: Svetlana, 1999.

Rashev, R. and V. Docheva. "Iurtoobrazna postroika v Pliska." *Problemi na prabălgarskata istoriia i kultura*, vol. 1 (1989) pp. 291–313.

Rashev, R. and S. Stanilov. "Kenotaf für einem Herrscher bei der ersten bulgarischen Hauptstadt Pliska." *Das Altertum*, vol. 44 (1998), pp. 67–72.

Raukar, T. "Land and society." In *Croatia in the Early Middle Ages. A Cultural Survey*, pp. 181–195. Ed. by I. Supičić. London: Philip Wilson Publishers and Zagreb: AGM, 1999.

Reimitz, H. "Conversion and control: the establishment of liturgical frontiers in Carolingian Pannonia." In *The Transformation of Frontiers from Late Antiquity to the Carolingians*, pp. 89–207. Ed. by W. Pohl, I. Wood, and H. Reimitz. Leiden, Boston, and Cologne: Brill, 2001.

Risos, A. "The Vlachs of Larissa in the 10th century." *Byzantinoslavica*, vol. 51 (1990), pp. 202–207.

Riveros, J. M. "Croatas y Serbios en el *De Administrando Imperio* de Constantino VII Porphyrogenito." *Bizantion Nea Hellás*, vols. 13–15 (1993–1996), pp. 55–79.

Roesler, R. "Über den Zeitpunkt der slavischen Ansiedlung an der unteren Donau." *Sitzungsberichte der kaiserlichen Akademie der Wissenschaften. Philosophische-historische Klasse*, vol. 73 (1873), pp. 77–126.

Romhanyi, B. "The role of the Cistercians in medieval Hungary: political activity or internal colonization?" *AMS* (1993–1994), pp. 180–204.

Róna-Tas, A. "Where was Khuvrat's Bulgharia?" *Acta Orientalia Academiae Scientiarum Hungaricae*, vol. 53 (2000), pp. 1–22.

Runciman, S. *A History of the First Bulgarian Empire*. London: G. Bell & Sons, 1930.

"The first crusaders' journey across the Balkan Peninsula." *Byzantion*, vol. 19 (1949), pp. 207–221.

Ruseva, V. "Mortality patterns and life expectancy in medieval skeleton populations from Bulgaria (VIII–X c. AD)." *AB*, vol. 7 (2003), pp. 77–84.

Rusu, A. A. "Die Frage der vom Deutschen Orden im Südosten Siebenbürgens errichteten Burgen." *Castrum Bene*, vol. 5 (1996), pp. 165–172.

Săbev, T. *Samostoina narodnostna cărkva v srednovekovna Bălgariia. Khristiianizatorski proces, osnovavane i văzkhod, avtokefaliia i mezhducărkovno polozhenie: cărkva i dărzhava, rolia i znachenie*. Sofia: Sinodalno izdatelstvo, 1987.

Sanders, G. D. R. "New relative and absolute chronologies for 9th to 13th century glazed wares at Corinth: methodology and social conclusions." In *Byzanz als Raum. Zu Methoden und Inhalten der historischen Geographie des östlichen Mittelmeerraumes*, pp. 153–173. Ed. by K. Belke, F. Hild, J. Koder, and P. Soustal. Vienna: Verlag der Österreichischen Akademie der Wissenschaften, 2000.

"Corinth." In *The Economic History of Byzantium from the Seventh through the Fifteenth Century*, pp. 647–654. Ed. by A. E. Laiou. Washington: Dumbarton Oaks Research Library and Collection, 2002.

Šanjek, F. *Les chrétiens bosniaques et le mouvement cathare, XIIe–XVe siècles*. Brussels, Paris, and Louvain: Nauwelaerts, 1976.

"La réforme grégorienne en Croatie sous le règne de Demetrius Zvonimir (1075–1089)." *SG*, vol. 14 (1991), pp. 245–251.

Saradi, H. "Aspects of early Byzantine urbanism in Albania." In *Hoi Albanoi sto mesaiona*, pp. 81–130. Ed. by Ch. Gasparis. Athens: Institouto Byzantinon Ereunon, 1998.

Savvides, A. G. C. "A note on the death of Leo Sgouros in AD 1208." *BMGS*, vol. 12 (1988), pp. 289–295.

"Morea and Islam, 8th–15th centuries." *Journal of Oriental and African Studies*, vol. 2 (1990), pp. 47–75.

Scărlătoiu, E. "La romanité balkanique. Origines et diffusion." *RESEE*, vol. 29 (1991), pp. 191–202; and vol. 30 (1992), pp. 11–17.

Schellewald, B. M. *Die Architektur der Sophienkirche in Ohrid*. Bonn: Rheinische Friedrich-Wilhelm-Univesität, 1986.

Schenker, A. M. *The Dawn of Slavic. An Introduction to Slavic Philology*. New Haven and London: Yale University Press, 1995.

Schreiner, P. "Das Christentum in Bulgarien vor 864." In *Das Christentum in Bulgarien und auf der übrigen Balkanhalbinsel in der Spätantike und im frühen Mittelalter*, pp. 51–57. Ed. by V. Giuzelev and R. Pillinger. Vienna: Verein "Freunde des Hauses Wittgenstein," 1987.

Schwartz, E. C. "Medieval ceramic decoration in Bulgaria." *Byzantinoslavica*, vol. 43 (1982), pp. 45–50.

Seibt, W. "Untersuchungen zur Vor- und Frühgeschichte der 'bulgarischen' Kometopulen." *Handes Amsorya*, vol. 89 (1975), pp. 66–98.

"Siegel als Quelle für Slawenarchonten in Griechenland." *Studies in Byzantine Sigillography*, vol. 6 (1999), pp. 27–36.

"Weitere Beobachtungen zu Siegeln früher Slawenarchonten in Griechenland." In *Byzantium, State and Society. In Memory of Nikos Oikonomides*, pp. 459–466. Ed. by A. Avramea, A. E. Laiou, and E. Chrysos. Athens: Institute for Byzantine Studies, 2003.

Sekelj-Ivančan, T. *Catalogue of Medieval Sites in Continental Croatia*. Oxford: Tempus Reparatum, 1995.

Semkov, G. "Der sozial-ökonomische Hintergrund der Bogomilen in Bulgarien und Byzanz wie auch der Patarener in Bosnien. Suite et fin." *Heresis*, vol. 4 (1985), pp. 37–62.

Shandrovskaia, V. S. "Iz istorii Bolgarii X–XI vv. po dannym sfragistiki." *Byzantinobulgarica*, vol. 7 (1981), pp. 455–467.

Shchepkin, V. N. *Savvina kniga*. St. Petersburg: Imperatorskaia Akademiia Nauk, Otdelenie russkogo iazyka i slovesnosti, 1903.

Shepard, J. "John Mauropous, Leo Tornicius and an alleged Russian army: the chronology of the Pecheneg crisis of 1048–1049." *JOB*, vol. 24 (1975), pp. 61–89.

"Symeon of Bulgaria – peacemaker." *GSU*, vol. 83 (1989), pp. 9–48.

"A marriage too far? Maria Lekapena and Peter of Bulgaria." In *The Empress Theophano: Byzantium and the West at the Turn of the First*

Millennium, pp. 121–149. Ed. by A. Davids. Cambridge: Cambridge University Press, 1995.

"Slavs and Bulgars." In *The New Cambridge Medieval History*, pp. 228–248. Ed. by T. Reuter. Vol. II. Cambridge: Cambridge University Press, 1998.

"Bulgaria: the other Balkan 'empire'." In *The New Cambridge Medieval History*, pp. 567–585. Ed. by T. Reuter. Vol. III. Cambridge: Cambridge University Press, 1999.

"Byzantium and the steppe-nomads: the Hungarian dimension." In *Byzanz und Ostmitteleuropa, 950–1453. Beiträge zu einer table-ronde des XIX Internationalen Congress of Byzantine Studies, Copenhagen 1996*, pp. 55–83. Ed. by G. Prinzing and M. Salamon. Wiesbaden: Otto Harrassowitz, 1999.

"The ruler as instructor, pastor, and wise: Leo VI of Byzantium and Symeon of Bulgaria." In *Alfred the Great. Papers from the Eleventh-Centenary Conferences*, pp. 339–358. Ed. by T. Reuter. Aldershot: Ashgate, 2003.

Sheppard, C. D. "Pre-Romanesque sculpture: evidence for the cultural evolution of the people of the Dalmatian coast." *Gesta*, vol. 23 (1984), pp. 7–16.

Shtereva, I. and M. Manolova. "About the problem of the origin of slip-coated ceramics from 11th–12th century Bulgaria." *AB*, vol. 5 (2001), pp. 57–63.

Silagi, G., ed. *Die "Gesta Hungarorum" des anonymen Notars. Die älteste Darstellung der ungarischen Geschichte*. Sigmaringen: Jan Thorbecke, 1991.

"Bishop Gerard (Gellért) of Csanád." In *Europe's Centre around A.D. 1000*, p. 417. Ed. by A. Wieczorek and H.-M. Hinz. Stuttgart: Theiss, 2000.

Simeonova, L. "Power in Nicholas Mysticus' letters to Symeon of Bulgaria. Notes on the political vocabulary of a tenth-century Byzantine statesman." *Byzantinoslavica*, vol. 54 (1993), pp. 89–94.

Diplomacy of the Letter and the Cross. Photios, Bulgaria, and the Papacy, 860s–880s. Amsterdam: Adolf Hakkert, 1998.

Simpson, C. "The Croats and the Glagolitic alphabet." *Medieval World*, vol. 7 (1992), pp. 17–23.

Sindik, D. I. "Stefan Nemanja i Kotor." In *Meždunarodni naučni skup "Stefan Nemanja-Sveti Simeon Mirotočivi. Istorija i predanje", Septembar 1996*, pp. 115–120. Ed. by J. Kalić. Belgrade: Srpska Akademija Nauka i Umetnosti, 2000.

Sindik, I. *Komunalno uredenje Kotora od druge polovine XII do početka XV stoljeća*. Belgrade: Naučna knjiga, 1950.

Sinos, S. *Die Klosterkirche der Kosmosoteira in Bera (Vira)*. Munich: C. H. Beck, 1985.

Smiljanić, F. "Kapitul kod Knina." *Radovi Filozofskog fakulteta u Zadru*, vol. 38 (1986–1987), pp. 53–95.

Sokol, V. "The archaeological heritage of the early Croats." In *Croatia in the Early Middle Ages. A Cultural Survey*, pp. 117–146. Ed. by I. Supičić. London: Philip Wilson Publishers and Zagreb: AGM, 1999.

Soulis, G. C. "On the Slavic settlement in Hierissos in the tenth century." *Byzantion*, vol. 23 (1953), pp. 67–72.

Soustal, P. "Bemerkungen zur byzantinisch-bulgarischen Grenze im 9. Jahrhundert." *Mitteilungen des Bulgarischen Forschungsinstitut in Österreich*, vol. 8 (1986), pp. 150–152.

Spinei, V. *Realităţi etnice şi politice în Moldova meridională în secolele X–XIII. Români şi turanici*. Iaşi: Junimea, 1985.

Moldavia in the 11th–14th Centuries. Bucharest: Editura Academiei Republicii Socialiste România, 1986.

"The Turkish nomadic population in Romanian countries in the 10th–14th centuries." In *Kongreye sunulan bildiriler X. Türk Tarih Kongresi, Ankara, 22–26 Eylül 1986*, pp. 981–989. Vol. III. Ankara: Türk Tarih Kurumu Basimevi, 1991.

"Les Petchénègues au nord du Bas-Danube aux Xe–XIe siècles." In *Actes du XIIe Congrès international des sciences préhistoriques et protohistoriques, Bratislava, 1–7 septembre 1991*, pp. 285–290. Ed. by J. Pavuj. Vol. IV. Bratislava: Institut Archéologique de l'Académie Slovaque des Sciences, 1993.

Ultimele valuri migratoare la nordul Mării Negre şi al Dunării de Jos. Iaşi: Helios, 1996.

The Great Migrations in the East and South East of Europe from the Ninth to the Thirteenth Century. Cluj-Napoca: Center for Transylvanian Studies and Braila: Istros, 2003.

Stanchev, K. and G. Popov. *Kliment Okhridski. Zhivot i tvorchestvo*. Sofia: Universitetsko izdatelstvo "Kliment Okhridski," 1988.

Stănescu, E. "Les 'Mixobarbares' du Bas-Danube au XIe siècle (quelques problèmes de la terminologie des textes)." *Nouvelles études d'histoire*, vol. 3 (1965), pp. 45–53.

Stanojev, N. *Nekropole X–XV veka u Vojvodini*. Novi Sad: Arheološko društvo Vojvodine, 1989.

Srednjovekovna seoska naselja od V do XV veka u Vojvodini. Novi Sad: Muzej Vojvodine, 1996.

"Les maisons du loess de Pannonie et des communautés du Moyen Age." In *The Rural House from the Migration Period to the Oldest Still Standing Buildings. Ruralia IV, 8.–13. September 2001, Bad Bederkesa, Lower Saxony, Germany*, pp. 333–338. Ed. by J. Klápšte. Prague: Institute of Archaeology, Academy of Sciences of the Czech Republic, 2002.

Stavrakos, C. "Die Vita des hl. Nikon Metanoeite als Quelle zur Prosopographie der Peloponnes im späten 10. Jahrhundert." *Südost-Forschungen*, vol. 58 (1999), pp. 1–7.

Stavridou-Zafraka, A. "The development of the theme organisation in Macedonia." In *Byzantine Macedonia: Identity, Image, and History. Papers from the Melbourne Conference, July 1995*, pp. 128–138. Ed. by J. Burke and R. Scott. Melbourne: Australian Association for Byzantine Studies, 2000.

Ştefan, Gh., I. Barnea, M. Comşa, and E. Comşa. *Dinogetia I. Aşezarea feudală timpurie de la Bisericuţa-Garvăn*. Bucharest: Editura Academiei Republicii Socialiste România, 1967.

Steindorff, L. *Die dalmatinischen Städte im 12. Jahrhundert. Studien zu ihrer politischen Stellung und gesellschaftlichen Entwicklung*. Cologne and Vienna: Böhlau, 1984.

"Die Synode auf der Planities Dalmae. Reichseinteilung und Kirchenorganisation im Bild der Chronik des Priesters von Dioclea." *Mitteilungen des Instituts für Österreichische Geschichtsforschung*, vol. 93 (1985), pp. 279–324.

Stepanov, C. *Vlast i avtoritet v rannosrednovekovna Bălgariia (VII–sr. XI v.)*. Sofia: Agató, 1999.

"The Bulgar title ΚΑΝΑΣΥΒΙΓΙ: reconstructing the notions of divine kingship in Bulgaria, AD 822–836." *Early Medieval Europe*, vol. 10 (2001), pp. 1–19.

Stephenson, P. "Manuel I Comnenus and Geza II: a revised context and chronology for Hungaro-Byzantine relations, 1148–1155." *Byzantinoslavica*, vol. 55 (1994), pp. 251–277.

"The Byzantine frontier at the Lower Danube in the late tenth and eleventh centuries." In *Frontiers in Question. Eurasian Borderlands, 700–1700*, pp. 80–104. Ed. by D. Power and N. Standen. New York: St. Martin's Press, 1999.

Byzantium's Balkan Frontier. A Political Study of the Northern Balkans, 900–1204. Cambridge: Cambridge University Press, 2000.

The Legend of Basil the Bulgar-Slayer. Cambridge and New York: Cambridge University Press, 2003.

Štih, P. *Studien zur Geschichte der Grafen von Görz. Die Ministerialen und Milites der Grafen von Görz in Istrien und Krain*. Vienna: Oldenbourg, 1996.

"Der ostadriatische Raum um das Jahr 1000." In *Europe around the Year 1000*, pp. 205–219. Ed. by P. Urbańczyk. Warsaw: Wydawnictwo DiG, 2001.

"Začetki in razmah listinskega pismenstva na ozemlju Slovenije do konca 11. stoletja." *Zgodovinski Časopis*, vol. 55 (2003), pp. 279–90.

Stipišić, J. "Hrvatski dvorski dignitar 'risarius'." *Zbornik Historijskog Zavoda Jugoslavenske Akademije Znanosti i Umjetnosti*, vol. 12 (1982), pp. 1–7.

"Croatia in diplomatic sources up to the end of the 11th century." In *Croatia in the Early Middle Ages. A Cultural Survey*, pp. 285–318. Ed. by I. Supičić. London: Philip Wilson Publishers and Zagreb: AGM, 1999.

Stoinev, Anani. *Sv. Ivan Rilski, oficialnoto khristiianstvo i bogomilstvoto*. Sofia: Far, 1991.

Stokes, A. D. "The background and chronology of the Balkan campaigns of Svyatoslav Igorevich." *SEER*, vol. 40 (1961–1962), pp. 44–57.

Stoliarik, E. S. *Essays on Monetary Circulation in the North-Western Black Sea Region in the Late Roman and Byzantine Periods (Late 3rd Century–Early 13th Century* AD*)*. Odessa: Polis, 1992.

Suić, M. "Prilog tumačenju natpisa kraljice Jelene." *SP*, vol. 14 (1984), pp. 15–39.

Sullivan, R. "Khan Boris and the conversion of Bulgaria: a case study of the impact of Christianity on a barbarian society." *Studies in Medieval and Renaissance History*, vol. 3 (1966), pp. 55–139.

Svoronos, N. "Recherches sur le cadastre byzantin et la fiscalité aux XIe et XIIe siècles: le cadastre de Thèbes." *Bulletin de Correspondance Hellénique*, vol. 83 (1959), pp. 1–166.

Sweeney, J. R. "Thomas of Spalato and the Mongols: a thirteenth-century Dalmatian view of Mongol customs." *Florilegium: Carleton University Annual Papers on Classical Antiquity and the Middle Ages*, vol. 4 (1982), pp. 156–183.

"Identifying the medieval refugee: Hungarians in flight during the Mongol invasion." In *Forms of Identity. Definitions and Changes*, pp. 63–76. Ed. by L. Löb, I. Petrovics, and G. E. Szönyi. Szeged: József Attila University Press, 1994.

Szádeczky-Kardoss, S. "Der awarisch-türkische Einfluss auf die byzantinische Kriegskunst um 600 (Anmerkungen zum Strategikon des Maurikios)." *Studia turco-hungarica*, vol. 5 (1981), pp. 63–71.

Avarica. Über die Awarengeschichte und ihre Quellen. Szeged: JATE, 1986.

"Die Nachricht des Isidorus Hispalensis und des spanischen Fortsetzers seiner 'Historia' über einen Slaweneinfall in Griechenland." In *Szlávok-Protobolgárok-Bizánc*, pp. 51–61. Ed. by N. Nikolov, S. Szádeczky-Kardoss, and T. Olajos. Szeged: József Attila University Press, 1986.

"The Avars." In *The Cambridge History of Early Inner Asia*, pp. 206–228. Ed. by D. Sinor. Cambridge and New York: Cambridge University Press, 1990.

"Vernachlässigte Quellenangaben zur Geschichte des ersten awarischen Khaganates." In *Varia Eurasiatica. Festschrift für Professor András Róna-Tas*, pp. 171–182. Szeged: Department of Altaic Studies, József Attila University Press, 1991.

Szameit, E. "Die Karantanen und Donauslawen im 8. Jahrhundert." In *Reitervölker aus dem Osten. Hunnen + Awaren. Burgenländische Landesausstellung 1996, Schloß Halbturn, 26. April–31. Oktober 1996*, pp. 320–325. Ed. by F. Daim, K. Kaus, and P. Tomka. Eisenstadt: Amt der Burgenländischen Landesregierung, 1996.

"Slawische Körpergräber des 8. Jh. im österreichischen Donauraum und ihre Beziehungen zum spätmerowingischen Kulturkreis." In *Ethnische und kulturelle Verhältnisse an der mittleren Donau vom 6. bis zum 11. Jahrhundert. Symposium Nitra 6. bis 10. November 1994*, pp. 215–226. Ed. by D. Bialeková and J. Zábojník. Bratislava: VEDA, 1996.

Székely, Z. "L'aspect de la culture matérielle des VIIIe–Xe siècles dans le sud-est de la Transylvanie." *Mitteilungen des archäologischen Instituts der Ungarischen Akademie der Wissenschaften*, vol. 1 (1972), pp. 125–128.

"Contribuţii la problema stabilirii secuilor în sud-estul Transilvaniei." *Crisia*, vol. 4 (1974), pp. 89–99.

"Pecenegii în sud-estul Transilvaniei." *Aluta*, vols. 17–18 (1988), pp. 197–210.

Szekeres, L. *Középkori települések Északkelet-Bácskában*. Ujvidék: Forum, 1983.

Szmoniewski, B. Sz. "Production of early medieval ornaments made of non-ferrous metals: dies from archaeological finds in north-east Romania." *Acta Archaeologica Carpathica*, vol. 37 (2002), pp. 111–135.

Szovák, K. "'Wer war der anonyme Notar?' Zur Bestimmung des Verfassers der *Gesta Hungarorum*." *Ungarn-Jahrbuch*, vol. 19 (1991), pp. 1–17.

Tachiaos, A. E. "Some controversial points relating to the life and activity of Cyril and Methodius." *Cyrillomethodianum*, vols. 17–18 (1993–1994), pp. 41–72.

Takács, M. "Einige Aspekte der Siedlungsgeschichte des südlichen Drittels des Donau-Theiss-Zwischenstromlandes von der awarischen Landnahme bis zum Ende des 11. Jahrhunderts." *AAASH*, vol. 51 (1999–2000), pp. 457–472.

Tănase, M. "L'expansion de Cîteaux dans le sud-est européen. Essai de localisation des possessions cisterciennes de Transylvanie." In *Crises et réformes dans l'Eglise de la Réforme grégorienne à la Préréforme. Actes du 115e Congrès national des sociétés savantes, Avignon, 1990, Section d'Histoire médiévale et de philologie*, pp. 79–90. Paris: Editions du Comité des Travaux Historiques et Scientifiques, 1991.

Tăpkova-Zaimova, V. "Les Mixobarbaroi et la situation politique et ethnique au Bas-Danube pendant la seconde moitié du XIe siècle." In *Actes du XIVe Congrès International des Etudes Byzantines, Bucarest, 6–12 septembre 1971*, pp. 615–619. Vol. II. Bucharest: Editura Academiei Republicii Socialiste România, 1975.

Tentiuc, I. *Populaţia din Moldova centrală în secolele XI–XIII.* Iaşi: Helios, 1996.

Teofilov, T. "Izsledvaniia vărkhu problema za stilovata rekonstrukciia na cărkvata 'Sv. Dimităr Solunski' văv Veliko Tărnovo." *Godishnik na muzeite ot Severna Bălgariia*, vol. 17 (1991), pp. 67–87.

Teteriatnikov, N. "Sanctuary design in the ninth- and tenth-century churches in Bulgaria: the question of origin." *GSU*, vols. 84–85 (1994), pp. 197–209.

The Chronicle of Theophanes Confessor. Byzantine and Near Eastern History AD *284–813*. English translation by C. Mango and R. Scott. Oxford: Clarendon Press, 1997.

Theophylact Simocatta. *History*. English translation by Michael Whitby and Mary Whitby. Oxford: Clarendon Press, 1986.

Thomson, F. J. "Cosmas of Bulgaria and his discourse against the heresy of Bogomil." *SEER*, vol. 54 (1976), pp. 263–269.

"John the Exarch's theological education and proficiency in Greek as revealed by his abridged translation of John of Damascus' 'De fide orthodoxa'." *Palaeobulgarica*, vol. 15 (1991), pp. 35–58.

"The Symeonic Florilegium – problems of its origin, content, textology and edition, together with an English translation of the Eulogy of Tzar Symeon." *Palaeobulgarica*, vol. 17 (1993), pp. 37–53.

"Has the Cyrillomethodian translation of the Bible survived?" In *Thessaloniki Magna Moravia*, pp. 149–163. Thessaloniki: St. Cyril and Methodios Center for Cultural Studies, 1999.

Tivchev, P. and G. Cankova-Petkova. "Au sujet des relations féodales dans les territoires bulgares sous la domination byzantine à la fin du XIe siècle et pendant la première moitié du XIIe siècle." *Byzantinobulgarica*, vol. 2 (1966), pp. 107–125.

Todorova, H. "Die frühmittelalterliche Siedlung auf der grossen Insel bei Durankulak." *Das Altertum*, vol. 26 (1980), pp. 234–236.

Tomičić, Ž. "Rezultati ranosrednjevjekovnih arheoloških istraživanja u Međimurju i varaždinskoj regiji." *Izdanja Hrvatskog arheološkog društva*, vol. 2 (1978), pp. 209–222.

"Prilog istraživanju kronologije srednjovjekovnoga groblja na položaju Lijeva bara u Vukovaru." *SP*, vol. 20 (1990), pp. 111–189.

"Neuere Erforschungen der Bijelo-Brdo-Kultur in Kroatien." *Prilozi Instituta za arheologiju u Zagrebu*, vol. 9 (1992), pp. 113–130.

Torbatov, S. "Quaestura exercitus: Moesia Secunda and Scythia under Justinian." *AB*, vol. 1 (1997), pp. 78–87.

Torcellan, M. *Le tre necropoli altomedioevali di Pinguente*. Florence: All'insegna di Giglio, 1986.

Totev, K. "Steatitovi ikoni na Sveti Georgi ot srednovekovna Bălgariia." In *Sbornik v chest na akad. Dimităr Angelov*, pp. 226–235. Ed. by V. Velkov,

Zh. Aladzhov, G. Bakalov, et al. Sofia: Izdatelstvo na Bălgarskata Akademiia na Naukite, 1994.

Totev, K., I. Chokoev, and E. Dermendzhiev. "Cărkvata 'Sv. Chetirideset Măchenici' văv Veliko Tărnovo spored poslednite arkheologicheski razkopki." In *Obshchestvo, ekonomika, kul'tura i isskusstvo slavian*, pp. 104–115. Ed. by V. V. Sedov. Moscow: Institut Arkheologii, Rossiiskaia Akademiia Nauk, 1998.

Totev, T. "Za obrabotkata na kost v srednovekovna Bălgariia." *Arkheologiia*, vol. 5 (1963), pp. 83–92.

"Srebărna chasha s nadpis ot Preslav." *IAI*, vol. 27 (1964), pp. 5–15.

"Bazilika pri Sakalova Mogila v Preslav." *Preslav. Sbornik*, vol. 2 (1976), pp. 38–61.

"Icônes peintes en céramique de 'Tuzlalăka' à Preslav." In *Culture et art en Bulgarie médiévale (VIIIe–XIVe siècles)*, pp. 65–73. Ed. by D. Angelov, I. Changova, G. I. Georgiev, et al. Sofia: Izdatelstvo na Bălgarskata Akademiia na Naukite, 1979.

Manastirăt v "Tuzlalăka" – centăr na risuvana keramika v Preslav IX–X v. Sofia: Izdatelstvo na Bălgarskata Akademiia na Naukite, 1982.

"Krăstovidna cărkva pod osnovite na Goliamata bazilika v Pliska (865–866)." In *Sbornik v pamet na prof. Stancho Vaklinov*, pp. 160–169. Ed. by V. Giuzelev. Sofia: Izdatelstvo na Bălgarskata Akademiia na Naukite, 1984.

"L'atelier de céramique peinte du monastère royal de Preslav." *CA*, vol. 35 (1987), pp. 65–80.

The Preslav Treasure. Shumen: Antos, 1993.

Great Preslav. Sofia: Professor Marin Drinov Academic Publishing House, 2001.

Tóth, S. L. "Hungarian–Bulgarian contacts in the ninth century." In *Hungaro-Bulgarica V. Szegedi Bolgarisztika*, pp. 71–78. Ed. by S. Szádeczky-Kardoss, T. Olajos, I. H. Tóth, and I. Ferincz. Szeged: Kiadja a JATE-Press, 1994.

"The territories of the Hungarian tribal federation around 950 (some observations on Constantine VII's 'Tourkia')." In *Byzanz und Ostmitteleuropa, 950–1453. Beiträge zu einer table-ronde des XIX Internationalen Congress of Byzantine Studies, Copenhagen 1996*, pp. 23–33. Ed. by G. Prinzing and M. Salamon. Wiesbaden: Otto Harrassowitz, 1999.

Trapp, E. "Die Viten des hl. Naum von Ochrid." *Byzantinoslavica*, vol. 35 (1974), pp. 161–185.

Trbuhović, L. "Avar finds from Sirmium and the surrounding region." In *Sirmium. Recherches archéologiques en Syrmie*, pp. 61–75. Vol. IV. Ed. by N. Duval, E. L. Ochsenschlager, and V. Popović. Belgrade: Institut Archéologique de Belgrade, Ecole Française de Rome, and the Research Foundation of the City University of New York, 1982.

Treadgold, W. "The Bulgars' treaty with the Byzantines in 816." *Rivista di studi bizantini e slavi*, vols. 4–5 (1985), pp. 213–220.

Tryjarski, E. "Alte und neue Probleme der runenartigen Inschriften Europas. Ein Versuch der Entzifferung der Texte aus Murfatlar und Pliska." In *Runen, Tamgas und Graffiti aus Asien und Osteuropa*, pp. 53–80. Ed. by K. Röhrborn and W. Veenker. Wiesbaden: Otto Harrassowitz, 1985.

Turlej, S. "The so-called Chronicle of Monemvasia. A historical analysis." *Byzantion*, vol. 68 (1998), pp. 446–468.

The Chronicle of Monemvasia. The Migration of the Slavs and Church Conflicts in the Byzantine Source from the Beginning of the 9th Century. Cracow: Towarzystwo Wydawnicze "Historia Iagellonica," 2001.

Vaillant, A. "Une homélie de Constantin le Prêtre." *Byzantinoslavica*, vol. 28 (1967), pp. 68–81.

Vaklinov, S. and S. Stanilov. *Kladenci. Rannosrednovekovno bălgarsko selishte*. Varna: Knigoizdatelstvo "Georgi Bakalov," 1981.

Văzharova, Zh. "Zur Frage der Etnogenese und der materiellen Kultur des bulgarischen Volkes (Zwei Nekropolen aus Nordostbulgarien)." In *Culture et art en Bulgarie médiévale (VIIIe–XIVe s.)*, pp. 5–30. Ed. by D. Angelov, I. Changova, G. I. Georgiev, et al. Sofia: Izdatelstvo na Bălgarskata Akademiia na Naukite, 1979.

Srednovekovnoto selishte s. Garvăn, Silistrenski okrăg (VI–XI v.). Sofia: Izdatelstvo na Bălgarskata Akademiia na Naukite, 1986.

Venedikov, I. "Legendata za Mikhail Kagan." *Preslav. Sbornik*, vol. 2 (1976), pp. 179–208.

Vergottini, G. de. "Venezia, e l'Istria nell'Alto Medioevo." In *Storia della civiltà Veneziana*, pp. 72–83. Ed. by V. Branca. Florence: Sansori, 1979.

Veselinović, R. L. "Starosrpsko naselie na Bostaništu kod Mošorina u Bačkoj (Prilog istoriji materijalne kulture Južnih Slovena X–XII veka)." *RVM*, vol. 2 (1953), pp. 5–58.

Vesely, J. M. "La sede e la sepoltura di San Metodio non erano a Sirmium." *Corso di cultura sull'arte ravennate e bizantina*, vol. 33 (1986), pp. 415–430.

Vida, T. and T. Völling. *Das slawische Brandgräberfeld von Olympia*. Rahden: Marie Leidorf, 2000.

Vilfan, S. "Zur Struktur der freisingischen Herrschaften südlich der Tauern im Frühmittelalter." In *Karantanien und der Alpen-Adria-Raum im Frühmittelalter*, pp. 209–222. Ed. by G. Hödl and J. Grabmeyer. Vienna, Cologne, and Weimar: Böhlau, 1993.

Vinski, Z. "Zu karolingischen Schwertfunden aus Jugoslawien." *Jahrbuch des Römisch-Germanischen Zentralmuseums*, vol. 30 (1983), pp. 465–501.

Vitlianov, S. "Das Schmiedehandwerk in Bulgarien vom VII.–XIV. Jh." *Slavia Antiqua*, vol. 32 (1989–1990), pp. 145–170.

"Feodalno imenie ot X–XI vek văv Vănshniia Grad na Pliska." In *Zwischen Byzanz und Abendland. Pliska, der östliche Balkanraum und*

Europa im Spiegel der Frühmittelalterarchäologie, pp. 63–66. Ed. by J. Henning. Frankfurt am Main: Johann Wolfgang Goethe Universität, 1999.

"Arkheologicheski danni za ikonomicheskiia oblik na Pliska." *Pliska–Preslav*, vol. 8 (2000), pp. 87–92.

Vokotopoulos, P. L. *He ekklesiastike architektonike eis ten dytiken sterean Hellada kai ten Epeiron. Apo tou telous tou 7ou mechri tou telous tou 10ou aionos.* Thessaloniki: Kentron Byzantinon Ereunon, 1975.

Vrana, J. *Vukanovo jevan delje*. Belgrade: Naučno delo, 1967.

Vroom, J. *After Antiquity. Ceramics and Society in the Aegean from the 7th to the 20th Century AC. A Case Study from Boeotia, Central Greece*. Leiden: Faculty of Archaeology, Leiden University, 2003.

Waldmüller, L. *Die Synoden in Dalmatien, Kroatien und Ungarn. Von der Völkerwanderung bis zum Ende der Arpaden (1311)*. Paderborn, Munich, Vienna, and Zürich: F. Schöningh, 1987.

Wasilewski, T. "Le thème maritime de la Dalmatie byzantine dans les années 805–822 et sa reconstitution par l'empereur Michel III." *Acta Poloniae Historica*, vol. 41 (1980), pp. 35–49.

Werner, J. "Zwei gegossene koptische Bronzefläschen aus Salona." *Vjesnik za arheologiju i historiju Dalmatinsku*, vols. 56–59 (1954–1957), pp. 115–128.

"Zur Zeitstellung der altkroatischen Grabfunde von Biskupija-Crkvina (Marienkirche)." *Schild von Steier. Beiträge zur steirischen Vor- und Frühgeschichte und Münzkunde*, vols. 15–16 (1979), pp. 227–237.

"Ein byzantinischer 'Steigbügel' aus Caričin Grad." In *Caričin Grad I. Les basiliques B et J de Caričin Grad, quatre objets remarquables de Caričin Grad, le trésor de Hajdučka Vodenica*, pp. 147–155. Ed. by N. Duval and V. Popović. Belgrade: Arheološki Institut and Rome: Ecole Française de Rome, 1984.

Der Grabfund von Malaja Pereščepina und Kuvrat, Kagan der Bulgaren. Munich: Verlag der Bayerischen Akademie der Wissenschaften, 1984.

Der Schatzfund von Vrap in Albanien. Beiträge zur Archäologie der Awarenzeit im mittleren Donauraum. Vienna: Verlag der Österreichischen Akademie der Wissenschaften, 1986.

"Neues zu Kuvrat und Malaja Pereščepina." *Germania*, vol. 10 (1992), pp. 430–436.

White, D. S. and J. R. Berrigan. *The Patriarch and the Prince. The Letter of Patriarch Photios of Constantinople to Khan Boris*. Brookline: Holy Cross Orthodox Press, 1982.

Wolff, R. L. "The 'Second Bulgarian empire'. Its origin and history to 1204." *Speculum*, vol. 24 (1949), pp. 167–206.

Wolfram, H. "Liudewit und Priwina. (Ein institutioneller Vergleich.)" In *Interaktionen der mitteleuropäischen Slawen und anderer Ethnika im 6.–10.*

Jahrhundert. Symposium Nové Vozokany 3.–7. Oktober 1983, pp. 291–296. Ed. by P. Šalkovský. Nitra: Archäologisches Institut der Slowakischen Akademie der Wissenschaften, 1984.

Salzburg, Bayern, Österreich: die Conversio Bagoariorum et Carantanorum *und die Quellen ihrer Zeit*. Vienna and Munich: R. Oldenbourg, 1995.

"Les Carantaniens, le premier peuple slave baptisé." In *Clovis, histoire et mémoire. Le baptême de Clovis, son écho à travers l'histoire*, pp. 279–287. Ed. by M. Rouche. Paris: Presses l'Université de Paris-Sorbonne, 1997.

"Moravien – Mähren oder nicht?" In *Svätopluk 894–1994. Materiály z konferencie organizovanej Archeologickym ústavom SAV v Nitre v spolupráci so Slovenskou historickou spoločnost'ou pri SAV. Nitra, 3.–6. október 1994*, pp. 235–245. Ed. by R. Marsina and A. Ruttkay. Nitra: Vydavatel' Archeologicky ústav Slovenskej akadémie vied v Nitre, 1997.

Yannopoulos, P. "Métropoles du Péloponnèse mésobyzantin: un souvenir des invasions avaro-slaves." *Byzantion*, vol. 63 (1993), pp. 388–400.

"La Grèce dans la Vie de S. Elie le Jeune et dans celle de S. Elie le Spéléote." *Byzantion*, vol. 64 (1994), pp. 193–221.

"Le rôle des Bulgares dans la guerre arabo-byzantine de 717/718." *VV*, vol. 55 (1994), pp. 133–153.

Zadnikar, M. "Typologie der romanischen Baukunst in Slowenien." In *Evolution générale et développements régionaux en histoire de l'art*, pp. 377–380. Ed. by G. Rózsa. Vol. 1. Budapest: Akadémiai kiadó, 1972.

"Die Babenberger und die 'Gruppe von Laško (Tüffer)' der romanischen Baukunst in Slowenien." In *1000 Jahre Babenberger in Österreicher. Stift Lilienfeld, 15. Mai–31. Okt. 1976*, pp. 507–511. Ed. by E. Zöllner. Vienna: Amt der Niederösterreichischen Landesregierung, 1976.

"Le bâtisseur bourguignon Michael en Slovénie." *Cîteaux: Commentarii Cistercienses*, vol. 31 (1980), pp. 267–271.

Romanika v Sloveniji. Tipologija in morfologija sakralne arhitekture. Ljubljana: Državna Založba Slovenije, 1982.

Zaharia, E. *Săpăturile de la Dridu. Contribuţii la arheologia şi istoria perioadei de formare a poporului român*. Bucharest: Editura Academiei Republicii Socialiste România, 1967.

Zaimov, I. "Eindeutige und umstrittene Stellen in der Bitolja-Inschrift des bulgarischen Selbstherrschers Ivan Vladislav (11. Jh.)." *Zeitschrift für Balkanologie*, vol. 13 (1978), pp. 194–204.

Zaimov, I. and M. Capaldo. *Suprasălski ili Retkov sbornik*. Sofia: Izdatelstvo na Bălgarskata Akademiia na Naukite, 1982.

Zaimov, I. and V. Tăpkova-Zaimova. *Bitolski nadpis na Ivan Vladislav, samodărzhec bălgarski. Starobălgarski pametnik ot 1015–1016 godina*. Sofia: Izdatelstvo na Bălgarskata Akademiia na Naukite, 1970.

Zajtay, I. "Le registre de Varad: un monument juridique du début du XIIIe siècle." *Revue historique du droit français et étranger*, vol. 32 (1954), pp. 527–562.

Zhekova, Zh. "Za Preslav sled văstanieto na Asenevci." *Preslav. Sbornik*, vol. 6 (2004), pp. 344–349.

Zimmermann, H. "Der deutsche Ritterorden in Siebenbürgen." In *Die geistlichen Ritterorden Europas*, pp. 267–298. Ed. by J. Fleckenstein and M. Hellmann. Sigmaringen: Jan Thorbecke, 1980.

"Die deutsch-ungarischen Beziehungen in der Mitte des 12. Jahrhunderts und die Berufung der Siebenbürger Sachsen." In *Von Schwaben bis Jerusalem. Facetten staufischer Geschichte*, pp. 151–165. Ed. by S. Lorenz and U. Schmidt. Sigmaringen: Jan Thorbecke, 1995.

"Die deutsche Südostsiedlung im Mittelalter." In *Deutsche Geschichte im Osten Europas. Land an der Donau*, pp. 11–88. Ed. by G. Schödl. Berlin: Siedler, 1995.

Der deutsche Orden im Burzenland. Eine diplomatische Untersuchung. Cologne, Vienna, and Weimar: Böhlau, 2000.

Živković, T. "The date of the creation of the theme of Peloponnese." *Symmeikta*, vol. 13 (1999), pp. 141–155.

Zuckerman, C. "Les Hongrois au pays de Lebedia: une nouvelle puissance aux confins de Byzance et de la Khazarie, ca. 836–889." In *To empolemo Byzantio (9os–12os ai.)*, pp. 51–74. Ed. by K. G. Tsiknakes. Athens: Idryma Goulandri-Horn, 1997.

INDEX

Cambridge Medieval Textbooks

Already published

Germany in the High Middle Ages *c.* 1050–1200
HORST FUHRMANN

The Hundred Years War
England and France at War *c.* 1300–*c.* 1450
CHRISTOPHER ALLMAND

Standards of Living in the Later Middle Ages:
Social Change in England, *c.* 1200–1520
CHRISTOPHER DYER

Magic in the Middle Ages
RICHARD KIECKHEFER

The Papacy 1073–1198: Continuity and Innovation
I. S. ROBINSON

Medieval Wales
DAVID WALKER

England in the Reign of Edward III
SCOTT L. WAUGH

The Norman Kingdom of Sicily
DONALD MATTHEW

Political Thought in Europe 1250–1450
ANTONY BLACK

The Church in Western Europe from the Tenth to the Early Twelfth Century
GERD TELLENBACH
Translated by Timothy Reuter

The Medieval Spains
BERNARD F. REILLY

England in the Thirteenth Century
ALAN HARDING

Monastic and Religious Orders in Britain 1000–1300
JANET BURTON

Religion and Devotion in Europe *c.* 1215–*c.* 1515
R. N. SWANSON

Medieval Russia, 980–1584
JANET MARTIN

The Wars of the Roses: Politics and the Constitution in England, *c.* 1437–1509
CHRISTINE CARPENTER

The Waldensian Dissent: Persecution and Survival, *c.* 1170–*c.* 1570
GABRIEL AUDISIO
Translated by Claire Davison

The Crusades, *c.* 1071–*c.* 1291
JEAN RICHARD
Translated by Jean Birrell

A History of Business in Medieval Europe, 1200–1550
EDWIN S. HUNT, JAMES MURRAY

Medieval Economic Thought
DIANA WOOD

Medieval Scotland
A. D. M. BARRELL

Roger II of Sicily
A Ruler between East and West
HUBERT HOUBEN
Translated by Graham A. Loud, Diane Milburn

The Carolingian Economy
ADRIAAN VERHULST

Women in Early Medieval Europe, 400–1100
LISA M. BITEL